The **Rough Guide** to

London

written and researched by

Rob Humphreys

with additional contributions by

Samantha Cook, Robin Lee and James Smart

www.roughguides.com

Contents

London for free colour section following p.144

The Thames colour section following p.400

Colour maps following p.512

◄◄ St Paul's Cathedral ◄ Old Royal Naval College, Greenwich

Introduction to

London

What strikes visitors more than anything else about London is the sheer size of the place. Stretching for more than thirty miles from east to west, and with a population of just under eight million, it's the largest capital in the EU. Ethnically and linguistically, it's also Europe's most diverse metropolis, offering cultural and culinary delights from right across the globe. Londoners tend to cope with all this by compartmentalizing their city, identifying with the neighbourhoods in which they work or live, and just making occasional forays "into town" or "up West", to the West End, London's shopping and entertainment heartland.

London dominates the national horizon, too: this is where most of the country's news and money are made, it's where the central government resides and, as far as its inhabitants are concerned, provincial life begins beyond the circuit of the city's orbital motorway. Londoners' sense of superiority causes enormous resentment in the regions, yet it's undeniable that the capital has a unique aura of excitement and success – in most walks of British life, if you want to get on, you've got to do it in London.

For the visitor, too, London is a thrilling place. And it's looking better than it has done for decades, thanks to the lottery- and millennium-driven investment that has seen virtually all London's world-class **museums**, **galleries** and **institutions** reinvented, from the Royal Opera House to the British Museum. The city boasts the world's largest modern art gallery in Tate Modern, the tallest observation wheel in the London Eye, and two fantastic

pedestrian bridges that have helped transform the south bank of the Thames into a magnet for visitors and Londoners alike.

As ever, London's traditional **sights** continue to draw in millions of tourists every year. Monuments from the capital's more glorious past are everywhere to be seen, from medieval banqueting halls and the great churches of Christopher Wren to the eclectic Victorian architecture of the triumphalist British Empire. There is also much enjoyment to be had from the city's quiet Georgian squares, the narrow alleyways of the City of London, the riverside walks, and the quirks of what is still identifiably a collection of villages. Even London's heavy traffic is offset by surprisingly large expanses of greenery: Hyde Park, Green Park and St James's Park are all within a few minutes' walk of the West End, while, further afield, you can enjoy the more expansive parklands of Hampstead Heath and Richmond Park.

You could spend days just **shopping** in London, too, mixing with the upper classes in the "tiara triangle" around Harrods, or sampling the offbeat weekend markets of Portobello Road, Brick Lane and Camden. The **music**, **clubbing** and **gay and lesbian** scenes are second to none, and mainstream **arts** are no less exciting, with regular opportunities to catch outstanding theatre companies, dance troupes, exhibitions and opera. The city's pubs have always had heaps of atmosphere, but its restaurants are now an attraction too, with everything from three-star Michelin establishments to low-cost, high-quality Chinese restaurants and Indian curry houses.

What to see

London has grown not through centralized planning but by a process of agglomeration, meaning that though the majority of the city's sights are situated to the north of the **River Thames**, which loops through the centre of the city from west to east, there is no single focus of interest. Villages and urban developments that once surrounded the core are now lost within the amorphous mass of Greater London, leaving London's highlights widely spread, and meaning that visitors should make mastering the public transport system, particularly the Underground (tube), a top priority.

If London has a centre, it's **Trafalgar Square**, home to Nelson's Column and the National Gallery. It's also as good a place as any to start exploring the city, especially as the area to the south of here, **Whitehall and Westminster**, is one of the easiest bits to discover on foot. This was the city's royal, political and ecclesiastical power-base for centuries, and you'll find some of London's most famous landmarks here: Downing Street, Big Ben, the Houses of Parliament and **Westminster Abbey**. The grand streets and squares of **St James's**, **Mayfair** and **Marylebone**, to the north of Westminster, have been the playground of the rich since the Restoration, and now contain the city's busiest shopping zones: Piccadilly, **Bond Street**, **Regent Street** and, most frenetic of the lot, **Oxford Street**.

East of Piccadilly Circus, **Soho**, **Chinatown** and **Covent Garden** are also easy to walk around and form the heart of the West End entertainment district, where you'll find the largest concentration of theatres,

The British Museum Great Court

cinemas, clubs, flashy shops, cafés and restaurants. Adjoining Covent Garden to the north, the university quarter of **Bloomsbury** is the traditional home of the publishing industry and location of the ever-popular **British Museum**, a stupendous treasure house that now boasts a wonderful central, covered courtyard. Welding the West End to the financial district, **Holborn** is a little-visited area, but offers some of central London's most surprising treats, among them the eccentric Sir John Soane's Museum and the secluded quadrangles of the Inns of Court.

A couple of miles downstream from Westminster, **The City** – or the City of London, to give it its full title – is simultaneously the most ancient and the most modern part of London.

▲ Guards marching along The Mall

Settled since Roman times, the area became the commercial and residential heart of medieval London, with its own Lord Mayor and its own peculiar form of local government, both of which survive (with considerable pageantry) to this day. The Great Fire of 1666 obliterated most of the City, and the resident population has dwindled to insignificance, yet this remains one of the great financial centres of the world, with the most prominent landmarks these days being the hi-tech offices of banks and insurance companies. However, the Square Mile boasts its share of historic sights too, notably the **Tower of London** and a fine cache of Wren churches that includes the mighty **St Paul's Cathedral**.

The **East End** and **Docklands**, to the east of the City, are equally notorious, but in entirely different ways. Impoverished and working-class, the East End is not conventional tourist territory, yet to ignore it is to miss out a crucial element of the real, multiethnic London. With its abandoned warehouses converted into overpriced apartment blocks for the city's upwardly mobile, Docklands is the converse of the down-at-heel East End, with the **Canary Wharf** tower, the country's tallest building, epitomizing the pretensions of the 1980s' Thatcherite dream.

The **South Bank**, **Bankside** and **Southwark** together make up the small slice of central London that lies south of the Thames. The Southbank Centre itself, London's little-loved concrete culture bunker, is enjoying a

Multiethnic London

With around three hundred languages spoken within its confines and all the major religions represented, London is Europe's most ethnically diverse city. First-, second- and third-generation immigrants make up over thirty percent of the population, while some claim that the majority of white Londoners are in fact descended from French Huguenot refugees. London has, of course, always been a **cosmopolitan** place. The first well-documented immigrants were invaders like the Romans, Anglo-Saxons, Vikings and Normans, while over the last four centuries, the city has absorbed wave after wave of foreigners fleeing persecution at home, or simply looking for a better life. However, it is the postwar period that stands out as the age of **immigration** par excellence. Initially, people came here from the Caribbean and the Indian subcontinent; today's arrivals are more likely to come from the world's war zones: Somalia, Afghanistan, Iraq.

Though London doesn't have the sort of ghettoization that's widespread in the US, certain areas have become **home from homes** for the more established communities. Brixton and Dalston are probably the most prominent Afro-Caribbean and African districts; Dalston and Haringey have the largest Turkish and Kurdish communities; Southall is predominantly Punjabi; Wembley is a Gujarati stronghold; Acton has a sizeable Polish community; Hoxton is a Vietnamese neighbourhood. The East End, London's top immigrant ghetto, has absorbed several communities over the centuries, and is currently the heart of Bengali London, while the Jewish community has more or less abandoned the East End and now has its most significant concentrations in Stamford Hill and Golders Green.

In general, these disparate groups live in peaceful coexistence and the traditions and customs they have brought with them have provided a vibrant contribution to London's cultural life, the most famous manifestation of which is the Notting Hill Carnival (see p.282).

new lease of life – thanks, in part, to the feel-good factor emanating from the graceful London Eye, which hangs over the Thames nearby. Bankside, the city's low-life district from Roman times to the eighteenth century, is also enjoying a renaissance, with a pedestrian bridge linking St Paul's with the former power station that is now home to **Tate Modern**, London's extraordinary museum of modern art.

In **Hyde Park** and **Kensington Gardens** you'll find the largest park in central London, a segment of greenery which separates wealthy west London from the city centre. The museums of **South Kensington** – the Victoria and Albert Museum, the Science Museum and the Natural History Museum – are a must, and if you have shopping on your agenda you may well want to investigate the hive of plush stores in the vicinity of Harrods, superstore to the upper echelons.

Some of the most appealing parts of north London are clustered around Regent's Canal, which skirts **Regent's Park** and serves as the focus for the capital's busiest weekend market, held around **Camden Lock**. Further out, in the chic literary suburbs of Hampstead and Highgate, there are unbeatable views across the city from half-wild **Hampstead Heath**, the favourite parkland of thousands of Londoners. The glory of southeast London is **Greenwich**, with its nautical associations, royal park and observatory (not to mention its Dome). Finally, there are plenty of rewarding day-trips up the Thames from **Chiswick** to **Hampton Court** and, beyond, to **Windsor**, an area that is liberally peppered with the stately homes and grounds of the country's royalty and former aristocracy.

Somerset House

When to go

Considering how temperate the London **climate** is, it's amazing how much mileage the locals get out of the subject. The truth is that summers rarely get really hot and the winters aren't very cold. In fact, it's impossible to say with any certainty what the weather will be like in any given month. May might be wet and grey one year and gloriously sunny the next; November stands an equal chance of being crisp and clear or foggy and grim. So, whatever time of year you come, be prepared for all eventualities, and bring a pair of comfortable shoes, as, inevitably, you'll be doing a lot of walking.

Average monthly temperatures and rainfall

	Jan	Feb	Mar	Apr	May	Jun	Jul	Aug	Sep	Oct	Nov	Dec
London												
Max/min (°C)	6/2	7/2	10/3	13/6	17/8	20/12	22/14	21/13	19/11	14/8	10/5	7/4
Max/min (°F)	43/36	44/36	50/37	56/43	62/46	69/53	71/57	71/56	65/52	57/45	50/41	44/39
Rainfall (mm)	54	40	37	37	46	45	57	59	49	57	64	48

20

things not to miss

It's not possible to see everything that London has to offer in one visit – and we don't suggest you try. What follows, in no particular order, is a selective taste of the city's highlights; from outstanding art collections and historic architecture to vibrant markets and picturesque parks, all arranged in five colour-coded categories. Each highlight has a page reference to take you straight into the Guide, where you can find out more.

01 **Tate Modern** Page **229** • One of the world's greatest modern art collections housed in a spectacularly converted, riverside power station.

02 **Double-decker bus** Page **39** • Take a ride on an old double-decker Routemaster bus, which run every fifteen minutes on the no. 9 and no. 15 routes, taking you past the Albert Hall, Trafalgar Square and St Paul's Cathedral.

03 **Sir John Soane's Museum** Page **153** • Part architectural set piece, part art gallery, the Soane museum is small and perfectly formed.

04 **London Eye** Page **224** • Londoners have taken to their new landmark, and there is certainly no better view, but book in advance.

05 **Kew Gardens** Page **345** • Kew boasts three hundred acres of beautiful botanic gardens by the River Thames, with the curvaceous Palm House as its centrepiece.

06 **Tower of London** Page **192** • Bloody royal history, Beefeaters, lots of armour, the Crown Jewels and ravens – and a great medieval castle.

07 **Borough Market**
Pages **235** & **444** • London's leading foodie market has loads of scrumptious fare spread out under the railway arches by Southwark Cathedral. Get there early to avoid the crowds and feast on all the free titbits as you browse.

08 **Houses of Parliament** Page **59** • See the "mother of all parliaments" at work from the public gallery or take a summertime tour.

09 **Somerset House** Page **147** ● Visit the art galleries, chill out by the dancing fountain, catch a film or (in winter) skate the night away at this wonderful riverside palace.

10 **London pubs** Page **396** ● Have a pint in one of London's many old and historic pubs.

11 **Hampton Court Palace** Page **356** ● Take a river boat to this sprawling red-brick affair on the banks of the Thames, the finest of London's royal palaces.

12 **Greenwich** Page **320** ● Soak up the naval history at the National Maritime Museum, and climb up to the Royal Observatory to enjoy the view over the river.

13 **Highgate Cemetery** Page **311** • The city's most atmospheric Victorian necropolis, thick with trees and crowded with famous corpses, with Karl Marx topping the bill.

15 **Victoria and Albert Museum** Page **257** • In terms of sheer variety and scale, the V&A is the greatest applied arts museum in the world.

14 **Spitalfields and Brick Lane** Page **203** • Visit the offbeat market stalls, shops, cafés and bars on the edge of the East End beyond Old Spitalfields Market.

16 **Walk along the South Bank** Page **220** • Starting at the London Eye, stroll along the bank of the Thames, and admire the vista of the north bank, all the way to Tower Bridge.

17 **National Gallery** Page **46** •
From the Renaissance to Picasso:
one of the world's great art galleries.

18 **Hampstead Heath** Page
307 • Fly kites, look across London
and walk over to Kenwood, for fine art, tea
and cakes.

19 **British Museum** Page **114**
• The spectacular Great Court and
the renovated Round Reading Room have
brought new life to the world's oldest and
greatest public museum.

20 **Shopping at Liberty** Page **436** • Just down the road from the scrum of Oxford
Circus, this beautiful department store, housed in a grand, mock-Tudor building, is
heaven for label aficionados and window-shoppers alike.

Basics

Basics

Getting there

Unless you're coming from elsewhere in Britain, or from northwest Europe, the quickest and easiest way to get to London is by plane. The city has five airports (see "Arrival" on p.22 for specific details on each) and is a major destination for most international airlines, so airfares tend to be keenly competitive.

How much you pay to fly to London depends on the **season**, with the highest fares charged from Easter to October, and around Christmas and New Year. With budget airlines, the earlier you book, the cheaper the prices tend to be.

Flights from the US and Canada

All major US and Canadian airlines run direct services **from North America to London**, Europe's busiest gateway. Two of London's airports – Heathrow and Gatwick – handle transatlantic flights, and in terms of convenience they're about equal.

Figure on around six hours' **flying time** from New York; it's an hour extra going the other way, due to headwinds. Add three or four hours more for travel from the West Coast. Most eastbound flights cross the Atlantic overnight, arriving the next morning; flying back, departure times tend to be morning or afternoon, arriving in the afternoon or evening of the same day.

Return **fares** (including taxes) from New York or Chicago (and even LA) are $400–500 low season, $500–800 high season; from Toronto C$600–800 low season, C$800–1000 high season; from Vancouver C$800–1000 low season, C$1000–1400 high season.

Flights from Australia and New Zealand

Flight time **from Australia and New Zealand to London** is at least 22 hours, and can be more depending on routes and transfer times. There's a wide variety of routes, with those touching down in Southeast Asia the quickest and cheapest on average. Given the length of the journey involved, you might be better off including a

night's stopover in your itinerary; some airlines include one in the price of the flight.

The cheapest direct scheduled flights to London are usually to be found on one of the Asian airlines. Average return **fares** (including taxes) from eastern gateways to London are A$1500–2000 in low season, A$2000–2500 in high season. Fares from Perth or Darwin cost around A$200 less. Return fares from Auckland to London range between NZ$2000 and NZ$3000 depending on the season, route and carrier.

By plane or train from Ireland

Travel from Ireland is quickest **by plane**, with the likes of Aer Lingus and Ryanair offering return tickets from Dublin, Derry, Cork or Shannon to London Stansted for as little as €70. From Belfast International, easyJet has return fares to London Stansted from around £60, if you book far enough in advance; flybe has similar fares from Belfast City to London Gatwick. A fully flexible fare can cost three or four times that amount, but will allow you to change your plans after purchasing the ticket.

Flying may be quick, but the **ferry and train** fares are pretty competitive and much more flexible, with Irish Railways (☎01/703 1884, ⊛www.irishrail.ie) offering return fares of around €80 from Dublin, and Northern Ireland Railways (☎028/9066 6630, ⊛www.translink.co.uk) offering returns from Belfast from £80. Journey time is eight hours from Dublin, ten from Belfast.

Agents and operators

ebookers UK ☎0800/082 3000, Ireland ☎01/488 3507; ⊛www.ebookers.com. Low fares on an extensive selection of scheduled flights and package deals.

North South Travel UK ☎01245/608291, ⓦwww.northsouthtravel.co.uk. Friendly, competitive travel agency, offering discounted fares worldwide. Profits are used to support projects in the developing world, especially the promotion of sustainable tourism.

STA Travel US ☎1-800/781-4040, Canada ☎1-888/427-5639, UK ☎0870/163 0026, Australia ☎1300/733035, New Zealand ☎0508/782872, South Africa ☎0861/781781; ⓦwww.statravel.com. Worldwide specialists in independent travel; also student IDs, travel insurance, car rental, rail passes, and more. Good discounts for students and under-26s.

Trailfinders UK ☎0845/058 5858, Ireland ☎01/677 7888, Australia ☎1300/780212; ⓦwww .trailfinders.com. One of the best-informed and most efficient agents for independent travellers.

Airlines

Aer Arann ⓦwww.aerarann.com
Aer Lingus ⓦwww.aerlingus.com
Air Canada ⓦwww.aircanada.com
Air New Zealand ⓦwww.airnz.co.nz
Air Transat ⓦwww.airtransat.com
American Airlines ⓦwww.aa.com
Asiana Airlines ⓦwww.flyasiana.com
bmi ⓦwww.flybmi.com
bmibaby ⓦwww.bmibaby.com
British Airways ⓦwww.ba.com
Cathay Pacific ⓦwww.cathaypacific.com
Continental Airlines ⓦwww.continental.com
Delta ⓦwww.delta.com
easyJet ⓦwww.easyjet.com
flybe ⓦwww.flybe.com
Gulf Air ⓦwww.gulfairco.com
KLM (Royal Dutch Airlines) ⓦwww.klm.com
Lufthansa ⓦwww.lufthansa.com
Malaysia Airlines ⓦwww.malaysiaairlines.com
Qantas ⓦwww.qantas.com.au
Royal Brunei ⓦwww.bruneiair.com
Ryanair ⓦwww.ryanair.com
Singapore Airlines ⓦwww.singaporeair.com
Thai Airways ⓦwww.thaiair.com
United Airlines ⓦwww.united.com
Virgin Atlantic ⓦwww.virgin-atlantic.com

Six steps to a better kind of travel

At Rough Guides we are passionately committed to travel. We feel strongly that only through travelling do we truly come to understand the world we live in and the people we share it with – plus tourism has brought a great deal of **benefit** to developing economies around the world over the last few decades. But the extraordinary growth in tourism has also damaged some places irreparably, and of course **climate change** is exacerbated by most forms of transport, especially flying. This means that now more than ever it's important to **travel thoughtfully and responsibly**, with respect for the cultures you're visiting – not only to derive the most benefit from your trip but also to preserve the best bits of the planet for everyone to enjoy. At Rough Guides we feel there are six main areas in which you can make a difference:

• Consider what you're contributing to the **local economy**, and how much the services you use do the same, whether it's through employing local workers and guides or sourcing locally grown produce and local services.
• Consider the **environment** on holiday as well as at home. Water is scarce in many developing destinations, and the biodiversity of local flora and fauna can be adversely affected by tourism. Try to patronize businesses that take account of this.
• Travel with a purpose, not just to tick off experiences. Consider **spending longer** in a place, and getting to know it and its people.
• Give thought to how often you **fly**. Try to avoid short hops by air and more harmful night flights.
• Consider **alternatives to flying**, travelling instead by bus, train, boat and even by bike or on foot where possible.
• Make your trips "**climate neutral**" via a reputable carbon offset scheme. All Rough Guide flights are offset, and every year we donate money to a variety of charities devoted to combating the effects of climate change.

Arrival

The majority of visitors arrive in London at one of its five airports, all but one of which can involve an expensive trip to the centre. Those arriving by train or bus are dropped right in the middle of the city, with easy access to public transport.

By plane

Flying into London, you'll arrive at Heathrow, Gatwick, Stansted, Luton or City airport, each of which is less than an hour from the city centre.

Heathrow

Heathrow (☎0870/000 0123, ⓦwww .heathrowairport.com) lies around fifteen miles west of central London, and is the city's busiest airport, with five terminals and three train/tube stations: one for terminals 1, 2 and 3, and separate ones for terminals 4 and 5. The fastest **trains** into London are the high-speed Heathrow Express services to Paddington station (daily 5am–11.30pm; journey 15–23min); tickets cost £16.50 one way or £32 return (more if you purchase your ticket on board the train). Heathrow Connect trains stop at some intermediate stations (Mon–Sat 5.30am–midnight, Sun 6am–midnight; every 30min; journey 25min) but tickets cost just £7 single and £14 return. An even cheaper alternative is to take the Piccadilly **Underground** line (☎020/7222 1234, ⓦwww.tfl.gov.uk), which connects the airport to numerous tube stations across central London (Mon–Sat 5am–11.30pm, Sun 6am–11.30pm; every 5min; journey 50min); tickets cost just £4 single, or, if you can buy a One-Day Travelcard (Zones 1–6) for £7.50 (see "City transport", p.24).

National Express **bus services** (☎0870/580 8080, ⓦwww.nationalexpress.com) run from Heathrow direct to Victoria Coach Station (5am–9.30pm every 15–25min; journey 40min–1hr); tickets cost £4 single, £8 return. From midnight, you can take night bus #N9 to Trafalgar Square for a bargain fare of £2; departures are every twenty minutes and journey time is just over an hour. **Taxis** are

plentiful, but will set you back between £50 and £70 to central London, and take around an hour (much longer in the rush hour).

Gatwick

Gatwick (☎0870/000 2468, ⓦwww.gatwick airport.com) is around thirty miles south of London, and has a train station at the South Terminal. Non stop Gatwick Express **trains** run between the airport and London Victoria (daily 4.30am–12.30am; every 15min; journey 30min); tickets cost around £17 single, £29 return. A cheaper option is to take a Southern train service to Victoria (every 15min; journey 35min), which stops at a couple of intermediate stations, or a First Capital Connect train to various stations within London (every 15–30min; journey 30–40min), including London Bridge and St Pancras; tickets for either cost around £10 single. easyBus (ⓦwww.easybus.co.uk) runs **buses** to Fulham Broadway tube (6.40am–11pm every 20min; 1hr 10min), with online tickets going for as little as £2 single (£10 if you buy on board). National Express buses run from Gatwick direct to central London (5am–9.30pm hourly; 1hr 30min); tickets cost around £7 single, £15 return. A **taxi** will set you back a ludicrous £90 or more, and take over an hour.

Stansted

Designed by Norman Foster, **Stansted** (☎0870/000 0303, ⓦwww.stanstedairport .com) is London's best-looking international airport, and lies roughly 35 miles northeast of the capital. The fastest **trains** are run by Stansted Express to Liverpool Street (5.30am–12.30am; every 15–30min; journey 45min), and cost £18 single, £30 return. easyBus (ⓦwww.easybus.co.uk) runs **buses** to Baker Street tube (daily 7am–1am; every 20min; 1hr 30min), with online tickets going for as little as £2 single (£10 if you buy on board). National Express (see p.22) runs buses 24 hours a day calling at various places in London en route to Victoria Coach Station (every 30min; journey 1hr 30min–1hr 45min), with tickets £10 single, £17 return. Terravision (☏01279/680028, ⓦwww.terravision.eu) also run coaches to Liverpool Street (daily 7am–1am every 30min; journey time 1hr 15min), with tickets £9 single, £13 return. A taxi will set you back £80 or more, and take at least an hour.

City Airport

City Airport (☏020/7646 0088, ⓦwww .londoncityairport.com), London's smallest, used primarily by business folk, is situated in the Royal Albert Docks, ten miles east of central London, and handles European flights only. The **Docklands Light Railway (DLR)** takes you straight to Bank in the City (Mon–Sat 5.30am–12.30am, Sun 7am–11.30pm; every 8–15min; journey 20min), where you can change to the tube; single tickets cost around £4. A taxi from the airport to the City's financial sector will cost around £20, and take half an hour or so.

Luton

Luton Airport (☏01582/405100, ⓦwww .london-luton.co.uk) is roughly thirty miles north of London and mainly handles charter flights. A **free shuttle bus** takes five minutes to transport passengers to Luton Airport Parkway station, which is connected by train to St Pancras (every 15–30min; journey 35–40min) and other stations in central

Train information

For up-to-date information on all train services and ticket prices from Gatwick, contact National Rail Enquiries (☏0845/748 4950, ⓦwww .nationalrail.co.uk).

London; single tickets cost around £11. All year round, 24 hours a day, **Green Line** and **easyBus** (ⓦwww.easybus.co.uk) run up to three buses an hour from Luton to Victoria Coach Station (every 15–30min; journey 1hr 20min), stopping at several locations en route, including Baker Street; tickets cost as little as £2 if you book in advance online, or as much as £12 single, £15 return. A taxi will cost in the region of £60 and take at least an hour to central London.

Arriving by train or bus

Eurostar (☏0870/160 6600, ⓦwww.eurostar .com) trains arrive at St Pancras International next door to King's Cross. Trains from the Channel ports arrive at Charing Cross or Victoria, while boat trains from Harwich arrive at Liverpool Street. Arriving by **train** (☏0845/ 748 4950, ⓦwww.nationalrail.co.uk) from elsewhere in Britain, you'll come into one of London's numerous mainline stations, all of which have adjacent Underground stations linking into the city centre's tube network. Coming into London by **coach** (☏0870/580 8080, ⓦwww.nationalexpress.com), you're most likely to arrive at Victoria Coach Station, a couple of hundred yards south down Buckingham Palace Road from Victoria train station and tube.

City transport

Thanks to London's first mayor, Ken Livingstone, the city's highly complex transport system definitely improved during the first eight years of this century. The congestion charge reduced traffic by thirty percent within central London, and much of the money was ploughed into improving the buses. That said, London still has one of the most expensive transport systems in the world.

Transport for London (TfL) provides excellent free maps and details of bus and tube services from its six **Travel Information Centres**: the most central one is at Piccadilly Circus tube station (daily 9.15am–7pm); there are other desks at the arrivals at Heathrow (terminals 1, 2 & 3), Victoria, Euston and Liverpool Street train stations, and Camden Town Hall, opposite King's Cross St Pancras. There's also a **24-hour helpline** and website for information on all bus and tube services (☎020/7222 1234, ⓦwww.tfl.gov.uk).

For transport purposes, London is divided into six concentric **zones** (plus a few extra in the northwest), with fares calculated depending on which zones you travel through: the majority of the city's accommodation, pubs, restaurants and sights lie in zones 1 and 2. If you cannot produce a valid ticket for your journey, or travel further than your ticket allows, you will be liable to a **Penalty Fare** of £50, reduced to £25 if you pay within 21 days. Try and avoid travelling during the **rush hour** (Mon–Fri 8–9.30am & 5–7pm), if possible, when tubes become unbearably crowded and hot, and some buses get so full they literally won't let you on.

The tube

Except for very short journeys, the **Underground** – or tube, as it's known to Londoners – is by far the quickest way to get about. Eleven different lines cross much of the metropolis, although London south of the river is not very well covered. Each line has its own colour and name – all you need to know is which direction you're travelling in: northbound, eastbound, southbound or westbound (this gets tricky when taking the Circle Line). As a precaution, it's also worth checking the final destination displayed on the front of the train, as some lines, such as the District and Northern lines, have several different branches.

Services are frequent (Mon–Sat 5.30am–12.30am, Sun 7.30am–11.30pm), and you rarely have to wait more than five minutes for a train between central stations. **Tickets** must be bought in advance from automatic machines or from a ticket booth in the station entrance hall. Single fares are outrageously expensive – a journey in the central zone costs an unbelievable £4 – so if you're intending to make more than one journey, an Oyster card, or a Travelcard is by far your best option (see opposite).

Buses

London's famous red double-decker **buses** are fun to ride on, but tend to get stuck in traffic jams, which prevents their running to a regular timetable. In the Pay Before You Board area in central London, and on all the extra-long "bendy buses", you must have a valid ticket before boarding, either an Oyster card, Travelcard, or a single ticket from the bus-stop ticket machines (which don't give out change); elsewhere, you can buy it from the driver. The standard walk-on fare is £2. If this is the type of journey you'll be making more than a few times, it might be worth buying a One-Day Bus Pass, which costs £3.80 and can be used on all buses any time anywhere in London.

A lot of bus stops are **request stops** (easily recognizable by their red sign), so if you don't stick your arm out to hail the bus you want, it will pass you by, and if you don't ring the bell for the bus to stop, it will just keep on going. Some buses run a 24-hour service, but most run between about 5am and

Oyster cards and tickets

The cheapest, easiest way to get about London is to use an **Oyster card**, London's transport smartcard, available from all tube stations and Travel Information Centres, and valid on the bus, tube, Docklands Light Railway (DLR), Tramlink, overground and all suburban rail services. You can use an Oyster card in one of two ways: you can use it simply to store a weekly/monthly/yearly Travelcard, or you can use it as a pay-as-you-go card – you can top-up your card at all tube stations and at most newsagents. As you enter the tube or bus, simply touch in your card at the card reader – if you're using pay-as-you-go, the fare will be taken off your card. If you're using the tube or train, you need to touch out again or a £4 maximum cash fare will be deducted. A pay-as-you-go Oyster operates daily price-capping so that when you've paid (slightly less than) the equivalent of a daily Travelcard, it will stop taking money off your card, though you still need to touch in (and out). Oyster cards are free for those purchasing monthly or yearly tickets; everyone else needs to hand over a £3 refundable deposit; visitors can buy a pay-as-you-go Oyster card for just £2.

If you don't have an Oyster card, you can still buy a paper **Travelcard** from machines and booths at all tube and train stations (and at many newsagents too – look for the sign). Anytime Day Travelcards start from £7.20 (zones 1 & 2); Off-Peak Travelcards are valid after 9.30am on weekdays and all day at the weekend, and cost £5.60 (zones 1 & 2), rising to £7.50 (zones 1–6). If you need to travel before 9.30am, it's worth considering an Anytime 3-Day Travelcard, which costs from £18.40 (zones 1 & 2), or a Weekly Travelcard for £25.80 (zones 1 & 2).

Children under 11 travel for free; children aged 11–15 travel free on all buses and trams and at child-rate on the tube; children aged 16 or 17 can travel at child-rate on all forms of transport. However, all children over 10 must have an Oyster photocard to be eligible for free travel – these should be applied for in advance online. Without a photocard, you can buy an Off-Peak Day Travelcard (zones 1–9) for children aged 11–15 for just £1, providing they're travelling with an adult.

midnight, with a network of **night buses** (prefixed with the letter "N") operating outside this period. Night-bus routes depart at approximately twenty- to thirty-minute intervals, more frequently on some routes and on Friday and Saturday nights. Tickets are £2 from central London, and Travelcards (see above) are valid until 4.30am. All stops are treated as request stops, so you must signal to get the bus to stop, and press the bell in order to get off.

Suburban trains

Large areas of London's suburbs are only served by the suburban **train** network. Wherever a sight can only be reached by train, we've indicated the nearest train station (and, if relevant, the central terminus from which trains depart). Oyster cards and Travelcards are valid on all suburban train services within Greater London. For information on services, phone National Rail Enquiries on ☎0845/748 4950, or visit ⊛www.nationalrail.co.uk.

The most useful train line to cross the capital is the **Overground**, which connects, among other places, Richmond and Stratford, via Hampstead Heath, Camden and Islington (Mon–Sat every 15min, Sun every 30min), and is destined to become the city's new orbital railway, and the First Capital Connect service (⊛www.thameslink .co.uk), which runs north–south via King's Cross, Blackfriars and London Bridge (Mon–Sat every 15min, Sun every 30min).

Docklands Light Railway

The **Docklands Light Railway**, or **DLR** (☎020/7363 9700), runs driverless trains from Bank in the City, and from Tower Gateway (close to Tower Hill tube and the Tower of London) overground to the financial centre of Docklands, plus other areas in the East End and also below ground to Greenwich and beyond. Oyster cards and Travelcards (see above) are valid on the network.

Boats

Unfortunately, **boat services** on the Thames are not integrated into the public transport system. If you have a valid Travelcard (either in paper or Oyster form), you're entitled to a 33 percent discount, but not if you have a pay-as-you-go Oyster card. Timetables and services are complex, and there are numerous companies and small charter operators – for a full list pick up a booklet from a TfL information centre (see p.24) or visit ⓦwww.tfl.gov.uk/river.

One of the largest companies is Thames Clippers (ⓦwww.thamesclippers.com), who run a regular **commuter service** (Mon–Fri 7am–11.30pm, Sat & Sun 9am–11.30pm; every 20–30min) between Waterloo and Greenwich (including the Dome), with some boats going as far as Woolwich. Typical fares are £5 single, with an unlimited hop-on, hop-off River Roamer day ticket costing £12, and a weekly ticket costing £36. A Rail Rover ticket (including unlimited travel on the DLR and hop-on, hop-off on City Cruises services) costs £13.50.

Other companies run boats upstream to Kew, Richmond and Hampton Court (see p.338). Look out, too, for the MV *Balmoral* and **paddle steamer** *Waverley*, which make regular visits to Tower Pier in the summer and autumn (☎0845/130 4647, ⓦwww .waverleyexcursions.co.uk).

Taxis

Compared to most capital cities, London's metered **black cabs** are an expensive option unless there are three or more of you. The minimum fare is £2.20, and a ride from Euston to Victoria, for example, costs around £12–15 (Mon–Fri 6am–8pm). After 8pm on

Congestion Charge

All vehicles entering central London on weekdays between 7am and 6.30pm are liable to a **congestion charge** of £8 per vehicle. Drivers can pay the charge online, over the phone and at garages and shops, and must do so before midnight the same day or incur a £2 surcharge – 24 hours later, you'll be liable for a £120 Penalty Charge Notice. Local residents, the disabled, motorcycles, minibuses and some alternative-fuel vehicles are exempt from the charge, but must register in order to qualify. For more details, visit ⓦwww.tfl.gov.uk.

weekdays and all day during the weekend, a higher tariff applies, and after 10pm, it's higher still. Tipping is customary. An illuminated yellow light over the windscreen tells you if the cab is available – just stick your arm out to hail it. London's cabbies are the best-trained in Europe; every one of them knows the shortest route between any two points in the capital, and they won't rip you off by taking another route. They are, however, a blunt and forthright breed, renowned for their generally reactionary opinions. To order a black cab in advance, phone ☎0871/871 8710, and be prepared to pay an extra £2.

Minicabs look just like regular cars and are considerably cheaper than black cabs, but they cannot be hailed from the street. All minicabs should be licensed and able to produce a Public Carriage Office licence on demand. There are hundreds of minicab firms in the phone book, but the best way to pick is to take the advice of the place you're

The London Pass

If you're thinking of visiting a lot of fee-paying attractions in a short space of time, it's worth considering buying a **London Pass** (ⓦwww.londonpass.com), which gives you free entry to a mixed bag of attractions including Hampton Court Palace, Kensington Palace, Kew Gardens, London Zoo, St Paul's Cathedral, the Tower of London and Windsor Castle, plus a whole host of other attractions. You can choose to buy the card with an All-Zone Travelcard thrown in; the extra outlay is relatively small, and this does include free travel out to Windsor. The pass costs around £39 for one day (£25 for kids), rising to £87 for six days (£60 for kids), or £46 with a Travelcard (£27 for kids) rising to £129 (£82 for kids). The London Pass can be bought online or in person from tourist offices and London's mainline train or chief underground stations.

at, unless you want to be certain of a woman driver, in which case book a cab from Ladycabs (☎020/7272 3300), or a gay/lesbian-friendly driver, in which case call Freedom Cars (☎020/7739 9080). Avoid illegal taxi touts, who hang around outside venues alongside licensed cabs, and always establish the fare beforehand, as minicabs are not metered.

Last, and definitely least, there's currently a plague of pedicabs or **bicycle taxis** in the West End. The oldest and biggest of the bunch are Bugbugs (☎020/7353 4028, ⓦwww.bugbugs.com), who have rickshaws operating Monday to Saturday from 7pm until the early hours of the morning. The rickshaws take up to three passengers and fares are negotiable, so you should always agree a price beforehand based on a fare of around £3–5 per person.

Driving

Given the traffic jams, parking hassle and pollution caused, **driving** in London – especially central London – is by far the worst transport option available. However, if you must drive, bear in mind the rules of the road (even if no one else does). Seatbelts are compulsory front and back and the speed limit is 30mph, unless it says otherwise.

Your biggest nightmare as a driver is undoubtedly **parking**. The basic rules are that double red and double yellow lines mean no waiting or stopping, as do the zigzag lines that you'll see near a pedestrian crossing. Single yellow and single red lines mean that you can park on them after 6pm or 7pm, and at the weekends, but times vary from borough to borough, so read the signs before leaving your vehicle. Parking at a meter or pay-and-display will cost you £4 an hour or more, usually up to a maximum of two hours, though again meters are often free in the evenings and at weekends. Parking meters are being phased out by some boroughs, in which case you'll need a mobile phone and credit card with you to pay for your parking. Finally, you can go to a car park – NCP are the largest operators ⓦwww.ncp.co.uk – which will cost you up to

£10 for two hours during the day. If you park your car illegally, you will get a Penalty Charge Notice (usually £80), possibly get clamped (another £80) or get towed away (£125 and upwards). If you suspect your vehicle has been towed away, phone the police on ☎020/7747 4747.

Cycling

Cycling is increasingly popular in London, not least because – in the centre, at least – it's by far the fastest way to get around. If you also use the tubes and trains, it can even be a good way to explore some of the suburbs. There are, however, restrictions on taking bikes on public transport: no bikes other than folding bikes are allowed on any part of the system (with a few minor exceptions) from Monday to Friday between 7.30am and 9.30am, and from 4pm to 7pm. Bikes are also restricted on the tube, being only allowed on the District, Circle, East London, Hammersmith & City and Metropolitan lines, plus certain overground sections of other tube lines. Bicycles are not allowed on the Docklands Light Railway, and restrictions on the suburban trains vary from company to company, so check before you set out.

London has been promised a free bike scheme like the one in Paris, but until then, the nearest thing is OYBike (☎020/7081 0742, ⓦwww.oybikes.com), a street-based **bike rental** outfit, which has bikes at over forty locations around the city (predominantly West London). In return for your credit-card details, you get a PIN which allows you to access the bikes: the first thirty minutes are free, after which it costs up to £8 a day. Other, more conventional bike-rental outfits include: London Bicycle Tour Company, on the South Bank at 1a Gabriel's Wharf, SE1 (☎020/7928 6838, ⓦwww.londonbicycle .com), which has hybrid and mountain bikes for rent at £3–4 an hour or £19 for the first day, £9 per day thereafter, £48 for the week; On Your Bike, 52–54 Tooley St, SE1 (☎020/7378 6669, ⓦwww.onyourbike.com), which has a whole range of bikes for rent for around £8–12 a day.

Festivals

London hosts an enormous number of festivals throughout the year, several of which are worth planning a trip around. The biggest street festival is still the Notting Hill Carnival, which takes place at the end of August and the longest-running event is still the Proms, whose series of classical music concerts takes place for around eight weeks over the summer. There are also regular free events held throughout the year on Trafalgar Square, funded by the Mayor of London. The list of events below really just skims the surface – for details of sporting events, see Chapter 32.

January

1 London Parade A procession of floats, marching bands, cheerleaders and clowns wends its way from Parliament Square, at noon, to Green Park. Admission charge for grandstand seats in Piccadilly, otherwise free. ⓦ www.londonparade.co.uk

Late London International Mime Festival Annual mime festival that takes place in the last two weeks of January at the South Bank Centre, the ICA and other funky venues. It pulls in some very big names in mime, animation and puppetry. ⓦ www.mimefest.co.uk

Late Chinese New Year Celebrations Soho's Chinatown, Leicester Square and even Trafalgar Square all erupt in a riot of dancing dragons and firecrackers – expect serious human congestion. Free. ⓦ www.chinatownchinese.co.uk

February

First Sunday Joseph Grimaldi Memorial Service Special church service for clowns, commemorating the great clown, at Holy Trinity Church, Beechwood Road, E8 (Dalston Kingsland or Junction Overground), with a clown show afterwards in the church hall. Free. ⓦ www.clownsinternational.com

Shrove Tuesday Pancake Day There are several places to enjoy a public pancake race: go to Brick Lane for frivolity, and the Guildhall for seriously silly costumes courtesy of the Poulterers' Guild. Free.

March

15 St Patrick's Day A parade sets off at noon and ends up at Trafalgar Square, where there's a festival of Irish culture; also plenty of events in the week building up to the day. Free. ⓦ www.london.gov.uk

Late Head of the River Race Less well known than the Oxford and Cambridge race, but much more fun, since there are over four hundred crews setting off at ten-second intervals and chasing each other from Mortlake to Putney. Free. ⓦ www.horr.co.uk

Late The Boat Race Since 1845 rowers from Oxford and Cambridge universities have battled it out over four miles from Putney to Mortlake. The pubs at prime vantage points pack out early. Free. ⓦ www.theboatrace.org

April

Late Alternative Fashion Week Lots of new designers and no exclusive guest lists at this week-long fashion show held in Spitalfields. ⓦ www.alternativearts.co.uk

Third or fourth Sunday London Marathon The world's most popular marathon, with around 40,000 masochists sweating the 26.2 miles from Greenwich to central London. A handful of world-class athletes enter each year, but most of the competitors are running for charity, often in ludicrous costumes. Free. ⓦ www.london-marathon.co.uk

May

May Bank Holiday weekend IWA Canal Cavalcade Lively three-day celebration of the city's inland waterways, held at Little Venice (near Warwick Avenue tube), with scores of decorated narrow boats, Morris dancers and lots of children's activities. Free. ⓦ www.waterways.org.uk

Sunday nearest May 9 May Fayre and Puppet Festival The gardens of St Paul's Church in Covent Garden play host to puppet booths to commemorate the first recorded Punch and Judy show in England, seen by diarist Samuel Pepys in 1662. Free. ⓦ www.alternativearts.co.uk

Sunday nearest May 11 Chestnut Sunday Parade of antique bicycles, classic cars, motorcycles and carriages along Chestnut Avenue, with the trees in full blossom, held in Bushy Park, near Hampton Court Palace. Free. ⓦ www.royalparks.gov.uk

Second Sunday Baishakhi Mela A colourful Bangla New Year open-air festival with street entertainment, fun fairs and lots of food on Brick Lane, Allen Garden and Weaver's Fields. Free. Ⓦ www.melafestival.com

Late Chelsea Flower Show The world's finest horticultural event on grounds near the Royal Hospital in Chelsea, is a solidly bourgeois affair. RHS members only on the first two days. Ⓦ www.rhs.org.uk/chelsea

June

Early Beating Retreat Annual military display on Horse Guards' Parade over three evenings, marking the old custom of drumming and piping the troops back to base at dusk. Soldiers on foot and horseback provide a colourful ceremony which precedes a floodlit performance by the Massed Bands of the Queen's Household Cavalry. Ⓦ www.army.mod.uk

Early Spitalfields Summer Festival Music recitals held over two weeks in Christ Church, Spitalfields and Wilton's Music Hall, off Cable Street. Ⓦ www .spitalfieldsfestival.org.uk

Until Aug Coin Street Festival Hugely varied, free festival of music, dance and performance, that takes place in and around the OXO Tower, just east of the South Bank Centre. Free. Ⓦ www.coinstreet.org

Second Saturday Trooping the Colour Celebration of the Queen's official birthday (her real one is on April 21) featuring massed bands, gun salutes, fly-pasts and crowds of tourists and patriotic Britons. The royal procession along the Mall allows you a glimpse for free, and there are rehearsals (minus Her Majesty) on the two preceding Saturdays. Ⓦ www.army.mod.uk

Late Meltdown Fortnight of groovy gigs, films and other events on the South Bank, chosen and presided over by a different seminal musician each year. Ⓦ www.southbankcentre.co.uk

July

Early Hampton Court Flower Show Six-day international flower extravaganza that's beginning to eclipse its sister show in Chelsea. RHS members only on the first two days. Ⓦ www.rhs.org.uk/hamptoncourt

Mid Doggett's Coat & Badge Race World's oldest rowing race from London Bridge to Chelsea, established by Thomas Doggett, an eighteenth-century Irish comedian, to commemorate George I's accession to the throne. Free. Ⓦ www.watermenshall.org

Mid Lambeth Country Show A traditional country show comes to Brixton's Brockwell Park, with traction engines, best-jam competitions, farm animals and a cider tent. Free. Ⓦ www.lambeth.gov.uk

Mid London Literature Festival The capital's chief wordfest is held over a fortnight at the Southbank Centre, with music, poetry and debate. Ⓦ www .southbankcentre.co.uk

Until early Sept Henry Wood Promenade Concerts Known as the Proms, this series of nightly classical concerts at the Royal Albert Hall (and elsewhere) is a well-loved British institution. For more info, see p.256. Ⓦ www.bbc.co.uk/proms

Until early Aug City of London Festival For over a month, churches (including St Paul's Cathedral), livery halls, corporate buildings and even the streets around the City play host to classical and jazz musicians, theatre companies and other guest performers. Ⓦ www.colf.org

Sunday nearest July 16 Italian Procession Big, boisterous Italian Catholic parade, party and stalls, which starts from St Peter's Italian Church on Clerkenwell Road and roams the streets of what used to be London's very own Little Italy (see p.157). Free. Ⓦ www.italianchurch.org.uk

A weekday Cart Marking Recalling a 1681 Act which restricted to 421 the number of horse-drawn carts allowed in the City, this arcane ceremony involves vintage vehicles congregating at 11am in Guildhall Yard in a branding ceremony organized by the Worshipful Company of Car Men. Free. Ⓦ www.thecarmen.co.uk

August

Early Great British Beer Festival A five-day binge organized by the Campaign for Real Ale (CAMRA). With up to five hundred brews to sample, the entrance fee is a small price to pay to drink yourself silly. Ⓦ gbbf.camra.org.uk

Early Carnival del Pueblo All-day Latino street party with a parade from Elephant & Castle and a festival in Burgess Park, with dancing and music from samba to hip-hop. Free. Ⓦ www.carnavaldelpueblo.co.uk

Mid London Mela Big open-air Asian festival of live music, dance and the arts, held in Gunnersbury Park, washed down with the best festival food in the capital. Free. Ⓦ www.londonmela.org

Late Notting Hill Carnival World-famous two-day street festival. Carnival is a tumult of imaginatively decorated floats, eye-catching costumes, thumping soundsystems, live bands, irresistible food and huge crowds. See p.282 for more details. Free. Ⓦ gbbf.camra.org.uk

September

Early Great River Race Hundreds of boats are rowed or paddled from Ham House, Richmond, down to Island Gardens on the Isle of Dogs. Starts are staggered and any number of weird and wonderful vessels take part. Ⓦ www.greatriverrace.co.uk

Mid Thames Festival The Mayor of London's very own family-orientated community festival with river races, a Thames beach, dancing, music and fireworks. Ⓦ www.thamesfestival.org

Late Car Free Day Always held on a weekday, and an excuse to exclude cars from bits of London and stage fun events. Definitely worth renting out a bike for the day. Free. ® www.tfl.gov.uk

Third Sunday Freewheel Another excuse to jump on a bike for this traffic-free ride around the capital – more than 50,000 people take part every year. Free. ® www.tfl.gov.uk

Third weekend Open House A once-a-year opportunity to peek inside over 650 buildings around London, many of which don't normally open their doors to the public. You'll need to book in advance for some of the more popular places. Free. ® www .londonopenhouse.org

Last Saturday Great Gorilla Run Don a gorilla suit and join (or simply watch) the thousand other gorillas running 7km through the City for gorilla conservation. Free. ® www.greatgorillas.org

Last Sunday Costermongers' Pearly Harvest Festival Parade Service Cockney festival at the Guildhall, with donkeys and carts, marching bands and Pearly Kings and Queens in their traditional pearl-button-studded outfits. Free. ® www.pearlysociety.co.uk

October

First Monday Judges' Service To mark the opening of the legal year the judiciary, in full regalia, attends a service at 10am in Westminster Abbey. Afterwards they process to the House of Lords for their "Annual Breakfast". Free.

Mid to late London Film Festival A two-week cinematic season with scores of new international films screened at the BFI Southbank and some West End venues. ® www.bfi.org.uk/lff

Late Return to Camden Town Ten-day festival of traditional Irish music, song and dance featuring a great line-up of performers as well as talks and workshops. ® www.returntocamden.org

Late State Opening of Parliament The Queen arrives by coach at the Houses of Parliament at 11am accompanied by the Household Cavalry and gun salutes. The ceremony itself takes place inside the House of Lords and is televised; it also takes place whenever a new government is sworn in. Free. ® www.parliament.uk

November

First Sunday London to Brighton Veteran Car Run In 1896 Parliament abolished the Act that required all cars to crawl along at 2mph behind someone waving a red flag. A rally was set up to mark the occasion, and more than a century later classic cars built before 1905 still set off from Hyde Park at sunrise and travel the 58 miles to Brighton along the A23 at the heady average speed of 20mph. Free. ® www.lbvcr.com

5 Bonfire Night In memory of Guy Fawkes – executed for his role in the 1605 Gunpowder Plot to blow up King James I and the Houses of Parliament – effigies of the hapless Fawkes are burned on bonfires all over the capital. See local listings or head for Alexandra Palace, which provides a good vantage point from which to take in several displays at once. Free.

Early London Jazz Festival Big ten-day international jazz fest held in all London's jazz venues, large and small. ® www.londonjazzfestival.org.uk

Second Saturday Lord Mayor's Show The Lord Mayor begins his or her day of investiture at Westminster, leaving there at around 9am for Guildhall. At 11.10am, the vast ceremonial procession, headed by a gilded coach, begins its journey from Guildhall to the Law Courts in the Strand, where the oath of office is taken at 11.50am. From there the coach and its train of 140-odd floats make their way back towards Guildhall, arriving at 2.20pm. After dark, there's a fireworks display on the Thames. Free. ® www.lordmayorsshow.org

Sunday nearest November 11 Remembrance Sunday A day of commemorative ceremonies for the dead and wounded of the two world wars and other conflicts. The principal ceremony, attended by the Queen and the prime minister, takes place at the Cenotaph in Whitehall, beginning with a march-past of veterans and building to a one-minute silence at the stroke of 11am. Free.

Until Dec Christmas Lights Assorted celebrities flick the switches, and Bond, Oxford and Regent streets are bathed in festive illumination from dusk to midnight until January 6. Also, each year since the end of World War II, Norway has acknowledged its gratitude to the country that helped liberate it from the Nazis with the gift of a mighty spruce tree that appears in Trafalgar Square in early December. Decorated with lights, it becomes the focus for carol singing versus traffic noise each evening until Christmas Eve. Free.

December

Until Jan Ice rinks have become all the rage. You can skate outside the Natural History Museum, at Somerset House, Marble Arch, Kew Gardens and elsewhere.

Christmas Day Serpentine Swim Brave (or foolhardy) members of the Serpentine Swimming Club have taken an icy 100yd plunge in the Serpentine Lido every year since 1864. Free. ® www .serpentineswimmingclub.com

New Year's Eve New Year is welcomed by thousands of revellers who get to enjoy a spectacular firework display centred on the London Eye. Transport for London runs free public transport all night, sponsored by various public-spirited breweries. Free. ® www.london.gov.uk

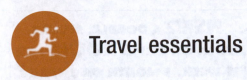

Travel essentials

Addresses

London addresses come with **postcodes** at the end. Each street name is followed by a letter or letters giving the geographical location of the street in relation to the City (E for "east", WC for "west central" and so on) and a number that specifies its location more precisely. Unfortunately, this number doesn't correspond to the district's distance from the centre (as in most cities). So W11 (Notting Hill) for example, is closer to the centre of town than W4 (Chiswick), and SE3 (Blackheath) lies beyond the remote-sounding SE10 (Greenwich). Full postal addresses end with a digit and two letters, which specify the individual block, but these are only used in correspondence.

Costs

The high cost of accommodation, and food and drink, make London a **very expensive** place to visit. The minimum expenditure for a couple staying in a budget hotel and eating takeaway meals, pizzas or other such basic fare would be in the region of at least £50 per person per day. You only have to add in the odd better-quality meal, plus some major tourist attractions, a few films or other shows, and you're looking at around £75–100 as a daily budget, even in decidedly average accommodation. For more details on the costs of accommodation and eating, see chapters 23 and 24.

Crime and personal safety

Although the traditional image of the friendly British "bobby" has suffered over the years by incidences of corruption and racism, in the normal run of events the **police** continue to be approachable, helpful and, for the most part, unarmed. If you're lost in London, asking a police officer is generally the quickest way to pinpoint your destination – police officers on street duty wear a distinctive domed hat with a silver tip. Like any other capital, London has its dangerous spots, but these tend to be obscure parts of the city where no tourist has any reason to be. The chief risk on London's streets is pickpocketing, and there are some virtuoso villains at work, especially on the big shopping streets and the Underground (tube). Carry only as much money as you need for the day, and keep all bags and pockets fastened.

Should you have anything stolen or be involved in an incident that requires reporting, go to the **local police station** or phone ☎0300/123 1212; the ☎999 number should only be used in emergencies. Central 24hr police stations include: Charing Cross, Agar St, WC2; Holborn, 10 Lambs Conduit St, WC1; Marylebone, 1–9 Seymour St, W1; West End Central, 27 Savile Row, W1; Ⓦwww.met.police.uk. The City of London Police are separate from the Metropolitan Police and have their headquarters at 182 Bishopsgate, EC2 ☎020/7601 2222, Ⓦwww.cityoflondon.police.uk. If there's an incident on public transport, call the British Transport Police on ☎0800/405040. If you have a complaint against the police, take the officer's number and report it to the Independent Police Complaints Commission (☎0845/300 2002, Ⓦwww.ipcc.gov.uk).

Disabled travellers

London is an old city, not well equipped for disabled travellers, though all public venues are obliged to make some effort towards accessibility. Even **public transport** is slowly improving, with most buses now wheelchair-accessible. The ancient tube and rail systems, designed, for the most part, in the nineteenth century, are still a trial for those with mobility problems. Major exceptions include the Docklands Light Railway, sections of the Jubilee Line, Tramlink and the Heathrow Express. However, TfL is committed to making 25 percent of all tube stations step-free by 2010 – a blue symbol on the tube map indicates a step-free

station. For a more detailed rundown, get hold of the free *Tube Access Guide* or use the TfL website to plan a step-free journey (Ⓦ www.tfl.gov.uk).

Tourism For All has lots of useful information on accessibility for visitors to London (Ⓣ 0845/124 9971, Ⓦ www.tourismforall .uk). Another valuable service is provided by **Artsline** (Ⓣ 020/7388 2227, Ⓦ www.artsline .org.uk), who can give up-to-date information and advice by phone on access to arts venues and events in London: theatres, cinemas, galleries and concert halls.

Discounts

Most attractions and many cinemas and theatres offer **concessions** for senior citizens, the unemployed, full-time students and under-16s, with under-5s being admitted free almost everywhere – proof of eligibility will be required in most cases.

Once obtained, youth/student ID cards soon pay for themselves in savings. Full-time students are eligible for the **International Student Identity Card** or **ISIC** (Ⓦ www .isiccard.com), which costs around £10 and entitles the bearer to reduced air, rail and bus fares, and discounts at museums, theatres and other attractions. If you're not a student, but you're 25 or younger, you can get an **International Youth Travel Card** or **IYTC**, which costs the same as the ISIC and carries the same benefits.

Electricity

Electricity supply in London conforms to the **EU standard** of approximately 230V. Sockets are designed for British **three-pin plugs**, which are totally different from those in the rest of the EU and North America.

Embassies and High Commissions

Australian High Commission Australia House, Strand, WC2 Ⓣ 020/7379 4334, Ⓦ www.australia .org.uk.
Canadian High Commission 1 Grosvenor Square, W1 Ⓣ 020/7528 6600, Ⓦ www.dfait-maeci.gc.ca.
Irish Embassy 17 Grosvenor Place, SW1 Ⓣ 020/7235 2171, Ⓦ www.embassyofireland.co.uk.
New Zealand High Commission New Zealand House, 80 Haymarket, SW1 Ⓣ 020/7930 8422, Ⓦ www.nzembassy.com.
South African High Commission South Africa House, Trafalgar Square, WC2 Ⓣ 020/7451 7299, Ⓦ www.southafricahouse.com.
US Embassy 24 Grosvenor Square, W1 Ⓣ 020/7499 9000, Ⓦ www.usembassy.org.uk.

Emergencies

Alcoholics Anonymous Ⓣ 0845/769 7555, Ⓦ www.alcoholics-anonymous.org.uk
Police, fire and ambulance Ⓣ 999
Rape crisis Ⓣ 020/8683 3300, Ⓦ www.rapecrisis .org.uk
Samaritans 24hr counselling helpline Ⓣ 0845/790 9090, Ⓦ www.samaritans.org; or drop-in (daily 9am–9pm) at 46 Marshall St, W1 Ⓣ 020/7734 2800; Piccadilly Circus or Oxford Circus tube.
Sexual Healthline Ⓣ 0800/567123, Ⓦ www .condomessentialwear.co.uk

Entry requirements

Citizens of all European countries – except Albania, Bosnia, Macedonia, Montenegro, Serbia and the former Soviet republics (other than the Baltic states) – can enter Britain with just a **passport**, for up to three months (indefinitely if you're from the EU). US, Canadian, Australian and New Zealand citizens can stay for up to six months, providing they have a return ticket and

---

English Heritage and National Trust

A few of London's historic properties come under the control of the private **National Trust** (Ⓣ 0844/800 1895, Ⓦ www.nationaltrust.org.uk), or the state-run **English Heritage** (Ⓣ 0870/333 1181, Ⓦ www.english-heritage.org.uk). These properties are denoted in the guide by "NT" or "EH" after the opening times. Annual membership for each organization is around £40 and allows free entry to their respective properties, though if you're only visiting London for a short time, it may not be worth it.

24 hour accident and emergency

Charing Cross Hospital, Fulham Palace Rd, W6 ☏020/8846 1234; Chelsea & Westminster Hospital, 369 Fulham Rd, SW10 ☏020/8746 8000; Guy's Hospital, Westminster Bridge Rd, SE1 ☏020/7188 7188; Royal Free Hospital, Pond St, NW3 ☏020/7794 0500; Royal London Hospital, Whitechapel Rd, E1 ☏020/7377 7000; St Mary's Hospital, Praed St, W2 ☏020/7886 6666; University College London Hospital, 235 Euston Rd, NW1 ☏0845/155 5000; Whittington Hospital, Highgate Hill, N19 ☏020/7272 3070.

adequate funds to cover their stay. Citizens of most other countries require a **visa**, obtainable from the British consular or mission office in the country of application.

Note that visa regulations are subject to frequent changes, so it's always wise to contact the nearest British embassy or High Commission before you travel. If you visit ⓦwww.ukvisas.gov.uk, you can download the full range of **application forms** and information leaflets and find out the contact details of your nearest embassy or consulate. In addition, an independent charity, the Immigration Advisory Service (IAS), County House, 190 Great Dover St, London SE1 4YB (☏0844/974 4000, ⓦwww.iasuk.org), offers free and confidential advice to anyone applying for entry clearance into the UK.

For **visa extensions**, you should write, before the expiry date given in your passport, to the UK Border Agency, Lunar House, 40 Wellesley Rd, Croydon CR9 2BY (☏0870/606 7766).

Health

For minor complaints, **pharmacists** (known as chemists in England) can dispense a limited range of drugs without a doctor's prescription. Most pharmacies are open standard shop hours, though some stay open later: Zafash, 233–235 Old Brompton Rd, SW5 ☏020/7373 2798, ⓦwww.zafash.com (Earl's Court tube), is open 24 hours; while Bliss, at 5–6 Marble Arch, W1 ☏020/3302 8345 (Marble Arch tube), is open daily 9am till midnight. In addition, every police station keeps a list of late-opening pharmacies.

EU citizens (and those of Iceland, Norway and Liechtenstein) are entitled to free medical treatment on production of an **EHIC** (European Health Insurance Card). Australia, New Zealand, Russia and several other

non-EU countries also have reciprocal health-care arrangements with the UK. If you need to see a doctor (GP), your hotel, hostel or host should be able to point you in the right direction. Alternatively, if it's an emergency, you can turn up at the **Accident and Emergency** (A&E) department of your local hospital, or phone for an ambulance (☏999). A&E services are free to all. You can also go to a **Minor Injuries Clinic** such as the one at St Bartholomew's Hospital, West Smithfield, EC1 ☏020/7601 7407, or get free medical advice from NHS Direct, the health service's 24-hour helpline ☏0845/4647, ⓦwww.nhsdirect.nhs.uk.

For an **emergency dentist** turn up as early as possible to the Dental Emergency Care Service at Guy's Hospital, St Thomas St (☏020/7188 7188), between 9am and 5pm Monday to Friday.

Insurance

Even though EU health-care privileges apply in the UK, it's as well to take out an insurance policy before travelling to cover against theft, loss and illness or injury. Non-EU citizens should check whether they are already covered before buying a new policy.

Internet access

Many hotels and hostels in London have internet access. After that, your best bet is a café with **wi-fi** like the café in Foyles bookshop at 113–119 Charing Cross Rd (Tottenham Court Road tube). Alternatively, to find an **internet café** (£2–5 per hr) log on to ⓦwww.easyinternetcafe.com. Some public libraries also offer free access.

Laundry

Most hotels offer a laundry service and most hostels have washing machines. Self-service

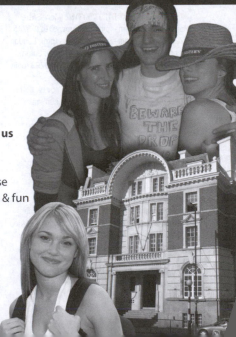

laundrettes exist all over London, although they are harder to find in the centre – there's one at 78 Marchmont St, WC1 (daily 6.30am–10.30pm; King's Cross tube). For a central dry cleaners, try Regent Dry Cleaners, 18 Embankment Place, WC2 ☏020/7839 6775 (Mon–Fri 8am–6.30pm; Embankment or Charing Cross tube).

Left luggage

Airports Gatwick: North Terminal ☏01293/502013 (daily 5am–9pm); South Terminal ☏01293/502014 (24hr). Heathrow ☏020/8759 3344: Terminal 1 (daily 6am–11pm); Terminal 2 (daily 5.30am–11pm); Terminal 3 (daily 6am–10pm); Terminal 4 & 5 (daily 5.30am–11pm). London City ☏020/7646 0000 (daily 6am–10pm). Luton ☏01582/405100 (24hr). Stansted ☏01279/663213 (4am–midnight).
Train stations Charing Cross ☏020/7930 5444 (daily 7am–11pm); Euston ☏020/7387 1499 (daily 7am–11pm); King's Cross ☏020/7837 4334 (daily 7am–11pm); Liverpool Street ☏020/7247 4297 (daily 7am–11pm); Paddington ☏020/7262 0344 (daily 7am–11pm); St Pancras ☏020/7833 1596 (Mon–Sat 6am–10pm, Sun 7am–10pm); Victoria ☏020/7963 0957 (daily 7am–midnight); Waterloo ☏020/7401 8444 (daily 7am–11pm).

Lost property

Airports Gatwick ☏01293/503162 (Mon–Sat 8am–7pm, Sun 8am–4pm); Heathrow ☏020/8745 7727 (Mon–Sat 8am–7pm, Sun 8am–4pm); London City ☏020/7646 0000 (daily 6am–10pm); Luton ☏01582/395219; Stansted ☏01279/663293 (daily 9.30am–4.30pm).
Buses ☏020/7222 1234, ⊛www.tfl.gov.uk (24hr).
Eurostar ☏0870/160 0052, ⊛www.eurostar .com.
Train stations ☏0870/000 5151, ⊛www .networkrail.co.uk: Euston ☏020/7387 8699 (Mon–Fri 9am–5.30pm); King's Cross ☏020/7278 3310 (Mon–Sat 9am–5pm); Liverpool Street ☏020/7247 4297 (Mon–Fri 9am–5.30pm); Paddington ☏020/7313 1514 (Mon–Fri 9am–5.30pm); St Pancras ☏020/7833 1596 (Mon–Sat 6am–10pm, Sun 7am–10pm); Victoria ☏020/7963 0957 (Mon–Fri 9am–5.15pm); Waterloo ☏020/7401 7861 (Mon–Fri 7.30am–7pm).
Transport for London Lost Property Office, 200 Baker St, NW1 ☏020/7918 2000, ⊛www.tfl.gov .uk (Mon–Fri 8.30am–4pm). Contact TfL about property lost on tubes or in black cabs. See map, p.97.

Mail

The postal service is pretty efficient. First-class **stamps** to anywhere in the UK currently cost 39p and should arrive the next day; second-class stamps cost 30p, taking three days; airmail to the rest of Europe costs 56p and should take three days; to the rest of the world stamps cost from 62p and should take five days. Stamps can be bought at post offices, and from newsagents and supermarkets, although they usually only sell books of four or ten first-class UK stamps.

For general postal enquiries phone ☏0845/774 0740 (Mon–Fri 8am–6pm, Sat 8am–1pm), or visit the website ⊛www .royalmail.com. Almost all London's **post offices** are open Monday to Friday 9am–5.30pm, Saturday 9am–noon. The exception is the Trafalgar Square Post Office (24/28 William IV St, WC2N 4DL; Mon–Fri 8.30am–6.30pm, Tues opens 9.15am, Sat 9am–5.30pm), to which **poste restante** mail should be sent. In the suburbs you'll find sub-post offices operating out of shops, but these are open the same hours as regular post offices, even if the shop itself is open for longer. To find out your nearest post office, contact ☏0845/722 3344, ⊛www .postoffice.co.uk (Mon–Fri 8.15am–6pm, Sat 8.30am–7pm).

Maps

The maps in this book should be adequate for sightseeing purposes. Alternatively, the Geographers' **A–Z map** series produces a whole range of street-by-street maps of London, from pocket-sized foldouts to giant atlases. Virtually every newsagent in London stocks them, but the best map shop in London is Stanford's, 12–14 Long Acre, WC2 (☏020/7836 1321, ⊛www.stanfords .co.uk). **Free maps** of the Underground and bus networks can be picked up at tourist offices and TfL information offices – see p.24. There's also the Rough Guide London Map, a comprehensive full-colour, waterproof and non-tearable map detailing restaurants, bars, shops and visitor attractions.

Media

The most useful listings magazine for visitors is **Time Out**, which comes out every Tuesday and has a virtual monopoly on listings. It carries critical appraisals of all the week's theatre, film, music, exhibitions, children's events and more. London's only proper daily **newspaper** is the reactionary *Evening Standard*. In addition, London is plagued by a rash of free newspapers, all similar in their inane tabloid content. Each of the London boroughs has a local paper, usually printed twice weekly and filled mostly with news of local crimes and cheap adverts. For a more whimsical look at London, look out for *Smoke*, an occasional mini-magazine of words and images inspired by the city.

Money

The currency in Britain is the **pound** sterling (£), divided into 100 pence (p). Coins come in denominations of 1p, 2p, 5p, 10p, 20p, 50p, £1 and £2. Notes come in denominations of £5, £10, £20 and £50. Many shopkeepers may not accept £50 notes – the best advice is to avoid having to use them. Very occasionally you may receive Scottish banknotes from £1 upwards: they're legal tender throughout Britain, but if you have any problems, go to the nearest bank and get them changed for English currency. At the time of writing, £1 was worth $1.50, €1.10, C$1.80, A$2 and NZ$2.60. For the most up-to-date exchange rates, contact the useful currency converter websites Ⓦwww.oanda.com or www.xe.com.

Credit/debit cards are by far the most convenient way to carry your money, and most hotels, shops and restaurants in London accept the major brand cards. There are ATMs all over the city and every area has a branch of at least one of the big-four high-street banks: NatWest, Barclays, Lloyds TSB and HSBC. The opening hours for most are Monday to Friday 9.30am–4.30pm, with some branches opening on Saturday mornings. Post offices charge no commission, and are therefore a good place to change money and cheques. Lost or stolen credit/debit cards should be reported to the police and the following numbers: Master-Card ⓉⒷ0800/964767, Visa ⓉⒷ0800/895082.

Opening hours and public holidays

Generally speaking, shop **opening hours** are Monday to Saturday 9am or 10am to 5.30pm or 6pm – with some places in central London staying open till 7pm, and later on Thursdays and Fridays (around 9pm) – and Sundays and Bank Holidays noon to 6pm. There are still plenty of stores that close completely on Sundays and Bank Holidays, and pretty much everything closes on Christmas Day. That said, numerous family-run corner shops stay open late every day of the year. The big supermarkets tend to open Monday to Saturday from 8am to 10pm, Sunday 10am or 11am to 4pm or 5pm. Note that many (gas/petrol) service stations in London are open 24 hours and have small shops.

Most **tourist attractions** and **museums** are typically open daily 10am to 6pm, occasionally with shorter hours on Sundays and public holidays (see box below). Most places are closed on December 25 and 26. Several museums now have late-night openings until 9pm or 10pm, typically one or two nights a week. Individual opening hours are given in the main text of this guide.

Phones

Public **payphones** are ubiquitous on the streets of London. Most take all coins from

Public holidays

You'll find all banks and offices closed on the following days, while everything else pretty much runs to a Sunday schedule (except on Christmas Day when everything shuts down): **New Year's Day** (January 1); **Good Friday** (late March/early April); **Easter Monday** (late March/early April); **Spring Bank Holiday** (first Monday in May); **May Bank Holiday** (last Monday in May); **August Bank Holiday** (last Monday in August); **Christmas Day** (December 25); **Boxing Day** (December 26). Note that if January 1, December 25 or December 26 falls on a Saturday or Sunday, the holiday falls on the following weekday.

UK operator services

Domestic operator ☎100
International operator ☎155

10p upwards, some take only phonecards and credit cards, and some take all three. Discount call cards with a PIN number are the cheapest way to make international calls.

If you're taking your **mobile/cellphone** with you, check with your service provider whether your phone will work abroad and what the call charges will be. Unless you have a tri- or quad-band phone, it's unlikely that a mobile bought for use in the US will work in London. Mobiles in Australia and New Zealand generally use the same system as the UK so should work fine.

London phone numbers are prefixed by the area code ☎020, separated from the subscriber number by a forward slash – this code can be omitted if dialling within London. However, some prefixes relate to the cost of calls rather than the location of the subscriber, and should never be omitted: numbers with ☎0800, 0808 and 0500 prefixes are free of charge (unless calling from a mobile); ☎0845 numbers are charged at local rates and ☎0870 up to the national rate, irrespective of where in the country you are calling from. Beware of premium-rate numbers which usually have the prefix ☎09, as these are charged at anything up to £1.50 a minute.

For **directory enquiries**, there are numerous companies offering the service, all with six-figure numbers beginning with ☎118. Whichever one you choose, the minimum charge you'll get away with is 40p. The best known is ☎118 118, but for a full rundown of numbers and prices, contact ☎0800/953 0720, ⊛www.118tracker.com. For an online UK phone directory, visit ⊛www.ukphonebook.com.

Tax

Most goods in Britain are subject to **Value Added Tax (VAT)**, which increases the cost of an item by 17.5 percent. Visitors from non-EU countries can save money through the **Retail Export Scheme** (tax-free shopping), which allows a VAT refund on goods taken out of the country. Note that not all shops participate in this scheme (those doing so will display a sign to this effect) and that you cannot reclaim VAT charged on hotel bills or other services. See ⊛www.hmrc.gov.uk for more details.

Time

Greenwich Mean Time (GMT) is used from the end of October to the end of March; for the rest of the year the country switches to **British Summer Time (BST)**, one hour ahead of GMT. GMT is five hours ahead of the US East Coast; eight ahead of the US West Coast; and nine behind Australia's East Coast.

Tipping

There are no fixed rules for **tipping**. However, there's a certain expectation in restaurants or cafés that you should leave a tip of ten percent of the total bill – check first, though, that service has not already been included. Taxi drivers also expect tips – add about ten percent to the fare – as do traditional barbers. The other occasion when you'll be expected to tip is in upmarket hotels where porters, bellboys and table waiters rely on being tipped to bump up their often dismal wages.

Tourist information

The chief **tourist office** in London is the Britain & London Visitor Centre, 1 Regent St, SW1 (April–Sept Mon 9.30am–6.30pm, Tues–Fri 9am–6.30pm, Sat 9am–5pm, Sun 10am–4pm; times vary slightly in winter and June–Sept; ⊛www.visitbritain.co.uk; Piccadilly Circus tube); there's also the London

Phoning home

To Australia ☎0061 + area code without the zero + number
To Ireland ☎00353 + area code without the zero + number
To New Zealand ☎0064 + area code without the zero + number
To South Africa ☎0027 + area code without the zero + number
To US and Canada ☎001 + area code + number

Information Centre, a tiny window in the tkts kiosk on Leicester Square, WC2 (daily 10am–6pm; ☎020/7292 2333, ⓦwww.londontown.com; Leicester Square tube).

Some **London boroughs** have tourist information offices, and every borough has its own tourism/leisure department, which can be consulted via the local council website. The most useful borough tourist offices are: Greenwich in the old Royal Naval College (daily 10am–5pm; ☎0870/608 2000); Richmond in the Old Town Hall on Whittaker Avenue (Mon–Sat 10am–5pm; May–Sept also Sun 10.30am–1.30pm; ☎020/8940 9125); and the City of London on the south side of St Paul's Cathedral (Mon–Sat 9.30am–5.30pm, Sun 10am–4pm; ☎020/7332 1456).

Tours and walks

Standard **sightseeing tours** are run by several rival bus companies, their open-top double-deckers setting off every thirty minutes from Victoria station, Trafalgar Square, Piccadilly and other conspicuous tourist spots. You can hop on and off several different routes as often as you like with The Original Tour (☎020/8877 1722, ⓦwww.theoriginaltour.com; daily 8.30am–6pm; every 15–20min; £24). Alternatively, you can climb aboard one of the bright-yellow World War II D-Day amphibious vehicles used by London Duck Tours (☎020/7928 3132, ⓦwww.londonducktours.co.uk), which offers a combined bus and boat tour (daily 9.30am–6pm or dusk; £20). After departing from behind County Hall, near the London Eye, you spend 45 minutes driving round the usual sights, before plunging into the river for a half-hour cruise; advance booking essential.

The cheapest option is to hop on a real **London double-decker** – the #11 bus from Victoria station, for example, will take you past Westminster Abbey, the Houses of Parliament, up Whitehall, round Trafalgar Square, along the Strand and on to St Paul's Cathedral. You can also take an old double-decker **Routemaster**, with open rear platform and roving conductor, on two "heritage" routes (daily every 15min 9.30am–6.30pm): #9 from the Royal Albert Hall to Aldwych and #15 from Trafalgar Square to Tower Hill.

Walking tours are infinitely more appealing and informative, mixing solid historical facts with juicy anecdotes in the company of a local specialist. Walks on offer range from a literary pub crawl round Bloomsbury to a roam around the East End. You'll find most of them detailed in *Time Out* magazine; as you'd imagine, there's more variety on offer in the summer months. Tours cost around £5 and take around two hours; normally you can simply show up at the starting point and join. If you want to plan – or book – walks in advance, contact the most reliable and well-established company, Original London Walks (☎020/7624 3978, ⓦwww.walks.com).

Websites

Aside from the aforementioned tourist authority and local borough websites, there's a vast quantity of useful London-related information online. Below are a handful of good general sites:

ⓦ**www.24hourmuseum.org.uk** Useful national website, with up-to-date information on virtually every single museum, large or small, in London.
ⓦ**www.derelictlondon.co.uk** Pictorial catalogue of the city's abandoned cinemas, pubs, theatres and even toilets, plus other forgotten derelict gems.
ⓦ**www.londonnet.co.uk** Virtual guide to London with useful up-to-date listings on eating, drinking and nightlife.
ⓦ**www.thegumtree.com** Very useful website aimed at expats living and working in London, or anyone who wants to buy or sell anything.
ⓦ**www.thisislocallondon.co.uk** Local news website with links to all the capital's local papers.

Working in London

All Swiss nationals and EEA citizens (except those from Bulgaria and Romania) can work in London without a permit, although citizens of Czech Republic, Estonia, Hungary, Latvia, Lithuania, Poland, Slovakia or Slovenia must register under the Worker Registration Scheme. Other nationals need a **work permit** in order to work legally in the UK, with eligibility worked out on a points-based system. There are exceptions to the above rules, although these are constantly changing, so for the latest regulations visit ⓦwww.ukvisas.gov.uk.

ABSOLUT ICEBAR LONDON

Made of crystal clear ice and maintained at a constant minus 5 degrees all year round, ABSOLUT ICEBAR is literally the UK's coolest bar.

Entrance tickets include a warm cape & gloves plus your first ABSOLUT vodka or fruit juice cocktail in your own glass made of pure Swedish ice.

Warm up afterwards with a delicious meal or cocktail in the contrasting warmth of belowzero restaurant + lounge on the lower ground floor.

Heddon Street, London W1B 4BN
⊖ Piccadilly Circus / Oxford Circus

For reservations call
020 7478 8910
www.absoluticebarlondon.com

belowzero
restaurant + lounge

The City

The City

1

Whitehall and Westminster

Political, religious and regal power has emanated from **Whitehall** and **Westminster** for almost a millennium. It was Edward the Confessor (1042–66) who first established Westminster as London's royal and ecclesiastical power base, some three miles west of the commercial City of London. The embryonic English parliament used to meet in the abbey and eventually took over the old royal palace of Westminster when Henry VIII moved out to Whitehall. Whitehall Palace burnt down in 1698 and was slowly replaced by government offices, so that by the nineteenth century Whitehall had become the "heart of the Empire", its ministries ruling over a quarter of the world's population. Even now, though the UK's world status has diminished and its royalty and clergy no longer wield much real power or receive the same respect, the institutions that run the country inhabit roughly the same geographical area: Westminster for the politicians, Whitehall for the ministers and civil servants.

Until the westward expansion of the City of London in the seventeenth century, Westminster was a more or less separate city. Today, the modern borough encompasses a much wider area than that covered in this chapter, including most of the West End and parts of the very wealthy districts of Mayfair and Belgravia, making its council one of the richest in the country. The monuments and buildings covered in this chapter include some of London's most famous landmarks – **Nelson's Column**, **Big Ben**, the **Houses of Parliament** and **Westminster Abbey**, plus two of the city's finest permanent art collections, the **National Gallery** and **Tate Britain**, and its finest architectural set piece, **Trafalgar Square**. This area is a well-trodden tourist circuit for the most part, though there are only a few shops or cafés and little commercial life (nearby Soho and Covent Garden are far better areas for this). It's also one of the easiest parts of London to walk round, with all the major sights within a mere half-mile of each other, and linked by one of London's most triumphant – and atypical – avenues, **Whitehall**.

Trafalgar Square

As one of the few large public squares in London, **Trafalgar Square** (Charing Cross tube) has been both a tourist attraction and the main focus for political demonstrations for over a century and a half. The first major demo was held in

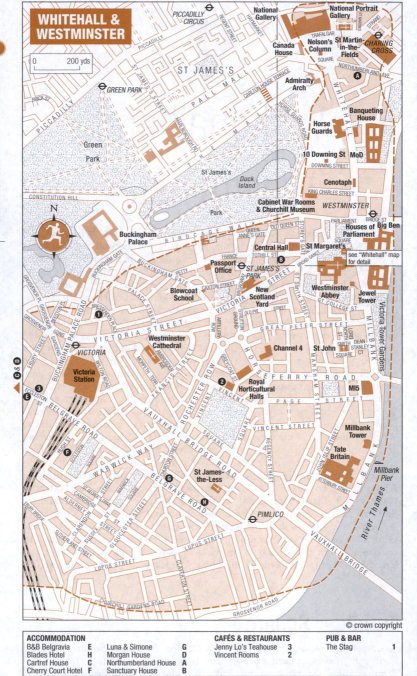

WHITEHALL & WESTMINSTER

0   200 yds

PICCADILLY CIRCUS

National Gallery

National Portrait Gallery

ST JAMES'S

PALL MALL

Green Park

Canada House

Nelson's Column

TRAFALGAR SQUARE

St Martin-in-the-Fields

CHARING CROSS

A

Admiralty Arch

Horse Guards

Banqueting House

St James's Park

Duck Island

Cabinet War Rooms & Churchill Museum

10 Downing St

MoD

Cenotaph

WESTMINSTER

CONSTITUTION HILL

N

Buckingham Palace

Houses of Parliament

Big Ben

see "Whitehall" map for detail

Central Hall

St Margaret's

Passport Office

St James's Park

Blewcoat School

New Scotland Yard

Westminster Abbey

Jewel Tower

Victoria Tower Gardens

VICTORIA

Westminster Cathedral

Channel 4

St John

MI5

Victoria Station

Royal Horticultural Halls

Millbank Tower

Tate Britain

St James-the-Less

Millbank Pier

PIMLICO

River Thames

VAUXHALL BRIDGE

C & D

E

F

G

H

1

2

3

B

A

© crown copyright

ACCOMMODATION

B&B Belgravia   **E**
Blades Hotel   **H**
Cartref House   **C**
Cherry Court Hotel   **F**

Luna & Simone   **G**
Morgan House   **D**
Northumberland House   **A**
Sanctuary House   **B**

CAFÉS & RESTAURANTS

Jenny Lo's Teahouse   **3**
Vincent Rooms   **2**

PUB & BAR

The Stag   **1**

www.roughguides.com

1848 when the Chartists assembled at the square to demand universal suffrage before marching to Kennington Common, and since then countless demos and rallies have been held. To keep an eye on the proceedings, a police phone box was built into one of the stone bollards in the southeast corner of the square, with a direct link to Scotland Yard.

Nowadays, most folk come here to see **Nelson's Column**, or to visit the **National Gallery**, though there are also various events, commemorations and celebrations staged here throughout the year. Each December, the square is graced with a giant Christmas tree covered in fairy lights, donated by Norway in thanks for Britain's support during World War II. Until recently, Trafalgar Square was also the city's traditional gathering point on **New Year's Eve**, though the focus has now shifted to the Thames, where a spectacular firework display is held each year.

The square

For centuries, Trafalgar Square was the site of the **King's Mews**, established in the thirteenth century by Edward I, who kept the royal hawks and the falconers here (the term "mews" comes from falconry: the birds were caged or "mewed up" there whilst changing their plumage). Chaucer was Clerk of the Mews for a time, and by Tudor times there were stables here, too. During the Civil War they were turned into Parliamentary barracks and later used as a prison for Cavaliers. In the 1760s, George III began to move the mews to Buckingham Palace, and by the late 1820s, **John Nash** had designed the new square (though he didn't live to see his plan executed). The Neoclassical National Gallery filled up the northern side in 1838, followed shortly afterwards by the central focal point, Nelson's Column. The famous bronze lions didn't arrive until 1868 and the fountains – built to deter the gathering of "urban mobs" – finally reached their present shape in the late 1930s. The development of the rest of the square was equally haphazard, though the overall effect is unified by the safe Neoclassical style of the buildings, and the square remains one of London's grandest architectural highlights.

Nelson's Column and the statues

Nelson's Column, raised in 1843 and now one of London's best-loved monuments, commemorates the one-armed, one-eyed admiral who defeated the French at the Battle of Trafalgar in 1805, but paid for it with his life. The sandstone statue which surmounts a 151-foot granite column is more than triple life-size but still manages to appear minuscule. The acanthus leaves of the capital are cast from British cannons, while bas-reliefs around the base – depicting three of Nelson's earlier victories as well as his death aboard HMS *Victory* – are from captured French armaments. Edwin Landseer's four gargantuan **bronze lions** guard the column and provide a climbing frame for kids (and demonstrators).

Keeping Nelson company at ground level, on either side of the column, are bronze **statues** of Napier and Havelock, Victorian major-generals who helped keep India British; against the north wall are busts of Beatty, Jellicoe and Cunningham, military leaders from the last century. To the right of them are the imperial standards of length – inch, foot and yard – "accurate at 62 degrees Fahrenheit", as the plaque says, and still in common usage by millions of Brits despite the efforts of the European Union. Above this is an equestrian statue of George IV (bareback, stirrup-less and in Roman garb), which he himself commissioned for the top of Marble Arch, but which was later erected here "temporarily". The **fourth plinth**, in the northwest corner, was originally earmarked for an equestrian statue of William IV. In the end, it remained empty until 1999, since when it has been used to display specially commissioned works of modern sculpture (Ⓦwww.london.gov.uk/fourthplinth).

Predating the entire square is the **equestrian statue of Charles I**, stranded on a traffic island to the south of the column. Completed in 1633 it was originally intended for a site in Roehampton, only to be sold off during the Commonwealth to a local brazier, John Rivett, with strict instructions to melt it down. Rivett made a small fortune selling bronze mementoes, allegedly from the metal, while all the time concealing the statue in the vaults of St Paul's, Covent Garden. After the Restoration, the statue was erected on the very spot where eight of those who had signed the king's death warrant were disembowelled in 1660, and within sight of the Banqueting House in Whitehall where Charles himself was beheaded. All distances from the capital are measured from this spot.

South Africa House and Canada House

There's an unmistakable whiff of empire about Trafalgar Square, with **South Africa House** (Ⓦwww.southafricahouse.com), erected in 1935 on the east side, complete with keystones featuring African animals, and **Canada House** (Mon–Fri 10am–6pm; free), constructed in warm Bath stone, opposite. Canada House was originally built in the 1820s, as a gentlemen's club and home for the Royal College of Physicians, by Robert Smirke – who also designed the British Museum – and, despite alterations over the years, it retains much of its original Neoclassical interior. You can see the ornate entrance lobby to the south of the building, browse through the Canadian press and then take in the excellent temporary exhibitions. Canadians can also send and receive emails from back home.

St Martin-in-the-Fields

At the northeastern corner of Trafalgar Square stands the church of **St Martin-in-the-Fields** (Mon–Wed 10am–7pm, Thurs–Sat 10am–10pm, Sun noon–7pm; free; Ⓣ020/7766 1100, Ⓦwww.stmartin-in-the-fields.org; Charing Cross tube), fronted by a magnificent Corinthian portico and topped by an elaborate tower and steeple – designed in 1721 by James Gibbs, it was subsequently copied widely in the American colonies. The barrel-vaulted interior features ornate, sparkling white Italian plasterwork and is best appreciated while listening to one of the church's **free lunchtime concerts** (Mon, Tues & Fri) or ticketed, candle-lit evening performances. As the official parish church for Buckingham Palace, St Martin's maintains strong royal and naval connections – there's a royal box on the left of the high altar, and one for the admiralty on the right. Down in the newly expanded **crypt** – accessible via an entrance north of the church – there's a licensed **café** (see p.378), shop, gallery and **brass-rubbing centre**.

National Gallery

Taking up the entire north side of Trafalgar Square, the sprawling Neoclassical hulk of the **National Gallery** (daily 10am–6pm, Wed till 9pm; free; Ⓣ020/7747 2885, Ⓦwww.nationalgallery.org.uk; Charing Cross tube) houses one of the world's greatest art collections. Unlike the Louvre or the Hermitage, the National Gallery is not based on a former royal collection, but was begun as late as 1824 when the government reluctantly agreed to purchase 38 paintings belonging to a Russian émigré banker, John Julius Angerstein.

Visiting the gallery

There are **four entrances** to the National Gallery: Wilkins' original Portico Entrance on Trafalgar Square, the Getty Entrance to the east, the Sainsbury Wing to the west, and the back entrance on Orange Street. The Getty Entrance and the Sainsbury Wing both have an **information desk**, which hands out free plans, and disabled access, with lifts to all floors. **Audioguides** are available for a "voluntary contribution" – much better, though, are the gallery's free **guided tours**, which set off from the Sainsbury Wing foyer (daily 11.30am & 2.30pm; 1hr). To the right of the Getty Entrance is the gallery's self-service *Espresso Bar*, beyond which lies the pricier *National Café* (which keeps longer hours). Pricier still are the *National Dining Rooms*, serving excellent British cuisine over in the Sainsbury Wing (☏020/7747 2525 for all three).

With more than a thousand paintings on permanent display in the main galleries, you can't possibly see everything in one day. You're also likely to discover rooms being rehung or paintings that have been removed: if you can't find a particular painting, ask the gallery staff. **Temporary exhibitions** are held in the basement of the Sainsbury Wing, or sometimes in the main galleries themselves, and often charge an admission fee. The gallery puts on lectures, films and talks, plus a programme of **live music** which takes place on Wednesday evenings.

Subsequently, the gallery's years of canny acquisition have produced a collection of more than 2300 paintings, but the collected works' virtue is not so much its size as the range, depth and sheer quality of its contents. As well as **Italian masterpieces** by the likes of Botticelli and Michelangelo, there are dazzling pieces by Velázquez and Goya, and an array of **Rembrandt** paintings that features some of his most searching portraits. In addition, the gallery has a particularly strong showing of **Impressionists**, with paintings by Monet, Van Gogh and Cézanne, plus several early Picassos. There are also showpieces of British art by Turner, Reynolds and Gainsborough, but for a wider range of British art – and many more Turners – you'll need to move on to Tate Britain (see p.71).

The collection was originally put on public display at Angerstein's old residence, on Pall Mall, until today's purpose-built edifice on Trafalgar Square was completed in 1838. A hostile press dubbed the gallery's diminutive dome and cupolas "pepperpots", and poured abuse on the Greek Revival architect, William Wilkins, who retreated into early retirement, and died a year later. A similar barrage of abuse broke out in the mid-1980s over plans for the new **Sainsbury Wing**. The winning design was dubbed by Prince Charles "a monstrous carbuncle on the face of a much-loved and elegant friend". So instead, the American husband-and-wife team of Venturi and Scott-Brown were commissioned to produce a softly-softly, postmodern adjunct, which playfully imitates elements of Wilkins' Neoclassicism and even Nelson's Column and, most importantly, got the approval of Prince Charles, who laid the foundation stone in 1988.

The Sainsbury Wing

Chronologically the gallery's collection begins in the **Sainsbury Wing**, which houses the National's oldest paintings dating from 1250 to 1500, mostly early Italian Renaissance masterpieces, with a smattering of early Dutch, Flemish and German works.

Giotto to Van Eyck

The gallery's earliest works are displayed in room 52, and include a depiction of the Pentecost attributed to **Giotto**, considered, even by his contemporaries, to

▲ National Gallery

be "the father of modern painting". There are also several panels by **Duccio**, a Sienese contemporary of Giotto, belonging to a monumental altarpiece that was carried in triumph from the artist's studio to the cathedral in 1311 with virtually the whole of Siena looking on. Room 53, meanwhile, features the extraordinarily vivid **Wilton Diptych**, one of the few English late medieval altarpieces to survive the Puritan iconoclasm of the Commonwealth. It was painted by an unknown fourteenth-century artist for the boy king Richard II, who is depicted being presented by his patron saints to the Virgin, Child and assorted angels.

Whatever you do, don't miss **Paolo Uccello**'s brilliant, blood-free *Battle of San Romano*, which dominates room 55. The painting commemorates a recent Florentine victory over her bitter Sienese rivals and once decorated a Medici bedroom as part of a three-panel frieze. Another Medici commission is *The Annunciation* by **Fra Filippo Lippi**, a beautifully balanced painting in which the poses of Gabriel and Mary carefully mirror one another, while the hand of God releasing the dove of the Holy Spirit provides the vanishing point.

Room 56 explores the beginnings of oil painting, which did away with the painstaking overpainting of egg-based tempera and allowed the artist to blend infinite gradations of pigment in the palette. The master of early oil painting was **Jan van Eyck**, whose intriguing *Arnolfini Portrait* is celebrated for its complex symbolism. The picture has often been interpreted as a depiction of a marriage ceremony, though the theory is now strongly criticized, and the "bride" is thought simply to be fashionably round-bellied, rather than actually pregnant.

Botticelli to Piero della Francesca

Several paintings by **Botticelli** hang in room 57, including two of the Nativity: the *Mystic Nativity* is unusual in that it features seven devils fleeing back into the Underworld, while in his *Adoration of the Kings*, Botticelli himself takes centre stage, as the best-dressed man at the gathering, resplendent in bright-red stockings and giving the audience a knowing look. Next door, in room 58, is his much-loved *Venus and Mars*, depicting a naked and replete Mars in deep postcoital sleep, watched over by a beautifully calm Venus, fully clothed and somewhat less overcome.

Further on, in room 62 hangs one of **Mantegna**'s best early works, *The Agony in the Garden*, which demonstrates a convincing use of perspective. Close by, the dazzling dawn sky in the painting on the same theme by his brother-in-law, **Giovanni Bellini**, shows the artist's celebrated mastery of natural light. Also in this room is one of Bellini's greatest portraits of the Venetian Doge *Leonardo Loredan*. Elsewhere, there are paintings from Netherlands and Germany, among them **Dürer**'s sympathetic portrait of his father (a goldsmith in Nuremberg), in room 65, which was presented to Charles I in 1636 by the artist's home town.

Finally, at the far end of the wing, in room 66, your eye will probably be drawn to **Piero della Francesca**'s monumental *Baptism of Christ*, one of his earliest surviving pictures, dating from the 1450s and a brilliant example of his immaculate compositional technique. Blindness forced Piero to stop painting some twenty years before his death, and to concentrate instead on his equally innovative work as a mathematician.

The main building

The collection continues in the gallery's **main building** with paintings from 1500 up to 1900. The account below follows the collection chronologically.

Veronese, Titian and Giorgione

The first room you come to from the Sainsbury Wing is the vast Wohl Room (room 9), containing mainly large-scale Venetian works. The largest of the lot is **Paolo Veronese**'s lustrous *Family of Darius before Alexander*, its array of colour-fully clad figures revealing the painter's remarkable skill in juxtaposing virtually the entire colour spectrum in a single canvas. Here, too, are all four of Veronese's slightly discoloured *Allegories of Love* canvases, designed as ceiling paintings, perhaps for a bedchamber.

More Venetian works hang in room 10, including **Titian**'s consummate *La Schiavona*, a precisely executed portrait within a portrait. His colourful early masterpiece *Bacchus and Ariadne*, and his much gloomier *Death of Actaeon*, painted some fifty years later, amply demonstrate the painter's artistic development and longevity. *The Virgin and Child* is another typical late Titian, with the paint jabbed on and rubbed in. Also here are two perplexing paintings attributed to the elusive **Giorgione**, a highly original Venetian painter, only twenty of whose paintings survive.

Bronzino, Michelangelo, Raphael and da Vinci

In room 8, **Bronzino**'s strangely disturbing *Venus, Cupid, Folly and Time* is a classic piece of Mannerist eroticism, once owned by François I, the decadent, womanizing, sixteenth-century French king. (Incidentally, Cupid's foot features in the opening animated titles of *Monty Python's Flying Circus*.) Here too is **Michelangelo**'s early, unfinished *Entombment*, which depicts Christ's body being carried to the tomb, and the National's major paintings by **Raphael**. These range from early works such as *St Catherine of Alexandria*, whose sensuous "serpentine" pose is accentuated by the folds of her clothes, and the richly coloured *Mond Crucifixion*, painted when the artist was a mere 21 years old, to later works like *Pope Julius II* – his (and Michelangelo's) patron – a masterfully percipient portrait of old age.

Boris Anrep's floor mosaics

One of the most overlooked features of the National Gallery is the mind-boggling **floor mosaics** executed by Russian-born Boris Anrep between 1927 and 1952 on the landings of the main staircase leading to the Central Hall (and now in need of some restoration). The *Awakening of the Muses*, on the halfway landing, features a bizarre collection of famous figures from the 1930s – Virginia Woolf appears as Clio (Muse of History) and Greta Garbo plays Melpomene (Muse of Tragedy). The mosaic on the landing closest to the Central Hall is made up of fifteen small scenes illustrating the *Modern Virtues*: Anna Akhmatova is saved by an angel from the Leningrad Blockade in *Compassion*; T.S. Eliot contemplates the Loch Ness Monster and Einstein's Theory of Relativity in *Leisure*; Bertrand Russell gazes on a naked woman in *Lucidity*; Edith Sitwell, book in hand, glides across a monster-infested chasm on a twig in *Sixth Sense*; and in the largest composition, *Defiance*, Churchill appears in combat gear on the white cliffs of Dover, raising two fingers to a monster in the shape of a swastika.

To continue with the Italians, skip through the next couple of rooms to room 2, which boasts **Leonardo da Vinci**'s melancholic *Virgin of the Rocks* (the more famous "*Da Vinci Code*" version hangs in the Louvre) and the "Leonardo Cartoon" – a preparatory drawing for a painting which, like so many of Leonardo's projects, was never completed. The cartoon was known only to scholars until the gallery bought it for £800,000 in the mid-1960s. In 1987, it gained further notoriety when an ex-soldier blasted the work with a sawn-off shotgun in protest at the political status quo.

Holbein, Cranach, Bosch and Bruegel

Room 4 contains several masterpieces by **Hans Holbein**, most notably his extraordinarily detailed double portrait, *The Ambassadors*. The French duo flank an open cabinet piled high with various objects: instruments for studying the heavenly realm on the upper shelf, those for contemplating the earthly life on the lower – note the anamorphic skull in the foreground. Among the other works by Holbein is his intriguing *A Lady with a Squirrel and a Starling*, and his striking portrait of the 16-year-old Christina of Denmark, part of a series commissioned by Henry VIII when he was looking for a potential fourth wife. Look out, too, for Holbein's contemporary, **Lucas Cranach the Elder**, whose *Cupid Complaining to Venus* is a none-too-subtle message about dangerous romantic liaisons – Venus's wonderfully fashionable headgear only emphasizes her nakedness.

Next door, in room 5, hangs the National's one and only work by **Hieronymus Bosch**, *Christ Mocked*, in which four manic tormentors (one wearing an Islamic crescent moon and a Jewish star) bear down on Jesus. Over in room 14, you'll also find the gallery's only **Bruegel**, the tiny *Adoration of the Magi*, with some very motley-looking folk crowding in on the infant; only the Black Magus looks at all regal.

Claude, Poussin and Dutch landscapes

Claude Lorrain's *Enchanted Castle*, in room 20, caught the imagination of the Romantics, supposedly inspiring Keats' *Ode to a Nightingale*, while the English painter **J.M.W. Turner** left specific instructions in his will for two of his Claude-influenced paintings to be hung alongside a couple of the French painter's landscapes. All four now hang in the octagonal room 15, and were slashed by a homeless teenager in 1982 in an attempt to draw attention to his plight. Claude's dreamy classical landscapes and seascapes, and the mythological scenes of **Poussin**, were favourites of aristocrats on the Grand Tour, and made both artists very famous in their time. Nowadays, though Poussin has a strong academic following, his works strike many people as empty and dull. Hardly surprising, then, that rooms 19 and 20, which are given over entirely to these two French artists, are among the quietest in the gallery.

Of the Dutch landscapes in rooms 21 and 22, those by **Aelbert Cuyp**'s stand out due to the warm Italianate light which suffuses his works, but the finest of all is, without a doubt, **Hobbema**'s tree-lined *Avenue, Middelharnis*. The market for such landscapes at the time was limited, however, and Hobbema quit painting at the age of just 30. **Jacob van Ruisdael**, Hobbema's teacher, whose works are on display nearby, also went hungry for most of his life.

Rembrandt, Vermeer and Rubens

Rooms 23 and 24 feature mostly works by **Rembrandt**, including the highly theatrical *Belshazzar's Feast*, painted for a rich Jewish patron. Look out also for two of Rembrandt's searching self-portraits, painted thirty years apart, with the melancholic *Self Portrait Aged 63*, from the last year of his life, making a strong contrast to the sprightly early work. Similarly, the joyful portrait of Saskia, Rembrandt's wife, from the most successful period of his life, contrasts with his more contemplative depiction of his mistress, Hendrickje, who was hauled up in front of the city authorities for living "like a whore" with Rembrandt. The portraits of Jacob Trip and his wife, Margaretha de Geer, are among the most painfully realistic depictions of old age in the entire gallery.

Room 25 harbours **de Hooch**'s classic *A Woman and her Maid in a Courtyard*, and a self-portrait by Carel Fabritius, one of Rembrandt's pupils. Fabritius died in the explosion of the Delft gunpowder store, the subject of another painting in the room. Also here is the seventeenth-century **van Hoogstraten Peepshow**, a box of tricks which reflects the Dutch obsession of the time with perspectival and optical devices. Two typically serene works by **Vermeer** hang nearby and provide a counterpoint to one another: each features a *Young Woman at a Virginal*, but where she stands in one, she sits in the other; she's viewed from the right and then the left, in shadow and then in light and so on.

Three adjoining rooms, known collectively as room 29, are dominated by the expansive, fleshy canvases of **Peter Paul Rubens**, the Flemish painter whom Charles I summoned to the English court. The one woman with her clothes on is the artist's future sister-in-law, Susanna Fourment, whose delightful portrait became known as *Le Chapeau de Paille* (*The Straw Hat*) – though the hat is actually made of black felt and decorated with white feathers. At the age of 54, Rubens married Susanna's younger sister, Helena (she was just 16), the model for all three goddesses posing in the later version of *The Judgement of Paris*. Also displayed here are Rubens' rather more subdued landscapes, one of which, the *View of Het Steen*, shows off the very fine prospect from the Flemish country mansion Rubens bought in 1635, earning himself the title Lord of Steen.

Velázquez, El Greco, Van Dyck and Caravaggio

The cream of the National Gallery's Spanish works are displayed in room 30, among them **Velázquez**'s *Rokeby Venus*, one of the gallery's most famous pictures. Velázquez is thought to have painted just four nudes in his lifetime, of which only the *Rokeby Venus* survives, an ambiguously narcissistic image that was slashed in 1914 by suffragette Mary Richardson, who loved the picture but was revolted by the way "men gaped at it all day". Slightly lost in this vast room is the masterpiece *Christ Driving Traders from the Temple*, by the Cretan painter **El Greco**. Its acidic colouring and angular composition are typical of his highly individual work.

Another Flemish painter summoned by Charles I was **Anthony van Dyck**, whose *Equestrian Portrait of Charles I*, in room 31, is a fine example of the work that made him a favourite of the Stuart court, romanticizing the monarch as a dashing horseman. Adjacent is the artist's double portrait of *Lord John and Lord Bernard Stuart*, two dapper young cavaliers about to set out on their Grand Tour in 1639, and destined to die fighting for the royalist cause shortly afterwards in the Civil War.

Caravaggio's art is represented in the vast room 32 by the typically salacious *Boy Bitten by Lizard*, and the melodramatic *Christ at Emmaus*. The latter was a highly influential painting: never before had biblical scenes been depicted with such naturalism – a beardless and haloless Christ surrounded by scruffy disciples. At the time it was deemed to be blasphemous, and, like many of Caravaggio's religious commissions, was eventually rejected by the customers. One of the most striking paintings in this room is Giordano's *Perseus turning Phineas and his Followers to Stone*, in which the hero is dramatically depicted in sapphire blue, with half the throng already petrified.

Turner to Tiepolo

Eighteenth-century French art by the likes of Fragonard, Boucher and Watteau is gathered together in room 33. There's a portrait of Louis XV's mistress in the year of her death and also a spirited self-portrait by the equally well-turned-out Elisabeth Louise **Vigée-Lebrun**, one of only three women artists in the whole National Gallery collection.

When the Tate Gallery opened in 1897, the vast bulk of the National's British art was transferred there, leaving just a few highly prized works behind. Among these are several superb late masterpieces by **Turner**, two of which herald the new age of steam: *Rain, Steam and Speed* and *The Fighting Téméraire*, in which a ghostly apparition of the veteran battleship from Trafalgar is pulled into harbour by a youthful, fire-snorting tug, a scene witnessed first-hand by the artist in Rotherhithe. Here, too, is **Constable**'s *Hay Wain*, probably the most famous British painting of all time, though it was just one of a series of landscapes that he painted in and around his father's mill in Suffolk, such as the irrepressibly popular *Cornfield*. There are landscapes, as well as the portraits, by **Thomas Gainsborough** – the actress Sarah Siddons is one of his finest "grand ladies", and his feathery, light technique is seen to superb effect in *Morning Walk*, a double portrait of a pair of newlyweds. **Joshua Reynolds**' contribution is a portrait, *Lady Cockburn and her Three Sons*, in which the three boys clamber endearingly over their mother.

More works by Gainsborough and Reynolds hang in room 35, including the only known self-portrait of the former with his family, painted in 1747 when he was just 20 years old. On the opposite wall are the six paintings from **Hogarth**'s *Marriage à la Mode*, a witty, moral tale that allowed the artist to give vent to his pet hates: bourgeois hypocrisy, snobbery and bad (ie Continental) taste. In the ornate, domed Central Hall (room 36) hangs Reynolds' dramatic portrait of the extraordinarily effeminate Colonel Tarleton.

Room 38 features **Canaletto**'s *Stonemason's Yard*, an unusual portrayal of everyday Venetian life compared to his usual glittery vistas of Venice (of which there are also several examples). In room 39, **Guardi**'s postcard snaps of Venice hang rather awkwardly alongside **Goya**'s gloomy portrait of the Duke of Wellington. Close by, in room 40, are examples of the airy draughtsmanship of **Tiepolo**, father and son, seen to best effect in the *Allegory with Venus and Time*, commissioned for the ceiling of a Venetian *palazzo*.

From Ingres to Picasso

Among the gallery's busiest section are the six magnificent rooms (41–46) of late nineteenth- and early twentieth-century paintings; rehangings are frequent, so it's difficult to say exactly which works will be displayed and where. In room 41, the most popular painting is **Paul Delaroche**'s slick and pretentious *Execution of Lady Jane Grey*, in which the blindfolded, white-robed, 17-year-old queen stoically awaits her fate. Nearby, don't miss **Gustave Courbet**'s languorous *Young Ladies on the Bank of the Seine*, innocent enough to the modern eye, scandalous when it was first shown in 1857 due to the ladies' "state of undress".

The National boasts several key works by **Manet**, including his famous *Music in the Tuileries Gardens*, and the unfinished *Execution of Maximilian*, one of three versions he painted – this one was cut into pieces during the artist's lifetime, then bought and reassembled by Degas after Manet's death. There are also canvases from every period of Monet's long life: from early works like *The Thames below Westminster* and *Gare St Lazare* to the late, almost abstract paintings executed in his beloved garden at Giverny.

Other major Impressionist works usually on display here include **Renoir**'s *Umbrellas*, **Seurat**'s classic pointillist canvas, *Bathers at Asnières* – one of the National's most reproduced paintings – and **Pissarro**'s *Boulevard Montmartre at Night*. There are also several townscapes from Pissarro's period of exile, when he lived in south London, during the Franco-Prussian War. There's a comprehensive showing of **Cézanne** with works spanning the great artist's long life. *The Painter's Father* is one of his earliest extant works, and was originally painted onto the walls of his father's house outside Aix. *The Bathers*, by contrast, is a very late work, whose angular geometry exercised an enormous influence on the Cubism of Picasso and Braque.

Van Gogh is represented by one of his famous, dazzling *Sunflowers* series, the beguiling *Van Gogh's Chair*, dating from his stay in Arles with Gauguin, and *Wheatfield with Cypresses*, which typifies the intense work he produced inside the asylum to which he was committed shortly before his suicide. Finally, look out for **Picasso**'s sentimental Blue Period *Child with a Dove*; Rousseau's imagined junglescape, *Surprised!*; Vuillard's *Young Girls Walking*, with its deliberately flat, decorative surfaces; and a trio of superb **Degas** canvases: *Miss La-La at the Cirque Fernando*, the languorous pastel drawing *After the Bath* and the luxuriant red-orange *La Coiffure*.

National Portrait Gallery

Around the east side of the National Gallery lurks the **National Portrait Gallery** (daily 10am–6pm, Thurs & Fri till 9pm; free; ☎020/7312 2463, Ⓦwww.npg.org.uk; Charing Cross tube), founded in 1856 to house uplifting depictions of the good and the great. Though it undoubtedly has some fine works among its collection of over 330,000 portraits, many of the studies are of less interest than their subjects. Nevertheless, it's interesting to trace who has been deemed worthy of admiration at any one time: aristocrats and artists in previous centuries, warmongers and imperialists in the early decades of the twentieth century, writers and poets in the 1930s and 1940s. The most popular part of the museum by far is the contemporary section, where the whole thing degenerates into a sort of thinking person's Madame Tussaud's, with photos and some very dubious portraits of today's celebrities.

The Tudors and Stuarts

To follow the collection chronologically, take the escalator to the **Tudor Galleries**, on the second floor. Here, you'll find Tudor portraits of pre-Tudor kings, a stout **Cardinal Wolsey** looking like the butcher's son he was and Holbein's larger-than-life cartoon of **Henry VIII**, showing the king as a macho buck against a modish Renaissance background. The most eye-catching canvas is the anamorphic portrait of his sickly young son and heir **Edward VI** in room 2, an illusionistic painting that must be viewed from the side. Nearby hangs the intriguing *Edward VI and the Pope*, in which the boy king is depicted casting down the pontiff and burning religious images. By contrast, the future **Bloody Mary** looks positively benign in a portrait celebrating her reinstatement to the line of succession in 1544.

Also in room 2 are several classic propaganda portraits of the formidable Elizabeth I and her various favourites. Further on hangs the only known painting of **Shakespeare** from life, a subdued image in which the Bard sports a gold-hoop earring; appropriately enough, it was the first picture acquired by the gallery. To keep to the chronology, you must turn left here into room 5, where the quality of portraiture goes up a notch thanks to the appointment of Van Dyck as court painter. Among the dressed-to-kill Royalists, **Oliver Cromwell** looks dishevelled but masterful, while an overdressed, haggard **Charles II** hangs in room 7 alongside his long-suffering Portuguese wife and several of his mistresses, including the orange-seller-turned-actress **Nell Gwynne**.

The Georgian period

The eighteenth century begins in room 9, with members of the **Kit-Kat Club**, a group of Whig patriots – including Robert Walpole – who met in a pub run by one Christopher Catling. The club was painted by one of its members, Godfrey Kneller, a naturalized German artist, whose self-portrait can be found in room 10. Next door, room 11 contains a hotchpotch of visionaries including a tartan-free **Bonnie Prince Charlie** and his saviour, the petite Flora MacDonald. Among the various artists, writers and musicians in room 12 are several fine self-portraits, including a dashing one of the Scot Allan Ramsay, and one by a very young Joshua Reynolds looking ahead to a bright future. Room 14 is dominated by a canvas depicting the dramatic death of **Pitt the Elder**, who collapsed in the

House of Lords having struggled in to plead for a tolerant attitude to the rebellious American colonies.

In room 17, you'll find a bold likeness of **Lord Nelson**, along with one of the many idealized portraits painted by the smitten George Romney of Nelson's mistress, **Lady Emma Hamilton**. Also here is a portrait of **George IV** and the twice-widowed Catholic woman, Maria Fitzherbert, whom he married without the consent of his father. His official wife, **Queen Caroline**, is depicted at the adultery trial in the House of Lords at which she was acquitted. Close by, Caroline is depicted again, with sleeves rolled up ready for her sculpture lessons, in an audacious portrait by Thomas Lawrence, who was called to testify on his conduct with the queen during the painting of the portrait.

The Romantics dominate room 18, with the ailing **John Keats** painted posthumously by Joseph Severn, in whose arms he died in Rome. Elsewhere, there's **Lord Byron** in Albanian garb, an open-collared **Percy Bysshe Shelley**, with his wife, Mary, nearby, and her mother, **Mary Wollstonecraft**, opposite.

The Victorians

Down on the first floor, the **Victorians** feature rather too many stuffy royals, dour men of science and engineering, and stern statesmen such as those lining the corridor of room 22. Centre stage, in room 21, is a comical statue of **Victoria and Albert** in Anglo-Saxon garb. The best place to head for is room 24, which contains a deteriorated portrait of the **Brontë sisters** as seen by their disturbed brother Branwell; you can still see where he painted himself out, leaving a ghostly blur between Charlotte and Emily. Nearby are the poetic duo, **Robert** and **Elizabeth Barrett Browning**, looking totally Gothic in their grim Victorian dress.

In room 26 is G.F. Watts' sensuous portrait of the 17-year-old actress **Ellen Terry**, whom he married the same year, though she was thirty years his junior – they separated after only a year. Meanwhile, over in room 28, it's impossible to miss the striking Edwardian portrait of **Lady Colin Campbell**, posing in a luxuriant black silk dress. Finally, in room 29, where there are some excellent **John Singer Sargent** portraits, and several works by students of the Slade: **Augustus John**, looking very confident and dapper at the age of just 22, his sister, **Gwen John**, **Walter Sickert** and **Philip Wilson Steer**, who founded the New English Arts Club, at which the last two portraits were originally exhibited.

The twentieth century and beyond

The **twentieth-century** collection begins in room 30, with Sargent's parade of World War I generals. The interwar years are then generously covered in room 31. The faces on display here are frequently rotated, but look out for Sickert's excellent small, smouldering portrait of **Churchill**, Augustus John's portrayal of a ruby-lipped Dylan Thomas and a whole host of works by, or depicting, the **Bloomsbury Group**.

Out on the Balcony Gallery, there's a who's who (or was who) of **Britain 1960–90**. Even here, amid the photos of the Swinging Sixties, there are usually a few genuine works of art by the likes of Leon Kossoff, R.B. Kitaj, Lucien Freud and Francis Bacon. The **Contemporary Galleries** occupy the ground floor, and are an unashamedly populist trot through the media personalities of the last two decades. As well as a host of photo portraits, you can sample such delights as Sam Taylor-Wood's video of David Beckham sleeping or Michael Craig Martin's LCD portrait of architect Zaha Hadid.

TRAFALGAR SQUARE & WHITEHALL

CAFÉS & RESTAURANTS		PUBS & BARS	
Café in the Crypt	2	The Chandos	1
Halfway 2 Heaven	4	Red Lion	5
National Dining Rooms	3	St Stephen's Tavern	6

Whitehall

Whitehall, the unusually broad avenue connecting Trafalgar Square to Parliament Square, is synonymous with the faceless, pinstriped bureaucracy charged with the day-to-day running of the country. Yet during the sixteenth and seventeenth centuries, it was, in fact, the chief London residence of the kings and queens of England. **Whitehall Palace** started out as the London seat of the Archbishop of York, but was confiscated and enlarged by Henry VIII after a fire at Westminster Palace forced the king to find alternative accommodation; it was here that he celebrated his marriage to Anne Boleyn in 1533, and here that he died fourteen years later. Described by one contemporary chronicler as nothing but "a heap of houses erected at diverse times and of different models, made continuous", it boasted some two thousand rooms and stretched for half a mile along the Thames. Not much survived the fire of 1698, and subsequently, the royal residence shifted to St James's and Kensington.

Since then nearly all the key governmental ministries and offices have migrated here, rehousing themselves on an ever-increasing scale. The **Foreign & Commonwealth Office**, for example, occupies a palatial Italianate building, built by George Gilbert Scott in 1868, and is well worth a visit if you can gain access (☎020/7008 1500). The process reached its apogee with the grimly bland **Ministry of Defence (MoD)** building, completed in 1957. Underneath the MoD is Britain's most expensive military bunker, Pindar, which cost over £125 million.

Banqueting House

The only sections of Whitehall Palace to survive the 1698 fire were Cardinal Wolsey's wine cellars (now beneath the Ministry of Defence) and Inigo Jones's **Banqueting House** (Mon–Sat 10am–5pm; £4.50; ☎020/3166 6154, ⓦhrp .org.uk; Charing Cross tube), the first Palladian building to be built in central London. Opened in 1622 with a performance of Ben Jonson's *Masque of Angers*, Banqueting House is still used for state occasions (and, as a result, may be closed at short notice). The one room open to the public is well worth seeing for the superlative ceiling paintings, commissioned by Charles I from **Rubens** and installed in 1635. A glorification of the divine right of kings, the panels depict the union of England and Scotland, the peaceful reign of James I and, finally, his apotheosis. To appreciate the paintings fully, it's worth getting hold of one of the free audioguides.

In 1649, **Charles I** walked through the Banqueting House for the last time and stepped onto the executioner's scaffold from one of its windows. He wore several shirts in case he shivered in the cold, which the crowd would take to be fear; once his head was chopped off, it was then sewn back on again for burial in Windsor – a very British touch. From the Restoration until 1859, "King Charles the Martyr" Holy Day (Jan 30) was a day of fasting, and his execution is still commemorated here on the last Sunday in January with a parade by the royalist wing of the Civil War Society.

Oliver Cromwell moved into Whitehall Palace in 1654, having declared himself Lord Protector, and kept open table in the Banqueting House for the officers of his New Model Army; he died here in 1658. Two years later **Charles II** celebrated the Restoration here, and kept open house for his adoring public – Samuel Pepys recalls seeing the underwear of one of his mistresses, Lady Castlemaine, hanging out to dry in the palace's Privy Garden. (Charles housed two mistresses and his wife here, with a back entrance onto the river for courtesans.)

Horse Guards and Household Cavalry Museum

Across the road, two mounted sentries of the Queen's Household Cavalry and two horseless colleagues are posted (daily 10am–4pm) to protect **Horse Guards**, a modest building begun in 1745 by William Kent, and originally the main gateway to St James's and Buckingham Palace. The black dot over the number two on the building's clock face denotes the hour at which Charles I was executed. The **Changing of the Guard** (see box, p.57) takes place behind the building on Horse Guards Parade.

Changing of the Guard

The Queen is colonel-in-chief of the seven **Household Regiments**: the Life Guards (who dress in red and white) and the Blues and Royals (who dress in blue and white) are the two Household Cavalry Regiments; while the Grenadier, Coldstream, Scots, Irish and Welsh guards make up the Foot Guards. The Foot Guards can only be told apart by the plumes (or lack of them) in their busbies (fur helmets), and by the arrangement of their tunic buttons. The three senior regiments (Grenadier, Coldstream and Scots) date back to the seventeenth century, as do the Life Guards and the Blues and Royals. All seven regiments still form part of the modern army as well as performing ceremonial functions such as the Changing of the Guard.

The **Changing of the Guard** takes place at two London locations: the Foot Guards hold theirs outside Buckingham Palace (April–July daily 11.30am; Sept–March alternate days; no ceremony if it rains), but the more impressive one is held on Horse Guards Parade, where a squad of mounted Household Cavalry arrives from Hyde Park to relieve the guards at the Horse Guards building on Whitehall (Mon–Sat 11am; Sun 10am) – alternatively, if you miss the whole thing, turn up at 4pm for the daily inspection by the Officer of the Guard, who checks the soldiers haven't knocked off early. If you want to see something grander, check out **Trooping the Colour**, and the **Beating Retreat**, which both take place in June (see p.29).

Round the back of Horse Guards, you'll also find the **Household Cavalry Museum** (daily: March–Sept 10am–6pm; Oct–Feb 10am–5pm; £6; ☎020/7930 3070, ⓦwww.householdcavalrymuseum.org.uk; Westminster tube), where you can try on a trooper's elaborate uniform, complete a horse quiz and learn about the regiments' history. With the stables immediately adjacent, it's a sweet-smelling place, and – horse-lovers will be pleased to know – you can see the beasts in their stalls through a glass screen. Don't miss the pocket riot act on display, which ends with the wise warning: "must read correctly: variance fatal".

Downing Street

Further down this west side of Whitehall is London's most famous address, **10 Downing Street** (ⓦwww.number10.gov.uk), the terraced house that has been the residence of the prime minister, or PM, since it was presented to the First Lord of the Treasury, Robert Walpole, Britain's first PM, by George II in 1732. With no. 11 – home of the Chancellor of the Exchequer (in charge of the country's finances) since 1806 – and no. 12, home of the government's Chief Whip (in charge of party discipline), it's the only remaining bit of the original seventeenth-century cul-de-sac, though all three are now interconnecting and house much larger complexes than might appear from the outside. The public have been kept at bay since 1990, when Margaret Thatcher ordered a pair of iron gates to be installed at the junction with Whitehall, an act more symbolic than effective – a year later the IRA lobbed a mortar into the street from Horse Guards Parade, coming within a whisker of wiping out the entire Tory cabinet.

Cabinet War Rooms and Churchill Museum

In 1938, in anticipation of Nazi air raids, the basement of the Treasury building on King Charles Street was converted into the **Cabinet War Rooms** (daily 9.30am–6pm; £12; ☎020/7930 6961, ⓦcwr.iwm.org.uk; Westminster tube),

Whitehall statues and the Cenotaph

The **statues** dotted along Whitehall recall the days of empire. Kings and military leaders predominate, starting outside Horse Guards with the Second Duke of Cambridge (1819–1904), a man who, as commander-in-chief of the British Army, was so resistant to military reform that he had to be forcibly retired, followed by the 8th Duke of Devonshire (1833–1908), who failed to rescue General Gordon from the Siege of Khartoum. Appropriately enough, **Lord Haig** (1861–1928), who was responsible for sending thousands to their deaths in World War I, faces the Cenotaph, his horse famously poised ready for urination. Before you get to the Cenotaph, there's a striking new memorial to the women who served in World War II, featuring seventeen uniforms hanging on a large bronze plinth.

At the end of Whitehall, in the middle of the road, stands Edwin Lutyens' **Cenotaph**, built in 1919 in wood and plaster to commemorate the Armistice, and rebuilt in Portland stone the following year. The stark monument, which eschews Christian imagery, is inscribed simply with the words "The Glorious Dead" – the lost of World War I, who, it was once calculated, would take three and a half days to pass by the Cenotaph marching four abreast. The memorial remains the focus of the **Remembrance Sunday** ceremony held on the Sunday nearest November 11. Between the wars, however, a much more powerful, two-minute silence was observed throughout the entire British Empire every year on November 11 at 11am, the exact time of the armistice at the end of World War I.

protected by a three-foot-thick concrete slab, reinforced with steel rails and tramlines. It was here that Winston Churchill directed operations and held cabinet meetings for the duration of World War II. By the end of the war, the six-acre site included a hospital, canteen and shooting range, as well as sleeping quarters; tunnels fan out from the complex to outlying government ministries, and also, it is rumoured, to Buckingham Palace itself, allowing the Royal Family a quick getaway to exile in Canada (via Charing Cross station) in the event of a Nazi invasion.

The rooms remain much as they were when they were abandoned on VJ Day, August 15, 1945, and make for an atmospheric underground trot through wartime London. To bring the place to life, pick up the museum's audioguide, which includes various eyewitness accounts by folk who worked here. When you get to Churchill's secret telephone hotline direct to the American president, signs direct to the **Churchill Museum**, which begins with his finest moment, when he took over as PM and Britain stood alone against the Nazis. You can hear snippets of Churchill's speeches and check out his trademark bowler, spotted bow tie and half-chewed Havana, not to mention his wonderful burgundy zip-up "romper suit". Fortunately for the curators, Churchill had an extremely eventful life and was great for a soundbite, so there are plenty of interesting anecdotes to keep you engaged.

Back in the Cabinet War Rooms, look out for Winnie's very modest emergency bedroom (though he himself rarely stayed here, preferring to watch the air raids from the roof of the building, or rest his head at the *Savoy Hotel*). Finally, you reach the Map Room, with its rank of multicoloured telephones, copious ashtrays, and floor-to-ceiling maps covering every theatre of war and showing the exact position of the front line on VJ Day.

Parliament Square

Parliament Square was laid out in the mid-nineteenth century to give the new Houses of Parliament and the adjacent Westminster Abbey a grander setting, though nowadays it functions primarily as a traffic roundabout. Statues of notables – Abraham Lincoln, Benjamin Disraeli and Jan Smuts, to name but a few – are scattered amid the swirling cars and buses, with Winston Churchill stooping determinedly in the northeast corner of the central green. At the beginning of Westminster Bridge, you can also spot Boudicca, depicted keeping her horses and daughters under control without the use of reins – the imperialist boast "regions Caesar never knew, thy posterity shall sway" adorns the plinth.

Houses of Parliament

The Palace of Westminster, better known as the **Houses of Parliament** (Westminster tube), is among London's best-known icons. The "mother of all parliaments", it's also the city's finest Victorian edifice, symbol of a nation once confident of its place at the centre of the world. Best viewed from the south side of the river, where the likes of Monet and Turner once set up their easels, the building's most famous feature is its ornate, gilded clock tower popularly known as **Big Ben**, at its most impressive when lit up at night. Strictly speaking, "Big Ben" refers only to the thirteen-ton bell that strikes the hour (and is

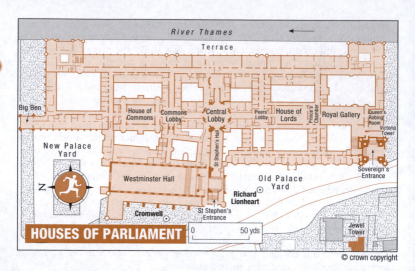

© crown copyright

broadcast across the world by the BBC), and takes its name from either the former Commissioner of Works, Benjamin Hall, or a popular heavyweight boxer of the time, Benjamin Caunt.

The original Palace of Westminster was built by **Edward the Confessor** in the eleventh century to allow him to watch over the building of his abbey. Westminster then served as the seat of all the English monarchs until a fire forced Henry VIII to decamp to Whitehall. The Lords have always convened at the palace, but it was only following Henry's death that the House of Commons moved from the abbey's chapter house into the palace's St Stephen's Chapel.

In 1834, a fire reduced the old palace to rubble. Save for Westminster Hall, and a few pieces of the old structure buried deep within the interior, everything you see today is the work of **Charles Barry**, who wanted to create something that expressed national greatness through the use of Gothic and Elizabethan styles. The resulting orgy of honey-coloured pinnacles, turrets and tracery is the greatest achievement of the Gothic Revival. Inside, the Victorian love of mock-Gothic detail is evident in the maze of over one thousand committee rooms and offices, the fittings of which were largely the responsibility of Barry's assistant, **Augustus Pugin**.

Westminster Hall

Virtually the only relic of the medieval palace is the bare expanse of **Westminster Hall**, on the west side of the complex. Built by William II in 1099, it was saved from the 1834 fire by the timely intervention of the PM, Lord Melbourne, who had the fire engines brought into the hall itself, and personally took charge of the firefighting. The sheer scale of the hall – 240ft by 60ft – and its huge oak hammerbeam roof, added by Richard II in the late fourteenth century, make it one of the most magnificent secular medieval halls in Europe.

Unless you're on a guided tour, you can only peer down from St Stephen's Porch, en route to the public galleries, at the bare expanse that has witnessed some nine hundred years of English history. The hall has been used for the lying-in-state of members of the Royal Family and a select few non-royals, but until 1821 every royal coronation banquet was also held here; during the ceremony, the Royal Champion would ride into the hall in full armour to challenge any who dared dispute the sovereign's right to the throne.

From the thirteenth to the nineteenth centuries the hall was also used as the country's highest court of law: **William Wallace** was forced to wear a laurel crown during his treason trial here; Thomas More was sentenced to be hanged, castrated and disembowelled (while still alive), though in the end was simply beheaded; **Guy Fawkes**, the Catholic caught in the cellars trying to blow up the House of Lords on November 5, 1605, was tried here and later hanged, drawn and quartered in Old Palace Yard. The trial of **Charles I** also took place here, but the king refused to take his hat off, since he did not accept the court's legitimacy. **Oliver Cromwell**, whose statue now stands outside the hall, was sworn in here as Lord Protector in 1653, only to have his head stuck on a spike above the hall after the Restoration – it remained there for several decades until a storm dislodged it. It now resides in a secret location at Cromwell's old college in Cambridge.

St Stephen's Hall and the Central Lobby

From St Stephen's Porch, the route to the parliamentary chambers passes through **St Stephen's Hall**, designed by Barry as a replica of the Gothic chapel built by Edward I, where the Commons met for nearly three hundred years until 1834. It was into this chamber that Charles I entered with an armed guard in 1642 in a vain attempt to arrest five MPs who had made a speedy escape down the river – "I see my birds have flown", he is supposed to have said. Shortly afterwards, the Civil War began, and no monarch has entered the Commons since. St Stephen's also witnessed the only assassination of a prime minister, when in 1812 Spencer Perceval was shot by a merchant whose business had been ruined by the Napoleonic Wars.

Visiting the Houses of Parliament

To watch proceedings in either the **House of Commons** – the livelier of the two – or the Lords, simply join the queue for the **public galleries** outside St Stephen's Gate. The public are let in slowly from about 4pm onwards on Mondays and Tuesdays, from around 1pm Wednesdays and Thursdays, and from 10am on Fridays: the whole procedure can take an hour or more. To avoid the queues, turn up an hour or so later, when the crowds have usually thinned, or on Friday morning, when the House is at its quietest. To find out exact "sitting times" and the dates of "recesses" (holiday closures), phone ☎020/7219 4272 or visit ⓦwww.parliament.uk.

Question Time – when the House of Commons is at its most raucous and entertaining – takes place in the first hour (Mon–Thurs) with **Prime Minister's Question Time** on Wednesday. To attend either, UK citizens must book in advance with their local MP (☎020/7219 3000). If Parliament is in session a Union flag flies from the southernmost tower, the Victoria Tower; at night there's a light above the clock face on Big Ben. (If an MP wants a taxi, a sign saying "taxi" flashes on the corner railings of Parliament Square.) Full explanatory notes on the procedures (and warnings about joining in or causing a disruption) are supplied to all visitors, but if you want to learn more about how Parliament works, visit the exhibition in the **Jewel Tower** (see p.63).

During the **Summer Opening** (Aug & Sept), there are regular **guided tours** (Mon–Sat 1hr 15min; £7). Visitors can book in advance (☎0870/906 3773), or simply head for the ticket office on Abingdon Green, opposite Victoria Tower. All year round, UK residents can take free guided tours of the palace, as well as up **Big Ben** (no under-11s); both need to be organized through your local MP (see above).

After a further wait you're shepherded through the bustling, octagonal **Central Lobby**, where constituents can "lobby" their MPs. In the tiling of the lobby Pugin inscribed the Latin motto "Except the Lord keep the house, they labour in vain that build it". In view of what happened to the architects, the sentiment seems like an indictment of parliamentary morality – Pugin ended up in Bedlam mental hospital and Barry died from overwork within months of completing the job.

The House of Commons

If you're going to listen to proceedings in the **House of Commons**, you'll be asked to sign a form vowing not to cause a disturbance and then led up to the Public Gallery. Protests from the gallery were, in fact, once a fairly regular occurrence: suffragettes have poured flour, farmers have dumped dung, Irish Nationalists have lobbed tear gas, and lesbians have abseiled down into the chamber. Since an incendiary bomb in May 1941 destroyed Barry's original chamber, what you see now is a rather lifeless postwar reconstruction. Barry's design was modelled on the palace's original St Stephen's Hall, hence the choir-stall arrangement of the MPs' benches. Members of the cabinet (and the opposition's shadow cabinet) occupy the two "front benches"; the rest are "backbenchers". To avoid debates degenerating into physical combat, MPs are not allowed to cross the red lines – which are exactly two swords' length apart – on the floor of the chamber during a debate, hence the expression "toeing the party line". The chamber is at its busiest during Question Time, though if too many of the 646 MPs turn up, a large number have to remain standing, as the House only has 427 seats. For much of the time, however, the chamber is almost empty, with just a handful of MPs present from each party.

The House of Lords

On the other side of the Central Lobby, a corridor leads to the **House of Lords** (or Upper House), a far dozier establishment peopled by unelected Lords and Ladies, plus a smattering of bishops. Their home boasts much grander decor than the Commons, full of regal gold and scarlet, and dominated by a canopied gold throne where the Queen sits for the state opening of Parliament in November. Directly in front of the throne, the Lord Chancellor runs the proceedings from the scarlet Woolsack, an enormous cushion stuffed with wool, which harks back to the time when it was England's principal export. Until 1999, there were a thousand-plus hereditary Lords (over a quarter of whom had been to Eton) who had the right to vote and debate in the House. Most rarely bothered to turn up, but in emergencies, they could be (and were) called upon by the Conservatives, to ensure a right-wing victory in a crucial vote. For the most part, the Lords have very little real power, as they can only advise and review parliamentary bills.

The royal apartments

If the House of Lords appeals, you can see more pomp and glitter by going on a **guided tour** (see p.61). You'll be asked to enter at the **Sovereign's Entrance** below Victoria Tower, where the Queen arrives in her coach for the state opening. Then, it's up the Royal Staircase to the Norman Porch, every nook of which is stuffed with busts of eminent statesmen. Next door is the **Queen's Robing Chamber**, which boasts a superb coffered ceiling and lacklustre Arthurian frescoes. As the name suggests, this is the room where the monarch dons the crown jewels before entering the Lords for the opening of Parliament. Beyond here you enter the **Royal Gallery**, a cavernous writing room for the House of Lords, hung with portraits of royals past and present, and two 45-foot-long frescoes of Trafalgar and Waterloo. Before entering the House of Lords itself, you pass through the **Prince's Chamber**, commonly known as the Tudor Room after the numerous portraits that line the walls, including Henry VIII and all six of his wives. The tour then takes you through both Houses, St Stephen's Hall and finally Westminster Hall (all described above), before you leave through New Palace Yard.

Jewel Tower and the Victoria Tower Gardens

The **Jewel Tower** (daily: April–Oct 10am–5pm; Nov–March 10am–4pm; EH; £3; ☎020/7222 2219; Westminster tube), across the road from the Sovereign's Entrance, is another remnant of the medieval palace. The tower formed the southwestern corner of the original exterior fortifications (there's a bit of moat left, too), and was constructed in 1365 by Edward III as a giant strongbox for the crown jewels. Nowadays, its three floors house an excellent exhibition on the history of Parliament, including a touch-screen tour of the palace and ending with a video on the procedural rigmarole that still persists there – well worth a visit *before* you enter Parliament.

To the south of Parliament's Victoria Tower are the leafy **Victoria Tower Gardens**, which look out onto the Thames. Visitors are greeted by a statue of Emmeline Pankhurst, leader of the suffragette movement, who died in 1928, the same year women finally got the vote on equal terms with men; medallions commemorating her daughter Christabel, and a WPSU Prisoners' Badge, flank the statue. Round the corner, a replica of Rodin's famous sculpture, *The Burghers of Calais*, makes a surprising appearance here, while at the far end of the gardens stands an exotic-looking, badly weathered, neo-Gothic fountain commemorating the abolition of slavery in 1834.

St Margaret's Church

To the north of the Jewel Tower, in the shadow of Westminster Abbey, is **St Margaret's Church** (Mon–Fri 9.30am–3.30pm, Sat 9.30am–1.30pm, Sun 2–5pm; free; Westminster tube), which has been the unofficial parliamentary church since 1614 when Puritan MPs decided to shun the elaborate liturgy of the neighbouring abbey. St Margaret's has also long been a fashionable church to get married in – Pepys, Milton and Shakespeare were followed in the twentieth century by Churchill and Mountbatten – and it gets a steady stream of visitors simply by dint of being so close to the abbey (and because it's free). The present building dates back to 1523, and its most noteworthy furnishing is the colourful Flemish stained-glass window above the altar, which commemorates the marriage of Henry VIII and Catherine of Aragon (depicted in the bottom left- and right-hand corners). Constructed in 1526, the window was never intended for St Margaret's, and was only bought by the church in 1758 to replace those smashed by the Puritans. The west window commemorates Walter Ralegh, who was beheaded in Old Palace Yard and buried in the old churchyard. Also interred here is William Caxton, who audited the parish accounts and set up the country's first printing press in the abbey close in 1476.

Westminster Abbey

The Houses of Parliament dwarf their much older neighbour, **Westminster Abbey** (hours can vary: Mon–Fri 9.30am–4.30pm, Wed until 6pm, Sat 9.30am–2.30pm; £12; ☎020/7654 4900, ⓦwww.westminster-abbey.org; Westminster tube), which squats uncomfortably on the western edge of Parliament Square. Yet this single building embodies much of the history of England: it has been the venue for every coronation since the time of William the Conqueror, and the site of just about every royal burial for some five hundred years between the reigns of Henry III and George II. Scores of the nation's most famous citizens are honoured here, too – though many of the stones commemorate people buried elsewhere – and the interior is cluttered with literally hundreds of monuments, reliefs and statues.

Legend has it that the first church on the site was consecrated by St Peter himself, who was rowed across the Thames by a fisherman named Edric, and who granted him a giant salmon as a reward. More verifiable is that there was a small Benedictine monastery here by the tenth century, for which **Edward the Confessor** built an enormous church. Nothing much remains of Edward's church, which was consecrated on December 28, 1065, just eight days before his death. The following January his successor, Harold, was crowned, and, on Christmas Day, William the Conqueror rode up the aisle on horseback, thus firmly establishing the tradition of royal coronation within the Confessor's church.

It was in honour of Edward (who had by now been canonized) that **Henry III** began to rebuild the abbey in 1245, in the French Gothic style of the recently completed Rheims Cathedral. The monks were kicked out during the Reformation, but the church's status as the nation's royal mausoleum saved it from any physical damage. In the early eighteenth century, Nicholas Hawksmoor designed

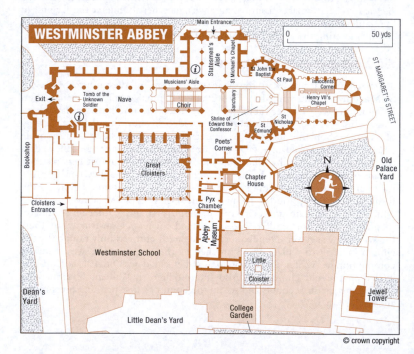

© crown copyright

Visiting the abbey

Once you've paid the hefty admission charge, head for the information desk and pick up a free plan. Locating some of the graves is tricky unless your Latin is good, so if you have any questions, ask the vergers in the black gowns, the marshals in red or the abbey volunteers in green. An **audioguide** to the abbey is available for free, and there are **guided tours**, which allow access to the Confessor's Tomb (Mon–Sat, times vary; ring ahead for details; 1hr 30min; £3). Note that you can visit the Chapter House and the cloisters (free admission), without buying an abbey ticket, by entering via Dean's Yard. Admission to the daily services at the abbey (check website for details) is, of course, free.

the quasi-Gothic west front, while the latest additions can be seen above the west door: a series of statues representing twentieth-century martyrs, from Dietrich Bonhöffer to Martin Luther King.

Statesmen's Aisle, the sanctuary and the north ambulatory

With over 3300 people buried beneath its flagstones and countless others commemorated here, the abbey is, in essence, a giant mausoleum. It has long ceased to be simply a working church, and admission charges are nothing new: Oliver Goldsmith complained about being charged three pence in 1765. A century or so later, so few people used the abbey as a church that, according to George Bernard Shaw, one foreign visitor kneeling in prayer was promptly arrested because the verger thought he was acting suspiciously. Despite protestations to the contrary, the abbey is now more a mass tourist attraction than a House of God.

The north transept, where you enter, is littered with overblown monuments to long-forgotten empire-builders and nineteenth-century politicians, and traditionally known as **Statesmen's Aisle**. The transept's best funereal art is tucked away in **St Michael's Chapel** to the east, where you can admire the remarkable monument to **Francis Vere** (1560–1609), one of the greatest soldiers of the Elizabethan period, made out of two slabs of black marble, between which lies Sir Francis; on the upper slab, supported by four knights, his armour is laid out, to show that he died away from the field of battle. The most striking grave, by Roubiliac, is that in which **Elizabeth Nightingale**, who died from a miscarriage, collapses in her husband's arms while he tries to fight off the skeletal figure of Death, who is climbing out of the tomb.

From the north transept, you can gain access to the central **sanctuary**, site of the coronations. The most precious work of art here is the thirteenth-century Italian **Cosmati floor mosaic**. It depicts the universe with interwoven circles and squares of Purbeck marble, glass, and red and green porphyry, though it's often covered by a carpet to protect it. The richly gilded high altar, like the ornately carved choir stalls, is, in fact, a neo-Gothic construction from the nineteenth century.

Continue into the **north ambulatory**, where the two side chapels now contain ostentatious Tudor and Stuart tombs that replaced the altarpieces that had graced them before the Reformation. One of the most extravagant tombs is that of Lord Hunsdon, which dominates the **Chapel of St John the Baptist**, and, at 36ft in height, is the tallest in the entire abbey. More intriguing, though, are the sarcophagi in the neighbouring **Chapel of St Paul**: one depicts eight "weepers", kneeling children along the base of the tomb – the two holding skulls predeceased their parents – while the red-robed Countess of

▲ Westminster Abbey

Sussex has a beautiful turquoise and gold porcupine (the family emblem) as her prickly footrest.

Henry VII's Chapel

At this point, you can climb the stairs and enter the Lady Chapel, better known as **Henry VII's Chapel**, the most dazzling architectural set piece in the abbey. Begun by Henry VII in 1503 as a shrine to Henry VI and as his own future resting place, it represents the final gasp of the English Perpendicular style, with its intricately carved vaulting, fan-shaped gilded pendants and statues of nearly one hundred saints, high above the choir stalls. The stalls themselves are decorated with the banners and emblems of the Knights of the Order of the Bath, established by George I. **George II**, the last king to be buried in the abbey, lies in the burial vault under your feet, along with Queen Caroline – their coffins were fitted with removable sides so that their remains could mingle.

Beneath the altar is the grave of Edward VI, the single, sickly son of Henry VIII, while behind lies the chapel's raison d'être, the black marble sarcophagus containing Henry VII and his spouse – their lifelike gilded effigies, modelled from death masks, are obscured by an ornate Renaissance grille by Pietro Torrigiano, who fled from Italy after breaking Michelangelo's nose in a fight. James I is also interred within Henry's tomb, while the first of the apse chapels, to the north, hosts a grand monument by Hubert le Sueur to James's lover, George Villiers, Duke of Buckingham, the first non-royal to be buried in this part of the abbey, who was killed by one of his own disgruntled soldiers. Le Sueur was also responsible for another overblown monument in the last of the apse chapels, to the south, in which four caryatids, holding up a vast bronze canopy, weep for Ludovic Stuart, another of James I's "favourites". The easternmost RAF Chapel sports a stained-glass window depicting airmen and angels in the Battle of Britain. Beneath it, a plaque marks the spot where Oliver Cromwell rested, briefly, until the Restoration, whereupon his mummified body was disinterred, dragged through the streets, hanged at Tyburn and beheaded.

Before descending the steps back into the ambulatory, pop into the chapel's north aisle, which is virtually cut off from the chancel. Here James I erected a huge ten-poster tomb to his predecessor, **Elizabeth I**. Unless you read the plaque on the floor, you'd never know that Elizabeth's Catholic half-sister, "Bloody Mary", is also buried here, in an unusual act of posthumous reconciliation. The far end of the north aisle, where James I's two infant daughters lie, is known as **Innocents' Corner**: Princess Sophia, who died aged three days, lies in an alabaster cradle, her face peeping over the covers, just about visible in the mirror on the wall; while Princess Mary, who died the following year aged 2, is clearly visible, casually leaning on a cushion. Set into the wall between the two is the Wren-designed urn containing (what are thought to be) the bones of the **Princes in the Tower**, Edward V and his younger brother, Richard (see p.194).

The south aisle of Henry VII's chapel contains more stellar tombs, including James I's mother, **Mary**, **Queen of Scots**, whom Elizabeth I had beheaded. James had Mary's remains brought from Peterborough Cathedral in 1612, and paid significantly more for her extravagant eight-postered tomb, complete with a terrifyingly aggressive, red Scots lion, than he had done for Elizabeth's (see above); the 27 hangers-on who are buried with her are listed on the nearby wooden screen. The last of the tombs here is that of **Lady Margaret Beaufort**, Henry VII's mother, her face and hands depicted wrinkles and all by Torrigiano. Below the altar, commemorated by simple modern plaques, lie yet more royals: **William and Mary**, **Queen Anne** and **Charles II**.

The Coronation Chair and Poets' Corner

As you leave Henry VII's Chapel, look out for Edward I's **Coronation Chair**, a decrepit oak throne dating from around 1300. The graffiti-covered chair, used in every coronation since 1308, was custom-built to incorporate the **Stone of Scone**, a great slab of red sandstone which acted as the Scottish coronation stone for centuries before Edward pilfered it in 1296. The stone remained in the abbey for the next seven hundred years, apart from a brief interlude in 1950, when some Scottish nationalists managed to steal it back and hide it in Arbroath. In a futile attempt to curry favour with the Scots before the 1997 election, the Conservatives returned the stone to Edinburgh Castle, where it now resides.

Behind the chair lies the tomb of **Henry V**, who died of dysentery in France in 1422 at the age of just 35, and was regarded as a saint in his day. Above him rises the highly decorative, H-shaped Chantry Chapel, where the body of Henry's wife, Catherine of Valois, was openly displayed for several centuries – Pepys records kissing her corpse on his 36th-birthday visit to the abbey. The chapel acts as a sort of gatehouse for the **Shrine of Edward the Confessor**, the sacred heart of the building, and site of some of the abbey's finest tombs, now only accessible on a guided tour (see p.65). With some difficulty, you can just about make out the battered marble casket of the Confessor's tomb and the niches in which pilgrims would kneel.

There are more bombastic Tudor and Stuart tombs in the side chapels of the south ambulatory, but, as with the royal tombs, these have been somewhat upstaged by **Poets' Corner**, in the south transept. The first occupant, **Geoffrey Chaucer**, was buried here in 1400, not because he was a poet, but because he lived nearby, and his battered tomb, on the east wall, wasn't built for another 150-odd years. When **Edmund Spenser** chose to be buried close to Chaucer in 1599, his fellow poets – Shakespeare may well have been among them – threw their own works and quills into the grave. Nevertheless, it wasn't until the eighteenth century that this zone became an artistic pantheon, since when the transept has been filled with tributes to all shades of talent.

Among those who are actually buried here, you'll find – after much searching – grave slabs or memorials for everyone from John Dryden and Samuel Johnson to **Charles Dickens** and Thomas Hardy (though his heart was buried in Dorset). Among the merely commemorated is the dandyish figure of **William Shakespeare**, erected in 1740 on one of the east walls. Even mavericks like Oscar Wilde, commemorated in the Hubbard window, are acknowledged here, though William Blake was honoured by a Jacob Epstein sculpture only in 1957, and Byron was refused burial for his "open profligacy", and had to wait until 1969 for a memorial.

Among the non-poets buried here is the German composer **Georg Friedrich Handel**, who spent most of his life at the English court, wrote the coronation anthem *Zadok the Priest*, which was first performed at George II's coronation, and has been performed at every subsequent one. Further along the same wall, the great eighteenth-century actor **David Garrick** is seen parting the curtains for a final bow. The one illiterate is old Thomas Parr, a Shropshire man who arrived in London as a celebrity in 1635 at the alleged age of 152, but died shortly afterwards, and whose remains were brought here by Charles II.

South choir aisle

Before you enter the cloisters, it's worth seeking out several wonderful memorials to undeserving types in the south choir aisle, though you may have to ask a verger to allow you to see them properly. The first is to Thomas Thynne, a Restoration rake, whose tomb incorporates a relief showing his assassination in his coach on Pall Mall by three thugs, hired to kill him by his Swedish rival in love. Further along lies Admiral Clowdisley Shovell, lounging in toga and wig. One of only two survivors of a shipwreck in 1707, he was washed up alive on a beach in the Scilly Isles, off southwest England, only to be killed by a fisherwoman for his emerald ring. Above Shovell is a memorial to the court portrait painter Godfrey Kneller, who declared, "By God, I will not be buried in Westminster…they do bury fools there." In the event, he has the honour of being the only artist commemorated in the abbey; the tomb is to his own design, but the epitaph is by Pope, who admitted it was the worst thing he ever wrote – which is just as well, as it's so high up you can't read it.

The cloisters

Doors in the south choir aisle lead to the **Great Cloisters** (daily 8am–6pm; free via Dean's Yard entrance), rebuilt after a fire in 1298 and paved with yet more funerary slabs, including, at the bottom of the ramp, that of the proto-feminist writer **Aphra Behn**, upon whose tomb "all women together ought to let flowers fall", according to Virginia Woolf, "for it was she who earned them the right to speak their minds."

At the eastern end lies the octagonal **Chapter House** (daily 10.30am–4pm; free), built in 1255 for Henry III's Great Council or putative parliament. The House of Commons continued to meet here until 1395, though the monks were none too happy about it, complaining that the shuffling and stamping wore out the expensive tiled floor. Despite their whingeing, the thirteenth-century decorative paving tiles have survived well, as have sections of the remarkable apocalyptic wall-paintings, which were executed in celebration of the eviction of the Commons. Be sure to check out the southern wall, where the Whore of Babylon rides the scarlet seven-headed beast from *The Book of Revelation*.

The nearby high-security **Pyx Chamber** (daily 10.30am–4pm; free) is one of the few surviving Norman sections of the abbey, along with the neighbouring **Abbey Museum** (daily 10.30am–4pm; free). The museum contains a real mixed bag of exhibits, from replica coronation regalia used during rehearsals to the ring given by Elizabeth I to her lover, the Earl of Essex. The most bizarre items, though, are the lifelike wood and wax royal funereal effigies (several of which are wigless), used in royal burials (1307–1660) instead of an open coffin, including that of Lady Frances Stuart, model for Britannia on the old penny coin, complete with her pet parrot, which died a few days after she did.

From the cloisters you can make your way via **Little Cloister**, where sick or elderly monks used to live, to the little-known **College Garden** (Tues–Thurs: April–Sept 10am–6pm; Oct–March 10am–4pm; free), a 900-year-old stretch of green, originally used as a herb garden by the monastery's doctor. The garden now provides a quiet retreat and a croquet lawn for pupils of Westminster School; brass-band concerts take place in the summer (July & Aug Wed 12.30–2pm).

The nave

It's only when you finally leave the cloisters that you get to enter the **nave** itself. Narrow, light and, at over a hundred feet in height, by far the tallest in the country, the nave is an impressive space. The first monument to head for is the **Tomb of the Unknown Soldier**, by the west door, with its garland of red poppies commemorating the million British soldiers who died in World War I. Close by is a large floor slab dedicated to **Winston Churchill**, though he chose to be buried in his family plot in Bladon, Oxfordshire.

A tablet in the floor near the Unknown Soldier marks the spot where **George Peabody**, the nineteenth-century philanthropist whose housing estates in London still provide homes for those in need, was buried for a month before being exhumed and removed to Massachusetts; he remains the only American to have been buried in the abbey. On the pillar by St George's Chapel, right by the west door, is a doleful fourteenth-century portrait of **Richard II**, painted at his coronation at the age of 10, and the oldest known image of an English monarch painted from life. Above the west door, **William Pitt the Younger**, prime minister at just 23, teaches Anarchy a thing or two, while History takes notes.

The dried and salted body of the explorer and missionary **David Livingstone** is buried in the centre of the nave – except for his internal organs, which, following the tradition of the African people in whose village he died, were buried in a box under a tree. To the left of the gilded neo-Gothic choir screen is a statue of **Isaac Newton**, who, although a Unitarian by faith, would no doubt have been happy enough to be buried in such a prominent position. Other scientists' graves cluster nearby, including non-believer **Charles Darwin**, who, despite being at loggerheads with the Church for most of his life over *On the Origin of Species*, was given a religious burial in the abbey.

In the far corner of the south aisle, the eighteenth-century marble memorial to **General Hargrave** by Roubiliac, has the deceased rising from the grave in response to the Last Trumpet; at the time there was a public outcry that such an undistinguished man – he was Governor of Gibraltar – should receive such a vast memorial. Another controversial grave is that of poet and playwright **Ben Jonson**, who, despite being a double murderer, was granted permission to be buried here, upright so as not to exceed the eighteen square inches he'd been allowed; his epitaph reads simply, "O Rare Ben Jonson". The so-called **Musicians' Aisle** lies to the east, beyond a barrier, so you'll need to ask a verger for access. In fact, just two musicians of great note are buried here: Ralph Vaughan Williams and Henry Purcell, who served as the abbey's organist. Of the statues lining the aisle, only the tireless anti-slavery campaigner **William Wilberforce**, slouching in his chair, is actually buried in the abbey.

Middlesex Guildhall and Central Hall

There are a couple of other buildings close to the abbey that deserve a mention. The first is **Middlesex Guildhall**, a wonderfully over-the-top Edwardian attempt at re-creating a medieval town hall, its facade replete with lugubrious gargoyles, statues and reliefs. Originally home to council offices, and more recently law courts, it has recently been redesigned by Norman Foster and now houses the UK's Supreme Court.

One block west, on Storey's Gate, the Methodists established their national headquarters, **Central Hall** (☎020/7222 8010, ⓦwww.c-h-w.com), in 1912. In order to avoid the Gothic of the abbey, and the Byzantine of the Catholic cathedral (see p.74), the Methodists opted for Edwardian Beaux-Arts – as a result, it looks rather like a giant continental casino, which is hardly appropriate given the Methodists' views on gambling and alcohol. Central Hall has been used over the years as much for political meetings as religious gatherings, and was the unlikely venue for the inaugural meeting of the **United Nations** in 1946. If there's no event on, you're free to wander round the building and – after donning black gloves – to look at the Historic Roll, a fifty-volume list of the folk who donated a guinea towards the cost of the building. Free **guided tours** are also available, and allow you to climb the stone balustrade atop the reinforced concrete dome.

Millbank to Victoria Street

The area south and west of Westminster Abbey, with **Millbank** to the east and St James's Park to the north, is home to various governmental ministries that can't quite fit into Whitehall. It's also a favourite place for MPs to have their London bases, and many of the restaurants and pubs in the area have "division bells", which ring eight minutes before any vote in the House of Commons. As for sights, the area boasts one of London's top public galleries, **Tate Britain**, and one of its most exotic churches, the Roman Catholic **Westminster Cathedral**.

Millbank

Running south from midway along the Victoria Tower Gardens, the busy riverside road of **Millbank** is dominated by the unprepossessing 1960s Millbank Tower, which reaches a height of 387ft. To the south, **Tate Britain** occupies the site of Millbank prison, which was built in the shape of a six-pointed star in 1816, according to the ideas of Jeremy Bentham. The prisoners, mostly awaiting transportation to Australia from the nearby quayside, were kept under constant surveillance, forbidden to communicate with each other for the first half of their sentence and put to work making mailbags and shoes – for its day, an extremely liberal regime. Nevertheless, very little natural light penetrated the three miles of labyrinthine passages, and epidemics of cholera and scurvy were commonplace. The prison closed down in 1890.

The green-and-beige postmodernist ziggurat across the water is Vauxhall Cross, the indiscreet Secret Intelligence Service or **MI6 headquarters** (ⓦ www.sis.gov .uk), designed in the 1990s by Terry Farrell. It has featured in several Bond films and is connected by tunnel to Whitehall. Such conspicuousness comes at a price, however, and in 2000, the building, known as "Legoland" to those who work there, was hit by a rocket attack courtesy of some dissident Irish-republican terrorists. **MI5** (ⓦ www.mi5.gov.uk), the UK's domestic Security Service, occupies the much more anonymous Thames House on the corner of Horseferry Road and Millbank.

Tate Britain

Originally founded in 1897 with money from Henry Tate, inventor of the sugar cube, **Tate Britain** (daily 10am–5.50pm; first Fri of month until 10pm; free; ⓣ 020/7887 8888, ⓦ www.tate.org.uk; Pimlico tube), on Millbank, is dedicated exclusively to British art from 1500 to the present day. In addition, the gallery has a whole wing devoted to Turner, as well as putting on large-scale temporary exhibitions (for which there is a charge) and sponsoring the **Turner Prize**, the country's most infamous modern-art award. Works by a shortlist of four artists under 50 are displayed in the gallery a month or two prior to the December prize-giving.

Tate currently follows a chronological, albeit thematic, approach in its permanent displays. Even with more than 25 rooms, what you see here is a tiny fraction of Tate's collection, and the paintings are frequently re-hung. At the moment, works from 1500 to around 1900 occupy rooms to the left (1–15); the twentieth-century galleries (16–29) are mostly to the right. What follows is a general rundown of the artists usually featured, plus some of the best works Tate owns, many of which stay on show more or less permanently.

British art from 1500 to 1900

The collection begins with richly bejewelled portraits of the Elizabethan and Jacobean nobility, the most striking being the *Cholmondeley Ladies*, who were born on the same day, married on the same day and "brought to bed" on the same day, but are not now thought to be twins. Despite a smattering of English talent, such as **William Dobson**, whose portrait of courtier *Endymion Porter* is usually on display, the Stuarts relied heavily on imported Dutch talent such as Van Dyck, Peter Lely – several of whose "lovelies" hang here – and the German

Visiting Tate Britain

The traditional **entrance** on Millbank leads up the steps to a small information desk beneath a glass-domed rotunda. A larger entrance with **disabled access** is on nearby Atterbury Street, and leads down to information desks and the cloakroom. Tate's Clore Gallery extension, which houses the Turner Bequest, can be reached via the modern-art galleries, but it also has its own entrance and information desk to the right of the original gallery entrance. There are free guided tours (Mon–Fri 11am, noon, 2 & 3pm, Sat & Sun noon & 3pm) and you can rent one of the gallery's multimedia guides for £3.50. If you're coming from, or going to, Tate Modern, there's a **Tate Boat** that plies between the two galleries (every 40min; 20min; ⓦ www .thamesclippers.com; £5).

Godfrey Kneller, who used to sign himself "Pictor Regis" such was the longevity of his royal patronage.

You can be guaranteed a good selection of works by the first great British artist, **William Hogarth**, including *O the Roast Beef of Old England*, a particularly vicious visual dig at the French, whom Hogarth loathed. **John Constable**'s most famous work, *Hay Wain*, hangs in the National Gallery, but the same location – Flatford Mill in his native Stour valley in Suffolk – features in many of the paintings displayed in Tate Britain. Another painter to look out for is **George Stubbs**, for whom "nature was and always is superior to art", and who portrayed animals – horses in particular – with a hitherto unknown anatomical precision.

Works by **Thomas Gainsborough** and **Joshua Reynolds** are sprinkled throughout the collection. Of the two, Reynolds, first president of the Royal Academy, was by far the more successful, elevating portraiture to pole position among the genres and flattering his sitters by surrounding them with classical trappings as in *Three Ladies adorning a Term of Hymen*. Gainsborough was equally adept at flattery, but preferred instead more informal settings, concentrating on colour and light, as with the portrait of dancer Giobanna Baccelli. At the outset of his career, Gainsborough was also a landscape artist, often painting the Stour valley in Suffolk, where he – like Constable – was born.

One room in the gallery is regularly devoted to the visionary works of the poet **William Blake**, who was considered something of a freak by his contemporaries. He rejected oil painting in favour of watercolours, and often chose unusual subject matter which matched his highly personal form of Christianity. He earned a pittance producing illuminated books written and printed entirely by himself, and painted purely from his own visions: "Imagination is My World; this world of Dross is beneath my notice", he wrote. He also executed a series of twelve large colour prints on the myth of the Creation, now considered among his finest works, several examples of which are normally on display here. Blake's works were originally intended for room 16, which is decorated by Boris Anrep's floor mosaics, accompanied by quotes from Blake's poem *The Marriage of Heaven and Hell*.

Tate is justifiably renowned for its vast collection of paintings by the **Pre-Raphaelites**, seven of whom formed their Brotherhood, the PRB, in 1848 in an attempt to re-create the humble, pre-humanist, pre-Renaissance world. One of the first PRB paintings to be exhibited was **Rossetti**'s *Girlhood of Mary Virgin*, which was well received by the critics, but his *Annunciation*, with its emaciated heroin-chic Virgin, the model for which was his sister, caused outrage. So too did **Millais**' *Christ in the House of His Parents*; Dickens described the figure of Jesus as "a hideous, wry-necked, blubbering, red-headed boy in a bed-gown". Millais also got into trouble for *Ophelia*, after his model, Elizabeth Siddal, caught a chill from lying in the bath to pose for the picture, prompting threats of a lawsuit from her father. Siddal later married Rossetti, and is also the model in his *Beata Beatrix*, painted posthumously, after she died of an opium overdose in 1862. Other classic PRB paintings in the collection are Arthur Hughes' *April Love*, Henry Wallis's Romantic hero *Chatterton*, John William Waterhouse's *The Lady of Shalott*, and Burne-Jones' *King Cophetua and the Beggar Maid*, all inspired by poems by Lord Tennyson.

Throughout Tate Britain, the term "British" is very loosely applied, so you'll find several works by the French artist, **James Tissot**, whose Impressionist take on English life (and, in particular, English ladies in frilly frocks) was very popular. Lord Leighton's *Bath of Psyche* is a typical piece of Victorian soft porn, the likes of which made him by far the most successful artist of his generation.

Other popular Victorian paintings to look out for include **John Singer Sargent**'s well-known *Carnation, Lily, Lily-Rose* and the American-born **Whistler**'s portrait of the precocious *Miss Cecily*, who looks as pissed off as she clearly felt after interminable sittings.

British art from 1900 to the present day

You'll find works by the same twentieth-century and contemporary British artists displayed in both Tate Modern and Tate Britain, so it's very hard to predict what will be on show here. Works by sculptors **Barbara Hepworth**, Jacob Epstein, Giacometti and **Henry Moore** usually feature prominently, while paintings by Walter Sickert and Francis Bacon crop up regularly. Vanessa Bell and Duncan Grant, from the Bloomsbury Group, are represented more often than not, and there are nearly always several paintings by **Stanley Spencer**, who saw his home village of Cookham, on the Thames, as paradise and depicted Christ preaching at the local regatta.

There's usually a good selection of work, too, by established living artists such as **Lucian Freud**, R.B. Kitaj, Frank Auerbach, **David Hockney** and op-art specialist Bridget Riley, as well as household names such as Rachel Whiteread, Tracey Emin, Chris Ofili and the ever-popular Anthony Gormley. Some less well-known artists to look out for include the Vorticist **David Bomberg**, who forged his own brand of Cubo-Futurism before World War I and pursued a more subdued Expressionism thereafter; **Ivon Hitchens**, whose distinctive use of blocks of colour harks back to the late works of Cézanne; and the self-taught St Ives painter **Alfred Wallis**.

The Clore Gallery: the Turner Bequest

J.M.W. Turner (1775–1851), possibly the greatest artist Britain has ever produced, bequeathed over a hundred oil paintings to the nation, and by the time his relatives had donated their share of the spoils, the total came to three hundred, plus a staggering 19,000 watercolours and drawings. Hence the world's largest Turner collection is housed here, in the adjoining Clore Gallery, a strangely childish building designed by James Stirling in 1987.

Turner was an extremely successful artist, exhibiting his first watercolours in the window of his father's barbershop in Maiden Lane, Covent Garden, while still a boy, and at the Royal Academy when he was just 15. Marine scenes appealed to Turner throughout his life, and one of the finest examples is *The Shipwreck*. Natural cataclysms also feature strongly in Turner's works, either for their own sake, as in *Deluge*, or as part of a grand historical painting like *Snow Storm: Hannibal and His Army Crossing the Alps*. Turner's only known self-portrait (he had no pretensions as a portraitist and was rather ashamed of his ruddy complexion) is usually on display, as are his personal belongings, such as his pocket watercolour kit and fishing rod, and his toothless death mask.

Paintings in the Turner galleries are regularly re-hung to draw out different themes from the artist's life and work, and sometimes even appear in the main galleries. Nevertheless, it's worth seeking out Turner's late works, great smudges of colour that seem to anticipate Monet in their almost total abandonment of linear representation. *Snow Storm – Steam Boat off a Harbour's Mouth* is a classic late Turner, a symbolic battle between the steam age and nature's primeval force. It was criticized at the time as "soapsuds and whitewash", though Turner himself claimed he merely painted what he saw, having been "lashed to a mast" for four hours.

Smith Square to Vincent Square and beyond

Two blocks south of Westminster Abbey lies the fine, early Georgian architectural ensemble of **Smith Square**, home to the **church of St John** (Ⓦ www .sjss.org.uk), a rare slice of full-blown Baroque completed in 1728. With its four distinctive towers topped by pineapples, it was dubbed the "footstool church" – the story being that Queen Anne, when asked how she would like the church to look, kicked over her footstool. Bombed in 1941, it has since been restored as a concert venue, but there's not much to see in its bare interior. To complete the Georgian experience, approach the square from **Lord North Street**, to the north, a perfectly preserved, early eighteenth-century terrace.

Another sight worth seeking out is the remarkable High Victorian church of **St James-the-Less** (Ⓦ www.sjtl.org), designed by George Edmund Street in the 1860s, which lies to the south of Vincent Square, on the far side of Vauxhall Bridge Road, amidst an unprepossessing 1960s housing estate. The red-and-black brickwork patterning on the exterior is exceptional, but pales in comparison to the red, black, cream and magenta tiling inside. The capitals of the church's rounded pillars hide biblical scenes amidst their acanthus-leaf foliage, and the font boasts similarly rich adornments, while above the chancel arch there's a wonderfully colourful fresco by G.F. Watts.

Westminster Cathedral

To the west of Vincent Square, just off Victoria Street, you'll find one of London's most surprising churches, the stripy neo-Byzantine concoction of the Roman Catholic **Westminster Cathedral** (Mon–Fri 7am–7pm, Sat 8am–7pm, Sun 8am–8pm; free; ☏020/7798 9055, Ⓦ www.westminstercathedral.org.uk; Victoria tube). Begun in 1895, it's one of the last and wildest monuments to the Victorian era: constructed from more than twelve million terracotta-coloured bricks, decorated with hoops of Portland stone, it culminates in a magnificent tapered campanile which rises to 274ft. From the small piazza to the northwest, you can admire the cathedral and the neighbouring mansions on Ambrosden Avenue, with their matching brickwork.

The **interior** is still only half-finished, and the domed ceiling of the nave – the widest in the country – remains an indistinct blackened mass, free of all decoration. To get an idea of what the place will look like when it's eventually completed, explore the series of **side chapels** – in particular the Holy Souls Chapel, the first one in the north aisle – whose rich, multicoloured decor makes use of over one hundred different marbles from around the world. Further down the north aisle is the Chapel of St George and the English Martyrs, where lies the enshrined body of St John Southworth, who was hanged, drawn and quartered as a traitor at Tyburn in 1654. Be sure, too, to check out the striking baldachin, held up by mustard-yellow pillars, and the low-relief Stations of the Cross sculpted by the controversial Eric Gill during World War I. The view from the **campanile** is definitely worth taking in as well, especially as you don't even have to slog up flights of steps, but can simply take a lift (daily 9.30am–12.30pm & 1–5pm; £3); the entrance is in the north aisle.

North of Victoria Street

In the 1860s, Victorian planners ploughed their way through the slums of Westminster to create **Victoria Street**, a direct link between Parliament and the newly built Victoria train station. The bland 1960s blocks that now line the street perfectly frame the London Eye. One tower block that deserves special mention is the Metropolitan Police headquarters, **New Scotland Yard**, on Broadway. The revolving sign alone should be familiar to many from countless TV detective serials and news reports.

Further down Broadway, at no. 55, is the austere **Broadway House**, home to Transport for London and St James's Park tube station, and the tallest building in London when it was built in 1929 by Charles Holden. It gained a certain notoriety at the time for its nude statues by Jacob Epstein, in particular the boy figure in *Day*, whose penis had to be shortened to appease public opinion. Round the corner, standing on its own in Caxton Street, is the former **Blewcoat School** (now a National Trust shop), a lovely little red-brick building built in 1709 by a local brewer as a charity school for the poor and used as such until 1926; a statue of a blue-coated charity boy still stands above the doorway.

There's more delightful Queen Anne architecture just to the north in **Queen Anne's Gate** and **Old Queen Street**, two exquisite streets, originally separated by a wall, whose position is indicated by a weathered statue of Queen Anne herself. Queen Anne's Gate is the older and more interesting of the two, each of its doorways surmounted by a rustic wooden canopy with pendants in the shape of acorns. It's worth walking round the back of the houses on the north side to appreciate the procession of elegant bow windows that look out onto St James's Park.

St James's

An exclusive little enclave sandwiched between St James's Park and Piccadilly, **ST JAMES'S** was laid out in the 1670s close to the royal seat of St James's Palace. Even today, regal and aristocratic residences overlook nearby **Green Park** and the stately avenue of **The Mall**; gentlemen's clubs cluster along Pall Mall and St James's Street; and jacket-and-tie restaurants and expense-account shops line **Jermyn Street**. Hardly surprising, then, that most Londoners rarely stray into this area, though plenty of folk frequent **St James's Park**, with large numbers heading for the Queen's chief residence, **Buckingham Palace**. If you're not in St James's for the shops, the best time to visit is on a Sunday, when the traffic is quieter, the nearby Mall is closed to traffic, and the royal chapels, plus the one accessible Palladian mansion, are open to the public.

St James's Park

St James's Park is the oldest of London's royal parks, having been drained and turned into a deer park by Henry VIII. It was redesigned and opened to the public by Charles II, who used to stroll through the grounds with his mistresses and courtiers, feed the ducks and even take a dip in the canal. By the eighteenth century, when some 6500 people had access to night keys for the gates, the park had become something of a byword for robbery and prostitution: diarist James Boswell was among those who went there specifically to be accosted "by several ladies of the town". The park's current landscaping was devised by Nash in the 1820s in an elegant style that established a blueprint for later Victorian city parks.

Today, the banks of the tree-lined lake are a favourite picnic spot for the civil servants of Whitehall and an inner-city reserve for wildfowl. James I's two crocodiles have left no descendants, alas, but the pelicans (which have resided here ever since a pair was presented to Charles II by the Russian ambassador) can still be seen at the eastern end of the lake, and there are exotic ducks, swans and geese aplenty. From the bridge across the lake there's a fine view over to Westminster and the jumble of domes and pinnacles along Whitehall – even the dull facade of **Buckingham Palace** looks majestic from here.

The Mall

The tree-lined sweep of **The Mall** – London's nearest equivalent to a Parisian boulevard – is at its best on Sundays, when it's closed to traffic. It was laid out in the first decade of the twentieth century as a memorial to Queen Victoria, and runs along the northern edge of St James's Park. The bombastic **Admiralty Arch** was erected to mark the entrance at the Trafalgar Square end of The Mall, while at the other end stands the ludicrous **Victoria Memorial**, Edward VII's

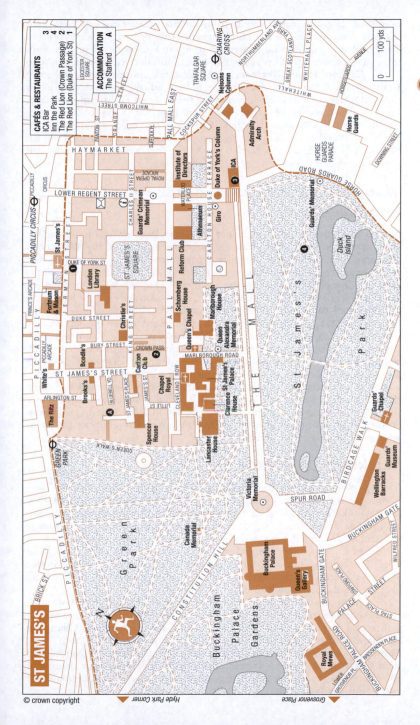

ST JAMES'S

CAFÉS & RESTAURANTS
ICA Bar 3
Inn the Park 4
The Red Lion (Crown Passage) 2
The Red Lion (Duke of York St) 1

ACCOMMODATION
The Stafford A

0   100 yds

© crown copyright

www.roughguides.com

77

CHARING CROSS

NORTHUMBERLAND AVE

GREAT SCOTLAND YARD

WHITEHALL PLACE

AVENUE

HORSE GUARDS AVENUE

Trafalgar Square

Nelsons Column

WHITEHALL

Admiralty Arch

Horse Guards

DOWNING STREET

HORSE GUARDS PARADE

HORSE GUARDS ROAD

Guards Memorial

Duck Island

St James's Park

BIRDCAGE WALK

Guards' Chapel

Guards' Museum

Wellington Barracks

BUCKINGHAM GATE

WILFRED STREET

PALACE STREET

STAG PLACE

STAFFORD PLACE

BRESSENDEN PLACE

LOWER GROSVENOR PL

BUCKINGHAM PALACE ROAD

Royal Mews

Buckingham Palace

Queen's Gallery

BUCKINGHAM GATE

Victoria Memorial

SPUR ROAD

Canada Memorial

CONSTITUTION HILL

Buckingham Palace Gardens

Green Park

QUEEN'S WALK

BRICK ST

PICCADILLY

Hyde Park Corner

The Ritz

ARLINGTON ST

PICCADILLY

GREEN PARK

Spencer House

Lancaster House

Clarence House

St James's Palace

CLEVELAND ROW

Chapel Royal

Queen Alexandra Memorial

MARLBOROUGH ROAD

THE MALL

Queen's Chapel

Marlborough House

Schomberg House

Reform Club

Athenaeum

CARLTON HOUSE TERRACE

Giro

ICA 3

Duke of York's Column

WATERLOO PLACE

Institute of Directors

ROYAL OPERA ARCADE

Guards' Crimean Memorial

PALL MALL

Carlton Club 2

CROWN PASS

BLUEBELL YD

JAMES'S PLACE

LITTLE ST

JAMES'S ST

ST JAMES'S STREET

Brooks's

White's

PICCADILLY ARCADE

PRINCES ARCADE

Berry Bros

BURY STREET

Christie's

DUKE STREET

KING STREET

ST JAMES'S SQUARE

London Library

Fortnum & Mason

JERMYN STREET

DUKE OF YORK ST

St James's

Guards' Crimean Memorial

PICCADILLY CIRCUS

LOWER REGENT STREET

CHARLES II STREET

HAYMARKET

PANTON ST

ORANGE STREET

WHITCOMB STREET

PALL MALL EAST

SUFFOLK PL

COCKSPUR STREET

LEICESTER SQUARE

PICCADILLY

Cleveland Row

Duke of York's Column

4

2

3

1

A

overblown 2300-ton marble tribute to his mother: *Motherhood* and *Justice* keep Victoria company around the plinth, which is topped by a gilded statue of *Victory*, while the six outlying allegorical groups in bronze confidently proclaim the great achievements of her reign. The Mall's most distinctive building is John Nash's **Carlton House Terrace**, whose graceful, cream-coloured Regency facade stretches away into the distance from Admiralty Arch. Among other things, it serves as the unlikely home of the **Institute of Contemporary Arts** or **ICA** (Mon noon–11pm, Tues–Sat noon–1am, Sun noon–10.30pm; free; ☎020/7930 0493, ⓦwww.ica.org.uk; Charing Cross tube), London's official headquarters of the avant-garde, so to speak, which moved here in 1968 and has put on a programme of regularly provocative exhibitions, films, talks and performances ever since.

Wellington Barracks, Guards' Chapel and Museum

Named after James I's aviary, which once stood here, Birdcage Walk runs along the south side of St James's Park, with the Neoclassical facade of the **Wellington Barracks**, built in 1833 and fronted by a parade ground, occupying more than half its length. Of the various buildings here, though, it's the modernist lines of the **Guards' Chapel** that come as the biggest surprise. Hit by a V1 rocket bomb on the morning of June 18, 1944 – killing 121 Sunday worshippers – the chapel was rebuilt in the 1960s. Inside, it's festooned with faded military flags, and retains the ornate Victorian apse, with Byzantine-style gilded mosaics, from the old chapel.

In a bunker opposite is the **Guards' Museum** (daily 10am–4pm; £3; ☎020/7414 3271, ⓦwww.theguardsmuseum.com; St James's Park tube), which displays the glorious scarlet-and-blue uniforms of the Queen's Foot Guards (see p.57). The museum also attempts to explain the Guards' complicated history, and gives a potted military history of the country since the Civil War. Among the exhibits here are a lock of Wellington's hair and a whole load of war booty, from Dervish prayer mats plundered from Sudan in 1898 to items taken from an Iraqi POW during the first Gulf War. The museum also displays (and sells) an impressive array of toy soldiers.

Buckingham Palace

The graceless colossus of **Buckingham Palace** (Aug & Sept daily 9.45am–6pm; advance booking fee £1.25 per ticket; £16.50; ☎020/7766 7300, ⓦwww .royal.gov.uk; Green Park tube), popularly known as "Buck House", has served as the monarch's permanent London residence only since Queen Victoria's reign. It began its days in 1702 as the Duke of Buckingham's city residence, built on the site of a notorious brothel, and was sold by the duke's son to George III in 1762. The building was overhauled by Nash in the late 1820s for the Prince Regent, and again by Aston Webb in 1913 for George V, producing a palace that's about as bland as it's possible to be.

For ten months of the year there's little to do here, with the Queen in residence and the palace closed to visitors – not that this deters the crowds who mill around the railings all day, and gather in some force to watch the **Changing of the Guard** (see box, p.57), in which a detachment of the Queen's Foot Guards marches to appropriate martial music from St James's Palace (unless it rains, that is). If the Queen is at home, the Royal Standard flies from the roof of the palace and four guards patrol; if not, the Union flag flutters aloft and just two guards stand out front.

Visiting the palace

Traditionally, unless you were one of the select thirty thousand invited to attend one of the Queen's three annual garden parties – the replacements for the society debutantes' "coming out" parties, which ceased to be royally sanctioned in 1958 – you had little chance of ever seeing inside Buckingham Palace. Since 1993, however, the hallowed portals have been grudgingly opened for two months of the year. **Timed tickets** can be purchased in advance or from the box office on the south side of the palace; queues vary enormously, but you may have some time to wait before your allocated slot.

The interior

Of the palace's 775 rooms you get to see the twenty or so grandest ones, and as the Queen and her family decamp to Scotland every summer, there's little sign of life. The visitors' entrance is via the **Ambassadors' Court** on Buckingham Palace Road, which lets you into the enormous **Quadrangle**, from where you can see the Nash portico, built in warm Bath stone, that used to overlook St James's Park.

Through the courtyard, you hit the **Grand Hall**, decorated like some gloomy hotel lobby, from where Nash's rather splendid winding, curlicued **Grand Staircase**, with its floral gilt-bronze balustrade and white plaster friezes, leads past a range of very fine royal portraits, all beautifully lit by Nash's glass dome. Beyond, the small Guard Room leads into the **Green Drawing Room**, a blaze of unusually bright green silk walls, framed by lattice-patterned pilasters, and a heavily gilded coved ceiling. It was here that the Raphael Cartoons used to hang, until they were permanently loaned to the V&A. The scarlet and gold **Throne Room** features a Neoclassical plaster frieze in the style of the Elgin Marbles, depicting the Wars of the Roses. The thrones themselves are disappointingly un-regal – just two pink his 'n' hers chairs initialled ER and P – whereas George IV's outrageous sphinx-style chariot seats, nearby, look more the part.

Nash originally designed a spectacular hammerbeam ceiling for the **Picture Gallery**, which stretches right down the centre of the palace. Unfortunately, it leaked and was eventually replaced in 1914 by a rather dull glazed ceiling. Still, the paintings on show here are excellent and include several Van Dycks, two Rembrandts, two Canalettos, a Poussin, a de Hooch and a wonderful Vermeer. Further on, in the East Gallery, check the cherub-fest in the grisaille frieze, before heading into the palace's rather overwrought **Ballroom**. It's here that the Queen holds her State Banquets, where the annual Diplomatic Reception takes place, and where folk receive their honours and knighthoods.

Having passed through several smaller rooms, you eventually reach the **State Dining Room**, whose heavily gilded ceiling, with its three saucer domes, is typical of the suite of rooms that overlooks the palace garden. Next door lies Nash's not very blue, but incredibly gold, **Blue Drawing Room**, lined with flock wallpaper interspersed with thirty fake onyx columns. The room contains one of George IV's most prized possessions, the "Table of the Grand Commanders", originally made for Napoleon, whose *trompe-l'oeil* Sèvres porcelain top features cameo-like portraits of the military commanders of antiquity.

Beyond the domed Music Room with its enormous semicircular bow window and impressive parquet floor, the **White Drawing Room** features yet another frothy gold and white Nash ceiling and a superb portrait of Queen Alexandra, wife of Edward VII. This room is also the incongruous setting for an annual royal prank: when hosting the reception for the diplomatic corps, the Queen and family emerge from a secret door behind a mirror to greet the ambassadors. Before you leave the palace, be sure to check out the Canova sculptures: *Mars and Venus* at the bottom of the Ministers' Staircase, and the pornographic *Fountain Nymph with Putto* in the Marble Hall. You exit via the palace gardens, the city's largest private gardens, and are finally ejected onto busy Grosvenor Place.

Queen's Gallery

A Doric portico on the south side of the palace forms the entrance to the **Queen's Gallery** (daily 10am–5.30pm; £8.50; ☏020/7766 7301, ⓦwww .royal.gov.uk; Victoria tube), which puts on temporary exhibitions drawn from the **Royal Collection**, a superlative array of art that includes works by Michelangelo, Raphael, Holbein, Reynolds, Gainsborough, Vermeer, Van Dyck, Rubens, Rembrandt and Canaletto, as well as the world's largest collection of Leonardo drawings, the odd Fabergé egg and heaps of Sèvres china. The Queen holds the Royal Collection, which is three times larger than the National Gallery, "in trust for her successors and the nation" – note the word order. However, with over seven thousand works spread over the numerous royal palaces, the Queen's Gallery, and other museums and galleries around the country, you'd have to pay a king's ransom to see the lot.

Royal Mews

A little further down Buckingham Palace Road, you'll find the **Royal Mews** (Easter–July & Oct daily except Fri 11am–4pm; Aug & Sept daily 10am–5pm; £7.50; ☏020/7766 7302, ⓦwww.royal.gov.uk; Victoria tube), built by Nash in the 1820s. The horses – or at least their backsides – can be viewed in their luxury stables, along with an exhibition of equine accoutrements, but it's the royal carriages, lined up under a glass canopy in the courtyard, that are the main attraction. The most ornate is the **Gold State Coach**, made for George III in 1762, smothered in 22-carat gilding, panel paintings by Cipriani, and weighing four

---

The Royal Family

Tourists still flock to see London's royal palaces, but the British public have become much less willing to foot the huge tax bill that goes to support the Royal Family (ⓦwww.royal.gov.uk) in the style to which they are accustomed. Matters came to a head over who should pay for the £50 million worth of repairs after the **1992 fire at Windsor Castle**. Misjudging the public mood, the Conservative government offered taxpayers' money to foot the entire bill. After a furore, the royals decided to raise some of the money by opening Buckingham Palace to the public for the first time (and by cranking up the admission charges on all the royal residences).

In addition, the Queen agreed to reduce the number of royals paid out of the Civil List, and, for the first time in her life, pay taxes on her personal fortune. Estimates of the **Queen's wealth** range from a modest £500 million (for her personal fortune) to £50 billion (if you include the assets she holds for the nation). Whatever the truth, she's certainly not hard up, and public subsidy of the richest woman in the world doesn't stop at the Civil List, as millions more are spent by government departments on luxuries such as the Royal Squadron (for air travel) and the Royal Train (estimated at around £30,000 per trip), not to mention the upkeep of the palaces.

The Queen's **Golden Jubilee** Year in 2002 was a rare PR success, but there have been plenty of subsequent royal gaffes to keep the tabloids and republicans happy. Yet despite the Royal Family's overall drop in popularity over the last couple of decades, none of the mainstream political parties currently advocates scrapping the monarchy. So the royal soap opera looks safe to run for many years to come.

tons, its axles supporting four life-size Tritons blowing conches. Eight horses are needed to pull it and the whole experience apparently made Queen Victoria feel quite sick; since then it has only been used for coronations and jubilees. The mews also house the Royal Family's fleet of five Rolls Royce Phantoms and three Daimlers, none of which is obliged to carry numberplates.

Lower Regent Street and Waterloo Place

Lower Regent Street, at the northeastern edge of St James's, was the first stage in John Nash's ambitious plan to link the Prince Regent's magnificent Carlton House with Regent's Park. Like so many of Nash's grandiose schemes, it never quite came to fruition, as George IV, soon after ascending the throne, decided that Carlton House – the most expensive palace ever to have been built in London – wasn't quite luxurious enough, and had it pulled down. Its Corinthian columns now support the main portico of the National Gallery.

Instead, Lower Regent Street opens into **Waterloo Place**, which Nash extended beyond Pall Mall once Carlton House had been demolished. At the centre of the square stands the **Guards' Crimean Memorial**, fashioned from captured Russian cannons, and commemorating the 2162 Foot Guards who died during the Crimean War – the horrors of battle were witnessed by Florence Nightingale (see p.226), whose statue graces one of the monument's pedestals.

Having dodged the traffic hurtling down Pall Mall and cutting the square in two, you come face to face with St James's two grandest gentlemen's clubs (see box, p.82): the former **United Services Club** (now the Institute of Directors), to the east, and the **Athenaeum**, to the west. Their almost identical Neoclassical designs are by Nash's protégé Decimus Burton: the better-looking is the Athenaeum, its portico sporting a garish gilded statue of the goddess Athena and, above, a Wedgwood-type frieze inspired by the Elgin Marbles, which had just arrived in London. The Duke of Wellington was a regular at the United Services Club, over the road, and the horse blocks – confusingly positioned outside the Athenaeum – were designed so the duke could mount his steed more easily.

Appropriately enough, a statue of that eminently clubbable man, **Edward VII** sits permanently on his horse between the two clubs. Behind the railings of nearby Waterloo Gardens, there's one of **Captain Scott**, sculpted by the widow he left behind after failing to complete the return journey from the South Pole. Beyond, overlooking St James's Park, is the "Grand Old" **Duke of York's Column**, erected in 1833, ten years before Nelson's more famous one, and paid for by stopping one day's wages of every soldier in the army that he marched "up the hill and down again", in the famous nursery rhyme.

Having pulled his old palace down, George IV had Nash build **Carlton House Terrace**, whose monumental facade now looks out onto St James's Park. Number 4, by the exquisitely tranquil Carlton Gardens, was handed to de Gaulle for the headquarters of the Free French during World War II; while nos. 7–9, by the Duke of York steps, served as the German embassy until World War II. Albert Speer designed the interior under the Nazis, while outside a tiny grave for *ein treuer Begleiter* (a true friend) lurks behind the railings near the column – it holds the remains of **Giro**, the Nazi ambassador's pet Alsatian, accidentally electrocuted in February 1934.

Pall Mall and around

Running west from Trafalgar Square across Waterloo Place, **Pall Mall** is renowned for its gentlemen's clubs, whose restrained Italianate and Neoclassical facades, fronted by cast-iron torches, still punctuate the street. It gets its bizarre name from the game of *pallo a maglio* (ball to mallet) – something like modern croquet – popularized by Charles II and played here and on The Mall. Crowds gathered here in 1807 when it became London's first gas-lit street – the original closely spaced lampposts (erected to reduce the opportunities for crime and prostitution) are still standing – but today's heavy traffic makes Pall Mall no fun to explore.

One block north is the peaceful enclave of **St James's Square**, laid out in the 1670s. Around the time of George III's birth at no. 31 in 1738, the square boasted no fewer than six dukes and seven earls, and over the decades it has maintained its exclusive air: no. 10 was occupied in turn by prime ministers Pitt the Elder, Lord Derby and Gladstone; at no. 16 you'll find the silliest-sounding gentlemen's club, the East India, Devonshire, Sports and Public Schools Club; no. 4 was the home of Nancy Astor, the first woman MP to sit in the House of Commons, in 1919; while no. 31 is where Eisenhower formed the first Allied HQ. The narrowest house on the square (no. 14) is home to the **London Library**, the oldest private library in the country, founded in 1841 by Thomas Carlyle, who got sick of waiting up to two hours for books to be retrieved from the British Library shelves only to find he couldn't borrow them (he used to steal them instead). It's open only to fee-paying members.

The square is no longer residential and, architecturally it's not quite the period piece it once was, but its proportions remain intact, as do the central **gardens**, which feature an equestrian statue of William III, depicted tripping over on the molehill that killed him at Hampton Court. In the northeastern corner, there's a small memorial marking the spot where police officer Yvonne Fletcher was

The gentlemen's clubs

The **gentlemen's clubs** of Pall Mall and St James's Street remain the final bastions of the male chauvinism and public-school snobbery for which England is famous. Their origins lie in the coffee- and chocolate-houses of the eighteenth century, though the majority were founded in the post-Napoleonic peace of the early nineteenth century by those who yearned for the life of the officers' mess; drinking, whoring and gambling were the major features of early club life. **White's** – the oldest of the lot, and with a list of members that still includes numerous royals (Prince Charles held his [first] stag party here), prime ministers and admirals – used to be the unofficial Tory party headquarters, renowned for its high gambling stakes, while, opposite, was the Whigs' favourite club, **Brooks's**. Bets were wagered over the most trivial of things to relieve the boredom – "a thousand meadows and cornfields were staked at every throw" – and in 1755 one MP, Sir John Bland, shot himself after losing £32,000 in one night.

In their day, the clubs were also the battleground of sartorial elegance, particularly **Boodle's**, where the dandy-in-chief Beau Brummell set the fashion trends for the London upper class and provided endless fuel for gossip. It was said that Brummell's greatest achievement in life was his starched neckcloth, and that the Prince Regent himself wept openly when Brummell criticized the line of his cravat. More serious political disputes were played out in clubland, too. The **Reform Club** on Pall Mall, from which Phileas Fogg set off in Jules Verne's *Around the World in Eighty Days*, was the gathering place of the liberals behind the 1832 Reform Act, and remains one of the more "progressive" – it's one of the few to admit women as members. The Tories, led by Wellington, countered by starting up the **Carlton Club** for those opposed to the Act – it's still the leading Conservative club, and still men-only (Mrs Thatcher was made a special member).

shot dead in 1984 during a raid on what was then the Libyan People's Bureau, at no. 5, by Libyan dissidents.

Back on Pall Mall, the unusual seventeenth-century facade of **Schomberg House**, rebuilt in the 1950s, is one of the few to stand out, thanks to its Dutch-style red brickwork and elongated caryatids; it was here in the 1780s that James Graham ran his Temple of Health and Hymen, where couples having trouble conceiving could try their luck in the "grand celestial bed". Next door, at no. 79, Charles II housed **Nell Gwynne**, so that the two of them could chat over the garden wall, which once backed onto the grounds of St James's Palace. It was from one of the windows overlooking the garden that Nell is alleged to have dangled her 6-year-old, threatening to drop him if Charles didn't acknowledge paternity and give the boy a title, at which Charles yelled out "Save the Earl of Burford!"; another, more tabloid-style version of the story alleges that Charles was persuaded only after overhearing Nell saying "Come here, you little bastard", then excusing herself on the grounds that she had no other name by which to call him.

St James's Palace

At the western end of Pall Mall stands **St James's Palace** (Green Park tube), built on the site of a lepers' hospital which Henry VIII bought in 1532. Bloody Mary died here in 1558 (her heart and bowels were buried in the Chapel Royal), and it was here that Charles I chose to sleep the night before his execution, so as not to have to listen to his scaffold being erected. When Whitehall Palace burnt down in 1698, St James's became the principal royal residence and even today every ambassador to the UK is accredited to the "Court of St James's", even though the court moved over to Buckingham Palace in 1837. The main red-brick gate-tower, which looks out onto St James's Street, is a survivor from Tudor times; the rest of the modest, rambling, crenel-lated complex was restored and remodelled by Nash, and now provides a home for Princess Anne and Princess Alexandra.

St James's Palace is off-limits to the public, with the exception of the **Chapel Royal**, which is open for services only (Oct to Easter Sun 8.30am & 11.15am); access is from Cleveland Row. Charles I took Holy Communion in the chapel on the morning of his execution, and here, too, the marriages of William and Mary, George III and Queen Charlotte, Victoria and Albert, and George V and Queen Mary, took place. One of the few remaining sections of Henry VIII's palace, it was redecorated in the 1830s, though the gilded strap-work ceiling matches the Tudor original erected to commemorate the brief marriage of Henry and Anne of Cleves (and thought to have been the work of Hans Holbein). The chapel's musical pedigree is impressive, with Tallis, Byrd, Gibbons and Purcell all having worked here as organists. Purcell even had rooms in the palace, which the poet Dryden used to use in order to hide from his creditors.

Clarence House

John Nash was also responsible for **Clarence House** (Aug & Sept daily 10am–5.30pm; £7.50; ☎020/7766 7303, ⓦwww.royal.gov.uk; Green Park tube), connected to the southwest wing of St James's Palace. Built in the 1820s for William IV and used as his principal residence, it was home to the Queen Mother, widow of George VI, until 2002, and is now the official London home of Charles and Camilla (ⓦwww.princeofwales.gov.uk). A handful of rooms can be visited over the summer when the royals are in Scotland. Visits must be booked in advance and are by **guided tour** only, and the rooms are pretty unremarkable, so apart from a peek behind the scenes in a working royal palace, or a few mementoes of the Queen Mum, the main draw is the twentieth-century British paintings on display by the likes of Walter Sickert and Augustus John.

Queen's Chapel and Marlborough House

On the other side of Marlborough Road is the **Queen's Chapel**, once part of St James's Palace but now in the grounds of Marlborough House, and open only for services (Easter Sun to July Sun 8.30am & 11.15am). A perfectly proportioned classical church, it was designed by Inigo Jones for the Infanta of Spain, intended child bride of Charles I, and later completed for his French wife, Henrietta Maria, who was also a practising Catholic. A little further down Marlborough Road is the glorious Art-Nouveau memorial to **Queen Alexandra** (wife of Edward VII), the last work of Alfred Gilbert (of Eros fame), comprising a bronze fountain crammed with allegorical figures and flanked by robust lampposts.

Marlborough House itself is hidden from Marlborough Road by a high, brick wall, and only partly visible from The Mall. Queen Anne sacrificed half her garden in granting this land to her lover, Sarah Jennings, Duchess of Marlborough, in 1709. The duchess, in turn, told Wren to design her a "strong, plain and convenient" palace, only to sack him later and finish the plans off herself. The highlight of the interior is the **Blenheim Saloon**, with its frescoes depicting the first duke's eponymous victory, along with ceiling paintings by Gentileschi transferred from the Queen's House in Greenwich. The royals took over in 1817, though the last one to live here was Queen Mary, wife of George V. Since 1965, the palace has been the Commonwealth headquarters, and can only be visited on a guided tour (Tues mornings for groups of ten or more; ☎020/7747 6491, ⓦwww.thecommonwealth.org; Green Park tube).

▲ Queen Alexandra memorial

Jermyn Street

Jermyn Street (pronounced "German Street"), which runs parallel with Piccadilly, has been, along with Savile Row in Mayfair, the spiritual home of English gentlemen's fashion since the advent of the clubs (see box, p.82). Its window displays and wooden-panelled interiors still evoke an age when mass consumerism was unthinkable, and when it was considered that gentlemen "should either be a work of art or wear a work of art", as Oscar Wilde put it. Those sort of Englishmen are now a dying breed, and these days Americans and Japanese tend to make up a large proportion of the customers.

Antiquated epithets are part of the street's quaint appeal: Taylor, a barber's at no. 74, still describe themselves as "Court hairdressers"; Foster & Son, a shoe shop at no. 85, style themselves as "Bootmakers since 1840"; while Geo. F. Trumper, at no. 20, is billed as a "Gentlemen's Perfumer". Floris, at no. 89, covers up the Royal Family's body odour with its ever-so-English fragrances, and Paxton & Whitfield, at no. 93, boasts an unrivalled selection of English and foreign cheeses. Lastly, at no. 21a, there's Bates the hatters, not quite as famous as Lock & Co at 6 St James's St, where the bowler hat was invented in 1850, but more memorable thanks to Binks, the stray cat which entered the shop in 1921 and never left, having been stuffed and displayed in a glass cabinet inside the shop, sporting a cigar and top hat. Notably, too, the shop has never had anything so vulgar as a sale.

Green Park

To the west of St James's Palace lies **Green Park**, laid out on the burial ground of the old lepers' hospital by Henry VIII. It was left more or less flowerless – hence its name (officially "The Green Park") – and, apart from the springtime swaths of daffodils and crocuses, it remains mostly meadow, shaded by graceful London plane trees. In its time, however, it was a popular place for duels (banned from neighbouring St James's Park), ballooning and fireworks displays. One such display was immortalized by Handel's *Music for the Royal Fireworks*, performed here on April 27, 1749, to celebrate the Peace of Aix-la-Chapelle, which ended the War of the Austrian Succession – over ten thousand fireworks were let off, setting fire to the custom-built Temple of Peace and causing three fatalities. The music was a great success, however.

Along the east side of the park runs the wide, pedestrian-only **Queen's Walk**, laid out for Queen Caroline, wife of George II, who had a little pavilion built nearby. At its southern end, there's a good view of **Lancaster House** (closed to the public), a grand Neoclassical palace built in rich Bath stone in the 1820s by Benjamin Wyatt, and used for government receptions and conferences since 1913. It was here that the end of white rule in Southern Rhodesia was negotiated in the late 1970s.

Just up from Lancaster House a sign in the garden announces Princess Diana's ancestral home, **Spencer House** (Feb–July & Sept–Dec Sun 10.30am–5.45pm; £9, no under-10s; ☎020/7499 8620, Ⓦwww.spencerhouse.co.uk; Green Park tube), one of London's finest Palladian mansions. Erected in the 1750s, its best-looking facade looks out over Queen's Walk onto Green Park, though access is from St James's Place. Inside, tour guides take you through nine of the state rooms, returned to something like their original condition by current owners, the Rothschilds. The Great Room features a stunning coved and coffered ceiling in green, white and gold, while the adjacent Painted Room is a feast of Neoclassicism, decorated with murals in the "Pompeian manner". The most outrageous decor, though, is to be found in Lord Spencer's Room, with its astonishing gilded palm-tree columns.

Mayfair

Along with neighbouring St James's and Marylebone, **Mayfair** emerged in the eighteenth century as one of London's first real residential suburbs. Sheep and cattle were driven off the land by the area's big landowners (the largest of whom are the Grosvenor family, whose head is the Duke of Westminster, Britain's third richest man) to make way for London's first major planned development: a web of brick-and-stucco terraces and grid-plan streets feeding into grand, formal squares, with mews and stables round the back. Mayfair quickly began to attract aristocratic London away from hitherto fashionable Covent Garden and Soho, and set the westward trend for upper-middle-class migration. The infamous fifteen-day fair, after which the area was named, bit the dust in 1764 after the newly ensconced wealthy residents complained of the "drunkenness, fornication, gaming and lewdness".

Nowadays, upmarket shops, offices, embassies and lavish hotels outnumber aristocratic pieds-à-terre, yet the social cachet of Mayfair's luxury apartments and mews houses has remained much the same. This is, after all, where the fictional Wooster – the perfect upper-class Englishman – and his faithful valet Jeeves, of P.G. Wodehouse's novels, lived. The borders of Mayfair, in particular, are among London's prime shopping streets, and it's here that Londoners mean when they talk of "going shopping up the West End". **Piccadilly** is no longer the fashionable promenade it once was, but a whiff of exclusivity still pervades **Bond Street** and its tributaries. **Regent Street** was created in 1812 as a new "Royal Mile" but took a while to catch on; **Oxford Street**, to the north, only came into its own early last century, though it now surpasses the lot for the sheer mass of people fighting their way down it.

Piccadilly Circus and around

Tacky and congested it may be, but **Piccadilly Circus** is, for many Londoners, the nearest their city comes to having a centre. A much-altered product of Nash's grand 1812 **Regent Street** plan, and now a major bottleneck, with traffic from Piccadilly, Shaftesbury Avenue and Regent Street all converging, it's by no means a picturesque place, and is probably best seen at night, when the spread of illuminated signs (a feature since the Edwardian era) gives it a touch of Times Square dazzle, and when the human traffic flow is at its most frenetic.

As well as being the gateway to the West End, this is also prime tourist territory, thanks mostly to the celebrated Shaftesbury Memorial, popularly

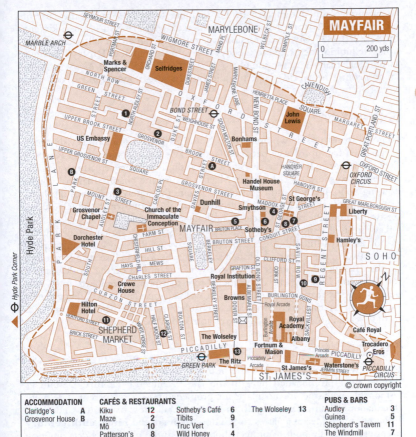

ACCOMMODATION		CAFÉS & RESTAURANTS						PUBS & BARS	
Claridge's	A	Kiku	12	Sotheby's Café	6	The Wolseley	13	Audley	3
Grosvenor House	B	Maze	2	Tibits	9			Guinea	5
		Mô	10	Truc Vert	1			Shepherd's Tavern	11
		Patterson's	8	Wild Honey	4			The Windmill	7

known as **Eros**. The fountain's aluminium archer is one of London's top tourist attractions, a status that baffles all who live here – when it was first unveiled in 1893, it was so unpopular that the sculptor, Alfred Gilbert, lived in self-imposed exile for the next thirty years. Despite his bow and arrow, the figure actually represents the *Angel of Christian Charity*, erected to commemorate the Earl of Shaftesbury, a Bible-thumping social reformer who campaigned against child labour.

Behind Eros, it's worth popping in to **The Criterion** restaurant, at no. 224 Piccadilly, just for a drink, so you can soak in probably the most spectacular Victorian interior in London, with Byzantine-style gilded mosaic ceiling.

Trocadero

Just east of the Circus, tacky **Trocadero** (daily 10am–midnight, Fri & Sat until 1am; Ⓦ www.londontrocadero.com; Piccadilly Circus tube) was originally an opulent restaurant, from 1896 until its closure in 1965. Since then, millions have been poured into this glorified amusement arcade, casino and multiplex cinema, in an unsuccessful attempt to find a winning formula. Among the current incumbents are **Amora** (Mon–Thurs 1pm–midnight, Fri–Sun 11am–midnight; ℡0871/230 9876, ⓦwww.amoralondon.com; £15), an erotic (allegedly educational) exhibition dedicated to the joys of sex, and a branch of **Ripley's Believe It or Not!** (daily 10am–midnight; £17.95; ℡020/3238 0022, ⓦwww.ripleys london.com), the world's largest odditorium, a sort-of waxwork version of a Victorian freak show.

Regent Street

Regent Street was drawn up by John Nash in 1812 as both a luxury shopping street and a triumphal way between George IV's Carlton House and Regent's Park to the north. It was the city's first stab at slum clearance, creating a tangible borderline to shore up fashionable Mayfair against the chaotic maze of neighbouring Soho. Today, it's still possible to admire the stately intentions of Nash's plan, even though the original arcading of the **Quadrant**, which curves westwards from Piccadilly Circus, is no longer there.

Regent Street enjoyed eighty years as Bond Street's nearest rival, before the rise of the city's middle classes ushered in heavyweight stores catering for the masses. Two of the oldest established stores can be found close to one another on the east side of the street: **Hamleys**, which claims to be the world's largest toy shop, and **Liberty**, the department store that popularized Arts and Crafts designs. Liberty features a central roof-lit well, surrounded by wooden galleries carved from the timbers of two old naval battleships; an overhead walkway leads to the eye-catching mock-Tudor extension, added in the 1920s.

Piccadilly

Piccadilly apparently got its name from the ruffs or "pickadills" worn by the dandies who promenaded here in the late seventeenth century. Despite its fashionable pedigree, it's no place for promenading in its current state, with three lanes of traffic careering down it nose to tail most of the day and night. Infinitely more pleasant places to window-shop are the **nineteenth–century arcades**, originally built to protect shoppers from the mud and horse dung on the streets, but now equally useful for escaping exhaust fumes.

Down to the Ritz

With the exception of the black modernist 1930s facade of **Waterstone's** multi storey flagship bookshop (originally built as Simpson's department store), there's nothing much to distract the eye along Piccadilly until you reach **St James's Church** (ⓦwww.st-james-piccadilly.org), Wren's favourite parish church (he built it himself). The church has rich furnishings, with the reredos, organ-casing and font all by the master sculptor **Grinling Gibbons**. St James's also runs a daily craft market in the churchyard, a café at the west end of the church, and puts on top-class, free lunchtime concerts.

Piccadilly may not be the shopping heaven it once was, but it still harbours several old firms that proudly display their royal warrants. **Hatchard's Bookshop**, at no. 187, was founded in 1797, as a cross between a gentlemen's club and a library, with benches outside for servants and daily papers for the gentlemen inside to peruse. Today, it's simply a branch of Waterstone's, elegant still, but with its old traditions marked most overtly by a large section on international royalty.

An even older institution is **Fortnum & Mason** (ⓦwww.fortnumandmason .com), the food emporium at no. 181, established in the 1770s by Charles

Fortnum, one of George III's footmen. Over the main entrance, the figures of its founders bow to each other on the hour as the clock clanks out the Eton school anthem – a kitsch addition dating from 1964. The store is most famous for its opulent food hall and its picnic hampers, first introduced as "concentrated lunches" for hunting and shooting parties, and now *de rigueur* for Ascot, Glyndebourne, Henley and other society events. Fortnum's is credited with the invention of the Scotch Egg in 1851, and was also the first store in the world to sell Heinz baked beans in 1886.

Further along Piccadilly, on the corner of Arlington Street, **The Wolseley** (Ⓦ www.thewolseley.com) is a superb Art Deco building, originally built as a Wolseley car showroom in the 1920s, now a café (see p.378). The most striking original features are the zigzag inlaid marble flooring, the chinoiserie woodwork and the giant red Japanese lacquer columns. Across St James's Street, with its best rooms overlooking Green Park, stands the **Ritz Hotel** (Ⓦ www.theritzhotel .co.uk), a byword for decadence since it first wowed Edwardian society in 1906. The hotel's design, with its two-storey French-style mansard roof and long arcade, was based on the rue de Rivoli in Paris.

Royal Academy

The **Royal Academy of Arts** (daily 10am–6pm, Fri until 10pm; £7–10; Ⓣ 020/7300 8000, Ⓦ www.royalacademy.org.uk; Green Park tube) occupies Burlington House, one of the few survivors from the ranks of aristocratic mansions that once lined the north side of Piccadilly. Rebuilding in the nineteenth century destroyed the original curved colonnades beyond the main gateway, but the complex has kept the feel of a Palladian *palazzo*. The academy itself was the country's first formal art school, founded in 1768 by a group of painters including Thomas Gainsborough and Joshua Reynolds. Reynolds

▲ Royal Academy

Monopoly

Although **Monopoly** was patented during the Depression by an American, Charles Darrow, the British really took to the game, and the UK version was the one used in the rest of the world outside of the US. In 1935, to choose appropriate streets and stations for the game, the company director of Waddington's in Leeds sent his son, Norman Watson, and his secretary, Marjorie Phillips, on a day-trip to London. She came up with an odd assortment, ranging from the bottom-ranking Old Kent Road (still as tatty as ever) to an obscure dead-end street in the West End (Vine Street), and chose only northern train stations. All the properties have gone up in value since the board's inception (six zeros need to be added to most), but Mayfair and Park Lane (its western border), the most expensive properties on the Monopoly board, are still aspirational addresses.

went on to become the academy's first president, and his statue now stands in the courtyard, palette in hand ready to paint the cars hurtling down Piccadilly.

The academy's alumni range from Turner and Constable to Hockney and Tracey Emin, though the college has always had a conservative reputation for both for its teaching and its shows. The most famous event in the RA's calendar is the **Summer Exhibition**, which first took place in 1769, and runs from June to mid-August each year. It's an odd event: anyone can enter paintings in any style, and the lucky winners get hung, in rather close proximity, and sold. In addition, RA "Academicians" are allowed to display six of their own works – no matter how awful. The result is a bewildering display, which gets annually panned by the critics.

As well as hosting exhibitions, the RA has a small selection of works from its own collection on **permanent display** in the white and gold John Madejski Fine Rooms (Tues–Fri 1–4.30pm, Sat & Sun 10am–6pm; free; free guided tours Tues, Thurs & Fri 1pm, Wed 1 & 3pm & Sat 11.30am). Highlights include a Rembrandtesque self-portrait by Reynolds, plus works by the likes of Constable, Hockney and Stanley Spencer. To see the gallery's most valuable asset, Michelangelo's marble relief, the *Taddei Tondo*, head for the glass atrium of Norman Foster's Sackler Galleries, at the back of the building.

Albany and Piccadilly's arcades

Another palatial Piccadilly residence which has avoided redevelopment is **Albany**, a plain, H-shaped Georgian mansion, designed by William Chambers, neatly recessed behind its own iron railings and courtyard, east of the Royal Academy. Built in the 1770s for Lord Melbourne, it was divided in 1802 into a series of self-contained bachelor "sets" for members of the nearby gentlemen's clubs too drunk to make it home. Only those who had no connections with trade, and did not keep a musical instrument or a wife, were permitted to live here, and over the years they have been occupied by such literary figures as Byron, J.B. Priestley, Aldous Huxley, Patrick Hamilton and Graham Greene.

Along the other side of the Royal Academy runs the **Burlington Arcade** (Mon–Sat 8am–7pm, Sun 11am–5pm; ⓦwww.burlington-arcade.co.uk), built in 1819 for Lord Cavendish, then owner of Burlington House, to prevent commoners throwing rubbish into his garden. Today, it's London's longest and most expensive nineteenth-century arcade, lined with mahogany-fronted jewellers, gentlemen's outfitters and the like. Upholding Regency decorum, it's still illegal to whistle, sing, hum, hurry or carry large packages or open umbrellas on this small stretch, and the arcade's beadles (known as Burlington Berties), in their Edwardian frock coats and gold-braided top hats, take the prevention of such criminality very seriously.

Neither of Piccadilly's other two arcades can hold a torch to the Burlington, though they are still worth exploring if only to marvel at the strange mixture of shops. The finer of the two is the **Piccadilly Arcade** (Ⓦwww.piccadilly -arcade.com), an Edwardian extension to the Burlington on the south side of Piccadilly whose squeaky-clean bow windows display, among other items, Wedgwood porcelain, Russian icons, model soldiers and buttons and badges supplied to Prince Charles. The **Princes Arcade**, to the east, exudes a more discreet Neoclassical elegance and contains Prestat (Ⓦwww.prestat.co.uk), purveyors of handmade, hand-packed chocolates and truffles to the Queen.

Bond Street and the squares

Bond Street runs more or less parallel to Regent Street, extending north from Piccadilly all the way to Oxford Street. It is, in fact, two streets rolled into one: the southern half, laid out in the 1680s, is known as Old Bond Street; its northern extension, which followed less than fifty years later, is known as New Bond Street. In contrast to their international rivals, rue de Rivoli and Fifth Avenue, both Bond streets are pretty unassuming architecturally – a mixture of modest Georgian and Victorian townhouses – but the shops that line them are among the flashiest in London. With so many retailers and offices around Piccadilly and Bond Street, Mayfair's residential heart has been pushed westwards into the backstreets north of Piccadilly. This area is dominated by Mayfair's two most grandiose squares, **Berkeley** and **Grosvenor**, named after the district's two big private landowners. Planned as purely residential, both have suffered over the years, and have nothing like the homogeneity of the Bloomsbury squares. Nevertheless, they are still impressive urban spaces, and their social lustre remains more or less untarnished.

Bond Street and around

Unlike its overtly masculine counterpart, Jermyn Street, **Bond Street** caters for both sexes, and although it has its fair share of old-established names, it's also home to flagship branches of multinational **designer clothes** outlets like Prada, Versace, Chanel and so on. This designer madness also spills over into **Conduit Street**, home to John Richmond, Issey Miyake, Vivienne Westwood and Moschino, as well as into neighbouring Dover Street, where Comme des Garçons have opened a vast indoor fashion bazaar at nos. 17–18.

In addition to fashion, Bond Street is renowned for its **auction houses** and **fine art galleries**. Visiting the auction houses is free and can be fun (see box, p.92), but even if you don't venture in, take a look at the doorway of **Sotheby's** at 34–35 New Bond St, topped by London's oldest outdoor sculpture, an Egyptian statue dating from 1600 BC. Bond Street's art galleries are actually outnumbered by those on neighbouring **Cork Street**. The main difference between the two is that the Bond Street dealers are basically heirloom offloaders, whereas Cork Street galleries sell largely contemporary art. Both have somewhat intimidating staff, but if you're interested, walk in (or ring the bell) and look around. They're only shops, after all.

Auction houses

A very Mayfair-style entertainment lies in visiting the area's trio of auction houses: **Sotheby's**, 34–35 New Bond St (℡020/7293 5000, ⓦwww.sothebys.com), was founded in 1744 and is the oldest of the three, though its pre-eminence only really dates from the last war; **Bonhams**, founded in 1793 (and now merged with Phillips), is at 101 New Bond St (℡020/7447 7447, ⓦwww.bonhams.com); and **Christie's**, founded in 1766, is actually over in St James's at 8 King St (℡020/7839 9060, ⓦwww.christies.com).

Viewing takes place from Monday to Friday, and also occasionally at the weekend, and entry to the galleries is free of charge, though if you don't buy a catalogue, the only information you'll glean is the lot number. Thousands of the works that pass through the rooms are of museum quality, and, if you're lucky, you might catch a glimpse of a masterpiece in transit between private collections. Anyone can attend the auctions themselves, though remember to keep your hands firmly out of view unless you're bidding.

Sotheby's is probably the least intimidating: there's an excellent **café**, and staff offer free valuations, if you have an heirloom of your own to check out. There's always a line of people unwrapping plastic bags under the polite gaze of valuation staff, who call in the experts if they see something that sniffs of real money. Christie's and Sotheby's, once quintessentially English institutions, are now under foreign control, with only Bonhams remaining British-owned. In 2002, Sotheby's and Christie's were found guilty of rigging the art market, defrauding sellers out of £290 million. Christie's escaped a fine because it confessed its sins, but Sotheby's was fined £12 million, and its former chairman jailed for a year.

Bond Street also has its fair share of perfumeries and **jewellers**, many of them long-established outlets that have survived the vicissitudes of fashion, and some, like De Beers, relatively recent arrivals. One of the most famous is **Asprey** (ⓦwww.asprey.com), at the corner of New Bond Street and Grafton Street, founded in 1781 by a family of Huguenot craftsmen, and now jewellers to the royals. The facade of the store features a wonderful parade of arched windows, flanked by slender Corinthian wrought-iron columns. Close by is "Allies", a popular double statue of **Winston Churchill and President Roosevelt** enjoying a chat on a park bench.

One Bond Street institution you can feel free to walk into is **Smythson** (ⓦwww.smythson.com), at 40 New Bond St, the bespoke stationers, founded in 1887, who made their name printing Big Game books for colonialists to record what they'd bagged out in Africa and India. At the back of the shop is a small octagonal museum encrusted with shells and mirrors, and a few artefacts: photos and replicas of the book of condolence Smythson created for JFK's funeral, and the cherry calf-and-vellum diary given to Princess Grace of Monaco as a wedding gift.

Royal Arcade and Albemarle Street

On the west side of Old Bond Street, a garish orange-and-white plasterwork entrance announces the **Royal Arcade**, a full-blown High Victorian shopping mall with tall arched bays and an elegant glass roof, designed so that the wealthy guests of **Brown's** (ⓦwww.brownshotel.com) in **Albemarle Street** could have a sheltered and suitably elegant approach to the shops on Bond Street. Apart from being a posh hotel opened in the 1830s by James Brown, Byron's former valet, *Brown's* was where the country's first telephone call was placed by **Alexander Graham Bell** in 1876, though initially he got a crossed line with a private telegraph wire. Also in Albemarle Street, at no. 50, are the offices of **John Murray**, the publishers of Byron and of the oldest British travel guides. It was here in 1824 that Byron's memoirs were burnt to cinders, after Murray persuaded Tom Moore, to whom they had been bequeathed, that they were too scurrilous to publish.

Further up Albemarle Street, at no. 21, is the weighty Neoclassical facade of the **Royal Institution** (Mon–Fri 9am–9pm; free; T020/7409 2992, W www .rigb.org; Green Park tube), a scientific body founded in 1799 "for teaching by courses of philosophical lectures and experiments the application of science to the common purposes of life". The RI is best known for its six Christmas Lectures, begun by Michael Faraday and designed to popularize science among schoolchildren, but it also houses an enjoyable interactive **museum** aimed at both kids and adults. In the basement, you can learn about the ten elements that have been discovered at the RI, and about the famous experiments that have taken place here: Tyndall's blue-sky tube, Humphry Davy's early lamps and Faraday's explorations into electromagnetism – there's even a reconstruction of Faraday's lab from the 1850s. The ground floor has displays on the fourteen Nobel Prize winners who have worked at the RI, while on the first floor, you can visit the semi circular hall where the Christmas Lectures take place and see some of the apparatus used in lectures over the decades.

Savile Row

Running parallel with New Bond Street, to the east, is another classic address in sartorial matters, **Savile Row**, *the* place to go for bespoke tailors since the early nineteenth century. Gieves & Hawkes (W www.gievesandhawkes.com), at no. 1, were the first tailors to establish themselves here back in 1785, with Nelson and Wellington among their first customers, while modernist Kilgour (W www .kilgour.eu), at no. 8, famously made Fred Astaire's morning coat for *Top Hat*, helping to popularize Savile Row tailoring in the US. Henry Poole & Co (W www.henrypoole.com), who moved to no. 15 in 1846, has cut suits for the likes of Napoleon III, Dickens, Churchill and de Gaulle, invented the short smoking jacket (originally designed for the future Edward VII), later popularized as the "tuxedo".

Savile Row also has connections with the pop world. **The Beatles** used to buy their suits from Tommy Nutter's House of Nutter established in 1968 at no. 35, and in the same year set up the offices and recording studio of their record label Apple at no. 3, until the building's near physical collapse in 1972. On January 30, 1969, The Beatles gave an impromptu gig (their last live performance) on the roof here, stopping traffic and eventually attracting the attentions of the local police – as captured on film in *Let It Be*.

Hanover Square and the Handel House Museum

Savile Row terminates at Conduit Street, where the funnel-shaped St George Street splays into **Hanover Square**, site of the old Hanover Square Rooms where Bach, Liszt, Haydn and Paganini all performed before the building's demolition in 1900. Halfway up **St George Street** stands the Corinthian portico of **St George's Church** (Mon–Fri 8am–4pm, Sun 8am–noon; W www.stgeorgeshanoversquare.org), much copied since, but the first of its kind in London when it was built in the 1720s. Nicknamed "London's Temple of Hymen", it has long been Mayfair's most fashionable church for weddings. Among those who tied the knot here are the Shelleys, Benjamin Disraeli, Teddy Roosevelt and George Eliot. Handel, a confirmed bachelor, was a warden here for many years and even had his own pew.

Handel and Hendrix

Born **Georg Friederic Händel** (1685–1759) in Halle, Saxony, Handel first visited London in 1711, composing *Rinaldo* in fifteen days flat. The furore it produced – not least when Handel released a flock of sparrows for one aria – made him a household name. The following year he was commissioned to write several works for Queen Anne, eventually becoming court composer to George I, his one-time patron in Hanover.

London quickly became Handel's permanent home: he anglicized his name and nationality and lived out the rest of his life here, producing all the work for which he is now best known, including the *Water Music*, the *Fireworks Music* and his *Messiah*, which failed to enthral its first audiences, but which is now one of the great set pieces of Protestant musical culture. George II was so moved by the *Hallelujah Chorus* that he leapt to his feet and remained standing for the entire performance. Handel himself fainted during a performance in 1759, and died shortly afterwards in his home (now a museum; see below); he is buried in Westminster Abbey. Today, Handel's birthday is celebrated with a concert at the Foundling Museum (see p.131), and an annual Handel Festival (Ⓦwww.london-handel-festival.com) takes place annually at St George's Church, Hanover Square (see p.93).

Two centuries later, **Jimi Hendrix** (1942–70) moved in next door to Handel's old address, and lived for eighteen months or so at 23 Brook St. Born in Seattle in 1942, Hendrix was persuaded to fly over to London in 1966 by The Animals. Shortly after arriving, he teamed up with two other British musicians, Noel Redding and Mitch Mitchell, and formed The Jimi Hendrix Experience. It was at the beginning of 1969 that Hendrix moved into Brook Street with his girlfriend, Kathy Etchingham; apparently he was much taken with the fact that it was once Handel's residence, ordering Kathy to go and buy the albums for him. It was also in London that Hendrix met his untimely death, on September 18, 1970. At around 7am, in a flat below the *Samarkand Hotel* in Notting Hill, after a gig at *Ronnie Scott's* in Soho, Hendrix swallowed nine sleeping pills, later vomiting in his sleep and slipping into unconsciousness. He was pronounced dead on arrival at St Mary's Hospital, Paddington, and is buried in Seattle.

Handel's former home, at 25 Brook St, now houses the **Handel House Museum** (Tues–Sat 10am–6pm, Thurs till 8pm, Sun noon–6pm; £5; ℡020/7495 1685, Ⓦwww.handelhouse.org; Bond Street tube). The composer used the ground floor as a shop where subscribers could buy scores, while the first floor was a rehearsal room. The museum has few original artefacts, but the house has been redecorated to how it would have looked in Handel's day. Further atmosphere is provided by the harpsichord students who often practise in the rehearsal room; to find out about the weekly recitals, visit the website. Access to the house is via the chic, cobbled yard at the back of the house.

Berkeley Square and around

Three blocks west of Old Bond Street, **Berkeley Square** is where, according to the music-hall song, nightingales sing (though it's probable they were, in fact, blackcaps). Laid out in the 1730s, only the west side of the square has any surviving Georgian houses to boast of, and nowadays any birds would have trouble being heard over the traffic. However, what saves the square is its wonderful parade of 200-year-old **London plane trees**. With their dappled, peeling trunks, giant lobed leaves and globular spiky fruits, these pollution-resistant trees are a ubiquitous feature of the city, and Berkeley Square's specimens are among the finest. The square also has royal connections, as the

Queen was born just off it, at 17 Bruton St, and then lived at 145 Piccadilly until 1936.

Just north of Berkeley Square, it's possible to see inside **Bourdon House**, a lovely Georgian mansion on the corner of Davies and Bourdon streets. Former private residence of the Duke of Westminster, the house is now the flagship store of **Alfred Dunhill** (ⓦ www.dunhill.com). Don't be put off by the intimidating staff, but head for the first floor, where a few items are displayed from the days of Dunhill Motorities, gadget suppliers to Rolls Royce, whose slogan was "everything but the motor". This wonderful range made hip flasks disguised as books, "Bobby Finders" for detecting police cars, in-car hookahs and even a motorist's pipe with a windshield for open-top toking.

Grosvenor Square and around

Grosvenor Square, to the northwest, is the largest of Mayfair's squares, and was known during World War II as "Little America" – General Eisenhower, whose statue now stands here, ran the D-Day campaign from no. 20. The American presence is still pretty strong, thanks to the Roosevelt Memorial, the 9/11 memorial garden dedicated to the 67 British victims of the 2001 attack, and the monstrously ugly and heavily guarded **US Embassy**, built in 1960, which occupies the entire west side of the square. The embassy is watched over by a giant gilded eagle plus a posse of armed police, as most weeks there's some demonstration or other against US foreign policy – albeit nothing to rank with 1968's violent protests against US involvement in Vietnam. Mick Jagger, so the story goes, was innocently signing autographs in his Bentley as the 1968 riot began, and later wrote *Street Fighting Man*, inspired by what he witnessed.

Eisenhower's initial pied-à-terre was a room painted "whorehouse pink" in **Claridge's**, the hotel for the rich and royal one block east of Grosvenor Square on Brook Street. *Claridge's* also served as the wartime hangout of the OSS, forerunner of the CIA, one of whose representatives held a historic meeting here in 1943 with Szmul Zygielbojm from the Jewish Board of the Polish government-in-exile. Zygielbojm was told that Roosevelt had refused his request to bomb the rail lines leading to Auschwitz; the following day he committed suicide.

The Cato Street Conspiracy

British history is disappointingly short on political assassinations: one prime minister, no royals and only a handful of MPs. One of the most dismal failures was the 1820 **Cato Street Conspiracy**, drawn up by sixteen revolutionaries in an attic off the Edgware Road. Their plan was to decapitate the entire Cabinet as they dined with Lord Harrowby at 44 Grosvenor Square. Having beheaded the Home Secretary and another of the ministers, they then planned to sack Coutts Bank, capture the cannon on the Artillery Ground, take Gray's Inn, Mansion House, the Bank of England and the Tower, torching the barracks in the process, and proclaiming a provisional government.

As it turned out, one of the conspirators was an *agent provocateur*, and the entire mob was arrested in the Cato Street attic on the night of the planned coup, February 23. In the melee, one Bow Street Runner was killed and eleven of the conspirators escaped. Eventually, the five ringleaders were hanged at Newgate, and another five were transported to Australia. Public sympathy for the uprising was widespread, so the condemned were spared being drawn and quartered, though they did have their heads cut off afterwards. (The hangman was later attacked in the streets and almost castrated.)

American troops stationed over here used to worship at the **Grosvenor Chapel** (Ⓦwww.grosvenorchapel.org.uk) two blocks south on South Audley Street, a building that formed the model for early settlers' churches in New England and still popular with the American community. The church's most illustrious corpse is radical MP John Wilkes ("Wilkes and Liberty" was the battle cry of many a mid-eighteenth-century riot). Behind the chapel are the beautifully secluded **Mount Street Gardens**, dotted with 200-year-old plane trees and enclosed by nineteenth-century red-brick mansions. At the far eastern end of the gardens is the back entrance to the **Church of the Immaculate Conception** (Ⓦwww.farmstreet.org.uk), on Farm Street, the Jesuits' London stronghold, built in ostentatious neo-Gothic style in the 1840s. Every surface is covered in decoration, but the reredos of gilded stone by Pugin (of Houses of Parliament fame) is particularly impressive.

Oxford Street

As wealthy Londoners began to move out of the City during the eighteenth century, in favour of the newly developed West End, so **Oxford Street** – the old Roman road to Oxford – gradually replaced Cheapside as London's main shopping street. Today, despite successive recessions and sky-high rents, this two-mile hotchpotch of shops is still one of the world's busiest streets, its Christmas lights switched on by the briefly famous, and its traffic controllers equipped with loud-hailers to prevent the hordes of Christmas shoppers from losing their lives at the busy road junctions.

East of Oxford Circus, the street forms a scruffy border between Soho and Fitzrovia (see Chapter 5). West of Oxford Circus is dominated by more upmarket stores, including the one great landmark, **Selfridges** (Ⓦwww .selfridges.com), a huge Edwardian pile fronted by giant Ionic columns, with the Queen of Time riding the ship of commerce and supporting an Art Deco clock above the main entrance. Opened in 1909 by Chicago millionaire Gordon Selfridge, Selfridges is credited with selling the world's first television set, as well as introducing the concept of the "bargain basement", "the customer is always right", the irritating "only ten more shopping days to Christmas" countdown, and the nauseous bouquet of perfumes from the cosmetics counters, strategically placed at the entrance to all department stores. Selfridge himself was a big spender, ran into trouble with the Inland Revenue and was eventually pensioned off – he died in poverty at the age of 90 in 1947.

Marylebone

o the north of Oxford Street lies **Marylebone**, once the outlying village of St Mary-by-the-Bourne (the bourne in question being the Tyburn stream) or St Marylebone (pronounced "marra-le-bun"). Samuel Pepys walked through open countryside to reach its pleasure gardens in 1668 and declared it "a pretty place". During the course of the next century, the gardens were closed and the village was swallowed up as its chief landowners – among them the Portlands and the Portmans – laid out a mesh of uniform Georgian streets and squares, much of which survives today. Marylebone may not have quite the pedigree and snob value of Mayfair, but it's still a wealthy

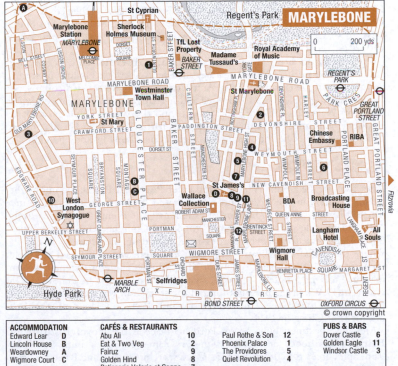

© crown copyright

ACCOMMODATION		CAFÉS & RESTAURANTS				PUBS & BARS	
Edward Lear	**D**	Abu Ali	**10**	Paul Rothe & Son	**12**	Dover Castle	**6**
Lincoln House	**B**	Eat & Two Veg	**2**	Phoenix Palace	**1**	Golden Eagle	**11**
Weardowney	**A**	Fairuz	**9**	The Providores	**5**	Windsor Castle	**3**
Wigmore Court	**C**	Golden Hind	**8**	Quiet Revolution	**4**		
		Patisserie Valerie at Sagne	**7**				

and aspirational area. It was here that The Beatles took up residence when they hit the big time in the 1960s, and it was here that Madonna lived with Guy Ritchie before the divorce.

Compared to the brashness of Oxford Street, Marylebone's backstreets are a pleasure to wander, especially the chi-chi village-like quarter around **Marylebone High Street**. The area's more conventional sights include the massively touristed **Madame Tussaud's**, on Marylebone Road, the free art gallery and aristocratic mansion of the **Wallace Collection**, and Sherlock Holmes' old stomping grounds around **Baker Street**.

Langham Place

North of Oxford Circus, Regent Street forms the eastern border of Marylebone, but stops abruptly at **Langham Place**, site of Nash's simple and ingenious little Bath-stone church, **All Souls**, built in the 1820s. The unusual circular Ionic portico and conical spire, which caused outrage in its day, are cleverly designed to provide a visual full stop to Regent Street and a pivot for the awkward twist in the triumphal route to Regent's Park. Behind All Souls lies the totalitarian-looking **Broadcasting House**, BBC radio headquarters since 1932. The figures of Prospero and Ariel (pun intended) above the entrance are by Eric Gill, who caused a furore by sculpting Ariel with overlarge testicles, and, like Epstein a few years earlier at Broadway House, was forced in the end to cut the organs down to size. Despite a refurbishment programme that's not set to finish until 2012, you can nevertheless sign up for a guided tour of Broadcasting House (monthly Sun; £6.50; ☏0370/903 0304, ⓦwww.bbc.co.uk/tours; Oxford Circus tube). Much more popular, however, are the regular tours of the **BBC TV Centre**, out in west London (Mon–Sat; £9.50; no under-10s; ☏0370/901 1227; White City tube).

Opposite Broadcasting House stands the **Langham Hotel**, built in grandiose Italianate style in the 1860s. It features in several Sherlock Holmes mysteries, and its former guests have included Antonín Dvořák (who courted controversy by ordering a double room for himself and his daughter to save money), exiled emperors Napoleon III and Haile Selassie, and the writer Ouida (aka Marie Louise de la Ramée), who threw outrageous parties for young Guards officers and wrote many of her bestselling romances in her dimly lit hotel boudoir.

Portland Place

After the chicane around All Souls, you enter **Portland Place**, laid out by the Adam brothers in the 1770s and incorporated by Nash in his grand route. Once the widest street in London, it's still a majestic avenue, lined exclusively with Adam-style houses, boasting wonderful fanlights and iron railings. Several embassies occupy properties here, including the Chinese at no. 49, where the exiled republican leader **Sun Yat Sen** was kidnapped and held incognito in 1896, on the orders of the Chinese emperor. Eventually Sun managed to send a note to a friend, saying "I am certain to be beheaded. Oh woe is me!". When the press got hold of the story, Sun was finally released; he went on to found the Chinese Nationalist Party and became the first president of China in 1911.

Arguably the finest building on Portland Place is the **Royal Institute of British Architects** or RIBA (Mon–Fri 8am–6pm, Tues until 9pm, Sat 9am–5pm; free; ☏020/7580 5533, ⓦwww.architecture.com; Regent's Park tube), at no. 66, with its sleek Portland-stone facade built in the 1930s amidst the remaining Adam houses. The main staircase remains a wonderful period piece, with its etched glass balustrades and walnut veneer, and with two large black marble columns rising up on either side. You can view the interior en route to the institute's first-floor exhibitions and café.

At the far end of Portland Place, Nash originally planned a giant "circus" as a formal entrance to Regent's Park (see p.289). Only the southern half – two graceful arcs of creamy terraces known collectively as **Park Crescent** – was completed, and it is now cut off from the park by the busy thoroughfare of Marylebone Road.

Wallace Collection

Just north of Oxford Street, minuscule Manchester Square has kept its peaceful Georgian appearance, thanks to its position away from the main traffic arteries. At its head is Hertford House, a miniature eighteenth-century French chateau transplanted to central London, which holds the splendid **Wallace Collection** (daily 10am–5pm; free; ☎020/7563 9500, ⓦwww.wallacecollection.org; Bond Street tube), a museum-gallery best known for its eighteenth-century French paintings and decorative art. The collection was originally bequeathed to the nation in 1897 by the widow of Richard Wallace, an art collector and the illegitimate son of the fourth Marquess of Hertford. The museum has preserved the feel of an old-fashioned institution, with exhibits piled high in glass cabinets and paintings covering every inch of wall space. However, it's the combined effect of the exhibits set amidst superbly restored period fittings – and a bloody great **armoury** – that makes the place so remarkable. Labelling can be pretty terse and paintings occasionally move about, so you might consider renting an audioguide.

Ground floor

The ground-floor rooms begin with the **Front State Room**, to the right as you enter, where the walls are hung with several fetching portraits by Reynolds, and Lawrence's typically sensuous portrayal of the author and society beauty, the Countess of Blessington, which went down a storm at the Royal Academy in 1822. The **Back State Room** houses the cream of the collection's spectacular Sèvres porcelain and gold snuff boxes, and, centre stage, a period copy of Louis XIV's desk, which was the most expensive piece of eighteenth-century French furniture ever made. On the other side of the adjacent Dining Room, in the **Billiard Room**, you'll find some outrageous, gilded oak and ebony Boulle furniture. From the Dining Room, you can enter the covered courtyard, home to *The Wallace* restaurant, and head down the stairs to the **Conservation Gallery** where folk of all ages can try on some medieval armour.

Back on the ground floor, the **Sixteenth-Century Gallery** displays works ranging from *pietre dure*, bronze and majolica to Limoges porcelain and Venetian glass. In the **Smoking Room**, a small alcove at the far end survives to give an idea of the effect of the original Minton-tiled decor Wallace chose for this room. The next three rooms house the extensive **European Armoury** bought *en bloc* by Wallace around the time of the Franco-Prussian War. (It was in recognition of the humanitarian assistance Wallace provided in Paris during that war that he received his baronetcy.) A fourth room houses the **Oriental Armoury**, collected by the fourth Marquess of Hertford, including a cabinet of Asante gold treasure, a sword belonging to Tipu Sultan and one of the most important Sikh treasures in Britain, the sword of Ranjit Singh (1780–1839).

First floor

The most famous paintings in the collection are on the first floor. Initially, however, the tone is set by **Boucher**'s sumptuous mythological scenes over the main staircase. In the **Boudoir**, off the landing, you'll find Reynolds' doe-eyed moppets, while in the gloriously camp, pink **Study**, amid Greuze's soft-focus studies of kids, there's a lovely self-portrait by Elisabeth Vigée-Lebrun, one of the most successful portraitists of pre-Revolutionary France. Next door, in the equally over-the-top, sky-blue **Oval Drawing Room**, one of Fragonard's coquettes flaunts herself to a smitten beau in *The Swing*, alongside more Boucher nudes – the soft porn of the *ancien régime*. There's plenty more Rococo froth in the other rooms on this floor, plus classic Grand Tour vistas from Canaletto and Guardi in the **West Room**.

In addition to all this French finery a good collection of Dutch paintings hangs in the **East Galleries**, including de Hooch's *Women Peeling Apples*, oil sketches by Rubens and landscapes by Ruisdael, Hobbema and Cuyp. Finally, you reach the largest room in the house, the **Great Gallery**, specifically built by Wallace to display his finest paintings, including works by Murillo and Poussin, several vast Van Dyck portraits, Rubens' *Rainbow Landscape* and **Frans Hals**' *Laughing Cavalier*. Here, too, are *Perseus and Andromeda*, a late work by **Titian**, and **Velázquez**'s *Lady with a Fan*. At one end of the room are three portraits of the actress Mary Robinson as Perdita: one by Romney, one by Reynolds and, best of the lot, **Gainsborough**'s deceptively innocent portrayal, in which she insouciantly holds a miniature of her lover, the 19-year-old Prince of Wales (later George IV), who is portrayed in a flattering full-length portrait by Lawrence. Look out, too, for **Rembrandt**'s affectionate portrait of his teenage son, Titus, who helped administer his father's estate after bankruptcy charges and died at the age of just 28.

Marylebone High Street and around

Marylebone High Street, which starts northeast of Manchester Square and finishes at Marylebone Road, is all that's left of the village street that once ran along the banks of the Tyburn stream. It's become considerably more upmarket since those bucolic days, though the pace of the street is leisurely by central London standards. A couple of shops, in particular, deserve mention: *Patisserie Valerie*, at no. 105, is decorated with the same mock-Pompeian frescoes that adorned it when it was founded in the 1920s (as *Maison Sagne*) by a Swiss pastry-cook; at no. 83 is Daunt, a purpose-built bookshop from 1910, which specializes in travel books, and has a lovely, long, galleried hall at the back, with a pitched roof of stained glass.

Despite its name, **St James's Church**, Spanish Place, is actually tucked away on neighbouring George Street, just off Marylebone High Street. A Catholic chapel was built here in 1791 thanks to the efforts of the chaplain at the Spanish embassy, though the present neo-Gothic building dates from 1890. Designed in a mixture of English and French Gothic, the interior is surprisingly large and richly furnished, from the white marble and alabaster pulpit to the richly gilded heptagonal apse. The Spanish connection continues to this day: Spanish royal heraldry features in the rose window, and there are even two seats reserved for the royals, denoted by built-in gilt crowns high above the choir stalls.

Marylebone Road

At the north edge of Marylebone High Street is **Marylebone Road**, a western extension of Euston Road, built in the 1750s to provide London with its first bypass. It remains one of London's major traffic arteries, and is no place for a stroll. There are, however, a couple of minor sights, such as **St Marylebone Church** and the **Royal Academy of Music**, and one major tourist trap, **Madame Tusssaud's**, that might bring you here. In addition, Marylebone Road is bisected by **Baker Street**, whose associations with the fictional detective Sherlock Holmes are, naturally, fully exploited.

St Marylebone Church

The traffic that pounds down Marylebone Road's six lanes unfortunately cuts off **St Marylebone Church** (Ⓦwww.stmarylebone.org.uk), built in 1813, from Nash's York Gate, which was designed as an alternative gateway to Regent's Park. The church crypt houses a small chapel, a healing centre, an NHS health centre and a café; the rest of the interior is only open fitfully for services and recitals, though the church's most attractive feature – the gilded caryatids holding up the beehive cupola on top of the tower – is visible from the High Street. It was at this church that **Elizabeth Barrett and Robert Browning** were secretly married in 1846 (there's a chapel dedicated to Browning), after which Elizabeth – 40 years old, a morphine addict, invalid and virtual prisoner in her father's house on Wimpole Street – returned home and acted as if nothing had happened. A week later the couple eloped to Italy, where they spent most of their married life.

Royal Academy of Music

On the other side of Marylebone Road from St Marylebone Church stands the **Royal Academy of Music** (Ⓣ020/7873 7300, Ⓦwww.ram.ac.uk; Baker Street tube), which was founded in 1823, and taught the likes of Arthur Sullivan, Harrison Birtwistle, Evelyn Glennie, Michael Nyman and Simon Rattle. As well as putting on free lunchtime and evening concerts, the academy houses a small **museum** (Mon–Fri 11.30am–5.30pm, Sat & Sun noon–4pm; free) at 1 York Gate. Temporary exhibitions are held on the ground floor, while upstairs, there are several violins by Stradivari, and a series of (mostly English) grand and square pianos. Listening-posts allow you to experience the instruments in live performance, and you can peek into the resident luthier's workshop.

Madame Tussaud's

The wax models at **Madame Tussaud's** (Mon–Fri 9.30am–5.30pm, Sat & Sun 9am–6pm; from £22; ☎0870/999 0046, Ⓦwww.madametussauds.com; Baker Street tube) have been pulling in the crowds ever since the good lady arrived in London from France in 1802 bearing the sculpted heads of guillotined aristocrats (she herself only just managed to escape the same fate – her uncle, who started the family business, was less fortunate). The entrance fee might be extortionate and the likenesses dubious, but you can still rely on finding London's biggest queues here – to avoid joining them, book online, or whizz round after 5pm for half-price.

There are **photo opportunities** galore throughout the first few sections, which are peppered with contemporary celebrities from the BBC to Bollywood. Keep your eyes out for the elderly and diminutive Madame Tussaud herself, and the oldest wax model, Madame du Barry, Louis XV's mistress, who gently respires as Sleeping Beauty – in reality she was beheaded in the French Revolution. The **Chamber of Horrors**, the most popular section of all, is irredeemably tasteless, and now features live, costumed actors who jump out at you in the dark (you can opt out of this). All the "great" British serial killers are here, and it remains the murderer's greatest honour to be included: Dennis Nilsen, a gruesome killer of young gay men in the 1980s, begged to be allowed to pose for Tussaud's while in prison. There's a reconstruction of John Christie's hanging, a tableau of Marat's death in the bath, and the very guillotine that lopped off Marie Antoinette's head, just for good measure.

Tussaud's also features the **Spirit of London**, an irreverent five-minute romp through the history of London in a miniaturized taxicab, taking you from Elizabethan times to a postmodern heritage nightmare of tourist tat (not unlike much of London today). The tour of Tussaud's ends with a short hi-tech presentation, on anything from recent Hollywood flicks to the cult of celebrity, projected onto a vast dome in the adjoining **Auditorium** (formerly the Planetarium).

Baker Street and around

Baker Street, which cuts across Marylebone Road, is synonymous with English literature's languid super-sleuth, Sherlock Holmes, who lived at no. 221b. The detective's address was always fictional, so you need to go to the **Sherlock Holmes Museum** (daily 9.30am–6pm; £6; ☎020/7935 8866, Ⓦwww.sherlock-holmes .co.uk; Baker Street tube), at no. 239 (the sign on the door says 221b), to find out more about the detective and his creator, Arthur Conan Doyle. Unashamedly touristy – you can have your photo taken in a deerstalker – the museum is nevertheless a competent exercise in period reconstruction, stuffed full of Victoriana and life-size models of characters from the books.

One last curiosity in this area is **Marylebone Station**, hidden in the backstreets north of Marylebone Road on Melcombe Place, where a delicate and extremely elegant wrought-iron canopy links the station to the former *Great Central Hotel* (now *The Landmark*). The last and most modest of the Victorian terminals, this was intended to be the terminal for the Channel tunnel of the 1880s, a scheme abandoned after only a mile or so of digging, when Queen Victoria got nervous about foreign invasions. The station now serves the Birmingham and Buckinghamshire commuter belt.

Soho and Fitzrovia

Soho gives you the best and worst of London: the porn joints that proliferated from the 1960s onwards still have a foothold, but the area also boasts a lively fruit-and-vegetable market, and a nightlife that has attracted writers and revellers of every sexual persuasion to the place since the eighteenth century. Despite regeneration, it has retained an unorthodox and slightly raffish air, born of an immigrant history as rich as that of the East End, while the area's most recent transformation has seen it become Europe's leading gay centre, with bars and cafés bursting out from the Old Compton Street area.

Bounded by Regent Street to the west, Oxford Street to the north and Charing Cross Road to the east, **Soho** remains very much the heart of London and one of the capital's most diverse and spicy areas. Conventional sights are few and far between, yet there's probably more street life here than anywhere else in the city – whatever the hour, there's always something going on. Most folk head to Soho to visit one of the district's cinemas or theatres, to have a drink in the latest trendy bars or to fill up at the innumerable cafés and restaurants that pepper the tiny area, from **Chinatown** to exclusive, Michelin-starred establishments in the backstreets.

Fitzrovia, the area immediately to the north, is much quieter than Soho, and has more in common with neighbouring Bloomsbury. Nevertheless, it has a bohemian pedigree similar to its raunchier southern neighbour, and undoubtedly functions as something of a Soho spillover. Tourist sights are again scarce, with just Pollock's Toy Museum and the odd architectural oddity to give you purpose.

Soho

When **Soho** – named after the cry that resounded through the district when it was a popular place for rabbit hunting – was built over in the seventeenth century, its streets were among the most sought-after addresses in the capital. Princes, dukes and earls built their mansions around Soho and Leicester squares, which became the centre of high-society nightlife, epitomized by Viennese prima donna Theresa Cornelys' wild masquerades, which drew "a riotous assembly of fashionable people of both sexes", a traffic jam of hackney chairs and a huge crowd of onlookers. By the end of the eighteenth century, however, the party was over, the rich moved west, and Soho began its inexorable descent into poverty and overcrowding. Even before the last aristocrats left, Soho had

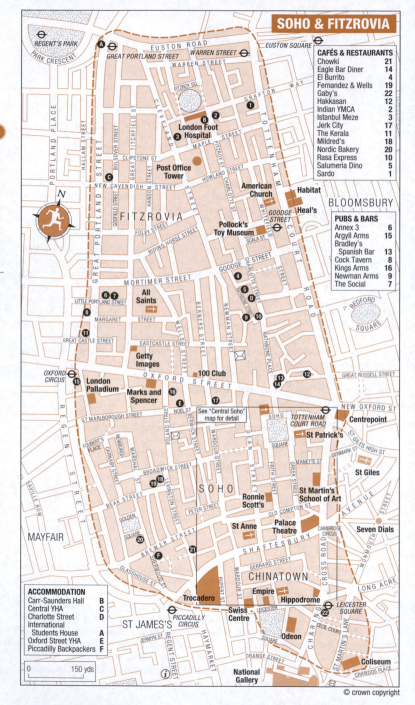

SOHO & FITZROVIA

CAFÉS & RESTAURANTS
Chowki	21
Eagle Bar Diner	14
El Burrito	4
Fernandez & Wells	19
Gaby's	22
Hakkasan	12
Indian YMCA	2
Istanbul Meze	3
Jerk City	17
The Kerala	11
Mildred's	18
Nordic Bakery	20
Rasa Express	10
Salumeria Dino	5
Sardo	1

PUBS & BARS
Annex 3	6
Argyll Arms	15
Bradley's	
Spanish Bar	13
Cock Tavern	8
Kings Arms	16
Newman Arms	9
The Social	7

ACCOMMODATION
Carr-Saunders Hall	B
Central YHA	C
Charlotte Street	D
International	
Students House	A
Oxford Street YHA	E
Piccadilly Backpackers	F

0   150 yds

© crown copyright

become one of the city's main dumping grounds for **immigrants**. French Huguenots were followed by Italians, Irish, Jews, and eventually the Chinese.

For several centuries, Soho has also been a favourite haunt of the capital's creative bohos and **literati**. It was at Soho's *Turk's Head* coffee shop, in 1764, that Joshua Reynolds founded "The Club", to give Dr Johnson unlimited opportunities for talking. Thomas de Quincey turned up in 1802, and was saved from starvation by a local prostitute, an incident later recalled in his *Confessions of an English Opium Eater*. Wagner arrived destitute in 1839, Marx lived in poverty here after the failure of the 1848 revolution, and Rimbaud and Verlaine pitched up after the fall of the Paris Commune in 1871. "Such noise and chaos. Such magnificent and terrible abandon. It's like stepping into the future", wrote Verlaine.

Soho's reputation for tolerance also made it an obvious place of refuge from dour, postwar Britain. Jazz and skiffle proliferated in the 1950s, folk and rock in the 1960s, and punk at the end of the 1970s. Soho's artistic (and alcoholic) cliques still gather here and the media, film and advertising industries have a strong presence. The attraction, though, remains in the unique mix of people who drift through Soho. There's nowhere else in the city where such diverse slices of London come face to face: businessmen, clubbers, drunks, theatregoers, fashion victims, market-stallholders, pimps, prostitutes and politicians. Take it all in, and enjoy – for better or worse, most of London is not like this.

Leicester Square

A short hop east of Piccadilly Circus, most Londoners tend to avoid **Leicester Square** unless they're heading for one of the cinemas. It's actually a fairly pleasant leafy square – at least by day – and was, in the eighteenth century, home to the fashionable "Leicester House set", headed by successive princes of Wales who didn't get on with their fathers at St James's. Busts of celebrities from those days can be found in the gardens, though most people are more impressed by the statues of Shakespeare and Charlie Chaplin, neither of whom have any real connection with the area. By night – and especially at weekends – Leicester Square resembles city centres across the country, a playground for the drunk and underdressed.

The square has been an **entertainment zone** since the mid-nineteenth century, when it boasted Turkish baths and music halls such as the grandiose Empire and, close by, the Hippodrome – designed by Frank Matcham in 1900 – edifices which survive today as cinemas and nightclubs. Movie houses moved in during the 1930s, a golden age evoked by the sleek black lines of the Odeon on the east side, and maintain their grip on the area. The aforementioned **Empire** is the favourite for London premieres – there are even handprints of the famous in the pavement by the southwestern corner of the garden railings, à la Hollywood.

One little-known sight, north of the square, in Leicester Place, is the modern Catholic church of **Notre-Dame de France**, heralded by an entrance flanked by two pillars decorated with biblical reliefs. The main point of interest inside is the Chapelle du St-Sacrement, which contains a series of frescoes by Jean Cocteau from 1960 and a mosaic by Boris Anrep.

Chinatown

The first Chinese immigrants were sailors who arrived here from the late eighteenth century onwards on the ships of the East India Company. London's first

▲ Chinatown

Chinatown grew up around the docks at Limehouse and eventually boasted over thirty Chinese shops and restaurants. Predominantly male, this closed community achieved a quasi-mythical status in Edwardian minds as a hotbed of criminal dives and opium dens, a reputation exploited in Sax Rohmer's novels (later made into films) featuring the evil Doctor Fu Manchu. Wartime bomb damage, postwar demolition and protectionist union laws all but destroyed Limehouse Chinatown. However, following the Communist takeover in China, a new wave of Chinese refugees began to buy up cheap property around **Gerrard Street**, establishing the nucleus of today's **Chinatown**.

Hemmed in between Leicester Square and Shaftesbury Avenue, this self-contained jumble of **shops**, **cafés** and **restaurants** makes up one of London's most distinct ethnic enclaves. Only a minority of the capital's Chinese live in the three small blocks of Chinatown, with its ersatz touches – telephone kiosks rigged out as pagodas and formal entrances or *paifang* – yet the area remains a focus for the community, a place to do business or the weekly shopping, celebrate a wedding or just meet up on Sundays for dim sum. Most Londoners come to Chinatown simply to eat, but if the mood takes you, you can easily while away several hours sorting through the Chinese trinkets, ceramics and ornaments in the various arts and crafts shops, or amassing the perfect ingredients for a demon stir-fry.

Charing Cross Road and Shaftesbury Avenue

Charing Cross Road, created in the 1880s as part of the Victorians' slum clearance drive, boasts the highest concentration of **bookshops** anywhere in London: chain and discounted stores north of Cambridge Circus; smaller, independent and secondhand stores to the south. One of the first to open here was **Foyles** (see p.439) at no. 119, where Éamon de Valera, George Bernard Shaw, Walt Disney and Arthur Conan Doyle were all once regular customers.

Two of the nicest places for secondhand-book browsing are **Cecil Court** and **St Martin's Court**, connecting the southern end of Charing Cross Road and St Martin's Lane. These short, civilized, paved alleys boast specialist bookshops, plus various antiquarian dealers selling modern first editions, old theatre posters, coins and notes, cigarette cards, maps and stamps.

At the southern end of St Martin's Lane stands the **Coliseum**, an extravagant variety theatre built in 1904 by Frank Matcham, where the likes of Lillie Langtry, Sarah Bernhardt and the Ballets Russes all performed. Now home to the English National Opera (see p.426), it remains London's largest theatre, its cutest feature the revolving illuminated globe that crowns the building.

Sweeping through the southern part of Soho, the gentle curve of **Shaftesbury Avenue** is the heart of the West End's **Theatreland**, with theatres and cinemas along its entire length. Built in the 1870s, ostensibly to relieve traffic congestion but with the dual purpose of destroying the slums that lay in its path, the street was ironically named after Lord Shaftesbury, whose life had been spent trying to help the likes of those dispossessed by the road. The most impressive theatre is the grandiose terracotta **Palace Theatre**, overlooking Cambridge Circus, which opened in 1891 as the Royal English Opera House; it folded after just one year, and, since the 1920s, has mostly hosted musicals. Just off Cambridge Circus, hidden away down West Street, is St Martin's Theatre, where Agatha Christie's record-breaking *Mousetrap* has been on non stop since 1952.

Central Soho

If Soho has a main drag, it has to be **Old Compton Street**, which runs parallel with Shaftesbury Avenue. The shops, boutiques and cafés here are typical of the area and a good barometer of the latest Soho fads. Several places have survived the vicissitudes of fashion, including *Patisserie Valerie*, opened by the Belgian-born Madame Valerie in 1926, the Algerian Coffee Store, the Italian deli, I Camisa & Son, Capital newsagents, The Vintage House off-licence, and Gerry's, whose spirit-window display is a paean to alcohol and includes a staggering range of Czech absinthe.

The liberal atmosphere of Soho has also made it a permanent fixture on the **gay scene** since the last century: gay servicemen frequented the *Golden Lion*, on Dean Street, from World War II until the end of National Service, while a succession of gay artists found refuge here during the 1950s and 1960s. Nowadays the scene is much more upfront, with gay bars, clubs and businesses jostling for position on Old Compton Street, and round the corner on Wardour Street.

Greek Street and Frith Street

The streets off Old Compton Street are lined with Soho institutions past and present, starting in the east with **Greek Street**, named after the Greek church that once stood nearby. The *Coach and Horses*, at no. 29, was lorded over for years by the boozy gang of writer Jeffrey Bernard, painter Francis Bacon and jazz man George Melly, as well as the staff of the satirical magazine, *Private Eye*. Parallel **Frith Street** is home to **Ronnie Scott's**, London's longest-running jazz club, founded in 1958 and still pulling in the big names. Opposite is *Bar Italia*, a tiny, quintessentially Italian café established in 1949, whose late-night hours make it a clubbers' favourite. It was in this building, appropriately enough for such a media-saturated area, that **John Logie Baird** made the world's first public television transmission in 1926. Next door, a plaque recalls that the 7-year-old Mozart stayed here in 1763, having wowed George III and London society.

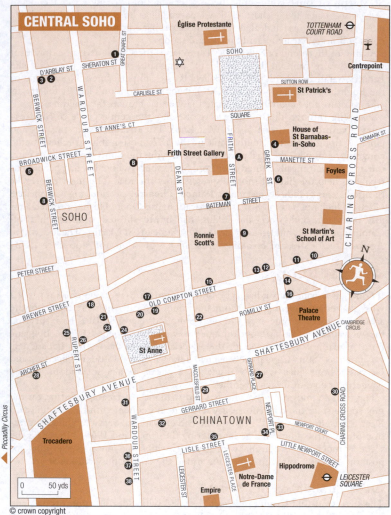

© crown copyright

5

SOHO AND FITZROVIA

Piccadilly Circus

CAFÉS & RESTAURANTS				PUBS & BARS				ACCOMMODATION	
Bar Italia	9	Mr Kong	35	79CXR	30	Friendly Society	23	Hazlitt's	A
Beatroot	8	Patara	6	The Admiral Duncan	15	G.A.Y. Bar	12	Soho Hotel	B
Breakfast Club	3	Royal Dragon	32	Balans	13	Green Carnation	4		
Comptons of Soho	20	Star at Night	1	BarCode Soho	28	LAB	10		
Kopi-Tiam	37	Stockpot	11	De Hems	27	Rupert Street	26		
Ku Bar	34	Thai Cottage	2	Dog & Duck	7	Shadow Lounge	18		
Leong's Legends	29	Tokyo Diner	33	Duke of Wellington	24	Trash Palace	36		
Maison Bertaux	14	Wong Kei	31	Escape	17	Village Soho	21		
Misato	38	Yauatcha	5	Freedom	16	The Yard	25		
Moaz Vegetarian	19			French House	22				

www.roughguides.com

Soho on record

Soho has been a popular meeting point for the capital's up-and-coming pop stars since the late 1950s, when the likes of Cliff Richard, Tommy Steele and Adam Faith used to hang out at the **2 i's coffee bar**, 59 Old Compton St, and perform at the rock'n'roll club in the basement. Marc Bolan, whose parents ran a market stall on Berwick Street, also worked at the café in the early 1960s. The Rolling Stones first met in a pub on Broadwick Street in early 1962 and, by the mid-1960s, were playing Soho's premier rock venue, the **Marquee**, originally at 90 Wardour St. David Bowie performed there (as David Jones) in 1965, Pink Floyd played their "Spontaneous Underground" sessions the following year, Led Zeppelin had their first London gig there in 1968, and Phil Collins worked for some time as a cloakroom attendant.

In November 1975, The Sex Pistols played their first gig at **St Martin's School of Art** on Charing Cross Road, during which Sid Vicious (in the audience, and not the band, at the time) made his contribution to dance history when he began to "pogo". The classic punk venue, however, was the **100 Club** on Oxford Street, where the Pistols, The Clash, Siouxsie, The Damned and The Vibrators all played. The Pistols used to rehearse in the studios on **Denmark Street**, London's tame version of New York's Tin Pan Alley, off Charing Cross Road. The Rolling Stones, The Kinks and Genesis all recorded songs there, and Elton John got his first job at one of the street's music publishers in 1963.

Soho Square

Soho Square is one of the few patches of green amid the neighbourhood's labyrinth of streets and alleys. It began life as a smart address, surrounded by the houses of the nobility and centred on an elaborate fountain topped by a statue of Charles II. Charles survives, if a little worse for wear, on one of the pathways, but the fountain is now an octagonal, mock-Tudor garden shed. As for the buildings around the square, they are a typical Soho mix: 20th Century-Fox; the Victorian Hospital for Sick Women (now a walk-in health centre); Paul McCartney's discreet corporate headquarters, mpl; the British Board of Film Classification (the national guardians of movie censorship); and the Football Association. There are also two square, red-brick churches: the Italianate **St Patrick's**, which serves the Irish, Italian and Chinese communities, and the **Église Protestante** (Protestant Church), sole survivor of London's once numerous Huguenot churches, concealed on the north side of the square; the tympanum relief depicts the French refugees crossing the Channel and being granted asylum by Edward VI.

Dean Street and Wardour Street

One block west of Frith Street runs **Dean Street**, home of the *Colony Club*, heart of the postwar bohemian drinking scene, and of the *Groucho Club*, where today's literati and media types preen themselves. Both clubs are members-only, but nearby *The French House*, at no. 49, is an open-to-all bohemian landmark. Once the plain old *York Minster* pub, it was bought by a Belgian, Victor Berlemont, in 1914, transformed into a French émigré haunt and frequented by de Gaulle and the Free French forces during World War II.

Soho's most famous Jewish immigrant was **Karl Marx**, who in 1850 stayed for six months with a Jewish lace dealer at no. 64, before moving into two "evil, frightful rooms" further down the street, on the top floor of no. 28, with his wife and maid (both of whom were pregnant by him) and four children, having been evicted from his first two addresses for failing to pay the rent. There's a plaque commemorating his stay (with incorrect dates), and the waiters at

Quo Vadis restaurant, the current occupants, will show diners round the rooms on request (☎020/7437 9585).

Neighbouring **Wardour Street**, a kind of dividing line between the busier eastern half of Soho and the marginally quieter western zone, is largely given over to the film and TV industry. Just north of Shaftesbury Avenue, there's a small park laid out on what used to be **St Anne's Church**, bombed in the last war, with only its tower now standing. The ashes of Dorothy L. Sayers are buried under the tower, and Baron von Neuhoff, a Westphalian adventurer who managed to get himself elected King of Corsica in 1736, is also interred here. His reign lasted eight months, after which he was forced to flee to try and raise more money and men to fight the Genoese. He lived out his exile on Dean Street and was eventually imprisoned for debt in 1750; when asked what assets he had, he declared "nothing but the Kingdom of Corsica".

Berwick Street, Broadwick Street and around

West of Wardour Street, the sex industry has a long history and firm foothold. It was at the **Windmill Theatre**, on Great Windmill Street, that the famous "Revuedeville" shows, featuring static nude performers (movement was strictly forbidden by the censor), were first staged in the 1930s. The shows continued pretty much uninterrupted right through World War II – the subject of the 2005 film *Mrs Henderson Presents* – eventually closing in 1964. Meanwhile, Paul Raymond's *Revue Bar* on Brewer Street opened in 1952 as a "World Centre of Erotic Entertainment", finally succumbing, in 2004, to competition from the slick **lap-dancing clubs** that have rejuvenated the West End sex industry.

Hidden in the very heart of Soho is the unlikely sight of **Berwick Street Market** (Mon–Sat 9am–6pm), one of the capital's cheapest fruit and

Soho vice

Prostitution is nothing new to Soho. Way back in the seventeenth and eighteenth centuries, prince and prole alike used to come here (and to Covent Garden) for paid sex. Several prominent courtesans were residents of Soho, their profession recorded as "player and mistress to several persons", or, lower down on the social scale, "generally slut and drunkard; occasionally whore and thief". *Hooper's Hotel*, a high-class Soho brothel which the Prince of Wales frequented, even got a mention in the popular, late eighteenth-century book *The Mysteries of Flagellation*. By Victorian times, the area was described as "a reeking home of filthy vice", where "the grosser immorality flourishes unabashed from every age downwards to mere children". And it was in Soho that Gladstone used to conduct his crusade to save prostitutes – managing "to combine his missionary meddling with a keen appreciation of a pretty face", as one perceptive critic observed.

By World War II, **organized gangs** like the notorious Messina Brothers from Malta controlled a huge vice empire in Soho, later taken over by one of their erstwhile henchmen, Bernie Silver, Soho's self-styled "Godfather". In the 1960s and 1970s, the sex trade threatened to take over the whole of Soho, aided and abetted by the police themselves, who were involved in a massive protection racket. The complicity between the gangs and the police was finally exposed in 1976, when ten top-ranking Scotland Yard officers were charged with bribery and corruption on a massive scale and sentenced to prison for up to twelve years. (Silver himself had been put inside in 1974.) The combined efforts of the Soho Society and Westminster Council has enormously reduced the number of sex establishments, but the area's vice days are not quite over yet.

vegetable markets, flanked by some of London's best specialist record shops and featured on the album cover of *(What's the Story) Morning Glory* by Oasis. The market ends at the crossroads with **Broadwick Street**, which features a replica of the water pump that caused the deaths of some five hundred Soho residents in the **cholera epidemic** of 1854. Dr John Snow, Queen Victoria's obstetrician, traced the outbreak to the pump, thereby proving that the disease was waterborne rather than airborne, as previously thought. No one believed him, however, until he removed the pump handle and effectively stopped the epidemic. The original pump stood outside the pub now called the *John Snow*, beside which there's a commemorative plaque and a red-granite kerbstone.

This part of Soho has its fair share of artistic and heretical associations too. It was at 74 Broadwick St that **William Blake** was born in 1757, above his father's hosiery shop, and where, from the age of 9, he had visions of "messengers from heaven, daily and nightly". He opened a print shop of his own next door to the family home, and later moved nearby to 28 Poland St, where he lived six years with his "beloved Kate" and wrote perhaps his most profound work, *The Marriage of Heaven and Hell*, among other poems. Poland Street was also **Shelley**'s first halt after having been kicked out of Oxford in 1811 for distributing *The Necessity of Atheism*, and **Canaletto** ran a studio just south on Beak Street for a couple of years while he sat out the Seven Years' War in exile in London. And it was in the *Old King's Arms* pub on Poland Street in 1781 that the **Ancient Order of Druids** was revived.

Carnaby Street and around

Until the 1950s, **Carnaby Street** (Ⓦ www.carnaby.co.uk) was a backstreet on Soho's western fringe, occupied, for the most part, by sweatshop tailors who used to make up the suits for Savile Row. Then, in 1954, Bill Green opened a shop called Vince (in neighbouring Newburgh St), selling outrageous clothes to the gay men who were hanging out at the local baths. He was followed by John Stephen, a Glaswegian grocer's son, who opened His Clothes in nearby Beak Street. In 1960, Stephen opened a branch on Carnaby Street and within a couple of years owned a string of trendy boutiques which catered for the new market in flamboyant men's clothing. By 1964 – the year of the official birth of the Carnaby Street myth – Mods, West Indian Rude Boys and other "switched-on people", as the *Daily Telegraph* noted, had begun to hang out in Carnaby Street. By the time Mary Quant sold her first miniskirt here, the area had become the epicentre of Swinging Sixties' London, and its street sign the capital's most popular postcard.

A victim of its own hype, Carnaby Street quickly declined into an avenue of overpriced tack. More recently, things have started to pick up again, especially at the top end of the street, and round the corner in Foubert's Place and **Newburgh Street**, where contemporary London fashion now has a firm foothold; elsewhere, chain stores and tourist shops remain firmly ensconced. Across Great Marlborough Street, at the top of Carnaby Street, stands the striking Art Deco **National Radiator Building**, with its sleek black-granite facade and gilded "65".

One last place you shouldn't miss, just off Great Marlborough Street, is the **Photographers' Gallery** (Tues–Sun 11am–6pm, Thurs & Fri until 8pm; free; ☎ 0845/262 1618, Ⓦ www.photonet.org.uk; Oxford Circus tube), now in new premises at 16–18 Ramillies St. Established in 1971, the gallery was the first of its kind in London, and hosts free temporary exhibitions that are invariably worth a visit, as are the bookshop and café.

Fitzrovia

Fitzrovia is the very much quieter northern extension of Soho, beyond Oxford Street. Like its neighbour, it has a raffish, cosmopolitan history, attracting its fair share of writers and bohemians over the last hundred years or so, including the Pre-Raphaelites and members of the Bloomsbury Group. That said, it's a lot less edgy than Soho, with just two real sights to visit – an ornate Victorian church on Margaret Street and Pollock's Toy Museum – and one unavoidable landmark, the former Post Office Tower.

All Saints, Margaret Street

Few London churches are as atmospheric as **All Saints** (🖐 www .allsaintsmargaretstreet.org.uk), built by William Butterfield in the 1850s, two blocks north of Oxford Street on Margaret Street. Patterned brickwork characterizes the entire ensemble of clergy house, choir school (Laurence Olivier sang here as a boy) and church, set around a small courtyard that's entered from the street through a pointed arch. The church interior, one of London's gloomiest, is best visited on a sunny afternoon when the light pours in through the west window, illuminating the fantastic variety of coloured marble and stone which decorates the place from floor to ceiling. Several of the walls are also adorned with Pre-Raphaelite Minton-tile paintings, the east window is a neo-Byzantine quasi-iconostasis with saintly images nestling in gilded niches, and the elaborate pulpit is like the entire church in miniature. Surrounded by such iconographical clutter, you would be forgiven for thinking you were in a Catholic church – but then that was the whole idea of the Victorian High Church movement, which sought to re-Catholicize the Church of England without actually returning it to the Roman fold.

Charlotte Street and around

After All Saints, the place to head for is **Charlotte Street**, Fitzrovia's main street since its heyday in the 1930s. In those days, it was home to the *Tour Eiffel*, where Wyndham Lewis and Ezra Pound launched the Vorticist magazine *Blast*; *L'Étoile*, further up, patronized by the likes of Dylan Thomas and T.S. Eliot; and *Bertorelli's*, where the Wednesday Club, including Eliot, John Berger and Christopher Isherwood, used to meet in the 1950s. The same crowd would get plastered in the nearby *Fitzroy Tavern* – from which the area got its sobriquet – along with rather more outrageous bohemians, like the hard-drinking Nina Hamnett, the self-styled "Queen of Bohemia", who used to boast that Modigliani once told her she had the best tits in Europe.

One block east, on Scala Street, is the highly atmospheric, doll's-house-like **Pollock's Toy Museum** (Mon–Sat 10am–5pm; £3; ☎020/7636 3452, 🖐 www.pollockstoymuseum.com; Goodge Street tube), housed above a wonderful toy shop. Its collections include a fine example of the Victorian paper theatres popularized by Benjamin Pollock, who sold them under the slogan "a penny plain, two pence coloured". The other exhibits range from vintage teddy bears to Sooty and Sweep, and from Red Army soldiers to wax dolls, filling every nook and cranny of the museum's six tiny, rickety rooms and the stairs – be sure to look out for the dalmatian, Dismal Desmond.

Exploring Fitzrovia, it's impossible to ignore the looming presence of the former **Post Office Tower** (officially known as the BT Tower), a glass-clad pylon designed in the early 1960s by a team of bureaucrats in the Ministry of

Works, which stands just west of Fitzroy Street, the extension of Charlotte Street. The city's tallest building until the NatWest Tower topped it in 1981, it's still a prominent landmark north of the river. Sadly, since a bomb attack by the Angry Brigade in 1971, the tower and its revolving restaurant have been closed to the public.

Fitzroy Square and around

Near the top of Fitzroy Street is **Fitzroy Square**, a Bloomsbury-style square begun by the Adam brothers in the 1790s and faced, unusually, with light Portland stone rather than the ubiquitous dark Georgian brickwork. Traffic is excluded, but few pedestrians come here either – except those hobbling to the London Foot Hospital – yet it's a square rich in artistic and revolutionary associations. The painter **Ford Madox Brown** had fortnightly singsongs at no. 37 with his Pre-Raphaelite chums, and illustrious guests such as Turgenev and Liszt. **Virginia Woolf**'s blue plaque can be seen at no. 29 (a house also lived in by George Bernard Shaw): her Bloomsbury mates considered it a disreputable neighbourhood, but she moved here with her brother in 1907, after taking the precaution of checking with the police. Later, in 1913, artist Roger Fry set up his Omega Studios at no. 33, padding the walls with seaweed to keep out the noise. The square enjoyed an even worse reputation in the 1890s when it was home to the International Anarchist School for Children, run by 60-year-old French anarchist Louise Michel. The police eventually raided the building and closed down the school after finding bombs hidden in the basement.

Fitzrovia's radical pedigree has a further presence in **Marie Stopes House**, nearby at 108 Whitfield St, originally opened as the pioneering Mothers' Clinic for Constructive Birth Control in 1921. A qualified paleobotanist, Stopes courted controversy by advocating birth control as an aid to women's sexual pleasure, after her first marriage remained unconsummated for five years. However, her espousal of eugenics – she was keen to reduce the size of working-class families in order to improve the nation's stock, and even invented her own cervical cap called "Pro-racial" – has left a cloud over her reputation.

One last revolutionary of note – the Venezuelan adventurer **General Francisco de Miranda** (1750–1816) – is commemorated with a statue at the eastern corner of the London Foot Hospital situated on the southern side of the square. De Miranda lived nearby for a few years at 58 Grafton Way, and in 1810 he met up in Fitzrovia with fellow revolutionary Simón Bolívar; de Miranda ended his days in a Spanish prison, while Bolívar went on to liberate much of South America.

Tottenham Court Road

It's been centuries since there was a stately mansion – the original Tottenham Court – at the northern end of **Tottenham Court Road**, which consistently makes a strong challenge for London's least prepossessing, central shopping street. A rash of stores flogging discount-priced electrical equipment pack out the southern end, while furniture-makers – the street's original vendors – from Habitat and Heal's to cheap sofa outlets, pepper its northern stretch. The London listings magazine *Time Out* has its base here, too.

6

The British Museum

Housed in London's grandest Greek Revival building, fronted by a giant Ionic colonnade and portico designed by Robert Smirke in the 1820s, **the British Museum** (daily 10am–5.30pm, Thurs & Fri until 8.30pm; free; ☎020/7323 8000, ⓦwww.britishmuseum.org; Tottenham Court Road tube) is one of the great museums of the world. With over seventy thousand exhibits ranged over several miles of galleries, it boasts one of the largest collections of antiquities, prints and drawings housed under one roof – over fourteen million objects (and growing). Its assortment of Roman and Greek art is unparalleled, its Egyptian collection is the best outside Egypt and there are fabulous treasures from Anglo-Saxon and Roman Britain, from Africa, China, Japan, India and Mesopotamia.

Visiting the British Museum

The BM has **two entrances**: the main entrance on Great Russell Street and a back entrance on Montague Place. The main entrance brings you straight into the museum's spectacular **Great Court**, with its startling glass-and-steel curved roof designed by Norman Foster. The centre of the Great Court is occupied by the domed **Round Reading Room** (closed until 2012), where Karl Marx wrote *Das Kapital*, and which once housed the British Library. You can usually pick up a free **museum plan** from the main information desk in the Great Court, but even equipped with a plan, it's easy enough to get confused – don't hesitate to ask the helpful and knowledge-able **museum staff**. The BM can get very crowded, particularly at weekends, so get here as early as possible. It's all a far cry from the museum's beginnings in 1759, when it was open for just three hours a day, entry was by written application, and tickets for "any person of decent appearance" were limited to ten per hour.

The BM can tire even the most ardent museum lover. J.B. Priestley, for one, wished "there was a little room somewhere in the British Museum that contained only about twenty exhibits and good lighting, easy chairs, and a notice imploring you to smoke". Short of such a place, the best advice is to visit the Enlightenment gallery and adjacent room 2, tick off the **highlights** (listed on p.118), or concentrate on one or two sections. Alternatively, join one of the BM's daily **guided tours**: Highlights tours (1hr 30min; £8) are led by professional guides, while the eyeOpener tours (30–40min; free) are led by trained volunteers, and concentrate on just one room. Look out, too, for the **Hands-On** desks (daily 11am–4pm), where you can handle some of the museum's artefacts. Another option is to pick up one of the **audio tours** (£3.50).

The museum's best **café and restaurant** is the *Gallery Café* beyond room 12; the *Court Café* in the Great Court itself is more snacky, though it has a spectacular setting; the *Court Restaurant* on the upper floor is pricier, and best booked in advance (☎020/7323 8990).

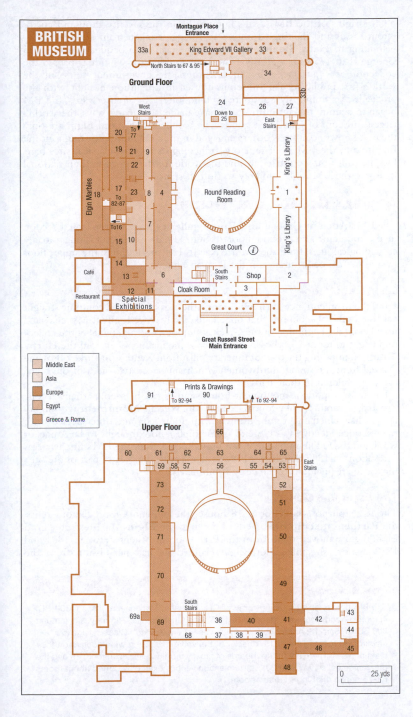

BRITISH MUSEUM

Ground Floor

Montague Place Entrance

33a   King Edward VII Gallery   33   33

North Stairs to 67 & 95

34

West Stairs

20   To 77
19   21   9
22
17   To 82-87
18   23   8   4
To16
15   10   7
14
13   6
Café
12   11
Restaurant   Special Exhibitions

24
Down to 25

26   27

East Stairs

King's Library

King's Library

1

33b

Elgin Marbles

Round Reading Room

Great Court   (i)

South Stairs   Shop   2
Cloak Room   3

Great Russell Street Main Entrance

Middle East
Asia
Europe
Egypt
Greece & Rome

Upper Floor

Prints & Drawings
91   90
To 92-94   To 92-94

66

60   61   62   63   64   65
59   58   57   56   55   54   53
East Stairs

73   52
72   51
71   50
70   49

South Stairs
69a   69   36   40   41   42   43
68   37   38   39   47   46   45   44
48

0   25 yds

The origins of the BM (as it's known) lie in the seventy thousand curios –from fossils and flamingo tongues to "maggots taken from a man's ear" – belonging to **Hans Sloane**, a Chelsea physician who bequeathed them to George II in 1753 for £20,000. The king couldn't (or wouldn't) pay, so the collection was purchased by an unenthusiastic government to form the world's first public secular museum, housed in a mansion bought with the proceeds of a dubiously conducted public lottery. Soon afterwards, the BM began to acquire the antiquities that have made it, in many ways, the world's largest museum of plundered goods. The "robberies" of Lord Elgin are only the best known; countless others engaged in sporadic looting throughout the Empire and the BM itself sent out archeologists to strip classical sites bare. Despite calls from countries around the world for the return of their national treasures, the BM looks unlikely to shift its stance.

Ancient Greece and Rome

The BM's **Ancient Greece and Rome galleries** make up the largest section in the museum. The ground floor (rooms 11–23) is laid out along broadly chronological lines, from the Bronze Age to Hellenistic times; the upper floor (rooms 69–73) concentrates on the Roman Empire.

Classical Greece

From the main entrance, turn left through the cloakroom, and continue straight past the twin half-columns that once flanked a beehive tomb at Mycenae and now herald the beginning of the Greek antiquities. The highlights of the collection begin in room 15, whose centrepiece is the marble relief from the **Harpy Tomb**, an imposing thirty-foot funerary pillar from Xanthos in Turkey. Its name derived from the strange birdwomen which appear on two sides of the relief, carrying children in their arms.

The most important monument from Xanthos can be seen, partially reconstructed, in room 17. The fourth-century BC **Nereid Monument** is a mighty temple-like chieftain's tomb, fronted with Ionic columns interspersed with figures, once identified as Nereids (sea nymphs), now thought to be Aurae, or wind goddesses. The monument was brought back from the BM's first overseas excavations in 1842 by Charles Fellows, along with the greater part of the site's moveable art (including the Harpy Tomb relief).

The Elgin Marbles

The large, purpose-built room 18 houses the museum's most famous relics, the **Parthenon sculptures**, better known as the **Elgin Marbles**, after Lord Elgin, who removed them from the Parthenon in Athens between 1801 and 1812. As British ambassador, Elgin claimed he had permission from the

Greek vases

The BM boasts an exhausting array of **Greek vases**: Mycenaean vases (1300 BC) in room 12 and Geometric (around 800 BC) and Athenian black-figure vases (around 600 BC) in room 13. Among the red-figure vases from Greece's Classical age (500 BC onwards) in rooms 14 and 15, check out the satyrs balancing wine coolers on their erect penises. There are further hoards of mostly red-figure vases in room 19 and the mezzanine gallery in room 20, not to mention various examples dotted about rooms 68–73 and in the King's Library (room 1).

▲ Elgin Marbles

Ottoman authorities (who ruled Greece at the time) to remove "any pieces of stone with inscriptions and figures". There were justifications for Elgin's action – a Venetian missile had caused considerable damage in 1687 when it landed on a pile of gunpowder the Turks had thoughtfully stored there – though it was criticized even at the time, most notably by Byron. The Greek government has asked for the sculptures to be sent back so they can be displayed, along with the rest of the sculptures, at the Acropolis Museum in Athens – so far, to no avail.

Despite their grand setting (and partly due to all the hype), first impressions of the marble friezes, carved between 447 and 432 BC under the supervision of the sculptor **Pheidias**, can be a little disappointing. The long, repetitive queues of worshippers lack the vigorous immediacy of high-relief sculptural friezes. To prepare yourself, head into the adjacent interpretive rooms to learn more about the context of the marbles. The main frieze, for example, would actually have been situated virtually out of sight behind the first set of columns, and, like most classical sculptures, would originally have been picked out in red, blue and gold paint.

Next, head for the traffic jam of horsemen on the north frieze, which is well preserved and exhibits superb compositional dexterity – it's worth remembering that the frieze is carved to a depth of only two inches, yet manages to convey a much greater feeling of perspective. Another superlative slice stands directly opposite, where the oxen are being led to the gods (said to have inspired Keats to write his *Ode on a Grecian Urn*). At each end of the room are the freestanding pedimental sculptures: the figures from the east pediment, which depict the extraordinary birth of Athena – she emerged full-grown and armed from the head of Zeus – are the most impressive, though most are headless.

The Tomb of Payava and the Mausoleum of Halikarnassos

Two of Lord Elgin's less defensible appropriations stand forlornly in room 19: a single column and one of the six caryatids from the portico of the **Erechtheion**, on the Acropolis. Further on, in room 20, is another large relic from Xanthos, the **Tomb of Payava**, built during the incumbent's lifetime in the fourth century BC; the reliefs on the tomb's steep roof would have been out of view of earthbound mortals, and are best viewed from the mezzanine (room 20a).

Room 21 contains fragments from one of the Seven Wonders of the Ancient World: two huge figures, an Amazonian frieze and a marble horse the size of an elephant from the self-aggrandizing tomb of **King Mausolus at Halikarnassos** (source of the word "mausoleum") from the fourth century BC. However, the real gem is the sculpted column drum, decorated in high relief, in room 22, from another Wonder, the colossal **Temple of Artemis at Ephesus**. The rest of the room is devoted to Hellenistic culture and features a fabulously delicate, gold oak wreath with a bee and two cicadas.

The upper floors

The remainder of the Greek and Roman collection is situated on the **upper floors** (rooms 69–73), best approached from the west stairs, which are lined with mosaic pavements from Halikarnassos. For the most part, the best stuff is displayed in room 70, and includes a dazzling display of silverware from Roman Gaul and an intriguing, warty, crocodile-skin suit of armour worn by a Roman follower of the Egyptian crocodile cult (cabinet 18). Whatever you do, don't miss the first-century AD **Warren Cup** (cabinet 12a), whose graphic depictions of gay sex were deemed too risqué to be shown to the public until the 1990s. Next to it stands the **Portland Vase**, made from cobalt-blue blown glass, and decorated with opaque white cameos. The vase was famously smashed into over two hundred separate pieces by a young Irishman in 1845, for which he was fined £3.

Middle East

The **Middle Eastern collection** covers all the lands east of Egypt and west of India. The majority of exhibits on the ground floor come from the Assyrian Empire; upstairs you'll find the Nimrud ivories, rich pickings from Mesopotamia, and the Oxus Treasure from ancient Persia.

Assyrian sculpture and reliefs

A colossal guardian lion, smothered in inscriptions, signals the beginning of the BM's remarkable collection of **Assyrian sculptures and reliefs** (room 6). Close by stands a small black obelisk carved with images of foreign rulers paying tribute to Shalmaneser III (858–824 BC), interspersed with **cuneiform inscriptions**. Ahead lies the Egyptian sculpture gallery (room 4), but to continue with Assyria, turn left and pass between the two awesome five-legged, human-headed winged lions that once flanked the doorway of the throne room in Nimrud, built by Ashurnasirpal II (883–859 BC). Beyond is a full-scale reconstruction of the colossal wooden **Balawat Gates** from the palace of Shalmaneser III, bound together with bronze strips decorated with low-relief friezes, depicting the defeat and execution of Shalmaneser's enemies.

The **Nineveh reliefs**, which begin in room 7, were originally brightly coloured, appearing rather like stone tapestries. There are some great snapshots of Assyrian life – a review of prisoners, a bull hunt and so on – but the most memorable scene, located towards the middle of the room, is of the soldiers swimming across the sea on inflated animal bladders. The reliefs in room 9 record the stupendous effort involved in transporting some gargantuan winged bulls from their quarry to the palace; they should be read from right to left. The Assyrians moved these carved beasts in one piece; not so the British, who cut the two largest winged bulls into four pieces before transporting them – the joins are still visible on the pair, which now stand at the northern entrance to room 10.

Room 10 itself is lined with even more splendid Assyrian friezes from King Sennacherib's palace in Nineveh. On one side the reliefs portray the chaos and carnage during the capture of the Judaean city of Lachish; the friezes were damaged, and Sennacherib's face smashed in, by Babylonian soldiers when the Assyrian capital later fell to its southern neighbours in 612 BC. On the other side are the **royal lion hunts** of Ashurbanipal (668–627 BC), which involved rounding up the beasts before letting them loose, one at a time, in an enclosed arena for the king's sport, a practice which effectively eradicated the species in Assyria; the succession of graphic death scenes features one in which the king slaughters the cats with his bare hands.

Mesopotamia and the Oxus Treasure

Upstairs, in room 59, are the Neolithic **Ain Ghazal statues**, the oldest large-scale representations of humans in the world, dating from the eighth millennium BC. Further on, in room 56, are some more of the BM's oldest artefacts, dating from Mesopotamia in the third millennium BC. The most extraordinary treasures hail from Ur, the first great city on earth, in modern-day Iraq: the enigmatic **Ram in the Thicket** (cabinet 28), a deep-blue lapis lazuli and white shell statuette of a goat on its hind legs, peering through gold-leaf branches; beside it, the equally mysterious **Standard of Ur**, a small hollow box showing scenes of battle on one side, with peace and banqueting on the other, all fashioned in shell, red limestone and lapis lazuli, set in bitumen; and (beside cabinet 9) the **Royal Game of Ur**, one of the earliest known board games.

In room 55, a selection of tablets scratched with infinitesimal cuneiform script includes lists, receipts, prescriptions, the **Flood Tablet**, a fragment of the Epic of Gilgamesh, the world's oldest story, and, in room 52, the **Cyrus Cylinder**, recounting the Persian leader's capture of Babylon in 539 BC. Finally, also in room 52, there's the **Oxus Treasure**, the most important surviving hoard of Persian goldwork from the Archaemenid Empire (550–330 BC), discovered in Tajikistan in 1877 and eventually picked up from the bazaar in Rawalpindi. The most celebrated pieces are the miniature four-horse chariot and the pair of armlets sprouting fantastical horned griffins.

Ancient Egypt

The BM's collection of **Egyptian antiquities**, ranging from Pre-dynastic times to Coptic Egypt, is one of the finest in the world, rivalled only by Cairo's and the New York Met's; the highlights are the **Rosetta Stone**, the vast hall of Egyptian sculpture and the large collection of **mummies**.

Egyptian sculpture

On the ground floor, just past the entrance to the Assyrian section (see p.118), two black-granite statues of **Amenophis III** (c.1417–1379 BC), whose rule coincided with the zenith of Egyptian power, guard the entrance to the BM's large hall of **Egyptian sculpture** (room 4). The name "Belzoni", scratched behind the left heel of the larger statue, was carved by the Italian circus strongman responsible for dragging some of the heftiest Egyptian treasures to the banks of the Nile. Further on, a colossal pink-speckled granite head of Amenophis III stands next to his enormous dislocated arm. Nearby are four seated statues of the goddess Sakhmet, the half-lion, half-human bringer of destruction, who was much loved by Amenophis III – each sports solar discs and clutches the *ankh*, the Egyptian symbol of life.

Centre stage in the Egyptian sculpture hall is the **Rosetta Stone**, a black basalt slab found in the Nile delta in 1799 by French soldiers. It was surrendered to the Brits in 1801, but it was a French professor, Champollion, who finally unlocked the secret of Egyptian hieroglyphs, by comparing the stone's three different scripts – ancient hieroglyphs, demotic Egyptian and Greek. North of here, another giant head and shoulders, made of two pieces of different-coloured granite, bears the hole drilled by French soldiers in an unsuccessful attempt to remove it from the mortuary temple of Rameses II. Moving towards the end of the room, make sure you seek out the bronze Gayer-Anderson cat goddess **Bastet**, with gold nose- and ear-rings, and the colossal granite scarab beetle by the exit.

The mummies and other funerary art

Climbing the west stairs brings you to room 61, where eleven large fragments of the colourful wall-paintings from the **tomb–chapel of Nebamun** from 1350 BC are displayed, depicting the idealized life of wealthy Egyptians of the period.

Next door, in room 62, you come to the popular **Egyptian mummy** collection, including numerous mummified corpses, embalmed bodies, and inner and outer **coffins** richly decorated with hieroglyphs. In one display cabinet, there are even mummies of various animals, including cats, apes, crocodiles, falcons and an eel, along with their highly ornate coffins. Also on display are colourful funerary **amulets**, which were wrapped with the mummy, and **heart scarabs**, which were placed on the chest of the mummy to prevent the deceased's heart from bearing witness against him or her after death. And don't miss the diminutive, glazed turquoise hippo, one of the museum's most popular items. The contents of Egyptian tombs included food, drink, clothing, furniture, weapons and dozens of **shabti figures** designed to perform any task the gods might require in the afterlife. In room 63, there are

Temporary exhibitions

The sheer volume of the BM's **prints and drawings**, everything from Botticelli to Bonnard, means there's only space for changing displays in rooms 90 and 91. Similarly, only a fraction of BM's collection of **coins and medals** can be shown at any one time in room 69a. In addition, the BM puts on large-scale **special exhibitions** on a wide range of themes in a temporary space within the Reading Room, for which there is an entrance charge.

miniature boats to provide transport in the afterlife, beer brewers, butchers and even an entire model granary.

At this point, pop into room 66 to admire the joyful depiction of the Battle of Adwa (1896), when **Ethiopia** trounced Italy, the Falasha (Jewish) dolls, the "chestlet" of beetle wings and the "Net of Solomon" used to trap demons. Lastly, the 5000-year-old sand-preserved corpse in room 64 (cabinet 15) always comes in for ghoulish scrutiny, and there's a limestone building block from the Great Pyramid of Cheops, another of the Seven Wonders of the Ancient World.

Europe

The BM fulfils its less controversial role as national treasure house of antiquities in the **Europe** section on the upper floor (rooms 41–51).

Prehistoric/Roman Britain

One of the BM's most sensational finds is the well-preserved leathery half-corpse **Lindow Man** (due to return to the BM in 2010), thought to have been clubbed and garrotted during a Druid sacrificial ceremony. Several impressive Iron Age treasure troves are displayed in room 51, chief among them the **Snettisham Hoard** (cabinet 19) of gold and silver torcs (neck-rings). The two most distinctive examples of **Celtic artistry** are the French Basse-Yutz wine flagons (room 50) made from bronze and inlaid with coral, with happy little ducks on the lip and rangy dogs for handles. Room 49 displays the best finds from **Roman Britain**, many, like the bronze head (and hand) of the Roman emperor Hadrian (cabinet 14), dredged out of the Thames. The most impressive display is the fourth-century AD **Mildenhall Treasure** (cabinet 22), a 28-piece silver tableware set, whose Great Dish is decorated with Bacchic images in low relief.

Europe: Medieval/Modern

From the south stairs, visitors entering room 40 are greeted by the incredible, fourteenth-century French **Royal Gold Cup** (cabinet 2), given by James I to the Constable of Castille, only to find its way back to England in later life – the scenes enamelled on its surface depict the gruesome story of St Agnes. Beyond lie the celebrated **Lewis chessmen** (cabinet 5), wild-eyed, thick-set, twelfth-century Scandinavian figures carved from walrus ivory, discovered in 1831 by a crofter in the Outer Hebrides. Room 41 houses a bewildering array of "Dark Age" treasures from all over the continent, most famously the Anglo-Saxon **Sutton Hoo Treasure**, which includes silver bowls, gold jewellery and an iron helmet bejewelled with gilded bronze and garnets, all buried along with a forty-oar open ship in East Anglia around 625 AD, and discovered by accident in 1939.

Room 47 brings you, with a bit of a jolt, into the **European nineteenth-century** section, and reflects the era's eclectic tastes, with everything from quasi-medieval jewellery to Neoclassical porcelain vases, much of it inspired by the BM itself. Look out for the Arts and Crafts De Morgan and Minton tiles and Christopher Dresser's outstanding geometric metalwork. In the adjacent room 48, the best of the museum's **twentieth-century exhibits** are displayed, including stunning examples of iridescent Tiffany glass, a copper vase by Frank Lloyd Wright and a lovely, chequered oak clock with a mother-of-pearl face, designed by the Scottish architect and designer Charles Rennie Mackintosh. There's also usually an impressive array of avant-garde Russian ceramics celebrating the 1917 revolution.

Renaissance and Baroque art fills room 46, with a bafflingly wide range of works from all over Europe (though much of it of British origin). Highlights include the Armada Service, a Tudor silver dining set, two pure-gold ice pails that belonged to Princess Diana's family, Cromwell's wax death mask and a collection of eighteenth-century Huguenot silver. The purple-walled chamber beyond (room 45) contains the **Waddesdon Bequest**, curiosities amassed by Baron Rothschild in the nineteenth century: a mixed bag of silver gilt, enamelware, glassware and hunting rifles. The three finest works are the Holy Thorn Reliquary (cabinet 1), with its wonderfully macabre depiction of the Resurrection; a Flemish sixteenth-century boxwood altarpiece (cabinet 8), just 6in high and carved with staggering detail; and the Lyte Jewel, which contains a miniature of James I by Hilliard (cabinet 4).

King's Library – Enlightenment

The **Enlightenment gallery** (room 1) runs the entire length of the east wing. Built to house George III's library (now the centrepiece of the British Library in St Pancras), it's like a snapshot of the BM of old, lined with antique display cases stuffed with books and artefacts, illustrating the acquisitive magpie tastes of the eighteenth-century colonial collector, epitomized by Hans Sloane himself, the BM's founder. Sloane's own collection features everything from priapic statuettes to a black obsidian mirror used by the magician, John Dee, to conjure up spirits (case 20). And he was not alone in falling for the bizarre and magical to augment his "cabinet of curiosities": the rhino-horn cup which protected the drinker from poison and the Japanese "merman" (case 14) – a dried monkey sewn onto a fish tail – are not atypical.

Displayed here, too, are some of the museum's earliest acquisitions, brought back from the far reaches of the expanding British Empire: a piece of bark cloth made by Fletcher Christian's Tahitian partner (case 22); Tipu Sultan's sword and ring, and a whole variety of Javanese puppets and dolls (case 23) collected by Stamford Raffles. Don't neglect to pop into the adjacent room 2, where some of the museum's **oldest exhibits** are usually displayed, like the 13,000-year-old ivory sculpture of swimming reindeer.

Time and Money

The BM has recently created a series of themed rooms, the largest of which is the Enlightenment gallery on the ground floor (see above). On the upper floor, the **Time** gallery (room 37) includes many of the BM's clocks and watches, which are also displayed in rooms 38 and 39. The centrepiece of room 37 is a sixteenth-century gilded brass clock from Strasbourg, based on the one that used to reside in the cathedral there; its series of moving figures includes the Four Ages of Man, who each strike one of the quarter-hours. The adjacent rooms resound to the tick-tocks and chimes of a hundred or more clocks, from pocket watches to grandfather clocks.

The **Money** gallery (room 68) traces the history of filthy lucre from the use of grain in Mesopotamia around 2000 BC, to the advent of coins in around 625 BC in Greek cities in Asia Minor. There are pound-coin moulds and punches (cabinet 14), a geometric lathe for old £1 notes (cabinet 16) and a wonderful Tiffany-designed National Cash Register till (cabinet 13). The largest denomination bill is the 1993 500,000 million Yugoslav dinar note (cabinet 17), but the most unusual exhibit is the one million dollar note issued by the Hong Kong "Bank of Hell" (cabinet 18), featuring the face of Harold Wilson, and designed to be burnt as an offering to keep the deceased happy in the afterlife.

Americas

The BM's two American galleries lie to the side of the themed gallery, **Living and Dying** (room 24), which features some spectacular large-scale exhibits, including Hoa Hakananai'a, the giant basalt Easter Island statue (originally painted red and white), and four modern apocalyptic papier-mâché skeletons from the Mexican Day of the Dead festival. Close by is the famous crystal skull, thought to have been Aztec when the BM bought it in 1897, but now known to be a fake.

Next door is the **North American gallery** (room 26), whose precise exhibits change regularly, due to the delicate, organic nature of the materials used. However, you can be sure to find feather headdresses, masks, basketry, bead and shell currency and zoomorphic stone pipes. From the Arctic, there are Inuit furs and skins, including a caribou-skin parka and bone sled, and from the Southwest, the ever-popular Pueblo pottery made by the Hopi.

The tiny **Mexican gallery** (room 27) covers a huge period of Mexican art from the second millennium BC to the sixteenth century AD. As you enter, you're greeted by an Aztec fire serpent, Xiuhcoatl, carved in basalt. On one side is a collection of Huaxtec female deities in stone, sporting fan-shaped headdresses; on the other are an Aztec stone rattlesnake cleverly lit and mirrored from below, the squatting figure of the sun-god, Xochipili, and the death-cult god, Mictlantecuhtli. A series of limestone Mayan reliefs from Yaxchilan, depicting blood-letting ceremonies, lines one wall and, elsewhere, there are some wonderful turquoise mosaic masks and figurines. Whatever you do, don't miss the brilliant colours of the Mixtec painted screen-fold book made of deerskin.

Africa

The BM's **Africa** collection is housed in the galleries known as lower-floor room 25. To the left, as you enter, there are **woodcarvings** from a whole range of African cultures: everything from a large stool from Cameroon to backrests from the Congo. Further to the left, you'll find the Yoruba royal palace doors, carved in high relief and depicting, among other things, lazy British imperialists arriving on a litter to collect taxes. Also on display is an entire cabinet of throwing knives from the Congo and the chilling "Tree of Life" sculpture made from decommissioned weapons from Mozambique.

To the right, there's a section on **masquerades**, with elaborate crocodile, buffalo, warthog and hippo masks from the last two centuries, and a video of contemporary initiation ceremonies in Nigeria. Perhaps the most famous of the BM's African exhibits are the so-called "**Benin Bronzes**" looted by the British in 1897. Confusingly, these are neither bronzes (they are, in fact, brass), nor from modern-day Benin, but from the former Benin Empire within modern-day Nigeria. Among the most impressive are the ornate sixteenth-century brass plaques, nine hundred of which once decorated the royal palace in Benin City. Other Benin exhibits, such as the eye-catching ivory leopards studded with copper gun caps, were actually commissioned by Europeans.

Asia

The BM's Chinese collection, though small compared with the museum's other departments, is unrivalled in the West, and the Indian sculpture is easily as good

China

The **Chinese collection** occupies the eastern half of room 33. Immediately striking are the pieces of garishly glazed **three-colour statuary**, particularly the three seated sages and central cabinet of horses, camels, kings, officials and fabulous beasts. However, it's the smaller pieces that hold the attention the longest: the central cabinet of miniature landscapes, in cabinet 56, popular among bored Chinese bureaucrats during the time of the Manchu Empire, or the incredible array of **snuff bottles** (cabinet 54), made from lapis lazuli, jade, crystal, tortoiseshell, quartz and amber. The Chinese invented **porcelain**, and it was highly prized both in China and abroad. There's a whole range on display here, but for an even more impressive collection of Chinese ceramics, head for room 95 (see below). Lastly, don't miss the Chinese jade, spanning seven thousand years, on display in the adjacent corridor (room 33b).

South and Southeast Asia

The other half of room 33 starts with a beautiful gilt-bronze statue of Tara, the goddess of good fortune, who was born from one of the tears wept by Avalokiteshvara (a companion of the Buddha, who stands on the east side of the marble well). She heralds the beginning of the **South and Southeast Asian** antiquities, a bewildering array of artefacts from places as far apart as India and Indonesia. It's worth seeking out cabinet 55 with its Tibetan depictions of tantric sex, its dakinis, fierce minor goddesses who dance on demons, and Chitipati, lord of the graveyard. Cabinet 39 features a whole set of ivory figures from Kandy, representing the local royal family and officials, including the all-important umbrella-bearer. Beyond are larger-scale **Indian stone sculptures**, featuring a bevy of intimidating goddesses such as Durga, depicted killing a buffalo demon with her eight hands (cabinet 25).

Korea and Chinese ceramics

The centrepiece of the BM's gallery devoted to **Korea** (room 67), up the north stairs from room 33, is a nail-free reconstruction of a *sarangbang* or scholar's study, a wonderfully serene, minimalist space set aside for the gentleman of the house. Among the other exhibits, which range from illuminated Buddhist manuscripts to contemporary Korean *objets d'art*, look out for the woven horsehair hats and bamboo fans used by dapper Korean gentlemen, the *paduk* gaming board (better known in the West as Go), and the seventeenth-century white porcelain "full-moon" jar, admired for both its irregularity and its Confucian austerity.

Next door is an entire room given over to **Chinese ceramics** (room 95), with nearly 1700 objects on display, dating from the third to the twentieth centuries. A few star exhibits get labels, like the "David vases", by the entrance, from 1351, in the blue-and-white Ming style that became so popular in Europe – touch-screen computers will help you identify the rest. What is so striking about many of the pieces is their apparent modernity – the bold single-colour porcelain wares at the far side of the room wouldn't look out of place in the 1960s, though in fact they date from the Ming and Qing dynasties. Among the most celebrated Chinese ceramics are the *Ru* wares whose "crackling" glaze was seen as a merit rather than a defect from the Song dynasty onwards.

Japan

The sensitive materials used in Japanese art mean that the items on display in the **Japan** (rooms 92–94) galleries change frequently. What you get is an educational sample laid out chronologically from the Neolithic Jomon period to the manga culture of contemporary Japan. In between, you get to inspect colourful Buddhist scrolls, Shinto shrines, nineteenth-century woodblock prints by artists such as Hokusai and Hiroshige, examples of *netsuke* (ornamental toggles) and *inro* (cases for holding small objects). Centre stage, there's a wonderfully ornate suit of Samurai armour, complete with the sort of horned helmet and mask that Darth Vadar might wear. There's also a section on the traditional tea ceremony alongside a reconstructed Urasenke teahouse, where the museum puts on regular demonstrations.

Islam

The museum's fairly modest **Islamic** collection is tucked away in room 34, by the Montague Place entrance. Among the highlights are the **Damascus and Iznik ceramics** in greens, tomato-reds and no fewer than five shades of blue. Also worth seeking out at the far end of the room, are the medieval astrolabes, celestial globes and a **geomantic instrument** used to tell the future. The most striking exhibit is a naturalistic **jade terrapin**, discovered in Allahabad in 1600; close by is a silver-filigree cosmetic box said to be from Tipu Sultan's palace, and a couple of jade Mughal hookah bases encrusted with lapis lazuli and rubies set in gold.

7

Bloomsbury

Bloomsbury gets its name from its medieval landowners, the Blemunds, who were probably given the estate by William the Conqueror. Nothing was built here, though, until the 1660s, when the Earl of Southampton laid out **Bloomsbury Square**, which John Evelyn thought "a noble square or piazza – a little towne". Through marriage, the Russell family, the earls and later dukes of Bedford, acquired much of the area, and established the other formal, bourgeois squares which remain the main distinguishing feature of Bloomsbury. The Russells named the grid-plan streets after their various titles and estates, and kept the pubs and shops to a minimum to maintain the tone of the neighbourhood.

In the twentieth century, Bloomsbury acquired a reputation as the city's most learned quarter, dominated by the dual institutions of the **British Museum** and **London University** and home to many of London's chief book publishers, but perhaps best known for its literary inhabitants. The **British Museum** is clearly Bloomsbury's main draw – it has its own chapter (see p.114) – but the real pleasure in Bloomsbury is simply strolling through its leafy squares which, though no longer the set pieces of Georgian architecture they once were, still provide some of the nicest picnic spots in central London.

Bloomsbury's northern border is formed by busy Euston Road, home to two middleweight museums: one literary, at the **British Library**, and one medical, courtesy of the **Wellcome Collection**. Finally, the area around **King's Cross Station** is undergoing massive redevelopment, spurred on by the arrival of Eurostar trains into **St Pancras**.

South of the British Museum

The Georgian streets of Museum Street and Bury Place, **south of the BM**, currently thrive on a mixture of antiquarian and secondhand print and book shops, and cafés and sandwich shops, while just round the corner, it's worth looking in at the window of **Jarndyce**, the booksellers at 46 Great Russell St, whose left window is renowned for its display of bizarre antiquarian books, with titles such as *Correctly English in Hundred Days* and *The Art of Faking Exhibition Poultry*.

Another place to go for a laugh is the **Cartoon Museum** (Tues–Sat 10.30am–5.30pm, Sun noon–5.30pm; £4; ☎020/7580 8155, ⓦwww.cartoon museum.org; Tottenham Court Road tube), housed in a former dairy at 35 Little Russell St, one block south of the BM. As well as putting on excellent temporary exhibitions, this small museum has a permanent display of over two hundred works spanning two centuries, beginning with Hogarth's moralistic engravings and the caricatures of Gillray, Rowlandson and Cruickshank. The

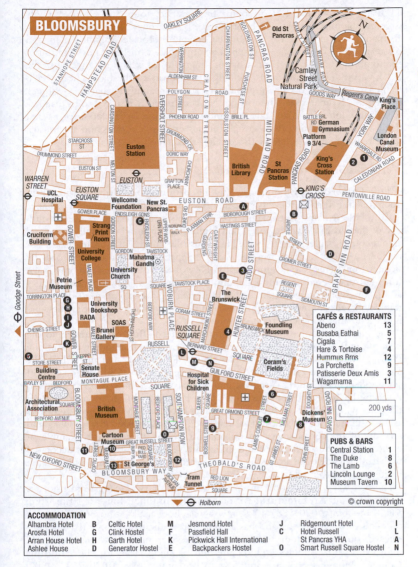

CAFÉS & RESTAURANTS
Abeno	13
Busaba Eathai	5
Cigala	7
Hare & Tortoise	4
Hummus Bros	12
La Porchetta	9
Patisserie Deux Amis	3
Wagamama	11

PUBS & BARS
Central Station	1
The Duke	8
The Lamb	6
Lincoln Lounge	2
Museum Tavern	10

© crown copyright

ACCOMMODATION
Alhambra Hotel	**B**	Celtic Hotel	**M**	Jesmond Hotel	**J**	Ridgemount Hotel	**I**
Arosfa Hotel	**G**	Clink Hostel	**F**	Passfield Hall		Hotel Russell	**L**
Arran House Hotel	**H**	Garth Hotel	**K**	Pickwick Hall International		St Pancras YHA	**A**
Ashlee House	**D**	Generator Hostel	**E**	Backpackers Hostel	**C**	Smart Russell Square Hostel	**N**
					O		

emphasis is very much on British cartoons from the likes of *Punch*, one of the earliest and longest-lasting satirical magazines, to *Private Eye*, which helped launch the careers of, among others, Ralph Steadman and Gerald Scarfe. The comic strips range from Ally Sloper, Britain's first regular comic-strip character who appeared in 1884, through D.C. Thompson (publisher of *Beano*), to *Viz*, the country's best-selling comic ever, which at its peak sold over a million copies each edition.

Set back from busy Bloomsbury Way, three blocks south of the BM, is Hawksmoor's **Church of St George's Bloomsbury** (Mon–Fri 1–2pm, Sat

11.30am–5pm, Sun 11.30am–6pm; free guided tour Sun 3pm; ⓦwww
.stgeorgesbloomsbury.org.uk), built to serve Bloomsbury's respectable residents.
Its main point of interest is the unusual steeple – Horace Walpole called it "a
masterpiece of absurdity" – a stepped pyramid based on Pliny's description of
the tomb of Mausolus at Halikarnassos (fragments of which now reside in the
BM), with lions and unicorns clinging precariously to the base. The tower is
topped by a statue of the unpopular German-speaking monarch, George I,
dressed in a Roman toga. The interior has been recently restored to its original,
gleaming-white Georgian state. Tall and wide, with a large clerestory, its best
features are the flaming pentecostal tongues on the keystones and an unusual
semicircular apse, complete with a scallop-shell recess.

The Bloomsbury squares

A little further along Bloomsbury Way lies **Bloomsbury Square**, laid out in
1665 and the first of the city's open spaces to be officially called a "square"
– sadly, little remains of its original or later Georgian appearance. At the south
end of the square, however, you'll find **Sicilian Avenue**, a beautifully preserved
architectural set piece from 1910. This unusually continental promenade leads
diagonally onto Southampton Row and is separated from the main roads by
slender Ionic screens. On Southampton Row itself, you can see the only **tram
lines** left uncovered in central London from what was, between World Wars I
and II, the world's largest tram system: to catch a glimpse, you must dodge the
traffic and peek through the wrought-iron railings to the tracks as they descend
into the former Kingsway tram subway.

The most handsome of the Bloomsbury squares is **Bedford Square**, to the
west of the BM. Some of Bloomsbury's best-known publishing houses – among
them Hodder & Stoughton, Bodley Head, Jonathan Cape and Chatto &
Windus – had their offices here until the mergers of the 1980s killed off most
small independent outfits. Architecturally, what you see now is pretty much as
it was in the 1770s when it was built by the Russells (who still own it), though
the gates which sealed the square from traffic have unfortunately been removed,
as have all but one of the mews that once accommodated the coaches and
servants of the square's wealthy inhabitants. Today, it's a perfect example of
eighteenth-century symmetry and uniformity: each doorway arch is decorated
with rusticated Coade stones; each side of the square is broken only by the
white-stuccoed central houses.

The best way to get a look inside one of Bloomsbury's Georgian mansions is
to head for the **Architectural Association** (term time Mon–Fri 10am–7pm,
Sat 10am–3pm; ☎020/7887 4000, ⓦwww.aaschool.ac.uk) at no. 36, which puts
on occasional exhibitions, and has a bookshop in the basement and a student
café/bar on the first floor, with a roof terrace open in fine weather. For more
information on London's architecture and planning, head for the **Building
Centre** (Mon–Fri 9.30am–6pm, Sat 10am–5pm; free; ☎020/7692 4000,
ⓦwww.buildingcentre.co.uk), at 26 Store St. Its centrepiece is a vast model of
London, including as-yet unrealized skyscrapers and the 2012 Olympic Village,
but it also hosts topical exhibitions on the future of London, and has a café and
bookshop.

The largest Bloomsbury square – indeed one of the largest in London – is
Russell Square, to the northeast of the BM. Apart from its monumental scale,
little remains of the Georgian scheme, though the gardens, with their gargantuan plane trees, are good for a picnic, and there's a café in the northeastern
corner. The Bloomsbury figure most closely associated with the square is

▲ Russell Hotel

T.S. Eliot, who worked at no. 24, then the offices of Faber & Faber, from 1925 until his death in 1965. The only architectural curiosity is the *Russell Hotel*, on the eastern side; twice as high as everything around it, it's a no-holds-barred Victorian terracotta fancy, concocted in a bewildering mixture of styles in 1898 by Fitzroy Doll.

Gordon Square (Mon–Fri 8am–8pm), one block north of Russell Square, with its winding paths and summer profusion of roses, remains one of Bloomsbury's quietest sanctuaries, a favourite with the local students. Looking like a miniature cathedral, in the southwest corner of the square, stands the strangely towerless neo-Gothic **University Church**, built in 1853 for the Catholic Apostolic sect (who encouraged the congregation to "speak in tongues") – the unbuilt tower was to have been nearly 300ft high. Gordon Square was once the centre of the Bloomsbury Group (see box, p.130): on the east side, where the Georgian houses stand intact, plaques mark the residences of Lytton Strachey (no. 51) and John Maynard Keynes (no. 46), while another (no. 50) commemorates the Bloomsbury Group as a whole.

One block east is **Tavistock Square**, laid out by Thomas Cubitt in the early nineteenth century. Though the west side of the square survives intact, the house at no. 52, where the Woolfs lived from 1924 until shortly before Virginia's suicide in 1941, and from which they ran the Hogarth Press, is no longer standing. It was here that Woolf wrote her most famous novels – *To the Lighthouse*, *Mrs Dalloway*, *Orlando* and *The Waves* – in a little studio decorated by her sister Vanessa and Duncan Grant. At the centre of the square's gardens is a statue of **Mahatma Gandhi**, whose presence has transformed the square into something of a garden for peace, with various trees and benches dedicated to the cause. That peace, however, was shattered on the morning of **July 7, 2005**, when a suicide bomber blew up bus #30 as it approached the northeast corner of the square, killing at least thirteen people. The blast occurred shortly after the city's tube system had been hit by three other terrorist bombs (see p.473).

The Bloomsbury Group

The **Bloomsbury Group** were essentially a bevy of upper-middle-class friends who lived in and around Bloomsbury, at that time "an antiquated, ex-fashionable area", in the words of Henry James. The group revolved around siblings Virginia, Vanessa, Thoby and Adrian Stephen, who moved into 46 Gordon Square in 1904. Thoby's Thursday-evening gatherings and Vanessa's Friday Club for painters attracted a whole host of Cambridge-educated types who subscribed to Oscar Wilde's theory that "aesthetics are higher than ethics". Their diet of "human intercourse and the enjoyment of beautiful things" was hardly revolutionary, but their behaviour, particularly that of the two sisters (unmarried, unchaperoned, intellectual and artistic), succeeded in shocking London society, especially through their louche sexual practices (most of the group swung both ways).

All this, though interesting, would be forgotten were it not for their individual work. In 1922, Virginia declared, without too much exaggeration, "Everyone in Gordon Square has become famous": Lytton Strachey was the first to make his name with a series of unprecedentedly frank biographies; Vanessa, now married to the art critic Clive Bell, became involved in Roger Fry's prolific design firm, **Omega Workshops**; and the economist John Maynard Keynes became an adviser to the Treasury. (He later went on to become the leading economic theorist of his day.) The group's most celebrated figure, Virginia, now married to Leonard Woolf, had become an established novelist; she and Leonard had also founded the **Hogarth Press**, which published T.S. Eliot's *Waste Land* in 1922.

Eliot was just one of a number of writers, such as Aldous Huxley, Bertrand Russell and E.M. Forster, who were drawn to the Bloomsbury set, but others, notably D.H. Lawrence, were repelled by the clan's narcissism and narrow-mindedness. Whatever their limitations, the Bloomsbury Group were certainly Britain's most influential intellectual coterie of the interwar years, and their appeal shows little sign of waning.

A short distance up Upper Woburn Place, not far from where the blast occurred, is the beautifully preserved Georgian terrace of **Woburn Walk**, designed in 1822 by Cubitt as London's first purpose-built pedestrianized shopping street. W.B. Yeats moved into no. 5 in 1895, shortly afterwards losing his virginity at the age of 31 to fellow writer Olivia Shakespear. He and Olivia had to go to Heal's to order a bed before they could consummate the relationship, and Yeats found the experience (of ordering the bed) deeply traumatic, as "every inch added to the expense". The same address was later occupied by the unrequited love of Yeats' life, Irish nationalist Maud Gonne, reputedly the most beautiful woman in Ireland, with, in Yeats' own words, "the carriage and features of a goddess".

East of Russell Square

East of Russell Square, the original Bloomsbury squares and streets here have been bashed about a bit. The chief tourist sight is **Dickens' House**, the only one of the writer's fifteen London addresses to survive intact. Medical institutions dominate the area, particularly around **Queen Square**, popularly known as "hospital square". One of the first to be established here was the Foundling Hospital, now home to the excellent **Foundling Museum**, and neighbouring **Coram's Fields**, shelter for London's most central city farm.

Foundling Museum and Coram's Fields

Halfway along Guilford Street stands the old entrance to the **Foundling Hospital**, founded in 1756 by **Thomas Coram**, a retired sea captain. Coram campaigned for seventeen years to obtain a royal charter for the hospital, having been shocked by the number of dead or dying babies left by the wayside on the streets of London during the gin craze. (At the time, 75 percent of London's children died before they were 5.) All that remains of the original eighteenth-century buildings is the alcove where the foundlings used to be abandoned and the whitewashed loggia which forms the border to **Coram's Fields** (daily 9am–7pm or dusk; free; ☎020/7837 6138, ⓦwww.coramsfields .org), an inner-city haven for children, with swings and slides, plus a whole host of hens, horses, sheep, goats and ducks. Adults are not allowed into the grounds unless accompanied by a child.

The **Foundling Museum** (Tues–Sat 10am–5pm, Sun 11am–5pm; £5; ☎020/7841 3600, ⓦwww.foundlingmuseum.org.uk; Russell Square tube), north of Coram's Fields, at 40 Brunswick Square, tells the fascinating story of the hospital. As soon as it opened, it was besieged, and forced to introduce a ballot system. After 1801 only illegitimate children were admitted, and even then only after the mother had given a verbal statement confirming that "her good faith had been betrayed, that she had given way to carnal passion only after a promise of marriage or against her will". Among the most tragic exhibits are the tokens left by the mothers in order to identify the children should they ever be in a position to reclaim them: these range from a heart-rending poem to a simple enamel pot label reading "ale".

One of the hospital's governors – he even fostered two of the foundlings – was the artist **William Hogarth**, who established an art gallery at the hospital to give his friends somewhere to display their works and to attract potential benefactors for the hospital. As a result the museum boasts works by artists such as Gainsborough and Reynolds, as well as Hogarth's splendid *March of the Guards to Finchley*. Upstairs, the Court Room, where the governors still hold their meetings, has been faithfully reconstructed, with all its fine stuccowork. The fireplace features a wonderful relief depicting the trades of navigation and agriculture, into which the foundling boys were apprenticed before being sent out to the colonies. (The girls went into service.) On the top floor, there's a room dedicated to **Georg Friedrich Handel**, who gave annual charity performances of the *Messiah*, wrote an anthem for the hospital (basically a rehash of the *Hallelujah Chorus*) and donated an organ for the chapel, the keyboard of which survives.

Dickens' House

Despite its plethora of blue plaques, Bloomsbury boasts just one literary museum, **Dickens' House** (Mon–Sat 10am–5pm, Sun 11am–5pm; £5; ☎020/7405 2127, ⓦwww.dickensmuseum.com; Russell Square tube), southeast of Coram's Fields at 48 Doughty St. Dickens moved here in 1837 – when it was practically on the northern outskirts of town – soon after his marriage to Catherine Hogarth, and they lived here for two years, during which time he wrote *Nicholas Nickleby* and *Oliver Twist*. Although Dickens painted a gloomy Victorian world in his books, the drawing room here, in which Dickens entertained his literary friends, was decorated (and has since been restored) in a rather upbeat Regency style. Letters, manuscripts and first editions, the earliest known portrait (a miniature painted by his aunt in 1830) and the reading copies he used during extensive lecture tours in Britain and the States are the rewards for those with more than a passing interest in the novelist. There's also a half-hour film of his life.

Charles Dickens

Few cities are as closely associated with one writer as London is with **Charles Dickens** (1812–70). The recurrent motifs in his novels have become the clichés of Victorian London – the fog, the slums and alleys, the prisons and workhouses, and of course the stinking river. Drawing on his own personal experience, he was able to describe the workings of the law and the conditions of the poor with an unrivalled accuracy.

Born in Portsmouth, the second of eight children, Dickens spent a happy early childhood in Chatham and then London. This was cut short at the age of 12 when his father was imprisoned in Marshalsea debtors' prison, and Charles was forced to work in a boot-blacking factory on the site of Charing Cross Station. The experience scarred him for life – he was hurt further when his mother forced him to keep the job even after his father's release – and was no doubt responsible for Dickens' strong philanthropic convictions. After two years as a solicitor's clerk at Gray's Inn, he became a parliamentary reporter and wrote *Sketches by Boz* (Dickens' journalistic pen name) and *The Pickwick Papers*, the two works that propelled him to fame and fortune in 1836.

The same year he married **Catherine Hogarth**, and there followed ten children – "the largest family ever known with the smallest disposition to do anything for themselves", as Dickens later described them – and sixteen novels, each published in monthly (or weekly) installments, which were awaited with bated breath by the Victorian public. Then in 1857, at the peak of his career, Dickens fell in love with the actress, **Ellen Ternan**; Dickens was 45, Ternan just 18. His subsequent separation from his wife, and his insistence that she leave the family house (while her sister Georgina and most of the children stayed), scandalized society and forced the author to retreat to Rochester.

Dickens died at his desk at the age of 58, while working on *The Mystery of Edwin Drood*. According to his wishes, there was no public announcement of his burial, though he was interred in Westminster Abbey (at Queen Victoria's insistence) rather than in Rochester (as he had requested). The twelve people present at the early-morning service were asked not to wear a black bow, long hatband or any other accessories of the "revolting absurdity" of Victorian mourning.

If you're on the Dickens trail, there are one or two other sights worth checking out: the Old Curiosity Shop (see p.153), on Lincoln's Inn Fields, the (possible) inspiration for Dickens' novel of the same name; the atmospheric Inns of Court (see p.150), which feature in several Dickens novels; "Nancy's Steps", where Nancy tells Rose Maylie Oliver's story in *Oliver Twist*, on the west side of London Bridge on the South Bank; and the evocative dockland area of Shad Thames (see p.240), where Bill Sykes has his hide-out.

London University

London only organized its own **University** (Ⓦ www.lon.ac.uk) in 1826, but was the first in the country to admit students regardless of race, class, religion or gender. The university started life in Bloomsbury, but it wasn't until after World War I that it really began to take over the area. Nowadays, the various colleges and institutes have spread their tentacles to form an almost continuous academic swathe from the British Museum all the way to Euston Road. Despite this, the university's piecemeal development has left it with only a couple of distinguishing landmarks in the form of **Senate House** and **University College**. Several of the university departments run their own small, specialist **museums and galleries**, scattered across the campus. Plans are afoot, however, to gather the UCL collections together under one roof at the Institute for Cultural Heritage, a new eight-floor building on Gordon Square, optimistically scheduled to open late in 2010.

Senate House and SOAS

Looming behind the British Museum is the skyscraper of **Senate House**, a "bleak, blank, hideous" building, according to Max Beerbohm, now housing the university library. Designed with Art Deco touches by Charles Holden in 1932, and austerely clad in Portland stone, it's best viewed from Malet Street. During the war it served as the Ministry of Information, where the likes of Evelyn Waugh, Graham Greene, Dorothy L. Sayers and George Orwell worked. Orwell later modelled the Ministry of Truth in *1984* on it: "an enormous pyramidal structure of glittering white concrete, soaring up, terrace after terrace, 300 metres into the air".

To the north, on Thornhaugh Street, is the **School of Oriental and African Studies** or **SOAS** (Ⓦwww.soas.ac.uk), which puts on fascinating temporary exhibitions of photography, sculpture and art, and has a permanent display of exotic treasures, at the rather snazzy **Brunei Gallery** (Tues–Sat 10.30am–5pm; free), funded by the immensely rich Sultan of Brunei. There's a tiny but excellent bookshop and a café on the ground floor, and a secluded Zen-like **roof garden**.

University College London

The oldest part of **University College London** or **UCL** (Ⓦwww.ucl.ac.uk) is the rather prosaically named **Main Building**, William Wilkins' Neoclassical edifice from the 1820s, with its handsome Corinthian portico and fine quadrangle, set back (and well hidden) from busy Gower Street. UCL is home to one of London's most famous art schools, the **Slade**, which puts on small, but excellent temporary exhibitions drawn from its collection of over ten thousand works of art, by the likes of Dürer, Rembrandt, Turner and Constable, as well as works by former students, such as Stanley Spencer, Paul Nash, Wyndham Lewis, Augustus John and Raymond Briggs. These are held at the **Strang Print Room** (Wed–Fri 1–5pm; free; ☎020/7679 2540; Euston Square tube), situated in the south cloister of the main quadrangle.

There's more artwork on display in the octagon beneath the Main Building's central dome, in an area known as the **Flaxman Gallery** – follow the signs to the library and ask the guards to let you through. John Flaxman (1755–1826) made his name producing Neoclassical funerary sculpture – his works feature prominently in Westminster Abbey and St Paul's – and the walls here are filled with scaled-down, high-relief, plaster models worked on by Flaxman himself for his marble monuments. The gallery's centrepiece is a dramatic, full-size plaster model of St Michael overcoming Satan.

Also on display, in the south cloisters of the Main Building, is the philosopher **Jeremy Bentham** (1748–1832), one of the university's founders. Bentham bequeathed his fully clothed skeleton so that he could be posthumously present at board meetings of the University College Hospital governors, where he was duly recorded as "present, but not voting". Bentham's **Auto-Icon**, topped by a wax head and wide-brimmed hat, is in "thinking and writing" pose as the philosopher requested, and can be seen in a hermetically sealed mahogany booth. Close by is a pair of watchful Egyptian lions, reconstructed from several thousand fragments belonging to the Petrie Museum (see p.133).

Petrie Museum of Egyptian Archeology

The **Petrie Museum of Egyptian Archaeology** (Tues–Fri 1–5pm, Sat 11am–2pm; free; ☎020/7504 2884, Ⓦwww.petrie.ucl.ac.uk; Euston Square/Goodge Street tube), on the first floor of the DMS Watson Building, down

Malet Place, has a couple of rooms jam-packed with antiquities, the bulk of them from excavations carried out in the 1880s by Flinders Petrie, UCL Professor of Egyptology. To the nonspecialist, the first room appears to contain little more than broken bits of pottery (a speciality of Professor Petrie's). Look more closely, however, and you'll also find the world's oldest dress, an understandably ragged, pleated garment worn by an Ancient Egyptian teenager around 3000 BC. More intriguing still is the very revealing, erotic bead-net dress made for a 10-year-old, from around 2400 BC, which would have made a seductive rattling sound when worn. In the second room, the cabinets are crammed full of tiny objects including weights and measures, *shabti* figures, combs, bottle stoppers, sandals, legs from a toy table, a mummified bird and a pair of tweezers. Look out, too, for the richly decorated wooden coffin of Nairytisitnefer from 750 BC, and the frog amulets, ivory spoons and bronze cat-goddess Bastet down the back stairs.

Grant Museum of Zoology

Another room piled high with exhibits – in this case skeletons – can be found in the **Grant Museum of Zoology** (Mon–Fri 1–5pm; free; ☎020/7679 2647, Ⓦ www.grant.museum.ucl.ac.uk; Goodge Street tube), on the ground floor of the Darwin Building, again accessible from Malet Place. The museum is named after Robert E. Grant (1793–1874), the university's first Professor of Zoology and Comparative Anatomy, a pre-Darwinian transmutationist who always wore full evening dress when delivering lectures and later risked his career by teaching evolution at UCL. Among the numerous specimens here, don't miss the walrus's penis bone, the skeletons of a dugong, a dodo, a quagga (an extinct zebra) and a thylacine (an extinct marsupial wolf).

Euston and around

The northern boundary of Bloomsbury is defined by **Euston Road**, laid out in 1756 as the city's first traffic bypass. This was the northern limit of the city until the mid-nineteenth century when the rival railway companies built Euston, King's Cross and St Pancras stations, termini serving the industrial boom towns of the north of England. Since those days, Euston Road has had some of the city's worst office architecture foisted on it, which, combined with the current volume of traffic, makes this an area for selective viewing only.

Amidst all the hubbub of Euston Road, it's easy to miss the depressingly functional **Euston Station**, descendant of London's first great train terminus, originally built with just two platforms way back in 1837. Philip Hardwick's original Neoclassical ensemble was demolished in the face of fierce protests in the 1960s – British Rail claimed it needed the space in order to lengthen the platforms, which it never did – and all that remains are the sad-looking lodge-houses, part of the Euston Arch.

Wellcome Collection

After a thorough refurbishment, the **Wellcome Collection** (Mon–Sat 10am–6pm, Thurs until 8pm, Sun 11am–6pm; free; ☎020/7611 2222, Ⓦ www .wellcomecollection.org; Euston tube) has reopened at 183 Euston Rd, with a series of excellent temporary exhibitions on topical scientific issues staged in the ground-floor gallery, where you'll also find an excellent café and bookshop. The permanent collection is on the first floor and begins with **Medicine Now**, which focuses on contemporary medical questions such as the body, genomes, obesity and malaria. Each subject area has an "art cube" which displays contemporary artists' responses to the issues: a giant jelly baby "clone" by Mauro Perucchetti; a map of the world traced out in mosquitoes by Alastair Mackie; and Chris Drury's collage of maps and an echocardiogram. Next door, **Medicine Man** showcases the weird and wonderful collection of historical and scientific artefacts amassed by the American-born pharmaceutical magnate Henry Wellcome (1853–1936). These range from Florence Nightingale's moccasins to a sign for a Chinese doctor's hung with human teeth, from erotic figurines and phallic amulets to Inuit snow goggles and a leper clapper – in other words, this section is an absolute must.

St Pancras New and Old churches

Euston Road's oldest edifice is **St Pancras New Church** (ⓦwww.stpancras church.org), built at enormous expense in the 1820s on the corner of Upper Woburn Place. Designed in Greek Revival style, it is notable for its octagonal tower, based on the Tower of the Winds in Athens, and for the caryatids, tacked onto the east end, which are modelled on the Erechtheion on the Acropolis – though the Euston Road ladies had to be truncated at the waist after they were found to be too tall. The best time to visit the interior, which features a dramatically lit Ionic colonnade in the apse, and some lovely Victorian stained glass, is during one of the free Thursday lunchtime recitals. There are also regular art exhibitions held in the atmospheric **Crypt Gallery** (ⓦwww.cryptgallery.org.uk; access from Duke's Road).

Allegedly the first parish church built in London, **Old St Pancras Church** lies hidden and neglected behind iron railings on raised ground behind St Pancras Station, up Midland Road. Apart from a little exposed Norman masonry and the sixth-century Roman altar stone, most of the church dates from the nineteenth century. Unfortunately, since Satanists attacked the church in 1985, access has been difficult outside of services. The **churchyard**, which is overlooked by the lugubrious Victorian Hospital for Tropical Diseases, was partially destroyed by the arrival of the railway, with the majority of graves being heaped around an ash tree under the supervision of Thomas Hardy. **John Soane's mausoleum** from 1816 – designed initially for his wife, and the inspiration for Giles Gilbert Scott's traditional red phone box – still stands in its original location, to the north of the church. Also buried here was Britain's great protofeminist, **Mary Wollstonecraft Godwin**, who died a few days after giving birth to her daughter, Mary. At the age of 16, the younger Mary was spotted visiting her mother's grave by the poet Percy Bysshe Shelley, who immediately declared his undying love, before eloping with her to Italy – both Marys are now buried in Bournemouth. A list of the graveyard's most illustrious corpses is inscribed on the monumental sundial erected by Baroness Burdett-Coutts, below which sits a statue of her collie dog, and there's a map of the prominent graves by the entrance.

British Library

As one of the country's most expensive public buildings, the **British Library** took flak from all sides during its protracted construction: few readers wanted to move out of the splendid Round Reading Room in the British Museum, where the library had been since the 1850s; the number of extra readers' seats was negligible and the extra shelving space inadequate; and, to top it all, the design was criticized by Prince Charles, who compared it to an academy for secret policemen. Yet, while it's true that architect Colin St John Wilson's penchant for red-brick brutalism is horribly out of fashion, the library has nevertheless proved popular both with the scholars who use it and the public who visit the library's superb galleries.

The new **piazza**, in front of the library, features Paolozzi's giant statue of Isaac Newton bent double over his protractor, inspired by William Blake – just one of a number of specially commissioned artworks in the library. Look out, too, for Bill Woodrow's *Book, Ball & Chain* sofa and R.B. Kitaj's unsettling giant tapestry, *If not, not*, both in the main foyer, and Patrick Hughes' optical illusion, *Paradoxymoron*, down in the basement cloakroom.

John Ritblat Gallery

The first of the three exhibition galleries to head for is the dimly lit **John Ritblat Gallery**, where a superlative selection of the BL's ancient manuscripts and precious books are permanently displayed. You can turn the pages of various texts – from the Mercator's 1570s atlas of Europe to Leonardo da Vinci's notebook – "virtually" on the touch-screen computers, thus allowing you to see much more than the double page displayed in the glass cabinets. One of the library's most prized possessions is the richly illustrated **Lindisfarne Gospels**, begun in 698 AD and seen by many as the apotheosis of Anglo-Saxon art – you can leaf through a facsimile near the exit. The sheer variety of sacred texts displayed is almost overwhelming: as well as numerous illuminated Bibles and Qur'ans (Korans), there are rules for Buddhist monks written on birch bark, a palm-leaf glorification of the Hindu goddess Jagannatha in the shape of a cow and several concertina-style folding books on the life of the Buddha. In the section on printing, you can see the ninth-century **Diamond Sutra**, an Indian Buddhist text written in Chinese and the world's earliest-dated printed document, along with the **Gutenberg Bible**, from 1454–55, the first Bible printed using movable type (and therefore capable of being mass-produced).

The most famous of the library's **historical documents** is probably King John's famous letter to his subjects in 1215, better known as the **Magna Carta**, displayed in a small room off the main gallery. Back in the main gallery, you can examine Thomas More's last letter to Henry VIII, Lady Jane Grey's prayer book given to the Lieutenant of the Tower moments before her execution, the logbook from HMS *Victory*, Scott's 1912 polar journal and Lenin's application for a British Library pass. Among the selection of **literary texts** are Shakespeare's First Folio from 1623, the original monthly instalments of Dickens' *David Copperfield* and the touchingly beautiful handwritten and illustrated copy of *Alice in Wonderland* given by Lewis Carroll to Alice Liddell. The British Library is also home to the **National Sound Archive**, so as well as examining James Joyce's maniacally scribbled *Finnegan's Wake*, you can also hear Joyce (and several other authors) reading extracts from their works. Similarly, in the **music** section, you can listen to works ranging from Bach and The Beatles and peruse the libretto used for the first performance of the *Messiah*.

The other galleries

Downstairs from the John Ritblat Gallery, the spacious **Pearson Gallery of Living Words** houses temporary exhibitions (for which there is sometimes an entrance charge), employing more of the library's wonderful texts, supplemented by items from the British Museum. Stamp lovers, meanwhile, should make their way up to the BL's gargantuan **Philatelic Collections**, made up of over eight million items, eighty thousand of which are displayed in vertical pull-out drawers just outside the John Ritblat Gallery. The Tapling Collection kicks off the proceedings, as it did the collection when it was bequeathed in 1891, and in drawer number one you'll find the famous "Penny Black", the birthmark of modern philately. After that you get a world tour of stamps from long-forgotten mini-kingdoms such as Mecklenburg-Schwerin and Nowanugger. Those with a political interest should head for the Bojanowicz Collection, which covers Polish stamps from 1939 to 1946, including ones from the German and Russian occupations, and even POW and displaced persons' camps. The Kay Collection consists of stamps from the colonies, but real boffins should head for the Turner Collection of railway letter stamps from the likes of the Pembroke & Tenby Railway.

St Pancras and King's Cross

The British Library has the misfortune of standing in the shadow of one of the most glorious of London's red-brick Victorian edifices, the former **Midland Grand Hotel**, whose majestic sweep of lancets, dormers and chimneypots forms the facade of **St Pancras Station**, London's swanky Eurostar terminus. Completed in 1876 by George Gilbert Scott, this masterpiece of neo-Gothic architecture enjoyed a brief heyday in the 1890s when the ratio of staff to guests was 3:1, but with few private bathrooms and no central heating, the hotel couldn't survive long into the modern age. For fifty years from 1935, it languished as underused British Rail offices, but has now been refurbished partly as private apartments and partly as a luxury hotel.

Compared to St Pancras, **King's Cross Station**, opened in 1850 as the terminus for the Great Northern Railway, is a mere shed. Legend has it that Boudicca's bones lie under platform 10 – the area used to be known as Battle Bridge, and was believed to have been the site of the final set-to between the Iceni and the Romans. More famously, the fictional **Harry Potter** and his wizarding chums leave for school on the Hogwarts Express each term from platform 9¾. The scenes from the films are, in fact, shot between platforms 4 and 5, though a station trolley is now half-embedded in the wall beside the side platforms of 9 and 10, providing a perfect photo opportunity for passing Potter fans.

The whole area beside and behind King's Cross is undergoing major redevelopment, with new flats, shops and a campus for the University of the Arts. Despite all this, one or two venerable structures survive, among them *Die Turnhalle* or the **German Gymnasium** (Wed & Thurs 10am–6.30pm, Fri 10am–2pm; free; Ⓦwww.kingscrosscentral.com), on St Pancras Road, built in the 1860s for the German Gymnastics Society and now housing a model of the new development and an exhibition on the history of King's Cross. Further north, beyond Camley Street Natural Park (see p.138), you can view George Gilbert Scott's ornate St Pancras waterpoint, which was moved to safety here and will eventually serve as a viewing tower. Nearby are the brooding skeletal **King's Cross Gasholders**, Victorian monsters that hark back to an era when nothing was too lowly to be given Neoclassical decoration, hence the wrought-iron Doric pillars and red triglyphs.

The oasis amongst all the redevelopment is **Camley Street Natural Park** (daily 10am–5pm; free; ☏020/7833 2311, ⓦwww.wildlondon.org.uk), transformed from a rubbish dump into a canalside wildlife haven, and run by the London Wildlife Trust. Pond, meadow and woodland habitats have been re-created and provide a natural environment for birds, butterflies, frogs, newts, toads and even the odd heron, plus a rich variety of plant life.

Kings Place and the London Canal Museum

A definite plus in the redevelopment of King's Cross has been the arrival of **Kings Place** (☏020/7842 4860, ⓦwww.kingsplace.co.uk), a glassy new arts centre overlooking the Regent's Canal, a short walk up York Way. As well as housing two state-of-the-art concert halls – home to the London Sinfonietta and the Orchestra of the Age of Enlightenment – the venue puts on regular art exhibitions, talks and events and has a swanky café and restaurant to boot. The most famous resident, however, is *The Guardian* newspaper, which occupies the southern portion of the building.

King's Place stands alongside Battlebridge Basin, which is packed with traditional narrowboats, and an appropriate location for the **London Canal Museum** (Tues–Sun 10am–4.30pm; £3; ☏020/7713 0836, ⓦwww .canalmuseum.org.uk), which you can access from New Wharf Road. The museum testifies to the hard life boat families had to endure and includes a restored "butty" (an engine-less narrowboat used for extra storage) and some of the unusual Measham Ware pottery and crockery that was popular with canalboat families. Other exhibits relate to the building itself, which was built as an ice house by Swiss-Italian entrepreneur Carlo Gatti, London's main ice trader in the nineteenth century. Gatti single-handedly popularized ice cream in London, supplying most of the city's vendors, who became known as "Hokey-Pokey Men" – a corruption of the street cry *Ecco un poco*, "Just try a little". Upstairs there's video footage of the canal from the 1920s and the 1990s.

Covent Garden and the Strand

Covent Garden's transformation from a workaday fruit and vegetable market into a fashionable *quartier* is one of the most miraculous and enduring developments of the 1980s. More sanitized and brazenly commercial than neighbouring Soho, it's a far cry from the district's heyday when **Covent Garden Piazza** was the great playground (and red-light district) of eighteenth-century London. The buskers in front of **St Paul's Church**, the theatres round about, and the **Royal Opera House** on Bow Street are survivors of this tradition, and on a balmy summer evening, **the piazza** is still an undeniably lively place to be.

As its name suggests, the **Strand**, just south of Covent Garden, once lay along the riverbank; its current form dates from the Victorians' creation of the Embankment to shore up the banks of the Thames. One showpiece river palace, **Somerset House**, remains, its courtyard graced by a lovely fountain in summer, and its chambers home to gallery and exhibition space, including the Courtauld's superb collection of Impressionist and Post-Impressionist paintings.

Covent Garden

Covent Garden (Ⓦ www.coventgardenlife.com) has come full circle: what started out in the seventeenth century as London's first luxury neighbourhood is once more an aspirational place to live, work and shop. Based around Inigo Jones's piazza – London's oldest planned square – the area had for years been a **market** for fruit, flowers and vegetables. When the market closed in 1974, only public protests averted yet another office development and ensured that the elegant Victorian market hall and its environs were restored to house shops, restaurants and arts-and-crafts stalls.

Boosted by buskers and street entertainers, Covent Garden is now one of London's major tourist attractions, and the streets to the north – in particular, Long Acre, Neal Street and Floral Street – are home to fashionable clothes shops, cafés and restaurants. Alongside them, a few tiny pockets of 1970s "alternative" culture survive, left over from the days of squats and cheap rentals. London's tourism revenues owe them a considerable debt – it was only their demonstrations, and mass protests, that saved the area.

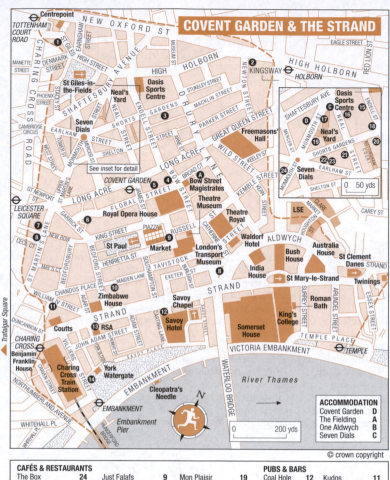

COVENT GARDEN & THE STRAND

CAFÉS & RESTAURANTS					
The Box	24	Just Falafs	9	Mon Plaisir	19
Canela	22	Kastner & Ovens	4	Poetry Café	3
Coffee, Cake & Kink	15	Masala Zone	5	Porterhouse	10
Food for Thought	21	Monmouth		Rock & Sole Plaice	18
J. Sheekey	7	Coffee Company	17	World Food Café	16

PUBS & BARS			
Coal Hole	12	Kudos	11
Cross Keys	20	Lamb & Flag	6
Detroit	23	Princess Louise	2
First Out	1	Retro Bar	13
Gordon's	14	The Salisbury	8

Most visitors are happy enough simply to wander around watching the street life, having a coffee and doing a bit of shopping, but there are a couple of specific sights worth picking out. One of the old market buildings houses the enjoyable **London Transport Museum**, while another serves as the public foyer for the **Royal Opera House** and boasts a great roof terrace overlooking the piazza.

The piazza

Covent Garden's **piazza** was laid out in the 1630s, when the Earl of Bedford commissioned Inigo Jones to design a series of graceful Palladian-style arcades based on the main square in Livorno, Tuscany, where Jones had helped build the cathedral. Initially it was a great success, its novelty value alone attracting a plutocratic clientele, but over time the tone of the place fell as the **market** (set up in the earl's back garden) expanded, and theatres, coffee houses and brothels began to proliferate.

By the onset of the nineteenth century, the market dominated the area, and so in the 1830s the piazza was cleaned up, slums were torn down and a proper market hall built in the Greek Revival style. A glass roof was added in the late Victorian era, but otherwise the building stayed unaltered until the market's closure in 1974 – when trade moved south of the river to Nine Elms in Vauxhall – and, after a battle, its 1980s renovation as a shopping arcade.

St Paul's Church

The piazza is overlooked from the west by **St Paul's Church** (ⓦwww.actors church.org). The Earl of Bedford allegedly told Jones to make St Paul's no fancier than a barn, to which the architect replied, "Sire, you shall have the handsomest barn in England". It's better known nowadays as the "**Actors' Church**", and is filled with memorials to thespians from Boris Karloff to Gracie Fields. The cobbles in front of the church's Tuscan portico – where Eliza Doolittle was discovered selling violets by Henry Higgins in George Bernard Shaw's *Pygmalion* – are now a legalized venue for buskers and street performers, who must audition for a slot.

The piazza's history of entertainment goes back to May 1662, when the first recorded performance of Punch and Judy in England was staged by Italian puppeteer Pietro Gimonde, and witnessed by Pepys. To celebrate this a **Punch and Judy Festival** is held on the second Sunday in May, in the gardens behind the church; for the rest of the year the **churchyard** provides a tranquil respite from the activity outside.

London Transport Museum

A former flower-market shed on the piazza's east side houses the ever-popular **London Transport Museum** (daily 10am–6pm, Fri until 9pm; adults £8, children under 16 free; ☎020/7379 6344, ⓦwww.ltmuseum.co.uk; Covent Garden tube). A surefire hit for families with kids under 10, it's less enthralling for the transport enthusiast, with space only for a handful of large exhibits.

Coffee houses and brothels

By the eighteenth century the piazza was known as "the great square of Venus", home to dozens of gambling dens, bawdy houses and so-called "bagnios". Some bagnios were plain Turkish baths, but most doubled as brothels, where courtesans stood in the window and, according to one contemporary, "in the most impudent manner invited passengers from the theatres into the houses".

London's most famous **coffee houses** were concentrated here, too, attracting writers such as Sheridan, Dryden and Aphra Behn. The rich and famous frequented places like the *Shakespeare's Head*, whose cook made the best turtle soup in town, and whose head waiter, John Harris, produced an annual "Who's Who of Whores".

The infamous *Rose Tavern*, on Russell Street (immortalized in a scene from Hogarth's *Rake's Progress*), was one of the oldest **brothels** in Covent Garden – Pepys mentions "frigging with Doll Lane" at the *Rose* in his diary of 1667 – and specialized in "Posture Molls", who engaged in flagellation and striptease, and were deemed a cut above the average whore. Food at the *Rose* was apparently excellent, too, and despite the frequent brawls, men of all classes, from royalty to ruffians, made their way there.

▲ Covent Garden piazza

Still, the story of London's transport is a fascinating one – to follow it chronologically, head for Level 2, where you'll find a reconstructed 1829 Shillibeer's Horse Omnibus, which provided the city's first regular horse-bus service, and a horse-drawn tram, first introduced in the 1860s. Level 1 tells the story of the world's first underground system and contains a lovely 1920s Metropolitan Line carriage, fitted out in burgundy and green with pretty, drooping lamps. Down on the ground floor, the museum's one double-decker electric **tram** is all that's left to pay tribute to the world's largest electric tram system, which was dismantled in 1952. Look out, too, for the first tube train, from the 1890s, whose lack of windows earned it the nickname "the padded cell". Most of the interactive stuff is aimed at kids, but visitors of all ages should check out the tube driver simulator.

The artistically inclined can buy reproductions of London Transport's stylish **maps and posters**, many commissioned from well-known artists, at the shop on the way out. Transport enthusiasts should check out the reserve collection at the **Museum Depot** in Acton (details on the website), which is open occasional weekends throughout the year.

Bow Street and Drury Lane

Covent Garden's dubious reputation was no doubt behind the opening of **Bow Street** magistrates' office in 1748. The first two magistrates were Henry Fielding, author of *Tom Jones*, and his blind half-brother John – nicknamed the "Blind Beak" – who, unusually for the period, refused to accept bribes. Finding "lewd women enough to fill a mighty colony", Fielding set about creating London's first police force, the **Bow Street Runners**. Never numbering more than a dozen, they were employed primarily to combat prostitution, and they continued to exist a good ten years after the establishment of the uniformed Metropolitan Police in 1829. Bow Street police station (which closed in 1989, followed by the magistrates court in 2006) had the honour of incarcerating Oscar Wilde after he was arrested for "committing indecent acts" in 1895 – he was eventually sentenced to two years' hard labour. In 1908 Emmeline

Pankhurst appeared here, charged with leafleting supporters to "rush" the House of Commons, and, in 1928, Radclyffe Hall's lesbian novel *The Well of Loneliness* was deemed obscene by Bow Street magistrates and remained banned in this country until 1949.

One block east of Bow Street runs **Drury Lane**, nothing to write home about in its present condition, but in Tudor and Stuart times a very fashionable address. During the Restoration, it became a permanent fixture in London's theatrical and social life, when the first **Theatre Royal, Drury Lane** was built in 1663 (the current one dates from 1812 and faces onto Catherine Street). It was here that women were first permitted to appear on stage in England (their parts having previously been played by boys), but critics were sceptical about their abilities and thought their profession little better than prostitution – most had to work at both to make ends meet (as the actress said to the bishop). The most famous was **Nell Gwynne** who played comic roles and eventually became Charles II's mistress, the first in a long line of Drury Lane actresses who made it into royal beds.

It was also at the Theatre Royal that **David Garrick**, as actor, manager and part-owner from 1747, revolutionized the English theatre, treating the text with more reverence, insisting on rehearsals and cutting down on improvisations. The rich, who had previously occupied seats on the stage itself, were confined to the auditorium, and the practice of refunding those who wished to leave at the first interval was stopped. Despite Garrick's reforms, the Theatre Royal remained a boisterous and often dangerous place of entertainment: George II and George III both narrowly escaped assassination attempts, and the orchestra often had cause to be grateful for the cage under which they were forced to play. The theatre has one other unique feature: two royal boxes, instigated in order to keep George III and his son, the future George IV, apart, after they had a set-to in the foyer. **Backstage tours** of the theatre are great fun and are led by actors (Mon–Sat 6pm; £9; ☎0870/890 6002).

Royal Opera House

The Corinthian portico of the **Royal Opera House** stands opposite the former magistrates' court. The original theatre witnessed the premieres of Goldsmith's *She Stoops to Conquer* and Sheridan's *The Rivals* before being destroyed by fire in 1808. To offset the cost of rebuilding, ticket prices were increased; riots ensued for 61 performances until the manager finally backed down. The current building dates from 1858, and is the city's main opera house, home to both the Royal Ballet and Royal Opera. A covered passageway connects the piazza with Bow Street, and allows access to the ROH box office, and upstairs to the beautiful wrought-iron-and-glass **Floral Hall** (daily 10am–3pm). Continuing up the escalators, you reach the *Amphitheatre* bar/restaurant, with a glorious terrace overlooking the piazza. **Backstage tours** of the opera house take place regularly and can be booked in advance (Mon–Fri 10.30am, 12.30 & 2.30pm, Sat 10.30am, 11.30am, 12.30 & 1.30pm; £9; tours last 1hr 30min; ☎020/7212 9389, Ⓦwww.royaloperahouse.org; Covent Garden tube).

North of the piazza

The network of streets to the north of Covent Garden piazza has been more or less colonized by designer clothes and shoe outlets, and the oddball shops that once characterized the entire neighbourhood are now few and far between. **Neal Street** is the busiest, with Floral Street, Long Acre, Shelton Street and Shorts Gardens also worth exploring.

Floral Street and Long Acre

The western half of **Floral Street** is dominated by three adjoining shops run by top-selling British designer Paul Smith, whose tongue-in-cheek window displays are always worth inspecting. One of the few quirky outlets left is the shop dedicated to Tintin, the Belgian boy-detective. Meanwhile, squeezed beside a very narrow alleyway off Floral Street is the **Lamb and Flag** pub, where the Poet Laureate, John Dryden, was beaten up in December 1679 by a group of thugs, hired most probably by his rival poet, the Earl of Rochester, who mistakenly thought Dryden was the author of an essay satirizing him.

Though it originally specialized in coach manufacture, **Long Acre**, to the north, has long been Covent Garden's main shopping street. The most famous shop on the street is **Stanford's**, the world's oldest and largest map shop (see p.440). Look out, too, for **Carriage Hall**, an old stabling yard originally used by coachmakers (now converted into shops), surrounded by cast-iron pillars and situated between Long Acre and Floral Street.

Freemasons' Hall

Looking east down the gentle curve of Long Acre, it's difficult to miss the austere, Pharaonic mass of the **Freemasons' Hall** (Mon–Fri 10am–5pm; free; ☎020/7395 9257, ⓦfreemasonry.london.museum; Covent Garden tube), built at 60 Great Queen St as a memorial to all the Masons who died in World War I. Whatever you may think of this reactionary, secretive, male-dominated organization, which enjoys a virtual stranglehold over institutions like the police and judiciary, the interior is worth a peek for the **Grand Temple** alone, whose pompous, bombastic decor is laden with heavy symbolism. To see the Grand Temple, sign up for one of the **guided tours** (Mon–Fri usually 11am, noon, 2, 3 & 4pm; free) and bring some ID with you. The Masonically curious might also take a look at the shop which sells Masonic merchandise: aprons, wands, rings and books about alchemy and the cabbala, as do several shops on Great Queen Street.

Neal Street, Neal's Yard and Seven Dials

Running north from Long Acre, **Neal Street** features some fine Victorian warehouses, complete with stair towers for loading and shifting goods between floors. The street is now dominated by designer shoe stores, with only a few alternative shops left: *Food for Thought*, the veggie café founded in 1971, is a rare survivor, as is **Neal's Yard**, a tiny little courtyard off Shorts Gardens, stuffed with cafés and prettily festooned with flower boxes and ivy.

West of Neal Street is **Seven Dials**, the meeting point of seven streets which make up a little circus, centred on a slender column topped by six tiny blue sundials (the seventh dial is formed by the column itself and the surrounding road). Erected in 1693, the column was torn down in 1773 when a rumour went about that treasure was hidden beneath it; it was re-erected in Weybridge, in Surrey, fifty years later; then, in 1989, a replica was built as a sort of roundabout with seats.

The Strand

The Strand remains the main road from Westminster to the City, but it's a shadow of its former self. Once famous for its riverside mansions, owned by bishops, noblemen and courtiers, by the 1890s, the Strand boasted more theatres than any other street in London, giving rise to the music-hall song *Let's All Go*

London for free

London can be an expensive place for locals and tourists alike, with some of the city's top tourist attractions – and in particular its royal palaces – charging a fortune for entry. However, there are lots of things to enjoy in the capital that are one hundred percent free, including many of the city's biggest museums and galleries. In addition, there are plenty of offbeat activities that don't cost a thing, from musical treats and street buskers to upmarket auctions and political sparring matches.

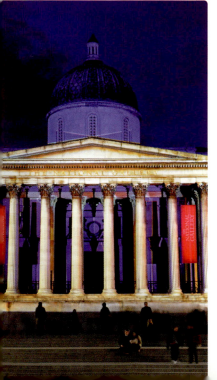

iTunes Festival, Roundhouse ▲

National Gallery ▼

Freeloading on culture

There's enough free **music** in London to keep you amused morning, noon and night. High-quality **buskers** can be found at twelve key tube stations, and, almost without fail, at Covent Garden, along the South Bank, and in the subway to the South Kensington museums. Free **lunchtime concerts** of classical music, usually chamber works or organ recitals, take place Monday to Friday at various churches, mostly in the City (see p.425). Late afternoon is the time to head for either St Paul's Cathedral or Westminster Abbey, where the choir perform **evensong** (Mon–Sat 5pm, Sun 3pm). After work, two good venues to catch live **foyer music** are the Royal Festival Hall and the Barbican – look out too for other regular musical spots at places like the National Gallery (Fri 6pm) and the V&A (Fri 6.30pm). Lastly, you'll find **free gigs** of every persuasion, rock, pop, folk, blues and jazz flagged up every night of the week in *Time Out*.

You can get to see an awful lot of art for free in London. For a start there are the well-known **permanent collections** of the National Gallery, National Portrait Gallery, Tate Britain and Tate Modern, all of which also offer free guided tours. Then, there's the often-overlooked Wallace Collection, where works by the likes of Rembrandt and Van Dyck are displayed in an exquisite eighteenth-century miniature chateau, just off Oxford Street. Unusually for an English Heritage property, the Neoclassical mansion of Kenwood House, on Hampstead Heath, also has free entry: here, you can admire more works by Rembrandt, Vermeer and Reynolds. Even the Courtauld Institute allows free entry to its superlative collection of Impressionist paintings once a week (Fri 10am–2pm).

Having exhausted the city's public art galleries, it's time to move on to the trendy **commercial galleries** of Hoxton and environs, where you can see oodles of contemporary art for free. Back in the West End, you can view more established modern artists, catch the odd heirloom before it's sold and, most intriguingly of all, check out the **auction houses**. During the week, at any of the big three – Sotheby's, Christie's or Bonhams – you can view hundreds of works of museum quality. You can even attend the auctions themselves; just keep your hands firmly out of view unless you're bidding.

Thanks to the Labour government, the permanent collections of the city's big **national museums** – such as the British Museum, the RAF Museum, and the South Kensington trio – are all free. In addition, however, these museums also offer a wide range of specialist talks, fun activities and archive films, most of which cost the visitor nothing. The Queen puts on her free bit of pageantry each day with the Changing of the Guard on Whitehall and elsewhere – she also gets out and about in her golden coach, at least once a year, to officially open Parliament. If you're more of a republican, there are still a surprising number of political meetings (and small-scale protests) that take place each week in the capital, and the original **free speech** spot, Speakers' Corner, is still going strong every Sunday morning. Finally, you might as well take advantage of London's wonderful green spaces, from the **royal parks** and the magnificent Heath to the tiny inner-city churchyards and splendidly overgrown cemeteries of the Victorian era. All – except Highgate – are free of charge and what's more they, too, often stage free events.

▲ Natural History Museum

▼ St James's Park

Chinese New Year celebrations ▲

Notting Hill Carnival ▼

London's top ten free festivals

▶▶ **London Parade** – if you've got any energy left after New Year's Eve, join the thousands taking part in the city's New Year's Day street parade. See p.28.

▶▶ **Chinese New Year** – from Chinatown down to Trafalgar Square, the city centre is given over to dragons and firecrackers. See p.28.

▶▶ **IWA Canal Cavalcade** – a three-day congregation of decorated narrow-boats and Morris Men at Little Venice, Regent's Canal's most picturesque spot. See p.28.

▶▶ **Coin Street Festival** – an eclectic series of free events and street parties held right through the summer months on the South Bank. See p.29.

▶▶ **Trafalgar Square Festival** – the Mayor's three-week free festival of live performances to keep the tourists happy in August.

▶▶ **Notting Hill Carnival** – the mother of all free festivals, Carnival attracts huge crowds – not for the faint-hearted but a must for the fun-loving soca fan. See p.282.

▶▶ **Thames Festival** – child-friendly outdoor festival featuring music, dance and fireworks, held on the South Bank. See p.29.

▶▶ **Open House** – not so much a festival, but a chance to get to see inside lots of the city's buildings, from private designer homes and studios to the Bank of England, for free. See p.30.

▶▶ **Lord Mayor's Show** – the city's annual chance to put on a big show of pageantry, with ceremonial processions and a fireworks display. See p.30.

▶▶ **New Year's Eve** – the focus has shifted now from Trafalgar Square to a spectacular, riverside display of fireworks with the London Eye as the backdrop. See p.30.

Down the Strand, and prompting Disraeli to declare it "perhaps the finest street in Europe". A hundred years later, the only surviving Thames palace is **Somerset House**, which houses gallery and exhibition space, and boasts a wonderful fountain-filled courtyard.

Along the Strand to Aldwych

The Strand begins at **Charing Cross Station**, fronted by the French Renaissance-style *Charing Cross Hotel*, built in the 1860s. Amid the taxis, in the station's cobbled forecourt, is a Victorian replica of the medieval **Charing Cross**, removed from nearby Trafalgar Square by the Puritans. The original thirteenth-century cross was the last of twelve erected by Edward I, to mark the overnight stops on the funeral procession of his wife, Eleanor, from Nottinghamshire to Westminster Abbey in 1290.

Opposite the station, on the corner of Agar Street, is the Edwardian-era former British Medical Association building, now **Zimbabwe House**. Few passers-by even notice the eighteen naked figures by Jacob Epstein that punctuate the second-floor facade, but at the time of their unveiling in 1908, they caused enormous controversy – "a form of statuary which no careful father would wish his daughter and no discriminating young man his fiancée to see", railed the press. When the Southern Rhodesian government bought the building in 1937 they pronounced the sculptures to be "undesirable" and a potential hazard to passers-by, and proceeded to hack at the genitals, heads and limbs of all eighteen, which remain mutilated to this day.

Further east on the opposite side of the Strand, the blind side-street of Savoy Court – the only street in the country where the traffic drives on the right – leads to **The Savoy**, London's grandest hotel, built in 1889 by Richard D'Oyly Carte. César Ritz was the original manager, Guccio Gucci started out as a dishwasher here, and the list of illustrious guests is endless: Monet and Whistler both painted the Thames from one of the south-facing rooms, Sarah Bernhardt nearly died here, and Strauss the Younger arrived with his own orchestra. It's worthwhile strolling up Savoy Court to check out the hotel's Art Deco foyer, the aluminium statue of John of Gaunt, and the equally outrageous 1930s fittings of the adjacent **Savoy Theatre**, whose profits helped fund the hotel. The theatre was built in 1881 to showcase Gilbert and Sullivan's comic operas, witnessing eight premieres, including *The Mikado*.

Nothing remains of John of Gaunt's medieval Savoy Palace, which stood here until it was burnt down in the 1381 Peasants' Revolt, though the **Savoy Chapel** (Tues–Thurs 11.30am–3.30pm, Fri 11.30am–1pm), hidden round the back of the hotel down Savoy Street, dates from the time when the complex was rebuilt as a hospital for the poor in 1505. The chapel is much altered, but it became a fashionable venue for weddings when the hotel and theatre were built next door – all three were the first of their kind in the world to be lit by electricity. And talking of lighting, don't miss the **Patent Sewer Ventilating Lamp**, erected in the 1880s halfway down Carting Lane, and still powered by methane collected in a U-bend in the sewers below.

Victoria Embankment

To get to the **Victoria Embankment**, from the Strand, head down Villiers Street, beside Charing Cross Station. Built between 1868 and 1874, the embankment was the inspiration of French engineer **Joseph Bazalgette**, whose project simultaneously relieved congestion along the Strand, and provided an extension for the tube, a new sewerage system, and a new stretch of riverside parkland – now filled with an eclectic mixture of statues and memorials from Robbie Burns to the Imperial Camel Corps. The 1626 **York Watergate**, in the Victoria Embankment Gardens to the east of Villiers Street, gives you an idea of where the banks of the Thames used to be: the steps through the gateway once led down to the river.

Less evidence remains of the Adam brothers' magnificent riverside development known as the **Adelphi**, a terrace of eleven houses supported by massive arches built between 1768 and 1772. Thoughtlessly demolished in 1936, there are nevertheless several Adam houses still standing between Victoria Embankment Gardens and the Strand. The most elaborate Adam house, at 6–8 John Adam St, is home to the "Society for the encouragement of Arts, Manufactures and Commerce", founded in 1754, and better known now as the Royal Society of Arts or **RSA**. On the first Sunday of the month, you can take a look inside the RSA (11am–1pm; free; Ⓦwww.rsa.org.uk; Charing Cross or Embankment tube), which contains a small display on the Adelphi and retains several original Adam ceilings and chimneypieces. The highlight, however, is The Great Room, with six paintings on *The Progress of Human Knowledge and Culture* by James Barry, forming a busy, continuous pictorial frieze around the room, punctuated by portraits of two early presidents by Reynolds and Gainsborough.

London's oldest monument, **Cleopatra's Needle**, languishes little noticed on the Thames side of the busy Victoria Embankment, guarded by two Victorian sphinxes (facing the wrong way). In fact, the sixty-foot-high, 180-ton stick of granite has nothing to do with Cleopatra – it's one of a pair erected in Heliopolis (near Cairo) in 1475 BC (the other one is in New York's Central Park) and taken to Alexandria by Emperor Augustus fifteen years after Cleopatra's suicide. This obelisk was presented to Britain in 1819 by the Turkish viceroy of Egypt, but nearly sixty years passed before it finally made its way to London. It was erected in 1878 above a time capsule containing, among other things, the day's newspapers, a box of hairpins, a railway timetable and pictures of the country's twelve prettiest women.

Benjamin Franklin House

From 1757 to 1775, **Benjamin Franklin** (1706–90) had "genteel lodgings" at 36 Craven St, on the other side of Charing Cross Station. Whilst Franklin was espousing the cause of the British colonies (as the US then was), the house served as the first de facto American embassy; eventually, he returned to America to help draft the Declaration of Independence and frame the US Constitution. Wisely, the curators have left the **Benjamin Franklin House** (Wed–Sun noon–5pm; £7; ℡020/7839 2006, Ⓦwww.benjaminfranklinhouse .org; Charing Cross or Embankment tube) pretty much empty, eschewing any attempt to install period furniture. Instead, aided by a costumed guide and a series of impressionistic audiovisuals, visitors are transported back to the time of Franklin, who lived here with his "housekeeper" in cosy domesticity, while his wife and daughter languished in Philadelphia. Note that you must book ahead for one of the 45-minute tours.

Aldwych

The wide crescent of **Aldwych**, forming a neat "D" with the eastern part of the Strand, was driven through the slums of this zone in the early twentieth century. A confident ensemble occupies the centre, with the enormous Australia House and India House sandwiching **Bush House**, home of the BBC's World

Service since 1940. Despite its thoroughly British associations, Bush House was actually built by the American speculator Irving T. Bush, whose planned trade centre flopped in the 1930s. The giant figures on the north facade and the inscription, "To the Eternal Friendship of English-Speaking Nations", thus refer to the friendship between the US and Britain, and are not, as many people assume, the World Service's declaratory manifesto.

Not far from these former bastions of Empire, up Houghton Street, lurks that erstwhile hotbed of left-wing agitation, the **London School of Economics**. Founded in 1895, the LSE gained a radical reputation in 1968, when a student sit-in in protest against the Vietnam War ended in violent confrontations that were the closest London came to the heady events in Paris that year. Famous alumni include Carlos the Jackal, Cherie Booth (wife of ex-Prime Minister Tony Blair) and Mick Jagger.

Somerset House

South of Aldwych stands **Somerset House** (daily 7.30am–11pm; free; ☎020/7845 4600, ⓦwww.somerset-house.org.uk; Temple or Covent Garden tube), sole survivor of the grandiose river palaces that once lined the Strand, its four wings enclosing a large courtyard rather like a Parisian *hôtel*. Although it looks like an old aristocratic mansion, the present building was, in fact, purpose-built in 1776 by William Chambers, to house numerous learned societies and governmental offices (including the Navy Office). Nowadays, Somerset House's granite-paved courtyard is a great place to relax thanks to its fab 55-jet **fountain** that spouts straight from the cobbles, and does a little syncopated dance every half-hour. The courtyard is also used for open-air performances, concerts, installations and, in winter, an ice rink.

The north wing houses the permanent collection of the **Courtauld Institute**, best known for its outstanding Impressionist and Post-Impressionist paintings. The south wing has a lovely riverside terrace (daily 8am–6pm, Thurs until 9pm) with a café-restaurant and the **Embankment Galleries** (daily 10am–6pm, Thurs until 9pm; £8), which host innovative special exhibitions on contemporary art and design. Before you head off to one of the collections, however, make sure you go and admire the Royal Naval Commissioners' superb gilded eighteenth-century barge in the **King's Barge House**, below ground level in the south wing.

Courtauld Institute

Founded in 1931 as part of the University of London, the **Courtauld Institute** (daily 10am–6pm; £5, free Mon 10am–2pm; ☎020/7848 2526, ⓦwww.courtauld.ac.uk) was the first body in Britain to award degrees in art history as an academic subject. It's much more famous, however, for its priceless art collection, whose virtue is quality rather than quantity. As well as its Impressionist and Post-Impressionist works, the Courtauld also owns a fine array of earlier works by the likes of Rubens, Botticelli, Bellini and Cranach the Elder.

The displays currently start on the **ground floor** with a small room devoted to medieval religious paintings from all over Western Europe, including a late, great polyptych by **Bernardo Daddi**, a pupil of Giotto, plus a few enamels and ivories. Next, you ascend the beautiful, semicircular staircase to the **first-floor galleries**, whose exceptional plasterwork ceilings recall their original use as the learned societies' meeting rooms. This is where the cream of the Courtauld's collection is currently displayed: rehangings have become more frequent, however, so ask if you can't find a particular painting. The Impressionists start off in room 2, with **Renoir**'s *La Loge*, **Degas**' *Two Dancers*, several **Monet** landscapes and a view of Lordship Lane by **Pissarro** from his days in exile in London. In room 3, there's a small-scale version of **Manet**'s bold *Déjeuner sur l'herbe*, and his atmospheric *A Bar at the Folies-Bergère*, a nostalgic celebration of the artist's love affair with Montmartre, painted two years before his death. There's a heap of **Cézanne**'s works, including one of his series of *Card Players*, and several magnificent, geometrical but lush landscapes, including, inevitably, one of his beloved *Montagne Sainte-Victoire*. In the same room, **Gauguin**'s Breton peasants *Haymaking* contrasts with his later Tahitian works, including the sinister *Nevermore*. Next door, in room 4, one of **Modigliani**'s celebrated nudes hangs alongside **Van Gogh**'s *Self-Portrait with Bandaged Ear*, painted shortly after his remorseful self-mutilation, following an attack on his housemate Gauguin.

In room 5, there's a large **Botticelli** altarpiece commissioned by a convent and refuge for former prostitutes; hence Mary Magdalene's pole position below the Cross. Amidst several splendid fifteenth-century Florentine *cassoni* (chests) – two with their original backrests – you can admire the masterful handling of colour and light in **Giovanni Bellini**'s *The Assassination of St Peter Martyr*. The Courtauld's large collection of works by **Rubens** fills room 6, ranging from oil sketches for church frescoes to large-scale late works, plus a winningly informal portrait of Jan Bruegel the Elder. Also in this room are **Pieter Bruegel the Elder**'s *Landscape with Flight into Egypt*, a small canvas once owned by Rubens, and **Lucas Cranach the Elder**'s *Adam and Eve*, one of the highlights of the collection, with the Saxon painter revelling in the visual delights of Eden.

The **second floor** is used primarily to display the Courtauld's twentieth-century works, which bring a wonderful splash of colour and a hint of modernism to the galleries. Unfortunately, there isn't the space to exhibit the entire collection, so it's impossible to say for definite what paintings will be on show at any one time. Room 8 is home to a dozen or so small sculptures by **Degas**, originally executed in clay and wax and only cast in bronze after his death – look out, too, for his *After the Bath*, a wonderfully intimate pastel evocation of female domesticity. In room 9, you hit the bright primary colours of the pioneers of **Fauvism**, such as Derain, Vlaminck, Braque, Bonnard and Dufy, which spill over into room 10. You'll also find a Japanese-influenced portrait of his wife by **Matisse**, and *Yellow Irises*, a rare early Picasso from 1901.

Beyond, a small room is devoted to **Roger Fry**, who organized the first Impressionist exhibitions in Britain, and went on to found the Omega Workshops in 1913 with Duncan Grant. Fry bequeathed his private collection to the Courtauld, including ceramics, an armchair, a spinet and some ancient Chinese bronzes, plus several paintings by Grant, his wife Vanessa Bell, and Fry himself. The last few rooms contain works by the likes of Kokoschka, Delaunay and Léger, and an outstanding array of works by **Kandinsky**, the Russian-born artist who was thirty when he finally decided to become a painter and moved to Munich. He's best known for his pioneering abstract paintings, such as *Improvisation on Mahogany* from 1910, where the subject matter is still just about discernible in the blocks of colour.

Further east down the Strand

Next door to Somerset House, the ugly concrete facade of **King's College** (part of the University of London) conceals Robert Smirke's much older buildings, which date from its foundation in 1829. Rather than entering the college itself, stroll down Surrey Street and turn right down Surrey Steps, which are in the middle of the old *Norfolk Hotel*, whose terracotta facade is worth admiring. Follow the signs to the **"Roman" Bath**, and you'll discover a fifteen-foot-long tub (actually dating from Tudor times at the earliest) with a natural spring that produces two thousand gallons a day. It was used in Victorian times as a cold bath (Dickens' David Copperfield "had many a cold plunge" here). The bath is visible through a window, but you can only get a closer look by appointment (℡020/8232 5050; April–Sept Wed 1–5pm; free).

Two historic churches survived the Aldwych development, and are now adrift amid the traffic of the Strand. The first is James Gibbs' **St Mary-le-Strand** (Mon–Sat 11am–4pm, Sun 10am–3pm; recitals Wed 1pm; free; Ⓦwww .stmarylestrand.org), his first commission, completed in 1724 in Baroque style and topped by a delicately tiered tower. Even in the eighteenth century, parishioners complained of the noise from the roads, and it's incredible that recitals are still given here. The entrance is flanked by two lovely magnolia trees, and the interior has a particularly rich plastered ceiling in white and gold. It was in this church that Bonnie Prince Charlie allegedly renounced his Roman Catholic faith and became an Anglican, during a secret visit to London in 1750.

In allusion to his own St Mary's, Gibbs placed a 115-foot tower on top of Wren's nearby **St Clement Danes** (daily 9am–4pm; Ⓦwww.raf.mod.uk /stclementdanes), whose bells play out the tune of the nursery rhyme *Oranges and Lemons* (Mon–Sat 9am, noon, 3pm & 6pm) – though St Clement's Eastcheap in the City is more likely to be the church referred to in the rhyme. The church was reduced to a smouldering shell during the Blitz (the pock marks are still visible in the exterior north wall). In the 1950s, St Clement Danes was handed over to the RAF – who contributed to the restoration costs – and it's now a very well kept memorial to those killed in the air battles of World War II. Glass cabinets in the west end of the church contain some poignant mementoes, such as a wooden cross carved from a door hinge in a Japanese POW camp. The nave and aisles are studded with over eight hundred squadron and unit badges, while heavy tomes set in glass cabinets record the 120,000 RAF service personnel who died.

In front of the church, the statue of **Gladstone** and his four female allegorical companions is flanked by two air chiefs: to the right, **Lord Dowding**, the man who oversaw the Battle of Britain; to the left, Arthur Harris, better known as **"Bomber Harris"**, architect of the saturation bombing of Germany that resulted in the slaughter of thousands of German civilians (and over 55,000 Allied airmen now commemorated on the plinth). Although Churchill was ultimately responsible, most of the opprobrium was left to fall on Harris, who was denied the peerage all the other service chiefs received, while his forces were refused a campaign medal. The decision to honour Harris with this privately funded statue, unveiled in 1992 on the anniversary of the bombing of Cologne, drew widespread protests in Britain and from Germany.

Further east along the Strand are two more architectural curiosities. At no. 216 stands **Twinings** tea shop (Mon–Fri 9.30am–4.45pm; ℡020/7353 3511, Ⓦwww.twinings.com; Temple or Holborn tube), founded in 1706 by Thomas Twining, tea supplier to Queen Anne. Its slender Neoclassical portico features two reclining Chinamen, dating from the time when all tea came from China. Several doors beyond, at no. 222, **Lloyd's Bank**'s Law Courts branch retains the extravagant decor of the short-lived *Palsgrave Restaurant*, which was built here in 1883. The foyer features acres of Doulton tiles, hand-painted in blues and greens, and a flying-fish fountain that was originally supplied with fresh water from an artesian well sunk 238ft below the Strand. The interior of walnut and sequoia wood panelling is worth a look, too, and features ceramic portrait panels. To continue east into Fleet Street, see p.167; for the Inns of Court, see p.150.

9

Holborn and the Inns of Court

ounded by Kingsway to the west, the City to the east, the Strand to the south and Theobald's Road to the north, **Holborn** (pronounced "Ho-bun") is a fascinating area to explore. Strategically placed between the royal and political centre of Westminster and the mercantile and financial might of the City, this wedge of land became the hub of the English legal system in the thirteenth century. Hostels, known as **Inns of Court**, were established where lawyers could eat, sleep and study law (which was not taught at the universities at the time).

Even today, every aspiring English barrister must study (and eat a required number of dinners) at one of the four Inns – **Inner Temple**, **Middle Temple**, **Lincoln's Inn** and **Gray's Inn** – in order to qualify and be called to the Bar. It's an old-fashioned system of patronage (you need contacts to get accepted at one of the Inns) and one that has done much to keep the judiciary overwhelmingly white, male and Oxbridge-educated.

Hidden away from the general hubbub of London, the Inns are nevertheless open to the public and make for an interesting stroll, their archaic, cobbled precincts exuding the rarefied atmosphere of an Oxbridge college, and sheltering one of the city's oldest churches, the twelfth-century **Temple Church**. On Lincoln's Inn Fields, Holborn boasts two of London's most enjoyable small museums: the **Sir John Soane's Museum**, with its architectural illusions and eclectic array of curios, and the **Hunterian Museum**, home of freakish medical curiosities.

Temple

Temple, the largest of the Inns of Court, consists of two Inns – **Middle Temple** and **Inner Temple** – both of which lie south of the Strand and Fleet Street. It's difficult to tell which Inn you're in, but the maze of courtyards and passageways is fun to explore – especially after dark, when the Temple is gas-lit – and a welcome haven from London's traffic. There are several points of access, simplest of which is Devereux Court, which leads south off the Strand, but at the weekend, you can only enter from Tudor Street to the east.

Medieval students ate, attended lectures and slept in the **Middle Temple Hall** (Mon–Fri 10–11.30am & 3–4pm, though access is not guaranteed; free), across Fountain Court, still the Inn's main dining room. The present building was

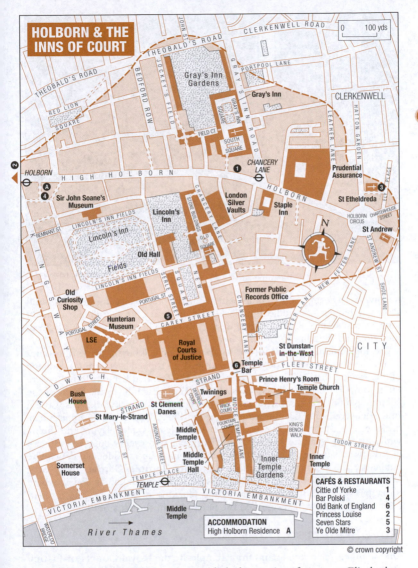

0   100 yds

CLERKENWELL ROAD

THEOBALD'S ROAD

JOHN'S ROAD

JOCKEY'S FIELD

BEDFORD ROW

Gray's Inn Gardens

GRAY'S INN SQUARE

PORTPOOL LANE

Gray's Inn

CLERKENWELL

THEOBALD'S ROAD

RED LION SQUARE

GRAY'S INN ROAD

FIELD CT

SOUTH SQUARE

LEATHER LANE

HATTON GARDEN

CHANCERY LANE ①

Prudential Assurance

HOLBORN ②

HIGH HOLBORN

HOLBORN

St Etheldreda ③

Ⓐ ④

Sir John Soane's Museum

REMNANT ST

London Silver Vaults

Staple Inn

HOLBORN CIRCUS

CHARTERHOUSE STREET

St Andrew

Lincoln's Inn

CHANCERY LANE

STONE BUILDINGS

N

FETTER LANE

ST ANDREW'S ST

LINCOLN'S INN FIELDS

Lincoln's Inn

Old Hall

OLD SQUARE

KINGSWAY

Fields

LINCOLN'S INN FIELDS

NEW SQUARE

SERLE STREET

Old Curiosity Shop

PORTUGAL ST

Hunterian Museum

CAREY STREET

Former Public Records Office

CHANCERY LANE

CITY

LSE

Royal Courts of Justice

St Dunstan-in-the-West

PORTUGAL STREET

FETTER LANE

SHOE LANE

Temple Bar ⑥

FLEET STREET

STRAND

ALDWYCH

Bush House

STRAND

FREDERICK COURT

Twinings

Prince Henry's Room

Temple Church

St Clement Danes

St Mary-le-Strand

SURREY ST

ARUNDEL STREET

BRICK COURT

MIDDLE TEMPLE LANE

Middle Temple

FOUNTAIN COURT

TEMPLE LANE

KING'S BENCH WALK

Inner Temple

TUDOR STREET

Somerset House

Middle Temple Hall

Inner Temple Gardens

TEMPLE PLACE

TEMPLE

VICTORIA EMBANKMENT

VICTORIA EMBANKMENT

WATERLOO BRIDGE

River Thames

Middle Temple

CAFÉS & RESTAURANTS
Cittie of Yorke	1
Bar Polski	4
Old Bank of England	6
Princess Louise	2
Seven Stars	5
Ye Olde Mitre	3

ACCOMMODATION
High Holborn Residence   A

© crown copyright

constructed in the 1560s and provided the setting for many Elizabethan masques and plays – including Shakespeare's *Twelfth Night*, which was premiered here in 1602. The hall is worth a visit for its fine hammerbeam roof, wood panelling and decorative Elizabethan screen, and the small wooden table said to have been carved from the hatch from Francis Drake's ship, the *Golden Hind*.

Despite wartime damage, the original round **Temple Church** – modelled on the Church of the Holy Sepulchre in Jerusalem – still stands, with its striking Purbeck marble piers, recumbent marble effigies of medieval knights and tortured grotesques grimacing in the spandrels of the blind arcading. At the

▲ Temple Church

northwestern corner of the choir, behind the decorative altar tomb of Edmund Plowden, builder of Middle Temple Hall, stairs lead up to a cell, less than 5ft long, in which disobedient knights were confined. The church features both in the book and the film of *The Da Vinci Code* by Dan Brown.

The millennium column, to the south of Temple Church, marks the point where the Great Fire of 1666 was extinguished; it's topped by a diminutive statue of two knights sharing a horse, a reference to the fact that Knights Templar were often too poor to have a horse each. **Inner Temple Hall**, to the south of the column, is a postwar reconstruction, as is clear from the brickwork. This was the Inn where Mahatma Gandhi studied law in 1888, living as a true Englishman, dressing as a dandy, dancing, taking elocution lessons and playing the violin, while his close associate Jawaharlal Nehru spent two even wilder years here a decade or so later, gambling, drinking and running up considerable debts. The public are also permitted to explore the **Inner Temple Garden** (May–Sept Mon–Fri noon–3pm), which slopes down to the Embankment and is where Shakespeare set the fictional scene of the plucking of red and white roses in *Henry VI Part One*, which signalled the beginning of the Wars of the Roses.

Royal Courts of Justice

On the other side of the Strand from Temple are the **Royal Courts of Justice** (Mon–Fri 9am–4.30pm; free; no cameras allowed; ☎020/7947 6000; Temple tube), home to the Court of Appeal and the High Court, where the most important civil cases are tried (criminal cases are heard at the Old Bailey). It was through the main portal and steps of this daunting Gothic Revival complex, designed in the 1870s, that the Guildford Four and Birmingham Six walked to freedom, and it's where countless public figures have battled it out with the tabloids. In the intimidating Main Hall, where bewigged barristers are busy on their mobiles, you can pick up a plan and a short guide to the complex, while the glass cabinets in the centre of the hall list which cases are being heard and where. In the minstrels' gallery, there's a small exhibition on the history of legal dress codes; if you continue heading north, you can leave via the Carey Street exit.

Lincoln's Inn Fields

To the north of the Law Courts lies **Lincoln's Inn Fields**, London's largest square. Originally simply pasture land and a playground for Lincoln's Inn students, it was used as a place of execution in Tudor times, Anthony Babington and his Catholic accomplices being hanged, drawn and quartered here for high treason in 1586. Laid out in the early 1640s, the square's most arresting statue is that of Margaret MacDonald (wife of the first Labour prime minister Ramsay MacDonald, who died at no. 3), amid a brood of nine children, commemorating her social work among the young. In the southwest corner of the square is one of London's few surviving timber-framed buildings, the sixteenth-century **Old Curiosity Shop** in Portsmouth Street (currently a shoe shop), which claims to be the inspiration for Dickens' sentimental tale of the same name.

Hunterian Museum

On the south side of the square, you'll find the **Hunterian Museum** (Tues–Sat 10am–5pm; free; ☎020/7869 6560, ⓦwww.rcseng.ac.uk; Holborn tube), on the first floor of the imposing Royal College of Surgeons building. First opened in 1813, the museum contains the unique specimen collection of the surgeon-scientist John Hunter (1728–93). Most of the exhibits consist of jars of pickled skeletons and body pieces – from the tibia of a young pig to the human tongue – prepared by Hunter himself, but the museum has even older exhibits, too, such as diarist John Evelyn's anatomical tables from the 1640s, in which arteries and nerves are displayed on wooden boards. Among the most prized exhibits are the skeleton of the "Irish giant", Charles Byrne (1761–83), who was seven feet ten inches tall, and the Sicilian dwarf Caroline Crachami (1815–24), who stood at only one foot ten and a half inches when she died at the age of 9. Upstairs, in the Science of Surgery gallery, you can have a go at simulated minimal-access surgery, and examine Joseph Lister's cumbersome carbolic-acid spray machine, known as the "donkey engine", with which he pioneered antiseptic surgery, performing operations obscured in a cloud of phenol (he even conducted a foggy operation on Queen Victoria – who had an abscess in the royal armpit – accidentally spraying her in the face in the process).

Sir John Soane's Museum

A group of buildings on the north side of the square houses the fascinating **Sir John Soane's Museum** (Tues–Sat 10am–5pm; free; ☎020/7405 2107, ⓦwww.soane.org; Holborn tube). Soane (1753–1837), a bricklayer's son who rose to be architect of the Bank of England, gradually bought up three adjoining Georgian properties here, altering them to serve not only as a home and office, but also as a place to stash his large collection of art and antiquities. No. 13, the central house with the stone loggia, is arranged much as it was in his lifetime, with an ingenious ground plan and an informal, treasure-hunt atmosphere, with surprises in every alcove. Few of Soane's projects were actually built, and his home remains the best example of what he dubbed his "poetry of architecture", using mirrors, domes and skylights to create wonderful spatial ambiguities.

The most unusual part of the house is the colonnaded **monument court**, built over the former stables at the back of the house. All around are antique busts and masonry; above is the wooden chamber on stilts from which Soane supervised his students. To your right is the **picture room**, whose false walls swing back to reveal another wall of pictures, which itself opens to reveal a window and a balcony looking down onto the crypt. The star paintings are **Hogarth**'s satirical *Election* series and his merciless morality tale *The Rake's Progress*.

The flagstoned **crypt** features a "monk's parlour", a Gothic folly dedicated to a make-believe padre, Giovanni, complete with tomb (containing Soane's wife's dog, Fanny), cloister and eerie medieval casts and gargoyles. The hushed sepulchral chamber continues the morbid theme with its wooden mummy case, a model of an Etruscan tomb (complete with skeleton), and the tombstones of Soane's wife and son. You then emerge into the colonnaded atrium, home to an Egyptian **sarcophagus**, rejected by the British Museum and bought by Soane.

Back on the ground floor, make your way to the **breakfast parlour**, which features all Soane's favourite architectural features: coloured skylights, a canopied dome and ranks of tiny convex mirrors. A short stroll up the beautiful cantilevered staircase brings you to the first-floor **drawing rooms**, whose airiness and bright colour scheme come as a relief after the ancient clutter of the downstairs rooms. Note that the museum is extremely popular on Saturdays, when there's a fascinating hour-long **guided tour** (£5) at 11am, and on the **candlelit evenings** held on the first Tuesday of the month (6–9pm).

Lincoln's Inn

On the east side of Lincoln's Inn Fields lies **Lincoln's Inn** (Mon–Fri 9am–6pm; ☎020/7405 1393; Holborn tube), the first, and in many ways the prettiest, of the Inns of Court; famous alumni include Thomas More, Oliver Cromwell and Margaret Thatcher. The oldest building is the fifteenth-century Old Hall (by appointment only), where the lawyers used to live and where Dickens set the case Jarndyce versus Jarndyce, the opening scene in *Bleak House*.

Beyond the Old Hall is the sixteenth-century **gatehouse** – best viewed from Chancery Lane – impressive for its age and bulk, not to mention its characteristic diamond-patterned brickwork. Adjacent is the **chapel** (Mon–Fri noon–2pm), built in 1620, with its unusual fan-vaulted open undercroft; on the first floor, the nave, rebuilt in 1880, hit by a Zeppelin in World War I and much restored since, still boasts its original ornate pews. North of the chapel lie the Palladian **Stone Buildings**, best appreciated from the manicured lawns of the Inn's gardens (Mon–Fri noon–2.30pm); the strange miniature castle near the garden entrance is the gardeners' tool shed, a creation of George Gilbert Scott, designer of London's old red telephone boxes.

Chancery Lane and Gray's Inn

Running along the eastern edge of Lincoln's Inn is legal London's main thoroughfare, **Chancery Lane**, home of the Law Society (the solicitors' regulatory body) and lined with shops where barristers, solicitors and clerks can buy their wigs, gowns, legal tomes, stationery and champagne. On the east side of Chancery Lane are the **London Silver Vaults** (Mon–Fri 9am–5.30pm, Sat 9am–1pm; free; ⦿ www.thesilvervaults.com; Chancery Lane tube), which began life as the Chancery Lane Safe Deposit for London's wealthy elite, but now house a strange, claustrophobic lair of subterranean shops selling every kind of silverware – mostly antique, mostly English and often quite tasteless.

The last of the four Inns of Court, **Gray's Inn** (Mon–Fri 10am–4pm; ☎020/7458 7800; Chancery Lane tube), lies hidden away off High Holborn, at the top of Chancery Lane; access is next to the venerable *Cittie of Yorke* pub. Established in the fourteenth century, the Inn took its name from the de Grey family, who owned the original mansion used as student lodgings; most of what you see today, however, was rebuilt after the Blitz. The **Hall** (by appointment only), with its fabulous Tudor screen and stained glass, witnessed the premiere of Shakespeare's *Comedy of Errors* in 1594. Unlike the south side, the north side of the Inn, taken up by the wide green expanse of **Gray's Inn Gardens**, is entirely and impressively visible through its wrought-iron railings from Theobald's Road; the gardens are open to the public weekday lunchtimes.

Holborn Circus

Heading east towards Holborn Circus, it's worth pausing to admire two remarkable buildings. The first, on the right, is **Staple Inn**, a former Inn of Chancery (a less prestigious version of the Inns of Court). Its overhanging half-timbered facade and gables date from the sixteenth century and are the most extensive in the whole of London; they survived the Fire, which stopped just short of Holborn Circus, but had to be extensively rebuilt after the Blitz. On the opposite side of the street stands the palatial, terracotta-red **Prudential Assurance Building**, begun in 1879 by Alfred Waterhouse. This fortress of Victorian capitalism has its very own Bridge of Sighs, harbours a dramatic memorial to the Prudential men who fell in the world wars and retains much of its original Doulton-tiled interior.

At **Holborn Circus** itself, the traffic swirls around London's politest statue, in which a cheerful Prince Albert doffs his hat to passers-by. Take the first left off Charterhouse Street, which runs northeast from the Circus, and you'll come to **Ely Place**, named after the Bishop of Ely, whose London residence used to stand here. Guarded by a beadle, lodge and wrought-iron gates, this patch is technically still outside the jurisdiction of the London authorities, but all that remains of the bishop's palace is its plain Gothic chapel, now **St Etheldreda's Church**, hidden halfway down this dead-end street on the left. At one time a Roman Catholic chapel to the Spanish ambassador and later used by Welsh non-conformists, St Etheldreda's has been an exclusive Catholic stronghold since 1874, attracting a fair number of worshippers from the City during the week, and foreign diplomats at the weekend. The main body of the church, though much restored, dates back to 1300, and is lined with niches sheltering statues of English martyrs; the atmospherically gloomy crypt contains a model of the pre-Reformation church complex.

Clerkenwell and Hoxton

A typical London mix of Georgian and Victorian townhouses, housing estates, old warehouses, loft conversions and art studios, **Clerkenwell** and **Hoxton** lie immediately to the north of the City. Both districts have been transformed over the last two decades into fashionable enclaves, and though they lie off the conventional tourist trail, there are a smattering of minor sights and more than enough nightlife to make them worth exploring. Clerkenwell boasts the vestiges of two pre-Fire-of-London priories and has a history of radicalism, exemplified by the **Marx Memorial Library**, where the exiled Lenin plotted revolution. Hoxton, meanwhile, is home to **Wesley's Chapel and House**, the spiritual heart of the Methodist movement, as well as the **Geffrye Museum** of domestic interiors and a whole host of **contemporary art galleries**.

Clerkenwell

Situated slightly uphill from the City and, more importantly, outside its jurisdiction, **Clerkenwell** (pronounced "Clarken-well") began life as a village serving the local monastic foundations (two of which survive to some extent). Following the Great Fire, the area was settled by craftsmen, including newly arrived French Huguenots, excluded from the City guilds. At the same time, the springs that give the place its name were rediscovered (and are still visible through the window of 14–16 Farringdon Lane), and Clerkenwell became a popular **spa resort** for a century or so.

During the nineteenth century, the district's population trebled, mostly through Irish and Italian immigration; the springs and streams became cholera-infested sewers, and Clerkenwell became an overpopulated **slum area** and the setting for Fagin's Den in *Oliver Twist*. Victorian slum clearances and wartime bombing took their toll, the population declined and the area's traditional trades – locksmithing, clockmaking, printing and jewellery – all but disappeared. The overall trend, now, is towards designer furniture and media companies, with trendy bars and restaurants catering for the area's new loft-dwelling residents.

Hatton Garden

Hatton Garden (Ⓦ www.hatton–garden.net), connecting Holborn Circus (see p.155) with Little Italy (see below), is no beauty spot, but, as the centre of the city's **diamond and jewellery trade** since medieval times, it's an intriguing place to visit during the week. As in Antwerp and New York, ultra-orthodox Hasidic Jews dominate the business here as middlemen (they are catered for by kosher cafés like the 24hr *Knosherie* on Greville St).

Near the top of Hatton Garden, there's a plaque commemorating **Hiram Maxim** (1840–1916), the American inventor who perfected the automatic gun named after him in the workshops at no. 57. East of Hatton Garden, off Greville Street, lies **Bleeding Heart Yard**, a key location in Dickens' *Little Dorrit*. The name refers to the gruesome 1626 murder of Lady Hatton, who sold her soul to the devil, so the story goes. One night, during a ball at nearby Hatton House, the devil came to collect, and all trace of her vanished except her heart, which was found bleeding and throbbing on the pavement. Parallel to Hatton Garden, be sure to take a wander through the **Leather Lane Market** (Mon–Fri 10.30am–2.30pm), an old market selling everything from fruit and vegetables to clothes and electrical gear.

Rosebery Avenue

Halfway up **Rosebery Avenue** – built in the 1890s to link Clerkenwell Road with Islington to the north – stands **Mount Pleasant Post Office**, Europe's largest sorting office, built on the site of the Coldbath Fields prison. A third of all inland mail passes through this building, and originally much of it was brought by the post office's own underground railway network, **Mail Rail**

Little Italy

In the late nineteenth century, London experienced a huge influx of Italian immigrants who created their own **Little Italy** in the triangle of land now bounded by Clerkenwell Road, Rosebery Avenue and Farringdon Road; craftsmen, artisans, street performers and musicians were later joined by ice-cream vendors, restaurateurs and political refugees. Between the wars the population peaked at around ten thousand Italians, crammed into overcrowded, insanitary slums. The old streets have long been demolished to make way for council and other low-rent housing, and few Italians live here these days; nevertheless, the area remains a focus for a community that's now spread right across the capital.

The main point of reference is **St Peter's Italian Church** (Ⓦ www.italianchurch.org .uk), built in 1863 and still the favourite venue for Italian weddings and christenings, as well as for Sunday Mass. It's rarely open outside of the daily mass, though you can view the World War I memorial in the main porch, and, above it, the grim memorial to the seven hundred Anglo-Italian internees who died aboard the *Arandora Star*, a POW ship which sank en route to Canada in 1940. St Peter's is the starting point of the annual Italian Procession, begun in 1883 and now a permanent fixture on the Sunday nearest July 16 (see p.29).

A few old-established Italian businesses survive here, too: the Scuola Guida driving school at 178 Clerkenwell Rd, and the deli, G. Gazzano & Son, at 167–169 Farringdon Rd. There's also a plaque to **Giuseppe Mazzini** (1805–72), the chief protagonist in Italian unification, above the Italian barbers at 10 Laystall St. Mazzini lived in exile in London for many years and was very active in the Clerkenwell community, establishing a free school for Italian children in Hatton Garden.

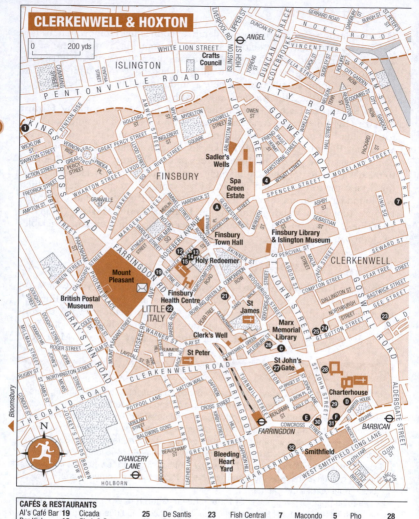

0   200 yds

WHITE LION STREET

Crafts
Council

ISLINGTON

ANGEL

PENTONVILLE ROAD

CITY ROAD

FINSBURY

Sadler's
Wells

Spa
Green
Estate

Finsbury
Town Hall

Finsbury Library
& Islington Museum

Holy Redeemer

CLERKENWELL

Mount
Pleasant

British Postal
Museum

LITTLE
ITALY

Finsbury
Health Centre

St James

Marx
Memorial
Library

Clerk's Well

St Peter

CLERKENWELL ROAD

St John's
Gate

Charterhouse

FARRINGDON

BARBICAN

Bloomsbury

N

CHANCERY
LANE

Bleeding
Heart
Yard

Smithfield

HOLBORN

CAFÉS & RESTAURANTS										
Al's Café Bar	19	Cicada	25	De Santis	23	Fish Central	7	Macondo	5	Pho	28
Bar Kick	10	Clark & Sons	15	Eyre Brothers	20	Golden Lion		Medcalf	13	Real Greek	8
Café Kick	12	Clerkenwell Kitchen	21	Flavours	16	Kurz & Lang	30	Moro	14	Saf	9

(Ⓦ www.mailrail.co.uk). Opened in 1927 and similar in design to the tube, the railway was fully automatic, sending driverless trucks of mail between London's sorting offices and train stations at speeds of up to 35mph. Unfortunately, all 23 miles of this two-foot-gauge railway was mothballed in 2003, with no immediate plans to reactivate it. Philatelists should head to the **British Postal Museum** (Mon–Fri 10am–5pm, Thurs until 7pm, plus selected Sat 10am–5pm; free; Ⓣ020/7239 2570, Ⓦwww.postalheritage.org.uk; Farringdon tube), alongside the sorting office on Phoenix Place, which puts on small exhibitions drawn from its vast archive.

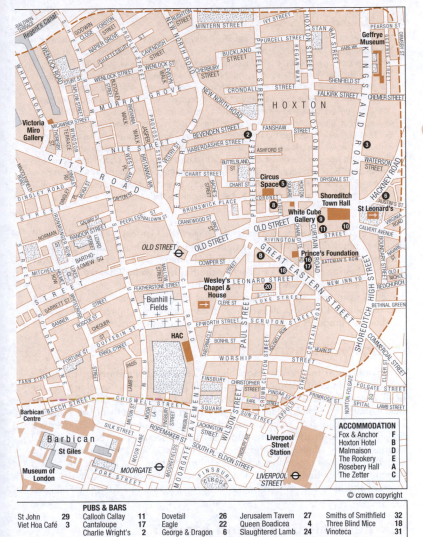

Regent's Canal

Victoria Miro Gallery

Geffrye Museum

HOXTON

Circus Space 5

Shoreditch Town Hall

White Cube Gallery 9

St Leonard's

OLD STREET

Prince's Foundation

Wesley's Chapel & House

Bunhill Fields

HAC

Barbican Centre

Barbican

St Giles

Museum of London

MOORGATE

Liverpool Street Station

LIVERPOOL STREET

© crown copyright

PUBS & BARS

St John	29	Calloo Callay	11	Dovetail	26	Jerusalem Tavern	27	Smiths of Smithfield	32
Viet Hoa Café	3	Cantaloupe	17	Eagle	22	Queen Boadicea	4	Three Blind Mice	18
		Charlie Wright's	2	George & Dragon	6	Slaughtered Lamb	24	Vinoteca	31

Opposite Mount Pleasant is **Exmouth Market** (Ⓦwww.exmouth-market .com), now at the epicentre of trendy Clerkenwell. Apart from a surviving pie-and-mash shop, the rest of the street has been colonized by modish shops, bars and restaurants, and there's now a small foodie market (Fri 11am–6pm & Sat 9am–4pm). A blue plaque at 56 Exmouth Market pays tribute to **Joey Grimaldi** (1778–1837), the "Father of Clowns", who first appeared on stage at nearby Sadler's Wells at the age of 3. The street's **Church of the Holy Redeemer** sports a fetching Italianate campanile, while the groin-vaulted interior features a large baldachin and stations of the cross – yet despite appearances, it belongs to the Church of England.

The People's Republic of Finsbury

The Borough of Finsbury was subsumed into Islington in 1965, but the former **Finsbury Town Hall** (now a dance academy) still stands, an attractive building from 1899, whose name is spelt out in magenta glass on the delicate wrought-iron canopy that juts out into Rosebery Avenue. As the plaque outside states, the district was the first to boast an Asian MP, **Dadabhai Nairoji**, who was elected (after a recount) as a Liberal MP in 1892 with a majority of five. In keeping with its radical pedigree, the borough went on to elect several Communist councillors and became known popularly as the "People's Republic of Finsbury". The council commissioned Georgian-born Berthold Lubetkin to design the modernist **Finsbury Health Centre** on Pine Street, off Exmouth Market, described by Jonathan Glancey as "a remarkable outpost of Soviet thinking and neo-Constructivist architecture in a part of central London wracked with rickets and TB". Lubetkin's later **Spa Green Estate**, the council flats further north on the opposite side of Rosebery Avenue from Sadler's Wells, featured novelties such as rubbish shutes and an aerofoil roof to help tenants dry their clothes.

At the end of the market, to the right, the Spa Field Gardens recall Clerkenwell's days as a fashionable spa, which began in 1683 when Thomas Sadler rediscovered a medicinal well in his garden and established a music house to entertain visitors. The well has since made a comeback at the **Sadler's Wells Theatre**, further up Rosebery Avenue, the seventh theatre on this site since 1683 and now one of London's main venues for visiting opera and ballet companies. A borehole sunk into the old well provides all the theatre's non-drinking supplies, helps cool the building and produces bottled drinking water for the punters.

Islington Museum

If you're keen to learn some more about Clerkenwell, Finsbury or the wider borough of Islington (for more on which see p.294), it's worth seeking out the newly established **Islington Museum** (Mon, Tues & Thurs–Sat 10am–5pm; free; T020/7527 2837; Angel tube), housed in the basement of the Finsbury Library, 245 St John St (access is down the steps on the north side). There's a dressing-up box for the kids and some fascinating sections on the area's radical politics for the adults. Highlights include the bust of Lenin, modelled by Lubetkin, that was erected in 1942 in Holford Square (see p.162), but had to be removed after the war, after it was targeted by vandals; you can also view some of the library books embellished by Joe Orton and Kenneth Halliwell (see p.295).

Clerkenwell Green and around

Poverty and overcrowding were the main features of nineteenth-century Clerkenwell, and **Clerkenwell Green** was well known in the press as "the headquarters of republicanism, revolution and ultra-non-conformity" and a popular spot for **demonstrations**. The most violent of these was the "Clerkenwell Riot" of 1832, when a policeman was stabbed to death during a clash between unemployed demonstrators and the newly formed Metropolitan Police Force. The "blue devils", as they were known, were at the height of their unpopularity, and the coroner reached a verdict of justifiable homicide. In 1871, a red flag was flown from a lamp post on the Green in support of the Paris Commune. London's first **May Day** march set off from here in 1890, and the tradition continues to this day. In 1900, the Labour Party was founded at a meeting on Farringdon Road and the Communist Party had its headquarters at nearby St John Street for many years, with the Party's *Daily Worker* (and later *Morning Star*) printed on Farringdon Road.

The oldest building on the Green is the former Welsh Charity School, at no. 37a, built in 1737 and now home to the **Marx Memorial Library** (Mon–Thurs 1–2pm or by appointment; closed Aug; free; ☎020/7253 1485, ⓦwww .marx-memorial-library.org; Farringdon tube). Headquarters of the left-wing London Patriotic Society from 1872, and later William Morris's Twentieth Century Press, this is where **Lenin** edited seventeen editions of the Bolshevik paper *Iskra* in 1902–03; the poky little back room where Lenin worked is maintained as a kind of shrine – even the original lino survives. Visitors are free to view the Lenin Room, an original copy of *Iskra* produced here, and the library's "workerist" *Hastings Mural* from 1935. The library itself, founded in 1933 in response to the book burnings in Nazi Germany, is open to members only.

The area north of the Green was once occupied by the Benedictine convent of St Mary. The buildings have long since vanished, though the current church of **St James** (Mon–Fri 10am–2pm; ⓦwww.jc-church.org), on Clerkenwell Close, is the descendant of the convent church. A plain, galleried eighteenth-century building decorated in Wedgwood blue and white, its most interesting features are the twin staircases for the galleries at the west end, both of which were fitted with wrought-iron guards to prevent parishioners from glimpsing any ladies' ankles as they ascended.

St John's Gate

The oldest of Clerkenwell's medieval religious establishments is the priory of the Order of St John of Jerusalem, whose Knights Hospitaller, along with the Knights Templar, were responsible for the defence of the Holy Land. The sixteenth-century **St John's Gate**, built in Kentish ragstone on the south side of Clerkenwell Road and originally forming the southern entrance to the complex, is the most visible survivor of the foundation. The priory was sacked in 1381 by Wat Tyler's poll-tax rebels on the lookout for the prior, Robert Hales, who was responsible for collecting the tax; Hales was eventually discovered at the Tower and beheaded on the spot. After the Reformation, the Knights moved to Malta and the Gate housed the Master of Revels, the Elizabethan censor, and later a coffee house run by Richard Hogarth, father of the painter, William.

Today, the gatehouse forms part of a **museum** (Mon–Fri 10am–5pm, Sat 10am–4pm; free; ☎020/7324 4005, ⓦwww.sja.org.uk/museum; Farringdon tube), whose main room traces the development of the Order before its expulsion in 1540 by Henry VIII. Elsewhere, there's masonry from the old priory, crusader coins and a small arms collection salvaged from the knights' armoury on Rhodes, where they were besieged and eventually expelled in 1523. Nowadays, the Order is best known for the **St John Ambulance**, a voluntary first-aid service, established in 1877, and described in the museum's interactive gallery. The cabinets of uniforms and pull-out drawers of cigarette cards, badges and medals are interspersed with touch-screen interviews with members past and present. Be sure to check out the Ashford Litter, a Victorian ambulance that was basically a stretcher on wheels with a protective hood.

To explore the gatehouse itself, including the mock-medieval Chapter Hall, and to visit the Grand Priory Church over the road, you must take a **guided tour** (Tues, Fri & Sat 11am & 2.30pm; £5 donation requested). Of the original twelfth-century church, all that remains is the **Norman crypt**, which contains

Virtually every Bolshevik leader spent at least some time in exile in London at the beginning of the twentieth century, to avoid the attentions of the Tsarist secret police. **Lenin** (1870–1924) and his wife, Nadezhda, arrived in April 1902 and found unfurnished lodgings at 30 Holford Square, off Great Percy Street, under the pseudonyms of Mr and Mrs Jacob Richter. Like Marx, Lenin did his studying in the British Library – L13 was his favourite desk.

The couple also entertained other exiles – including **Trotsky**, whom Lenin met for the first time at Holford Square in October 1902 – but Lenin's most important job was his editing of *Iskra* with Yuli Martov (later the Menshevik leader) and Vera Zasulich (one-time revolutionary assassin). The paper was set in Cyrillic script at a Jewish printer's in the East End and run off on the Social Democratic Federation presses on Clerkenwell Green.

In May 1903, Lenin left to join other exiles in Geneva, though over the next eight years he visited London on five more occasions. The Holford Square house was destroyed in the war, so, in 1942, the local council erected a (short-lived) **monument** to Lenin (now in the Islington Museum). A blue plaque at the back of the hotel on the corner of Great Percy Street commemorates the site of 16 Percy Circus, where Lenin stayed in 1905 whilst attending the third RSDLP congress.

two outstanding monuments: a sixteenth-century Spanish alabaster effigy of a Knight of St John, and the emaciated effigy of the last prior, who is said to have died of a broken heart in 1540 after hearing of the Order's dissolution. Above ground, the curve of the church's walls – it was circular, like Temple Church – is traced out in cobblestones on St John's Square.

Charterhouse

Southeast of St John's Gate lies **Charterhouse**, founded in 1371 as a Carthusian monastery. The Carthusians were one of the few religious orders in London to put up any resistance to the Dissolution of the Monasteries, for which the prior was hanged, drawn and quartered at Tyburn, and his severed arm nailed to the gatehouse as a warning to the rest of the community, several more of whom were later martyred. The gatehouse, on Charterhouse Square, which retains its fourteenth-century oak doors, is the starting point for the exhaustive two-hour **guided tours** (April–Aug Wed 2.15pm; £10; ☎020/7251 5002) that are the only way to visit the site; advance booking is essential.

Very little remains of the original buildings, as the monastery was rebuilt as a Tudor mansion after the Dissolution. The monks lived in individual cells, each with its own garden and were only allowed to speak to one another on Sundays; three of their tiny cells can still be seen in the west wall of **Preachers' Court**. The larger of the two enclosed courtyards, **Masters' Court**, retains the wonderful Great Hall, which boasts a fine Renaissance carved screen and a largely reconstructed hammerbeam roof, as well as the Great Chamber where Elizabeth I and James I were once entertained. The **Chapel**, with its geometrical plasterwork ceiling, is half-Tudor and half-Jacobean, and contains the marble and alabaster tomb of **Thomas Sutton**, whose greyhound-head emblem crops up throughout the building. It was Sutton, deemed "the richest commoner in England" at the time, who bought the place in 1611 and converted it into a charity school for boys (now the famous public school in Surrey) and an **almshouse** for gentlemen – known as "brothers" – forty of whom continue to be cared for here.

Hoxton

Despite the area's lack of obvious aesthetic charm, over the last decade or so **Shoreditch** has been colonized by artists, designers and architects and transformed into one of the city's most vibrant artistic enclaves. At the same time it has been rejacketed: what was once Shoreditch is now better known as **Hoxton**, previously a much smaller neighbourhood confined to the north of Old Street. Whatever its real name, the area is, in actual fact, rich in literary and artistic associations. It was here that James Burbage established the country's **first public theatre** – called simply the Theatre – in 1576 (he subsequently took it down and reassembled it on Bankside as the Globe). There are a couple of specific sights – **Wesley's Chapel and House** and the **Geffrye Museum** of period interiors – but the majority of folk come here for the area's **bars** (listed on p.400), **clubs** (p.412) and **art galleries**.

Wesley's Chapel and House

Just south of the Old Street roundabout (and tube), and striking an unusual note of calm on busy City Road, is the largely Georgian ensemble of **Wesley's Chapel and House** (Mon–Sat 10am–4pm, Sun 12.30–1.45pm; free; ☏020/7253 2262, ⓦwww.wesleyschapel.org.uk; Old Street tube), set around a cobbled courtyard. A place of pilgrimage for Methodists from all over the world, the chapel was designed in 1778 by George Dance and heralded the coming-of-age of the followers of **John Wesley** (1703–91), who had started out in a small foundry east of the present building. The name "Methodist" was a term of abuse used by Wesley's fellow Oxford students, but it wasn't until his "conversion" at a prayer meeting in Aldersgate (marked by a plaque outside the Museum of London) in 1738, and later expulsion from the Anglican Church, that he decided to become an independent field preacher. More verbal and even physical abuse followed – Wesley was accused of being a papist spy and an illegal gin distiller – but by the time of his death there were more than 350 Methodist chapels serving over 130,000 worshippers.

The **chapel** forms the centrepiece of the complex, though it is uncharacteristically ornate for a Methodist place of worship, with its powder-pink columns of French jasper and its superb, Adam-style gilded plasterwork ceiling, not to mention the colourful Victorian stained glass depicting, among other things, Wesley's night-time conversion, with his brother still in his dressing gown. The chapel has often attracted well-heeled weddings: one Margaret Hilda Roberts got married to divorcé Denis Thatcher here in 1951, and later paid for the new communion rail.

The **Museum of Methodism** (same hours) in the basement tells the story of Wesley and Methodism, and there's even a brief mention of Mrs Mary Vazeille, the 41-year-old, insanely jealous, wealthy widow he married, and who eventually left him. Wesley himself lived his last two years in the Georgian **house** to the right of the main gates, and inside you can see bits of his furniture and his deathbed, plus an early shock-therapy machine with which he used to treat members of his congregation. Wesley's **grave** is round the back of the chapel, in the shadow of a modern office block.

Bunhill Fields

Appropriately enough, **Bunhill Fields** (April–Sept Mon–Fri 7.30am–7pm, Sat & Sun 9.30am–7pm; Oct–March Mon–Fri closes 4pm), the main burial ground for Dissenters or Nonconformists (practising Christians who were not members of the Church of England), lies across the road from Wesley's Chapel. Following bomb damage in the last war, most of the graveyard is fenced off, though you can still stroll through on the public footpaths under a canopy of giant London plane trees. The three most famous graves have been placed in the central paved area: the simple tombstone of poet and artist **William Blake** stands next to a replica of writer **Daniel Defoe**'s, while opposite lies the recumbent statue of **John Bunyan**, seventeenth-century author of *The Pilgrim's Progress*.

Hoxton Square and around

The geographical focus of Hoxton's transformation is **Hoxton Square**, situated northeast of Old Street tube: a strange and not altogether happy assortment of light industrial units, many now artists' studios, arranged around a leafy, formal square. The chief landmark here is the **White Cube** gallery (Tues–Sat 10am–6pm; free; Ⓦ www.whitecube.com; Old Street tube), a sort of miniature Tate Modern: it's an old piano factory, with a glass roof plonked on the top, and represents the likes of Damien Hirst, Tracey Emin and Sam Taylor-Wood. A couple of blocks west is the intimate cobbled square of **Hoxton Market**, home to Circus Space (Ⓦ www.thecircusspace.co.uk), a college for jugglers and acrobats housed in the former Shoreditch Electric Light Station, an old refuse destructor which sports the motto *E pulvere lux et vis* (Out of the dust, light and power).

▲ White Cube

The area's two architectural landmarks deserve a brief mention. The most prominent is **St Leonard's**, the Neoclassical church at the junction of Old Street, Shoreditch High Street and Kingsland Road. Though it's usually closed, you can sometimes take a look inside on a Sunday morning and admire the memorial to Elizabeth Benson on the southeast wall, which depicts two skeletons tearing at the Tree of Life. Just up Old Street is the former **Shoreditch Town Hall** (Ⓦ www.shoreditchtownhall.org.uk), a self-confident Victorian edifice, whose tower features Progress, torch and battleaxe in hand, and, in the pediment, Hope and Plenty, reclining beside the Shoreditch motto "More Light, More Power", adopted in recognition of the borough's progressive policy of creating power from rubbish incineration.

Geffrye Museum

Hoxton's chief attraction is the **Geffrye Museum** (Tues–Sat 10am–5pm, Sun noon–5pm; free; ☎ 020/7739 9893, Ⓦ www.geffrye-museum.org.uk; Old Street tube), housed in a grandiose enclave of eighteenth-century ironmongers' almshouses, set back from Kingsland Road. In 1911, at a time when the East End furniture trade was centred on Shoreditch, the almshouses were converted into a museum for the "education of craftsmen". The Geffrye remains, essentially, a furniture museum, with the almshouses rigged out as period living rooms of the urban middle class, ranging from the oak-panelled seventeenth century, through refined Georgian to cluttered Victorian. You'll also pass through the original central Georgian **chapel**, with its tiny Neoclassical apse and archetypal stone-coloured wood panelling; round the back of the chapel, an enclosed balcony overlooking the garden serves as a reading room.

Further on is the museum's twentieth-century **extension**, with four "snapshots in time", beginning with an Edwardian drawing room in understated Arts and Crafts style, and finishing off with a minimalist 1990s loft conversion. The extension also houses a pleasant licensed **café–restaurant**, serving inexpensive British food, and hosts excellent temporary exhibitions on the lower ground floor. Out the back, the **gardens** show the transition in horticultural tastes from the seventeenth-century knot gardens to today's patio garden, culminating in a pungent, walled **herb garden** (April–Oct only).

To get a feel of what the living conditions in the **almshouses** were like, one of them has been restored to its original condition and can now be visited on the first Saturday of the month, and the first and third Wednesday of the month; numbers are limited, visits are by timed entry only and tickets cost £2.

11

The City

The **City** is where London began. Long established as the financial district, it currently stretches from Temple Bar in the west to the Tower of London in the east – administrative boundaries that are only slightly larger than those marked by the Roman walls and their medieval successors. However, in this **Square Mile** (as the City is often called) you'll have to dig hard to find leftovers of London's early days: four-fifths of the area burnt down in the Great Fire of 1666. What you see on the ground is mostly the product of three fairly recent building phases: the Victorian construction boom; the overzealous reconstruction that followed the Blitz; and the building frenzy that began in the 1980s, which has seen over half the City's office space rebuilt.

When you consider what's happened here, it's amazing that anything has survived to bear witness to the City's 2000-year history. Yet Wren's spires still punctuate the skyline, and his masterpiece, **St Paul's Cathedral**, remains one of London's geographical and touristic pivots. To the east, the **Tower of London**, begun shortly after the Norman Conquest, survives (and is covered in Chapter 12). Other relics, such as the City's few existing medieval alleyways, Wren's **Monument** to the Great Fire and London's oldest synagogue and church, are less conspicuous, and even the locals have problems finding the more modern attractions of the **Museum of London** and the **Barbican** arts complex. It's also worth checking out some of the Square Mile's modern architecture, including Richard Rogers' mould-breaking **Lloyd's Building**, and Norman Foster's eye-catching **Gherkin**.

The biggest change of all, though, has been in the City's **population**. Until the eighteenth century, the vast majority of Londoners lived and worked in or around the City; nowadays, while more than 300,000 commuters spend the best part of Monday to Friday here, only nine thousand actually live here, most of them cooped up in the Barbican complex. The result of this demographic shift is that the City is only fully alive during office hours, with many pubs, restaurants and even some tube stations and tourist sights closing down at the weekend.

The one unchanging aspect of the City is its special status, conferred on the area by William the Conqueror to appease the powerful burghers, and extended and reaffirmed by successive rulers ever since. Nowadays, with its own Lord Mayor, its Beadles, Sheriffs and Aldermen, its separate police force and its select electorate of freemen and liverymen, the City is an anachronistic, one-party mini-state. It's run by the **Corporation of London** (ⓦwww .cityoflondon.gov.uk), an unreconstructed old-boy network whose medievalist pageantry camouflages the very real power and wealth that it holds. Its anomalous status is all the more baffling when you consider that the area was once the cradle of British democracy: it was the City that traditionally stood up to bullying sovereigns.

The City's churches

The City of London is crowded with **churches** (ⓦ www.visitthecity.co.uk) – well over forty at the last count, the majority of them built or rebuilt by Christopher Wren after the Great Fire. Prompted by the decline in the City's population, the Victorians demolished a fair few, but there are still a vast number. The **opening times** given in the text should be taken with a pinch of salt, since most churches rely on volunteers to keep their doors open. As a general rule, weekday lunchtimes are the best time to visit the City's churches, many of which put on free lunchtime concerts. Below is a list of the six most interesting City churches:

St Bartholomew-the-Great Cloth Fair. This is the oldest surviving pre-Fire church in the City and by far the most atmospheric. It's also the only church in the country to charge an entrance fee. See p.178.

St Mary Abchurch Abchurch Lane. Uniquely for Wren's City churches, the interior features a huge, painted, domed ceiling, plus the only authenticated Gibbons reredos. See p.186.

St Mary Aldermary Queen Victoria Street. Wren's most successful stab at Gothic, with fan vaulting in the aisles and a panelled ceiling in the nave. See p.184.

St Mary Woolnoth Lombard Street. Hawksmoor's only City church, sporting an unusually broad, bulky tower and a Baroque clerestory that floods the church with light from its semicircular windows. See p.186.

St Olave Hart Street. Built in the fifteenth century, and one of the few pre-Fire Gothic churches in the City. See p.190.

St Stephen Walbrook Walbrook. Wren's dress rehearsal for St Paul's, with a wonderful central dome and plenty of original woodcarving. See p.185.

Fleet Street

Fleet Street offers one of the grandest approaches to the City, thanks to the view across to Ludgate Hill and beyond to St Paul's Cathedral, but it's best known for its associations with the printed press and particularly the newspaper industry (see box, p.171).

Temple Bar and around

Temple Bar, at the western end of Fleet Street, is the latest in a long line of structures marking the boundary between Westminster and the City of London. It began as a simple chain between two posts but by the 1670s a Wren-designed triumphal arch stood here. The heads of executed traitors were displayed on the arch until the mid-eighteenth century – one could even rent a telescope for a closer look. Then, in 1878, the arch was removed to ease traffic congestion, exiled to a park in Hertfordshire, only to be re-erected near St Paul's (see p.172). The current monument, topped by a winged dragon, marks the spot where the sovereign must ask for the Lord Mayor's permission to enter the City, a tradition that began when Elizabeth I passed through on her way to St Paul's to give thanks for the defeat of the Armada.

The western part of Fleet Street was spared from the Great Fire, which stopped at the junction with Fetter Lane, just short of **Prince Henry's Room** (Mon–Fri 11am–2pm; free; ⓦ www.cityoflondon.gov.uk/phr; Blackfriars or Temple tube), a fine Jacobean house with timber-framed bay windows on the first floor, and the gateway to Inner Temple at street level. Originally a pub, later a waxworks, the first-floor room now contains material relating to the diarist Samuel Pepys (see box, p.170), who was born and baptized in the area. Even if

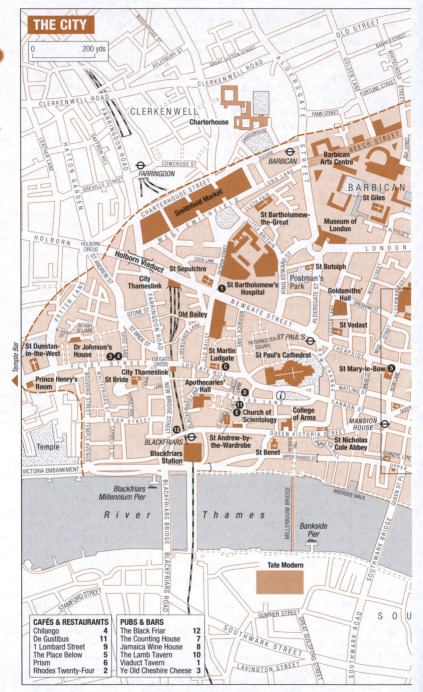

THE CITY

0   200 yds

CLERKENWELL ROAD

CLERKENWELL

Charterhouse

AYLESBURY ST

GREAT SUTTON STREET

CLERKENWELL ROAD

CLERKENWELL GREEN

OLD STREET

BARBICAN

Barbican
Arts Centre

BARBICAN

St Giles

Museum of
London

LEATHER LANE

HATTON GARDEN

SAFFRON HILL

FARRINGDON ROAD

GREVILLE STREET

COWCROSS ST

FARRINGDON

CHARTERHOUSE STREET

Smithfield Market

WEST SMITHFIELD

CLOTH FAIR

St Bartholomew-
the-Great

LITTLE BRITAIN

LONG LANE

FANN STREET

BEECH STREET

SILK STREET

HOLBORN

HOLBORN
CIRCUS

Holborn Viaduct

St Sepulchre

City
Thameslink

Old Bailey

COCK LANE

GILTSPUR ST

St Bartholomew's
Hospital

NEWGATE STREET

Postman's
Park

St Botolph

KING EDWARD ST

Goldsmiths'
Hall

GRESHAM ST

St Vedast

LONDON WALL

ALDERSGATE STREET

ST ALPHAGE'S

WOOD STREET

ALDERMANBURY

FETTER LANE

GOUGH
SQUARE

W HARD
COURT

STONE ST

FARRINGDON ROAD

SHOE LANE

St Dunstan-
in-the-West

Dr Johnson's
House

Prince Henry's
Room

FLEET STREET

City Thameslink

St Bride

LIMEBURNER LANE

WARWICK LANE

OLD BAILEY

LUDGATE
CIRCUS

LUDGATE HILL

St Martin
Ludgate

ST PAUL'S

PATERNOSTER
SQUARE

St Paul's Cathedral

NEW CHANGE

CHEAPSIDE

St Mary-le-Bow

BOW LANE

MILK STREET

Temple Bar

BOUVERIE STREET

WHITEFRIARS ST

NEW BRIDGE STREET

BRIDE LANE

ST BRIDE ST

Apothecaries'
Hall

BLACKFRIARS LANE

SEACOAL LANE

CARTER LANE

Church of
Scientology

College
of Arms

WATLING ST

CANNON ST

MANSION
HOUSE

QUEEN

TEMPLE

Temple

TUDOR STREET

TEMPLE AVENUE

CARMELITE ST

QUEEN VICTORIA STREET

St Andrew-by-
the-Wardrobe

St Benet

St Nicholas
Cole Abbey

UPPER THAMES ST

SKINNERS LANE

UPPER

QUEEN ST PL

VICTORIA EMBANKMENT

BLACKFRIARS

Blackfriars
Station

BLACKFRIARS BRIDGE

BLACKFRIARS ROAD

Blackfriars
Millennium Pier

River   Thames

MILLENNIUM BRIDGE

RIVERSIDE WALK

Bankside
Pier

SOUTHWARK BRIDGE

QUEEN ST PL

Tate Modern

SOU

STAMFORD STREET

SUMNER STREET

SOUTHWARK STREET

GREAT GUILDFORD STREET

LAVINGTON STREET

CAFÉS & RESTAURANTS		PUBS & BARS	
Chilango	4	The Black Friar	12
De Gustibus	11	The Counting House	7
1 Lombard Street	9	Jamaica Wine House	8
The Place Below	5	The Lamb Tavern	10
Prism	6	Viaduct Tavern	1
Rhodes Twenty-Four	2	Ye Old Cheshire Cheese	3

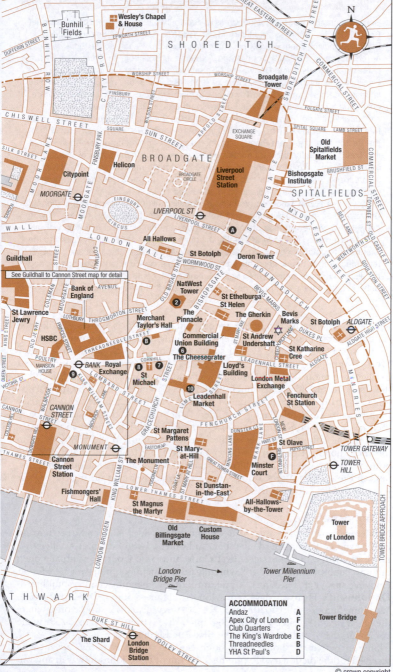

ACCOMMODATION

Andaz	A
Apex City of London	F
Club Quarters	C
The King's Wardrobe	E
Threadneedles	B
YHA St Paul's	D

© crown copyright

Samuel Pepys

Born to a humble tailor and a laundress in Salisbury Court, off Fleet Street, **Samuel Pepys** (1633–1703) was baptized in St Bride's (see opposite) and buried in St Olave's, having spent virtually his entire life in London. Family connections secured an education at St Paul's School and Pepys, a scholarship to Cambridge and a career in the civil service. He was an MP, served as Secretary to the Admiralty, and was instrumental in the establishment of a professional British navy. In 1679 he was imprisoned for six weeks in the Tower on suspicion of treason, but returned to office, only to be forced out again in 1689, following the overthrow of James II.

Of course, it's not Pepys' career, but his **diaries**, written between 1660 and 1669, that have immortalized him. This rollicking journal includes eyewitness accounts of the Restoration, the Great Plague and the Great Fire, giving an unparalleled insight into London life at the time. Ultimately, Pepys emerges from the pages, warts and all, as an eminently likeable character, who seems almost imperturbable – he gives as much space to details of his pub meals as he does to the Great Fire, and finishes most entries with his catchphrase "and so to bed".

Pepys was also a notorious womanizer, detailing his philanderings in his diary in Spanish so as to avoid detection by his French Huguenot wife. Nevertheless he was caught *in flagrante* with one of her best friends, and his slow reconciliation with his spouse is recorded in a novelist's detail, the diary ending in 1669 as they sail off to the Continent to patch things up. In the event, his wife died later that year and he never remarried. Pepys bequeathed his vast library to his old college in Cambridge, and his diaries lay there undiscovered until the nineteenth century, when they were finally published (with the erotic passages omitted) for the first time in 1825.

you've no interest in Pepys, the wood-panelled room is worth a look as it contains a very fine Jacobean plasterwork ceiling and original stained glass.

Opposite Prince Henry's Room stands the church of **St Dunstan-in-the-West** (Mon–Fri 11am–2pm; ☎020/7405 1929, ⓦwww.stdunstaninthewest.org), whose distinctive neo-Gothic tower and lantern dominate this top end of the street. To the side is the much earlier clock temple, erected by the parishioners in thanks for escaping the Great Fire; within the temple, the legendary British giants Gog and Magog, in gilded loincloths, nod their heads and clang their bells on the hour. The statue of Queen Elizabeth I, in a niche in the vestry wall, and the crumbling statues of the legendary King Lud and his two sons in the vestry porch, originally stood over Ludgate, the gateway into the City at the bottom of Fleet Street. The church's unusual, octagonal, neo-Gothic interior, built in the 1830s, features a huge wooden iconostasis, used during the regular Romanian Orthodox services.

Dr Johnson's House

Numerous narrow alleyways lead off the north side of Fleet Street beyond Fetter Lane, concealing legal chambers and offices. Two of the narrow alleyways that lead north off Fleet Street – Bolt Court and Hind Court – eventually open out into cobbled Gough Square, which features a statue of Johnson's cat, Hodge, enjoying an oyster. The square's one authentic eighteenth-century building is **Dr Johnson's House** (May–Sept Mon–Sat 11am–5.30pm; Oct–April Mon–Sat 11am–5pm; £4.50; ☎020/7353 3745, ⓦwww.drjohnsonshouse.org), where the great savant, writer and lexicographer lived from 1748 to 1759 while compiling the 41,000 entries for the first English dictionary.

Johnson rented the house on Gough Square with the £1575 advance he received for the dictionary. Despite his subsequent fame, Johnson was in and out of debt all his life – his famous philosophical romance, *Rasselas*, was written in less than a week to raise funds for his mother's funeral. The house itself is a lovely Georgian period piece peppered with quotes by the great man and portraits of his contemporaries, including Johnson's servant Francis Barber, to whom he left most of his wordly goods. On the second floor, you can watch a video on Johnson's life, after which you get to see the open-plan attic, in which Johnson and his six clerks put together the dictionary, and where kids can try on some replica Georgian garb.

Ludgate Circus

Fleet Street terminates at **Ludgate Circus**, built in the 1870s to replace a bridge over the **River Fleet**, which had already been buried under the roads after a drunken butcher got stuck in the river mud and froze to death. The Fleet marked the western boundary of the Roman city, and was once an unmissable feature of the landscape, as the tanneries and slaughterhouses of Smithfield used to turn the water red with entrails. The western bank of the Fleet was the site of the notoriously inhumane **Fleet Prison**, whose famous incumbents included the poet John Donne, imprisoned here for marrying without his father-in-law's consent. Until 1754, Fleet Prison was renowned for its clandestine "**Fleet Marriages**", performed by priests (or impostors) who were imprisoned there for debt. These marriages, in which couples could marry without a licence, attracted people of all classes, and took place in the prison chapel until 1710, when they were banished to the neighbouring taverns, the fee being split between clergyman and innkeeper.

The Fleet Street press

Fleet Street's associations with the printed press began in 1500, when Wynkyn de Worde, William Caxton's apprentice (and the first man to print italics), moved the Caxton presses here from Westminster to be close to the lawyers of the Inns of Court (his best customers) and to the clergy of St Paul's, the city's largest literate group. In 1702, the world's first daily newspaper, the now defunct **Daily Courant**, began publishing here, and by the nineteenth century, all the major national and provincial dailies had moved to the area. Then in 1985, Britain's first colour tabloid, *Today*, appeared, using computer technology that rendered the Fleet Street presses obsolete. It was left to media tycoon Rupert Murdoch to take on the printers' unions in a bitter year-long dispute that changed the face of the newspaper industry for ever.

The press headquarters that once dominated the area have all now relocated, leaving just a handful of small publications and a few architectural landmarks to testify to 500 years of printing history. The former **Daily Telegraph** building, at nos. 135–141, is one of London's few truly Art Deco edifices, built in a Greco-Egyptian style in 1928, with a striking polychrome clock and a great stone relief above the doorway depicting Mercury's messengers sending news around the world. It was upstaged a few years later, however, by the city's first glass curtain-wall construction, the former **Daily Express** building at no. 127, with its sleek black Vitrolite facade. It's worth peering inside the cinema-like foyer, which features a silver-leaf sunburst ceiling, ocean-wave floor tiles, shiny silver serpent handrails, and remarkable chrome and gold relief panels extolling the British Empire.

The best source of information about Fleet Street's history is the little exhibition in the crypt of **St Bride's Church** (Mon–Fri 9am–5pm, Sat 11am–3pm; ☏020/7427 0133, ⊛www.stbrides.com), the "journalists' and printers' cathedral", situated behind the former Reuters building. The church also boasts Wren's tallest, and most exquisite, spire (said to be the inspiration for the traditional tiered wedding cake).

St Paul's Cathedral

St Paul's Cathedral (Mon–Sat 8.30am–4pm; £11; ☎020/7236 4128, ⓦwww.stpauls.co.uk; St Paul's tube), topped by an enormous lead-covered dome, has been a London icon since the Blitz, when it stood defiantly unscathed amid the carnage (as in the famous wartime propaganda photo). It remains a dominating presence in the City, despite the encroaching tower blocks; its showpiece west facade is particularly magnificent, fronted by a wide flight of steps, a double-storey portico and two of London's most Baroque towers. Westminster Abbey, St Paul's long-standing rival, has the edge when it comes to celebrity corpses, pre-Reformation sculpture, royal connections and sheer atmosphere. St Paul's, by contrast, is a soulless but perfectly calculated architectural set piece, a burial place for captains rather than kings, and a popular wedding venue for the privileged few (including, most famously, Charles and Diana). The current building is the fifth church on this site, its immediate predecessor being **Old St Paul's**, a huge Gothic cathedral built by the Normans, whose 489-foot spire (destroyed by lightning in 1561) was one of the wonders of medieval Europe. The **Great Fire** caused irreparable damage to Old St Paul's, and Christopher Wren was given the task of building a replacement – just one of over fifty church commissions he received in the wake of the blaze. Hassles over money plagued the project throughout – at one point Parliament withheld half of Wren's salary because they felt the work was proceeding too slowly. Wren remained unruffled and rose to the challenge of building what was, in effect, the world's first Protestant cathedral, completing the commission in 1710 during the reign of Queen Anne, whose statue still stands in front of the west facade.

The interior

Queen Victoria thought the **nave** "dirty, dark and undevotional", though since the destruction of the stained glass in the Blitz, it is once again light and airy, as Wren intended. Burials are confined to the crypt, and memorials were only permitted after 1790 when overcrowding at Westminster Abbey had become intolerable. Unfortunately, what followed was a series of overblown funerary monuments to the military victims of the Napoleonic Wars. Some are simply ludicrous, like the virtually naked statue of Captain Burges, in the south aisle, holding hands with an angel over a naval cannon; others are mildly offensive, such as the monument to Thomas Fanshaw Middleton, first Protestant Bishop of India, depicted baptizing "heathen" locals. The best of the bunch are Flaxman's **Nelson** memorial, in the south transept, with its seasick lion, and, in the north aisle, the

Visiting the cathedral

Admission charges are nothing new at St Paul's – they were first introduced in 1709, before the cathedral was even finished. Once inside, pick up a free plan, and simply ask the vergers if you're having trouble locating a particular monument. Alternatively, **audioguides** are available for £4, and there are regular **guided tours** (1hr 30min; £3), plus a behind-the-scenes triforium tour (☎020/7246 8357; £12). It's worth attending one of the cathedral's **services**, if only to hear the choir, who perform during most evensongs (Mon–Sat 5pm), and on Sundays at 10.15am, 11.30am and 3.15pm. Strictly speaking, on Sundays St Paul's is only open for services and consequently there's no admission charge. However, in between services, you're free to wander round the cathedral and crypt (though not the galleries).

bombastic bronze and marble monument – the cathedral's largest – to the **Duke of Wellington**, begun in 1857 but only topped with the statue of the duke astride his faithful steed, Copenhagen, in 1912. Both men are buried in the crypt.

The best place from which to appreciate the glory of St Paul's is beneath the **dome**, which was decorated (against Wren's wishes) by Thornhill's monochrome trompe-l'oeil frescoes, now rather upstaged by the adjacent gilded spandrels. St Paul's most famous work of art, *however*, hangs in the north transept: the crushingly symbolic *Light of the World* by the Pre-Raphaelite **Holman Hunt**, depicting Christ knocking at the handleless, bramble-strewn door of the human soul, which must be opened from within. The original is actually in Keble College, Oxford, though this copy was executed by the artist himself, some fifty years later in 1900.

By far the most richly decorated section of the cathedral is the **chancel**, in particular the spectacular, swirling, gilded Byzantine-style mosaics of birds, fish, animals and greenery, from the 1890s. The intricately carved oak and limewood choir stalls, and the imposing organ case, are the work of Grinling Gibbons. The north choir-aisle contains Henry Moore's *Mother and Child* sculpture and allows you to admire Jean Tijou's ornate black-and-gold **wrought-iron gates** that separate the aisles from the high altar. The latter features an extravagant Baroque baldachin, held up by barley-sugar columns and wrapped round with gilded laurel, created after the war to a design by Wren. Behind the high altar stands the **American Memorial Chapel**, dedicated to the 28,000 Americans based in Britain who lost their lives in World War II (check out the space rocket hidden in the carved wooden foliage of the far right-hand panel, a tribute to America's postwar space exploration). Leaving via the south choir-aisle, you'll find the upstanding shroud of **John Donne**, poet, preacher and one-time Dean of St Paul's, the only complete effigy to have survived from the previous cathedral.

The galleries

From the south transept, a series of stairs lead to the dome's three **galleries**, and they're well worth the climb. The initial 259 steps take you to the **Whispering Gallery**, so called because of its acoustic properties – words whispered to the wall on one side are audible 100ft away on the other, though it's often so busy you can't hear much above the hubbub. Another 119 steps up bring you to the exterior **Stone Gallery**, around the base of the dome, while the final 152 steel steps take you inside the dome's inner structure to the **Golden Gallery**, just below the golden ball and cross which top the cathedral. The views of the City and along the Thames are unbeatable – you should be able to identify the distinctive white facade of Wren's London house, next door to the Globe Theatre, from which he could contemplate his masterpiece. Before you ascend the last flight of stairs, be sure to look through the peephole in the floor, which looks down onto the monochrome marble floor beneath the dome, a truly terrifying sight.

The crypt

The entrance to the cathedral's vast **crypt** is on your left as you leave the south choir-aisle. The whitewashed walls make this one of the least atmospheric mausoleums you could imagine – a far cry from the nineteenth century, when visitors were shown around the tombs by candlelight.

The crypt boasts as many painters and architects as Westminster Abbey has poets, most of them stuffed into the southern aisle, known as **Artists' Corner**. Appropriately enough, it was Wren himself who started the trend, with a tomb inscribed: "*lector, si monumentum requiris, circumspice*" (reader, if you seek his monument, look around). Close to Wren are the graves of

▲ St Paul's Cathedral

Reynolds, Turner, Millais, Holman Hunt, Lord Leighton and Alma-Tadema; nearby there's a bust of Van Dyck, whose monument perished along with Old St Paul's. Over in the north aisle is the grave of Alexander Fleming, the discoverer of penicillin.

The crypt's two star tombs – those of **Nelson** and **Wellington** – occupy centre stage. Wellington's porphyry and granite monstrosity is set in its own mini-chapel, surrounded by memorials to illustrious British field marshals, while Nelson lies in a black marble sarcophagus originally designed for Cardinal Wolsey and later intended for Henry VIII and his third wife, Jane Seymour. As at Trafalgar Square, Nelson lies close to later admirals Jellicoe and Beatty (the last person to be buried in the cathedral, in 1936). Beyond are the cathedral shop, a café and the exit.

Paternoster Square and around

The Blitz destroyed Paternoster Row, immediately to the north of St Paul's, which had been the centre of the book trade since 1500. The postwar office complex that replaced it was torn down in the 1980s and supplanted by the softer, post-classical development of **Paternoster Square**, centred on a Corinthian column topped by a gilded urn, and, since 2004, home to the London Stock Exchange. One happy consequence of the square's redevelopment is that **Temple Bar**, the last surviving City gateway which once stood at the top of Fleet Street (see p.167), found its way back to London after a century of languishing in a park in Hertfordshire. Designed by Wren himself, the triumphal arch now forms the entrance to Paternoster Square from St Paul's, with the Stuart monarchs, James I and Charles II, and their consorts, occupying the niches.

St Paul's Churchyard, to the northeast of the cathedral, was also destroyed in the war. The churchyard's most famous feature was Paul's Cross – also known as "Pol's Stump" – where proclamations and political speeches were made from a wooden pulpit. Heretics were regularly executed on this spot, and in 1519 Luther's works were publicly burnt here, before Henry VIII changed sides and demanded the "preaching down" of papal authority from the same spot. The cross was destroyed by Cromwell and his followers, and is now commemorated by a column erected in 1910, topped by a gilded statue of St Paul, and diplomatically inscribed "amid such scenes of good and evil as make up human affairs, the conscience of the church and nation through five centuries found public utterance".

Blackfriars to Southwark Bridge

Most folk heading south from St Paul's are aiming for the Millennium Bridge (see p.231), Tate Modern and Bankside. However, instead of simply heading for the bridge, it's worth taking time to venture into the City's backstreets and alleyways, or go for a stroll along the Riverside Walk which now extends all the way from Blackfriars railway bridge to Tower Bridge.

Blackfriars

Blackfriars, where a Dominican monastery stood until the Dissolution, was once a fashionable district – Ben Jonson had a house here, as did Shakespeare, and, later, Van Dyck. Destroyed in the Great Fire, the area suffered little from wartime bombing and remains a warren of alleyways, courtyards and narrow streets, conveying something of the plan of the City before the Victorians, the German bombers and the 1960s brutalists did their worst. Wandering down Creed Lane and St Andrew's Hill, you'll come to the least costly of Wren's churches, St Andrew-by-the-Wardrobe (Mon–Fri 10am–4pm), named for the royal depot for furniture and armour once situated here. The nave is usually locked, but you can look through from the vestry at the simple, light interior, with its oak wood-panelling and attractive white plasterwork. To the north, off Carter Lane, you'll find various unexpected little streets and courtyards – like Wardrobe Place – that present a slice of the pre-Blitz City. Down the cobbles of Blackfriars Lane is the Apothecaries' Hall, prettiest of the City Livery Companies (see box, p.182), with a tiny doorway leading to a pastel-shaded seventeenth-century court. Round the corner in Blackfriars Court, near the site of the old monastery, is *The Black Friar*, which boasts a fantastically ornate Arts and Crafts pub interior (see p.400).

East to Cannon Street

Just below St Andrew-by-the-Wardrobe, the Church of Scientology (daily 9am–10pm; free; ☎020/7246 2700, ⓦwww.scientology-london.org; Blackfriars tube) has its multi-million-pound London headquarters at 146 Queen Victoria St. Built in the 1860s for the British and Foreign Bible Society, to look like an Italian *palazzo*, the building itself is worth admiring, and, if you're prepared to put up with the slightly creepy attendants, there's also a whole exhibition on L. Ron Hubbard, the American pulp-fiction writer and hypnotist who founded the Scientology cult.

A short way east stands the surprising little red-brick mansion of the College of Arms (Mon–Fri 10am–4pm; free; ☎020/7248 2762, ⓦwww.college-of -arms.gov.uk; Blackfriars tube), originally built round a courtyard in the 1670s but subsequently opened up to the south with the building of the new road.

Dick Whittington

The City's Lord Mayor is elected on an annual basis, and the most famous Lord Mayor of the lot is **Dick Whittington** (c.1350–1423) of pantomime fame. The third son of a wealthy Gloucestershire family, Whittington was an apprentice mercer, dealing in silks and velvets, who rose to become one of the richest men in the City by the age of just 21. He was an early philanthropist, establishing a library at Greyfriars' monastery and a refuge for single mothers at St Thomas' Hospital, and building one of the city's first public lavatories, a unisex 128-seater known as "Whittington's Night Soil House of Easement". The pantomime story appeared some 200 years after Whittington's death, though quite how he became the fictional ragamuffin who comes to London after hearing the streets are paved with gold, no one seems to know. Traditionally, Whittington is leaving London with his knapsack and cat, when he hears the Bow Bells ring out "Turn again, Whittington, thrice Lord Mayor of London" (he was, in fact, mayor on four occasions and was never knighted as the story claims). The theory on the cat is that it was a common name for a coal barge at the time, and Whittington is thought to have made much of his fortune in the coal trade. There's a statue on Highgate Hill commemorating the very spot where Dick allegedly heard the Bow Bells, and a stained-glass window in St Michael Paternoster Royal, on Skinner's Lane, near where he lived.

The Earl Marshal's Court – featuring a gallery, copious wooden panelling and a modest throne – is the only room open to the public, unless you apply to trace your family or study heraldry in the college library. Amid the roar of traffic, Wren's Dutch-looking church of **St Benet** (now a Welsh Church; only open first Mon in month 11am–3.30pm or for its Welsh-language services Sun 11am & 2.30pm), opposite, with its distinctive chequered quoins, completes this vignette of seventeenth-century London.

There are several more Wren churches in the vicinity, the best of which is **St James Garlickhythe** (Mon–Fri 10.30am–4pm; free; Ⓦ www.stjames garlickhythe.org.uk; Mansion House tube), on Upper Thames Street, named after the garlic that used to be sold at a nearby wharf. Damaged in the Blitz, and again in 1991 when a crane crashed through the south rose window, the interior nevertheless remains much as Wren designed it, with the highest roof in the City after St Paul's, generously lit by clear arched windows in the clerestory, an arrangement which earned it the nickname of "Wren's Lantern".

Newgate to Smithfield

The area to the northwest of St Paul's is one of the most interesting parts of the City. The financial and business sectors play a more minor role here, the three most important institutions being the criminal court at the **Old Bailey**, on the site of the old **Newgate Prison**; **St Bartholomew's**, the only hospital still to occupy its original medieval site; and the meat market at **Smithfield**, last of the ancient City markets.

Old Bailey

London's Central Criminal Court is better known as the **Old Bailey** (Mon–Fri 10am–1pm & 2–5pm; Ⓣ 020/7248 3277, Ⓦ www.hmcourts-service.gov.uk; St Paul's tube) after the street on which it stands, which used to form the outer wall of the medieval city. The court's pompous, domed, Edwardian building – "Defend the Children of the Poor & Punish the Wrongdoer" the entrance proclaims – is topped by a gilded statue of Justice, unusually depicted without blindfold, holding her sword and scales. The country's most serious criminal court cases take place here, and have included, in the past, the trials of Lord Haw-Haw, the Kray twins, the Angry Brigade (see p.298), the Guildford Four and Birmingham Six "IRA bombers", and all Britain's multiple murderers. You can watch the proceedings from the visitors' gallery (no under-14s), but you're not allowed to take anything into the court and there's no cloakroom. It's worth venturing inside, however, if only to see the Grand Hall, with its swirling marble floor and walls, succession of domes, and grandiloquent frescoes.

The site of the Old Bailey was originally occupied by **Newgate Prison**, which began life as a small lock-up above the medieval gateway into the City and was burnt down during the 1780 Gordon Riots, only to be rebuilt as "a veritable Hell, worthy of the imagination of Dante", as one of its more famous inmates, Casanova, put it. Earlier well-known temporary residents included Thomas Malory, who wrote *Le Morte d'Arthur* while imprisoned here for murder (among other things); Daniel Defoe, who was put inside for his *The Shortest Way with Dissenters*; Ben Jonson, who served time for murder; and Christopher Marlowe, who was on a charge of atheism.

St Bartholomew's Hospital

North of the Old Bailey on Giltspur Street lies **St Bartholomew's Hospital** (Ⓦ www.bartsandthelondon.nhs.uk; St Paul's tube) – affectionately known as Bart's. The oldest hospital in London, Bart's began as an Augustinian priory and hospice in 1123, founded by Rahere, court jester to Henry I, on the

Public executions and body snatchers

After 1783, when hangings at Tyburn were stopped, **public executions** drew the crowds to Newgate, with more than 100,000 turning up on some occasions. The last public beheading took place here in 1820 when five Cato Street Conspirators (see p.95) were hanged and decapitated with a surgeon's knife. It was in hanging, however, that Newgate excelled, its most efficient gallows dispatching twenty criminals simultaneously. Unease over the "robbery and violence, loud laughing, oaths, fighting, obscene conduct and still more filthy language" that accompanied public hangings drove the executions inside the prison walls in 1868. The night before an execution, a handbell was tolled outside the condemned's cell, while the jailer recited the Newgate verse, bellowing the last two lines: "All you that in the condemned hole do lie/Prepare you, for tomorrow you shall die.... And when St Sepulchre's bell in the morning tolls/The Lord above have mercy on your souls." Until Newgate got its own bell, the "Great Bell of Old Bailey" was in the church of **St Sepulchre** (Tues 5–7pm, Wed 11am–3pm, Thurs noon–2pm; Ⓦ www.st-sepulchre .org.uk), and tolled the condemned to the scaffold at eight in the morning. The handbell and verse are displayed inside the church, opposite the Old Bailey.

The bodies of the executed were handed over to the surgeons of St Bartholomew's for dissection, but body snatchers also preyed on non-criminals buried in the St Sepulchre churchyard. Such was the demand for corpses that relatives were forced to pay a night watchman to guard the graveyard in a specially built watch-house – which still stands to the north of the church – in order to prevent the "Resurrection Men" from retrieving their quarry. Successfully stolen stiffs were taken to the nearby *Fortune of War* tavern, on Pie Corner, at the junction of Cock Lane, to be sold to the surgeons. Today, Pie Corner is marked by a gilded overfed cherub known as **Fat Boy**, who commemorates the "staying of the Great Fire", which, when it wasn't blamed on the Catholics, was ascribed to the sin of gluttony, since it had begun in Pudding Lane and ended at Pie Corner.

orders of St Bartholomew, who appeared to him in a vision while he was in malarial delirium on a pilgrimage to Rome. The priory was dissolved by Henry VIII, but in 1546, with just two weeks left to live, Henry agreed to re-found the hospital.

There's a statue of Henry in the main gateway, built in 1702, and one of a lame man and a melancholic man above the broken pediment. Further along, you can make out shrapnel marks left from a 1916 Zeppelin air raid. Through the gateway on the left stands the church of **St Bartholomew-the-Less** (daily 7am–8pm), sole survivor of the priory's four chapels. The tower and vestry are fifteenth-century, the octagonal interior is neo-Gothic, though it does contain a Tudor memorial to Elizabeth I's surgeon. Beyond the church lies three-quarters of the courtyard created for the hospital by James Gibbs in the mid-eighteenth century, including the **Great Hall** and the **Grand Staircase**, its walls decorated with biblical murals that were painted free of charge by Hogarth, who was born and baptized nearby and served as one of the hospital's governors.

You can get a glimpse of the staircase from inside **St Bartholomew's Museum** (Tues–Fri 10am–4pm; free), on the left, under the archway into the courtyard. Among the medical artefacts, there are some fearsome amputation instruments, a pair of leather "lunatic restrainers", some great jars with labels such as "poison – for external use only", and a cricket bat autographed by W.G. Grace, who was a student at Bart's in the 1870s. To see the Great Hall join one of the fascinating weekly **guided tours** (Fri 2pm; £5), which take in the surrounding area as well; the meeting point is the Henry VIII Gate.

St Bartholomew-the-Great

Hidden in the backstreets north of the hospital is London's oldest and most atmospheric parish church, **St Bartholomew-the-Great** (Mon–Fri 8.30am–5pm, Sat 10.30am–1.30pm, Sun 8.30am–1pm & 2.30–8pm; mid-Nov to mid-Feb Tues–Fri closes 4pm; £4; ☎020/7606 5171, ⓦwww.greatstbarts.com; Barbican tube). Begun in 1123 as the priory's main church, it was partly demolished in the Reformation, and gradually fell into ruins: the cloisters were used as a stable, there was a Nonconformist boys' school in the triforium, a coal and wine cellar in the crypt, a blacksmith's in the north transept and a printing press (where Benjamin Franklin worked for a while) in the Lady Chapel. From 1887, what was left of the old church was restored, the chequered patterning patched up and the flintwork that now characterizes the exterior added. Much beloved of film companies (*Shakespeare in Love* and *Four Weddings and a Funeral* both shot scenes here), in 2007 it became the first parish church in the country to charge an entrance fee.

To get an idea of the scale of the original church, approach it through the half-timbered Tudor **gatehouse**, on Little Britain Street, which was discovered after the aforementioned Zeppelin raid. A wooden statue of St Bartholomew stands in a niche, holding the knife with which he was flayed; below is the thirteenth-century arch which once formed the entrance to the nave. The churchyard now stands where the nave itself would have been, and one side of the **cloisters** survives to the south. The rest is a confusion of elements, including portions of the transepts and, most impressively, the **chancel**, where thick Norman pillars separate the main body from the ambulatory. There are various pre-Fire monuments, the most prominent being Rahere's tomb, which shelters under a fifteenth-century canopy north of the altar, with an angel at his feet and two canons kneeling beside him reading from the prophets. Beyond the ambulatory lies the large Lady Chapel, mostly nineteenth-century, though with original stonework here and there.

Smithfield

The ground was covered, nearly ankle-deep with filth and mire; a thick steam perpetually rising from the reeking bodies of the cattle, and mingling with the fog.

Charles Dickens, *Oliver Twist*

Blood and guts were regularly spilled at **Smithfield** long before the meat market was legally sanctioned here in the seventeenth century. Open ground outside the City walls (its name is a corruption of "Smooth Field"), it was used as a horse fair in Norman times, and later for jousts and tournaments. In 1381, the poll-tax rebels under **Wat Tyler** assembled here to negotiate with the boy-king Richard II. At the meeting Lord Mayor Walworth pulled Tyler from his horse and stabbed him, after which he was bustled into Bart's for treatment, only to be dragged out by the king's men and beheaded.

Smithfield subsequently became a venue for **public executions**. The Scottish hero, William Wallace, was dragged behind a horse from the Tower, then hanged, drawn and quartered here in 1305, and the Bishop of Rochester's cook was boiled alive in 1531, but the local speciality was burnings. These reached a peak during the reign of "Bloody" Mary in the 1550s, when hundreds of Protestants were burnt at the stake for their beliefs, in revenge for the Catholics who had suffered a similar fate under Henry VIII, and Edward VI; a plaque on the side of Bart's commemorates some of those who died. Even more popular than the public executions was **St Bartholomew's Fair**, established by Rahere in order to fund Bart's. Rahere himself used to perform juggling tricks, while Pepys reports seeing a horse counting sixpences and, more reliably, a puppet show of Ben Jonson's play *Bartholomew Fair*. Predictably enough, it was the Victorians who closed it down to protect public morals.

The meat **market**, with which Smithfield is now synonymous, grew up as a kind of adjunct to the fair. Live cattle continued to be herded into Smithfield until 1852, when the fair was suppressed and the abattoirs moved out to Islington. A new covered market hall was erected in 1868, along with the "Winkle", a spiral ramp at the centre of West Smithfield, linked to the market's very own (now defunct) tube station. Smithfield subsequently tripled in size and remains London's main meat market – the action starts around 4am and is all over by noon.

Barbican

The City's only large residential complex is the ugly concrete ghetto of the **Barbican**, built on the heavily bombed Cripplegate area. It's a classic 1970s urban dystopia, a maze of pedestrian walkways and underground car parks,

> ### Postman's Park
>
> Opposite the former General Post Office building, southeast of Smithfield, lies **Postman's Park**, one of the most curious and little-visited corners of the City. Here, in 1900, in the churchyard of St Botolph, Aldersgate, the painter and sculptor George Frederick Watts paid for a national memorial to "heroes of everyday life", a patchwork of majolica tiles inscribed with the names of ordinary folk who had died in the course of some act of bravery. It exhibits the classic Victorian sentimental fascination with death, and makes for macabre but compelling reading: "Drowned in attempting to save his brother after he himself had just been rescued" or "Saved a lunatic woman from suicide at Woolwich Arsenal station, but was himself run over by the train".

pinioned by three 400-foot tower blocks. At the centre of the complex is the **Barbican Arts Centre** (Ⓦwww.barbican.org.uk), home to the London Symphony Orchestra, two performance spaces, a three-screen cinema, a rooftop garden, a public library and an art gallery. Sadly, the arts centre's obtusely confusing layout continues to prove user-repellent; just finding the main entrance on Silk Street is quite a feat, even for Londoners. The complex's solitary prewar building is the heavily restored early Tudor church of **St Giles-without-Cripplegate** (Mon–Fri 10am–4pm; free; Ⓣ020/7638 1997, Ⓦwww .stgilescripplegate.com), now bracketed between a pair of artificial lakes. It was here that Oliver Cromwell was married in 1620 and John Milton buried in 1674 – he was subsequently exhumed in 1793, his teeth knocked out as souvenirs and his corpse exhibited to the public until the novelty wore off.

Museum of London

Hidden in the southwestern corner of the Barbican complex is the **Museum of London** (daily 10am–5.50pm; free; Ⓣ020/7001 9844, Ⓦwww.museum oflondon.org.uk; Barbican or St Paul's tube), whose permanent galleries are basically an educational trot through London's past from prehistory to the present day, illustrated by the city's major archeological finds and some great scale models. The real strength of the museum, however, lies in the excellent temporary exhibitions, gallery tours, lectures, walks and videos it organizes throughout the year.

The permanent displays start on the upper floor (where visitors enter), with a section on **London Before London**. Here, you'll find a cave-bear skull from half a million years ago, Neolithic flint tools, not to mention a lion skull, a hippo's tooth, an auroch's skull and an elephant's foot. The **Roman London** section includes the Bucklersbury mosaic floor, discovered during Victorian road-building projects and now displayed in a mock-up of a wealthy Roman dining room. There are also gold coins, marble busts from the Temple of Mithras (see p.184), and mock-up Roman shop displays. Highlights in the **Medieval London** section include a reconstructed Saxon home, a model of Old St Paul's and a wonderfully over-the-top video on the Black Death.

The museum's post-1666 galleries are all undergoing redevelopment until 2010, after which you should once more be able to see Nelson's Sword of Honour, a pair of Wellington's boots, and the **Lord Mayor's Coach**, which rivals the Queen's in sheer weight of gold decoration.

Guildhall and around

Situated at the geographical centre of the Square Mile, **Guildhall** (daily 10am–5pm; Oct–April closed Sun; free; Ⓣ020/7606 3030, Ⓦwww.cityoflondon .gov.uk; Bank tube) was the seat of the City administration for over eight hundred years, and remains the headquarters of the Corporation of London. Architecturally, it no longer exudes quite the municipal wealth it once did, having been badly damaged in both the Great Fire and the Blitz, its courtyard scarred by the addition of a 1970s concrete cloister and wing. To visit the **Great Hall** you must approach from the reception on the west side of the courtyard, not the quasi-Indian porch, tacked on in the eighteenth century. Venue in 1553 for the high-treason trials of Lady Jane Grey and her husband, Lord Dudley, and, three years later, for Archbishop Cranmer, the Great Hall is still used for various state functions. The interior is basically a postwar reconstruction of the fifteenth-century original, complete with a minstrels' gallery from which statues of the pagan giants Gog and Magog look down.

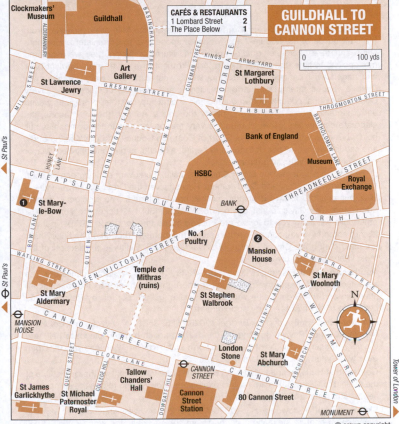

Guildhall Art Gallery

On the east side of the courtyard stands the **Guildhall Art Gallery** (Mon–Sat 10am–5pm, Sun noon–4pm; £2.50, free Fri and after 3.30pm; ☏020/7332 3700), a neo-Gothic pastiche purpose-built in 1999 by one of the Gilbert Scott family. As you might expect, there's plenty of pomp and pageantry, especially in the main gallery, where you'll find lots of dull, official portraits of royals, aldermen and mayors. Also hiding up here is a marble statue of **Margaret Thatcher**, now surrounded by a protective glass cabinet after the head was knocked off by a protester in 2002. The centrepiece of the gallery is the gigantic and very dramatic *Defeat of the Floating Batteries at Gibraltar*, by **John Singleton Copley**, depicting the Brits magnanimously saving the drowning enemy from flaming barques during the 1782 Siege of Gibraltar. Commissioned by the Corporation, poor old Copley had to redo the entire thing when the garrison officers insisted on having more prominence.

More intriguing is the gallery's wide range of paintings depicting **London subjects** – bygone vistas of old London, postwar bomb sites and so on – which are sprinkled throughout the rooms. On the ground floor, you'll also find a small sample of works by the English artist **Matthew Smith** (1879–1959), who

The City Livery Companies

The hundred or so **City Livery Companies** in the Square Mile are descended from the craft guilds of the Middle Ages, whose purpose was to administer apprenticeships and take charge of quality control, in return for which they were granted monopolies. In time, the guilds began to build themselves ever more opulent halls and staged lavish banquets at which they would wear elaborate "livery" (or uniforms). Despite various attempts to introduce democracy over the centuries, the Livery Companies remain deeply undemocratic and anomalous, but their prodigious wealth and charitable works have helped pacify the critics. As with the freemasons, the elaborate ceremonies serve to hide the very real power that these companies still hold. Liverymen still dominate the Court of Common Council, the City's ruling body, and as Aldermen, they take it in turns to be first a Sheriff, and eventually Lord Mayor – a knighthood is virtually guaranteed.

The City boasts numerous Livery Company halls, many with enticing names such as the Tallow Chandlers and Cordwainers. Few survived the Great Fire, fewer still the Blitz, but a handful are worth visiting for their ornate interiors. The problem is gaining **admission**. The City's tourist office (☎020/7332 1456) has tickets to some halls; other halls will allow you to join a pre-booked group tour for around £5 per person. It's not something you can do on the spur of the moment, though some Livery halls are used during the City of London Festival (see p.29). Below is a selection of the most interesting City Livery halls:

Apothecaries' Hall Blackfriars Lane ☎020/7236 1189, ⊛www.apothecaries.org. The seventeenth-century courtyard is open to the public, but entry to the magnificent staircase and the Great Hall – with its musicians' gallery, portrait by Reynolds and collection of leech pots – is by appointment.

Fishmongers' Hall London Bridge ☎020/7626 3531, ⊛www.fishhall.co.uk. A prominent Greek Revival building on the riverfront, with a grand staircase hall, and the very dagger with which Mayor Walworth stabbed Wat Tyler (see p.179). Open days twice yearly; Mon 10.30am & 2.30pm; £5.

Goldsmiths' Hall Foster Lane ☎020/7606 7010, ⊛www.thegoldsmiths.co.uk. One of the easiest to visit as there are regular exhibitions allowing you to see the sumptuous central staircase built in the 1830s. Free.

Skinners' Hall 8 Dowgate Hill ☎020/7236 5629, ⊛www.skinnershall.co.uk. The seventeenth-century staircase and courtroom survive, while the wood-panelled hall contains a wonderful series of Frank Brangwyn murals from 1902. Open days three times yearly; £5.

Tallow Chandlers' Hall 4 Dowgate Hill ☎020/7248 4726, ⊛www.tallowchandlers .org. Set back from the street around an attractive courtyard, the Candlemakers' Company retains its seventeenth-century courtroom, complete with original seating. By appointment only.

Vintners' Hall 68 Upper Thames St ☎020/7236 1863, ⊛www.vintnershall.co.uk. The oldest hall in the City, dating from 1671, with a period-piece staircase with "fabulously elaborate balusters". By appointment only.

was heavily influenced by Cézanne's late works and Matisse's Fauvist phase. Some of the best works are in the **Victorian galleries**, which are packed floor to ceiling with works by prosperous artists such as G.F. Watts, Alma–Tadema and Lord Leighton. A few exceptional paintings are worth seeking out: **Constable**'s full-sized oil sketch of *Salisbury Cathedral*, characterized by loose brushwork and an air of foreboding; **Holman Hunt**'s *The Eve of St Agnes* (inspired by Keats' poem), painted while he was still a student at the RA, and bought by the gallery's first director out of his own pocket; and **Rossetti**'s *La Ghirlandata*, a typically lush portrait, in intense blues and greens, of a model who's a dead ringer for Jane Morris, with whom the artist was infatuated.

During the gallery's construction a **Roman amphitheatre**, dating from around 120 AD, was discovered. The foundations of the amphitheatre's eastern entrance are all that remain, displayed in the basement, but they give you a hint of the vast size of the original arena, which would have held up to six thousand. (The outline of the amphitheatre is marked out on the pavement in the Guildhall courtyard.)

Clockmakers' Museum

From the Guildhall reception, on the west side of the courtyard, you can reach the **Clockmakers' Museum** (Mon–Sat 9.30am–4.30pm; free; ☎020/7332 1868, ⓦwww.clockmakers.org), run by the Worshipful Company of Clockmakers. Here, you'll find everything from Tudor pocket watches to grandfather clocks, which ring out in unison on the hour. Highlights include an orrery clock, a rolling ball clock (of the kind invented by William Congreve), a water clock, the ghoulish skull watch, once believed to have been given by Mary Queen of Scots to her maid-of-honour and the watch used by Edmund Hillary on Everest. Of particular interest is the collection of marine chronometers including the earliest known clock made by **John Harrison** (1693–1776), along with his brother, when he was only 20, his personal pair-case watch, and the prototype for the H4 clock that won him the Longitude Prize (see p.327). Pride of place, though, goes to H5, tested by George III himself at Richmond observatory, which won Harrison (more or less) the full prize money. Next to the clock museum is the Guildhall **library**, which puts on small temporary exhibitions, and the excellent Guildhall **bookshop**, specializing in books on London.

St Lawrence Jewry

Across the courtyard from the Guildhall stands Wren's church of **St Lawrence Jewry** (Mon–Thurs 8am–1pm; recitals Mon & Tues 1pm), whose smart interior reflects its role as the official Corporation of London church. Opened in 1677 in the presence of Charles II, but gutted during the Blitz, the church's handsome, wide, open-plan interior is well worth a peek for its richly gilded plasterwork ceiling. As the name indicates, this was once the site of London's **Jewish ghetto**. Old Jewry, the street two blocks east, was the nucleus of the quarter, containing a synagogue that was confiscated by the City authorities in 1272, shortly before the bloody expulsion of the entire community by Edward I.

Cheapside and Bow Lane

Cheapside, south of the Guildhall, was once the City's foremost medieval marketplace. Nowadays only the names of the nearby streets – Bread Street, Milk Street, Honey Lane, Poultry – recall its former prominence, which faded when the shops and their customers began to move to the West End from the eighteenth century onwards. The only distinguishing feature of Cheapside is Wren's church of **St Mary-le-Bow** (Mon–Thurs 7am–6pm, Fri 7am–4pm; ⓦwww.stmarylebow.co.uk), whose handsome tower features each of the five classical orders, a granite obelisk and a dragon weather vane. The tower also contains postwar replicas of the famous "Bow Bells", which sounded the 9pm curfew for Londoners from the fourteenth to the nineteenth centuries, and within whose earshot all true Cockneys are born. The original interior was totally destroyed in the Blitz and contains little of interest, but the church crypt is home to a veggie café, *The Place Below* (see p.386).

Down the side of St Mary-le-Bow runs **Bow Lane**: narrow, pedestrianized, and jam-packed at weekday lunchtimes with office workers heading for its sandwich bars and pubs. At its southern end lies the church of **St Mary Aldermary** (Mon–Fri 11am–3pm; Ⓦ www.stmaryaldermary.co.uk), whose interior is a rare foray into the perpendicular Gothic style by Wren, based on the original church – the plaster fan-vaults and saucer domes in the aisles are the highlight.

Just to the east, in the shadow of an office block on the other side of Queen Victoria Street, are the remains of a **Temple of Mithras**, discovered in 1954. Mithraism was a male-only cult popular among the Roman legions before the advent of Christianity. Its Persian deity, Mithras, is always depicted slaying a cosmic bull, while a scorpion grasps its genitals and a dog licks its wounds – the bull's blood was seen as life-giving, and initiates had to bathe in it. The foundations of the third-century temple give little impression of what the building would have been like – the rich finds and reconstruction in the Museum of London offer a better idea.

One of London's most esoteric sights is the **London Stone**, a small block of limestone lodged behind an iron grille set low into the exterior wall of 111 Cannon St, at the corner of St Swithin's Lane. To some it is London's omphalos, its geomantic centre; to the uninitiated, it looks more like a lump of Roman masonry. Whatever your reaction to this bizarre relic, it has been around for some considerable time, certainly since the 1450 Peasants' Revolt, when the Kentish rebel Jack Cade struck it, declaring himself "Lord of the City".

Bank and around

Bank lies at the heart of the City's finance sector and is the busy meeting point of eight streets. It's an impressive architectural set piece, overlooked by a handsome collection of Neoclassical buildings – among them the Bank of England, the Royal Exchange and Mansion House – each one faced in Portland stone.

By far the most graceful of the trio is the **Royal Exchange**, twice destroyed by fire since it was first built in 1570 at the personal expense of the "King's Merchant", Thomas Gresham (his gilded grasshopper flies from the roof), as a meeting place for City merchants. The current building, fronted by a massive eight-column portico and a very convenient set of steps for lunching office workers, was built in the 1840s. Nowadays, the building is filled with super swish shops especially around the inner courtyard, with its beautifully tiled floor, glazed roof and half-columns in three classical orders.

Mansion House, the Lord Mayor's sumptuous Neoclassical lodgings during his or – on only one occasion so far – her term of office, is now open to the public for guided tours (Tues 2pm; £6). Designed in 1753 by George Dance, the building's grandest room is the columned "Egyptian" Hall, with its barrel-vaulted, coffered ceiling. Also impressive is the vast collection of gold and silver tableware, the mayor's 36-pound gold mace and the pearl sword given by Elizabeth I and held out to the sovereign on visits to the City. Scattered about the rooms are an impressive array of Dutch and Flemish paintings by the likes of Hals, Ruisdael, Cuyp, Hobbema and de Hooch. Places are allocated on a first-come, first-served basis, so turn up at the Walbrook entrance in good time.

London's financial community first grew up around **Lombard Street**, off Bank, named after the region of northern Italy from which most of the bankers and goldsmiths originated. Most UK banks had their head offices here until the 1980s – only Lloyd's now remains. It's actually worth visiting the former Midland Bank headquarters, now a branch of **HSBC** at 27–32 Poultry; built by Edwin Lutyens between the wars, it features magnificent green African verdite

London's loos

Down gleaming walls of porc'lain flows the sluice
That out of sight decants the kidney juice
Thus pleasuring those gents for miles around
Who, crying for relief, once piped the sound
Of wind in alleyways...

This celebratory ode was composed by Josiah Feable for the opening, in 1855, of the first public flush lavatories, which were situated outside the Royal Exchange. There was a charge of one penny (hence the euphemism) and the toilets were gents-only – ladies had to hold theirs in until 1911, when new lavatories were built.

square columns, walnut counters, flying-saucer hanging lights and really comfy sofas. Many of the City's most sumptuous banking halls now serve as pubs and restaurants: one of the best is *The Counting House*, 50 Cornhill, with a gloriously flamboyant Victorian interior (see p.401).

Bank of England

Established by William III in 1694 to raise funds for his costly war against France, the **Bank of England**, the so-called "Grand Old Lady of Threadneedle Street", wasn't erected on its present site until 1734. The bank was attacked during the 1780 Gordon Riots, but never sacked thanks to the bank's clerks who melted down their inkwells into bullets. Subsequently a detachment of the Foot Guards, known as the Bank Picquet, was stationed outside until 1973. Security remains pretty tight at the bank, which still acts as a giant safe-deposit box, storing the official gold reserves of many of the world's central banks (though Britain's were moved to the Federal Reserve Bank of New York during World War II).

The windowless, outer curtain wall, which wraps itself round the 3.5-acre island site, is pretty much all that remains of John Soane's late eighteenth-century design. However, you can view a reconstruction of Soane's Bank Stock Office, with its characteristic domed skylight, in the **museum** (Mon–Fri 10am–5pm; free; ℡020/7601 5545, ⓦwww.bankofengland.co.uk; Bank tube), whose entrance is on Bartholomew Lane. The exhibition traces the history of the bank, banknotes and banking in general. Beyond, beneath a reconstruction of Herbert Baker's interwar rotunda (wrecked in the Blitz), you can caress a 13kg gold bar, worth over £250,000, and, elsewhere, view specimens of every note issued by the Royal Mint over the centuries (including a million pound note).

Bank's churches

Along the north side of the Bank of England, in Lothbury, is the tiny Wren church of **St Margaret Lothbury** (Mon–Fri 7am–5.15pm; ℡020/7606 4878, ⓦwww.stml.org.uk), whose plain interior harbours some of the finest furnishings of any City church. The most eye-catching is the magnificent screen, designed by Wren (for a different church, as it happens) and consisting of delicate, intertwined spiral columns either side of the main entrance, which features a segmental pediment and a huge eagle. Also worth a closer look is the wonderful hexagonal pulpit and tester, laden with carved putti, birds, fruit and flowers.

Along the west wall of Mansion House runs Walbrook, a street named after the shallow stream which provided Roman London with its fresh water. Here, you'll find the church of **St Stephen Walbrook** (Mon–Thurs 10am–4pm,

Fri 10am–3pm; ⓦststephenwalbrook.net), the Lord Mayor's official church and Wren's most spectacular after St Paul's. Faced with a fairly cramped site, Wren created a church of great space and light, with sixteen Corinthian columns arranged in clusters around a central coffered dome, which many regard as a practice run for his cathedral. The furnishings are mostly original, but the modern beech-wood pews jar, as does Henry Moore's altar, an amorphous blob of Travertine stone – nicknamed "The Camembert" – placed centrally right under the dome. The Samaritans were founded here by the local rector in 1953, and their first helpline telephone serves as a memorial in the church's southwest corner.

Hidden from the bustle of Bank itself, a short distance down King William Street, stands **St Mary Woolnoth** (Mon–Fri 9.30am–4.30pm), one of Nicholas Hawksmoor's six idiosyncratic London churches. The main facade is very imposing, with its twin turrets, Doric pillars and heavy rustication. Inside, in a cramped but lofty space, Hawksmoor manages to cram in a cluster of three big Corinthian columns at each corner, which support an ingenious lantern lit by semicircular clerestory windows. The most striking furnishing is the altar canopy, held up by barley-sugar columns and studded with seven golden cherubic faces. The church's projecting clock gets a brief mention in T.S. Eliot's *The Waste Land*.

A complete contrast to Hawskmoor's church is provided by Wren's **St Mary Abchurch** (Tues 10.30am–2.30pm), set in its own courtyard (the paved-over former graveyard) on Abchurch Lane, off King William Street. Nothing about the dour red-brick exterior prepares you for the interior, which is dominated by a vast dome fresco painted by a local parishioner and lit by oval lunettes, with the name of God in Hebrew centre stage. The lime-wood reredos, festooned with swags and garlands, and decorated with gilded urns and a pelican, is a Grinling Gibbons masterpiece.

Bishopsgate to the Tower

Financial institutions predominate in the easterly section of the Square Mile between Bishopsgate and the Tower, many of them housed in the brashest of the City's new architecture. In fact, the area's two most obvious landmarks are both temples of Mammon: the groundbreaking **Lloyd's Building** and the unmissable **Gherkin**. These, plus the Victorian splendour of **Leadenhall Market**, the oldest **synagogue** in the country, several pre-Fire churches and Wren's famous **Monument** to the Great Fire make for an especially interesting sector of the City to explore.

Liverpool Street and Broadgate

At the top of Bishopsgate stands **Liverpool Street Station**, the City's busiest terminal, renowned for its vibrantly painted wrought-iron Victorian arches. The station's Liverpool Street entrance features the **Kindertransport memorial**, depicting some of the Jewish children who arrived at the station from Nazi Germany, without their parents, shortly before war broke out. To the north and west of the station are the traffic-free piazzas of the **Broadgate** complex, built on a relatively human scale in the late 1980s. Richard Serra's rusting steel sheets act as a kind of gateway to the **Broadgate Circle**, whose arena is used as an open-air ice rink in winter and as a performance space in summer. The piazza to the west is decorated with the dismal sculptural commuters of *Rush Hour*. Continuing north to **Exchange Square**, built above the rail tracks themselves, you'll find a cascading waterfall, the hefty *Broadgate Venus* by Fernando Botero, and Xavier Corbero's *Broad Family* of obelisks, one of whose "children" reveals a shoe.

Bishopsgate

The northern end of **Bishopsgate** is dominated by bombastic office blocks – far more distinguished, though, is the faïence facade of the diminutive **Bishopsgate Institute** (Ⓦwww.bishopsgate.org.uk), a graceful Art-Nouveau building designed in 1894 by Harrison Townsend, across the road from Liverpool Street Station. (Townsend also designed the excellent Whitechapel Art Gallery and the wonderful Horniman Museum.)

South of the train station, the church of **St Botolph-without-Bishopsgate** (Mon–Fri 8am–5.30pm; Ⓦwww.botolph.org.uk) is named after the Anglo-Saxon abbot who cared for travellers. It's been restored seven times since the current building was erected in 1728, lastly after it was damaged by an IRA bomb in 1993, and the church's coved ceiling, with its undersized dome and lantern, added in 1828, currently looks as good as new. The churchyard contains an old charity school, decorated with a uniformed boy and girl, and a small ceramic and terracotta Turkish bathhouse (now an Italian restaurant).

On the opposite side of Bishopsgate, hemmed in by office blocks, is the "humble rag-faced front" of the pre-Fire church of **St Ethelburga** (Fri 11am–3pm; ☎020/7496 1610, Ⓦwww.stethelburgas.org). All but totally destroyed by IRA bombs in the early 1990s, the church now functions as a centre for reconciliation and peace, hosting regular events and workshops. Another pre-Fire church that suffered extensive damage in the IRA blasts is the late Gothic church of **St Helen** (Mon–Fri 9.30am–12.30pm & Mon, Wed & Fri 2–5pm; ☎020/7283 2231, Ⓦwww.st-helens.org.uk), set back to the east of Bishopsgate. With its undulating crenellations and Baroque bell turret, it's an intriguing building, incorporating the original Benedictine nunnery church and containing five grand pre-Fire tombs. Since the bomb, the floor level has been raised, the church screens shifted, a new organ gallery added and the seating rearranged to focus on the pulpit, in keeping with the church's current evangelical bent.

The Gherkin and Lloyd's

South of St Helen's is a bleak piazza overlooked by the giant 1960s Commercial Union skyscraper (now known confusingly as St Helen's), the first building in the city to top St Paul's. Nearby is Norman Foster's iconic, glass-diamond-clad **Gherkin**, officially known as 30 St Mary Axe. At 590ft, it's very tall, but most Londoners like it for its cheeky shape, and at street level it's a very modest building. You can't go up it, but you can grab a bite to eat on the ground floor.

At the southeast corner of the piazza is the medieval church of **St Andrew Undershaft**, named after the maypole which stood outside until it was torn

---

City skyscrapers

The economic recession notwithstanding, the City skyline is about to sprout a whole new generation of **skyscrapers**. Since 1980, the City's tallest building has been Tower 42, designed as the **NatWest Tower** by Richard Seifert (in the shape of the bank's logo, and over 600ft high). However, this looks set to be topped, first by **The Cheesegrater**, Richard Rogers' 737-foot triangular-shaped office block at 122 Leadenhall St, then by the **Heron Tower**, a 660-foot skyscraper with a 144-foot mast at 110 Bishopsgate, designed by Kohn Pedersen Fox, and finally by **The Pinnacle** (945ft), a swirling helter-skelter of a tower (with a restaurant on the top floor) at 22–24 Bishopsgate, also by Kohn Pedersen Fox. The City will then have outreached Canary Wharf, but it will still be ousted for the prize of the country's tallest building by Renzo Piano's 1017-foot **Shard**, near London Bridge (see p.237).

down as an object of pagan idolatry in 1549 by the curate from neighbouring St Katharine Cree. Inside is the tomb of John Stow, the humble tailor who wrote the first detailed account of the City in 1598. A memorial service is held here in April, during which the Lord Mayor replaces the quill pen in the tailor's hand; at other times, contact St Helen's.

Opposite St Andrew Undershaft, on Leadenhall Street, stands the **Lloyd's Building**, completed by Richard Rogers in 1984. "A living, breathing machine" of a building, it's a vertical version of Rogers' Pompidou Centre, a jumble of blue-steel pipes with glass lifts zipping up and down the exterior. It's a bizarre leap into the modern by this most conservative of City institutions – the portico of its previous, much more sedate building, from 1925, can still be seen to the west. Some things never change, though, and the building is still guarded by porters in antiquated waiters' livery, in recognition of Lloyd's modest origins in a coffee house. Lloyd's started out in shipping and is now the largest insurance market in the world. Lloyd's famous **Lutine Bell**, brought here from a captured French frigate that sank in 1799, was traditionally struck, once for bad news, twice for good, but now only tolls to commemorate disasters.

Just south of Lloyd's is **Leadenhall Market**, whose graceful Victorian cast-ironwork is richly painted in cream and maroon, with each of the four entrances to the covered arcade topped by an elaborate stone arch. Inside, the traders cater mostly for the lunchtime City crowd, their barrows laden with exotic seafood and game, fine wines, champagne and caviar, while the surrounding shops and bars remain busy until the early evening.

▲ Leadenhall Market

Bevis Marks Synagogue

Hidden away behind a red-brick office block in a little courtyard off Bevis Marks, at the north end of St Mary Axe, is the **Bevis Marks Synagogue** (Mon 10.30am–12.30pm, Tues & Wed 11am–1pm, summer Fri 11am–1pm; guided tours Wed & Fri noon, Sun 11.15am; £2; ☎020/7626 1274, ⓦwww.bevismarks .org.uk; Aldgate tube). Built in 1701 by Sephardic Jews who had fled the Inquisition in Spain and Portugal, this is the country's oldest surviving synagogue, and its roomy, rich interior gives an idea of just how wealthy the community was at the time. Although it seats over six hundred, it is only a third of the size of its prototype in Amsterdam, where many Sephardic Jews initially settled. The Sephardic community has since moved out to Maida Vale and Wembley, and the congregation has dwindled, though the synagogue's magnificent array of chandeliers makes it very popular for candle-lit Jewish weddings.

St Katharine Cree to Aldgate

Close by Bevis Marks, just past Creechurch Lane, a plaque commemorates the even larger **Great Synagogue** of the Ashkenazi Jews, founded in 1690 but destroyed by bombs in 1941. At the southern end of Creechurch Lane is the church of **St Katharine Cree** (Mon–Fri 10.30am–4pm), built in 1630, and a rare example of its period. It's a transitional building with Neoclassical elements, such as the Corinthian columns of the nave and, above, a Gothic clerestory and ribbing. At the east end is a very lovely, seventeenth-century stained-glass Catherine-wheel window.

The only place in the City where you can still witness the human scrum of share dealing – known as "open-outcry" – is at the **London Metal Exchange** (noon–12.45pm, 12.45pm–1.30pm, 3.30–4.15pm & 4.15–5pm; free; ☎020/7264 5555, ⓦwww.lme.com; Aldgate tube), at 56 Leadenhall St, where metals – and even plastic – but not silver and gold, are traded. To visit the public viewing gallery, you must fill in a security form and book at least four weeks ahead.

East along Aldgate, on the site of the City gateway, stands **St Botolph-without-Aldgate** (Mon–Thurs & Sun 10am–3pm; ⓦwww.stbotolphs.org .uk; Aldgate tube), designed in 1741 by George Dance. Its bizarre interior, remodelled last century, features blue-grey paintwork, gilding on top of white plasterwork, some dodgy modern art, a batik reredos and a stunning, modern stained-glass rendition of Rubens' *Descent from the Cross* on a deep-purple background. Situated at the edge of the East End, this is a famously campaigning church, active on issues like gay priests and social exclusion.

Monument to the Tower

In the 1670s, Wren's **Monument** (daily 9.30am–5.30pm; £2; ☎020/7626 2717; Monument tube), commemorating the Great Fire of 1666 (see box, p.466) used to tower above the surrounding buildings. Nevertheless, this plain 202-foot Doric column, crowned with spiky gilded flames, remains the tallest isolated stone column in the world; if it were laid out flat it would touch the site of the bakery where the fire started, east of Monument. The bas-relief on the base depicts Charles II and the Duke of York in Roman garb conducting the emergency relief operation. The 311 steps to the gallery at the top – plagued by suicides until a cage was built around it in 1842 – once guaranteed an incredible view; nowadays it's dwarfed by the surrounding buildings.

Signs from the Monument will point you in the right direction for another Wren edifice, the church of **St Magnus-the-Martyr** (Tues–Fri 10am–4pm, Sun 10am–1pm; ⓦwww.stmagnusmartyr.org.uk), whose octagonal spire used

London Bridge

Unreal City

Under the brown fog of a winter dawn,

A crowd flowed over London Bridge, so many,

I had not thought death had undone so many.

The Waste Land T.S. Eliot

At rush hour, you can still see Eliot's "undead" trudging to work across **London Bridge**, which was, until 1750, the only bridge across the Thames. The Romans were the first to build a permanent crossing here, a structure succeeded by a Saxon version that was pulled down by King Olaf of Norway in 1014, and commemorated in the popular nursery rhyme *London Bridge is Falling Down*. It was the medieval bridge, however, that achieved world fame: built of stone and crowded with timber-framed houses, it became one of London's greatest attractions. At the centre stood the richly ornate Nonsuch House, decorated with onion domes and Dutch gables, and a chapel dedicated to Thomas Becket; at the Southwark end was the Great Gatehouse, on which the heads of traitors were displayed, dipped in tar to preserve them. The houses were removed in the mid-eighteenth century, and a new stone bridge erected in 1831 – that one now stands in of Lake Havasu City, in the Arizona desert, having been bought in the 1960s by a guy who, so the story goes, thought he'd purchased Tower Bridge. The present concrete structure – without doubt the ugliest yet – dates from 1972.

to greet travellers arriving across old London Bridge. Now it stands forlorn by busy Lower Thames Street, though the Anglo-Catholic interior holds, in T.S. Eliot's words, "an inexplicable splendour of Ionian white and gold". In addition, there's a wooden pier from an old Roman wharf in the porch, and a great model of the old London Bridge in the vestry.

Along the river from St Magnus is **Old Billingsgate Market**, a handsome Victorian market hall that once housed London's chief wholesale fish market. It's difficult to imagine the noise and smell of old Billingsgate, whose porters used to carry the fish in towers of baskets on their heads, and whose wives were renowned for their bad language even in Shakespeare's day: "as bad a tongue… as any oyster-wife at Billingsgate" (*King Lear*). Next door stands the Neoclassical **Custom House**, from 1825, which has been collecting duties from incoming ships since around 1275.

Up **Lovat Lane**, one of the City's most atmospheric cobbled streets, stands **St Mary-at-Hill** (Mon–Fri 11am–4pm; Ⓦ www.stmary-at-hill.org), the old fishermen's church, rebuilt by Wren after the Great Fire. The church was badly damaged by fire in 1988, but has since made a phoenix-like recovery, allowing you to once more admire its beautiful white-stuccoed dome and lantern, held up by four fluted composite columns – the box pews, pulpit and reredos are yet to be restored. Continuing north up St Mary-at-Hill brings you to **Eastcheap**, along which several admirable Victorian Gothic facades have survived (no. 33 is particularly fancy). If you're looking for a secluded spot, however, head for the garden in the nave of the ruined church of **St Dunstan-in-the-East**, off St Dunstan's Hill, further east, which retains its distinctive Wren-designed crown steeple.

Saved from the Fire, but left as an empty shell by the Blitz, the ragstone Gothic church of **St Olave** (Mon–Fri 9am–5pm), Hart Street, was dubbed "St Ghastly Grim" by Dickens after the skulls and crossbones and vicious-looking spikes adorning the 1658 entrance to the graveyard on Seething Lane, a short stroll from St Dunstan's. Samuel Pepys lived in Seething Lane for much of his life, and he and his wife, Elizabeth, are both buried here amidst the pre-Fire brasses and monuments – Elizabeth's monument was raised by Pepys himself; Pepys' own is Victorian.

At the bottom of Seething Lane, across noisy Lower Thames Street, stands another pre-Fire church, **All Hallows-by-the-Tower** (Mon–Sat 10am–5pm, Sun 1–5pm; ⓣ020/7481 2928, ⓦwww.ahbtt.org.uk; Tower Hill tube). Only the red-brick tower (from which Pepys watched the Great Fire) survived the Blitz; the rest of the church is a postwar neo-Gothic pastiche wrought in concrete. The furnishings are fascinating, however, and include lots of maritime memorials, model ships, two wings of a Flemish triptych from around 1500, and, best of all, the exquisitely carved Gibbons lime-wood font cover, in the southwest chapel. Close by is an arch from the original seventh-century church; remains of a tessellated Roman pavement can also be found in the tiny crypt. All Hallows also has some superb pre-Reformation brasses, and offers brassrubbing.

12

Tower of London and around

The area around **Tower Hill** is choked with tourists who flock here to see one of London's most famous landmarks, Tower Bridge and the adjacent Tower of London (March–Oct Mon & Sun 10am–5.30pm, Tues–Sat 9am–5.30pm; Nov–Feb closes 4.30pm; £16.50; ☎0844/482 7777, ⒲hrp.org.uk; Tower Hill tube), a superbly fortified castle begun shortly after the Norman Conquest. Despite all the attendant hype and heritage claptrap, the Tower remains one of London's most remarkable buildings, site of some of the goriest events in the nation's history, and somewhere all visitors and Londoners should explore at least once. Sitting beside the river, at the eastern edge of the old city walls, the Tower is chiefly famous as a place of imprisonment and death, yet it's also variously been used as a royal residence, armoury, mint, menagerie, observatory and – a function it still serves – a safe-deposit box for the Crown Jewels. And, finally, it's easy to forget that the Tower is, above all, the most perfectly preserved medieval fortress in the country.

A brief history

Begun as a simple watchtower, built by **William the Conqueror** to keep an eye on the City, the Tower had evolved into a palace-fortress by 1100. The inner curtain wall and towers were built under Henry III, while the outer fortifications, and an even wider moat, were added by Edward I, on his return from the Crusades, which means that most of what's visible today was already in place by 1307, the year of Edward's death. The Tower has been besieged on a number of occasions – firstly, in 1191, when Bishop Longchamp surrendered to Prince John after only three days – but sacked only once, during the 1381 Peasants' Revolt, when the Archbishop of Canterbury, among others, was lynched.

The Tower's **first prisoner**, the Bishop of Durham, arrived in 1101, having been found guilty of extortion, and promptly escaped from the window of his cell by a rope, having got the guards drunk. Gruffydd ap Llywelyn, heir to the Welsh throne, attempted a similar feat in 1244, with less success: "his head and neck were crushed between his shoulders…a most horrid spectacle." Incidentally, the **most famous escapee** from the Tower was the Jacobite Earl of Nithsdale, who, the night before his execution in 1716, managed to get past the guards dressed as his wife's maid (despite his red beard), and lived for another thirty years in exile in Rome.

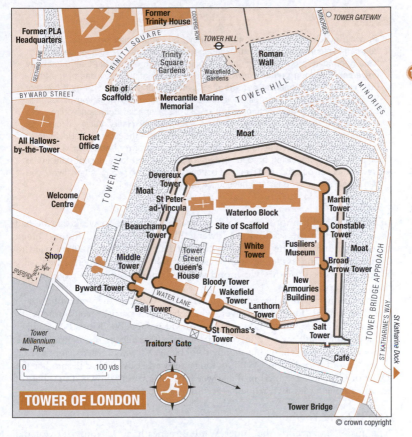

Following the Restoration in 1660, the general public were admitted for the first time to view the **coronation regalia** and the impressive displays of arms and armour – by the end of Victoria's reign, there were half a million visitors annually. Nevertheless, during both world wars, the Tower was still used to hold prisoners: **Roger Casement**, the Irish nationalist, was held here briefly before his trial and hanging in 1916, but the last VIP inmate was **Rudolf Hess**, Hitler's deputy, who flew secretly into Britain to sue for peace in May 1941 and was held here for a few days. The **last execution** took place on August 14, 1941, when Josef Jakobs, a German spy who (like Hess) had broken his ankle parachuting into Britain, was given the privilege of being seated before the firing squad.

Bell Tower and Traitors' Gate

Visitors enter the Tower by the Middle Tower and the Byward Tower, in the southwest corner. Two of the first victims of the Reformation – Thomas More and John Fisher – were incarcerated nearby in the **Bell Tower**, from whose dinky wooden belfry a bell would toll to signal an execution. More was initially allowed writing materials, but later they were withdrawn; Fisher was kept in worse conditions ("I decay forthwith, and fall into coughs and diseases

To avoid queuing (and to save some money), buy your ticket online or by phone. You can explore the Tower complex independently, or with an audioguide (£4), but it's a good idea to get your bearings by joining up with one of the free, theatrically irreverent, hour-long **guided tours**, given every thirty minutes by one of the forty-odd, eminently photogenic **Beefeaters** – it's also the only way to visit the Chapel of St Peter-ad-Vincula. These self-assured ex-servicemen are best known for their scarlet-and-gold Tudor costumes, but unless it's a special occasion you're more likely to see them in dark-blue "undress". Formed by Henry VIII as a personal bodyguard, they're officially known as Yeoman Warders – the nickname "Beefeaters" was coined in the seventeenth century, when it was a term of abuse for a well-fed domestic servant. Talking of food, there's a spacious and fairly decent **café** in the New Armouries building, and plenty of benches on which to picnic. Alternatively, you can obtain a re-entry pass and have lunch outside the Tower.

of my body, and cannot keep myself in health") and was so weak that he had to be carried to the scaffold on Tower Hill. The 20-year-old future Queen Elizabeth I arrived here in 1554, while her half-sister Queen Mary tried to find incriminating evidence against her. Catholic Mass was performed daily in Elizabeth's cell for the two months of her imprisonment, but she refused to be converted.

Most prisoners were delivered through **Traitors' Gate**, on the waterfront, which forms part of **St Thomas's Tower**, which has been partially reconstructed to re-create the atmosphere of Edward I's **medieval palace**. The King's Bedchamber has a beautiful little oratory in one of the turrets, while in the oratory of the Throne Room, the "saintly but slightly daft" Henry VI was murdered at prayer on the orders of Edward IV in 1471. Not long afterwards, Edward had his brother, the Duke of Clarence, executed in the Tower for high treason, drowned in a butt of malmsey wine (at his own request – according to Shakespeare).

The Bloody Tower

The main entrance to the Inner Ward is beneath a 3.5-ton, 700-year-old portcullis, which forms part of the **Bloody Tower**, so called because it was here that the 12-year-old Edward V and his 10-year-old brother, Richard, were accommodated "for their own safety" in 1483 by their uncle, Richard of Gloucester (later Richard III), following the death of their father, Edward IV. Of all the Tower's many inhabitants, few have so captured the public imagination as the **Princes in the Tower**. According to Thomas More, they were smothered in their beds, and buried naked at the foot of the White Tower. In 1674, workmen discovered the skeletons of two young children close to the Tower; they were subsequently buried in Innocents' Corner in Westminster Abbey.

The Bloody Tower's other illustrious inmate – even more famous in his time than the princes – was **Walter Ralegh**, who spent three separate periods here. His first stay was in 1592, after he had impregnated and secretly married one of Elizabeth I's ladies-in-waiting without the Queen's permission; his second spell began in 1603, when he was found guilty of allegedly plotting against James I. He spent nearly thirteen years here growing and smoking tobacco (his most famous import), composing poetry, concocting potions in his distillery and writing his *History of the World*, which outsold even Shakespeare, despite being banned by James I for being "too saucy in censuring princes". When Ralegh complained that the noise of the portcullis kept him awake at night, he was moved to much worse accommodation. In 1616 he was released and sent off to Guyana to discover gold, on condition that he didn't attack the Spanish; he broke his word and was sent straight back to the Tower on his return in 1618. For six weeks he was imprisoned in "one of the most cold and direful dungeons", before being beheaded at Westminster.

Ralegh's study is re-created on the ground floor, while his sleeping quarters upstairs, built to accommodate his wife, children and three servants, now house an exhibition on the Princes in the Tower and on the poisoning of the poet **Thomas Overbury**. Confined to the Bloody Tower in 1613 on a flimsy charge by James I, after falling out with one of the king's favourites, Robert Carr, Overbury was slowly poisoned to death with arsenic concealed within the tarts and jellies sent by Carr's wife. Arrested, tried and condemned to death, Carr and his wife were themselves incarcerated in the Tower for five years before being pardoned. The Lieutenant of the Tower was less fortunate, and was hanged for failing to protect his prisoners.

The White Tower

William the Conqueror's central hall-keep, known as the **White Tower**, is the original "Tower", begun in 1076. Whitewashed (hence its name) in the reign

▲ Tower of London

The Royal Menagerie and the ravens

The **Royal Menagerie** began in earnest in 1235 when the Holy Roman Emperor presented three "leopards" to Henry III; the keeper was initially paid sixpence a day for the sustenance of the beasts (they were, in fact, lions), and one penny for himself. They were put on public display and joined some years later by a polar bear from the King of Norway and an elephant from the King of France. James I was particularly keen on the menagerie, and used to stage regular animal fights on the green, but the practice was stopped in 1609 when one of the bears killed a child. In 1704, six lions, two leopards, three eagles, two Swedish owls "of great bigness", two "cats of the mountains" and a jackal were recorded. Visitors were advised not to "play tricks" after an orang-utan threw a cannonball at one and killed him.

The menagerie was transferred to the newly founded London Zoo in the 1830s, leaving the Tower with just its ravens, descendants of early scavengers attracted by waste from the palace kitchens. They have been protected by royal decree since the Restoration, and have their wings clipped so they can't fly away – legend says that the Tower (and therefore the kingdom) will fall if they do, though the Tower was in fact briefly raven-less during the last war after the Tower suffered heavy bombing. While the ravens may appear harmless, they are vicious, territorial creatures best given a wide berth. They live in coops in the south wall of the Inner Ward, have individual names and even have their own graveyard in the dry moat near the main entrance.

of Henry III, it was later returned to its Kentish ragstone exterior by Wren, who added the large windows. Of the tower's four turrets, topped by stylish Tudor cupolas, only three are square: the fourth is rounded in order to encase the main spiral staircase, and for a short while was used by Charles II's royal astronomer, Flamsteed, before he moved to Greenwich. The main entrance to the Tower is the original one, high up in the south wall, out of reach of the enemy, and accessed by a wooden staircase which could be removed during times of siege.

The four floors of arms and armour displayed within the tower represent a mere smidgen of the **Royal Armouries** (the majority of which resides in Leeds), which have been on display since the time of Charles II. Whatever your interests, you should pay a visit to the first-floor **Chapel of St John**, a beautiful Norman structure completed in 1080, making it the oldest intact ecclesiastical building in London. It was here that Henry VI's body was buried following his murder in 1471; that Henry VII's queen, Elizabeth of York, lay in state surrounded by eight hundred candles, after dying in childbirth and that Lady Jane Grey came to pray on the night before her execution. Today, the once highly decorated blocks of honey-coloured Caen limestone are free of all ecclesiastical excrescences, leaving the chapel's smooth curves and rounded apse perfectly unencumbered.

On the ground floor, is the **Line of Kings**, a display first recorded in 1660, originally depicting the monarchs of England on horseback. Also on show here is a suit of armour for a man six feet nine inches tall (once thought to have been John of Gaunt) and one for a boy just three feet one and a half inches high (allegedly Richard, Duke of York). Among the most striking armour displayed is the colossal **Holbein-designed garniture** of 1540 made for Henry VIII (and famous for its protruding codpiece), the Japanese armour presented to King James I by the Shogun of Japan and Charles I's unusual gold-leaf suit. Visitors exit via the basement, which contains artillery and the gnarled, melted relics salvaged from the Tower after a fire in 1841, some of which were sold to the public and later made into candelabra and the like.

Tower Green

Being beheaded at Tower Hill (as opposed to being hanged, drawn and quartered) was a privilege of the nobility; being beheaded on **Tower Green**, the stretch of lawn to the west of the White Tower, was an honour conferred on just a handful of people, whose names are recorded on a ghastly new glass monument at the centre of the green. It was an arrangement that suited both parties: the victim was spared the jeering crowds of Tower Hill, and the monarch was spared bad publicity. Among the victims were: Lord Hastings, executed immediately after his arrest on the orders of Richard III, who swore he wouldn't go to dinner until Hastings was beheaded; Anne Boleyn (Henry VIII's second wife), accused of incest and adultery, who was dispatched cleanly and swiftly with a French long sword rather than the traditional axe, at her own insistence; 19-year-old Catherine Howard (Henry VIII's fifth wife and Anne's cousin), convicted of adultery and beheaded along with her lady-in-waiting, who was deemed an accomplice; 16-year-old Lady Jane Grey, who was Queen for just nine days; and the Earl of Essex, one-time favourite of Elizabeth I. The bloody, headless corpses of these "traitors", and the many more executed on Tower Hill, were all buried in the plain Tudor **Chapel of St Peter-ad-Vincula**, north of the scaffold site, accessible only on the Beefeaters' tours.

Close by the chapel is the **Beauchamp Tower**, which accommodated only the wealthiest of prisoners and boasts a better class of graffiti: Lord Dudley, husband of Lady Jane Grey, even commissioned a stonemason to carve the family crest on the first floor. On the far side of the green is the **Queen's House** (closed to the public), built in the last years of Henry VIII's reign and distinguished by its swirling timber frames. These were the most luxurious cells in the Tower, and were used to incarcerate the likes of Catherine Howard and Anne Boleyn, who had also stayed there shortly before her coronation. Lady Jane Grey was cooped up here in 1553, and in the following year it was from here she watched the headless torso of her husband, Lord Dudley, being brought back from Tower Hill, only hours before her own execution. In 1688, William Penn, the Quaker and founder of Pennsylvania, was confined to the Queen's House, where he penned his most popular work, *No Cross, No Crown*.

The Crown Jewels

The castellated **Waterloo Block**, north of the White Tower, now holds the **Crown Jewels**, the major reason so many people flock to the Tower. The Jewels include the world's three largest cut diamonds, but only a few of the exhibits could be described as beautiful – assertions of status and wealth are more important considerations. Queues can be long, and you only get to view the rocks from moving walkways. The vast majority of exhibits postdate the Commonwealth, when most of the royal riches were melted down for coinage or sold off. Before you reach the walkway, you'll see the twelfth-century **Coronation Spoon**, the oldest piece of regalia. The first piece along the walkway is St Edward's Crown, used in every coronation since the Restoration. The world's largest diamond, the 530-carat "First Star of Africa" or **Cullinan I** is set into the Sceptre with the Cross, while the legendary 105.6-carat **Koh-i-Nûr** (Mountain of Light) is set into the Queen Elizabeth, the Queen Mother's Crown from 1937. The most famous crown is the **Imperial State Crown**, worn by the Queen on state occasions, and sparkling with 2868 diamonds (including the 317-carat "Second Star of Africa", Cullinan II), seventeen sapphires, eleven emeralds, five rubies and 273 pearls.

Tower ceremonies

The Ceremony of the Keys is a 700-year-old, seven-minute floodlit ceremony. At 9.53pm daily, the Chief Yeoman Warder, accompanied by the Tower Guard, locks the Tower gates, and as he attempts to return to the Inner Ward, the following exchange then takes place: "Halt. Who comes there?" "The Keys." "Whose Keys?" "Queen Elizabeth's Keys." "Pass, Queen Elizabeth's Keys. All's well." To find out how to witness this long-running drama, visit the website.

Gun Salutes are fired by the Honourable Artillery Company at 1pm at Tower Wharf on royal birthdays and other special occasions.

The Constable's Dues occurs whenever a large Royal Navy ship moors alongside the Tower; the ship's captain and his escort march through the Tower and present a barrel of rum to the Constable of the Tower.

The Ceremony of the Lilies and Roses is carried out every year on May 21 by the provosts of Eton and King's College, Cambridge, who place white lilies and roses (their respective emblems) on the spot where King Henry VI, founder of both institutions, was murdered in 1471.

The Beating of the Bounds ceremony takes place once every three years on Ascension Day (forty days after Easter), outside the walls of the Tower. It used to be little boys who were beaten, but now it's the 29 stones that mark the limits of the Tower's jurisdiction that are thrashed with willow wands by local children, while the Chief Yeoman Warder gives the order "Whack it, boys! Whack it!"

The Salt Tower to the Martin Tower

Visitors can walk along the eastern section of the Tower walls, starting at the **Salt Tower**, which features more prisoners' graffiti, including a stunningly detailed zodiac carved by Hugh Draper, incarcerated in 1561 on a charge of sorcery. The **Martin Tower**, at the far end of the wall walk, was once the home of Henry Percy, the Earl of Northumberland, who moved in here in 1605 having rejected another suite of cells because of their smell and lack of shade. He had good reason to be choosy, since he was serving life imprisonment for failing to inform the king of the Gunpowder Plot. One of the richest men in the country, Percy employed his own cook, and paid for a bowling alley as well as for the walls near his cell to be paved for his daily stroll. Like Walter Ralegh (held at the same time in the Bloody Tower), Percy brought a library with him, plus three eminent scholars to assist him with his astrological and alchemical studies. When he was finally released in 1621, after paying a large fine, he was given a royal salute from the Tower guns.

The Martin Tower now houses an interesting exhibition entitled **Crowns and Diamonds**, which relates the story of the Cullinan diamonds. The most famous attempt to steal the Crown Jewels took place in the Martin Tower, in 1671, when "Colonel" **Thomas Blood**, an Irish adventurer, made an attempt to make off with the lot, disguised as a parson. He was caught with the crown under his habit, the orb in one of his accomplices' breeches and the sceptre about to be filed in half. Charles II, good-humoured as ever, met and pardoned the felon, and even awarded him a pension and made him welcome at court.

Last, and probably least, there's the **Fusiliers' Museum** (£1), which tells the story of the Royal Fusiliers, who were founded in the 1680s in a desperate attempt by James II to hold on to his throne. The museum trots through the regiment's various campaigns, displays its medals and spoils from across the Empire, and lists its most famous alumni, although it neglects to mention that East End gangsters, the Kray twins (see p.208), were once Fusiliers.

Tower Hill

Perhaps it's fitting that traffic-blighted **Tower Hill** to the northwest of the Tower should be such a god-awful place, for it was here that the Tower's convicted "traitors" were executed. Sometimes the tables were turned: during the 1381 Peasants' Revolt, rioters broke into the Tower, dragged out the Lord High Treasurer (the man responsible for the hated poll tax), and hacked him to death, along with the Archbishop of Canterbury. The first official beheading took place in 1388 and the last in 1747, when the 80-year-old Jacobite Lord Lovat was dispatched. Lovat's beheading drew such a crowd that one of the spectators' stands collapsed, killing several bystanders, at which Lovat exclaimed: "The more mischief, the better sport." The Duke of Monmouth, beheaded for his rebellion against James II, suffered the most botched execution: it took Jack Ketch (who lives on in Punch & Judy shows) five blows of the axe to sever his head, and even then the job had to be finished off with a surgeon's knife. Hangings continued for another thirty-odd years, ending with the execution of two prostitutes and a one-armed soldier arrested for attacking a Catholic-run pub in the 1780 Gordon Riots.

The actual spot for the executions, at what was the country's first permanent scaffold, is marked by a plaque on the west side of Trinity Square Gardens, to the northwest of the Tower. Close by stands the **Mercantile Marine Memorial**, designed by Edwin Lutyens, smothered with the names of the twelve thousand civilians of the merchant navy who died in World War I, and subsequently enlarged to commemorate the 24,000 merchant seamen who died in World War II. The marine theme is continued in the buildings overlooking the gardens: the gargantuan temple-like former headquarters of the **Port of London Authority** (soon to be a hotel), an Edwardian edifice that exudes imperial confidence, with Neptune adorning the main tower; and, to the east, the elegant Neoclassical former headquarters of **Trinity House** (Ⓦ www.trinityhouse.co.uk), the organization that oversees the upkeep of the lighthouses of England, Wales, the Channel Islands and Gibraltar – check out the reliefs of mermen, cherubs and lighthouses on the main facade, and the splendid gilded nautical weather vane.

Continuing east, you'll find perhaps the most impressive remaining section of London's **Roman walls** in the forecourt of the *Grange Hotel*, on Coopers Row, and in Wakefield Gardens, close to Tower Hill tube station, along with an eighteenth-century copy of a Roman statue of Emperor Trajan, saved from a Southampton scrapyard by a local vicar.

Tower Bridge

Tower Bridge ranks with Big Ben as the most famous of all London landmarks. Completed in 1894, its neo-Gothic towers are clad in Cornish granite and Portland stone, but conceal a frame of Scottish steel, which, at the time, represented a considerable engineering achievement, allowing a road crossing that could be raised to give tall ships access to the upper reaches of the Thames. The raising of the bascules (from the French for "seesaw") remains an impressive sight, and an event that takes place around a thousand times a year – visit the website for details. If you buy a ticket (daily: April–Sept 10am–6.30pm; Oct–March 9.30am–6pm; £6; Ⓣ 020/7403 3761, Ⓦ www.towerbridge.org.uk; Tower Hill tube), you get to walk across the elevated walkways linking the summits of the towers, and visit the Tower's Engine Rooms, on the south side of the bridge, where you can see the now-defunct, giant coal-fired boilers which drove the hydraulic system until 1976, and play some interactive engineering games.

The East End

The East End of London is the hell of poverty. Like an enormous, black, motionless, giant kracken, the poverty of London lies there in lurking silence and encircles with its mighty tentacles the life and wealth of the City and of the West End...

J.H. Mackay, *The Anarchists* (1891)

Few places in London have engendered so many myths as the **East End** (a catch-all title which covers just about everywhere east of the City, but has its historic heart closest to the latter). Its name is synonymous with slums, sweatshops and crime, epitomized by antiheroes such as Jack the Ripper and the Kray twins, and with rags-to-riches success stories of a whole generation of Jews who were born in these cholera-ridden quarters and then moved to wealthier pastures. Old East Enders will tell you that the area's not what it was – and it's true, as it always has been. The East End is constantly changing, as newly arrived **immigrants** assimilate and move out.

The first immigrants were **Huguenots**, French Protestants fleeing from religious persecution in the late seventeenth century, who bequeathed the word "refugee" (from the French, *réfugié*). They were welcomed by all except the apprentice weavers whose work they undercut. Some settled in Soho, but the majority settled in Spitalfields, where they were operating some twelve thousand silk looms by the end of the eighteenth century. Within three generations the Huguenots were almost entirely assimilated, and the **Irish** became the new immigrant population. Irish labourers, ironically enough, played a major role in building the area's Protestant churches, and later were crucial to the development of the docks. The perceived threat of cheap Irish labour provoked riots in 1736 and 1769, and their Catholicism made them easy targets during the 1780 Gordon Riots.

It was the influx of **Jews** escaping pogroms in eastern Europe and Russia that defined the character of the East End in the late nineteenth century. The Bishop of Stepney complained in 1901 that his churches were "left like islands in the midst of an alien sea". The same year, the MP for Stepney helped found the East End's first organized racist movement, the British Brothers League, whose ideology foreshadowed the British Union of Fascists, led by Oswald Mosley and famously defeated at the **Battle of Cable Street** (see p.204). The area's Jewish population has now dispersed throughout London, though the East End remains a deprived area. Despite the millions that have been poured into the nearby Docklands development, and the proximity of the wealth of the City, unemployment and housing problems persist. There remains an undercurrent of racism in the area, directed, for the most part, against the extensive **Bangladeshi** community, who came here in the 1960s and 1970s.

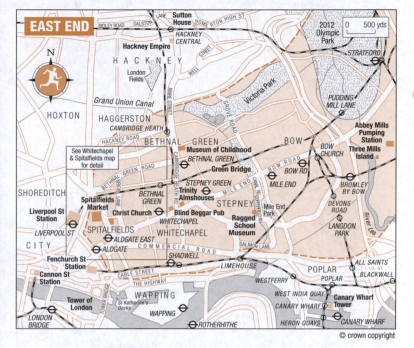

The districts of **Whitechapel**, and in particular **Spitalfields**, within sight of the sleek tower blocks of the financial sector, represent the old heart of the East End. If you visit just one area in the East End, it should be this zone, which preserves mementoes from each wave of immigration. Most visitors come for the **Sunday markets**: Petticoat Lane for cheap clothes, **Brick Lane** for bric-a-brac, fashion and cheap curries, **Columbia Road** for flowers and plants, and **Spitalfields** for arts, crafts and organic food. These apart, the area is not an obvious place for sightseeing, and certainly no beauty spot – Victorian slum clearances, Hitler's bombs and postwar tower blocks have left large areas looking bleak. However, there's a lot of history in the East End, and one or two specific points of interest, including a smattering of **museums**, most of them open to the public free of charge. As for the future, one part of the East End that is set to be totally transformed is the lower Lea Valley, a former industrial area between Bow and Stratford, where the **2012 Olympic Park** is being constructed (see p.210).

Petticoat Lane (Middlesex Street) and around

Heavily bombed in the Blitz, **Petticoat Lane** (daily except Sat 9am–2pm) is not one of London's prettiest streets, but it has a rich history: the Huguenots sold the petticoats that gave the market and the street its name; the authorities renamed it Middlesex Street in 1830 to avoid the mention of ladies' underwear (though the original name has stuck) and tried to prevent Sunday trading here (it was finally sanctioned by law in 1936). In the Victorian era the market grew into one of London's largest, and by the end of the century it was known as the Jews' Market, and stood at the heart of the Jewish East End, a "stronghold of

▲ Geffrye Museum

WHITECHAPEL & SPITALFIELDS

HOXTON

St Leonard

Old Truman Brewery

Dennis Severs' House

SPITALFIELDS

19 Princelet St

Liverpool St Station

Old Spitalfields Market

Jamme Masjid

Bishopsgate Institute

School

Sandys Row

Christ Church

East London Mosque

Royal London Hospital

Toynbee Hall

Fieldgate St

Institute of Cell & Molecular Sciences

Women's Library

Whitechapel Art Gallery

Whitechapel Bell Foundry

WHITECHAPEL

Bevis Marks

ALDGATE

Angel Alley

ALDGATE EAST

© crown copyright

0   400 yds

CAFÉS & RESTAURANTS						PUBS & BARS	
Arkansas Café	15	Frizzante @ City Farm	1	Rosa's	13	Joiner's Arms	2
Brick Lane Beigel Bake	6	Jones Dairy	3	St John Bread and Wine	14	Loungelover	7
Café 1001	12	Lahore Kebab House	20	Sweet & Spicy	18	Ten Bells	16
Café Naz	17	Les Trois Garçons	8	Tayyab's	19	Vibe Bar	9
E. Pellicci	5	Rootmaster	11	Wild Cherry	4	Water Poet	10

hard-sell Judaism…into which no missionary dared to set foot", according to novelist Israel Zangwill. It remains the city's number-one cheap clothes market, with a smaller lunchtime version in the week (Mon–Fri) on neighbouring Wentworth Street.

North of Petticoat Lane are further reminders of the old Jewish community: the **Soup Kitchen for the Jewish Poor**, on Brune Street, which opened in 1902 and closed in 1992 (the undulating stone lettering and the Christian and Jewish dates are still clearly visible) and the **Sandys Row synagogue**, an old Huguenot chapel converted in 1870 for Dutch Jews and one of the few working synagogues left in the East End. The surrounding network of narrow streets is fascinating to walk around – unique survivors that give a strong

The Women's Library

In the 1840s, the Victorians decided it was time to do something about "the great unwashed" and a grandly named Committee for Promoting the Establishment of Baths and Wash-Houses for the Labouring Classes was set up. Among the plushest public baths were the Goulston Square Wash Houses, opened by Prince Albert himself: "a penny for a cold bath, two for a hot bath for up to four children under eight". The grey-brick facade of the old wash houses survives on Old Castle Street, south of Wentworth Street, but the interior has been transformed into a new home for the **Women's Library**, which puts on excellent exhibitions covering a wide range of social issues on the ground floor (Mon–Fri 9.30am–5.30pm, Thurs until 8pm, Sat 10am–4pm; free; ☏020/7320 2222, ⊛www.thewomenslibrary.ac.uk). The actual library (Tues–Fri only) was set up by the suffragette Millicent Fawcett in 1926 and specializes in women's history; it also puts on regular talks and events, and has a café on the first floor.

impression of the old East End. From the bakery at 12 Widegate St, with its high-relief ceramic friezes, cross Sandys Row, and walk down Artillery Passage into **Artillery Lane**, which boasts a superb Huguenot shop front at no. 56. Incidentally, the ballistic connection dates from the reign of Henry VIII, when the Royal Artillery used to hold gunnery practice here.

Old Spitalfields Market and around

Old Spitalfields Market (⊛www.visitspitalfields.com), once the capital's premier fruit and vegetable market, moved out to Stratford in 1991. After a decade of mixed community use, the western, 1920s half of the market was replaced by an anonymous glass-box redevelopment courtesy of Norman Foster. Part of the original facade survives on the north side of Brushfield Street; on the south side, the old fruiterers' shops are occupied by modishly retro businesses, such as Verde & Co, author Jeanette Winterson's deli venture. The market (Mon–Fri 10am–4pm, Sun 9am–5am) continues to thrive in the original red-brick and green-gabled 1893 building, to the east (see p.444), but much of the scene has moved east to Brick Lane.

Looking down Brushfield Street and facing the market from across Commercial Street, is **Christ Church** (Tues 11am–4pm, Sun 1–4pm; ☏020/7247 7202, ⊛www.christchurchspitalfields.org.uk; Liverpool Street tube), a characteristically bold Georgian church designed by Hawksmoor. The church's main features are its huge 225-foot-high broach spire and giant Tuscan portico, raised on steps and shaped like a Venetian window (a central arched opening flanked by two smaller rectangles), a motif repeated in the tower and doors. Inside, there's a forest of giant columned bays, a hexagonal, embossed ceiling, with a lion and a unicorn playing peekaboo on the top of the chancel beam and, opposite, London's largest Georgian organ. The church's restoration has saved it from falling down; sadly, it's also removed all the atmosphere the old decaying interior once had.

Dennis Severs' House, 18 Folgate Street

North of the market, at **18 Folgate Street** (☏020/7247 4013, ⊛www .dennissevershouse.co.uk), you can visit the house where the American artist **Dennis Severs** lived until his death in 1999. Severs created a theatrical experience which he described as "passing through a frame into a painting". The house

William the Conqueror invited the first **Jews** to England in 1066. After a period of relatively peaceful coexistence and prosperity, the small community increasingly found itself under attack, milked by successive monarchs and forced eventually to wear a distinguishing mark or *tabula* on their clothing. The Crusades whipped up further religious intolerance, the worst recorded incident taking place in 1189, when thirty Jews were killed by a mob during the coronation of Richard I. In 1278 Edward I imprisoned the entire community of around six hundred on a charge of "clipping coins" (debasing currency by shaving off bits of silver from coins), executing 267 at the Tower, and finally in 1290 expelling the rest.

For nearly four centuries thereafter, Judaism was outlawed in England. Sephardic (ie Spanish or Portuguese) Jews fleeing the Inquisition began arriving from 1540 onwards, though they had to become, or pretend to be, Christians until 1656, when Oliver Cromwell granted Jews the right to meet privately and worship in their own homes. The Jews who arrived immediately following this **Readmission** were in the main wealthy merchants, bankers and other businessmen. As a beacon of (relative) tolerance and economic prosperity, London quickly attracted further Jewish immigration by poorer Sephardi families and, increasingly, Ashkenazi settlers from eastern and central Europe.

By far the largest influx of **Ashkenazi Jews** arrived after fleeing pogroms that followed the assassination of Tsar Alexander II in 1881. The more fortunate were met by relatives at the Irongate Stairs by Tower Bridge; the rest were left to the mercy of the boarding-house keepers or, after 1885, found shelter in the Jewish Temporary Shelter. They found work in the sweatshops of the East End: cabinetmaking, shoemaking and, of course, tailoring – by 1901, over 45 percent of London's Jews worked in the garment industry.

Perhaps the greatest moment in Jewish East End history was the **Battle of Cable Street**, which took place on October 4, 1936, when Oswald Mosley and three thousand of his black-shirted fascists attempted to march through the East End. More than twice that number of police tried to clear the way for Mosley with baton charges and mounted patrols, but they were met with a barrage of bricks and stones from some 100,000 East Enders chanting the slogan of the Spanish Republicans: "*No pasaran*" (They shall not pass). Eventually the police chief halted the march – and another East End legend was born. A mural on the side of the old Shadwell town hall on Cable Street commemorates the event.

After World War II, more and more Jews moved out to the suburbs of North London, and the largest Orthodox Jewish communities are now to be found in Golders Green and Stamford Hill.

is entirely candle-lit and log-fired, and decked out as it would have been two hundred years ago. Visitors are free to explore the ten rooms, and are left with the distinct impression that someone has literally just popped out. The house cat prowls, there's the smell of food, and the sound of horses' hooves on the cobbled street outside. "The Experience" takes place on Sundays (noon–4pm; £8), and on Mondays following the first and third Sunday (noon–2pm; £5); for the Monday evening "Silent Night" you must book ahead (times vary; £12).

Brick Lane and beyond

Crossing the eastern end of Fournier Street, **Brick Lane** was the main location for the brick kilns that helped rebuild the City after the Great Fire. By 1900, this was the high street of the unofficial Jewish ghetto, but since the 1960s, Brick Lane has been at the heart of the Bengali community. Racism has been a problem for each wave of immigrants, but nowadays it's bohemian gentrification, followed by City developers, that are probably the greatest threat. For the moment, however, the southern half of Brick Lane remains pretty staunchly Bangladeshi: bright-coloured sari fabrics line the clothes-shop windows, bhangra music emanates from the shops and, in the evening, waiters from the numerous restaurants try to cajole you into their establishments.

The changing ethnic make-up of this part of Brick Lane is most clearly illustrated in the **Jamme Masjid** (Great Mosque) on the corner of Fournier Street. Established in 1743 as a Huguenot church, it became a Wesleyan chapel in 1809, the ultra-Orthodox Spitalfields Great Synagogue in 1897, and since 1976 has served as a mosque. Another example, a little further south, is **Christ Church primary school**, whose pupils are mostly Muslim; a hundred years ago they were mainly Jewish, as the Star of David on one of the drainpipes testifies. If you want to dig deeper into the area's past, contact **19 Princelet Street** (occasional open days; free; ☏020/7247 5352, ⓦwww.19princeletstreet.org.uk; Liverpool Street tube), where there's a permanent exhibition on Spitalfields' rich history of immigration. The building itself houses a wonderfully evocative disused synagogue, built by Polish Jews in the 1860s and hidden behind the Georgian facade. The attic was home to the mysterious real-life main character in Rachel Lichtenstein's *Rodinsky's Room* (see p.477).

The Old Truman Brewery and the markets

A red-brick chimney halfway up Brick Lane heralds the **Old Truman Brewery** (ⓦwww.trumanbrewery.com), founded back in 1666 and once the largest in the world. It's now a creative centre for music, fashion, art and IT and forms the focal point of Brick Lane's current gentrification. In **Dray's Lane**, the old stables have been turned into shops for independent designers and artists; cafés abound, including a vegan one in a bus (see p.387); and on Sundays, the market stalls that once filled Spitalfields now camp out in the outbuildings.

▲ Columbia Road flower and plant market

North of the brewery and railway Cheshire Street is the epicentre of **Brick Lane's Sunday market** (8am–2pm), selling everything from cheap hardware to fruit and veg and CDs. The shops tend to sell vintage clothing or are quirky one-offs like the self-consciously old-fashioned Labour and Wait at no. 18, or the neighbouring F–Art, and Shelf, which sell designer *objets*.

There's more trendification in the small-scale Victorian terraces north of Brick Lane. The **Columbia Road flower and plant market** (Sun 8am–2pm) is the descendant of the market that once occupied a huge cathedralesque Gothic Revival building financed in 1869 by Baroness Burdett-Coutts, who was appalled at the dishonesty of Cockney costermongers. The Archbishop of Canterbury and the Duke of Wellington were present at the grand opening, but the high-handed philanthropy behind the scheme – the great hall was daubed with uplifting inscriptions such as "Speak every man truth with his neighbour" – was resented by the traders. The market flopped and was handed back to the baroness within five years; it was finally pulled down in 1960.

Whitechapel Road

The East End institution that draws in more outsiders than any other is the **Whitechapel Art Gallery** (Wed–Sun 11am–6pm, Thurs until 9pm; free; ☎020/7522 7888, ⓦwww.whitechapel.org; Aldgate East tube), housed in a beautiful, crenellated 1899 Arts and Crafts building by Charles Harrison Townsend. The gallery was founded by one of the East End's many Victorian philanthropists, **Samuel Barnett**. His motives may have been dubious – "The principle of our work is that we aim at decreasing not suffering but sin", he

Anarchists in the East End

Founded in 1886, the **Freedom Press** (Mon–Sat noon–6pm, Sun noon–4pm; ☎020/7247 9249, ⓦwww.freedompress.org.uk; Aldgate East tube), a small anarchist bookshop and printing press in Angel Alley, by the side of the Whitechapel Art Gallery, is the lone survivor of an East End tradition of radical politics that reached its height at the end of the nineteenth century. For a roll call of famous anarchists, check out the stainless-steel portrait gallery in Angel Alley. East End anarchism found a strong following among the Jewish community especially, and supporters of the *Arbeter Fraint* newspaper staged atheist demonstrations outside Orthodox synagogues on the Sabbath, as well as making other gestures like ostentatiously smoking and eating ham sandwiches. In 1907, delegates to the Fifth Congress of the Russian Social Democratic Labour Party staged a meeting on the corner of Fulbourne Street attended by Lenin, Stalin, Trotsky, Gorky and Litvinov, and the Jubilee Street Anarchist Club later loaned £1700 to the Bolsheviks (paid back in full by the Soviet government after the revolution).

The event for which the anarchists are best remembered, however, is the **Siege of Sidney Street**, which took place in January 1911. A gun battle occurred after a routine police enquiry at the back of a jeweller's on Houndsditch, and left one Russian anarchist and three policemen dead. Over the next few weeks, all but three of the anarchist gang were arrested; following a tip-off, the three were eventually cornered in a building on Sidney Street. A further gun battle ensued: a detachment of Scots Guards and two cannons were deployed, and the Home Secretary, Winston Churchill, arrived on the scene to give orders. By lunchtime the house was in flames, leaving two charred bodies in the burnt-out shell. However, the ringleader, nicknamed Peter the Painter, vanished without trace, to join the likes of Jack the Ripper as an East End legend.

once claimed – but the legacy of his good works is still discernible across the East End. The gallery now puts on innovative exhibitions of contemporary art, as well as hosting the biennial East End Academy, a chance for local artists to get their work shown to a wider audience.

Whitechapel Road also boasts the most visible symbol of Muslim presence in the East End, the Saudi-financed **East London Mosque** (ⓦ www.eastlondon mosque.org.uk), a gaudy red-brick 1980s building which seats two thousand; it stands in marked contrast to the tiny **Fieldgate Street Great Synagogue**, behind the mosque, dating from 1899. Neither building is open to the public. Nearby, you can pay a quick visit to the small exhibition in the nearby **Whitechapel Bell Foundry** (Mon–Fri 9am–4.15pm; free; guided tours occasionally Sat 10am & 2pm, £10; no under-14s; ☎ 020/7247 2599, ⓦ www .whitechapelbellfoundry.co.uk; Whitechapel tube), part of which occupies the short terrace of Georgian houses on the corner of Fieldgate Street. Big Ben, the Liberty Bell, the Bow Bells and numerous English church bells (including those of Westminster Abbey) all hail from the foundry, established in 1570.

Past Vallance Road, the street widens at the beginning of **Whitechapel Market** (Mon–Sat 8am–6pm), once one of the largest hay markets in London, now given over to everything from nectarines to net curtains, and including a large number of stalls catering for the local Bengali and Somali communities. In the 1890s, this was where casual workers used to gather to be selected for work in the local sweatshops, earning it the Yiddish nickname *Hazer Mark*, or "pig market". Nearby, on the other side of Vallance Road, stood the Pavilion Theatre, one of several East End theatres that used to put on Yiddish shows for the thousands of newly arrived Jews. Raucous and irrev- erent, Yiddish theatre was frowned upon by the Anglicized Jews, the *Jewish Chronicle* stating that Yiddish was "a language we should be the last to encourage any efforts to preserve". The sole reminder of those days is the Edward VII monument at the centre of the market, erected by the local Jewish community in 1911.

It was on the Mile End Road that Joseph Merrick, better known as the **Elephant Man**, was discovered in a freak show in 1884 by Dr Treves, and subsequently admitted as a patient to the **Royal London Hospital** on Whitechapel Road. He remained there, on show as a medical freak, and was eventually allowed to live there until his death in 1890, at the age of just 27. There's an interesting twenty-minute documentary on Merrick, and a small section displaying, among other things, the veil and hat he wore, in the **Hospital Museum** (Mon–Fri 10am–4.30pm; free; ⓦ www.bartsandthelondon .nhs.uk; Whitechapel tube) on Newark Street. The museum also covers the history of the hospital and of nursing and medicine in general, with a section on Edith Cavell, who trained here before assisting Allied soldiers to escape from occupied Belgium; she was eventually arrested and shot as a spy by the Germans in 1915.

At the eastern end of Whitechapel Road stands the handsome, gabled entrance to the former Albion Brewery, where the first bottled brown ale was produced in 1899. Next door is the **Blind Beggar**, the East End's most famous pub since March 8, 1966, when Ronnie Kray walked into the crowded bar and shot gangland rival George Cornell for calling him a "fat poof". This murder spelt the end of the infamous Kray Twins, Ronnie and Reggie, both of whom were sentenced to life imprisonment, though their well-publicized gifts to local charities created a Robin Hood image that still persists.

The Whitechapel murders

In eight weeks between August and November 1888, five prostitutes were stabbed to death in and around Whitechapel. Few of the letters received by the press and police, which purported to come from the murderer, are thought to have been genuine (including the one which coined the nickname **Jack the Ripper**), and the murderer's identity remains a mystery to this day. At the time, it was assumed he was a Jew, probably a *shochet* (a ritual slaughterman), since the mutilations were obviously carried out with some skill. The theory gained ground when the fourth victim was discovered outside the predominantly Jewish Working Men's Club off Commercial Road, and for a while it was dangerous for Jews to walk the streets at night for fear of reprisals.

Ripperologists have trawled through the little evidence there is to produce **numerous suspects**, none of whom can be conclusively proven guilty. The most celebrated suspect is the Duke of Clarence, eldest son of the future Edward VII, an easy if improbable target, since he was involved in a scandal involving a male brothel and was a well-known homosexual. Crime writer Patricia Cornwell spent over a million dollars trying (and failing) to prove conclusively that the Ripper was the painter Walter Sickert, who exhibited an unhealthy fascination with the murders. The man who usually tops the lists, however, was a cricket-playing barrister named Druitt whose body was found floating in the Thames some weeks after the last murder, though, as usual, there is no evidence linking him with any of them.

The one **positive outcome** of the murders was that they focused the attention of the rest of London on the squalor of the East End. Philanthropist Samuel Barnett, for one, used the media attention to press for improved housing, streetlighting and policing to combat crime and poverty in the area. Today, the murders continue to be exploited in gory, misogynistic detail by the likes of Madame Tussaud's and the London Dungeon, while guided walks retracing the Ripper's steps set off every week throughout the year.

Mile End Road

Beyond Cambridge Heath Road, Whitechapel Road becomes the **Mile End Road**. The first section, known as the Mile End Waste, is punctuated at the western end by a bust, and at the eastern by a more dramatic statue, of the most famous East End philanthropist, **William Booth**. It was here, one June evening in 1865, that Booth, moved by the sight of the crowds at the pubs and gin palaces, made his first impromptu public speech. Later on he set up a tent on Vallance Road and began in earnest the missionary work that eventually led to the foundation of the quasi-military **Salvation Army** in 1878. In contrast to many Victorian philanthropists, Booth never accepted the divisive concept of the deserving and undeserving poor – "if a man was poor, he was deserving". Booth railed against the laissez-faire economic policies of his era, while attending to the immediate demands of the poor, setting up soup kitchens and founding hostels, which, by the time of his death in 1912, had spread right across the globe. Booth is buried in Abney Park Cemetery (see p.297).

Another East End philanthropist, **Frederick Charrington**, used to try his best to steer the local inhabitants away from their sinful ways at this very spot. Heir to the eponymous local brewery, Charrington was, rather surprisingly, a tireless temperance campaigner, who in 1886 established a vast Assembly Hall on the **Mile End Waste**, capable of seating five thousand, with a Coffee Palace and a "pure" book salon. He tried unsuccessfully to close down the neighbouring music hall by marching up and down outside with sandwich boards reading "The Wages of Sin is Death" and, more effectively, used to keep vigil outside brothels, threatening to publish the names of those who entered.

There are two unusual architectural features worth mentioning on the Waste. The biggest surprise is the **Trinity Almshouses**, a quaint courtyard of cottages with a central chapel, built in 1695 for "Twenty-eight decay'd Masters and Commanders and the widows of such". Further up, on the same side of the street, stands a large Neoclassical former department store, sporting a central domed tower, its facade of Ionic half-columns sliced in two by a small two-storey shop that used to belong to a Jewish watchmaker called **Spiegelhalter**. This architectural oddity is the result of a dispute between Spiegelhalter and his affluent Gentile neighbour, Thomas Wickham, who was forced to build his new store around the watchmaker's shop after he refused to be bought out.

Ragged School Museum

To the south of the Mile End Road, on the bombed-out remains of Copperfield Road, the **Ragged School Museum** (Wed & Thurs 10am–5pm, first Sun of month 2–5pm; free; ☎020/8980 6405, ⓦwww.raggedschoolmuseum.org.uk; Mile End tube) occupies a Victorian canalside warehouse originally used to store lime juice. Accommodating more than one thousand pupils from 1877 to 1908, this was the largest of London's numerous Ragged Schools, institutions that provided free education and two free meals daily to children with no means to pay the penny a week charged by most Victorian schools. This particular Ragged School was just one of innumerable projects set up by the East End's most irrepressible philanthropist, the diminutive and devout **Dr Thomas Barnardo**, whose tireless work for the children of the East End is the subject of the ground-floor exhibition. Upstairs, there's a reconstructed Victorian schoolroom, where period-dressed teachers, cane in hand, take today's schoolkids through the rigours of a Victorian lesson, and on the top floor you can see two contrasting mock-up kitchens from the 1890s and the 1950s. There are also further displays on the nearby docks and local sweatshops, and a canalside café back on the ground floor.

Three Mills Island

As it continues east, the Mile End Road becomes Bow Road and eventually crosses the A102 and the River Lea. The reason to head out here is to visit the eighteenth-century architectural ensemble of **Three Mills Island**, an artificial island in the River Lea. Despite its name, there are now only two mills remaining, the most distinctive of which is the Clock Mill, with its conical oasts – kilns used to dry out grain – and its pretty white clock tower. Opposite stands the Dutch-style **House Mill** (May–Oct Sun 1–4pm; £3; ☎020/8980 4626, ⓦwww.housemill.org.uk; Bromley-by-Bow tube), built in 1776, and now open for guided tours, which explain the milling process and show you the surviving mill wheels which were driven by the tide. On the first Sunday of the month (March–Dec), the mill is open from 11am and there's also a craft market. Beyond the mills are later gin-distillery buildings, most of which have now been converted into television and film studios.

Visible to the northeast of the island is the new **Abbey Mills Pumping Station**, sporting a gleaming metal pitched roof, and, adjacent, its much more famous Victorian predecessor, a glorious Gothic-Italianate edifice nicknamed the "Cathedral of Sewage". The latter was built in the 1860s by Joseph Bazalgette and Edwin Cooper, and was originally flanked by two twin chimneys

2012 Olympics

The focus of the 2012 **Olympic Games** (⊛ www.london2012.com) will be the **Olympic Park**, situated in a most unlikely East End backwater by the River Lea, just north of Three Mills Island and the Abbey Mills Pumping Station between Hackney Wick and Stratford. The centrepiece of the park will be an 80,000-seat Olympic Stadium, which will become a 25,000-seat athletics stadium after the games. Close by, there'll be a 20,000-seat aquatic centre, a 3000-seat velodrome and an outdoor BMX track, a 15,000-seat hockey complex and several other multi-sports arenas. The Olympic Village, housing nearly 18,000 athletes, will also be here, and will be converted to public housing after the games.

The rest of the events will take place in and around London, mostly in existing venues: Wimbledon will obviously host the tennis; Wembley Stadium some of the football; ExCel, by Royal Victoria Dock, will be used for a whole host of sports from boxing to table tennis; and Eton's rowing centre will serve for some canoeing and kayaking events as well as for skulling. The Dome will finally serve a useful purpose by hosting the gymnastics and basketball finals, along with a smaller temporary venue for rhythmic gymnastics and badminton, and Earl's Court will host the volleyball. Equestrian events are scheduled for Greenwich Park, while Hyde Park will host the triathlon and Regent's Park the road cycling. Archery will take place at Lord's Cricket Ground, shooting at the Royal Artillery Barracks in Woolwich and – the one piece of planning that's really grabbed the headlines – beach volleyball will be staged on Horse Guards Parade. Only sailing, mountain biking and the canoeing slalom will take place any great distance from the capital.

The games will certainly generate employment, and provide some badly needed housing for a deprived area, though it's difficult to judge how great the long-term benefits will really be. Despite protestations to the contrary, the environmental costs will be great, and council taxes in London – already among the highest in the country – are set to rise to pay for the privilege. On the positive side, East London's transport infrastructure will improve: Stratford International will be linked by train with St Pancras in seven minutes, and with Paris in just over two hours; the East London Line will be extended north into Hackney and south to Crystal Palace; and the Docklands Light Railway will reach Woolwich.

decorated in Moorish style, which were sadly demolished during World War II. Visible to the southeast of Three Mills are seven ornate, Grade II–listed wrought-iron **Victorian gasholders**, built on the site of a rocket factory set up in the 1820s by William Congreve.

Victoria Park

Victoria Park (daily 7am–dusk; bus #277 from Mile End tube or bus #8 from Liverpool Street tube), London's first public park – as opposed to royal park – was opened in the heart of the East End in 1845, after a local MP presented Queen Victoria with a petition of thirty thousand signatures. The only large open space in the area, "Viccy Park" immediately became a favourite spot for **political rallies**: Chartists congregated here in their thousands in 1848; Suffragette supporters of the ELFS gathered here, under the leadership of Sylvia Pankhurst; it even had its own Speakers' Corner attended by the likes of George Bernard Shaw and William Morris.

The park boasts the world's oldest **model boat club**, the Victoria Model Steam Boat Club, which meets on most summer Sunday mornings. Look out, too, for the **Dogs of Alcibiades**, two snarling sculpted beasts based on the Molossian hounds kept by the Athenian statesman and presented by Lady

Regnart in 1912. The much larger eastern section of the park contains an extraordinarily lavish Gothic-cum-Moorish **drinking fountain**, decorated with oversized cherubs and paid for by Baroness Burdett-Coutts in 1861 – it hasn't functioned for years. At the park's eastern edge are two alcoves from old London Bridge, brought here in 1860.

Museum of Childhood

The **Museum of Childhood** (daily 10am–5.45pm; free; ☎020/8980 2415, Ⓦwww.vam.ac.uk/moc), a branch of the V&A, is situated just across Cambridge Heath Road from Bethnal Green tube station. The elegant, open-plan wrought-iron hall was, in fact, part of the original V&A building, and was transported here from South Kensington in the late 1860s in order to bring art to the East End. The emphasis has changed since those pioneering days, and although the wide range of exhibits means that there's something here for everyone, the museum's most frequent visitors are children, with plenty of hands-on exhibits and special kids' events at weekends and during school holidays.

To the right as you enter, are the clockwork and moving **toys** – bring your 20p pieces for the bigger exhibits – everything from classic robots to a fully functioning model railway, early computer games, and wooden toys – there's often a queue for the replica Victorian rocking horse. At the back, the museum has a great collection of marionettes and puppets, which brings you into the doll and figures section, ranging from teddies and Smurfs to Inuit dolls. The most famous exhibits are the remarkable antique **dolls' houses** dating back to 1673: they are displayed upstairs, where you'll also find antique dolls and prams, a play area for very small kids, the ever-popular Albert and the Lion, and a space for temporary exhibitions.

Docklands

A whole people toil at the unloading of the enormous ships, swarming on the barges, dark figures, dimly outlined, moving rhythmically, fill in and give life to the picture. In the far distance, behind the interminable lines of sheds and warehouses, masts bound the horizon, masts like a bare forest in winter, finely branched, exaggerated, aerial trees grown in all the climates of the globe.

Gabriel Mourey (1865–1943)

T
he architectural embodiment of Thatcherism according to its critics or a blueprint for inner-city regeneration to its free-market supporters – the **Docklands** development has always provoked extreme reactions. Despite the catch-all name, however, Docklands is far from homogeneous. **Canary Wharf**, with its Manhattan-style skyscrapers, is only its most visible landmark, and is by no means typical of the area; warehouse conversions, industrial-estate sheds, left-over council housing, and Costa del Thames apartments in a whole travesty of styles, are more indicative. **Wapping**, the most easily accessible district, has retained and restored much of its original Victorian warehouse architecture, while the Royal Docks, further east, are still in the process of being developed. Travelling through on the **Docklands Light Railway (DLR)**, the area comes over as a fascinating open-air design museum, not a place one would choose to live or work necessarily – most people stationed here see it as removed from the rest of London – but a spectacular sight nevertheless.

From the sixteenth century onwards the **Port of London** was the key to the city's wealth. The "legal quays" – roughly the area between London Bridge and the Tower – were crowded with as many as 1400 seagoing vessels forced to wait for up to six weeks to be unloaded, with some 3500 cutters, barges and punts jostling between their hulls. It was to relieve such congestion that, from 1802 onwards, London constructed the largest enclosed **cargo-dock system** in the world. Each dock was surrounded by forty-foot-high walls, patrolled by its own police force and geared towards a specific cargo. Casual dockers gathered at the dock gates each morning for the "call-on", a human scrummage to get selected for work. This mayhem was only stopped after World War II, when the Dock Labour Scheme was introduced, and by then it was too late. Since the mid-nineteenth century, competition from the railways had been eroding the river traffic, and with the development of container ships and the movement of the port downriver to Tilbury in the 1960s, the old city docks began to wind down.

In 1981, the **London Docklands Development Corporation (LDDC)** was set up to regenerate the area, with the unfortunate slogan of "Looks like Venice, works like New York". By the time the LDDC was wound up in 1998, it had

Visiting Docklands

Nothing will convey to the stranger a better idea of the vast activity and stupendous wealth of London than a visit to these warehouses, filled to overflowing with interminable stores of every kind of foreign and colonial products; to these enormous vaults, with their apparently inexhaustible quantities of wine; and to these extensive quays and landing-stages, cumbered with huge stacks of hides, heaps of bales, and long rows of casks…Those who wish to taste the wines must procure a tasting-order from a wine merchant. Ladies are not admitted after 1pm. Visitors should be on their guard against insidious effects of "tasting" in the heavy, vinous atmosphere.

Baedeker (1905)

Sadly, visits to the docks are no longer as intoxicating. You can, however, view Docklands from a distance on one of the boats that course up and down the Thames (see p.26). For a close-up you should take the driverless, overhead **Docklands Light Railway** or **DLR** (see p.25). If you're heading for Greenwich, and fancy taking a boat back into town, it might be worth considering a Rail & River Rover ticket (£13.50), which gives you unlimited travel on the DLR and City Cruises services between Greenwich and Westminster. Alternatively, you can now **walk** the two miles from Wapping to Canary Wharf along, or close to, the river bank, by following the **Thames Path**; there are also several pedestrian bridges linking the different quays around Canary Wharf. Note that bicycles are not allowed on the DLR, though you can walk them through the Greenwich Foot Tunnel.

achieved more than many thought possible, though it's certainly easy to criticize its approach – ad hoc planning, and a lack of basic amenities, of open green spaces, of civic architecture or public buildings, and of consultation with the local community. Today, however, construction is continuing apace, with the end result destined to be, as one critic aptly put it, "a chain of highly polarized ghettos epitomizing the gulf between the rich and poor, home-owner and tenant". For the local community's views on the Docklands, visit Ⓦwww.wharf.co.uk.

Wapping

Once famous for its boatyards and its 36 riverside pubs (a handful of which remain), **Wapping** changed forever with the construction of the enclosed docks in the early nineteenth century. Cut off from the rest of the East End by the high walls of the docks, its inhabitants crowded into unsanitary housing, the area became notorious for its thieves, attracted by the opportunities of rolling drunk sailors and poorly guarded warehouses. With the demise of the docks, Wapping became an early candidate for regeneration, but restoration and renovation of existing property rather than demolition and redevelopment has been the rule. Thus something of Wapping's Victorian atmosphere has been preserved, and, as it lies just a short walk east of the Tower, this is easily the most satisfying part of Docklands to explore.

St Katharine Docks

St Katharine Docks (Ⓦwww.skdocks.co.uk) were built in the late 1820s immediately east of the Tower – in the process some 11,300 people were made homeless, and the medieval hospital of St Katharine was demolished. Having specialized in luxury goods such as ivory, spices, carpets and cigars, the docks were very badly bombed in the Blitz and, in the early 1970s, were turned into a luxury yacht marina.

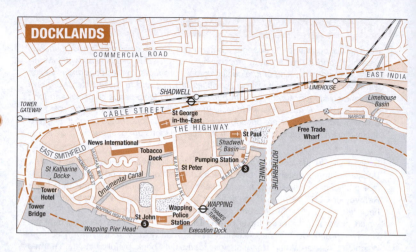

Much of the original warehouse architecture has gone, but the docks' redeeming qualities are the old **swing bridges**, the one or two old sailing ships and Dutch barges that moor here, and the **Ivory House** warehouse, with its clock tower and wrought-iron colonnade, at the centre of the three basins. Built in 1854, at its peak this warehouse received over two hundred tons of ivory annually (that's four thousand dead elephants), plus hippopotamus and walrus teeth and even mammoth tusks from Siberia. Halfway along East Smithfield, you can see the original gates with elephants on the pillars, and on the corner of Thomas More Street, a section of the **original dock wall** survives, plus the main entrance to the former London Docks, with two Neoclassical Customs and Excise offices from 1805.

A steady stream of tourists passes through the docks, heading for the *Dickens Inn*, an eighteenth-century timber-framed brewery warehouse that was air-lifted in 1969 from its original site several hundred yards to the east. Roughly at the centre of the docks is the ugly **Coronarium chapel** (now a *Starbucks*), built for Queen Elizabeth II's Silver Jubilee, and situated as near as possible to the old church of St Katharine's, which was itself owned by the Crown.

News International to St George-in-the-East

East down the busy Highway lies the headquarters of Rupert Murdoch's **News International**, a complex dubbed "Fortress Wapping", on account of its high walls, barbed wire and security cameras. Murdoch was one of the first capitalist barons to give Docklands his blessing, sacking his entire workforce of printers and journalists when he moved his newspapers – *The Times*, *Sunday Times*, *The Sun* and *News of the World* – out here in 1986, thus sparking one of the most bitter trade-union disputes of the Thatcher era. Mounted police engaged in violent skirmishes with protesters for nearly a year – no prizes for guessing who won.

Close by stands **Tobacco Dock**, a huge warehouse built in 1814 and initially used to store tobacco and wine (sheepskin, cork and molasses came later). A fascinating combination of timber and early cast-iron framing, it was converted into a shopping complex in 1990 by postmodernist Terry Farrell, but the place has been empty for years.

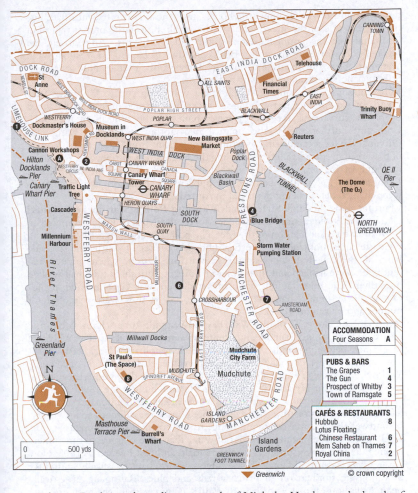

ACCOMMODATION
Four Seasons   A

PUBS & BARS
The Grapes   1
The Gun   4
Prospect of Whitby 3
Town of Ramsgate   5

CAFÉS & RESTAURANTS
Hubbub   8
Lotus Floating
  Chinese Restaurant 6
Mem Saheb on Thames 7
Royal China   2

Greenwich ▼   © crown copyright

Tobacco Dock is a short distance south of Nicholas Hawksmoor's church of **St George-in-the-East** (daily 9am–5pm; Ⓦ www.stgite.org.uk), built in 1726 on the north side of the busy Highway. As bold as any of Hawksmoor's buildings, it boasts four "pepperpot" towers above the nave, built to house the staircases to the church's galleries, and a hulking west-end tower topped by an octagonal lantern. Within, it comes as something of a shock to find a miniature modern church squatting in the nave, but that's all the parish could come up with following the devastation of the Blitz.

Beginning south of Tobacco Dock, a tree-lined **canal walk** – all that remains of the huge Western Dock that once stood here – will take you effortlessly back to Wapping High Street.

Wapping High Street to Shadwell Basin

If you arrive on **Wapping High Street** expecting the usual parade of shops, you're in for a big surprise. Traditionally, the business of Wapping took place on the river; thus tall brick-built warehouses, most now converted into flats, line the Thames side of the street, while to the north, in a stark contrast typical of Docklands, lie the council estates of the older residents. (Alf Garnett, the bigoted dockworker of the 1960s BBC comedy *Till Death Us Do Part*, lived in Wapping.) Few tourists make it out here, but it's only a ten-minute walk from St Katharine Docks, and well worth the effort.

Five minutes' walk along the High Street will bring you to **Wapping Pier Head**, former entrance to the London Docks, now grassed over but still flanked by grand, curvaceous Regency terraces built for the officials of the Dock Company. Further east is the unusual neo-Gothic former tea warehouse, **Oliver's Wharf**, a trailblazing apartment conversion from 1972, with a couple of preserved overhead gangways crossing the High Street just beyond. You'll also find one of the few surviving stairs down to the river beside the *Town of Ramsgate* pub (see p.402); beneath the pub are the dungeons where convicts were chained before being deported to Australia.

Further along the High Street stands **Wapping Police Station**, headquarters of the world's oldest uniformed police force, the Marine Police, founded in 1798 and now a subdivision of the Met. The police boatyard is a 1960s building which features funky, abstract, vertical fibreglass friezes. Down by the riverside here, at the low-water mark, was **Execution Dock**, where pirates and mutineers were hanged and then hung in a gibbet until three tides had washed over them. The most famous felon to perish here was Captain Kidd, pirate-catcher-turned-pirate, hanged in 1701; the last victims were executed for murder and mutiny in 1830.

Further east, along **Wapping Wall**, beyond Wapping tube station, you'll find the finest collection of nineteenth-century warehouses left in the whole of Docklands, beginning with the gargantuan Metropolitan Wharf, its wrought-iron capstan cranes and pulleys still clearly in evidence. At the far end of Wapping Wall is the venerable *Prospect of Whitby* pub (see p.402), and, opposite, the ivy-clad red-brick **London Hydraulic Pumping Station**, built in the 1890s and once chief supplier of hydraulic power to the whole of central London, powering the likes of the bascules of Tower Bridge; it now houses a restaurant and art gallery.

Shadwell Basin, over the swing bridge to the north of the Pumping Station, is one of the last remaining stretches of water that once comprised three interlocking docks, known simply as London Docks and first opened in 1805. Now a water-sports centre, it's enclosed on three sides by characteristically gimmicky new housing finished off in primary reds and blues. Rising up majestically behind the houses to the north is **St Paul's** (Ⓦ www.stpaulsshadwell.org), the "sea captains' church", with a Baroque tower.

Limehouse

East of Wapping, **Limehouse** was a major shipbuilding centre in the eighteenth and nineteenth centuries, hub of London's canal traffic and the site of the city's first **Chinatown**, a district sensationalized in Victorian newspapers as a warren of opium and gambling dens, by the likes of Oscar Wilde, Arthur Conan Doyle, Sax Rohmer, and Dickens: "Down by the docks the shabby undertaker's shop will bury you for next to nothing, after the Malay or Chinaman has stabbed you for nothing at all." Wartime bombing and postwar road schemes all but obliterated Limehouse; the only remnants of the Chinese community are the street names: Canton, Mandarin, Ming and Pekin among them.

Heading east from Wapping to Limehouse, the Thames Path passes below the Legoland ziggurat apartments of **Free Trade Wharf**, eventually bringing you out on **Narrow Street**, Limehouse's sleepy main thoroughfare. Continuing past the giant herring-gull sculpture, several excellent pubs and the entrance to the packed Limehouse Basin, you'll come to Hawksmoor's **St Anne's Church**, rising up beyond the DLR, to the north. Begun in 1714, and dominated by a gargantuan west tower, topped by an octagonal lantern, it boasts the highest church clock in London. The interior was badly damaged by fire in 1850, though it does contain a superb organ built for the Great Exhibition the following year. In the graveyard Hawksmoor erected a pyramidal structure carved with masonic symbols, now hopelessly eroded; opposite is a war memorial with relief panels depicting the horrors of trench warfare.

Back on the waterfront, the Thames Path continues inexorably towards the Isle of Dogs. A pedestrian bridge carries the path over the entrance to the tidal inlet of **Limekiln Dock**, overlooked to the north by a picturesque gaggle of listed warehouses, and to the south by the gargantuan Dundee Wharf development, sporting a huge grey free-standing pylon of balconies. Beyond lies the mock-Egyptian development that houses the *Four Seasons Hotel* (see p.373). The Thames Path will eventually plough its way right round the Isle of Dogs, but for now it's still a bit stop-start once you get past Canary Wharf Pier.

Isle of Dogs

The Thames begins a dramatic horseshoe bend at Limehouse, thus creating the **Isle of Dogs**. The origin of the peninsula's strange name has been much debated: it could be a corruption of ducks, or of dykes, or, in fact, refer to the royal kennels which once stood here. In 1802, London's first enclosed trade docks were built here to accommodate rum and sugar from the West Indies, and later expanded, boosting the population to 21,000 by 1901. The demise of the docks was slow in coming, but rapid in its conclusion: in 1975, there were still eight thousand jobs; five years later the docks were closed. Now at the heart of the new Docklands, the Isle of Dogs reaches its apotheosis in **Canary Wharf**, home to Britain's three tallest buildings. Yet while some ninety thousand workers trek to Canary Wharf each weekday, the rest of the "island" remains surreally lifeless, an uneasy, socially divided community comprised of drab council housing, encompassed by a horseshoe of crass, super-rich, riverside developments.

Canary Wharf

The strip of land in the middle of the former West India Docks, **Canary Wharf** was originally a destination for rum and mahogany, and later tomatoes and bananas (from the Canary Islands, hence the name). It's the easiest bit of the Isle of Dogs to explore on foot, though the whole place feels a bit like a stage-set, a spotlessly clean business quarter policed by security guards, with make-believe streets like Wren Steps and Chancellor Passage. The most famous building is Cesar Pelli's stainless-steel **Canary Wharf Tower** (closed to the public) – at 800ft, the highest building in the country (for the moment at least – see p.187). Officially known as **One Canada Square**, the tower is flanked by Norman Foster's glassy HSBC and Pelli's Citigroup skyscrapers, both of which are 656ft high.

Arriving by boat, bus or foot at Canary Wharf, you approach from Westferry Circus, the double-decker roundabout park at the western end of the tree-lined West India Avenue. This, in turn, leads to Cabot Square, centred on a graceful fountain, and, beyond, to the colonnaded offices that terminate at Canada Square. **Arriving by DLR** at Canary Wharf is even more spectacular, with the rail line cutting right through the middle of the office buildings, spanned by Pelli's parabolic steel-and-glass canopy. **Arriving by tube**, you get probably the best

▲ Canary Wharf

close-up view of the Pelli tower from the forest of public clocks on West Plaza, right outside Norman Foster's stingray-like entrance to the tube.

West India Quay and around

North of Cabot Square, you can cross a floodlit floating bridge to **West India Quay**, probably the most pleasant new development on the Isle of Dogs. Here, the last two surviving Georgian warehouses of the West India Docks now house flats, bars, restaurants and the Museum of Docklands (see p.218). Out on the water, look out for the **SS Robin** (℡020/7538 0652, Ⓦwww.ssrobin.com), the world's oldest complete steamship, originally launched at the East India Dock in 1890 and now a photographic gallery and café.

Immediately to the west of the warehouses is the old entrance to the West India Docks, heralded by the **Ledger Building** (now a pub), which sports a dinky Doric portico and, round the corner, a splendidly pompous plaque commemorating the opening of the docks from 1800. Opposite, across Hertsmere Road, stands a small, circular, domed building, the surviving one of two guardhouses that flanked the main entrance to the docks; behind it lies the former cooperage, now the **Cannon Workshops**.

To the northeast, behind the Ledger Building, are more little-known remnants of the old docks, among them the stately **Dockmaster's House**, built in 1809 as the Excise Office and now an Indian restaurant, with a smart white balustrade. Behind here, on Garford Street, there's a prim row of **Dock Constables' Cottages**, built in pairs in 1802, with the one for the sergeant slightly detached. Before you reach them, you'll pass **Grieg House**, a lovely yellow-and-red-brick building, built in 1903 as part of the Scandinavian Seamen's Temperance Home, with a little cupola and lovely exterior mouldings.

Museum in Docklands

If you've any interest in the history of the docks or the Thames, then a visit to the **Museum in Docklands** (daily 10am–6pm; £5; ℡020/7001 9844, Ⓦwww .museumindocklands.org.uk; West India Quay DLR) is well worth it. Housed in a warehouse built in 1803 for storing rum, sugar, molasses, coffee and cotton, the museum takes a conventional chronological approach, beginning on the top floor, where you'll find a great model of old London Bridge, one side depicting it in 1440, the other around 1600. Also here is the Rhinebeck Panorama, an eight-foot-long watercolour showing the "legal quays" in the 1790s, just before the enclosed docks eased congestion. On the floor below, there are diverse sections on slavery, frost fairs and whaling, a reconstructed warren of late nineteenth-century shops and cobbled streets called "Sailortown", plus mock-ups of a cooperage, a bottling vault and a tobacco-weighing office. Look out, too, for the model of Brunel's *Leviathan*, the fascinating wartime film reel and the excellent even-handed coverage of the docks' postwar history. Those with kids should head for Mudlarks, where children can learn a bit about pulleys and ballast, drive a DLR train or simply romp around the soft play area.

South of Canary Wharf

Points of interest elsewhere on the Isle of Dogs are few and far between, but one or two monuments are worth pointing out. One of Docklands' more playful monuments is Pierre Vivant's **Traffic Light Tree**, west of Heron Quays, which features a cluster of traffic signals all flashing madly – a strangely confusing sight for drivers after dark. Impossible to miss, to the southwest, is **Cascades**, a wedge of high-rise triangular apartments that's become something of a Docklands landmark. Equally unavoidable is **Millennium Harbour**, a gated development whose weatherboarded top-floor penthouses jut out like air-traffic-control towers.

The only other slice of the Isle of Dogs worth exploring on foot is **Island Gardens**, in the far south, from which Christopher Wren used to contemplate his masterpieces, the Royal Naval College and the Royal Observatory, across the river in Greenwich and accessible either via the DLR or the 1902 **Greenwich Foot Tunnel**.

If you'd rather explore a little more of Docklands, head west along the river or Westferry Road until you come to **Burrell's Wharf**, a residential development based around the industrial relics of the old Millwall Ironworks, built in the 1830s. The boiler-house chimney survives, as does the Italianate Plate House, where the steel plates for Isambard Kingdom Brunel's 19,000-ton steamship, the *Great Eastern* (aka the *Leviathan*), were manufactured. Built at a cost of £1 million, the *Leviathan* was four times larger than any other ship in the world at the time, but enjoyed a working life of just sixteen years as a passenger liner and cable-layer. The timber piles of the ship's 1857 launching site can still be seen, a little further upstream from Burrell's Wharf.

Trinity Buoy Wharf

Hidden away to the east of East India Dock, **Trinity Buoy Wharf** is the most bizarre little enclave. Built in 1803, it is home to London's only lighthouse, one of a pair built by Trinity House for experiments in optics and used by, among others, Michael Faraday. The wharf itself is also home to several innovative offices and flats, fashioned out of old shipping containers, an original 1940s American mobile diner where you can get a bite to eat, and a whole array of interesting boats, including an old lightship. In the lighthouse itself, there's a musical installation called **Longplayer** (first weekend of month 11am–5pm; Dec–March closes 4pm; free; ⊛longplayer.org), a twenty-minute recording of Tibetan singing bowls, manipulated to create a 1000-year-long loop, and due to play until December 31, 2999. The wharf is a ten-minute walk from East India DLR station, at the end of Orchard Place, where the Bow Creek winds its way into the Thames.

15

The South Bank

For centuries London stopped southwards at the Thames; the **South Bank** was a marshy, uninhabitable place, a popular place for duck-shooting, but otherwise seldom visited. Then, in the eighteenth century, wharves began to be built along the riverbank, joined later by factories, so that by 1905 the *Baedeker* guidebook characterized Lambeth (covered in this chapter) and Southwark (covered in the next chapter) as "containing numerous potteries, glass-works, machine-factories, breweries and hop-warehouses". Slums and overhead railway lines added to the grime until 1951, when a slice of **Lambeth**'s badly bombed riverside was used as a venue for the Festival of Britain, the site eventually evolving into the **Southbank Centre**, a concrete arts complex forever criticized by Londoners.

Recently, however, more and more visitors (and locals) have discovered that the South Bank has, in fact, got a lot going for it. Since most of London sits on the north bank of the Thames, the views from the South Bank are the best. Even more importantly, you can explore the whole area on foot, free from the traffic noise and fumes that blight so much of central London, and then continue east along the riverside walkway into the regenerated districts of Bankside and Southwark. What helped kick-start the South Bank's rejuvenation was the arrival of the spectacular **London Eye**, the world's largest observation wheel, followed by the state-of-the-art **BFI IMAX cinema**; the renovation of the distinctive **OXO Tower** building; and the rejuvenation of **Hungerford Bridge**, which was flanked by a majestic symmetrical double-suspension footbridge.

Other popular attractions in the area include the London Aquarium, situated close to the London Eye, and, further inland, the **Imperial War Museum**, which harbours the country's only permanent exhibition devoted to the Holocaust. To find out about the latest events and exhibitions on the South Bank (and in neighbouring Southwark) visit Ⓦwww.london-se1.co.uk.

Southbank Centre and around

In 1951, the South Bank Exhibition, on derelict land south of the Thames, formed the centrepiece of the national **Festival of Britain**, an attempt to revive morale postwar by celebrating the centenary of the Great Exhibition (when Britain really did rule over half the world). The most striking features of the site were the Ferris wheel (now reincarnated as the London Eye), the saucer-shaped Dome of Discovery (inspiration for the Millennium Dome), the Royal Festival Hall (which still stands) and the cigar-shaped steel and aluminium Skylon tower.

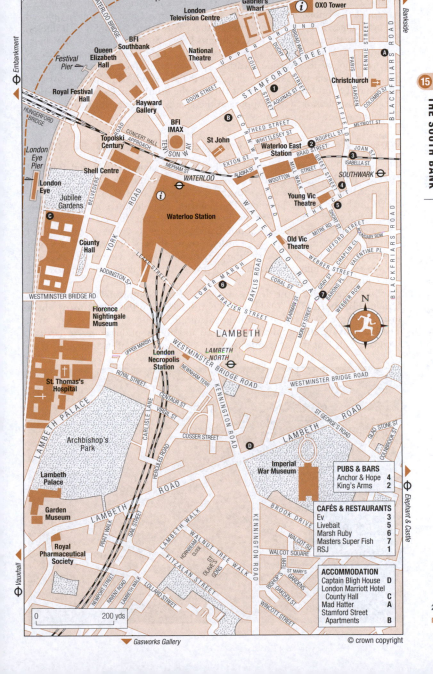

River Thames

⊖ *Blackfriars*

Bankside

Doggett's
Coat & Badge

RIVERSIDE WALK

Gabriel's
Wharf

ⓘ OXO Tower

London
Television Centre

WATERLOO BRIDGE

BFI
Southbank

National
Theatre

UPPER GROUND

BROAD WALL

DUCHY

STAMFORD STREET

RENNIE STREET

BLACKFRIARS ROAD

Ⓐ

Christchurch

Queen
Elizabeth
Hall

COIN STREET

AQUINAS ST

PARIS GARDEN

COLOMBO ST

*Festival
Pier*

Royal Festival
Hall

DOON STREET

❶

Ⓑ

MEYMOTT ST

HATFIELDS

Hayward
Gallery

CONCERT HALL APPROACH

THEED STREET

Topolski
Century

BFI
IMAX

St John

WHITTLESEY ST

ROUPELL ST

❷

JOAN ST

HUNGERFORD BRIDGE

BELVEDERE ROAD

TENISON WAY

MEPHAM ST

St John

EXTON ST

Waterloo East
Station

BRAD STREET

GREET STREET

ISABELLA ST

*London
Eye
Pier*

WATERLOO

ALASKA ST

WOOTTON STREET

SOUTHWARK ⊖

London
Eye

Shell Centre

Jubilee
Gardens

Ⓒ

YORK ROAD

Waterloo Station

MITRE RD

❹

❺

Young Vic
Theatre

SHORT ST

UFFORD STREET

BOUNDARY ROW

County
Hall

ADDINGTON ST

LEAKE STREET

Old Vic
Theatre

GRAY'S PL

CHAPLIN CL

VALENTINE PL

WEBBER STREET

WEBBER ROW

N

WESTMINSTER BRIDGE RD

LOWER MARSH

BAYLIS ROAD

CORAL ST

FRAZIER STREET

HERCULES ROAD

PEARMAN ST

BARONS PL

❼

Florence
Nightingale
Museum

UPPER MARSH

WESTMINSTER BRIDGE ROAD

❻

LAMBETH

MORLEY ST

WESTMINSTER BRIDGE ROAD

London
Necropolis
Station

NEWNHAM TERR

*LAMBETH
NORTH* ⊖

St. Thomas's
Hospital

ROYAL STREET

CENTAUR ST

VIRGIL ST

KENNINGTON ROAD

ST GEORGE'S ROAD

GLADSTONE ST

COLOMBO ST

LAMBETH PALACE ROAD

CARLISLE LANE

COSSER STREET

Ⓓ

LAMBETH ROAD

Archbishop's
Park

Imperial
War Museum

BROOK DRIVE

PUBS & BARS
Anchor & Hope 4
King's Arms 2

Lambeth
Palace

WALNUT TREE WALK

SAIL STREET

PRATT WALK

LAMBETH WALK

FITZALAN STREET

HORSEMAN CLOSE

OLIVE RD

WALCOT SQ

WALCOT SQUARE

CAFÉS & RESTAURANTS
Ev 3
Livebait 5
Marsh Ruby 6
Masters Super Fish 7
RSJ 1

Garden
Museum

LAMBETH ROAD

Royal
Pharmaceutical
Society

NEWPORT STREET

LAMBETH HIGH ST

BARON ROAD

BISHOPS TERR

ST MARY'S
GARDENS

LOLLARD STREET

WINCOTT STREET

OAKDEN ST

ACCOMMODATION
Captain Bligh House D
London Marriott Hotel
  County Hall C
Mad Hatter A
Stamford Street
  Apartments B

⊖ *Vauxhall*

⊖ *Elephant & Castle*

Gasworks Gallery

© crown copyright

0 200 yds

The great success of the festival eventually provided the impetus for the creation of the **Southbank Centre** (Ⓦ www.southbankcentre.co.uk), comprising the Royal Festival Hall, Queen Elizabeth Hall, the Purcell Room and the Hayward Gallery. Unfortunately, however, it failed to capture the imagination of the public in the same way, and became London's much unloved culture bunker. The low point came in the 1980s when hundreds of homeless lived under the complex in a "Cardboard City". Since then, there have been considerable improvements, and the centre's unprepossessing appearance is softened, too, by its riverside location, its avenue of trees, fluttering banners, occasional buskers and skateboarders, and the weekend secondhand bookstalls outside BFI Southbank. The nearest **tube** to the Southbank Centre is Waterloo, but the most pleasant way to approach the area is via Hungerford Bridge from Embankment or Charing Cross tube.

Royal Festival Hall to the National Theatre

The only building left from the 1951 Festival of Britain is the **Royal Festival Hall** or RFH, one of London's main concert venues, whose auditorium is suspended above the open-plan foyer – its curved roof is clearly visible above the main body of the building. The interior furnishings remain fabulously period, and exhibitions and events in the foyer are generally excellent, making this one of the most pleasant South Bank buildings to visit. You can also kill time before a concert in the little-known **Poetry Library** (Tues–Sun 11am–8pm; free; Ⓦ www.poetrylibrary.org.uk) on Level 5, where you can either browse or, by joining (membership is free), borrow from the library's vast collection of poetry since 1912.

Architecturally, the most depressing parts of the Southbank Centre are the **Queen Elizabeth Hall** (QEH) and the more intimate **Purcell Room**, which share the same foyer and are built in uncompromisingly brutalist 1960s style. The **Hayward Gallery**, which sits behind and on top of this concrete garbage, is equally repellent from the outside, with the exception of its strange rooftop

▲ National Theatre

neon sculpture. Tucked underneath Waterloo Bridge is **BFI Southbank** (ⓦwww.bfi.org.uk), which screens London's most esoteric films, hosts a variety of talks, lectures and mini-festivals and also runs **Mediathèque** (Tues–Sun 11am–8pm; free), where you can settle into one of the viewing stations and choose from a selective archive of British films, TV programmes and documentaries.

On the far side of Waterloo Bridge, looking like a multistorey car park, is Denys Lasdun's **National Theatre** (ⓦwww.nationaltheatre.org.uk), an institution first mooted in 1848 but only finally realized in 1976. Again, it tends to receive flak from architectural critics, though the three auditoriums within are superb, and, in fairness to Lasdun, nobody told him that the concrete exterior would receive a zero maintenance budget. The National offers excellent **backstage tours** (daily 1hr 15min; £6; ☎020/7452 3400) for which it's advisable to book in advance.

Gabriel's Wharf and the OXO Tower

Beyond the National Theatre, the riverside promenade brings you eventually to **Gabriel's Wharf**, an ad hoc collection of lock-up craft shops, brasseries and bars that has a small weekend craft market. It's a pleasant extension to the Southbank Centre's own, rather limited facilities, and one for which Coin Street Community Builders (ⓦwww.coinstreet.org) must be thanked. With the population in this bomb-damaged stretch of the South Bank down from fifty thousand at the beginning of the century to four thousand in the early 1970s, big commercial developers were keen to step in and build hotels and office blocks galore. They were successfully fought off, and instead the emphasis has been on projects that combine commercial and community interests.

Coin Street's most high-profile project has been the restoration of the landmark **OXO Tower**, an old power station that was converted into a meat-packing factory in the 1930s by Liebig Extract of Meat Company, best known in Britain as the makers of OXO stock cubes. To get round the local council's ban on illuminated advertisements, the company cleverly incorporated the letters into the windows of the main tower, and then illuminated them from within. The building contains an exhibition space on the ground floor (Tues–Sun 11am–6pm), plus flats for local residents, sandwiched between a series of retail-workshops for designers on the first and second floors, and a swanky restaurant, bar and brasserie on the top floor. To enjoy the view, however, you don't need to eat or drink here: you can simply take the lift to the eighth-floor **public viewing gallery** (daily 10am–10pm).

BFI IMAX to Waterloo

At the southern end of Waterloo Bridge, the eye-catching glass-drum of the hi-tech **BFI IMAX** (ⓦwww.bfi.org.uk) rises up from the old "Bull Ring" beneath the roundabout. Boasting the largest screen in the country, it's definitely worth experiencing a 3D film here at least once, but as with all IMAX cinemas, it suffers from the fact that very few movies are shot on 70mm film.

An unusual and little-known sight on the South Bank is **Topolski Century** (Mon–Sat 11am–7pm, Sun noon–6pm; free; ☎020/7620 1275, ⓦwww.topolskicentury.org.uk; Waterloo tube), hidden under the arches on the north side of Hungerford Bridge on Concert Hall Approach. This enormous work, by Polish-born artist Feliks Topolski (1907–89), consists of a series of murals, painted floor to ceiling on panels, telling the story of

Topolski's life and that of the twentieth century. Painted from 1975 until the artist's death, it depicts many of the seminal events and the leading figures of the century, as well as containing a more light-hearted section entitled "One Hundred Hippies", featuring Mick Jagger and members of Hawkwind.

On the south side of Hungerford Bridge, overlooking Jubilee Gardens, is the Stalinist-looking **Shell Centre** (officially and poetically entitled The Downstream Building). Built in the 1950s – and the tallest building in London at the time – it's still owned and operated by oil giant Shell, which started life as an East End sea-shell shop in 1833. An overhead walkway leads through the Shell Centre to **Waterloo Station**, originally built in 1848, its later Edwardian facade slightly lost behind the railway bridge on Mepham Street. Along the western edge of the old station is the snake-like, curving roof of the former **Waterloo International**, designed by Nicholas Grimshaw, and the London terminus for Eurostar trains from 1993 to 2007.

On the other side of the tracks, at 121 Westminster Bridge Rd, is the early twentieth-century facade and entrance of the former **London Necropolis Station**, without doubt the city's most bizarre train terminus. It was originally opened in 1854 following one of London's worst outbreaks of cholera, and trains from this station took their hearse-carriages to Brookwood Cemetery in Surrey (at the time, the world's largest cemetery). Brookwood Station had separate platforms for Anglicans and Nonconformists and a licensed bar – "Spirits served here", the sign apparently read – but the whole operation was closed down after bomb damage in World War II.

London Eye

Despite being little more than ten years old, the **London Eye** (daily: June & Sept 10am–9pm; July & Aug 10am–9.30pm; Oct–May 10am–8pm; £17; ℡0870/500 0600, ⓦwww.ba-londoneye.com; Waterloo or Westminster tube) is already one of the city's most famous landmarks. Standing an impressive 443ft high, it's the largest Ferris wheel in Europe, weighing over two thousand tons, yet as simple and delicate as a bicycle wheel. It's constantly in slow motion, which means a full-circle "flight" in one of its 32 pods (one for each of the city's boroughs) should take around thirty minutes – that may seem a long time, though in fact it passes incredibly quickly. Not surprisingly, you can see right out to the very edge of the city – bring some binoculars if you can – where the suburbs slip into the countryside, making the wheel one of the few places (apart from a plane window) from which London looks a manageable size. Book in advance (and online to save money), as on arrival, you'll still have to queue to be loaded on.

County Hall

Continuing south, the colonnaded crescent of **County Hall** (ⓦwww.london countyhall.com) is the only truly monumental building on the South Bank. Designed to house the London County Council, it was completed in 1933 and enjoyed its greatest moment of fame as the headquarters of the GLC (Greater London Council), under the Labour leadership of Ken Livingstone, or "Red Ken", as the right-wing press called him at the time. The Tories moved in swiftly, abolishing the GLC in 1986, and leaving London as the only European city without an elected authority. In 2000, Livingstone had the last laugh when he was successfully elected to become London's first mayor, and head of the new Greater London Authority (GLA), housed in City Hall, near Tower Bridge. The building's tenants are constantly changing, but it's currently home to, among other things, several hotels and restaurants, an aquarium and an amusement arcade. None of the attractions that have gravitated here is an absolute must, and several have fallen by the wayside, but they prosper (as do the buskers round here) by feeding off the captive audience milling around the London Eye.

London Aquarium

The most enduring County Hall tenant is the **Sea Life London Aquarium** (Mon–Fri 10am–6pm, Sat & Sun 10am–7pm; £15.25; ⓣ020/7967 8000, ⓦwww .sealife.co.uk/london; Waterloo or Westminster tube), housed in the basement across two subterranean levels. With some super-large tanks, and everything from dog-face puffers and piranhas to robot fish (seriously), this is an attraction that's pretty much guaranteed to please kids. Impressive in scale, the aquarium has had a multi-million pound facelift and now boasts a thrilling Shark Walk as well as a replica blue whale skeleton encasing an underwater walkway. Ask at the main desk or check the website for the times of the daily presentations.

Dalí Universe

Three giant surrealist sculptures outside County Hall herald the **Dalí Universe** (daily 10am–6.30pm; £12; ⓣ020/7620 2720, ⓦwww.daliuniverse.com; Waterloo or Westminster tube). With two museums (in the US and Spain) already devoted to the Catalan artist Salvador Dalí (1904–89), some might question the need for a third. On the other hand, his popularity shows no sign of waning, and as a supreme self-publicist himself – even his moustache was a work of art – he would definitely have approved of the project. The museum has gone out of its way to appear as wacky as its star, but you can't help feeling that he would have done something altogether more outrageous.

There's no denying Dalí was an accomplished and prolific artist, but you'll be disappointed if you come expecting to see his "greatest hits" – those are scattered across the globe. The majority of the works displayed here are little-known bronze and glass sculptures, and various drawings from the many illustrated books he published, ranging from Ovid to the Marquis de Sade. That said, all his trademark themes are here: melting clocks, lots of Freudian allusions, phalluses and naked Venuses. Aside from these, there's one of the numerous Lobster Telephones which Edward James commissioned for his London home, a copy of his famous Mae West lips sofa and the oil painting from the dream sequence in Hitchcock's movie *Spellbound*.

Lambeth

South of Westminster Bridge, you leave the South Bank proper behind (and at the same time lose the crowds) and head upstream to what used to be the village of Lambeth (now a borough stretching as far south as Brixton). Vestiges of village atmosphere are notably absent, but there are a few minor sights worth considering, such as **Lambeth Palace** and the **Garden Museum**. It's also from this stretch of the riverbank that you get the best views of the Houses of Parliament. Inland lies London's most even-handed military museum, the **Imperial War Museum**, which has a moving permanent exhibition devoted to the Holocaust.

Florence Nightingale Museum

On the south side of Westminster Bridge, a series of red-brick Victorian blocks and modern accretions make up **St Thomas' Hospital**, which moved here after being ejected from its Georgian premises by London Bridge in 1862, when the railway came sweeping through Southwark. At the hospital's north-eastern corner, off Lambeth Palace Road, is the **Florence Nightingale Museum** (daily 10am–5pm; £5.80; ℡020/7620 0374, Ⓦwww.florence-nightingale.co.uk; Lambeth North, Waterloo or Westminster tube), celebrating the devout woman who revolutionized the nursing profession by establishing the first school of nursing at St Thomas' in 1860 and publishing her *Notes on Nursing*, emphasizing the importance of hygiene, decorum and discipline. The exhibition gives a strictly orthodox and uncritical account, but hits just the right note by putting the two years she spent in the Crimea in the context of a lifetime of tireless social campaigning. Exhibits include the white lantern that earned her the nickname "The Lady with the Lamp", a reconstruction of a Crimean military hospital ward and a slightly disappointing twenty-minute slide show.

Lambeth Palace

A short walk south of St Thomas' stands the imposing red-brick Tudor Gate of **Lambeth Palace** (by appointment Feb–Nov; ℡020/7898 1200, Ⓦwww.archbishopofcanterbury.org; Lambeth North or Westminster tube), London residence of the archbishop of Canterbury since 1197. Guided tours take place regularly, but you'll need to apply in writing.

The most impressive room is, without doubt, the **Great Hall** (now the library), with its very late Gothic, oak hammerbeam roof, built after the Restoration by Archbishop Juxon, who made his money in the slave trade, hence the African heads on his coat of arms (and on the bookshelves). On display here are some of the library's most valuable books – a Gutenberg Bible, the Nuremberg Chronicle, "mad" King George III's medical reports – and the grubby leather gloves allegedly handed to Juxon by Charles I on the scaffold. Upstairs, the **Guard Room** boasts an even older, arch-braced timber roof from the fourteenth century, and is the room where Thomas More was brought for questioning before being sent to the Tower (and subsequently beheaded).

Among the numerous portraits of past archbishops, look out for works by Holbein, Van Dyck, Hogarth and Reynolds. The final point on the tour is the **palace chapel**, where the religious reformer and leader of the Lollards, John Wycliffe, was tried (for the second time) in 1378 for "propositions, clearly heretical and depraved". The door and window frames date back to Wycliffe's day, but the place is somewhat overwhelmed by the ceiling frescoes added in the 1980s, telling the story of the Church of England. Best of all is the fact that you can see the choir screen and stalls put there in the 1630s by Archbishop Laud, and later used as evidence of his Catholic tendencies at his trial (and execution) in 1645.

Garden Museum

Just to the south of Lambeth Palace is the Kentish ragstone church of St Mary-at-Lambeth, now home to the **Garden Museum** (daily 10.30am–5pm; closed first Mon of month; £6; ℡020/7401 8865, Ⓦwww.gardenmuseum.org.uk; Westminster/Lambeth North/Vauxhall tube). You can visit the church's shop and café for free – what's more you can take your tea and cake out into the small graveyard, which is now laid out as a **seventeenth-century knot garden**.

Two interesting sarcophagi lurk among the foliage. The first, featuring a sculpted eternal flame, is the resting place of one-time Lambeth resident **Captain Bligh**, commander of the *Bounty* in 1787 when it set off to transport breadfruit trees from Tahiti to the West Indies. On the way home the crew mutinied and set Bligh and eighteen others adrift in a small open boat, with no map and few provisions. Using just a sextant, Bligh navigated the craft 3600 miles to the Indonesian island of Timor, a journey of 48 days. He later became governor of New South Wales, where his subjects once again rebelled, and on his return to England was promoted to vice-admiral.

The **Tradescant memorial** is more unusual, depicting a seven-headed griffin contemplating a skull, and several crocodiles sifting through sundry ruins flanked by gnarled trees. Gardener to James I and Charles I, John Tradescant was a tireless traveller in his search for new plant species, and set up a museum of curiosities known as "Tradescant's Ark" in Lambeth in 1629. Among the many exhibits were the "hand of a mermaid…a natural dragon, above two inches long…blood that rained on the Isle of Wight…and the Passion of Christ carved very daintily on a plumstone". The less fantastical pieces formed the nucleus of Oxford's Ashmolean Museum.

Back in the church, the museum itself puts on excellent exhibitions on a horticultural theme in the ground-floor galleries, and has a small permanent exhibition in the "belvedere", reached by a new wooden staircase. There's a tiny section on Tradescant, including one of his curiosities – a "vegetable lamb" that's in fact a Russian fern – plus a few dibbers and grubbers, and some pony boots designed to prevent damage to your lawn.

Imperial War Museum

From 1815 until 1930, the domed building at the east end of Lambeth Road was the infamous lunatic asylum of Bethlehem Royal Hospital, better known as **Bedlam**. (Charlie Chaplin's mother was among those confined here – the future comedian was born and spent a troubled childhood in nearby Kennington.) When the hospital was moved to Beckenham on the southeast outskirts of London, the wings of the 700-foot-long facade were demolished, leaving just the central building, now home to the **Imperial War Museum** (daily 10am–6pm; free; ☏020/7416 5000, ⓦ www.iwm.org.uk; Lambeth North tube), by far the capital's best military museum.

The treatment of the subject is impressively wide-ranging and fairly sober, once you've passed through the Large Exhibits Gallery, with its militaristic display of guns, tanks, fighter planes and a giant V-2 rocket. On the **lower ground floor**, the array of documents and images attesting to the human damage of the last century of war is underlined by a clock which adds two more casualties every minute to its grand total. In addition to the static displays, a good deal of stagecraft is used to convey the misery of combat, with a walk-through World War I trench, and a re-creation of the Blitz in which you wander from an air-raid shelter through bomb-ravaged streets, accompanied by blaring sirens and human voices.

One gallery to head for is **The Children's War**, on the first floor, which focuses on the plight of kids during World War II. With over a million children evacuated to the countryside in September 1939, and some 130,000 losing at least one parent during the course of the war, there are some very moving life stories recounted here. One of the most popular exhibits is the perfectly re-created **1940s House**, a typical two-storey terraced house complete with Morrison shelter in the dining room. Also on the first floor is the **Secret War** gallery, which follows the clandestine activities of MI5, MI6 and the SOE (the wartime equivalent of MI6) – expect exploding pencils, trip wires and spy cameras – though it's marred by an unrealistically glowing account of the SAS operations in the Gulf War.

The museum's **art galleries**, on the second floor, display a changing selection of works by war artists. One painting that's on permanent display is *Gassed*, by John Singer Sargent, a painter better known for his portraits of society beauties; alongside it are three other canvases, on a similarly grand scale, by Paul Nash, Stanley Spencer and Henry Lamb. Also on this floor is the **Crimes Against Humanity gallery**, which features a harrowing half-hour film on genocide and ethnic violence in the last century (not recommended for under-16s). Look out, too, for the excellent programme of talks, films, concerts, poetry readings and temporary exhibitions (for which there's usually an admission charge).

The Holocaust Exhibition

Many people come to the Imperial War Museum specifically to see the **Holocaust Exhibition** (not recommended for under-14s), which you enter from the third floor. Taking a fairly conventional, sober approach to the subject, the museum has made a valiant attempt to avoid depicting the victims of the Holocaust as nameless masses, by focusing on individual cases, and interspersing the archive footage with eyewitness accounts from contemporary survivors.

The exhibition pulls few punches, bluntly stating that the pope failed to denounce the anti-Jewish **Nuremberg Laws**, that writers such as Eliot and Kipling expressed anti-Semitic views, and that at the 1938 Evian Conference, the European powers refused to accept any more Jewish refugees. Despite the restrictions of space, there are sections on the extermination of the gypsies, Nazi euthanasia, pre-Holocaust Yiddish culture and the persecution of the Slavs. The **genocide**, which began with the *Einsatzgruppen* and ended with the gas chambers, is catalogued in painstaking detail, while the problem of "proving" the Final Solution is also addressed, in a room that emphasizes the complexity of the Nazi bureaucracy, which, allied to an ideology of extermination, made the Holocaust not just possible but inevitable.

The centrepiece of the museum is a vast, all-white, scale model of (what is, in fact, only a very small slice of) **Auschwitz-Birkenau**, showing what happened to the two thousand Hungarian Jews who arrived at the camp from the town of Beregovo in May 1944. The significance of this transport is that, uniquely, photographs, taken by the SS, of the selection process meted out on these particular arrivals managed to survive the war. In the alcoves overlooking the model, which has a pile of discarded possessions from the camps as its backdrop, survivors describe their first impressions of Auschwitz. This section is especially harrowing, and it's as well to leave yourself enough time to listen to the reflections of camp survivors at the end, as they attempt to come to terms with the past.

Southwark

I n Tudor and Stuart London, the chief reason for crossing the Thames, to what is now **Southwark** (Ⓦwww.visitsouthwark.com), was to visit the disreputable Bankside entertainment district around the south end of London Bridge. Four hundred years on, Londoners have rediscovered the habit of heading for the area, thanks to a wealth of new attractions – with the charge led by the mighty **Tate Modern** on Bankside – that now pepper the riverside from Blackfriars Bridge to Tower Bridge.

In the shadow of the Tate is **Shakespeare's Globe Theatre**, a reconstruction of one of the Elizabethan theatres for which Southwark was once famous. Close by, the **Millennium Bridge** provides a wonderful pedestrian link from the City and St Paul's. Further east, you'll find a replica of Drake's Tudor galleon, the **Golden Hinde**, and, in **Southwark Cathedral**, some of the city's best-preserved Gothic architecture. At this point, the shops, cafés and stalls of nearby **Borough Market**, which has become something of a gourmet food haven, provide a welcome refuelling stop.

East of London Bridge lies **Bermondsey** and the beginning of the south-bank Docklands development, less well known than Canary Wharf, but more innovative architecturally. The wartime cruiser **HMS Belfast** sits in what was once the busiest section of the Thames, with **City Hall**, the headquarters for London's mayor and assembly, on the riverbank nearby. Further inland, on Tooley Street, there are regular queues outside the ever-popular **London Dungeon**.

East of Tower Bridge is the thriving little warehouse development of **Butler's Wharf**, centred on the excellent **Design Museum**. Further east still, **Rotherhithe** clings onto its old seafaring identity despite the demise of its once extensive enclosed docks.

Bankside

Little remains above ground to remind you of Southwark's pre-industrial golden age of entertainment under the Tudors and Stuarts. The **Clink Prison Museum** and the rebuilt **Shakespeare's Globe Theatre** go some way towards remedying this, as do **Southwark Cathedral** and the *George Inn*, London's last surviving galleried coaching inn, but nowadays the area's biggest attraction by far is **Tate Modern**, the modern art museum housed in the former Bankside power station.

Bankside started out as a Roman **red-light district**, and its brothels continued to do a thriving illegal trade until 1161, when they were licensed by royal decree. This measure imposed various rules and restrictions on the prostitutes, who could now be fined three shillings for "grimacing to passers-by", but were given Sunday mornings off in order to attend church. The women wore

Blackfriars' Station
Cannon Street Station
TOWER HILL
TOWER GATEWAY
See Bankside & Pool of London map for detail
Tower of London
OXO Tower
Globe Theatre
Tate Modern
MILLENNIUM BRIDGE
BLACKFRIARS BRIDGE
SOUTHWARK BRIDGE
LONDON BRIDGE
EAST SMITHFIELD
St Katharine Dock
STAMFORD STREET
HMS Belfast
Southwark Cathedral
SOUTHWARK
UPPER GROUND
HOPTON ST
SUMNER ST
PARK ST
SOUTHWARK STREET
LONDON BRIDGE
Hay's Galleria
TOOLEY STREET
Butler's Wharf
SHAD THAMES
Design Museum
FOOTBRIDGE
Waterloo East Station
BLACKFRIARS ROAD
UNION STREET
City Hall
ST THOMAS ST
GAINSFORD ST
ELIZABETH ST
SHAD THAMES
MILL STREET
THE CUT
GREAT SUFFOLK STREET
Guy's Hospital
London Bridge Station
BERMONDSEY STREET
JAMAICA ROAD
St George
BOROUGH
Leather Market
Fashion & Textile Museum
LONG LANE
WATERLOO ROAD
LAMBETH ROAD
ST GEORGES ROAD
BOROUGH ROAD
BRIDGE ROAD
LONDON ROAD
SOUTHWARK BRIDGE RD
BOROUGH HIGH STREET
GREAT DOVER STREET
TOWER BRIDGE ROAD
Antique Market
GRANGE ROAD
BERMONDSEY
Imperial War Museum
ELEPHANT & CASTLE
NEWINGTON CAUSEWAY
NEW KENT ROAD
OLD KENT ROAD
SOUTHWARK
NEWINGTON BUTTS
WALWORTH ROAD
Cuming Museum

South London Gallery

red-and-white-striped caps and white aprons, and were known as "Winchester Geese", since the land was owned by the Bishop of Winchester. The Church made a small fortune out of the rent until Henry VIII closed the bawdy houses down. In Elizabethan times, Bankside once more became the most nefarious area in London, known as "Stew's Bank" for its brothels or "stewhouses", and studded with **bull- and bear-pits**. Pepys recalls seeing "some good sport of the bulls tossing of the dogs; one into the very boxes", but opinion was by then inclining towards Evelyn's description of the sport as a "rude and dirty pastime" and in 1682 the last bear- garden was closed down.

   Theatres – another disreputable institution banned in the City – also flourished on Bankside, with no fewer than four during the reign of James I: the Swan, built in 1587, with Edward Alleyn (founder of Dulwich College) as the lead actor and Christopher Marlowe as its main playwright; the **Rose**, built in 1595, its foundations still extant on Park Street; the Hope, built in 1613, which doubled as a bear garden and theatre; and the **Globe**, the Burbages' theatre (originally built in Shoreditch in 1576, re-erected in 1599 on Park Street), where Shakespeare put on his greatest plays, now reconstructed on New Globe Walk. The theatres lasted barely half a century before being closed down by the Puritans, who considered them "chapels of Satan". With the Restoration, the focus of the theatre scene, and its accompanying vices, moved to Covent Garden, and Southwark faded from the limelight.

Tate Modern

Bankside is dominated by the awesome **Tate Modern** (daily 10am–6pm, Fri & Sat until 10pm; free; ☎020/7887 8888, Ⓦwww.tate.org.uk; Southwark tube), an absolute must for anyone visiting or living in London. Originally designed as an oil-fired power station by Giles Gilbert Scott, this austere, brick-built

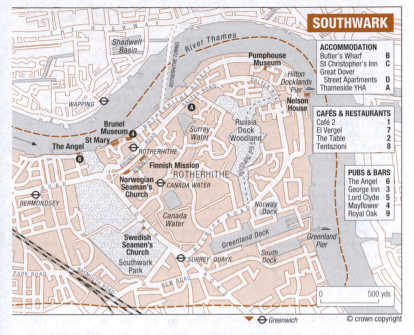

"cathedral of power" was closed down in 1981. It was then transformed by the Swiss architects Herzog & de Meuron and opened to the public in 2000. The masterful conversion has left plenty of the original industrial feel, while providing wonderfully light and spacious galleries to show off Tate's impressive collection of international twentieth-century artists, including Monet, Duchamp, Moore, Matisse, Mondrian, Picasso, Pollock, Rothko and Warhol.

The collection

Tate's collection dates back as far as 1900, so, in amongst all the attention-grabbing conceptual stuff, you'll find some early twentieth-century paintings, looking terribly old-fashioned in their gilded frames: **Monet**'s *Water-lilies*, several works by **Bonnard**, **Cézanne** and **Vuillard**, plus the odd jaunty paper collage by **Matisse**, executed towards the end of his life when he was wheelchair-bound.

You can be pretty sure of catching perennial Tate favourites like **Mark Rothko**'s abstract "Seagram Murals". Commissioned by the swanky *Four Seasons* restaurant in New York, they were withheld by Rothko, who decided he didn't wish his art to be a mere backdrop to the recreation of the wealthy. The gallery usually displays a replica of **Marcel Duchamp**'s seminal *Fountain*, a (disappointingly clean) urinal signed "R. Mutt, 1917" which was the world's first "readymade", a non-art object which becomes "art" only because it sits in a museum. Taking this idea one stage further, **Kurt Schwitters** put together works such as an "assemblage of discarded rubbish and printed ephemera", for as he himself said, "everything the artist spits is art" – a philosophy that logically led to Piero Manzoni's can of "Artist's Shit".

There's always a smattering of works by the major Surrealists: **Miró**, **Magritte**, **Dalí** and the dreamlike de Chirico, as well as the utopian geometry of

Visiting Tate Modern

The gallery is worth visiting for its architecture alone, so to appreciate it fully, approach from the Millennium Bridge, since the river crossing gives you an unobstructed view. From the bridge, the nearest entrance is the **North Entrance** underneath the chimney, which brings you out at Level 2. The best way to enter, however, is via the ramp at the **West Entrance**, allowing you to fully appreciate the stupefying enormity of the main **turbine hall**, which sits on Level 1, below the Thames, yet rises to a height of 115ft, and is used to display large-scale installations. Level 1 is also where you'll find the **information desk**, and, on the opposite side, the museum's **cloakroom** and giant **bookshop**.

Escalators from this floor lead straight up to Level 3, which, along with Level 5, contains the **permanent collection**; Level 4 is used for large-scale **special exhibitions**, for which there is an entrance fee. In the permanent collection, Tate Modern's curators have eschewed the old chronological approach, and gone instead for hanging (and re-hanging) works according to -isms. You'll need stamina to wade through more than one level in any one visit, so if there's something you really want to see, go there first before you run out of energy. There are **free guided tours** (daily at 11am, noon, 2 & 3pm), and you can rent **multimedia guides** for £2.

There's a pricey **restaurant and bar** on Level 7, with a great view over the river, and a more reasonably priced **café** on Level 2. There's also a **Tate Boat**, which takes twenty minutes to ply between Tate Britain and Tate Modern (every 40min; £5).

Mondrian and the De Stijl movement, plus several abstract expressionist works by **Jackson Pollock** and examples of **Pop Art** by Andy Warhol and Roy Lichtenstein. Look out, too, for **Joseph Beuys**, whose bizarre choice of materials derives directly from his wartime experiences, when his plane crashed in the Crimea and he was saved by local Tartars, who cocooned him in felt and fat. Tate owns works from every period of **Picasso**'s life, including *Weeping Woman*, which is both a portrait of his lover Dora Maar and a heartfelt response to the Spanish Civil War.

Other highlights to look out for are Yves Klein's totally blue paintings, Lucio Fontana's slashed canvases, and **Carl André**'s infamous "Bricks" (officially entitled *Equivalent VIII*), seen by many critics, at the time Tate acquired it in 1972, as evidence of the nadir of modern art. A more recent work that captured a lot of interest is **Michael Craig Martin**'s glass of water on a shelf, called *An Oak Tree*, exhibited complete with the artist's defence of the work. The sculptures scattered throughout the gallery are top-class, too: early African-style Cubist busts by Picasso and **Modigliani**, emaciated, elongated figures by **Giacometti** and smooth, organic works by **Henry Moore** and Barbara Hepworth.

The Millennium Bridge

The first new bridge to be built across the Thames in London since Tower Bridge opened in 1894, the sleek, stainless-steel **Millennium Bridge** is London's sole pedestrian-only crossing. A suspension bridge of innovative design – the high-profile triumvirate responsible were sculptor Anthony Caro, architect Norman Foster and engineers Ove Arup – it famously bounced up and down when it first opened in 2000 and had to be closed for another two years for repairs. It still wobbles a bit, but most people are too busy enjoying the spectacular views across to St Paul's Cathedral and Tate Modern to notice.

There's usually a few surprises, too: sections on Soviet graphics and interwar documentaries or neon sculptures and video installations, not to mention plenty of artists or artistic movements about which you may know very little. You'll also find quite a bit of overlap with Tate Britain, with works by British artists like **Stanley Spencer**, **Francis Bacon** and Paul Nash, plus living artists like **David Hockney**, **Lucian Freud** and Sarah Lucas, featuring in both galleries.

Shakespeare's Globe Theatre

Dwarfed by Tate Modern, but equally remarkable in its own way, **Shakespeare's Globe Theatre** (☎020/7902 1400, ⓦwww.shakespeares-globe.org; Southwark or London Bridge tube) is a more or less faithful reconstruction of the polygonal playhouse where most of the Bard's later works were first performed. The theatre, which boasts the first new thatched roof in central London since the Great Fire, puts on plays by Shakespeare and his contemporaries, using only natural light and the minimum of scenery. The season runs from May to September, and the performances so far have managed to be both fun, historically authentic and, more often than not, critically acclaimed. For more details, see p.430.

To find out more about Shakespeare and the history of Bankside, the Globe's stylish **exhibition** (daily: mid-April to mid-Sept 9am–noon & 12.30–5pm; mid-Oct to mid-April 10am–5pm; £10.50), to the west of the theatre, is well worth a visit. It details the long campaign by the single-minded American actor Sam Wanamaker (1919–93) to have the Globe rebuilt, but it's the interactive exhibits that hit the spot. You can have a virtual play on period musical instruments such as the crumhorn or sackbut, prepare your own edition of Shakespeare and feel the thatch, hazelnut shell and daub used to build the theatre. There are even booths in which you can record and compare your own rendition of key speeches with those of the stage greats, plus the odd live demo on the exhibition's stage. Visitors also get taken on an informative half-hour **guided tour** round the theatre itself; during the summer season, you get to visit the exhibition and the nearby Rose Theatre instead for a reduced fee (see box below).

Vinopolis

Housed in the former wine vaults under the railway arches on Clink Street, **Vinopolis** (Thurs–Sat noon–10pm, Sun noon–6pm; £20 and up; ☎0870/241 4040, ⓦwww.vinopolis.co.uk; London Bridge tube) is a strange fish: part wine bar-restaurant, part wine retailers (there's a branch of the excellent Majestic Wines round the back), part museum. The focus of the complex is the "Wine Odyssey", a light-hearted, rather disjointed, trot through the world's wine regions with an audioguide. The visual gags – you get to tour round the Italian

---

The Rose Theatre

The discovery of the remains of the **Rose Theatre** (☎020/7261 9565, ⓦwww .rosetheatre.org.uk), the Globe's great rival, beneath an office block on Park Street in 1989, helped enormously in the reconstruction of the Globe. The outline of the theatre can clearly be traced in the foundations, but most of the remains are currently flooded to preserve them until sufficient funds can be found for a full excavation. Close by the Rose exhibition, there's a plaque showing where the Globe actually stood, before it was destroyed in a fire started by a spark from a cannon during a performance of Shakespeare's *Henry VIII*. Tours of the Rose Theatre form part of the package offered by the Globe exhibition on summer afternoons (see above).

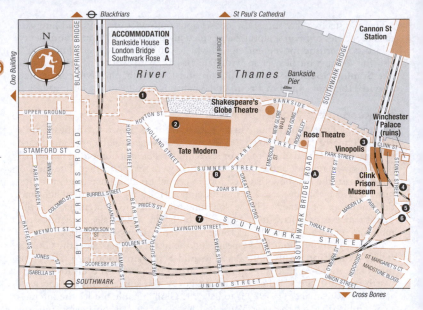

vineyards on a Vespa – are a bit lame, and tickets are pricey, but do include five wine tastings; you can also upgrade your ticket to include more tastings of wine and other alcoholic drinks. The staff diligently use spittoons, but most visitors seem quite happy to get slowly inebriated.

Clink Street

Round the corner from Vinopolis, in the suitably dismal confines of dark and narrow Clink Street, is the **Clink Prison Museum** (Mon–Fri 10am–6pm, Sat & Sun 10am–9pm; £5; ℡020/7403 0900, ⓦwww.clink.co.uk; London Bridge tube), built near the site of the former Clink Prison, and the origin of the expression "in the clink". The prison began as a dungeon for disobedient clerics under the Bishop of Winchester's Palace – the rose window of the palace's Great Hall has survived just east of the prison – and later it became a dumping ground for heretics, debtors, prostitutes and a motley assortment of Bankside lowlife, before being burnt to the ground during the 1780 Gordon Riots. The exhibition features a handful of prison-life tableaux and dwells on the torture and grim conditions within, but, given the rich history of the place, it is a disappointingly lacklustre display.

Further east down Clink Street, in St Mary Overie Dock, sits an exact replica of the **Golden Hinde** (Mon–Sat 10am–5.30pm, Sun 10am–5pm, but phone ahead; £6; ℡020/7403 0123, ⓦwww.goldenhinde.com; London Bridge tube), the galleon in which Francis Drake sailed around the world from 1577 to 1580. This version was launched in 1973, and circumnavigated the world for the next twenty years, before eventually settling here in Southwark. The ship is surprisingly small and, with a crew of eighty-plus, must have been cramped, to say the least. There's a lack of interpretive panels, so it's worth trying to coincide with one of the regular tours, during which costumed guides show you the ropes, so to speak, and demonstrate activities such as firing a cannon or using the ship's toilet. Always phone ahead, though, to check that a group hasn't booked the place up.

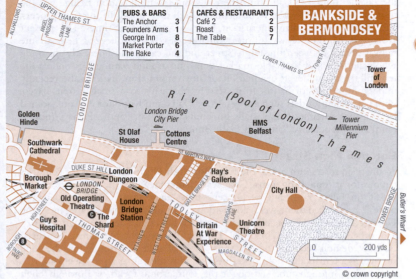

PUBS & BARS	
The Anchor	3
Founders Arms	1
George Inn	8
Market Porter	6
The Rake	4

CAFÉS & RESTAURANTS	
Café 2	2
Roast	5
The Table	7

BANKSIDE & BERMONDSEY

© crown copyright

Southwark Cathedral

East of Clink Street, just before London Bridge, stands **Southwark Cathedral** (Mon–Fri 7.30am–6pm, Sat & Sun 8.30am–6pm; free; Ⓦ www.southwark .anglican.org/cathedral; London Bridge tube), built in the thirteenth century as the Augustinian priory church of St Mary Overie. It's a minor miracle that the church survived the nineteenth century, which saw the east-end chapel demolished to make way for London Bridge, railways built within a few feet of the tower and some very heavy-handed Victorian restoration. As if in compensation, the church was given cathedral status in 1905, and has since gone from strength to strength – if you're feeling peckish, the cathedral refectory serves tasty food.

Of the original thirteenth-century **interior**, only the choir and retrochoir now remain, separated by a beautiful, high, stone Tudor screen; they are probably the oldest Gothic structures left in London and were used by the Bishop of Winchester as a court – those sentenced ended up in the Clink. The cathedral contains numerous intriguing **monuments**: from a thirteenth-century oak effigy of a knight, to one dedicated to the 51 people who died when the *Marchioness* pleasure boat collided with a barge on the Thames in 1989. Others include the brightly painted tomb of poet John Gower, Chaucer's contemporary, in the north aisle, his head resting on the three books he wrote – one in Latin, one in French and one in English. The quack doctor Lionel Lockyer has a humorous epitaph in the north transept, and, nearby, there's a chapel dedicated to John Harvard, who was baptized here in 1607. In the south aisle, an early twentieth-century memorial to Shakespeare (he was a worshipper in the church and his brother is buried here) depicts the Bard in green alabaster lounging under a stone canopy. Above the memorial is a postwar stained-glass window featuring a whole cast of characters from the plays.

Borough Market

Medieval Southwark, also known as **The Borough**, was London's first suburb, clustered round the southern end of London Bridge, London's only bridge over the Thames until 1750, and thus the only route south. London Bridge was the most obvious place for the Kent farmers to sell their goods to the City grocers, and there's been a thriving market here since medieval times. The present **Borough Market** (Ⓦwww.boroughmarket.org.uk) is squeezed beneath the railway arches between the High Street and the cathedral. The early-morning wholesale fruit and vegetable market winds up around 9am and is one of the few still trading under its original Victorian wrought-iron shed. It's also recently undergone a transformation from scruffy obscurity to a small foodie haven, with permanent outlets such as Neal's Yard Dairy and Konditor & Cook, joined by gourmet daytime market stalls on Thursdays (11am–5pm), Fridays (noon–6pm) and, particularly, Saturdays (9am–4pm).

Borough High Street

As the main road south out of the City, **Borough High Street** was for centuries famous for its **coaching inns**. Chaucer's Canterbury pilgrims set off from *The Tabard* (in Talbot Yard), but by Dickens' time "these great rambling queer old places", as he called them, were closing down. The only extant coaching inn is the **George Inn**, situated in a cobbled yard east off the High Street, dating from 1677 and now owned by the National Trust. Unfortunately, the Great Northern Railway demolished two of the three original galleried fronts, but the lone survivor is a remarkable sight nevertheless, and is still run as a pub (see p.402).

Opposite Borough tube station, at the southernmost end of Borough High Street, is **St George the Martyr**, built in the 1730s, with four clock faces: three white and illuminated at night; one black and pointing towards Bermondsey, whose parishioners refused to give money for the church. To the north of St George's, a wall survives from the **Marshalsea**, the city's main debtors' prison, where Dickens' father (and family) was incarcerated for six months in 1824.

Redcross Way

Running parallel with Borough High Street, one block to the west, is **Redcross Way**, a little-visited backstreet that hides a couple of remarkable sights. The first is **Red Cross Garden**, the row of cottage-style model dwellings established by the social reformer (and founder of the National Trust) Octavia Hill, to house the workers of a local rag factory. The row of houses faces onto a miniature village green, recently restored complete with village pond and even a maypole. Meanwhile, on the opposite side of the street, is the site of the **Cross Bones cemetery** (Ⓦwww.crossbones.org.uk). It was on this unconsecrated land that the prostitutes who worked on Bankside were buried, and later, the local poor were interred. Local residents have turned the gates, leading to the plot of land, into an impromptu shrine of messages and tokens to those buried, and the plan is eventually to establish a Garden of Remembrance.

Old Operating Theatre Museum and Herb Garret

The most educative and the strangest of Southwark's museums is the **Old Operating Theatre Museum and Herb Garret** (daily 10.30am–5pm; closed mid-Dec to early Jan; £5.60; ☎020/7188 2679, Ⓦwww.thegarret.org.uk; London Bridge tube) on St Thomas Street. Built in 1821 up a spiral staircase at the top of a church tower, where the hospital apothecary's herbs were stored, this women's operating theatre was once adjacent to the women's ward of St Thomas' Hospital (now in Lambeth). Despite being gore-free, the museum is as stomach-churning as the nearby London Dungeon, for this theatre dates from the pre-anaesthetic era.

The surgeons who used this room would have concentrated on speed and accuracy (most amputations took less than a minute), but there was still a thirty percent mortality rate, with many patients simply dying of shock, and many more from bacterial infection (about which very little was known). This much is clear from the design of the theatre itself, which has no sink and is made almost entirely of mahogany and pine, a breeding ground for bacteria. Sawdust was sprinkled on the floor to soak up the blood and prevent it dripping onto the congregation in the church below. In the herbarium section, you can read up on the medicinal uses of the herbs stored and have a go at making your own pills.

Opposite the museum stands **Guy's Hospital**, founded in 1726 by Thomas Guy, a governor of St Thomas' Hospital, with the money he made in the City. The hospital retains several of its original eighteenth-century buildings, in particular the courtyard on St Thomas Street, and a pretty little **Hospital Chapel**, on the west side of the courtyard, with raked balconies on three sides, and cheerful light-blue paintwork throughout. You can wander in to admire the giant marble and alabaster tomb of the founder, who's depicted welcoming a new patient to the hospital, though in fact Guy died a year before the first patients were admitted.

Bermondsey

Famous in the Middle Ages for its Cluniac abbey, **Bermondsey**, the area east of London Bridge, changed enormously in the nineteenth century. In 1836, the London and Greenwich Railway – the city's first – was built through the district, supported by 878 brick arches stretching for four miles, and used for storing goods. The area became famous for its wharves, its tanneries and its factories. So much of the city's food – in particular teas, wines, grain, butter, bacon and cheese – was stored here that it was nicknamed "London's Larder". Bermondsey also became infamous for some of the worst social conditions in Victorian London, as Charles Kingsley discovered: "O God! What I saw! People having no water to drink but the water of the common sewer which stagnates full of…dead fish, cats and dogs."

Badly bombed in the Blitz, the wharves never really recovered and, by the 1960s, the docks had closed down. They have since undergone a Docklands-style regeneration, and, as at Wapping, on the other side of the river, much of the original warehouse architecture has been preserved. **HMS Belfast**, the cruiser moored near City Hall, is the only permanent maritime link (see p.238). Nearby the curvaceous dock of Hay's Wharf, originally built to accommodate tea clippers like the *Cutty Sark*, has been filled in, covered with glass and steel barrel-vaulting, and transformed into the **Hay's Galleria**, a shopping precinct whose Christmas Shop, near the entrance on Tooley Street, is a must if you've got children. The area's most popular attraction, however, is the Hammer-horror **London Dungeon**, tucked under the railway arches under London Bridge Station (see p.237). And ready to steal the limelight from all the above is the **Shard** (Ⓦwww.shardlondonbridge.com), Renzo Piano's tapered tower block, due for completion right outside London Bridge Station, in 2012 and, at over 1000ft, destined to become Britain's tallest building.

London Dungeon

Housed beneath the railway arches of London Bridge Station, on Tooley Street, is the **London Dungeon** (daily: Easter to mid-July, Sept & Oct 10.30am–5.30pm; mid-July to Aug 9.30am–7.30pm; Nov–Easter 10.30am–5pm; £22, or £17 online; Ⓣ020/7403 7221, Ⓦwww.thedungeons.com; London Bridge tube), an orgy of Gothic horror and one of the city's major crowd-pleasers – to avoid queuing (and save money), buy your ticket online. Young teenagers and the credulous probably get the most out of the life-sized waxwork tableaux of folk being hanged, drawn, quartered and tortured, the general hysteria boosted by actors dressed in period garb. Visitors are led into the labyrinth, an old-fashioned mirror maze, before being herded through a series of live action scenarios, then sent off on the "Boat Ride to Hell", condemned to a free-fall hanging in "Drop Ride to Doom", and compelled to endure the "Jack the Ripper Experience", an exploitative trawl through postmortem photos and wax mock-ups of the victims. To escape, you have to endure the "Great Fire of London", in which visitors are forced to walk through a revolving tunnel of flames.

Britain at War Experience

Further east along Tooley Street is **Winston Churchill's Britain at War Experience** (daily: April–Oct 10am–5pm; Nov–March 10am–4.30pm; £11.45; ℡020/7403 3171, ⓦwww.britainatwar.co.uk; London Bridge tube), an illuminating insight into the stiff-upper-lip London mentality during the Blitz. It begins with a rickety elevator ride down to a mock-up of a tube air-raid shelter (minus the stale air and rats), in which a contemporary newsreel cheerily announces "a great day for democracy" as bombs drop indiscriminately over Germany. This is just a prelude to the museum's hundreds of wartime artefacts, posters and old shop fronts, all looking a bit worn around the edges, but still fascinating. You can sit in an Anderson shelter beneath the chilling sound of the V-1 "doodlebugs", tune in to contemporary radio broadcasts and walk through the chaos of a just-bombed street – pitch-dark, noisy and smoky.

HMS Belfast

Permanently moored opposite Southwark Crown Court, the camouflage-painted **HMS Belfast** (daily: March–Oct 10am–6pm; Nov–Feb 10am–5pm; £10.70; ℡020/7940 6300, ⓦhmsbelfast.iwm.org.uk; London Bridge tube) is an 11,550-ton Royal Navy cruiser. Launched in Belfast in 1938, the *Belfast* spent the first two years of the war in the Royal Naval shipyards, after being hit by a mine in the Firth of Forth. It later saw action in the 1943 Battle of North Cape and assisted in the D-Day landings before being decommissioned after the Korean War, and becoming an outpost of the Imperial War Museum.

The fun bit is exploring the maze of cabins and scrambling up and down the vertiginous ladders of the ship's seven confusing decks, which could accommodate a crew of over nine hundred. Be sure to check out the punishment cells, in the most uncomfortable part of the ship, and to make it down to the airlocked Boiler Room, a spaghetti of pipes and valves, from which there was very little chance of escape in the event of the ship being hit. If you want to know more about the cruiser's history, head for the Exhibition Flat in Zone 5; next door, in the Life at Sea room, you can practise your Morse code and knots, and listen to accounts of naval life on board.

City Hall

East of the *Belfast*, overlooking the river, is Norman Foster's startling glass-encased **City Hall** (Mon–Fri 8am–8pm, plus occasional weekends; ℡020/7983 4000, ⓦwww.london.gov.uk), which looks like a giant car headlight or fencing mask. Headquarters for the Greater London Authority and the Mayor of London, visitors are welcome to stroll up the helical walkway, visit the café and watch proceedings from the second floor. For access to "London's Living Room" on the ninth floor, which boasts the best views over the Thames,

▲ City Hall

contact City Hall. Before you leave the area, be sure to check out Fiona Banner's shiny black *Full Stops*, 3D renditions styled in different fonts and wrought in bronze.

Bermondsey Street

Bermondsey Street, once the area's high street, has been transformed over the last decade into a trendy strip of cafés, pubs and shops. This was also once the heart of the tanning industry – hence Tanner Street, Morocco Street (where much of the leather came from) and Leathermarket Road, which leads to the former **Leather Hide and Wool Exchange** of 1878, decorated with roundels depicting the process of tanning. Next door is the former Leather Market, built in 1833 and now converted into workshops, including one where you can watch **glassblowing** demonstrations (Mon–Fri 10am–1 & 2–5pm; free).

The **Fashion and Textile Museum** (Wed–Sun 11am–6pm; £5; ☎020/7407 8664, ⓦ www.ftmlondon.org) is the lifelong dream of Zandra Rhodes, fashion *grande dame extraordinaire*. Designed by Mexican architect Ricardo Legorreta, and daubed in Rhodes' favourite colours of pink and orange, the FTM (a former cash-and-carry warehouse) is an arresting sight on the otherwise drab Bermondsey Street. Rhodes opened her first boutique in the 1960s, and reached the peak of her popularity during the punk era. Her own sartorial taste hasn't changed much in the intervening years, but thankfully FTM's exhibitions are more wide-ranging – from designer tea cosies to 1970s fashion – and are often drawn from her own vast collection.

At the far end of the street, the Bermondsey **antique market** takes place on Friday mornings. The market is also known confusingly as the New Caledonian Market, since it's the descendant of the prewar flea market that used to take place off Islington's Caledonian Road.

Butler's Wharf and beyond

Butler's Wharf, immediately east of Tower Bridge, is one of the densest networks of Victorian warehousing left in London and one of the most enjoyable parts of Docklands to explore. The best place to start is on Tower Bridge itself (see p.199), the only place from where you can get a really good view of the old **Anchor Brewhouse**, which produced Courage ales from 1789 until 1982. A cheery, ad hoc sort of building, with a boiler-house chimney at one end and malt-mill tower and cupola at the other, it has been sensitively converted into apartments. Next door is the original eight-storey **Butler's Wharf**, the largest warehouse complex on the Thames when it was built in 1873. Closed down in the 1970s, it became London's largest artists' colony, home to everyone from Derek Jarman to Sid Vicious. Nowadays, its flats, shops and restaurants form part of Terence Conran's gastronomic empire, but the wide promenade on the riverfront is open to the public.

Shad Thames, the narrow street at the back of Butler's Wharf, has kept the wrought-iron overhead gangways by which the porters used to transport goods from the wharves to the warehouses further back from the river; it's one of the most atmospheric alleyways in the whole of Docklands. For a totally different ambience, head for **Horsleydown Square**, to the south of Shad Thames, where terracotta-rendered flats, with striking blue balconies, overlook a piazza centred on a fountain encrusted with naked women, whose belongings are sculpted around the edge. Also worth a look, two blocks south on Queen Elizabeth Street, is the **Circle**, a modern take on the Victorian "circus", its street facades smothered in shiny cobalt-blue tiles.

Design Museum

East of Butler's Wharf is Terence Conran's superb riverside **Design Museum** (daily 10am–5.45pm; £7; ☎0870/833 9955, ⓦwww.designmuseum.org; Tower Hill tube), at the eastern end of Shad Thames. The stylish white edifice, a Bauhaus-like conversion of an old 1950s warehouse, is the perfect showcase for mass-produced industrial design from classic cars to Tupperware. The museum hosts a series of special exhibitions (up to four at any one time) on important designers, movements or single products. The museum shop is great for design classics and innovations, and the small coffee bar in the foyer serves delicious cakes and is a great place to relax; there's also the superb *Blue Print Café* on the top floor.

St Saviour's Dock and beyond

East of the Design Museum, a stainless-steel footbridge takes you across **St Saviour's Dock**, a tidal inlet overlooked by swanky warehouse offices. Incredible though it may seem, it really is still possible to smell the spices – cinnamon, nutmeg and cloves, mostly – which were stored here until the 1970s, especially in the last section of Shad Thames after a shower of rain. The footbridge takes you over to **New Concordia Wharf** on Mill Street, one of the first warehouse conversions in the area, completed in 1984. Next door stands **China Wharf**, one of the most photographed postmodernist buildings in Docklands, with its stack of semicircular windows picked out in red.

The area to the east of **Mill Street** was dubbed by the Victorian press "the very capital of cholera". In 1849, the *Morning Chronicle* described it thus: "Jostling with unemployed labourers of the lowest class, ballast heavers, coal-whippers, brazen women, ragged children, and the very raff and refuse of the river, [the visitor] makes his way with difficulty along, assailed by offensive sights and smells from the narrow alleys which branch off." This was the location of Dickens' fictional Jacob's Island, a place with "every imaginable sign of desolation and neglect", where Bill Sikes met his end in *Oliver Twist*.

If you want to continue east on foot to Rotherhithe, you can follow a route alongside the river, stopping en route at **The Angel**, a pub once frequented by Pepys and Captain Cook, which now stands all alone on Bermondsey Wall, with great views over to Wapping. Close by are the foundations of Edward III's moated manor house, begun in 1353, and the "Leaning Tower of Bermondsey", a precariously tilting riverside house downstream from the pub.

Rotherhithe

Rotherhithe, the thumb of marshy land jutting out into the Thames east of Bermondsey, has always been slightly removed from the rest of London. It was a thriving shipbuilding centre even before the construction of the Surrey Commercial Docks in the nineteenth century. However, no other set of London dockyards took such a hammering in the Blitz, and the immediate postwar decades were years of inexorable decline. The docks have since been reclaimed for new housing estates and more upmarket Docklands developments.

The bit of Rotherhithe worth visiting, however, is the heart of the old eighteenth-century seafaring village around **St Mary's Church**, which stands in its own leafy square, northwest of the tube station. The church itself is unremarkable, but it has rich maritime associations: several of the furnishings are made from the timber of the *Fighting Temeraire*, the veteran of Trafalgar which ended its days in a Rotherhithe breaker's yard (Turner's painting of its last voyage hangs in the National Gallery), and the master of the *Mayflower* was buried here. The *Mayflower* was Rotherhithe-owned and-crewed, and set off from outside the *Mayflower* pub in 1620 to transport the Pilgrim Fathers to the New World. (The ship had to call in at Plymouth for repairs after being damaged in the English Channel.) The pub (see p.403), north of the church, is a rickety white weatherboarded building, badly damaged in the last war, and a minor pilgrimage site for Americans.

Brunel Museum

East of St Mary's, down Tunnel Street, you'll find the **Brunel Museum** (daily 10am–5pm; £2; ☏020/7231 3840, ⓦ www.brunel-museum.org.uk; Rotherhithe tube), a brick-built shed that marks the site of the Thames Tunnel, the world's first

---

Scandinavian seamen's missions

One of the more unusual legacies of Rotherhithe's seafaring past is the trio of Scandinavian seamen's missions – a reminder of the former dominance of the timber trade in the nearby Surrey Docks – which survive to the south of the tube station, around Albion Street. The most prominent is the **Norwegian Seamen's Church**, by the approach road to the Rotherhithe Tunnel, which flies the Norwegian flag and features a longboat atop its weather vane. Albion Street itself still has a Scandinavian bent – even the nearby public toilets are bilingual – and further down you'll find the well-maintained **Finnish Seamen's Mission**, built in modernist style in 1958, with a freestanding belfry that looks more like a fire-station practice tower. The 1960s **Swedish Seamen's Church**, further south at 120 Lower Rd, completes the trio but is architecturally undistinguished.

under-river tunnel. It was begun in 1825 by Marc Brunel and his more famous son, Isambard, to link Rotherhithe with Wapping, using technology which was invented by Brunel senior and whose basic principles have been used for all subsequent tunnelling. Plagued by periodic flooding, labour unrest, fatalities and lack of funds, the tunnel took eighteen years to construct and was nicknamed "The Great Bore" by the press.

The circular working shaft, which housed an engine to pump water out of the tunnel, survives to the east of the engine house, but funds ran out before the spiral ramps, which would have allowed horse-drawn vehicles actually to use the tunnel, could be built. Instead, in 1843, the tunnel was opened to pedestrians as a tourist attraction, pulling in two million visitors in its first year. It was visited by Queen Victoria herself, who knighted Brunel junior, but soon became the haunt of whores and "tunnel thieves". Since 1869 it has formed part of the East London Railway (now the London Overground) and remains the most watertight of all the rail tunnels under the Thames. As well as telling the tunnel's fascinating story, the museum displays some of the old souvenirs sold in Victorian times.

Surrey Docks and Rotherhithe Street

The once marshy land of Rotherhithe peninsula, east of the old village, was chosen as the site for London's first wet dock, the Howland Great Dock, built in 1696 to take on any extra repair work and refitting emanating from the Royal Dockyards in nearby Deptford. Later renamed Greenland Dock, it became part of the network known as **Surrey Commercial Docks**. The main trade was timber, which was piled into stacks up to 80ft high by porters nicknamed "Flying Blondins" (after the tightrope walker), who wore distinctive leather pads on their heads and shoulders to protect them from splinters. The docks took a pounding in the Blitz, and on one particular occasion, 350,000 tons of timber were set ablaze in one of the largest fires ever seen in Britain.

Rotherhithe Street, which hugs the riverbank, is the longest street in London at around a mile and a half. It's mainly residential, a mixture of new Docklands developments and council housing, but the Thames Path, which runs parallel to it for most of the way, is pleasant enough to walk or cycle along, with great views over to Limehouse and Canary Wharf. Halfway along the street, you can learn more about the area's history at the **Pumphouse Museum** (Mon–Fri 10am–4pm; free; ☎020/7231 2976, ⓦwww.thepumphouse.org.uk; bus #C10 from Canada Water or Rotherhithe tube), housed in an old pumphouse on Lavender Street. Further along, you can catch a boat back into town or on to Greenwich, from the Nelson Dock Pier beside the *Hilton* hotel. If you've time to kill, check out the three-masted schooner (now a restaurant) built in the 1950s as a training ship for the French navy, and nearby **Nelson House**, a beautiful Georgian house built for one of the wealthy owners of Nelson Dock.

Hyde Park and Kensington Gardens

Londoners tend to see their city as grimy and built-up, but most visitors are amazed at how green and pleasant so much of the centre is, with three royal parks – St James's Park, Green Park and Hyde Park – forming a continuous grassy belt that stretches for four miles. **Hyde Park**, together with its westerly extension, **Kensington Gardens**, is the largest of the trio, covering a distance of a mile and a half from Speakers' Corner in the northeast to Kensington Palace in the southwest. In between, you can jog, swim, fish, sunbathe or mess about in boats on the Serpentine, cross the park on horseback or mountain bike, or view the latest in modern art at the Serpentine Gallery. At the end of your journey, you've made it to one of London's most exclusive districts, the Royal Borough of Kensington and Chelsea, covered in the next two chapters.

Hyde Park

Seized from the Church by Henry VIII to satisfy his desire for yet more hunting grounds, **Hyde Park** (daily 5am–midnight; ☏020/7298 2100, Ⓦwww.royalparks.gov.uk) was first opened to the public by James I, when refreshments available included "milk from a red cow". Under Charles II, the park became a fashionable gathering place for the beau monde, who rode round the circular drive known as the Ring, pausing to gossip and admire each other's equipages. Its present appearance is mostly due to Queen Caroline, an enthusiast for landscape gardens, who spent a great deal of George II's money creating the park's main feature, the **Serpentine** lake.

Hangings, muggings and duels, the 1851 Great Exhibition and numerous public events have all taken place here – and it's still a popular gathering point or destination for political demonstrations, as well as the location of **Speakers' Corner**, of which more below. For the most part, however, Hyde Park is simply a leisure ground – a wonderful open space that allows you to lose all sight of the city beyond a few persistent tower blocks. In addition, the southeast corner of the park contains two conventional tourist attractions: **Apsley House**, housing a museum to the Duke of Wellington, and the triumphal **Wellington Arch**, which you can now climb.

© crown copyright

N

MAYFAIR

ORCHARD ST
SOUTH AUDLEY STREET
CURZON ST

PARK LANE

Wellington
Arch

Achilles

HYDE PARK
CORNER

Apsley House

PORTMAN ST
OLD QUEBEC ST
Marble Arch

MARBLE ARCH
EDGWARE ROAD

Speakers'
Corner

Holocaust
Memorial

KNIGHTSBRIDGE

Reformers'
Tree

Tyburn
Convent

BAYSWATER ROAD
NORTH CARRIAGE DRIVE
THE RING

Hyde   Park

SOUTH CARRIAGE DRIVE

Hyde Park
Barracks

BROMPTON ROAD

Victoria Gate

NORTH RIDE
WEST CARRIAGE DRIVE

Rima

The Serpentine

KNIGHTSBRIDGE

MONTPELIER
SQUARE

BROOKS ST

Pet
Cemetery

Kensington

Gardens

Lido

RUTLAND
GATE

WEST
BOURNE ST

Italian
Garden

Diana
Memorial
Fountain

ENNISMORE GARDENS

Malborough
Gate

LANCASTER
GATE

The Long Water

Prince of
Wales Gate

ENNISMORE GDNS

CRAVEN TERRACE

Lancaster
Gate

Peter Pan

Physical Energy

KENSINGTON ROAD

PRINCE'S
GARDENS

LANCASTER
MEWS

Speke
Monument

Serpentine Gallery

EXHIBITION

KNIGHTSBRIDGE

LEINSTER TERRACE

NORTH WALK

Albert Memorial

KENSINGTON GORE

Royal Albert
Hall

PRINCE CONSORT ROAD

PORCHESTER TERRACE

Kensington

QUEENSBOROUGH TERR.

INVERNESS TERR.

Gardens

QUEENS GATE

QUEENSWAY

Round
Pond

BAYSWATER ROAD

BROAD   WALK

Princess of
Wales Playground

Elfin Oak

Kensington
Palace

PALACE GATE

PALACE AVENUE

PARK
PLACE

ORME COURT

PETERSBURGH   PLACE

PALACE GREEN

ACCOMMODATION
Baglioni   C
Columbia   B
Smart Hyde
Park Inn   A

PUB & BAR
The Quebec   1

HYDE PARK & KENSINGTON GARDENS

0   200 yds

OXFORD STREET
Marble Arch

MARBLE ARCH

NEW QUEBEC ST
SEYMOUR ST

PARK
STREET
PARK LANE
UPPER GROSVENOR STREET
GREEN STREET
NORTH ROW
WOODS MEWS
UPPER BROOK STREET

GROSVENOR PLACE

Bayswater

High Street Kensington

Museums

www.roughguides.com

Marble Arch and Speakers' Corner

Marble Arch, in the treeless northeastern corner of the park and at the west end of Oxford Street, is the most historically charged spot in Hyde Park, as it marks the site of **Tyburn gallows**, the city's main public execution spot until 1783, when the action moved to Newgate. There's a plaque on the traffic island at the bottom of Edgware Road/Bayswater Road marking the approximate site of the gallows, where around fifty thousand lost their lives. Of these, some 105 were Catholics, martyred during the Reformation, in whose memory the **Tyburn Convent** (daily 6.30am–8.30pm; ⓦ www.tyburnconvent.org.uk; Marble Arch tube) was established at 8 Hyde Park Place in 1902. It's run by a group of cloistered French Benedictine nuns who are happy to show visitors round the basement shrine (10.30am, 3.30pm & 5.30pm; free), which contains a mock-up of the Tyburn gibbet over the main altar, and various pictures and relics of the martyrs. The house next door to (and now part of) the convent, no. 10, is London's smallest, measuring just three and a half feet across.

The **Marble Arch** itself, now stranded on a ferociously busy traffic island, was designed in 1828 by John Nash as a triumphal entrance for Buckingham Palace. The sculpted friezes intended to adorn it ended up on the palace, while the equestrian statue of George IV, intended to surmount it, was carted off to Trafalgar Square. When the palace was extended in the 1840s, the arch was moved to form an entrance to Hyde Park, its upper chambers used as a police observation post. During the 1855 riot (see below), a detachment of police emerged, like the Greeks from the Trojan Horse, much to the surprise of the demonstrators.

In 1855 an estimated 250,000 people gathered in the park to protest against the Sunday Trading Bill (Karl Marx was among the crowd and thought it was the

Tyburn gallows

For nearly five hundred years, **Tyburn** was the capital's main **public execution** site. Dressed in their best clothes, the condemned were processed through the streets in a cart (the nobility were allowed to travel in their own carriages) from Newgate Prison, often with the noose already in place. They received a nosegay at St Sepulchre, opposite the prison, and then a pint of ale at various taverns along the route, so that most were blind drunk by the time they arrived at the three-legged gibbet known as the "Tyburn Tree" or the "Triple Tree", which could dispatch over twenty people at one go.

The condemned were allowed to make a speech to the crowd and were attended by a chaplain, though according to one eighteenth-century spectator he was "more the subject of ridicule than of serious attention". The same witness describes how the executioner, who drove the cart, then tied the rope to the tree: "This done he gives the horse a lash with his whip, away goes the cart and there swings my gentleman kicking in the air. The Hangman does not give himself the trouble to put them out of their pain but some of their friends or relations do it for them. They pull the dying person by the legs and beat his breast to dispatch him as soon as possible."

Not all relatives were so fatalistic, however, and some would attempt to support the condemned in the hope of a last-minute reprieve, or of reviving the victim when they were cut down. Fights frequently broke out when the body was cut down, between the relatives, the spectators (who believed the corpse had miraculous medicinal qualities), and the surgeons (who were allowed ten corpses a year for dissection). The executioner, known as "**Jack Ketch**" after the famous London hangman (see p.199), was allowed to take home the victim's clothes, and made further profit by selling the hanging rope by the inch. Following the 1780 Gordon Riots, the powers-that-be took fright at unruly gatherings like Tyburn, and in 1783 the Tyburn Tree was demolished.

beginning of the English Revolution), and ever since it has been one of London's most popular spots for political demos. In 1872 the government licensed free assembly at **Speakers' Corner**, a peculiarly English Sunday-morning tradition that continues to this day, featuring an assembly of ranters and hecklers. The largest demonstration in London's history took place here in February 2003 when over a million people turned up to try and stop the war against Iraq.

Hyde Park Corner

A better place to enter the park is at **Hyde Park Corner**, the southeast corner, where **Wellington Arch** (Wed–Sun: April–Oct 10am–5pm; Nov–March 10am–4pm; EH; £3.20; Hyde Park Corner tube) stands in the midst of another of London's busiest traffic interchanges. Inside, you can view an exhibition on the history of the arch, and of London's outdoor sculpture, and take a lift to the top of the monument (once London's smallest postwar police station) where the exterior balconies offer a bird's-eye view of the swirling traffic.

Designed by a youthful Decimus Burton in 1828 to commemorate Wellington's victories in the Napoleonic Wars, the arch originally served as the northern entrance to Buckingham Palace. Positioned opposite Burton's delicate Hyde Park Screen, the arch once formed part of a fine architectural ensemble with Apsley House, Wellington's London residence, and St George's Hospital to the west. Unfortunately the symmetry was destroyed when the arch was repositioned in 1883 to line up with Constitution Hill – named after the "constitutional" walks that Charles II used to take here. The arch's original statue was an enormous equestrian portrayal of the "Iron Duke" erected in 1846 while he was still alive. The duke was taken down in 1883, and eventually replaced by Peace and her four-horse chariot, erected in 1912.

The replacement (ground level) statue for Wellington is much smaller, and stands opposite his erstwhile residence, **Apsley House** (see p.246). He is depicted seated astride his faithful steed, Copenhagen, which carried the field marshal for sixteen hours during the Battle of Waterloo; the horse eventually died in 1836 and was buried with full military honours at the duke's country pile in Hampshire. Close by are two powerful war memorials erected in 1925: the first, the **Machine Gun Corps Memorial**, features the naked figure of David leaning on Goliath's sword and the chilling inscription, "Saul hath slain his thousands, but David his tens of thousands"; the larger of the two, the **Artillery Memorial**, includes a 9.2-inch howitzer rendered in Portland stone, realistic relief depictions of the brutality of war, and the equally blunt epitaph, "Here was a royal fellowship of death".

Apsley House: the Wellington Museum

Known during the Iron Duke's lifetime as Number One, London, **Apsley House** (Tues–Sun: April–Oct 11am–5pm; Nov–March 11am–4pm; EH; £5.40; Hyde Park Corner tube) was once an immensely desirable residence, but nowadays, overlooking a very busy roundabout, it would be poor reward for any national hero. The interior isn't what it used to be either, but in this case it's Wellington himself who's to blame. Built and exquisitely decorated by Robert Adam in the 1770s for Baron Apsley, it was remodelled by Benjamin Wyatt after Wellington bought the place in 1817. Wyatt faced the red-brick exterior with Bath stone and more or less got rid of the Adam interiors. As a result, the house is very much as it would have been in Wellington's day, and the current duke still lives in the attic.

The house is worth visiting for the **art collection** alone. Wellington acquired the collection in 1813 after the Battle of Vittoria, when he seized the baggage train of Napoleon's brother, who was fleeing for France with two hundred paintings belonging to the King of Spain. The best pieces, including works by de Hooch, Van Dyck, Goya, Rubens and Murillo, cover the red walls of the **Waterloo Gallery** on the first floor, where sliding mirrors cover the windows. The most prized works of all are a trio by Velázquez – *The Water-Seller of Seville*, *Portrait of a Gentleman* and *Two Young Men Eating at a Humble Table* – though Wellington preferred Correggio's *Agony in the Garden*, the key for which he used to carry round with him, so he could take the picture out of its frame and dust it fondly.

Like several of the other rooms, the gallery was originally hung with yellow satin, which, as one of the duke's friends lamented, "is just the very worst colour he can have for the pictures and will kill the effect of the gilding". It was here that Wellington held his annual veterans' **Waterloo Banquet**, using the thousand-piece silver-gilt Portuguese service, now displayed in the rather lugubrious Dining Room at the other end of the house. Most of the Waterloo portraits are, in fact, hung in the adjacent Striped Drawing Room, which is decorated like a military tent in the manner of Napoleon's Loire chateau, Malmaison.

Canova's famous, more than twice life-sized, **nude statue of Napoleon** stands at the foot of the main staircase, having been bought by the government for the duke in 1816. It was disliked by the sitter, not least for the tiny figure of Victory in the emperor's hand, which appears to be trying to fly away. In the dimly lit Plate and China Room, also on the ground floor, you can view numerous gifts to the duke, including a 400-piece Prussian dinner service decorated with scenes of Wellington's life, and the bizarre Egyptian service, which was originally a divorce present from Napoleon to Josephine; unsurprisingly, she rejected it and

The Iron Duke

Perhaps if the **Duke of Wellington** had died, like Nelson, at his moment of greatest triumph, he too would enjoy an unsullied posthumous reputation. Instead, he went on to become the epitome of the outmoded, reactionary conservative, earning his famous nickname, the "Iron Duke", not from his fearless military campaigning, but from the iron shutters he installed at Apsley House after his windows were broken by demonstrators rioting in favour of the 1832 Reform Bill, to which the duke was vehemently opposed.

Born **Arthur Wesley** in Dublin in 1769 – the same year as Napoleon – he was educated at (but hated) Eton and the French military academy at Angers. He campaigned out in India, helping to defeat Tipu Sultan, and eventually becoming Governor of Mysore. After continued military success in his Napoleonic campaigns, he eventually became Duke of Wellington in 1814, shortly before achieving his most famous victory of all at Waterloo.

With great reluctance he became **prime minister** in 1828, "a station, to the duties of which I am unaccustomed, in which I was not wished, and for which I was not qualified…I should have been mad if I had thought of such a thing". Despite his own misgivings, his government passed the Catholic Relief Act – allowing Catholics to sit in Parliament – thus avoiding civil war in Ireland, but splitting the Tory ranks. Accused of popery by the Earl of Winchelsea, Wellington challenged him to a duel in Battersea Park; the duke fired and missed, while the earl shot into the air and apologized for the slur.

Wellington's opposition to the Reform Bill brought down his government and allowed the Whigs (under Earl Grey, of tea fame) to form a majority government for the first time in sixty years. Despite retiring from public life in 1846, he was on hand to organize the defence of the capital against the Chartists in 1848, and strolled across to the Great Exhibition every day in 1851. Two million people lined the streets for his funeral in 1852 (more than for anyone before or since), and he has more outdoor statues (and pubs named after him) in London than any other historical figure. Despite this, his greatest legacy is, of course, the **Wellington boot**, originally made of leather, now rubber.

⓱

Louis XVIII ended up giving it to the duke. In the basement there's plenty of Wellingtonia, a goodly selection of cruel, contemporary caricatures and a pair of the famous boots.

Achilles and Rotten Row

Behind Apsley House, a pair of frothy, rather silly, silvery gates marks the Queen Elizabeth Gate, and the beginning of the park proper. Close by, overlooking the back of Apsley House, is the 33-ton bronze **Achilles** statue, designed by Richard Westmacott and cast from captured French cannon. It was erected in 1822 on behalf of "the women of Great Britain", who acted as fundraisers for the statue, and commemorates the Duke of Wellington's achievements. As the country's first public nude statue it caused outrage, especially since many thought it a portrait of the duke himself. In actual fact, it represents neither the duke nor Achilles, but is a copy of one of the horse-tamers from the Monte Cavallo in Rome. William Wilberforce led a campaign to have the statue removed for decency's sake; a fig leaf was placed in the appropriate place as a compromise.

From the gates, two roads set off west to Kensington: South Carriage Road, which is open to cars, and **Rotten Row**, thought to be a corruption of *route du roi* (king's way), since it was established by William III as a bridle path linking Westminster and Kensington. William had three hundred oil lamps hung from the trees to try to combat the increasing number of highwaymen active in the park, thus making Rotten Row the first road in the country to be lit at night. The measure was only partly successful – George II himself was later mugged here. To the south of Rotten Row, the **Hyde Park Barracks** are difficult to miss, thanks to Basil Spence's hideous high-rise design. Early in the morning, you might catch sight of the Household Cavalry exercising in the park, and at around 10.30am daily (Sun 9.30am) they set off for the Horse Guards building in Whitehall for the Changing of the Guard (see p.57).

The Serpentine

Rotten Row remains a bridle path, so pedestrians should wander through the pretty flower gardens to the north instead. Beyond lies the **Serpentine lake**, created in 1730 by damming the Westbourne, a small tributary of the Thames, in order that Queen Caroline might have a spot for the royal yachts to mess about on. A miniature re-enactment of the Battle of Trafalgar was staged here in 1814, and two years later Shelley's pregnant wife, Harriet Westbrook, drowned herself in the lake after the poet had eloped with the 16-year-old Mary Wollstonecraft. The popular **Lido** (May–Sept daily 10am–6pm; £3.75; ☎020/7706 3422, ⓦwww.serpentinelido.com) is situated on the south bank, alongside the lovely Lido café, and rowing boats and pedalos can be rented (March–Oct daily 10am–5pm or dusk; £4 per person, per half-hour; ☎020/7262 1330) from the boathouse on the north bank.

Royal Gun Salutes

At noon on February 6 (Accession Day), April 21 (Queen's Birthday), June 2 (Coronation Day) and June 10 (Duke of Edinburgh's Birthday), and at 11am on the Queen's official birthday (a variable date in June), the Royal Horse Artillery wheel out cannons and the park resounds to a 41-round **Royal Gun Salute**. If a date falls on a Sunday, then the salute takes place the next day. There are further gun salutes for London state visits, the State Opening of Parliament (at 11.08am) and two, two-gun salutes on Remembrance Sunday at 11am and 11.02am.

To the west of the Lido is the entrance to the **Diana Memorial Fountain** (daily: March & Oct 10am–6pm; April–Aug 10am–8pm; Sept 10am–7pm; Nov–Feb 10am–4pm; free). Less of a fountain, and more of a giant oval-shaped mini-moat, the intention was to allow children to play in the running water, but, after three people suffered minor injuries, the fountain has been fenced off and supplied with security guards, making it rather less fun for kids, who are now only allowed to dabble their feet.

To the north of the Serpentine is a Jacob Epstein monument, a relief of **Rima**, a naked, female, South American version of Tarzan, which provoked such hostility when it was unveiled in 1925 that it was tarred and feathered on two separate occasions. The monument is dedicated to the naturalist and writer **W.H. Hudson**, who wrote the Victorian adventure novel *Green Mansions*, in which Rima is one of the main protagonists.

Kensington Gardens

The more tranquil half of the park, west of the West Carriage Drive, is known as **Kensington Gardens** (daily 6am to dusk; ℡020/7298 2141, ⓦwww.royal parks.gov.uk) and is, strictly speaking, a separate entity from Hyde Park, though the only difference is that Kensington Gardens is locked at night. More exclusive because of the proximity of royalty at Kensington Palace, the gardens were first opened to the public in George II's reign, but only on Sundays and only to those in formal dress, not including sailors, soldiers or liveried servants. Unrestricted access was only granted in Victoria's reign, by which time, in the view of the Russian ambassador's wife, the park had already been "annexed as a middle-class rendezvous. Good society no longer [went] there except to drown itself."

The Long Water

The upper section of the Serpentine – beyond the bridge – is known as the **Long Water**, and is by far the prettiest section of the lake. It narrows until it reaches the lovely **Italian Gardens**, a group of five fountains, laid out symmetrically in front of a pumphouse disguised as an Italianate loggia. To the east, by Victoria Gate, lies the odd little **Pet Cemetery**, begun in the 1880s when Mr and Mrs J. Lewis Barnes buried their Maltese terrier, Cherry, here. When the Duke of Cambridge buried his wife's pet hound at the same spot after it had been run over on Bayswater Road, it became *the* place to bury your pooch; three hundred other cats and dogs followed, until the last burial in 1967. The cemetery – "perhaps the most horrible spectacle in Britain", according to George Orwell – is no longer open to the public, though you can peep over the wall.

The best-known of all Hyde Park's outdoor monuments is **Peter Pan**, the fictional character who enters London along the Serpentine and whose statue stands by the west bank of the Long Water; fairies, squirrels, rabbits, birds and mice scamper round the pedestal. It was in Kensington Gardens that the author, J.M. Barrie, used to walk his dog, and it was here that he met the five pretty, upper-class Llewellyn Davies boys, who wore "blue blouses and bright red tam o'shanters", were the inspiration for the "Lost Boys", and whose guardian he eventually became. Barrie himself paid for the statue, which was erected in secret during the night in 1912.

The rough-hewn muscleman struggling with his horse, to the southwest of Peter Pan, is G.F. Watts' **Physical Energy**, a copy of the Rhodes memorial in Cape Town; to the north is a granite obelisk raised to **John Hanning Speke**, who was the first non-African to find the source of the Nile, and who died in 1864 after accidentally shooting himself rather than the partridge he was aiming at. In the far northwestern corner is the top-quality **Princess of Wales Playground**, which features a ship stuck in sand, paving gongs and other groovy playthings. Just outside the entrance is the **Elfin Oak**, a gnarled stump from Richmond Park, carved with little animals and mystical creatures by children's-book illustrator Ivor Innes in the late 1920s.

To the south of all this statuary stands the **Serpentine Gallery** (daily 10am–6pm; free; ☎020/7402 6075, ⓦwww.serpentinegallery.org; South Kensington tube), built as a tearoom in 1908 because the park authorities thought "poorer visitors" might otherwise cause trouble if left without refreshments. An art gallery since the 1960s, it has a reputation for lively, and often controversial, contemporary art exhibitions, and contains an excellent bookshop. In more recent years the gallery has commissioned a different architect each year to design a temporary **pavilion** for its summer-only teahouse extension.

Albert Memorial

Completed in 1876 by George Gilbert Scott, the **Albert Memorial** (March–Dec first Sun of month 2pm & 3pm; 45min guided tours £4.50; ☎020/7495 0916; South Kensington tube), on the south side of Kensington Gardens, is as much a hymn to the glorious achievements of Britain as to its subject, Queen Victoria's husband (who died of typhoid in 1861), whose gilded image sits under its central canopy, clutching a catalogue for the 1851 Great Exhibition. The pomp of the monument is overwhelming: the spire, inlaid with semiprecious stones and marbles, rises to 180ft, a marble frieze around the pediment is cluttered with 169 life-sized figures (all men) in high relief, depicting poets, musicians, painters, architects and sculptors from ancient Egypt onwards; the pillars are topped with bronzes of Astronomy, Chemistry, Geology and Geometry; mosaics show Poetry, Painting, Architecture and Sculpture; four outlying marble groups represent the four continents; and other statuary pays homage to Agriculture, Commerce and other aspects of imperial economics. Albert would not have been amused: "I can say, with perfect absence of humbug, that I would rather not be made the prominent feature of such a monument… it would upset my equanimity to be permanently ridiculed and laughed at in effigy", he once claimed.

Kensington Palace

On the western edge of Kensington Gardens stands **Kensington Palace** (daily: March–Oct 10am–6pm; Nov–Feb 10am–5pm; £12.50; ☎020/3166 6000, ⓦwww.hrp.org.uk; Queensway or High Street Kensington tube), a modestly

Visiting KP

The most handsome facade of KP – as it's fondly known in royal circles – faces south, behind a flamboyant statue of William III, given to Edward VII by the Kaiser. The public entrance is on the east side, and must be approached from the **Round Pond**, where George I used to keep his edible turtles, and the Broad Walk, a favourite rollerblading avenue; both are overlooked by a flattering statue of Queen Victoria sculpted by her daughter, Princess Louise. You buy your tickets in the gloomy **Red Saloon** on the ground floor, where the 18-year-old Victoria held her first Privy Council meeting, just hours after William IV's death on June 20, 1837. To the north of the palace there's a café in Hawksmoor's **Orangery**, built for Queen Anne as a summer dining room, and decorated with carving and statues by Grinling Gibbons.

The Great Exhibition and the Crystal Palace

East of the Albert Memorial was the site of the **Great Exhibition** of the Works and Industry of All Nations, held between May 1 and October 15, 1851. The idea originated with Henry Cole, a minor civil servant in the Record Office, and was taken up enthusiastically by Prince Albert despite opposition from snooty Kensington residents, who complained it would attract an "invasion of undesirables who would ravish their silver and their serving maids". A competition to design the exhibition building produced 245 rejected versions, until Joseph Paxton, head gardener to the Duke of Devonshire, offered to build his "**Crystal Palace**", a wrought-iron and glass structure some 1848ft long and 408ft wide. The acceptance of Paxton's radical proposal was an act of faith by the exhibition organizers, since such a structure had never been built, and their faith was amply rewarded – a team of two hundred workers completed the building in just four months.

As well as showing off the achievements of the British Empire it was also a unique opportunity for people to enjoy the products of other cultures. Thousands of exhibits were housed in the Crystal Palace, including the Koh-i-Noor diamond (displayed in a birdcage), an Indian ivory throne, a floating church from Philadelphia, a bed which awoke its occupant by ejecting him or her into a cold bath, false teeth designed not to be displaced when yawning, a fountain running with eau de Cologne, and all manner of china, fabrics and glass.

To everyone's surprise, six million people came to visit it, and the exhibition made a profit, which was used to buy 87 acres of land south of Kensington Road, for the creation of a "Museumland" where "the arts and sciences could be promoted and taught in a way which would be of practical use to industry and make Britain the leading country of the industrialized world". The Crystal Palace itself was dismantled after the exhibition and rebuilt in southeast London in 1854, where it served as a concert hall, theatre, menagerie and exhibition space, only to be entirely destroyed by fire in 1936.

proportioned, Jacobean brick mansion bought as an out-of-town residence by William and Mary in 1689 because the king's asthma and bronchitis were aggravated by Whitehall's damp and fumes. Wren, Hawksmoor and later William Kent were called in to embellish the place, though the palace was actually chief royal residence for barely fifty years.

The palace is best known today as the place where **Princess Diana** lived until her death in 1997. In the weeks following the princess's death, literally millions of flowers, mementoes, poems and gifts were deposited at the palace gates. Visitors get to see some of Diana's dresses, but they don't get to see Diana's rooms, which were on the west side of the palace, where the dukes and duchesses of Kent and Gloucester all still live.

Royal Ceremonial Dress Collection

The **Royal Ceremonial Dress Collection** kicks off with a tableau of a 1920s debutante getting ready to be presented at court, and an ambassador kitted out in full court dress. The displays change from year to year but usually you get to see a few of the **Queen's dresses** – from the glamorous 1950s ball gowns, smothered in sequins and pearls, to her more suspect later penchant for apricot- and peach-coloured frocks – and a selection of **Princess Diana's dresses**. You also get to look round 1A, the apartment where the Queen's sister, **Princess Margaret**, lived until her death in 2002. To be honest, the place has been stripped bare of virtually all furnishings, except for a few rather peculiar portraits of Margaret, and the hagiographical exhibition shies away from anything seamy and dwells instead on her status as an amateur conchologist.

▲ Kensington Palace

State apartments

Little of Wren's work survives in the **King's Apartments**, and the most interesting rooms are mostly designed by William Kent, beginning with the impressive **King's Staircase**, with its Irish black marble steps, its Tijou wrought-iron balustrade and trompe-l'oeil crowds of courtiers and yeomen. Another great Kent creation is the "grotesque"-style painting on the ceiling of the **Presence Chamber**, which also features a lovely pear-wood Gibbons overmantle with weeping putti. Two rooms further on, the **Cupola Room**, with its monstrously ugly clock occupying centre stage, features another wonderful trompe-l'oeil fresco, which gives the effect of a coffered dome.

Another two rooms on, **Queen Victoria's Bedroom** is a bit of a contrast, since it was totally redecorated in 1836. Victoria was born in the decaying palace in 1819, and spent her dull, sad childhood cooped up here with her strict mother, the Duchess of Kent, who slept in the same room. According to her diary, her best friends were the palace's numerous "black beetles", though it's clear from the Indian clubs that she was also into keep-fit. The palace's grandest room is the **King's Gallery**, whose red damask walls are hung with paintings by, among others, Tintoretto. Also of interest is the wind dial above the fireplace, connected to the palace weather vane, built for William III and still fully functioning

The **Queen's Apartments**, which follow, are, by contrast, much more modest, wood-panelled rooms hung with Dutch works reflecting the tastes of William and Mary. The best room is the **Queen's Bedchamber**, decked out in deep-blue velvet, with a four-poster bed that belonged to Queen Mary of Modena, James II's second wife. It was here that the diminutive Queen Anne died of gout; the toilet on which George II died of a heart attack, brought on by constipation, is, however, no longer in existence. **Queen Mary's Closet** was the scene of a furious quarrel between Queen Anne and her lover, the Duchess of Marlborough, after which they never saw each other again. The last room on the tour is **Queen Mary's Gallery**, once magnificently decorated with 154 pieces of Oriental porcelain, now reduced to a mere handful, and lined with royal portraits. At the far end is one by Peter Lely, of Anne Hyde, mistress and later wife of the future James II; they officially married after she was already pregnant, causing something of a royal scandal even in the libidinous Restoration period.

18

South Kensington, Knightsbridge and Chelsea

O ther districts go in and out of fashion, but the Royal Borough of Kensington and Chelsea, particularly the area to the south of Hyde Park, has been in vogue ever since royalty moved into Kensington Palace in the late seventeenth century. Aside from the shops around Harrods in **Knightsbridge**, however, the popular tourist attractions lie in **South Kensington**, where three of London's top free **museums** – the Victoria and Albert, Natural History and Science museums – stand on land bought with the proceeds of the 1851 Great Exhibition. The following half-century saw the entire borough transformed from fields, farms and private estates into street after street of ostentatious, whitewashed Italianate terraces, grandiose red-brick mansions and mews houses. This is prime London real estate (among the world's most expensive) and heartland of the privately educated, wealthy offspring of the middle and upper classes and the rich and famous.

Chelsea, bordering the river to the south, also has royal connections, though these date mostly from Tudor times and have left few tangible remains. Since the nineteenth century, however, when artists and writers began to move here in significant numbers, Chelsea's character has been more bohemian than its neighbours. In the 1960s, the **King's Road** carved out its reputation as London's catwalk, while in the late 1970s it was the unlikely epicentre of the punk explosion. Nothing so risqué goes on in Chelsea now, though its residents like to think of themselves as a cut above the purely moneyed types of Kensington.

South Kensington

To everyone's surprise, the 1851 Great Exhibition was not only an enormous success, but actually yielded a profit, with which Prince Albert and his committee bought 87 acres of land in **South Kensington**. Institutions and

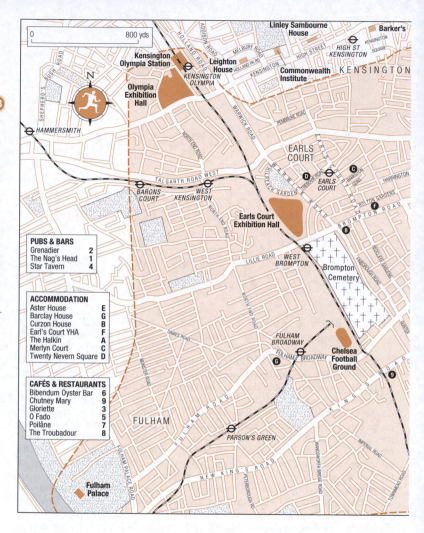

museums, whose purpose was to "extend the influence of Science and Art upon Productive Industry", were to be established here to form a kind of "**Museumland**". Albert died of typhoid in 1861 at the age of just 41, and never saw his dream fully realized, but "Albertopolis", with its remarkable cluster of **museums and colleges**, plus the vast Albert Hall, now stands as one of London's most enlightened examples of urban planning.

With the founding of "Museumland", the surrounding area was transformed almost overnight into one of the most fashionable in town – a status it retains today. South Ken, as it's known, has acquired further cachet thanks to its **French connections**, with a French school and crèche, a couple of bookshops, a deli and several genuine patisseries and brasseries clustered around the **Institut Français** (Ⓦwww.institut-francais.org.uk) on Queensberry Place, which maintains an interesting programme of theatre, cinema and exhibitions.

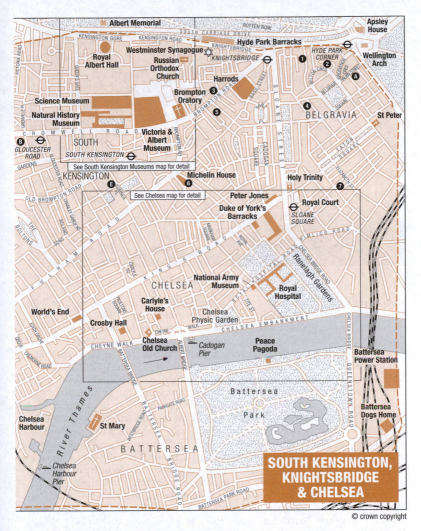

© crown copyright

A further French sight worth checking out is the gorgeous Art Deco **Michelin House**, a short walk to the south down Brompton Road. Faced in white faïence and decorated with tyres and motoring murals by French artists in 1911, its ground floors now house the shop, café, oyster bar and restaurant of *Bibendum*, all run by Terence Conran.

Royal Albert Hall and around

The funds raised on the death of the Prince Consort in 1861 were squandered on the Albert Memorial (see p.250), and it took considerable effort by Henry Cole, his collaborator on the Great Exhibition, to get funding to complete the **Royal Albert Hall**, on Kensington Gore. Plans for this splendid iron- and glass-domed auditorium had been drawn up during the prince's lifetime, with

▲ Royal Albert Hall

an exterior of red brick, terracotta and marble that was already the hallmark of South Ken architecture. The hall was finally completed in 1871 and has been the venue for everything from Miss World to pop gigs. It's also the venue for London's most democratic classical music festival, the annual Henry Wood Promenade Concerts, better known as the **Proms** (see p.256). Daytime **guided tours** of the hall (daily except Wed 10.30am–3.30pm; £8; ☎020/7838 3105, ⓦwww.royalalberthall.com; South Kensington or High Street Kensington tube) depart from the South Porch at Door 12 and last around an hour.

Behind the hall, flanked by the monumental **South Steps**, is a memorial to the Great Exhibition, featuring the Prince Consort. Predating the Royal Albert Hall (which Albert turns his back on), it originally stood amid the gardens and pavilions of the Royal Horticultural Society, which were replaced in the 1880s by the colossal **Imperial Institute** building. Of this only the 287-foot **Queen's Tower** (closed to the public) remains, stranded amid the modern departments of Imperial College, the University of London's science faculty. On the north side of this complex is the neo-Gothic **Royal College of Music**, whose students have included Ralph Vaughan Williams and Benjamin Britten. The college also houses a museum (term-time Tues–Fri 2–4.30pm; free; ☎020/7591 4842, ⓦwww.rcm.ac.uk) containing a collection of over seven hundred instruments, mostly European, dating from the fifteenth to the twentieth centuries.

Several other educational institutions congregate near the Albert Hall, as was Albert's intention. The most striking architecturally is the former **Royal College of Organists** to the west of the Albert Hall, a strange neo-Jacobean confection, designed for free in 1875 by Henry Cole's eldest son and laced with cream, maroon and sky-blue sgraffito. Also on the west side of the Albert Hall is the headquarters of the **Royal College of Art** (ⓦwww.rca.ac.uk), a seven-storey 1960s block which belies its foundation by Prince Albert; past students have included Henry Moore and Tracey Emin; student art exhibitions are held during term-time on the ground floor (daily 10am–6pm; free).

To the east of the Albert Hall is the **Royal Geographical Society** (Mon–Fri 10am–5pm; free; ☎020/7591 3000, ⓦwww.rgs.org; South Kensington tube), a wonderful brick-built complex in the Queen Anne style, with statues of two of the society's early explorers, David Livingstone and Ernest Shackleton, occupying niches along the outer wall. The society gives regular talks, maintains a remarkable library and map room and puts on special exhibitions (entrance on Exhibition Road).

There are strong Polish connections in the South Kensington area, as exemplified by the **Sikorski Museum** (Mon–Fri 2–4pm, also first Sat of month 10am–4pm; free; ☎020/7589 9249, ⓦwww.sikorskimuseum.co.uk; South Kensington tube) and Polish Institute, east of the Royal Geographical Society at 20 Prince's Gate. World War II militaria form the bedrock of the museum, along with the personal effects of General Wladyslaw Sikorski, the prewar prime minister who fled to London in 1939, only to die in a mysterious plane accident in 1943. The absence of a non-Communist leader of Sikorski's standing after the war was lamented by exiled Poles for the next forty years.

Another East European connection is contained within the **Westminster Synagogue** (by appointment ☎020/7584 3741, ⓦwww.westminstersynagogue .org), in Kent House, a spacious Victorian mansion in Rutland Gardens, off Kensington Road. The synagogue arrived here in 1963, and occupies the first floor, while the third floor houses a museum of Torah scrolls, 1564 of which were rescued, after having been gathered from all over Czechoslovakia by the Nazis for their planned "Museum of an Extinct Race". Hundreds have since been restored and sent out to Jewish communities in America, Israel and throughout Europe, but the remainder are displayed here.

Brompton Oratory

London's most flamboyant and atmospheric Roman Catholic church, the **Brompton Oratory** (ⓦwww.bromptonoratory.com), stands just east of the Victoria and Albert Museum. The first large Catholic church to be built since the Reformation, it was begun by the young and unknown Herbert Gribble in 1880 and modelled on the Gesù church in Rome, "so that those who had no opportunity of going over to Italy to see an Italian church had only to come here to see a model of one". The ornate Italianate interior, financed by the Duke of Norfolk, is filled with gilded mosaics and stuffed with sculpture, much of it genuine Italian Baroque from the Gesù church and Siena cathedral, notably the seventeenth-century apostles in the nave and the main altar, and the reredos of the Lady Chapel. The pulpit is a superb piece of neo-Baroque from the 1930s, with a high cherub count on the tester. True to its architecture, the church practises a "rigid, ritualized, smells-and-bells Catholicism", as one journalist put it, with daily Mass in Latin, and some very high-society weddings throughout the year.

Victoria and Albert Museum (V&A)

For variety and scale, the **Victoria and Albert Museum** (daily 10am–5.45pm, Fri until 10pm; free; ☎020/7942 2000, ⓦwww.vam.ac.uk; South Kensington tube) is the greatest museum of applied arts in the world. The range of exhibits on display means that whatever your taste, there's bound to be something to grab your attention: the finest collection of Italian sculpture outside Italy, the world's largest collection of Indian art outside India, plus extensive Chinese, Islamic and Japanese galleries; a gallery of twentieth-century *objets d'art* to rival the Design Museum; and more Constable paintings than Tate Britain. In addition, the V&A's temporary shows – for which you have to pay – are among the best in Britain.

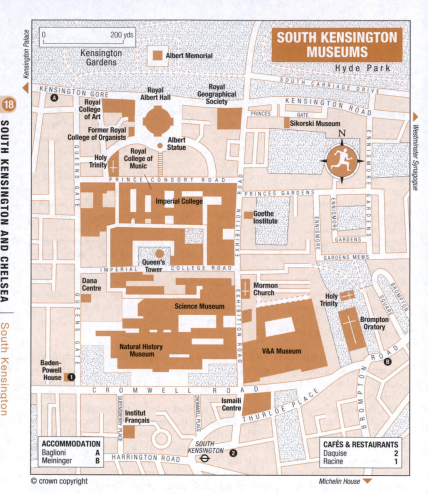

SOUTH KENSINGTON MUSEUMS

ACCOMMODATION
Baglioni   A
Meininger   B

CAFÉS & RESTAURANTS
Daquise   2
Racine   1

© crown copyright

Michelin House ▼

The V&A began life in 1852 as the Museum of Manufactures – it being Albert's intention to help bolster Britain's industrial dominance by inspiring factory workers, students and craftspeople with examples of excellence in applied art and design. Queen Victoria laid the foundation stone of the present, deeply colonial building in 1899 (the last major public engagement of her life); ten years later Aston Webb's imposing main entrance, with its octagonal cupola, flying buttresses and pinnacles, was finished. The side entrance on Exhibition Road, originally built in 1873 for the School of Naval Architects, is equally ornate, with its terracotta arcading and Minton tiles.

Raphael Cartoons, Fashion and Musical Instruments

The most famous of the V&A's many exhibits are the **Raphael Cartoons** (room 48a) – from the Italian *cartone* meaning a large piece of paper – to the left of the main entrance. They comprise seven vast, full-colour paintings in distemper, which are, in fact, designs for tapestries ordered by Pope Leo X for the Sistine Chapel. The pictures – based on episodes from the New Testament – were bought by the future Charles I in 1623. They were subsequently reproduced in countless tapestries and engravings and became more familiar and influential than any of the artist's paintings. Alongside the paintings is an example of one of the tapestries woven at Mortlake – there are further examples in Hampton Court Palace.

At the far end of the room stands the **Retable of St George**, a huge fifteenth-century gilded altarpiece from Valencia, centred on a depiction of James I of Aragon defeating the Moors at the Battle of Puig in 1237. More alarming, though, are the bloodthirsty side panels, which feature the gross tortures endured by St George, with him having nails driven through his body before being placed in a cauldron of molten lead, dragged naked through the streets and finally beheaded and sawn in half.

Directly opposite the Cartoons room, the V&A uses the dimly lit Costume Court for its **Fashion** displays (room 40) from 1850 onwards, but the focus nowadays is very much on special exhibitions usually featuring contemporary designers. A flight of stairs leads to the museum's (strangely silent) collection of **Musical Instruments** (room 40a), chosen for their decorative rather than musical qualities (and only very occasionally open).

Asia

East of the Costume Court, there's a string of superb galleries, kicking off with **South Asia** (room 41), where a fraction of this world-class collection is displayed, much of it derived from London's old East India Company Museum. The most popular exhibit is **Tippoo's Tiger**, a life-sized wooden automaton of a tiger mauling an officer of the East India Company; the innards of the tiger feature a miniature keyboard which simulates the groans of the dying soldier. It was made for the amusement of Tipu Sultan, who was killed when the British took Seringapatam in 1799, and whose watch, telescope, brooch and sword are also displayed here. Close by is the **Golden Throne**, revered by the Sikh community as it belonged to **Ranjit Singh**, the last Sikh emperor, and was taken by the British when they annexed the Punjab in 1849. Next to it is a conical turban decorated with quoits, which can be taken off and hurled at your enemy. Elsewhere, there's a superb white nephrite-jade wine cup, carved in the shape of a shell, made for the Mogul emperor Shah Jahan.

The **Islamic Middle East** gallery (room 42), next door, has, as its centrepiece, the silk-and-wool **Ardabil Carpet**, the world's oldest Persian carpet dating from 1540: copies have variously adorned the floors of 10 Downing Street and Hitler's Berlin office. Unusually, on the west side of the gallery, there are several oil paintings of female acrobats, a harem's tea party and several full-length portraits from the Qajar dynasty in nineteenth-century Iran.

In the **China** gallery (room 44), the range of materials, from jade to rhino horn, lacquer to lapis lazuli, is more striking than any individual piece, though

Visiting the V&A

As Baedeker noted in 1905, "it can hardly be claimed that the arrangements of the [museum] are specially perspicuous". Beautifully but haphazardly displayed across a seven-mile, four-storey maze of rooms, the V&A's treasures are impossible to survey in a single visit. The free **floor plans** can help you decide which areas to concentrate on, but it's easy to get lost so you may prefer one of the museum's hourly, free Introductory or British Galleries **tours**.

Future plans

Like most big museums, the V&A is in a state of flux, with galleries opening and closing throughout the year. The **Gilbert Collection** of silver and gold, micromosaics and snuffboxes will arrive at the V&A (Level 3, rooms 70–73) as of summer 2009. The encyclopaedic **Ceramics** galleries (Level 6, rooms 133–145), should be open by 2010, as should the ground-floor **Medieval and Renaissance** galleries, housing such treasures as the twelfth-century Thomas Becket casket, the Norman master-piece of gilt bronzework, the **Gloucester Candlestick**, and Giambologna's marble statue *Samson Slaying a Philistine*.

the pair of top-hatted gentlemen carved in marble stand out in the parade of Buddhas near the entrance – they are thought to represent Korean envoys. At the main entrance to the adjacent **Japan** gallery (room 45) is an incredible bronze incense burner, decorated with life-sized peacocks. Amidst the wealth of silk, lacquer and samurai armour, look out for the tiny, elaborately carved, jade and marble *netsuke* (belt toggles) portraying such quirky subjects as "spider on aubergine", "starving dog on a bed of leaves" and "badger dressed in a lotus leaf".

Cast Courts

Two enormous **Cast Courts** (rooms 46a & 46b), filled with plaster casts of famous works of art and architecture, were created at the outset of the V&A so that ordinary Londoners could experience the glories of classical and ancient art. These barrel-vaulted, glass-roofed rooms remain an astonishing sight. In room 46a, a copy of the colossal Trajan's Column from the forum in Rome, sliced in half to fit in the room, towers over the rest of the plaster casts, which include the Brunswick Lion and a full-scale painted replica of the entire portal of the cathedral of Santiago de Compostela, set around the ill-fitting doors of Hildesheim cathedral. Over in room 46b, a life-sized replica of Michelangelo's *David* (complete with large detachable fig-leaf, now displayed at the back of the plinth, used to save visiting royalty from embarrassment) stands opposite Verrocchio's smaller bronze of the same subject alongside the pulpits of Pisa cathedral and baptistry, and Ghiberti's celebrated bronze doors from the baptistry in Florence, framed by the central doorway of Bologna's San Petronio.

Sculpture

Although spread over several floors, the bulk of the V&A's Sculpture collection is on the ground floor (rooms 21–24), where you'll find Bernini's life-sized fountain sculpture, *Neptune and Triton*, and Giambologna's expressively brutal *Samson Slaying a Philistine*, amidst a whole series of top-notch Italian pieces. Other highlights include Donatello's *Chellini Madonna*, a bronze roundel given by the artist to his doctor in lieu of payment, Canova's depiction of Theseus astride the Minotaur, and his head of Helen of Troy about which Byron wrote an eight-line paean. **Auguste Rodin** donated several sculptures to the V&A in 1914, including a number of full-scale works such as his beautifully wrought *The Fallen Angel*, a swirling mass of rippling bronze, and his sensuous *Cupid and Psyche*, in which the lovers emerge half-hewn from the white marble. Look out, too, for G.F. Watts's sensuous *Clytie*, a torso by Meštrovic, and several strikingly simple works by Eric Gill.

Round the corner (rooms 17–20), the museum displays its impressive collection of Buddhist sculpture, from serene, gilded-copper seated figures from Tibet and Nepal to an entire Burmese shrine. There's also a corridor of **small-scale sculpture** on Level 3 in room 111, ranging from medieval religious ivories and alabaster relief panels to images of Christ and the Apostles rendered in lime-wood by German sculptors and a whole collection of works by Gilbert Bayes, who worked at Doulton, the ceramics company. (Bayes's Art Deco Doulton frieze from the company's headquarters in Lambeth is displayed in room 127.)

British Galleries

The superbly designed **British Galleries** are a joy to visit. The first series of rooms covers **Britain 1500–1760** (Level 2, rooms 52–58), and begins in room 58 with Tudor times. Highlights include Torrigiani's bust of Henry VII, Holbein's miniature of Anne of Cleves, with its original ivory case, and the **Howard Grace Cup**, a medieval ivory cup associated with Thomas Becket, but given a Tudor silver-gilt makeover and crowned by a tiny St George and the dragon. At the other end of the scale is the **Great Bed of Ware**, a king-sized Elizabethan oak four-poster in which 26 butchers and their wives are said to have once spent the night, and which gets a mention in Shakespeare's *Twelfth Night*. Other specific items to look out for include the **Dark Jewel** given to Francis Drake by Queen Elizabeth I, the tapestries embroidered by **Mary, Queen of Scots** during her incarceration, James II's wonderfully camp wedding suit and the amazing high-relief lime-wood *Stoning of St Stephen* by Gibbons.

The galleries also contain a number of **period interiors** saved in their entirety from buildings that have since been demolished. These include a Jacobean panelled room from Bromley-by-Bow, a Georgian parlour from Henrietta Street in Covent Garden and a heavily gilded Rococo Music Room from St James's Square. Towards the end, you should pass Roubiliac's marble statue of **Handel**, carved in 1738 and the first statue in Europe of a living artist. It originally stood in the then-fashionable Vauxhall Gardens in south London, and caused a great stir in its day, with the composer depicted as Apollo slouching in inspired disarray, one shoe dangling from his foot.

Britain 1760–1900 continues upstairs (Level 4, rooms 118–125), with a Chippendale four-poster made for the actor David Garrick, and paintings by

---

The world's first museum café

Whatever you do, make sure you pay a visit to the V&A Café in the museum's original refreshment rooms, the **Morris, Gamble & Poynter Rooms**, at the back of the main galleries.

Embellished by Edward Poynter with a wash of decorative blue tiling depicting the months and seasons of the year, the eastern **Poynter Room**, where the hoi polloi ate, was finished in 1881 and originally known as the Grill Room – the grill, also designed by Poynter, is still in place and was in use until 1939. On the opposite side, the dark-green **Morris Room** (William Morris's first public commission), completed in 1868, accommodated a better class of diner. The decorative detail is really worth taking in – gilded Pre-Raphaelite panels and Burne-Jones stained glass, embossed olive-branch wallpaper and a running cornice frieze of dogs chasing hares.

The largest and grandest of the rooms lies between the two. The **Gamble Room**, completed in 1878 by the museum's own team of artists, boasts dazzling, almost edible decor, with mustard, gold and cream-coloured Minton tiles covering the walls and pillars from floor to ceiling. Fleshy Pre-Raphaelite nudes hold up the nineteenth-century chimneypiece from Dorchester House, while a ceramic frieze of frolicking cherubs accompanies a quote from Ecclesiastes, spelt out in decorative script around the cornice.

Gainsborough and Constable. Again, period interiors are a big feature of the collection: Adam's Venetian-red Glass Drawing Room from Northumberland House and the fan-vaulted Strawberry Room from Lee Priory in Kent, which was inspired by Walpole's Gothic Revival masterpiece in Twickenham, Strawberry Hill. You'll also find plenty of outpourings from the **Arts and Crafts movement**, starting with a cabinet painted with medieval scenes by William Morris, inspired by Walter Scott's novels. Other highlights to look out for include *La Belle Iseult*, Morris's only known painting (of his future wife), and a whole room on the Scottish School, including several tables and chairs from Glasgow tearooms designed by Charles Rennie Mackintosh.

Twentieth-century, Silver, Stained Glass and Ironwork

The relatively small **Twentieth Century** collection (Level 3, rooms 74–75) is, nevertheless, stuffed with high-quality artefacts: furniture by Otto Wagner, Charles Rennie Mackintosh, Bauhaus and the Wiener Werkstätte co-op; Constructivist fabrics and crockery; and a range of works by Finnish modernist supremo Alvar Aalto. Special exhibitions are staged here too, and in the adjacent National Art Library.

The centrepiece of the vast **Silver** galleries (Level 3, rooms 65–70a) is the giant **Jerningham Wine Cooler**, smothered with images of Bacchic revelry. The nearby "Discovery Area" is the fun section, where you can rub or stamp a hallmark, and flick through the museum's photo store of contemporary artists working in silver. Before you leave, don't miss the three, virtually life-sized, slightly comical, silver lions at the far end of the room.

Round the corner, there's a wonderful gallery of **Sacred Silver and Stained Glass** (rooms 83–84). The stained glass, all beautifully backlit, dates from around 1140 to the present day, while the silver includes reliquaries, crosses, crowns and medieval shrines from all over Christian Europe.

Still further on, it's worth persevering to the V&A's **Ironwork** collection, a display of keys, locks, gates and grilles, ranged along a vast corridor (Level 3, rooms 113–114e). At the centre is George Gilbert Scott's Hereford Screen, an eight-ton neo-Gothic monster of copper and ironwork that was pulled out of the city's cathedral in 1967. Nearby, there are two great cabinets filled with every kind of tin, from a Huntley & Palmers biscuit-dispensing machine to a money box in the shape of a tea caddy.

Paintings

The V&A's collection of **Paintings** (Level 3, rooms 81, 82, 87 & 88) includes minor works by Blake, Corot, Degas, Delacroix, Rembrandt, Tintoretto and Botticelli, a study for Ingres' *Odalisque*, a Tiepolo sketch, some Fantin-Latour flowers and several Pre-Raphaelite works, the best of which is Rossetti's verdant, emerald-green *The Day Dream*, one of his last great works. The V&A owns over four hundred works by John Constable, bequeathed by his

---

The Ceramic Staircase and the Leighton Frescoes

Whilst you're on Level 3, make sure you see the spectacular Minton tiles of the **Ceramic Staircase**, designed by Frank Moody. Note the ceramic memorial to Henry Cole, the work of his niece, who has rendered her uncle in mosaic with "Albertopolis" in relief above. Look out too for the grandiose **Leighton Frescoes**, which used to look down onto the Cast Courts from on high; now, stuck in the corridor on Level 3 between rooms 107 and 109, you can at least see them close up.

daughter, including famous views of Salisbury Cathedral (in the British Galleries) and Dedham Mill, and full-sized preparatory oil paintings for *The Hay Wain* and *The Leaping Horse*, plus a whole host of his alfresco cloud studies and sketches. There are also several works by **Turner**, including a dreamy view of East Cowes Castle, painted for the castle's owner, John Nash, and **Gainsborough's Showbox**, in which he displayed the oil-on-glass landscapes he executed in the 1780s. Room 90 is used for temporary exhibitions of prints and drawings, and room 90a displays **portrait miniatures** by Holbein, Hilliard and others.

Theatre

The V&A's **Theatre and Performance** galleries (Level 3, rooms 103–106) contain a vast collection of objects formerly in the Theatre Museum in Covent Garden. The display areas are divided into themes – producing, rehearsing, promotion and so on – and cover every theatrical genre from music hall to straight theatre, plus a surprisingly large amount of pop memorabilia. You may not learn much about the history of London theatre, but you do get to see some great individual exhibits, from the rotating hook, tunic and shorts used by Pansy Chinery in her teeth-spinning act to Pink Floyd's Azimuth Co-ordinator, which could produce an early form of surround sound. Perhaps the best section is "costume and make-up" where you can examine Tom Thumb's waistcoat, Adam Ant's self-made Prince Charming get-up, Elton John's lurex Bicycle John outfit from the height of glam rock and an exact replica of Kylie Minogue's dressing room circa 2007.

Jewellery

The V&A's justifiably popular **Jewellery** galleries (Level 3, rooms 91–93) display everything from a Bronze Age gold collar from Ireland to contemporary jewellery made from recycled materials. Amongst the earlier pieces, there are some pretty impressive gold papal rings – giant knuckle-dusters made from rock crystal – and some lovely gilded pomanders used to ward off evil. Specific highlights to look out for, further on, include the emeralds and diamonds given by Napoleon to his adopted daughter in 1806, the emeralds and rubies from Seringapatam captured in 1799, and the rare Siberian amethysts given by Tsar Alexander I to the wife of the Third Marquess of Londonderry (in cabinet 24). Elsewhere, there are Art Nouveau pieces by René Lalique (cabinet 26), Arts and Crafts works by May Morris and the ostentatious personal jewellery of the eccentric Edith Sitwell (cabinet 29). Check out cabinet 56, too, for the Fabergé cigarette cases, the spectacular Manchester Tiara from 1903 and the whole series of semiprecious carved animals that belonged to Queen Alexandra.

Architecture and Glass

The V&A's **Architecture** gallery (Level 4, rooms 127–128) puts on special exhibitions, but also has a permanent display of architectural models in room 128. It's an eclectic array of realized and unrealized projects – everything from a fifteenth-century mosque and a Le Corbusier villa, to Spiral (Daniel Libeskind's now-shelved extension for the V&A), and Bluewater, Britain's largest mall. Beyond, lies the small hi-tech **Glass Gallery** (Level 4, room 131), with its spectacular modern glass staircase and balustrade. The beauty and variety of the glass on display is staggering, and ranges from the Greek and Roman world to *objets d'art* by contemporary artists.

Science Museum

The **Science Museum** (daily 10am–6pm; free; ☎0870/870 4868, ⓦwww
.sciencemuseum.org.uk; South Kensington tube) on Exhibition Road is undeniably impressive, filling seven floors with items drawn from every conceivable area
of science. The spectacular, hi-tech **Wellcome Wing** dragged the museum into
the twenty-first century, and nearly all the old galleries have since been
redesigned and made more accessible to the nonspecialist. The museum also puts
on populist special exhibitions (for which you have to pay), often timed to
coincide with the latest special-effects movie.

The ground floor

The **Energy Hall** focuses on the advent of the Industrial Revolution, and
features models of the world's first steam engines. The largest exhibit is the
bright red Burnley mill engine, whose enormous wheel used to drive 1700
looms and worked *in situ* until as late as 1970. Beyond lies the **Space** exhibition,
which follows the history of rockets from tenth-century China and Congreve's
early nineteenth-century efforts, through the V-1 and V-2 wartime bombs, right
up to the Apollo landings. There's a great, full-size replica of the Apollo 11
landing craft which deposited US astronauts on the moon in 1969.

Beyond, **Making the Modern World** displays iconic inventions of modern
science and technology. These include *Puffing Billy*, the world's oldest surviving
steam locomotive, used for hauling coal in 1815, and Robert Stephenson's
Rocket of 1829, which pulled the Manchester–Liverpool passenger service.
Other ground-breaking inventions on display include a Ford Model T, the
world's first mass-produced car, and a gleaming aluminium Lockheed 10A
Electra airliner from 1935, which signalled the birth of modern air travel. Less
glamorous discoveries, such as the brain scanner, occupy the sidelines, along
with disasters such as the drug thalidomide.

Wellcome Wing

The darkened, ultra-purple **Wellcome Wing** beckons you on. The displays on
the ground floor, **Antenna** and **Talking Points**, change regularly in order to
cover contemporary science issues while they are topical. **Pattern Pod**,
meanwhile, is for under-8s, and is basically a lot of interactive hi-tech fun. Kids
can experiment with water ripples, footprints and the Penrose tessellation, and
groove away in the multicoloured human shadow box.

On Floor 1, **Who am I?** is a guaranteed winner, as it concentrates on humans
themselves. You can morph yourself into the opposite sex, watch a sperm race,
and test the gender of your brain. Down the middle of the gallery are traditional
static displays and reading matter that delve more deeply into the issues raised.

Visiting the Science Museum

Your first stop should be the **information desk**, in the Energy Hall, where you can
pick up a museum plan and find out about the day's events and demonstrations;
you can also sign up for a free **guided tour** on a specific subject. To visit the IMAX
3D cinema, it's best to book ahead (☎0870/870 4771; £8). Refreshment pit-stops
include the *Revolution Café* off the Energy Hall, and the funky *Deep Blue Café* in the
Wellcome Wing, plus several picnic areas. The museum's **Dana Centre** (☎020/7942
4040, ⓦwww.danacentre.org.uk), on Queen's Gate, puts on free talks, discussions
and events aimed at adults.

Floor 3 contains **In Future**, where you can play frivolous but fun multi-player educational games, and vote on contemporary socio-scientific questions, such as "Should you be able to choose the gender of your child?"

The basement: hands-on galleries

The basement houses two hands-on galleries perfect for children under 11. In the misleadingly entitled **Garden**, 3- to 6-year-olds don waterproofs to experiment with lock gates, and hard hats to play with pulleys. The imaginatively entitled **Things** is aimed at the natural curiosity of 7- to 11-year-olds about unidentifiable objects. A longer attention span and a fair bit of reading are involved, and there are the usual problems with crowds at the weekend and with the durability of the exhibits.

Floors 1 and 2

The **Challenge of Materials**, ranged around the balcony on the first floor, is an extremely stylish exhibition – the glass-floored suspension bridge is particularly cool – covering the use of materials ranging from aluminium to zerodur (used for making laser gyroscopes). As well as the excellent hands-on displays, there are aesthetically pleasing exhibits as diverse as a Bakelite coffin and an Axminster-carpet morning gown designed by Vivienne Westwood.

The most popular section on Floor 2 is **Energy**, with its "do not touch" electric-shock machine that absolutely fascinates kids. Much of it is thought-provoking stuff – you can play computer games to reduce your carbon emissions – and the rest comprises more conventional displays, everything from a bird oil lamp to a clay stove from contemporary Kenya.

Elsewhere on Floor 2, there are sections on **Computing** and **Mathematics** now renamed "histories", as they were designed some years ago. Taking up quite some space are Charles Babbage's gargantuan Difference Engine 1, the world's first computer built in 1832, and his unrealized second version, which the museum completed in 1991.

Finally, you reach the little-visited **Ships** section, with its interminable glass cabinets of model vessels, from the *Great Harry* and the *Mayflower* to the *Great Eastern* and the *Cutty Sark*, not to mention Townsend Thoresen's ill-fated *Spirit of Free Enterprise*, which sank in the Zeebrugge disaster of 1987. Look out too for the model of the old London docks, at the point of their demise in the 1960s.

Floor 3

Floor 3 is now mobbed by kids having enormous fun at the **Launch Pad**, the museum's chief interactive gallery where they can experiment with water, waves, light and sound and build a catenary arch (and knock it down again); "explainers" are on hand to try and impart some educational input.

If you're looking for peace and quiet, head for the exquisite scientific instruments, chiefly created by George Adams for George III, in **Science in the Eighteenth Century**. Close by, **Health Matters** dwells thoughtfully on modern medical history from the introduction of mass vaccination to the challenge of finding a cure for HIV.

Heading towards the Wellcome Wing, you eventually reach the giant hangar of **Flight**, festooned with aircraft of every description from a Spitfire to a modern executive jet. Look out for the scaled-down model of the Montgolfier balloon which recorded the first human flight in 1783, and the full-size model of the flimsy contraption in which the Wright brothers made their epoch-making power-assisted flight in 1903.

Floors 4 and 5

On the floor above, **Glimpses of Medical History** features an attractive series of dioramas of medical operations, and larger mock-ups of surgeries and dentists' and chemists' premises through the ages, starting with Neolithic trepanning and finishing up with the gore-free spectacle of an open-heart operation circa 1980.

The best section here – and arguably of the whole museum – is Wellcome's **Science and Art of Medicine** gallery. Using an anthropological approach, this is a visual and cerebral feast, galloping through ancient medicine, medieval and Renaissance pharmacy, alchemy, quack doctors, royal healers, astrology and military surgery. Offbeat artefacts include African fetish objects, an Egyptian mummy, numerous masks, an eighteenth-century Florentine model of a female torso giving birth, and George Washington's dentures.

Natural History Museum

Alfred Waterhouse's purpose-built mock-Romanesque colossus, with its 675-foot terracotta facade built in 1880, ensures the status of the **Natural History Museum** (daily 10am–5.50pm; free; ☎020/7942 5000, ⓦwww.nhm .ac.uk; South Kensington tube) as London's most handsome museum. Its vast collections derive from a bequest by Hans Sloane to the British Museum, separated off in the 1860s after a huge power struggle. The founding director, Richard Owen, was an amazing figure, who arranged expeditions around the globe to provide everything from butterflies to dinosaurs for the museum's cabinets. Nowadays, the museum struggles manfully with the task of remaining an important resource for serious zoologists, and a major tourist attraction for the families with kids who flock here to check out the dinosaur collection.

Blue and Green zones

The **Central Hall** is dominated by "Dippy", a replica **Diplodocus** skeleton, 85ft from tip to tail, while the "side chapels" are filled with "wonders" of the natural world – a model of a sabre-toothed tiger, a stuffed Great Bustard, a dodo skeleton

▲ Natural History Museum

Visiting the museum

The museum is divided into four **colour-coded zones**, but all you really need to know is that the Red Zone is the old Geology Museum linked to the rest of the museum by the Birds section, and the Orange Zone is the new Darwin Centre. If the queues are long for the **main entrance** (as they can be at the weekend and school holidays), you're better off heading for the Red Zone's **side entrance** on Exhibition Road. There's a **café** behind the stairs in the Central Hall, a sandwich bar in the Red Zone and a **picnic area** in the basement, or you can head out to the Wildlife Garden (April–Oct). As well as large special exhibitions (for which there's a charge), the museum also puts on lots of **free tours**, talks, discussions, workshops and performances and in the winter there's an ice rink in front of the building.

and so on. It's also worth pausing here to take in the architecture of this vast "nave", whose walls are decorated with moulded terracotta animals and plants.

In Dinosaurs (Blue Zone), a raised walkway leads straight to the highlight for many kids, the grisly life-sized animatronic dinosaur tableau, currently a roaring *Tyrannosaurus rex*. The rest of the displays are less theatrical and more informative, with massive-jawed skeletons and more conventional models.

The old-fashioned **Mammals** section (Blue Zone) is filled with stuffed animals and plastic models and dominated by a full-sized model of a blue whale juxtaposed with its skeleton. It usually goes down well enough with younger children, but it's showing its age somewhat. Upstairs on the first-floor balconies, the story of mammals continues with an investigation into the emergence of bipeds among the **Primates** (Green Zone).

The other firm favourite with kids is the insect and arthropod room, known as **Creepy Crawlies** (Green Zone). Filled with giant models of bugs, arachnids and crustaceans, plus displays on the life cycle of the wasp and other unlovely creatures, it's here that you'll find the museum's only live exhibits, a colony of leaf-cutter ants from Trinidad, which feed on a fungus that they grow on the leaves they've gathered.

The **Ecology** (Green Zone) gallery takes you through the basics of green politics – the food chain, recycling, the ozone layer and the greenhouse effect. Meanwhile down in the basement is the excellent futuristic **Investigate** (Mon–Fri 2.30–5pm; Sat & Sun 11am–5pm; during school holidays daily 11am–5pm), aimed at children aged 7 to 14, for which you need to obtain a timed ticket. Kids get to choose a tray of specimens and then play at being scientists, using microscopes, scales, a computer and various tools of the trade to examine and catalogue the items before them. There are one or two simpler hands-on exhibits too, as well as several plant species to look at.

Up on the first floor, **Minerals** (Green Zone) features serried ranks of glass cabinets, culminating in a darkened chamber called The Vault. Here, the cream of the museum's rocks reside: a meteorite from Mars, a golden nugget weighing over 1000lb, one of the largest uncut emeralds in the world and the Star of South Africa, found in 1869, which triggered the South Africa diamond rush. Don't miss the 1300-year-old slice of **Giant Sequoia**, on the top floor, and whilst you're there, admire the view down onto the Central Hall and the moulded monkeys clinging to the arches.

Darwin Centre (Orange Zone)

Despite its enormous size, the museum displays just a fraction of its collection of zoological and plant specimens. Visitors can now view a selection of these bits and bobs in the giant, glass-encased, concrete cocoon of the Darwin Centre, which houses 200 scientists, 28 million insect and 6 million plant specimens. Among the more bizarre items pickled in the glass jars are a 50-year-old piece of algae from Mauritius, a partially digested human head from a sperm whale's stomach and a brown rat found during the building's construction. To see behind the scenes and even talk to one of the museum's scientists about their work, you need to sign up for an **Explore tour** (daily 3pm & 4.15pm; 45min) – book on the day at the information desk.

Red Zone

From Exhibition Road, you enter the vast, darkened hall of the **Red Zone**, with the solar system and constellations writ large on the walls. Boarding the central escalator will take you through a partially formed globe to the top floor and **The Power Within**, an exhibition on volcanoes and earthquakes. The most popular section is the 1995 Kobe earthquake simulator, where you enter a mock-up of a Japanese supermarket and see the soy-sauce bottles wobble, while watching an in-store video of the real event. Despite the museum's protestations, the whole thing seems in very poor taste. On the same floor is **Restless Surface**, an interactive display on the earth's elements, soil and rock erosion and, of course, global warming.

Down one floor, **From the Beginning** covers the geological history of the planet from the Big Bang to the present day. The display ends with a crystal ball, which predicts the earth's future (bleak, but probably not within our lifetime). More alluring is **Earth's Treasury**, a dimly lit display of lustrous minerals and crystals, gemstones and jewels. Exhibits include rocks that shine in UV light, carved artefacts such as a lapis lazuli necklace, and even some recently discovered kryptonite (the mineral that weakens Superman).

Finally, **Earth Today and Tomorrow** (on the ground floor) is a look at how we are running down the earth's non-renewable natural resources, and polluting the planet in the process. Ironically, one of the chief sponsors is Rio Tinto, the distinctly environmentally unfriendly mining company.

Knightsbridge and around

Knightsbridge is irredeemably snobbish, revelling in its reputation as the swankiest shopping area in London, with designer stores all the way down Sloane Street, and its pretty little mews streets, built to house servants and stables, but now inhabited by the rich themselves. However, most people come to Knightsbridge for just one reason: to visit Harrods, London's most famous department store. **Belgravia**, over to the east and strategically close to Buckingham Palace, is London's chief embassy land, with at least 25 scattered amongst the grid-plan stuccoed streets. All in all, it's a pretty soulless place, and not one in which you're likely to want to spend much time, although there are one or two lovely pubs hidden in the various mews.

Harrods

Housed in a grandiose 1905 terracotta building on Brompton Road, which turns into a palace of fairy lights at night, **Harrods** (Mon–Sat 10am–8pm, Sun noon–6pm; ☎020/7730 1234, ⓦwww.harrods.com; Knightsbridge tube) has come a long way since it started out as a family-run grocer's in 1849. Nowadays, it's spread over 7 floors, 4.5 acres, employs over 5000 staff, and welcomes over 15 million customers a year. If you are coming to visit, note that a "clean and presentable" **dress code** is enforced and backpacks have to be carried or placed in the left luggage (£2.50). Once here, however, you can avail yourself of the first-floor "luxury washrooms" and splash on a range of perfumes for free.

Obviously, you can buy most of what the shop stocks more cheaply if you can do without the distinctive olive-green Harrods carrier bag, but the store does have a few sections on the ground floor that are architectural sights in their own right. Chief among these is the **Food Hall**, with its exquisite Arts and Crafts tiling. Thanks to the current owner, Mohamed Al Fayed, there's now an Egyptian Hall, with its pseudo-hieroglyphs and sphinxes, and an Egyptian Escalator, with a **Di and Dodi fountain shrine** at its base. Here, to the strains of Mahler (and the like), you can contemplate photos of the ill-fated couple, and, preserved in an acrylic pyramid, a used wine-glass from the couple's last evening and the engagement ring Dodi allegedly bought for Di the previous day. Another memorial has been erected at Door Three, a bronze statue entitled *Innocent Victims*, depicting the couple dancing on a beach and clutching an albatross.

Chelsea, Battersea and Fulham

Until the sixteenth century, **Chelsea** was nothing more than a tiny fishing village on the banks of the Thames. It was Thomas More who started the upward trend by moving here in 1520, followed by members of the nobility, including Henry VIII himself. In the eighteenth century, Chelsea acquired its riverside houses along Cheyne Walk, which gradually attracted a posse of literary and intellectual types. However, it wasn't until the late nineteenth century that the area began to earn its reputation as London's very own Left Bank.

In the 1960s, Chelsea was at the forefront of "Swinging London", with the likes of David Bailey, Mick Jagger, George Best and the "Chelsea Set" hanging out in the boutiques and coffee bars. Later **King's Road** became a fashion parade for hippies, as well as witnessing the birth of punk. These days, Chelsea is very far from the cutting edge, with franchise fashion rather than avant-garde fashion the order of the day. The area's other aspect, oddly enough considering its reputation, is a **military** one, with the former Chelsea Barracks, the Royal Hospital (home of old soldiers known as the Chelsea Pensioners) and the National Army Museum.

Further west, Chelsea becomes rather more down-to-earth, a transition signalled by the presence of the local football ground, Stamford Bridge. Beyond here lies **Fulham**, whose main point of interest is Fulham Palace, at the very end of the King's Road. To the south, across the river, Chelsea aspirants have now colonized previously working-class **Battersea**, an area dominated by the brooding presence of the derelict Battersea Power Station.

Sloane Square

Sloane Square is a leafy nexus on the very eastern edge of Chelsea, centred on a Venus fountain, featuring a relief of Charles II and Nell Gwynne. On the

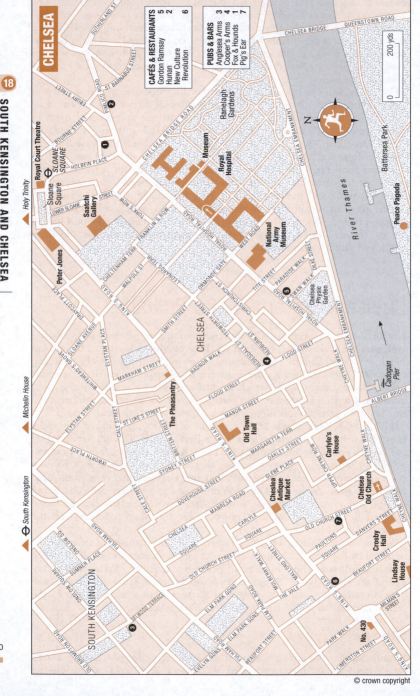

CHELSEA

CAFÉS & RESTAURANTS
Gordon Ramsay 5
Hunan 2
New Culture Revolution 6

PUBS & BARS
Anglesea Arms 3
Cooper's Arms 4
Fox & Hounds 1
Pig's Ear 7

© crown copyright

east side of the square, beside the tube station, stands the Victorian **Royal Court Theatre**, a bastion of new theatre writing since John Osborne's *Look Back in Anger* sent tremors through the establishment in 1956. On the opposite side is **Peter Jones**, a department store housed in London's finest glass-curtain building, built in the 1930s, which curves its way seductively into the King's Road.

Round the corner in Sloane Street is another architectural masterpiece, **Holy Trinity** (Mon–Sat 8.30am–5.30pm, Sun 8.30am–1.30pm; Sloane Square tube), created in 1890, and probably the finest Arts and Crafts church in London. The east window is the most glorious of the furnishings, a vast 48-panel extravaganza designed by Edward Burne-Jones, and the largest ever made by Morris & Co. Holy Trinity is very High Church, filled with the smell of incense and statues of the Virgin Mary, and even offering confession.

King's Road

The **King's Road**, Chelsea's main artery, was designed as a royalty-only thoroughfare by Charles II, in order – so the story goes – to avoid carriage congestion en route to Nell Gwynne's house. Lesser mortals could travel down it on production of a special copper pass but it wasn't opened to the public until 1830. This prompted a flurry of speculative building that produced the series of elegant, open-ended squares – Wellington, Markham, Carlyle and Paultons – which still punctuate the road.

If you don't fancy walking down the King's Road, buses #11 and #22 run the length of it, and buses #19 and #319 run from Sloane Square partway down and then south across Battersea Bridge. On the south side of the road, a short stroll from Sloane Square, are the former **Duke of York's Barracks**, now housing shops and cafés. The main building, built in 1801 and fronted by a solid-looking Tuscan portico, houses the **Saatchi Gallery** (daily 10am–6pm; free; ☎020/7823 2363, ⓦwww.saatchi-gallery.co.uk; Sloane Square tube), which puts on changing exhibitions of contemporary art in its fifteen whitewashed rooms. (Charles Saatchi, the collector behind the gallery, was the man whose clever advertising campaigns kept Mrs Thatcher in power in the 1980s.)

A little further down on the same side is **Royal Avenue**, the first of the picturesque squares that open out onto the King's Road. This particular one is rather like a Parisian *place*, with plane trees and gravel down the centre, and was originally laid out in the late seventeenth century as part of William III's ambitious (and unrealized) scheme to link Kensington Palace with the Royal Hospital to the south. The next square along is Wellington Square, suspected fictional London address of James Bond, Ian Fleming's spy hero – no. 30 is thought to have been the location of his "comfortable ground-floor flat".

The most famous address on the King's Road is **no. 430**, a modest little shop, a mile from Sloane Square, where the designer Vivienne Westwood and her then-boyfriend Malcolm McLaren opened a Teddy Boy – revival store called Let It Rock, located, with a neat sense of irony, right next door to the Chelsea Conservative Club. In 1975 they changed tack and renamed the shop Sex, stocking it with proto-punk fetishist gear, with simulated burnt limbs in the window. It became a magnet for the likes of John Lydon and John Simon Ritchie, better known as Johnny Rotten and Sid Vicious, and was renamed Seditionaries – the rest, as they say, is history. Now known as World's End, the shop, with its landmark backward-running clock, continues to flog Westwood's eccentric designer clothes.

Royal Hospital Chelsea

Among the most nattily attired of all those parading down the King's Road are the scarlet- or navy-blue-clad Chelsea Pensioners, army veterans from the nearby **Royal Hospital** (April–Sept daily 10am–noon & 2–4pm; Oct–March closed Sun; free; T020/7881 5200, Wwww.chelsea-pensioners.co.uk; Sloane Square tube), founded by Charles II in 1682. Designed by Wren, the hospital's plain, red-brick wings and grassy courtyards became a blueprint for institutional and collegiate architecture across the Empire. On Founder's Day (May 29), the Pensioners, wearing their traditional tricorn hats, festoon Grinling Gibbons' gilded statue of Charles with oak leaves to commemorate the day after the disastrous 1651 Battle of Worcester, when the future king hid in an oak tree to escape his pursuers.

The public are welcome to visit the hospital's austere **chapel**, with its huge barrel vault and Sebastiano Ricci's colourful apse fresco *Resurrection*, in which Jesus patriotically bears the flag of St George. Opposite lies the equally grand, wood-panelled **dining hall**, where the three hundred or so Pensioners still eat under portraits of the sovereigns and Antonio Verrio's vast allegorical mural of Charles II and his hospital. In the Secretary's Office, designed by John Soane, on the east side of the hospital, there's a small **museum**, displaying Pensioners' uniforms, medals and two German bombs.

The playing fields to the south, from which you get the finest view of the hospital, are the venue for the annual **Chelsea Flower Show** (see p.29). To the east is the last remnant of one of London's most famous pleasure gardens, **Ranelagh Gardens**, now a pleasant little landscaped patch used mostly by the Chelsea Pensioners, but open to the public too. A couple of information panels in the gardens' Soane-designed shelter show what the place used to look like when Canaletto painted it in 1751. The main feature was a giant rotunda, where the beau monde could promenade to musical accompaniment – the 8-year-old Mozart played here. Shortly after it opened in 1742, Walpole reported that "you can't set your foot without treading on a Prince or Duke". Fashion is fickle, though, and the rotunda was eventually demolished in 1805.

National Army Museum

The concrete bunker next door to the Royal Hospital houses the **National Army Museum** (daily 10am–5.30pm; free; T020/7730 0717, Wwww.national -army-museum.ac.uk; Sloane Square tube). There are plenty of interesting histor- ical artefacts, plus an impressive array of uniforms and medals, but for a more balanced view of war, you're better off visiting the Imperial War Museum.

To follow the museum chronologically, start in the basement with **The Making of Britain** (1066–1783), which concentrates on the Civil War and the origins of the professional British Army, before heading for **Changing the World** (1784– 1904), a none-too-critical look at the British Empire. Here you can see a vast spot-lit model of the Battle of Waterloo (at 7pm before the Prussians arrived to save the day). The skeleton of Marengo, Napoleon's charger at the battle, the saw used to amputate the Earl of Uxbridge's leg, a paper lantern used by Florence Nightingale, and Richard Caton-Woodville's famous painting of *The Charge of the Light Brigade* are among the highlights of this section.

World Wars has sections on just about every conflict zone of the two global conflicts from a slice of the Somme to the POW camps of the Far East. **Fighting for Peace**, on the top floor, starts with a good section on National Service, inviting you to inspect a soldier's kit, learn how to drill and try on a

Wilde about Chelsea

John Singer Sargent, Augustus John, James Whistler and Bertrand Russell all lived at one time or another in Tite Street, which runs alongside the National Army Museum, but the street's most famous resident was writer and wit **Oscar Fingal O'Flahertie Wills Wilde** (1856–1900), who moved into no. 1 in 1880 with an old Oxford chum, Frank Miles, only to be asked to leave the following year by the latter (under pressure from his father, Canon Miles), after the hostile reception given to Wilde's recently published poetry. Four years later, Wilde moved back into the street to no. 34, with his new bride Constance Lloyd. By all accounts he was never very good at "playing husband", though he was happy enough to play father to his two boys (when he was there). It was in Tite Street, in 1891, that Wilde first met **Lord Alfred Douglas**, son of the Marquis of Queensberry and known to his friends as "Bosie", who was to become his lover, and eventually to prove his downfall.

At the height of Wilde's fame, just four days after the first night of *The Importance of Being Earnest*, the marquis left a visiting card for Wilde, on which he wrote "To Oscar Wilde, posing as a somdomite [sic]". Urged on by Bosie, Wilde unsuccessfully sued Queensberry, losing his case when the marquis produced incriminating evidence against Wilde himself. On returning to the *Cadogan Hotel* on Sloane Street, where Bosie had rooms, Wilde was arrested by the police, taken to Bow Street police station, charged with homosexual offences and eventually sentenced to **two years' hard labour**. Bankrupt, abandoned by Bosie and separated from his wife, he served his sentence in Pentonville, Wandsworth and later Reading jail. On his release he fled abroad, travelling under the pseudonym of Sebastian Melmoth, and died three years later from a syphilitic infection. He is buried in Paris's Père Lachaise cemetery.

uniform, but overall it's really little more than a propaganda exercise for the postwar armed forces. Next door in the **Art Gallery**, however, there are some excellent military portraits by the likes of Reynolds, Gainsborough, Romney and Lawrence, not to mention a suave self-portrait by a uniformed Rex Whistler, who died in action shortly after D-Day.

Chelsea Physic Garden

The **Chelsea Physic Garden** (April–Oct Wed–Fri noon–5pm, Sun noon–6pm; July & Aug also Wed until 10pm; plus occasional winter weekend openings; £8; ☎020/7352 5646, ⊛www.chelseaphysicgarden.co.uk; Sloane Square tube) lies at the western end of Royal Hospital Road. Founded in 1673 by the Royal Society of Apothecaries, this is the oldest botanical garden in the country after Oxford's: the first cedars grown in this country were planted here in 1683, cotton seed was sent from here to the American colonies in 1732, England's first rock garden was constructed here in 1773, and the walled garden contains Britain's oldest olive tree. Unfortunately, it's a rather small garden, and a little too close to Chelsea Embankment to be a peaceful oasis, but keen botanists will enjoy it nevertheless. At the entrance (on Swan Walk) you can take a map with a list of the month's most interesting flowers and shrubs. A statue of Hans Sloane, who presented the Society with the freehold, stands at the centre of the garden; behind him there's a teahouse, serving afternoon tea and delicious home-made cakes.

Cheyne Walk

Chelsea Physic Garden marks the beginning of **Cheyne Walk** (pronounced "chainy"), whose quiet riverside locale and succession of Queen Anne and

Georgian houses drew artists and writers here in great numbers during the nineteenth century. Since the building of the Embankment and the increase in traffic, however, the character of this peaceful haven has been lost. Novelist Henry James, who lived at no. 21, used to take "beguiling drives" in his wheelchair along the Embankment; today, he'd be hospitalized in the process. An older contemporary of James, Mary Ann Evans (better known under her pen name George Eliot), moved into no. 4 – the first blue plaque you come to – in December 1880, five months after marrying an American banker 21 years her junior. Three weeks later she died of a kidney disease. In the 1960s, Mick Jagger and Keith Richards graced this section of Cheyne Walk with their presence, at no. 48 and no. 3 respectively.

Chelsea Old Church and Crosby Hall

At the end of Cheyne Walk's gardens, there's a garish, gilded statue of **Thomas More**, "Scholar, Saint, Statesman", a local who used to worship in nearby **Chelsea Old Church** (Tues–Thurs 2–4pm; ℡020/7795 1019, ⓦwww .chelseaoldchurch.org.uk; bus #19 or #319 from Sloane Square tube), where he built his own private chapel in the south aisle (the hinges for the big oak doors are still visible). More is best known for his martyrdom in 1535, though he himself showed little mercy to heretics – he even had some tied to a tree in his Chelsea back garden and flogged. Badly bombed in the last war, the church nevertheless contains an impressive number of monuments. Chief among them is Lady Cheyne's memorial (thought to be by Bellini) and More's simple canopied memorial to his first wife, Jane, in which he himself hoped to be buried. In the event, his torso ended up in the Tower chapel, while his head was secretly buried in Canterbury by his daughter, Margaret Roper. More's second wife, Alice, is also buried here.

More's house on Cheyne Walk was destroyed in 1740 by Hans Sloane, but in 1910 **Crosby Hall**, part of a fifteenth-century wool merchant's house once owned by More, was transferred bit by bit from the City to the corner of Danvers Street, west of the church. Once occupied by the future Richard III (and mentioned by Shakespeare), it's now a private residence and its fine hammerbeam roof can no longer be viewed.

Beyond Crosby Hall

The continuation of Cheyne Walk, beyond Crosby Hall, is no less rich in cultural associations. Mrs Gaskell was born in 1810 at no. 93, while the Brunels, Marc and Isambard, both lived at no. 99. The painter James Whistler, who lived at ten different addresses in the 41 years he spent in Chelsea, lived for a time at no. 96, the house where the Provisional IRA and the British government met secretly in 1972, to discuss peace, some five months after Bloody Sunday. The Brunels' and Whistler's old residences form part of **Lindsey House**, built in 1674 on the site of Thomas More's farm – it's occasionally possible to visit the entrance hall, garden room and gardens (phone ℡020/7447 6605 for more details). Last but not least, the reclusive J.M.W. Turner lived at no. 118 for the last six years of his life under the pseudonym Booth, and painted many a sunset over the Thames.

Carlyle's House

A short distance from Cheyne Walk, at 24 Cheyne Row, is **Carlyle's House** (April–Oct Wed–Fri 2–5pm, Sat & Sun 11am–5pm; NT; £4.90; ℡020/7352 7087; bus #19 or #319 from Sloane Square tube), where the Scottish historian

Brompton Cemetery

Brompton Cemetery (daily: summer 8am–8pm; winter 8am–4pm; ⓦ www.royalparks .gov.uk; West Brompton tube), on the Fulham Road, is the least overgrown of London's "Magnificent Seven" Victorian graveyards. Laid out on a grid plan in 1840 and now overlooked by the east stand of Chelsea Football Club, the cemetery's leafy central avenue leads south to an octagonal chapel. Here, you'll find the grave of Frederick Leyland, president of the National Telephone Company: designed by Edward Burne-Jones, it's a bizarre copper-green jewel box on stilts, smothered with swirling wrought-ironwork. Before you reach the chapel, eerie colonnaded catacombs, originally planned to extend the full length of the cemetery, open out into the Great Circle, a forest of tilted crosses.

Few really famous corpses grace Brompton, but enthusiasts might like to seek out Suffragette leader Emmeline Pankhurst; Henry Cole, the man behind the Great Exhibition and the V&A; Fanny Brawne, the love of Keats' life; and John Snow, Queen Victoria's anaesthetist, whose chloroform-fixes the monarch described as "soothing, quieting and delightful beyond measure". Long Wolf, a Sioux Indian chief, was a temporary resident here, after he died while on tour entertaining the Victorian masses with Colonel "Buffalo Bill" Cody. His body has since been returned to his descendants in America.

Thomas Carlyle set up home with his wife, Jane Welsh Carlyle, in 1834. Carlyle's full-blooded and colourful style, best illustrated by his account of the French Revolution, brought him great fame during his lifetime – a statue was erected to the "Sage of Chelsea" on Cheyne Walk less than a year after his death in 1881, and the house became a museum just fifteen years later. That said, the intellectuals and artists who visited Carlyle – among them Dickens, Tennyson, Chopin, Mazzini, Browning and Darwin – were attracted as much by the wit of his strong-willed wife, with whom Carlyle enjoyed a famously tempestuous relationship. The house itself is a typically dour Victorian abode, kept much as the Carlyles would have had it – the historian's hat still hangs in the hall. Among the artefacts are an eightieth birthday card signed by the historian's famous chums, a letter from Disraeli offering a baronetcy and Carlyle's reply, refusing it. The top floor contains the garret study where Carlyle tried in vain to escape the din of the street and the neighbours' noisy roosters, in order to complete his final magnum opus on Frederick the Great.

Battersea

Since the 1980s, aspiring Chelsea types have been colonizing the cheaper terraces and mansions across the river in **Battersea**, otherwise known as "South Chelsea". For the best part of last century, however, Battersea was a staunchly working-class enclave. In 1913 it elected the country's first black mayor, John Richard Archer, and in the 1920s returned Shapurji Saklatvala as its MP – first for the Labour Party, then as a Communist. Saklatvala was always in the news: he was banned from entry into the US and even to his native India. He was also the first person to be arrested during the 1926 General Strike, after a speech in Hyde Park urging soldiers not to fire on striking workers, for which he received a two-month prison sentence.

Poverty was one of the main reasons behind the establishment of **Battersea Park** (ⓦ www.batterseapark.org; bus #19 or #319 from Sloane Square tube), opened in 1853 and connected to Chelsea by the Albert Bridge, one of the prettiest to span the Thames, especially when lit up with fairy lights at night. The

18

Fulham Palace

It's worth venturing as far as the New King's Road by Putney Bridge in order to visit **Fulham Palace** (Mon & Tues noon–4pm, Sat 11am–2pm, Sun 11.30am–3.30pm; free; Putney Bridge tube; ☎020/7736 8140, ⓦwww.fulhampalace.org), in Bishop's Park. Once the largest moated site in England, it was the residence of the Bishop of London from 704 to 1973. The oldest section of the present-day complex is the modestly-scaled Tudor courtyard, patterned with black diamonds; the most recent is William Butterfield's neo-Gothic chapel, which, with the other period interiors, can only be seen on the **guided tours** that take place on the second and fourth Sundays and every third Tuesday at 2pm (£5). At other times, you can visit the small **museum** which traces the complex history of the building, and displays a few archeological finds, including a mummified rat. In the palace grounds there's a lovely herb garden, with a Tudor gateway and a maze of miniature box hedges, but sadly no sign of the moat, which was filled in in 1921.

park itself is best known nowadays for its two-tier **Peace Pagoda**, erected in 1985 by Japanese Buddhists. Made from a combination of reconstituted Portland stone and Canadian fir trees, the pagoda shelters four large gilded Buddhas. The park's **fountain lake**, to the southwest, is impressive in summer (mid-March to mid-Nov daily 10am–4pm) and there's a small family-run **Children's Zoo** (daily 10am–5pm; £6.50; ⓦwww.batterseaparkzoo.co.uk), established during the 1951 Festival of Britain, and home to monkeys, lemurs, mynah birds, otters and meerkats.

The old village of Battersea was originally centred on **St Mary's Church** (ⓦwww.stmarysbattersea.org.uk), half a mile upstream. In 1775, when the current church was built, Battersea was a peaceful place with a population of less than two thousand, among them Catherine Boucher, who married the poet and visionary William Blake in the church in 1782. Another painter associated with St Mary's is Turner, who used to sit in the oriel vestry window and paint the clouds and sunsets (his favourite chair is now reverently preserved in the chancel).

Most Londoners know Battersea for just two things: its Dogs Home and its Power Station. **Battersea Dogs and Cats Home** (Mon–Fri 1–4pm, Sat & Sun 10.30am–4pm; ⓦwww.battersea.org.uk) moved to 4 Battersea Park Rd in 1871 as the "Home for Lost Dogs and Cats"; cats are still catered for, as well as dogs, with over 16,000 passing through their doors each year. To the north stands **Battersea Power Station**, Giles Gilbert Scott's awesome cathedral of power from 1933, which looks like an upturned table and featured (along with an inflatable flying pig) on the Pink Floyd album cover *Animals*. Closed down in 1983, every plan for subsequent resurrection has ended in failure – for the latest, visit ⓦwww.batterseapowerstation.org.uk.

High Street Kensington to Notting Hill

Despite the smattering of aristocratic mansions and the presence of royalty in Kensington Palace, the village of **Kensington** remained surrounded by fields until well into the nineteenth century, when the rich finally began to seek new stomping grounds away from the West End. The Great Exhibition and its legacy of museums in South Kensington brought further cachet to the area, and prompted a building frenzy that boosted the borough's population from 44,000 in 1851 to 175,000 by 1901. Kensington village has disappeared entirely now in the busy shopping district around Kensington High Street, and the chief attractions are the wooded **Holland Park** and the former artists' colony clustered around the exotically decorated **Leighton House**.

Once slummy, now swanky, **Bayswater** and **Notting Hill** to the north were for many years the bad boys of the borough, dens of vice and crime comparable to Soho. Gentrification has changed them out of all recognition, though they remain more cosmopolitan districts, with a strong Arab presence and vestiges of the African–Caribbean community who initiated and still run the Notting Hill **Carnival**, one of Europe's largest street festivals, held on August Bank Holiday weekend.

Kensington High Street and around

The village of Kensington was centred to the north of St Mary Abbots church, but once the area was transformed into a residential suburb in the nineteenth century, **Kensington High Street**, to the south, became the area's commercial centre. The street itself is nothing special, but in the quieter backstreets, you'll find one or two hidden gems like **Holland Park**, the former gardens of an old Jacobean mansion, and **Leighton House**, the perfect Victorian artist's pad.

High Street Kensington

Kensington High Street – better known as **High Street Ken** – is dominated architecturally by the twin presences of George Gilbert Scott's neo-Gothic church of **St Mary Abbots** (whose 250-foot spire makes it London's tallest parish church) and the Art Deco colossus of **Barkers** department store, remodelled in the 1930s. A little-known feature of the High Street is Europe's largest

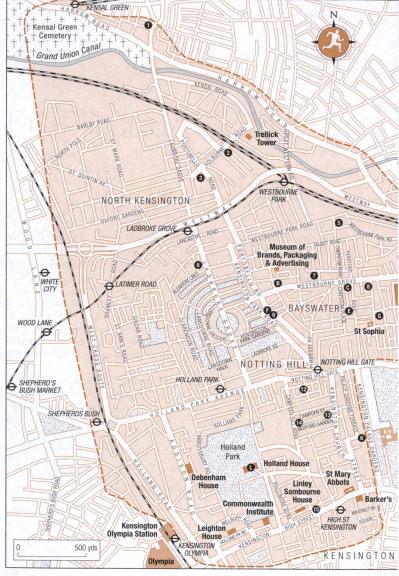

Roof Gardens (☎020/7937 7994, Ⓦwww.roofgardens.virgin.com), which tops the former Derry & Toms department store, another 1930s colossus, situated next door to Barkers. To check the gardens are open, phone ahead; to gain access, head for the side entrance on Derry Street and take the lift. The nightclub at the centre of the garden is pretty tacky, but the mock-Spanish convent, the formal gardens, the four flamingoes, sundry ducks and the views across the rooftops are surreal.

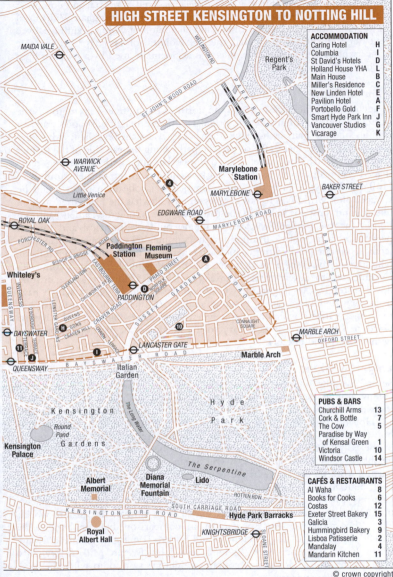

HIGH STREET KENSINGTON TO NOTTING HILL

ACCOMMODATION

Caring Hotel	H
Columbia	I
St David's Hotels	D
Holland House YHA	L
Main House	B
Miller's Residence	C
New Linden Hotel	E
Pavilion Hotel	A
Portobello Gold	F
Smart Hyde Park Inn	J
Vancouver Studios	G
Vicarage	K

PUBS & BARS

Churchill Arms	13
Cork & Bottle	7
The Cow	5
Paradise by Way of Kensal Green	1
Victoria	10
Windsor Castle	14

CAFÉS & RESTAURANTS

Al Waha	8
Books for Cooks	6
Costas	12
Exeter Street Bakery	15
Galicia	3
Hummingbird Bakery	9
Lisboa Patisserie	2
Mandalay	4
Mandarin Kitchen	11

© crown copyright

On the south side of the High Street lies **Kensington Square**, an early piece of speculative building laid out in 1685. Luckily for the developers, royalty moved into Kensington Palace shortly after its construction, and the square soon became so fashionable that it was dubbed the "old court suburb". By the nineteenth century, the courtiers had moved out and the bohemians had moved in: Thackeray wrote *Vanity Fair* at no. 16; the Pre-Raphaelite painter Burne-Jones lived at no. 41; the actress Mrs Patrick Campbell, for whom George Bernard Shaw wrote *Pygmalion*, lived at no. 33; and composer Hubert Parry (of *Jerusalem* fame) gave music lessons to Vaughan Williams at no. 17. John Stuart Mill, philosopher and champion of women's suffrage, lived next door, and it was here that the first volume of Thomas Carlyle's sole manuscript of *The French Revolution* was accidentally used by a maid to light the fire.

Holland Park

Hidden away in the backstreets to the north of High Street Kensington is the densely wooded **Holland Park**, popular with the neighbourhood's army of nannies and au pairs, who take their charges to the excellent adventure playground. To get there, take one of the paths along the east side of the former **Commonwealth Institute**, a bold 1960s building with a startling tent-shaped Zambian copper roof. The park is laid out in the former grounds of **Holland House** – only the east wing of the Jacobean mansion could be salvaged after World War II, but it gives an idea of what the place used to look like. A youth hostel is linked to the east wing (see p.266); the garden ballroom houses the spectacular *Belvedere* restaurant; outdoor theatrical and musical performances take place throughout the summer (ⓦwww.operahollandpark .com), continuing a tradition which stretches back to the first Lady Holland, who put on plays here in defiance of the puritanical laws of Cromwell's Commonwealth. Several formal gardens are laid out before the house, drifting down in terraces to the arcades, *Garden Ballroom* and *Ice House*, which have been converted into a café, a restaurant and an art gallery. The most unusual of the formal gardens, which are peppered with modern sculpture, is the **Kyoto Garden**, a Japanese-style sanctuary to the northwest of the house, complete with koi carp and peacocks.

Leighton House

Several wealthy Victorian artists rather self-consciously founded an artists' colony around the fringes of Holland Park, and a number of their highly individual mansions are still standing. First and foremost is **Leighton House**, 12 Holland Park Rd (due to reopen 2010; ⓦwww.rbkc.gov.uk/leighton housemuseum), the "House Beautiful" built for Frederic Leighton, president of the Royal Academy and the only artist to be made a peer (albeit on his deathbed). "It will be opulence, it will be sincerity", the artist opined before starting work on the house in the 1860s. The big attraction is its domed Arab Hall, built in 1877: based on the banqueting hall of a Moorish palace in Palermo, it has a central black marble fountain, and is decorated with Saracen tiles, gilded mosaics and latticework drawn from all over the Islamic world. The other rooms are less spectacular in comparison, but are hung with excellent paintings by Lord Leighton and his Pre-Raphaelite friends, Edward Burne-Jones, Lawrence Alma-Tadema and John Everett Millais. Skylights brighten the upper floor, which contains Leighton's vast studio, where he used to hold evening concerts.

Beyond Leighton House

Leighton's neighbours included artists G.F. Watts and Holman Hunt, Marcus Stone, illustrator of Dickens, and, in the most outrageous house of all, architect William Burges, who designed his own medieval folly, the **Tower House**, at 29 Melbury Rd. Further afield, at 8 Addison Rd, is the Arts and Crafts **Debenham House** (ⓦwww.debenhamhouse.com), designed by Halsey

Ricardo in 1906 for the department-store Debenham family. The exterior of the latter is covered with peacock-blue and emerald-green tiles and bricks; the interior, which features a wonderful neo-Byzantine domed hall, is even more impressive. Sadly, both houses are closed to the public.

Two blocks north of Kensington High Street at 18 Stafford Terrace, is **Linley Sambourne House** (guided tours Wed 11.15am, Sat & Sun 11.15am, 1, 2.15 & 3.30pm; £6; ☏020/7602 3316, ⓦwww.rbkc.gov.uk/linleysambournehouse; High Street Kensington tube), where the successful *Punch* cartoonist lived until his death in 1910. A grand, though fairly ordinary stuccoed terrace house by Kensington standards, it's less a tribute to the artist (though it does contain a huge selection of Sambourne's works) and more a showpiece for the Victorian Society, which helps maintain the house in all its cluttered, late-Victorian excess, complete with stained glass, heavy furnishings and lugubrious William Morris wallpaper. The guided tours are great fun, last ninety minutes and, in the afternoons, are led by an actor in period garb; there are also occasional evening tours which re-create a night in with the Sambournes.

Bayswater and Paddington

It wasn't until the removal of the gallows at Tyburn (see p.245) that the area to the north of Hyde Park began to gain respectability. The arrival of the Great Western Railway at Paddington in 1838 further encouraged development, and the gentrification of **Bayswater**, the area immediately north of the park, began with the construction of an estate called Tyburnia. These days Bayswater is mainly residential, and a focus for London's widely dispersed Arab community, who are catered for by some excellent restaurants and cafés along the busy **Edgware Road**.

Paddington and around

The area's main focus is **Paddington Station** on Praed Street, one of the world's great early train stations, its cathedral-scale wrought-iron sheds designed by Isambard Kingdom Brunel in 1851. An earlier wooden structure was the destination of Victoria and Albert's first railway journey in 1842. The train, pulled by the engine *Phlegethon*, travelled at an average speed of 44mph, which the prince consort considered excessive – "Not so fast next time, Mr Conductor", he is alleged to have remarked. To the north and east of Paddington is **Paddington Basin**, built as the terminus of the Grand Union Canal in 1801. Now regenerated, it's worth exploring if only to admire the trio of funky footbridges which span the water. Funkiest of the lot is the **Rolling Bridge**, a hydraulic gangway that coils up into an octagon rather like a curled-up woodlouse – it curls up every Friday at noon. If you follow the basin to the northwest, you'll reach Little Venice in St John's Wood.

One block east of Paddington up Praed Street is St Mary's Hospital, home of the **Fleming Museum** (Mon–Thurs 10am–1pm; £2; ☏020/7886 6528, ⓦwww.medicalmuseums.org/museums/alex.htm; Paddington tube), on the corner of Norfolk Place, where the young Scottish bacteriologist Alexander Fleming accidentally discovered penicillin in 1928. A short video, a small exhibition and a reconstruction of Fleming's untidy lab tell the story of the medical discovery that saved more lives than any other during the last century. Oddly enough, it aroused little interest at the time, until a group of chemists in Oxford succeeded in purifying penicillin in 1942. Desperate for good news in wartime, the media made Fleming a celebrity, and he was eventually awarded the Nobel Prize, along with several of the Oxford team.

Queensway

Bayswater's main drag is **Queensway**, a cosmopolitan street with Middle Eastern cafés, and, just up Moscow Road, the beautifully ornate Greek Orthodox Cathedral of **St Sophia** (Ⓦwww.stsophia.org.uk), boasting mosaics by Boris Anrep. Queensway is best known, however, for **Whiteley's**, opened in 1885 as the city's first real department store or "Universal Provider" with the boast that it could supply "anything from a pin to an elephant". The present building opened in 1907, and in the same year was the scene of the murder of the store's founder, William Whiteley, by a man claiming to be his illegitimate son. Whiteley's also had the dubious distinction of being Hitler's favourite London building – he planned to make it his HQ once the invasion was over. The store closed in 1981, and now houses shops, restaurants and a multiscreen cinema, but the original wrought-iron staircase, centaurs' fountain and glass-domed atrium all survive.

Notting Hill

Notting Hill is home to London's most popular market, **Portobello Road**, and its most famous annual street festival, the **Notting Hill Carnival**. It's also one of the city's most affluent neighbourhoods, characterized by leafy avenues, private garden squares, trendy shops and white stuccoed mansions. Back in the 1950s, however, it was described as "a massive slum, full of multi-occupied houses, crawling with rats and rubbish". Along with Brixton in south London, it was one of the main neighbourhoods settled by Afro-Caribbean immigrants,

Notting Hill Carnival

When it emerged in the 1960s, Notting Hill Carnival was little more than a few church-hall events and a carnival parade by Trinidadians. Today Carnival, held over the August Bank Holiday weekend, still belongs to West Indians (from all parts of the city), but there are participants too from London's Latin American and Asian communities, and Londoners of all descriptions turn out to watch the bands and parades, drink Red Stripe, eat curry goat and generally hang out.

The main sights of Carnival are the **costume parades**, which take place on the Sunday (for kids) and Monday (for adults) from around 10am until just before midnight. The parade makes its way around a three-mile route, and consists of big trucks which carry the soundsystems and *mas* (masquerade) bands, behind which the masqueraders dance in outrageous costumes. Most of the *mas* bands play a variety of soca or calypso featuring steel bands – the "pans" of the **steel bands** are one of the chief sounds of Carnival and have their own contest on the Saturday at Horniman's Pleasance, off Kensal Road by the canal. As well as the parade, there are several stages for live music and numerous soundsystems where you can catch reggae, ragga, drum'n'bass, jungle, garage, house and much more.

Over the last decade or so, the Carnival has been fairly relaxed, considering the huge numbers of people it attracts. However, this is not an event for you if you're at all bothered by crowds – you can be wedged stationary during the parades – and very loud music. It's also worth taking more than usual care with yourself and your belongings. The static soundsystems are switched off at 7pm each day – if there's going to be any trouble it tends to come after that point or if you feel at all uneasy, head home early.

Getting to and from the Carnival is quite an event in itself. Ladbroke Grove tube station is closed for the duration, while other stations have restricted hours or are open only for incoming visitors.

▲ Portobello Road

invited over to work in the public services. Tensions between the black families who'd moved into the area and the young white working-class "Teddy Boys" were exploited by far-right groups. And for four days in August 1958, Pembridge Road became the epicentre of the UK's first **race riots**.

The following year, the **Notting Hill Carnival** (see opposite) was begun as a response to the riots; in 1965 it took to the streets and has since grown into one of Europe's biggest street festivals. In the 1970s and early 1980s, tensions between the black community and the police came to a head at carnival time, but strenuous efforts on both sides have meant that such conflict has generally been avoided in the last two decades. However, there are still plenty of doubters among the area's wealthier and mostly white residents, most of whom switch on the alarm system and leave town for the weekend.

Portobello Road

Portobello Road is a meandering, beguiling street that starts just down Chepstow Road from the tube and is famed for its market (see p.444), at its busiest on Saturdays. A short distance up the road stands the **Electric Cinema** (Ⓦ www.the-electric.co.uk), London's oldest movie house, which opened in

1910 on the corner of Blenheim Crescent. In Blenheim Crescent itself, at no. 13–15, you'll find the Travel Bookshop (run by Hugh Grant in the movie *Notting Hill*); his house was nearby at 280 Westbourne Park Rd.

Continuing up Portobello Road, under the **Westway** flyover and east into Golborne Road, you come face-to-face with the awesome **Trellick Tower**, built by Ernö Goldfinger in 1973 and, despite its brutalist concrete appearance, still popular with its residents. Golborne Road is known for its Portuguese and Moroccan cafés, giving the road some of the bohemian feel of old Notting Hill, and making it the perfect place to wind up a visit to the market.

Museum of Brands, Packaging and Advertising

Despite its rather unwieldy title, it's definitely worth popping into the **Museum of Brands, Packaging and Advertising** (Tues–Sat 10am–6pm, Sun 11am–5pm; £5.80; ☎020/7908 0880, ⓦwww.museumofbrands.com; Notting Hill Gate tube), hidden away in Colville Mews, off Lonsdale Road, one block east of Portobello Road. The museum houses an awesome array of old British shop displays through the decades, based on the private collection of Robert Opie, a Scot whose compulsive collecting disorder has left him with ten thousand yoghurt pots alone. From Victorian ceramic pots of anchovy paste to the alcopops of the 1990s, the displays provide a fascinating social commentary on the times. Look out for the militarization of marketing during the last two world wars, with their bile beans "for radiant health and a lovely figure" and V for Victory mugs, and clock the irony of the glamorous early cigarette adverts or the posters for Blackpool "for happy, healthy holidays".

Kensal Green Cemetery

Within easy walking distance of Portobello Road, on the other side of the railway tracks, gasworks and the Grand Union Canal, is **Kensal Green Cemetery**, the first of the city's commercial graveyards, opened in 1833 to relieve the pressure on overcrowded inner-city churchyards. Highgate may be the most famous of the "Magnificent Seven" Victorian cemeteries, but Kensal Green has by far the best funerary monuments. It's still owned by the founding company and remains a functioning cemetery, with services conducted daily in the central Greek Revival chapel. **Guided tours** of the cemetery (March–Oct Sun 2pm; Nov–Feb first & third Sun 2pm; £5; ☎020/8960 1030, ⓦwww.kensalgreen.co.uk; Kensal Green tube) include a visit to the **catacombs** (bring a torch) on the first and third Sunday of the month.

The graves of the more famous incumbents – Thackeray, Trollope and the Brunels – are less interesting architecturally than those arranged on either side of the Centre Avenue, which leads from the easternmost entrance on Harrow Road. Vandals have left numerous headless angels and irreparably damaged the beautiful Cooke family monument, but still worth looking out for are Major-General Casement's bier, held up by four grim-looking turbaned Indians, circus manager Andrew Ducrow's conglomeration of beehive, sphinx and angels, and artist William Mulready's neo-Renaissance extravaganza. Other interesting characters buried here include Charles Wingfield, who invented lawn tennis; Mary Seacole, the "black Florence Nightingale"; Charles Blondin, the famous tightrope walker; Carl Wilhelm Siemens, the German scientist who brought electric lighting to London; and "James" Barry, Inspector-General of the Army Medical Department, who, it was discovered during the embalming of the corpse, was in fact a woman. Playwright Harold Pinter was buried here and Queen singer Freddie Mercury was cremated here, but his ashes were scattered in Bombay.

North London: Camden, Regent's Park, Hampstead and beyond

E verything north of the Marylebone and Euston roads was, for the most part, open countryside until the mid-nineteenth century, and is now largely built up, right the way up to the "green belt" created in the immediate postwar period to try and limit the continuing urban sprawl. This chapter concentrates on just a handful of the former satellite villages, now subsumed into the general mass of north London. Most of north London is easily accessible by tube; in fact, it was the expansion of the tube that encouraged the forward march of bricks and mortar in the outer suburbs.

The first section of the chapter traces the route of the **Regent's Canal**, built in 1820 on the city's northern periphery. Along the way, the canal passes one of London's finest parks, **Regent's Park**, framed by Nash-designed architecture and home to London Zoo. The canal forces its way into Londoners' consciousness only at **Camden**, a rakish place even today, whose weekend market is one of the city's big attractions – a warren of stalls selling funky wares, street fashion, books, music and ethnic art.

Few visitors to the capital head out to neighbouring **Islington**, which has its own flourishing antiques trade, and **Hackney**, further east, with its ethnically diverse population, thus missing out on two of north London's defining areas. The real highlights, though, for visitors and residents alike, are **Hampstead** and **Highgate**, elegant, largely eighteenth-century developments which still reflect their village origins. They have the added advantage of proximity to one of London's wildest patches of greenery, **Hampstead Heath**, where you can enjoy stupendous views, kite flying and outdoor bathing, as well as high art at the Neoclassical country mansion of **Kenwood House**.

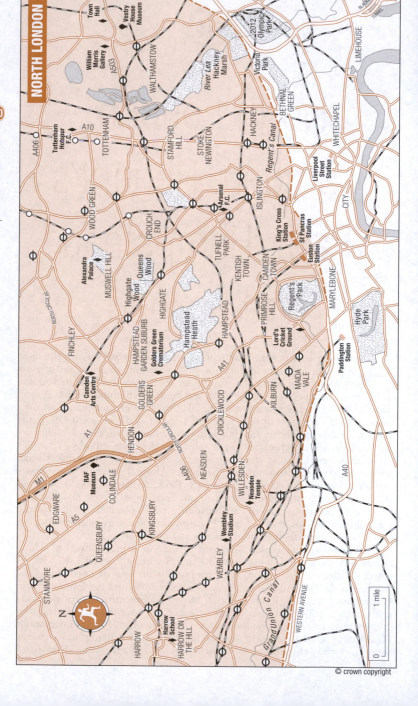

© crown copyright

Also covered, at the end of this chapter, are a few sights in more far-flung suburbs: the nineteenth-century utopia of **Hampstead Garden Suburb**; the Orthodox Jewish suburb of **Golders Green**; the **RAF Museum** at Hendon; and the spectacular **Hindu temple** in Neasden.

Regent's Canal

The **Regent's Canal**, completed in 1820, was constructed as part of a direct link from Birmingham to the newly built London Docks. After an initial period of heavy usage it was overtaken by the railway, and never really paid its way as its investors had hoped. By some miracle, however, it survived, and its nine miles, 42 bridges, twelve locks and two tunnels stand as a reminder of another age. The lock-less stretch of the canal **between Little Venice and Camden Town** is the busiest, most attractive section, tunnelling through to Lisson Grove, skirting Regent's Park, offering views of London Zoo, and passing straight through the heart of Camden Market. It's also the one section that's served by scheduled narrowboats (see below). Alternatively, you can cycle, walk or jog along the towpath.

St John's Wood

The Regent's Canal starts out from the west in the smart, residential district of **St John's Wood**, which was built over in the nineteenth century by developers hoping to attract a wealthy clientele with a mixture of semidetached Italianate villas, multi-occupancy Gothic mansions and white stucco terraces. Edwin Landseer (of Trafalgar Square lions fame), novelist George Eliot and Mrs Fitzherbert, the uncrowned wife of George IV, all lived here, while current residents include knights Richard Branson and Paul McCartney and supermodel Kate Moss.

To catch a canal boat to Camden, head for the triangular leafy basin known as **Little Venice**, a nickname coined by one-time resident and poet Robert Browning. The title may be far-fetched, but the willow-tree Browning's Island is one of the prettiest spots on the canal, and the houseboats and barges moored hereabouts are brightly painted and strewn with tubs of flowers. While you're here, try and catch a traditional marionette performance on the **Puppet Theatre Barge** (Ⓦwww.puppetbarge.com), moored on the Blomfield Road side of the basin, a unique and unforgettable experience;

Regent's Canal by boat

Three companies run daily **boat services** on the Regent's Canal between Camden and Little Venice, passing through the Maida Hill tunnel. The narrowboat *Jenny Wren* (April–Oct only; ℡020/7485 4433, Ⓦwww.walkersquay.com) starts off at Camden, goes through a canal lock (the only company to do so) and heads for Little Venice, while Jason's narrowboats (℡020/7286 3428, Ⓦwww.jasons.co.uk) start off at Little Venice; the London Waterbus Company (April–Sept daily; Oct Thurs–Sun only; Nov–March Sat & Sun only, weather permitting; ℡020/7482 2660, Ⓦwww.londonwaterbus.com) sets off from both places and calls in at London Zoo en route. Whichever you choose, you can board at either end; **tickets** cost around £9 return, and journey time is 45 minutes one-way.

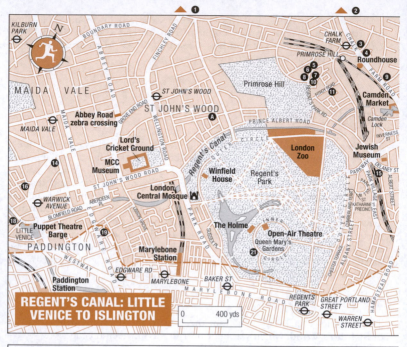

REGENT'S CANAL: LITTLE
VENICE TO ISLINGTON

0   400 yds

CAFÉS & RESTAURANTS		Garden Café	21	Odette's	10
Afghan Kitchen	25	M. Manze	24	Ottolenghi	20
Alpino	26	Mandalay	19	Pasha	23
Black Cap	13	Mango Room	12	Primrose Patisserie	7
Camden Arts Centre	1	Manna	5	Trojka	6
Elk in the Woods	27	Marine Ices	3		

performances take place every weekend and daily at 3pm throughout the
school holidays (except Aug).

Lord's Cricket Ground

The Regent's Canal was bad news for Thomas Lord, who had only recently
been forced to shift his cricket ground due to the construction of what is now
Marylebone Road. Once more he upped his stumps and relocated, this time
to St John's Wood Road, where **Lord's**, as the ground is now known, remains
to this day. The ground is the home of the **MCC** (Marylebone Cricket Club),
founded in 1787, and the most hallowed institution in the game, boasting a
very long members waiting list (unless you're exceptionally famous or rich).
Its politics were neatly summed up by Viscount Monckton, who said, "I have
been a member of the Committee of the MCC and of a Conservative cabinet,
and by comparison with the cricketers, the Tories seem like a bunch of
Commies."

A match ticket allows you free access to the **MCC museum**, the world's
oldest sports museum, which houses the minuscule pottery urn containing the
Ashes (along with the complex tale of this odd trophy), numerous historic balls,
bats and bails, and a sparrow which was "bowled out" by Jehangir Khan at
Lord's in 1936. At other times, you have to visit the museum as part of a **guided**

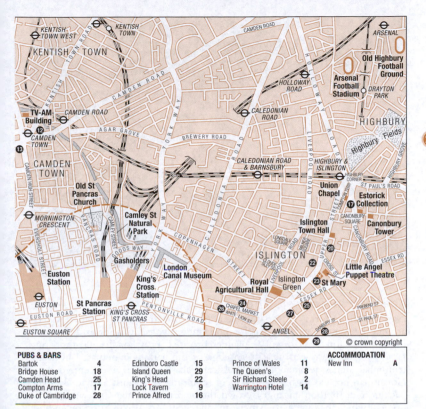

© crown copyright

tour (daily except match & preparation days: Mon–Fri noon & 2pm, Sat & Sun 10am, noon & 2pm; £14; ☏020/7616 8595, Ⓦwww.lords.org), which sets off from the Grace Gates at the southwest corner of the ground. On the tour, you also get to see the famous Long Room (from which the players walk onto the pitch), Lord's Real Tennis Court, the various stands and the futuristic Media Centre, cruelly nicknamed "Cherie Blair's Smile".

Regent's Park

As with almost all of London's royal parks, we have Henry VIII to thank for **Regent's Park** (daily 5am to dusk; ☏020/7486 7905, Ⓦwww.royalparks.gov .uk), which he confiscated from the Church for yet more hunting grounds. However, it wasn't until the reign of the Prince Regent (later George IV) that the park began to take its current form – hence its official title, The Regent's Park – and the public weren't allowed in until 1845 (and even then for just two days of the week). According to John Nash's 1811 master plan, the park was to be girded by a continuous belt of terraces, and sprinkled with a total of 56 villas, including a magnificent pleasure palace for the prince himself, linked by Regent Street to Carlton House in St James's. Inevitably, the plan was never fully realized, but enough was built to create something of the idealized garden city that Nash and the Prince Regent envisaged.

▲ Little Venice

The eastern terraces

Nash's terraces form a near-unbroken horseshoe of cream-coloured stucco around the Outer Circle. By far the most impressive is **Cumberland Terrace**, intended as a foil for George IV's planned private tea pavilion. Its 800-foot-long facade, hidden away on the eastern edge of the park, is punctuated by Ionic triumphal arches, peppered with classical alabaster statues and centred on a Corinthian portico with a pediment of sculptures set against a vivid sky-blue background. In 1936 an angry crowd threw bricks through the windows of no. 16, which belonged to American divorcée Mrs Wallis Simpson, whose relationship with Edward VIII was seen as a national calamity.

Fifty-two more statues depicting British worthies were planned for the even longer facade of **Chester Terrace**, to the south, but Nash decided the ridicule they provoked was "painful to the ears of a professional man" and ditched them. Nevertheless, Chester Terrace is worth walking down if only to take in the splendid triumphal arches at each end, which announce the name of the terrace in bold lettering; the northern one features a bust of Nash.

To the north of Cumberland Terrace, the neo-Gothic **St Katharine's Precinct** provides a respite from the Grecian surroundings, though not one Nash was at all happy with. The central church serves the Danish community, who have erected a copy of the imposing tenth-century **Jelling Stone** in an alcove to the right.

Nash could build equally well on a much more modest scale, as in **Park Village West**, a secluded network of winding streets and culs-de-sac off Albany Street, on the other side of Gloucester Gate, in the northeast corner of the park. The houses, Nash's last work for Regent's Park, feature copious ornamental urns and black lattice pergolas, and range from mock-Athenian cottages to Tudor and Italianate villas.

The Inner Circle and the western periphery

Of the numerous villas planned for the park itself, only eight were built, and of those just two have survived around the **Inner Circle**: St John's Lodge, to the north, and **The Holme**, Decimus Burton's first-ever work (he was 18 at the time), picturesquely sited by the Y-shaped **Boating Lake**. Within the Inner Circle is the Open Air Theatre (see p.430), and **Queen Mary's Gardens**, by far the prettiest section of the park. A large slice of the gardens is taken up with a glorious rose garden, featuring some four hundred varieties, surrounded by a ring of ramblers.

On the western edge of the park, the curved end wings and quirky octagonal domes of **Sussex Place** stand out among the other, more orthodox, Nash terraces. A further surprise on the skyline is the shiny copper dome and minaret of the **London Central Mosque** (☏020/7725 2213, ⓦwww.iccuk.org), an entirely appropriate addition given the Prince Regent's taste for the Orient (as expressed in the Brighton Pavilion). Non-Muslim visitors are welcome to look in at the information centre, and glance inside the hall of worship, which is packed out with a diversity of communities during Friday lunchtime prayers.

A little further up the Outer Circle, there's a trio of modern neo-Nash villas by Quinlan Terry that reflect the conservative tastes of the current Prince of Wales. On the opposite side of the road is **Winfield House**, a dull 1930s replacement for Decimus Burton's Hertford House, built by the heiress to the Woolworth chain, Countess Haugwitz-Reventlow (better known as Barbara Hutton), who gifted Winfield House to the US government during World War II and went on to marry Cary Grant; it's now the American ambassador's residence.

London Zoo

The lion sits within his cage,
Weeping tears of ruby rage,
He licks his snout, the tears fall down
And water dusty London town.

The Zoo, Stevie Smith

The northeastern corner of the park, beyond acres of football pitches, is occupied by **London Zoo** (daily: March–Oct 10am–5.30pm; Nov–Feb

The Beatles in London

Since the Fab Four lived in London for much of the 1960s, it's hardly surprising that the capital is riddled with Beatle associations. The prime Beatles landmark is, of course, the **Abbey Road** zebra crossing featured on the album cover, located near the EMI studios, where the group recorded most of their albums. To get there, walk down Grove End Road from St John's Wood tube, and then turn right into Abbey Road – and remember to bring three friends plus another to take the photos. Incidentally, Paul McCartney still owns the house at 7 Cavendish Ave, which he bought in 1966, two blocks east of the zebra crossing.

One (short-lived) nearby curiosity was the **Apple Boutique**, opened by The Beatles at 94 Baker St, Marylebone, in December 1967 as a "beautiful place where you could buy beautiful things". The psychedelic murals that covered the entire building were whitewashed over after a lawsuit by the neighbours, and eight months later The Beatles caused even more pandemonium when they gave the shop's entire stock away free in the closing-down sale.

Other Beatles locations include the old **Apple headquarters** in Savile Row, Mayfair, where the 1969 rooftop concert took place, while Macca has his current office on Soho Square. Real devotees of the group, however, should get hold of a copy of the exhaustive book by David Heron and Norman Maslov, *The Beatles' England*. Alternatively, sign up for a Beatles tour, run by The Original London Walks (☏020/7624 3978, ⓦwww.walks.com).

10am–4pm; £14; ☎020/7722 3333, ⓦwww.zsl.org/zsl-london-zoo; Camden Town tube). Founded in 1826 with the remnants of the royal menagerie (see p.196), the enclosures here are as humane as any inner-city zoo could make them, and kids usually enjoy themselves. In particular they love Animal Adventure, the new children's zoo (and playground) where they can actually handle the animals, and the regular "Animals in Action" live shows. The invertebrate house, now known as BUGS, the gorilla kingdom and the walk-through rainforest and monkey forest are also guaranteed winners.

The zoo boasts some striking architectural features, too, such as the 1930s modernist, spiral-ramped, concrete former penguin pool (where Penguin Books' original colophon was sketched), designed by the Tecton partnership, led by Berthold Lubetkin, who also made the zoo's Round House. The Giraffe House, by contrast, was designed in Neoclassical style by Decimus Burton, who was also responsible for the mock-Tudor Clock Tower. Other landmark features are the mountainous Mappin Terraces, from just before World War I, and the colossal tetrahedral aluminium-framed tent of Lord Snowdon's modern aviary.

Prince Albert Road and Primrose Hill

Nash intended the Regent's Canal to run right through the middle of the park, but potential residents objected to canal-faring families ploughing through their well-to-do neighbourhood. Instead, the canal curves its way along the northern edge, passing right through London Zoo. Equally visible from the canal are the millionaire apartment buildings of **Prince Albert Road**, which boast unrivalled views across the park. Nash left the park's north side open so folk might enjoy "the many beautiful views towards the villages of Hampstead and Highgate", and it was left to twentieth-century architects to fill in the gaps with a wild variety of high-rise flats, some clad in Edwardian pomp, others with package-holiday-hotel balconies.

Halfway along Prince Albert Road, the mansions stop to reveal the small northern extension of Regent's Park, known as **Primrose Hill**, which commands a great view of central London from its modest summit. To the east is the much sought-after residential area of Primrose Hill, which has attracted numerous successful literati and artists over the years: H.G. Wells, W.B. Yeats, Friedrich Engels, Kingsley Amis and Morrissey have all lived here. You might catch the present denizens such as Jamie Oliver, Ewan McGregor, Alan Bennett or Martin Amis browsing the bookshops and galleries on **Regent's Park Road**, which skirts Primrose Hill to the east. Ted Hughes and Sylvia Plath lived in a flat at 3 Chalcot Square, just east of Regent's Park Road, and it was nearby at 23 Fitzroy Rd, the house that Yeats once lived in, that Plath committed suicide in 1963.

Camden Town

Until the canal arrived, **Camden Town** wasn't even a village, but by Victorian times it had become a notorious slum area, an image it took most of the past century to shed. In the meantime, it attracted its fair share of artists, most famously the Camden Town Group formed in 1911 by Walter Sickert, later joined by the likes of Lucian Freud, Frank Auerbach and Leon Kossoff. These days, you're more likely to bump into young foreign tourists heading for the market, and as-yet-unknown bands on the lookout for members of the local music industry.

For all the gentrification of the last thirty years, Camden retains a gritty aspect, compounded by the various railway lines that plough through the area, the

Camden Market

Camden Market was confined to Inverness Street until the 1970s, when the focus shifted to the disused warehouses around Camden Lock. The tiny crafts market which began in the cobbled courtyard by the lock has since mushroomed out of all proportion, with stalls on both sides of Camden High Street and Chalk Farm Road. More than 100,000 shoppers turn up here each weekend and Camden Lock and the Stables Market now stay open all week long. The overabundance of cheap leather goods, hats, trainers, incense and naff jewellery at **Camden Market** (Ⓦwww .camdenlock.net) is compensated for by the sheer variety of what's on offer, from bootleg tapes to furniture, along with a mass of clubwear and street fashion that may or may not make the transition to mainstream stores. For all its tourist popularity, this is a market that remains a genuinely offbeat placeTo avoid the crowds, which can be overpowering in the summer, aim to come either early (before 10am) or late (say, after 4pm), or on a Friday. The nearest tube is Camden Town, though this is exit-only at peak times at the weekend; Chalk Farm tube is only ten minutes' walk up Chalk Farm Road from Camden Lock.

canal and the large shelter for the homeless on Arlington Road. Its proximity to three mainline stations has also made it an obvious point of immigration over the years, particularly for the Irish, but also for Greek Cypriots during the 1950s. The **market**, however, gives the area a positive lift, especially at weekends, and is now the district's best-known attribute.

Camden Lock

If you've already seen enough jangly earrings for one day, stand on the bowed iron footbridge by **Camden Lock** itself, and admire the castellated former lock-keeper's house, to the west. The flight of three locks to the east begins the canal's descent to Limehouse and the Thames; you can catch a boat in the opposite direction, to Little Venice, from the lock inlet (see p.287). Here too are the covered basins of the Interchange Warehouse, which in turn are linked by a disused railway line to the **Camden Catacombs**, built in the nineteenth century as stables for the pit ponies that used to shunt the railway wagons.

The stabling extended as far north as the brick-built **Roundhouse** (Ⓦwww .roundhouse.org.uk), on Chalk Farm Road, now a youth arts centre and performance venue, but originally built in 1846 as an engine repair shed for 23 goods engines, arranged around a central turntable. Within fifteen years the engines had outgrown the building, and for the next century it was used for storing booze. In 1964, Arnold Wesker established the place as a political theatre venue, and two years later, the Roundhouse began to stage rock gigs – everyone from Hendrix and The Doors to The Ramones and Kraftwerk – and other nonconformist happenings. In 1966, it staged a launch party for the underground paper, *International Times*, at which Pink Floyd and Soft Machine both performed, later hosting a Dialectics of Liberation conference organized by R.D. Laing, not to mention performances by the anarchist Living Theatre of New York, which featured a naked cast.

Camden Town also boasts a few modern architectural curiosities, from Piers Gough's **Glass Building**, with its undulating bile-green facade on Jamestown Road, to Terry Farrell's corrugated steel-clad former **TV-AM Building**, over the High Street on Hawley Crescent. Now occupied by MTV, the building retains its giant blue-and-white egg cups on the canal facade, from breakfast television days.

Jewish Museum

Despite having no significant Jewish associations, Camden is home to London's **Jewish Museum** (☎020/7284 1997, ⓦwww.jewishmuseum.org.uk), at 129 Albert St, just off Parkway. The purpose-built premises were under reconstruction at the time of writing, to enable the museum's social-history collection to be housed alongside its collection of Judaica. The latter includes treasures from London's Great Synagogue on Duke's Place in the City, burnt down by Nazi bombers in 1941, and a sixteenth-century Venetian Ark of the Covenant. There's also a video and exhibition explaining Jewish religious practices and the history of the Jewish community in Britain. More compelling are the temporary exhibitions, discussions and concerts put on by the museum.

Islington

Since the 1960s and 1970s, **Islington**'s picturesque but dilapidated Regency and early Victorian squares and terraces have been snapped up by professionals and City types and comprehensively renovated. The impact of this gentrification, however, has been relatively minor on the borough as a whole, which stretches as far north as Highgate Hill, and remains one of the city's poorest. On the other hand, the main drag, **Upper Street**, has changed enormously: the arrival of its antique market – confusingly known as **Camden Passage** – running parallel on the east side, coincided with the new influx of cash-happy customers, and its pubs and **restaurants** reflect the wealth of its new residents. For entertainment, Islington boasts the long-established *King's Head* **pub theatre**, the Little Angel **puppet theatre** and the ever-popular Almeida plus several comedy and live-music venues (see chapters 27 & 30). All of which makes Islington one of the liveliest areas of north London in the evening – a kind of off-West End.

Upper Street and around

Looking at the traffic fighting its way along **Upper Street**, it's hard to believe that "merry Islington", as it was known, was once a spa resort to which people would flock from the City to drink the pure water and breathe the clean air. Today, the district has fewer green spaces than any other London borough – one of the few being the minuscule **Islington Green**, a short distance along Upper Street from Angel tube. At the apex of the green stands a weathered statue of **Hugh Myddelton**, the Welsh jeweller to James I, who revolutionized London's water supply by drawing fresh water direct from springs in Hertfordshire via an aqueduct known as the **New River**. From 1612 until the late 1980s Myddelton's New River continued to supply most of north London with its water – the succession of ponds to the northeast of Canonbury Road is a surviving fragment of the scheme.

Twice a week, the pavements to the east of the green are occupied by the antique stalls of the **Camden Passage market** (Wed & Sat; ⓦwww.camden passageislington.co.uk; Camden Town tube). The antique shops in the market's narrow namesake and the surrounding streets stay open all week. A total contrast to the antique market can be found at **Chapel Street market** (Tues–Sun 9.30am–3.30pm, Thurs till 1pm), a short distance up Liverpool Road, on the other side of Upper Street. Selling cheap clothes, fruit and veg and Arsenal football memorabilia, it's a salutary reminder of Islington's working-class roots.

Royal Agricultural Hall and Liverpool Road

On the other side of the green from Camden Passage, the ugly modern glass frontage of the Business Design Centre hides the former **Royal Agricultural Hall**, built in 1862 and known locally as the "Aggie". As well as hosting agricultural and livestock exhibitions, it used to host the World's Fair, the Grand Military Tournament, Cruft's Dog Show and such marvels as Urbini's performing fleas. During World War II, however, it was requisitioned by the government for use by the Post Office, who remained in residence until 1971. The interior is still magnificent, but the best exterior view is now from **Liverpool Road**, where two large brick towers rise up either side of the roof, like a Victorian train station.

Walking along these sections of Upper Street and Liverpool Road, it's impossible not to be struck by one of the quirky architectural features of Islington – the raised pavements which protected pedestrians from splattered mud. Such precautions were especially necessary in Islington, which was used as a convenient grazing halt for livestock en route to Smithfield.

From St Mary's to Highbury Fields

Back on Upper Street, past the green, is **St Mary's Church**, originally built in the 1750s. Only the steeple survived the Blitz, though the light, spacious 1950s interior is an interesting period piece, with six fluted Egyptian-style columns framing the sanctuary. The churchyard opens out into Dagmar Passage, where in 1961 a former temperance hall was converted into the **Little Angel Puppet Theatre** (Ⓦ www.littleangeltheatre.com). The archway at the end of Dagmar Terrace brings you out onto **Cross Street**, Islington's loveliest street, with eighteenth-century houses sloping down to Essex Road and raised pavements on both sides. If you've a penchant for Deco-style buildings, head north up Essex Road, where the former **Carlton Cinema** (currently boarded up) was built in 1929 in mock-Egyptian style, using brightly coloured Hathernware tiles.

Back on Upper Street, north of **Islington Town Hall**, a handsome 1920s Neoclassical Portland-stone building, is the fancifully extravagant **Union Chapel**

Orton in Islington

Playwright **Joe Orton** and his lover **Kenneth Halliwell** lived together for sixteen years, spending the last eight years of their lives in a top-floor bedsit at 25 Noel Rd, to the east of Upper Street, where the Regent's Canal emerges from the Islington tunnel. It's ironic that the borough council has seen fit to erect a plaque on the house commemorating the couple, when it was instrumental in pressing for harsh prison sentences after both men were found guilty of stealing and defacing local library books in 1962. (A few of the wittily doctored books are now on display at the **Islington Museum** – see p.160.)

Six months in prison worked wonders for Orton's writing, as he himself said: "Being in the nick brought detachment to my writing." It also brought him success, with irreverent comedies like *Loot*, *Entertaining Mr Sloane* and *What the Butler Saw* playing to sell-out audiences in the West End and on Broadway. Orton's meteoric fame and his sexual profligacy drove Halliwell to despair, however, and on August 9, 1967, Halliwell finally cracked – beating Orton to death with a hammer and then killing himself with a drug overdose. Their ashes were mixed together and scattered over the grass at **Golders Green Crematorium** (see p.314). Apart from the local public toilets, Orton's favourite hangout was the appropriately entitled *Island Queen* pub, at the end of Noel Road.

(Ⓦwww.unionchapel.org.uk), built in 1888 at the height of the Congregational-ists' popularity and now an innovative independent concert venue. Its lugubrious, spacious, octagonal interior is designed like a giant Gothic auditorium, with raked seating and galleries capable of holding 1650 rapt worshippers with the pulpit centre stage. To the north of Highbury Corner, at the top of Upper Street, lies the largest open space in the entire borough, **Highbury Fields**, where over 200,000 people gathered in 1666 to escape the Great Fire, and which is now overlooked on two sides by splendid Georgian terraces.

Canonbury Square

East of Compton Terrace is Islington's most perfect Regency set piece, **Canonbury Square**, centred on a smartly maintained flower garden, but blighted by traffic ploughing up Canonbury Road. In 1928, **Evelyn Waugh** moved into the first floor of no. 17 with his wife Evelyn Gardiner (they called themselves "He-Evelyn" and "She-Evelyn"). In those days, the square was nothing like as salubrious as it is now. In fact, it was precisely the square's squalor that appealed to **George Orwell**, who moved into the top floor of no. 27 in 1944, with his wife and son, having been bombed out of his digs in St John's Wood; he later used it as the prototype for Winston Smith's home in *1984*.

Immediately to the northeast of the square stands the last remaining relic of Islington's bygone days as a rural retreat, the red-brick **Canonbury Tower**, originally part of a Tudor mansion built for the prior of St Bartholomew in the City. The very top floor boasts three Elizabethan interiors, with carved oak panelling and fireplaces carved with Freemasonic and Rosicrucian symbols from when the rooms were used by Renaissance man Francis Bacon. The tower is currently occupied by the Canonbury Masonic Research Centre, who will occasionally show visitors round (Ⓣ020/7226 6256, Ⓦwww.canonbury.ac.uk).

Estorick Collection of Modern Italian Art

Islington's most intriguing attraction is the **Estorick Collection of Modern Italian Art** (Wed, Fri & Sat 11am–6pm, Thurs 11am–8pm, Sun noon–5pm; £5; Ⓣ020/7704 9522, Ⓦwww.estorickcollection.com; Highbury & Islington tube), which occupies a Georgian mansion on Canonbury Square, with the entrance on Canonbury Road. The most exciting works in the gallery are those of the early Italian Futurists, although their founding manifesto of 1909 urged followers to "divert the canals to flood the museums!" Futurism's mouthpiece was Filippo Marinetti, a rich boy with a penchant for crashing fast cars, and, as evidenced by the photos, an eye for natty waistcoats, complete with appliqué hands patting the pockets.

The permanent collection, spread out over the two upper floors, ranges from the rainbow colours of *Music* by Luigi Russolo (inventor of the *intonarumori* – a sort of avant-garde hurdy-gurdy), which is firmly Futurist, to a couple of portraits by Modigliani, and a typically melancholic canvas by Symbolist painter, Giorgio de Chirico. One of the strangest works is Medardo Rosso's wax sculpture *Woman with a Veil*, from 1893, which had a profound influence on the Futurists. Other highlights include Giacomo Balla's *Hand of the Violinist*, a classic Futurist study of movement, speed and dexterity, and Gino Severini's Cubist *Dancer*. The gallery also features paintings by lesser-known Italian artists such as Giorgio Morandi, Massimo Campigli, Mario Sironi and Zoran Music, as well as works by Italy's two leading postwar sculptors, Emilio Greco and Marino Marini. Excellent temporary exhibitions are also held here on the lower floors, and there's a pleasant Italian café that spills out into the back courtyard in good weather.

Hackney and beyond

The borough of **Hackney** (Ⓦ www.myhackney.co.uk) stretches from the East End edge of the City to the north London suburb of **Stamford Hill**. One of the most ethnically diverse of all London boroughs, it comes as no surprise that the country's longest-serving black woman MP, Diane Abbott, has her constituency in Hackney. The fact that the borough has tourist signposts comes as a surprise to many visitors, yet Hackney repays selective visits: **Stoke Newington** is a haven of inexpensive restaurants and laid-back cafés and **central Hackney** is famous for the former music hall of the Hackney Empire, with the red-brick Tudor mansion of **Sutton House** a short stroll away.

Stoke Newington

Stoke Newington (or "Stokey") is probably the most immediately appealing area of Hackney, though like much of the borough, it's off the tube map, so you need to catch a bus (#73 or #476 from Angel tube) or train (Stoke Newington train station from Liverpool St) to reach it. Stokey's best attribute is **Church Street**, a more or less franchise-free, former village high street of little independent shops and restaurants.

The whole area was, for several centuries, a haven for Nonconformists (Christians who were not members of the Anglican church), who were denied the right to live in the City. When Bunhill Fields (see p.163) became overcrowded, **Abney Park Cemetery** (Ⓦ www.abney-park.org.uk), north of Church Street, became the "Campo Santo of English non-Conformists", in the words of the 1903 brochure. The most famous grave is that of William Booth, founder of the Salvation Army (see p.208), by the Church Street entrance, but the romantically overrun cemetery was originally planted as an arboretum, and is now an inner-city wildlife reserve (not to mention a gay cruising area). A **visitors' centre** (Mon–Fri

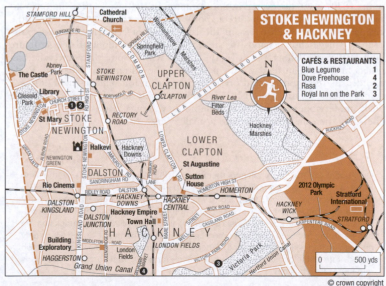

© crown copyright

▲ Abney Park Cemetery

9.30am–4.30pm, Sun noon–3pm) is housed in one of the Egyptian-style lodges at the main entrance, on busy Stoke Newington High Street.

The most famous Dissenter to live in Stokey was **Daniel Defoe**, who wrote *Robinson Crusoe* on the corner of what is now Defoe Road and Church Street; his gravestone is displayed in the Hackney Museum – stolen from Bunhill Fields in the 1870s, it was discovered in Southampton in 1940. Stoke Newington's two main churches on Church Street, both dedicated to **St Mary**, reflect the changes wrought on this area in the last couple of centuries: the sixteenth-century village church stands to the north, opposite a more urbane structure built by George Gilbert Scott in the 1850s, with a spire that outreached all others in London in its day. This pair marks the entrance to **Clissold Park**, founded in 1889 and centred on a porticoed mansion built in the 1790s as a country house for the Quaker Hoare banking family: it's now the park café. The duck and terrapin pond in front of the house was once part of the New River; elsewhere there are goats, deer and a small aviary.

The Angry Brigade

On August 20, 1971, six alleged members of the **Angry Brigade** – at the time Britain's only home-grown urban terrorist group – were arrested at 359 Amhurst Rd, off Stoke Newington High Street, along with (according to the police) a small arsenal of weapons and explosives. The police attempted to link the Angries with the explosives (despite a total lack of forensic evidence) and a total of 25 bomb attacks on the homes of Tory politicians and other members of the Establishment, during which only one person had been slightly injured. After one of the longest criminal trials in English history, four of the accused were sent to prison for conspiracy to cause explosions and four were acquitted.

Stamford Hill and the Lea Valley

Stamford Hill, northeast of Clissold Park, is home to a tight-knit Yiddish-speaking community of ultra-Orthodox Hasidic Jews, one of Hackney's oldest immigrant populations. The most visually striking aspect of the community is the men's attire – frock coats, white stockings and elaborate headgear – which derives from that worn by the Polish nobility of the period. The shops on Stamford Hill and Dunsmure Road, running west, are where the Hasidim buy their kosher goods, and on Sundays, large families take the air at **Springfield Park**, opened in 1905 "to change the habits of the people and to keep them out of the public houses". To reach the park from Stamford Hill, walk across Clapton Common, and down Spring Hill. En route, be sure to check out the four winged beasts (characters from the Book of Revelation) at the base of the spire of the **Cathedral Church of the Good Shepherd** on the corner of Rookwood Road, built for the sect of Spiritual Free Lovers known as the Agapemonites in 1892. Six thousand gathered outside the church in 1902 to throw rotten tomatoes at the womanizing local vicar, who had declared himself the Second Messiah, and drive him into the nearby Clapton Pond to see if he could walk on water. The park itself boasts an awesome view east across the Lea Valley, and has a decent **café** (Ⓦwww.sparkcafe.co.uk) in the White Lodge Mansion by the pond.

On the other side of the river lie the **Walthamstow Marshes**, a valuable stretch of wetland that's alive with butterflies and warblers in the summer. If you follow the river southwards, you will eventually reach the **Middlesex Filter Beds** (Sat & Sun: Easter–Sept 10am–6pm; Oct–Easter 10am–4pm; summer holidays also Mon–Fri 10am–5pm; free), originally built in 1852 on the south side of Lea Bridge Road. Today, drained of most of their water, the filter beds serve as a nature reserve – in the spring check out the noisy frogs in the pond by the main culvert. Beyond, to the south, lie the **Hackney Marshes**, best known as the venue for Sunday League football matches, beyond which is the area earmarked for the London 2012 Olympics (see p.210).

Mare Street and around

The old parish of **Hackney** (and the modern borough) is centred around **Mare Street**, whose main claim to fame is the ornate terracotta **Hackney Empire** (Ⓦwww.hackneyempire.co.uk), one of the last surviving variety theatres in London, built in typically extravagant style by Frank Matcham in 1899. The Empire stands at the centre of Hackney's "cultural quarter", with **Hackney Town Hall**, built in a very restrained 1930s Art Deco style and set back from Mare Street, next door. Opposite, stands the equally austere Methodist hall and the old library, refurbished in 2001 as *Ocean* music venue.

Beside the town hall stands the borough's new library and the **Hackney Museum** (Tues, Wed & Fri 9.30am–5.30pm, Thurs 9.30am–8pm, Sat 10am–5pm; free; Ⓣ020/8356 3500, Ⓦwww.hackney.gov.uk/cm-museum; Hackney Central overground). As well as excellent temporary exhibitions, the museum has an interesting permanent display with lots of personal accounts from local residents. Specific exhibits to look out for include the "upside-down" map of the borough and the Saxon log boat found in Springfield Park, thought to have been a ferry for taking folk across the River Lea.

On the north side of the railway bridge, Mare Street is still discernibly a village high street, known, for obvious reasons, as the **Narroway**, and overlooked by the dumpy fifteenth-century tower of the former parish church of **St Augustine**, and next to it, the Old Town Hall originally built in 1802. Head east across the graveyard behind the tower and down the Georgian terrace of Sutton Place and you'll come to **Sutton House** (Feb to mid-Dec Thurs–Sun 12.30–4.30pm; NT; £2.90; ☎020/8986 2264; Hackney Central overground). Built in 1535 for Ralph Sadleir, a rising star at the court of Henry VIII, the house takes its name from Thomas Sutton, founder of Charterhouse, who lived in an adjacent building (he is buried at Charterhouse, minus his entrails, which you've probably just walked over in the graveyard). The National Trust have done their best to adapt to unfamiliar surroundings and have preserved not just the exquisite Elizabethan "linenfold" wooden panelling, but also a mural left by squatters in 1986. In addition to showing its rambling complex of period rooms, the house puts on classical concerts, hosts contemporary art exhibitions, and even runs a café.

Walthamstow

On the other side of the River Lea and the marshes from Hackney, the chief reason to head out to **Walthamstow** is to visit the William Morris Gallery, but there are one or two other points of interest. **Walthamstow Market** (Mon–Sat 9am–4pm, Sat till 5pm), stretching for well over a mile along the old High Street, north of the tube station, claims to be the country's longest street market. For a traditional East End snack, head for *Manzes*, at no. 76, one of London's finest pie-and-mash shops, with its traditional tiled walls and ceiling.

From the tube, head east down St Mary Road, then Church End, to the heart of the old village, a surprising oasis of calm. On your right as you reach the end of Church End is the **Vestry House Museum** (Wed–Sun 10am–5pm; free; ☎020/8509 1917; Walthamstow Central tube), built in 1730 and at one time the village workhouse. Later on, it became the police station, and a reconstructed police cell from 1861 is one of the museum's chief exhibits. Pride of place, however, goes to the tiny Bremer car, Britain's first-ever internal combustion engine automobile, designed in 1892 by local engineer Fred Bremer, 20-year-old son of German immigrants. Victorian times are comprehensively covered, while the temporary exhibitions tend to cover contemporary topics. The other point of interest here is the fifteenth-century half-timbered **Ancient House**, a short walk up Church Lane.

Civic Centre and the William Morris Gallery

Walthamstow's two other sights are a five-minute walk north past the concrete-encased church of St Mary's, and up The Drive and its continuation, Hurst Road. First is the local **Civic Centre**, set back from Forest Road around a huge open courtyard. Designed in an unusual 1930s Scandinavian style, it is, without doubt, London's grandest town-hall complex. Indeed, there's a touch of Stalinism about the severe Neoclassical central portico and in the exhortation above the adjacent Assembly Hall: "Fellowship is life and the lack of fellowship is death." Sadly, construction of the law courts that would have completed the ensemble was interrupted by the war, but this remains one of the most startling public buildings in London.

To the west of the Civic Centre, along Forest Road, stands a lovely Georgian mansion with two big bay windows, now known as the **William Morris Gallery** (Wed–Sun 10am–5pm; free; ☎020/8527 3782, ⊛www1.waltham forest.gov.uk/wmg; Walthamstow Central tube). This was the Morris family home from 1848 until the death of William Morris's father, a successful businessman in the City, in 1856. Poet, artist, designer and socialist, Morris (1834–96) was one of the most fascinating characters of Victorian London.

Closely associated with both the Pre-Raphaelite and Arts and Crafts movements, he went on to set up Morris & Co, whose work covered all areas of applied art: glasswork, tiles, metalwork, curtains, furniture, calligraphy, carpets, book illumination and (perhaps most famously) wallpaper.

The ground floor contains a modest array of every kind of Morris's very varied work, and also hosts temporary exhibitions. Disappointingly, there are only passing references to Morris's stormy personal life: he married Jane Burden, a working-class girl whom Dante Rossetti picked up at an Oxford theatre and later reclaimed as his lover. Upstairs, there's a small collection of paintings by his later followers and Pre-Raphaelite chums. Edward Burne-Jones shows his mastery of gouache in *St George and the Dragon*, while Ford Madox Brown does the same for pure watercolour in his richly textured portrait, *Jacopo Foscari in Prison*. As is clear from his *Portrait of Alexa Wilding*, Rossetti was so obsessed with Jane Burden that although the model for *The Loving Cup* was a "Chelsea laundry-maid", she looks just like "Janey".

As well as being a successful capitalist – the company's flagship store was on Mayfair's Hanover Square – Morris also became one of the leading political figures of his day, active in the Socialist League with Eleanor Marx, and publishing several utopian tracts, most famously *News from Nowhere*, in which he suggests that the Houses of Parliament be used as "a storage place for manure" (you can buy a copy in the bookshop for the tube journey back). You can see several other works by Morris elsewhere in London: at the V&A, Holy Trinity Church, and the Red House.

Hampstead

Perched on a hill to the west of Hampstead Heath, **Hampstead** village developed into a fashionable spa in the eighteenth century, and was not much altered thereafter. Its sloping site, which deterred Victorian property speculators and put off the railway companies, saved much of the Georgian village from destruction. Later, it became one of the city's most celebrated literary *quartiers* and even now it retains its reputation as a bolt hole of the high-profile intelligentsia and discerning pop stars. You can get some idea of its tone from the fact that the local Labour MP is currently the actor-turned-politician Glenda Jackson.

The steeply inclined **High Street**, lined with trendy clothes shops and arty cafés, flaunts the area's ever-increasing wealth without completely losing its charm, though the most appealing area is the precipitous network of alleyways, steps and streets west of Heath Street. Proximity to the Heath is, of course, the real joy of Hampstead, for this mixture of woodland, smooth pasture and landscaped garden is quite simply the most exhilarating patch of greenery in London.

Holly Bush to the Admiral's House

If you wander into the backstreets north of Hampstead tube, you will probably end up at the small triangular green on **Holly Bush Hill**, where the white weatherboarded **Romney House** stands (closed to the public). In 1797, painter George Romney converted the house and stables into London's first purpose-built studio house, though he spent only two years here before returning to the Lake District and the wife he had abandoned thirty years earlier. Later, it served as Hampstead's Assembly Rooms, where Constable used to lecture on landscape

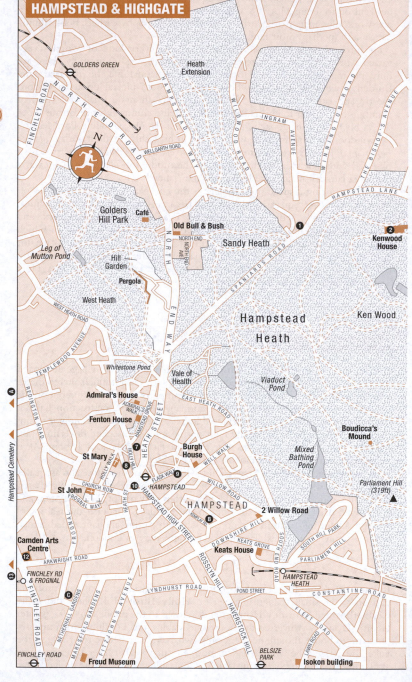

HAMPSTEAD & HIGHGATE

▲ Hampstead Garden Suburb

GOLDERS GREEN

Heath
Extension

FINCHLEY ROAD

NORTH END ROAD

WELLGARTH ROAD

WILDWOOD ROAD

INGRAM

WINNINGTON ROAD

THE BISHOP'S AVENUE

AVENUE

HAMPSTEAD LANE

N

Golders
Hill Park   Café

Old Bull & Bush ●1   ●2 Kenwood
House

Leg of
Mutton Pond

NORTH END

NORTH END
AVE.

Sandy Heath

SPANIARDS ROAD

Hill
Garden

Pergola

West Heath

WEST HEATH ROAD

Hampstead

Heath

Ken Wood

NORTH END WAY

TEMPLEWOOD AVENUE

Whitestone Pond

Vale of
Health

EAST HEATH ROAD

Viaduct
Pond

REDINGTON ROAD

Admiral's House

ADMIRAL'S
WALK

HAMPSTEAD GROVE

HEATH STREET

Boudicca's
Mound

Fenton House

Hampstead Cemetery

●A

●7

Burgh
House

WELL WALK

Mixed
Bathing
Pond

St Mary

HOLLY HILL

●8

STATION RD

FLASK WALK

WILLOW ROAD

●9

HAMPSTEAD

●10

HEATH ST

HAMPSTEAD HIGH STREET

CHURCH ROW

St John

FROGNAL WALK

2 Willow Road

Parliament Hill
(319ft)
▲

SOUTH END ROAD

HAMPSTEAD

●B

KING'S RD

DOWNSHIRE HILL

South Hill Park

FROGNAL

Camden Arts
Centre

ARKWRIGHT ROAD

●12

Keats Grove

Keats House

ROSSLYN HILL

PARLIAMENT HILL

PARLIAMEN HILL

●13

FINCHLEY RD
& FROGNAL

●C

NETHERHALL GARDENS

MARESFIELD GARDENS

FITZJOHN'S AVENUE

LYNDHURST ROAD

Pond Street

HAMPSTEAD
HEATH

CONSTANTINE ROAD

FINCHLEY ROAD

HAVERSTOCK HILL

FLEET ROAD

LAWN ROAD

FINCHLEY ROAD

Freud Museum

BELSIZE
PARK

Isokon building

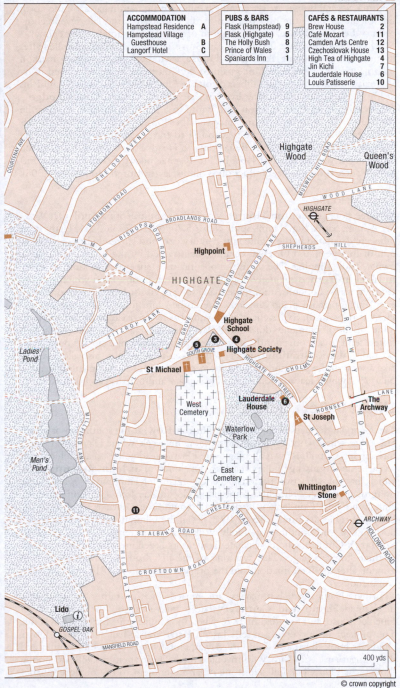

ACCOMMODATION
Hampstead Residence   A
Hampstead Village
    Guesthouse   B
Langorf Hotel   C

PUBS & BARS
Flask (Hampstead)   9
Flask (Highgate)   5
The Holly Bush   8
Prince of Wales   3
Spaniards Inn   1

CAFÉS & RESTAURANTS
Brew House   2
Café Mozart   11
Camden Arts Centre   12
Czechoslovak House   13
High Tea of Highgate   4
Jin Kichi   7
Lauderdale House   6
Louis Patisserie   10

20

Highgate
Wood

Queen's
Wood

WOOD LANE

HIGHGATE

SHEPHERDS HILL

Highpoint

HIGHGATE

Highgate
School

Highgate Society

St Michael

Lauderdale
House

The
Archway

St Joseph

West
Cemetery

Waterlow
Park

Ladies'
Pond

East
Cemetery

Whittington
Stone

Men's
Pond

ARCHWAY

St ALBANS ROAD

CROFTDOWN ROAD

Lido

GOSPEL OAK

MANSFIELD ROAD

0   400 yds

painting. Several houses are set grandly behind wrought-iron gates, on the north side of the green – the one you can hardly see at all is the late seventeenth-century **Fenton House**, now a museum of musical instruments (see below).

Beyond Fenton House, up Hampstead Grove, is Admiral's Walk, so-called after its most famous building, **Admiral's House**, a whitewashed Georgian mansion with nautical excrescences. Once painted by Constable, it was later lived in by Victorian architect George Gilbert Scott, of Albert Memorial fame. Until his death in 1933 John Galsworthy lived in the adjacent cottage, **Grove Lodge** – "[it] wasn't cheap, I can tell you", he wrote to a friend on arrival – where he completed *The Forsyte Saga* and received the 1932 Nobel Prize, which was presented to him here since he was too ill to travel abroad. Opposite is **The Mount**, a gently sloping street descending to Heath Street, which has changed little since it was depicted in *Work* by Pre-Raphaelite artist (and local resident) Ford Madox Brown – a reproduction is on display in Burgh House (see p.306).

Fenton House

All three floors of **Fenton House** (March Sat & Sun 2–5pm; April–Oct Wed–Fri 2–5pm, Sat & Sun 11am–5pm; NT; £5.70; ☎020/7435 3471; Hampstead tube) are decorated in the eighteenth-century taste and currently house a collection of European and Oriental ceramics bequeathed by the house's last private owner, Lady Binning. The house also contains a superb collection of **early musical instruments**, chiefly displayed on the top floor – from which you can see right across London. Among the many spinets, virginals and clavichords is an early English grand piano and an Unverdorben lute from 1580 (one of only three in the world). Experienced keyboard players are occasionally let loose on some of the instruments during the day; **concerts** also take place, although tickets tend to sell out months in advance; alternatively, sign up for one of the occasional **demonstration tours** (£10). Tickets for the house also allow you to take a stroll in the beautiful orchard, kitchen garden and formal **garden** (garden only; £1), which features some top-class topiary and herbaceous borders.

Church Row and around

The Georgian terraces of tree-centred **Church Row**, at the south end of Heath Street, are where City gents would stay for the week when Hampstead was a thriving spa. Church Row is also the nearest Hampstead comes to an architectural set piece, and forms a grand approach to the church of **St John-at-Hampstead**, which has an attractive period-piece Georgian interior and a romantically overgrown cemetery. The chest-tomb of the clockmaker John Harrison lies in the churchyard; John Constable is buried in the southeastern corner; Hugh Gaitskill, Labour Party leader from 1955 to 1963, lies in the Churchyard Extension to the northeast. If you continue up Holly Walk past the extension, you'll come to **St Mary's Church**, whose Italianate facade is squeezed into the middle of a row of three-storey cottages. This was one of the first Catholic churches built in London after the Reformation, and the original facade from 1816 was much less conspicuous.

Further Hampstead luminaries are buried in the rather more neatly maintained **Hampstead Cemetery** half a mile west, on the other side of Finchley Road, and founded in 1876 when the Churchyard Extension was full. The pioneer of antiseptic surgery Joseph Lister, music-hall star Marie Lloyd, children's book illustrator Kate Greenaway, Hollywood actress Lilli Palmer and the Hungarian Laszlo Biro, who invented the ballpoint pen in 1938, are among those buried here. The full-size stone organ monument to the obscure Charles

Hampstead Who's Who

Over the years, countless writers, artists and politicos have been drawn to Hampstead, which has more blue plaques commemorating its residents than any other London borough. **John Constable** lived here in the 1820s, trying to make ends meet for his wife and seven children and painting cloud formations on the Heath, several of which hang in the V&A. **John Keats** moved into Well Walk in 1817, to nurse his dying brother, then moved to a semidetached villa, fell in love with the girl next door, bumped into Coleridge on the Heath, and in 1821 went to Rome to die; the villa is now a museum (see p.307). In 1856, **Karl Marx** finally achieved bourgeois respectability when he moved into Grafton Terrace, a new house on the south side of the Heath. **Robert Louis Stevenson** stayed here when he was 23 suffering from tuberculosis, and thought it "the most delightful place for air and scenery".

Author **H.G. Wells** lived on Church Row for three years just before World War I. In the same period, the photographer **Cecil Beaton** was attending a local infants' school, and was bullied there by author **Evelyn Waugh** – the start of a lifelong feud. The composer **Edward Elgar**, who lived locally, became a special constable during the war, joining the Hampstead Volunteer Reserve. **D.H. Lawrence**, and his German wife Frieda, watched the first major Zeppelin raid on London from the Heath in 1915 and decided to leave. Following the war, Lawrence's friend and fellow writer, **Katherine Mansfield**, lived for a couple of years in a big grey house overlooking the Heath, which she nicknamed "The Elephant". Actor **Dirk Bogarde** was born in a taxi in Hampstead in 1921. **Stephen Spender** spent his childhood in "an ugly house" on Frognal, and went to school locally. **Liz Taylor** was born in Hampstead in 1932, and came back to live here in the 1950s during her first marriage to Richard Burton.

In the 1930s, Hampstead's modernist **Isokon Flats**, on Lawn Road, became something of an artistic hangout, particularly its drinking den, the *Isobar*: architect **Walter Gropius**, and artists **Henry Moore**, **Ben Nicholson** and his wife **Barbara Hepworth** all lived here (Moore moved out in 1940 when his studio was bombed and retired to Herefordshire). Another tenant, **Agatha Christie**, compared the exterior to a giant ocean liner; others were less impressed. Local resident **Ian Fleming** even conducted a campaign to stop architect **Ernö Goldfinger** from building his modernist house at 2 Willow Rd (now a National Trust property; see p.307) and named James Bond's adversary after him. **Mohammed Ali Jinnah** abandoned India for Hampstead in 1932, living a quiet life with his daughter and sister, and working as a lawyer. **George Orwell** lived rent-free above Booklovers' Corner, a bookshop on South End Road, in 1934, in return for services in the shop in the afternoon; *Keep the Aspidistra Flying* has many echoes of Hampstead and its characters. **Sigmund Freud** spent the last year of his life in Hampstead, having reluctantly left Austria, following the Nazi Anschluss; his house is now a museum (see p.306). Artist **Piet Mondrian** also escaped to Hampstead from Nazi-occupied Paris, only to be bombed out a year later, after which he fled to New York. Nobel Prize-winning writer **Elias Canetti** was another refugee from Nazi-occupied Europe, as was **Oskar Kokoschka** who, along with photomontage artist John Heartfield, was given assistance by the Hampstead-based Artists Refugee Committee, set up by local Surrealist artist, Roland Penrose. **General de Gaulle** lived on Frognal with his wife and two daughters and got some first-hand experience of Nazi air raids.

Ruth Ellis, the last woman to be hanged in Britain in 1955, shot her lover outside the *Magdala Tavern* by Hampstead Heath train station. **Sid Vicious** and **Johnny Rotten** lived in a squat on Hampstead High Street in 1976. **John le Carré** lived here in the 1980s and 1990s and set a murder in *Smiley's People* on Hampstead Heath. Of the current residents, one of the oldest is **Michael Foot**, the former Labour leader, now in his nineties, who lives in a house he bought with his redundancy cheque from Beaverbrook. Actors Hugh Grant and Stephen Fry, writer Doris Lessing, and pop stars Robbie Williams and George Michael both have homes here.

Barritt is the most unusual piece of funerary art, while the most unlikely occupant is Grand Duke Mikhail Mikhailovitch of Russia, uncle to the last tsar, Nicholas II.

Freud Museum

One of the most poignant of London's house museums is the **Freud Museum** (Wed–Sun noon–5pm; £5; ☎020/7435 2002, ⓦwww.freud.org.uk; Finchley Road tube), in the leafy suburban streets of south Hampstead at 20 Maresfield Gardens. Having fled Vienna after the Anschluss, **Sigmund Freud** arrived in London in the summer of 1938, and was immediately Britain's most famous Nazi exile. He had been diagnosed as having cancer way back in 1923 (he was an inveterate cigar-smoker) and given just five years to live. He lasted sixteen, but was a semi-invalid when he arrived in London, and rarely left the house except to visit his pet dog, Chun, who was held in quarantine for nearly a year. On September 21, 1939, Freud's doctor fulfilled their secret pact and gave his patient a lethal dose of morphine.

The ground-floor study and library look exactly as they did when Freud lived here (they are modelled on his flat in Vienna); the large collection of antiquities and the psychiatrist's couch, sumptuously draped in opulent Persian carpets, were all brought here from Vienna in 1938. Upstairs, where the Freud archive now resides, there's some old footage of the family, while another room is dedicated to his favourite daughter, Anna, herself an influential child analyst, who lived in the house until her death in 1982. Sigmund's architect son, Ernst, designed a loggia at the back of the house so that Freud could sit out and enjoy the garden; it has since been enclosed and serves as the museum shop, which flogs Freudian merchandise such as a "Brainy Beanie" – Freud himself as a cuddly toy – and stocks a superb range of books.

Towards the Heath

It only takes five minutes or so to walk from the tube to the Heath, but en route, there are a handful of sights worth visiting: **Burgh House**, housing the local museum; the modernist townhouse of **2 Willow Road**; and **Keats' House** where the poet once lived.

This part of Hampstead recalls the period in the eighteenth century when Hampstead became a thriving spa, known briefly as **Hampstead Wells**. Three-penny containers of the local spring water were sold in the pedestrianized alleyway of **Flask Walk** (hence its name), while bottling took place at *The Flask* pub (see p.405); Flask Walk opens out into **Well Walk**, where the Victorian Chalybeate Well commemorates the springs.

Burgh House

The Queen Anne mansion of **Burgh House** (Wed–Sun noon–5pm; free; ☎020/7431 0144, ⓦwww.london-northwest.com/burghhouse; Hampstead tube), on New End Square, off Well Walk, dates from the halcyon days of Hampstead Wells, and was at one time occupied by Dr Gibbons, the physician who discovered the spring's medicinal qualities. Surrounded by council housing, exhibitions are staged on the ground floor, and there's a modest museum upstairs, with special emphasis on such notable locals as Constable and Keats. Other curiosities include a reproduction of Ford Madox Brown's painting *Work*, a modernist Isokon plywood chair, found in a Hampstead skip by a local councillor, and the hat from Stanley Spencer's portrait of the artist Daphne Charlton, which was painted at the Charltons' house at 40 New End Square.

The *Buttery* tearoom (Wed–Sun 11am–5.30pm) in the basement has outdoor seating in the summer on a lovely terrace.

2 Willow Road

Hampstead's newest attraction is **2 Willow Road** (March & Nov Sat 11am–5pm; April–Oct Thurs & Fri noon–5pm, Sat 11am–5pm; NT; £5.30; ☎020/7435 6166; Hampstead tube), a modernist red-brick terraced house, built in the 1930s by the Hungarian-born architect **Ernö Goldfinger**, best known for his controversial Trellick Tower. When Goldfinger moved in, in 1937, this was a state-of-the-art house, its open-plan rooms flooded with natural light and much of the furniture designed by Goldfinger himself. Strangely for a modernist, Goldfinger changed little in the house in the following sixty years, so what you see is a 1930s avant-garde dwelling preserved in aspic, a house at once both modern and old-fashioned. An added bonus is that the rooms are packed with *objets trouvés* and works of art by the likes of Léger, Duchamp, Max Ernst, Henry Moore and Man Ray. Before 3pm, visits are by hour-long guided tour only (noon, 1 & 2pm); after 3pm the public has unguided, unrestricted access.

Keats' House

Hampstead's most lustrous figure is celebrated at **Keats' House** (Tues–Sun 1–5pm; £3.50; ☎020/7435 2062; Hampstead tube), an elegant, whitewashed Regency double villa on Keats Grove, a short walk south of Willow Road. The consumptive poet moved here in 1818 after his brother Tom had died of the same illness. Inspired by the peacefulness of Hampstead and by his passion for girl-next-door Fanny Brawne (whose house is also part of the museum), Keats wrote some of his most famous works here before leaving for Rome, where he died in 1821. In the pretty front garden, as you approach the house, you pass a deeply uninspiring plum tree, which replaces the much larger specimen in whose shade Keats is said to have sat for two or three hours before composing *Ode to a Nightingale*. The neat, rather staid interior contains books and letters, an anatomical notebook from Keats' days as a medical student at Guy's Hospital, Fanny's engagement ring and the four-poster bed in which the poet first coughed up blood, and proclaimed "that drop of blood is my death warrant". There are regular events – poetry readings, performances and talks – on Wednesday evenings.

Hampstead Heath

Hampstead Heath, north London's "green lung", is the city's most enjoyable public park. Little of the original heathland survives, but the Heath nevertheless packs in a wonderful variety of bucolic scenery, from the formal **Hill Garden** and rolling green pastures of **Parliament Hill** to the dense woodland of **West Heath** and the landscaped grounds of **Kenwood**. As it is, the Heath was lucky to survive the nineteenth century intact, for it endured more than forty years of campaigning by the Lord of the Manor, Thomas Maryon Wilson, who introduced no fewer than fifteen parliamentary bills in an attempt to build over it. It wasn't until after Wilson's death in 1871 that 220 acres of the Heath passed into public ownership. The Heath now covers over eight hundred acres, and is run by the Corporation of London (see p.166).

Parliament Hill and the Ponds

Parliament Hill, the Heath's southernmost ridge, is perhaps better known as Kite Hill, since this is north London's premier spot for kite flying, especially busy at weekends when some serious equipment takes to the air. The parliamentary connection is much disputed by historians, so take your pick: a Saxon parliament met here; Guy Fawkes' cronies gathered here in vain to watch the Houses of Parliament burn; the Parliamentarians placed cannon here during the Civil War to defend London against the Royalists; and the Middlesex parliamentary elections took place here in the seventeenth century. Whatever the reason for the name, the view over London is unrivalled.

The Heath is the source of several of London's lost rivers – the Tyburn, Westbourne and Fleet – and home to some 28 natural ponds, three of which are used as **Bathing Ponds**: single-sex men's and ladies' ponds, on the Highgate side; mixed bathing on the Hampstead side (see p.308).

To the Vale of Health

To the northwest of Parliament Hill is a fenced-off **Tumulus**, where, according to one tradition, Queen Boudicca was buried after she and ten thousand other Brits had been massacred at Battle Bridge; another legend says she's buried under Platform 10 in King's Cross Station. Due west lies the picturesque **Viaduct Pond**, named after its red-brick bridge, which is also known as Wilson's Folly. It was built as part of Thomas Maryon Wilson's abortive plans to drive an access road through the middle of the Heath to his projected estate of 28 villas.

Below, to the west, beyond the Viaduct Pond, an isolated network of streets nestles in the **Vale of Health**, an area that was, in fact, a malarial swamp until the late eighteenth century. Literary lion Leigh Hunt moved to this quiet backwater in 1816, after serving a two-year prison sentence for calling the Prince Regent "a fat Adonis of fifty", among other things; Hunt was instrumental in persuading Keats to give up medicine for poetry. Other artistic residents have included Nobel Prize-winner Rabindranath Tagore, who lived here in 1912, and Stanley Spencer, who stayed here with the Carline family and married their daughter Hilda in the 1920s. D.H. Lawrence spent a brief, unhappy period here in 1915: in September of that year his novel *The Rainbow* was banned for obscenity, and by December, Lawrence and his wife, Frieda von Richthofen, whose German origins were causing the couple immense problems with the authorities, had resolved to leave the country.

West Heath, Hill Garden and Golders Hill Park

Northwest of the Vale of Health is the busy road junction around **Whitestone Pond**, which marks the highest point in north London (440ft), overlooked by the faux-ancient *Jack Straw's Castle* pub. To the west lies **West Heath**, a densely wooded, boggy area with a thick canopy of deciduous trees sloping down towards Childs Hill; it's a very peaceful place for a stroll and a popular cruising area for gay men. A track leads northwest from *Jack Straw's Castle*, across West Heath, over to **The Hill Garden** (daily 8.30am to dusk), the Heath's most secretive and romantic little gem. Originally an extension to the grounds of nearby Hill House, built by Lord Leverhulme in 1906 (and now converted into flats), the garden's most startling feature is the 800ft-long zigzag **Pergola**, whose Doric columns support a host of climbers including a wonderfully gnarled wisteria. The pergola is elevated some 15ft above the ground in order to traverse a public footpath that Lord Leverhulme tried in vain to have removed.

The path across West Heath eventually leads to the more municipal landscaped gardens of **Golders Hill Park** (daily 7.30am to dusk). The central section of the park is taken up by animal enclosures containing pygmy goats and wallabies, and a series of impeccably maintained aviaries, home to cranes and other exotic birds; to the north, closer to the entrance, is a beautifully kept walled garden and pond. Before you leave the park, make sure you try some of the café's wonderful Italian ice cream, courtesy of *Arte Gelato*.

Spaniards Road runs from Whitestone Pond along the eastern edge of **Sandy Heath**, a triangle of oak and beech woodland to the south of the Extension, where sand was quarried until the nineteenth century. At the northeastern end of Spaniards Road, cars struggle to avoid oncoming traffic as the road squeezes between the old tollhouse and the **Spaniards Inn**, an eighteenth-century coaching inn thought to have been used by the highwayman Dick Turpin as a hiding place and vantage point for sizing up the coaches leaving town.

Kenwood House

The Heath's most celebrated sight is **Kenwood House** (daily 11.30am–4pm; EH; free; ☎020/8348 1286; bus #210 from Archway or Golders Green tube), whose beautiful off-white Neoclassical facade faces south to catch the sun. Set in its own magnificently landscaped grounds (daily: summer 8am–8pm; winter 8am–4pm), the house dates from the seventeenth century, but was later remodelled by Robert Adam for the Earl of Mansfield, the most powerful jurist in the country. Mansfield, who sent 102 people to the gallows and sentenced another 448 to transportation, was a deeply unpopular character and one of the prime targets of the Gordon rioters in 1780, who ransacked his Bloomsbury house. A crowd also made their way towards Kenwood, but they were waylaid by the canny landlord of the nearby *Spaniards Inn* (an ex-butler of Mansfield's), who plied them with free drink until soldiers arrived to disperse the mob.

The house is now home to a superb collection of seventeenth- and eighteenth-century art from the English, Dutch and French schools. First off, head for the Dining Room, where a superb late self-portrait by **Rembrandt** shares space with marvellous portraits by Franz Hals, Van Dyck and Ferdinand Bols, and **Vermeer**'s delicate *Guitar Player*. Of the house's many wonderful period interiors, the most spectacular is Adam's sky-blue and gold **Library**, its book-filled apses separated from the central entertaining area by paired columns. The *pièce de résistance* is the tunnel-vaulted ceiling, decorated by Antonio Zucchi, who fell in love with and married Kenwood's other ceiling painter, Angelica Kauffmann.

Upstairs, you'll find more paintings, including William Larkin's full-length portraits, possibly of a Jacobean wedding party, with twin ladies in slashed silver brocade dresses, the arrogant Richard Sackville, a dissolute aristocrat resplendent in pompom shoes, and his much nicer brother, Edward, sporting earrings festooned with ribbons. Don't miss the room of shoe buckles, jewellery and portrait miniatures bequeathed by local collectors. Back downstairs in the Music Room, you'll find more masterful portraits by **Gainsborough**, most strikingly the diaphanous *Countess Howe*, caught up in a bold, almost abstract landscape, plus several by **Reynolds**, including his whimsical *Venus Chiding Cupid for Learning to Cast Accounts*.

Kenwood has splendid azaleas and rhododendrons to the west, and a huge grassy amphitheatre to the south, which slopes down to a lake. The lawn is a favourite picnic spot, while the provision-less can head for the excellent *Brew House Café* in the old coachhouse.

Highgate

Northeast of the Heath, and fractionally lower than Hampstead (appearances notwithstanding), **Highgate** lacks the literary cachet of Hampstead, but makes up for it with London's most famous **cemetery**, resting place of, among others, Karl Marx. It also retains more of its village origins, especially around **The Grove**, Highgate's finest row of houses, set back from the road in pairs overlooking the village green, and dating back to 1685. Their most famous one-time resident is the poet **Samuel Taylor Coleridge**, who lived at no. 3 from 1816, with a certain Dr Gillman and his wife. With Gillman's help, Coleridge got his opium addiction under control and enjoyed the healthiest, if not necessarily the happiest, period of his life, until his death here in 1834.

Coleridge was initially buried in the local college chapel, but in 1961 his remains were reburied in **St Michael's Church**, in South Grove. Its spire is a landmark, but St Michael's is much less interesting architecturally than the grandiose, late seventeenth-century Old Hall next door, or the two tiny ramshackle cottages opposite, built for the servants of one of the luxurious mansions that once characterized Highgate. Arundel House, which stood on the site of the Old Hall, was where **Francis Bacon**, the Renaissance philosopher and statesman, is thought to have died, having caught a chill while trying to stuff a chicken full of ice during an early experiment in refrigeration.

Up and down the High Street

Highgate gets its name from the tollgate – the highest in London and the oldest in the country – that stood where the *Gatehouse* pub now stands on **Highgate High Street**. The High Street itself, though architecturally pleasing, is packed out with franchises and estate agents, and marred by heavy traffic, as is its northern extension, North Road. If you persevere with North Road, however, you'll pass **Highgate School**, founded in 1565 for the local poor but long since established as an exclusive fee-paying public school, housed in suitably impressive Victorian buildings. T.S. Eliot was a master here for a while, and famous poetical alumni, known as Cholmeleians after the founder Sir Roger Cholmeley, include Gerard Manley Hopkins and John Betjeman.

Further up North Road, on the left, are the whitewashed high-rises of **Highpoint 1** and **2**, seminal early essays in modernist architecture designed by Berthold Lubetkin and his Tecton partnership from the late 1930s. Highpoint 1, the northernmost of the two blocks, was conceived as workers' housing, with communal roof terraces and a tearoom. The locals were outraged so Highpoint 2 ended up being luxury apartments, the caryatids at the entrance a joke at the expense of his anti-modernist critics. Lubetkin also designed himself a penthouse apartment on the roof in the style of a Georgian dacha, with views right across London, where he lived until 1955.

In the other direction, Highgate High Street slopes down into **Highgate Hill**, with still more amazing views down towards the City. Halfway down the hill stands the Roman Catholic church of St Joseph or "Holy Joe", whose green copper dome is a prominent Highgate landmark. Beside the church is **Waterlow Park**, named after Sydney Waterlow, who donated it in 1889 as "a garden for the gardenless". Waterlow also bequeathed **Lauderdale House** (Ⓦ www.lauderdalehouse.co.uk), a much-altered sixteenth-century building, which is thought to have been occupied at one time by Nell Gwynne and her infant son, and which now houses a decent café and restaurant that spill out into the terraced gardens. The park itself, occupying a dramatic sloping site, is an amalgamation of several house gardens, and is one of London's finest landscaped parks, providing a through route to Highgate Cemetery. Further down Highgate Hill, you'll find the **Whittington Stone**, with cat, marking the spot where Dick Whittington miraculously heard the Bow Bells chime (see p.176).

Highgate Cemetery

Ranged on both sides of Swain's Lane and receiving far more visitors than Highgate itself, **Highgate Cemetery** (☎020/8340 1834, ⓦhighgate-cemetery .org; Highgate or Archway tube) is London's most famous graveyard. Opened in 1839, it quickly became the preferred resting place of wealthy Victorian families, who could rub shoulders here with numerous intellectuals and artists. As long as prime plots were available, business was good and the cemetery could afford to employ as many as 28 gardeners to beautify the place. But as the cemetery filled, funds dried up and the whole place fell prey to vandals. In 1975, the old (west) cemetery was closed completely and was taken under the wing of the Friends of Highgate Cemetery. Nowadays, you have to take a guided tour to visit the West Cemetery, though you can still wander freely in the less dramatic east cemetery – both sections have entrance charges.

West Cemetery

The old, overgrown **West Cemetery** (March–Nov Mon–Fri 2pm, Sat & Sun hourly 11am–4pm; Dec–Feb Sat & Sun hourly 11am–3pm; £5; no under-8s) is the ultimate Hammer-horror graveyard, and one of London's most impressive sights, with its huge vaults and eerie statuary.

Dickens could have been the most famous corpse here, but only his estranged wife and daughter lie in the family tomb – despite the author's wishes to be buried privately and without ostentation, he was posthumously overruled by Queen Victoria, who insisted on his being buried in Westminster Abbey. Instead, the most famous names here are Charles Chubb (of the locks), Charles Cruft (of the Dog Show) and Michael Faraday, who, as a member of the obscure Sandemanian sect, is buried along the unconsecrated north wall. There's no guarantee your tour will cover these tombs, but you're more than likely to be shown the lion that snoozes above the tomb of menagerist George Wombwell, and the faithful and watchful dog (confusingly called Lion) that lies on bare-knuckle fighter Thomas Sayers' grave. Another popular destination is the **Rossetti family tomb**, resting place of Elizabeth Siddall, the Pre-Raphaelites' favourite model and wife of Dante Gabriel Rossetti, who buried the only copy of his many love poems along with her. Seven years later he changed his mind and had the poems exhumed and published. The poet Christina Rossetti, Dante's sister, is also buried in the vault.

The cemetery's spookiest section is around **Egyptian Avenue**, entered through an archway flanked by Egyptian half-pillars, known as the "Gateway to the City of the Dead". The avenue slopes gently upwards to the Circle of Lebanon, at the centre of which rises a giant cedar. The circular Egyptian-style sunken catacombs here include the tomb of the lesbian novelist Radclyffe Hall (her lover, Mabel Batten, is also buried here). Above are the **Terrace Catacombs**, and the cemetery's most ostentatious mausoleums, some of which accommodate up to fifteen coffins; the largest – based on the tomb of Mausolus at Halicarnassus – is that of Julius Beer, one-time owner of the *Observer* newspaper.

Alexandra Palace

Built in 1873 on the commanding heights of Muswell Hill, **Alexandra Palace** (Ⓦ www.alexandrapalace.com) is now London's only surviving example of a Victorian "People's Palace", since its more famous rival, Crystal Palace, burnt down in 1936 (see p.320). However, the history of "Ally Pally" is almost as tragic as that of Crystal Palace. Sixteen days after the official opening, the whole place burnt down and, despite being rebuilt within two years and boasting a theatre, a reading room, an exhibition hall and a concert room with one of the largest organs in the world, it was a commercial failure. During World War I more than seventeen thousand German POWs passed through its gates, and in 1936 the world's first television transmission took place here. It was the venue for the "14 Hour Technicolour Dream" in 1967, organized by the *International Times* and featuring performances by, among others, Pink Floyd and Soft Machine. The palace was rebuilt again after another devastating fire in 1980, but it continues to struggle to make itself viable commercially. In addition to the annual round of shows, there's a pub, the appropriately named *Phoenix Bar*, with great views, a garden centre and an indoor ice rink open daily, as well as regular funfairs in the holidays.

This section of the cemetery provided inspiration for Bram Stoker's *Dracula*, and was at the centre of a series of bizarre incidents in the early 1970s. Graves were smashed open, cadavers strewn about, and the High Priest of the British Occult Society, Allan Farrant, was arrested, armed with a stake and crucifix with which he hoped to destroy "the Highgate Vampire". He was eventually sentenced to four years' imprisonment, after being found guilty of damaging graves, interfering with corpses and sending death-spell dolls to two policemen.

East Cemetery

What the **East Cemetery** (April–Oct Mon–Fri 10am–5pm, Sat & Sun 11am–5pm; Nov–March closes 4pm; £3) lacks in atmosphere, it makes up for by the fact that you can wander at will through its maze of circuitous paths. The most publicized occupant is, of course, **Karl Marx**, who spent more than half his life in London, much of it in bourgeois Hampstead. Marx himself asked for a plain and simple grave topped by a headstone, but by 1954 the Communist movement had decided to move his tomb to a more prominent position and erect the vulgar bronze bust that now surmounts a granite plinth bearing the words "Workers of all lands, unite", from *The Communist Manifesto*. He has been visited here by Khrushchev, Brezhnev and just about every postwar Communist leader in the world.

Buried along with Marx are his grandson, wife and housekeeper, Helene Delmuth, whom he got pregnant. Engels accepted paternity to avoid a bourgeois scandal and only told Marx's daughter, Eleanor, on his deathbed in 1895. Eleanor committed suicide a few years later after discovering her common-law husband had secretly married someone else. Her ashes were finally placed in the family vault in 1954, having been seized from the Communist Party headquarters in London by the police in 1921. Lesser-known Communists such as Yusef Mohamed Dadoo, chairman of the South African Communist Party until his death in 1983, cluster around Marx. Not far away is **George Eliot**'s grave and, behind it, that of her lover, George Henry Lewes.

Golders Green, Hendon and Neasden

North and west of Hampstead is suburbia good and proper, but there are one or two specific reasons for venturing so far into residential London: **Hampstead Garden Suburb**, an offshoot of Golders Green, is the city's original garden suburb; the **RAF Museum** in Hendon has probably the country's finest collection of military aircraft; and the **Hindu temple** in Neasden – the largest outside India – has to be seen to be believed.

Golders Green

If the East End is the spiritual home of working-class Jews, **Golders Green**, northwest of Hampstead, is its middle-class equivalent. A hundred years ago this whole area was open countryside but, like much of suburbia, it was transformed overnight by the arrival of the tube in 1907. Before and after World War II, the area was heavily colonized by Jews moving out of the old East End ghetto around Spitalfields or fleeing as refugees from the Nazis. Nowadays, Golders Green, along with Stamford Hill, is one of the most distinctively Jewish areas in London. The Orthodox community has a particularly strong presence here and there's a profusion of kosher shops beyond the railway bridge on Golders Green Road, at their busiest on Sundays.

Hampstead Garden Suburb

Much of Golders Green is architecturally bland, the one exception being **Hampstead Garden Suburb** (Ⓦwww.hgs.org.uk), begun in 1907 to the north of the Hampstead Heath Extension. This model housing development was a product of the utopian dream of Henrietta Barnett, wife of the philanthropist who established Toynbee Hall in the East End. In the Barnetts' view, the only long-term solution to social reform was to create a mixed social environment where "the poor shall teach the rich, and the rich, let us hope, shall help the poor to help themselves". Yet from the start the suburb was socially segregated, with modest artisan dwellings to the north, middle-class houses to the west and the wealthiest villas overlooking the Heath to the south. As a social engineering experiment it was a failure – the area has remained a thoroughly middle-class ghetto – but as a blueprint for suburban estates it has been enormously influential.

The formal entrance to the suburb is the striking Arts and Crafts gateway of shops and flats on Finchley Road (nearest tube Golders Green). From here, ivy-strewn houses, each with its own garden encased in privet, yew and beech hedges, fan out eastwards along tree-lined avenues towards the deliberately "non-commercial" **Central Square**, laid out by Edwin Lutyens in a neo-Georgian style he dubbed "Wren-aissance". (Pubs, shops, cinemas and all commercial buildings were, and still are, excluded from the suburb.) Lutyens also designed the square's twin churches: the Nonconformist Free Church, sporting an octagonal dome, and the Anglican St Jude's-on-the-Hill – the finer of the two – with its steeply pitched roof and spire, and its unusual 1920s murals within. East of the central green is the Lutyens-designed **Institute**, with its clock tower, now occupied by an adult education centre and Henrietta Barnett Girls' School. From the square, you could walk south along cherry-tree-lined Heathgate, which ends at the Heath Extension.

Golders Green Crematorium and Jewish Cemetery

West of Hampstead Garden Suburb, down Meadway and then Hoop Lane, is the **Golders Green Crematorium** (daily: summer 9am–6pm; winter 4pm), where over 300,000 Londoners have been cremated since 1902. More famous names have been scattered over the crematorium's unromantically named Dispersal Area than have been buried at any single London graveyard: Boris Anrep, Enid Blyton, Seán O'Casey, Charles Rennie Mackintosh, H.G. Wells, Kathleen Ferrier, Joe Orton, Don Revie, Peter Sellers, Peggy Ashcroft, Joyce Grenfell, Marc Bolan, Keith Moon, Bram Stoker and Prajadhipok, the former King of Thailand; Neville Chamberlain, Rudyard Kipling, Henry James and T.S. Eliot were cremated here, but their ashes lie elsewhere. Finding a particular memorial plaque among the serene red-brick chapels and arcades is no easy task, so it's best to enquire at the office in the main courtyard. The Ernst George Columbarium is where you'll find the ashes of Anna Pavlova; Freud and his wife Martha are contained within one of Freud's favourite Greek red-figure vases in an adjacent room, with their daughter Anna in her own urn close by.

On the opposite side of Hoop Lane is a **Jewish Cemetery** (daily except Sat 8.30am–5pm or dusk), founded in 1895 before the area was built up. The eastern section, to your right, is for Orthodox Sephardic Jews, whose tombs are traditionally laid flat with the deceased's feet pointing towards Jerusalem. To the left are the upright headstones of Reform Jews, including the great cellist Jacqueline du Pré, and Lord Hore-Belisha, Minister of Transport in the 1930s, who gave his name to "Belisha beacons" (the yellow flashing globes at zebra crossings for pedestrians).

Hendon: the RAF Museum

One of the most impressive collections of historic military aircraft in the world is lodged at the **RAF Museum** (daily 10am–6pm; free; Colindale tube; ☎020/8205 2266, ⓦwww.rafmuseum.org.uk), in the former Hendon Aerodrome beside the M1 motorway. Start your tour in the **Grahame-White Factory** (daily 10am–noon), which displays the museum's oldest aircraft including several flimsy World War I biplanes, or head straight for the **Historic Hangars**, dominated by a vast 1920s Southampton reconnaissance flying boat. Be sure to check out the Hoverfly, the first really effective helicopter, and, of course, the most famous British plane of all time, the Spitfire. By the exit you'll find a Harrier jump jet, the world's first vertical takeoff and landing aircraft, labelled with a text extolling its role in the Falklands War.

The most chilling section is the adjacent **Bomber Hall**, where you're greeted by a colossal Lancaster bomber, similar to those used in Operation Upkeep, the mission carried out by Squadron 617 (and immortalized in the film *The Dambusters*), about which there's a ten-minute documentary. To the museum's credit, the assessment of Bomber Command's wartime policy of blanket-bombing gives both sides of the argument. The video of the "precision bombing" conducted during the 1991 Gulf War is given rather less even-handed treatment. Two other exhibits deserve special mention: the crumbling carcass of a Halifax bomber, recovered from the bottom of a Norwegian fjord, and the clinically white Valiant, the first British aircraft to carry thermonuclear bombs.

Those with children should head for the hands-on **Aeronauts** gallery, which teaches the basic principles of flight and airplane construction. In **Milestones of Flight**, south off Bomber Hall, you get to see a century's worth of aircraft from an early airship gondola to the state-of-the-art Eurofighter Typhoon.

Across the car park is **Battle of Britain Hall** (daily noon–6pm), which contains a huge Sunderland flying boat, a V-1 flying bomb and a V-2 rocket. The focus of the hall, though, is *Our Finest Hour*, an unashamedly jingoistic fifteen-minute audiovisual on the aerial battle fought between the RAF and the Luftwaffe during the autumn of 1940.

Neasden: the Swaminarayan temple

The lotus blooms in splendour, but its roots lie in the dirt.

Hindu proverb

Perhaps the most remarkable building in the whole of London lies just off the busy North Circular, in the glum suburb of Neasden. Here, rising majestically above the dismal interwar housing like a mirage, is the **Shri Swaminarayan Mandir** (daily 9am–6pm; free; Ⓣ020/8965 2651, Ⓦwww.mandir.org; Neasden tube), a traditional Hindu temple topped with domes and *shikharas*, erected in 1995 in a style and scale unseen outside of India for over a millennium. The building's vital statistics are incredible: three thousand tons of Bulgarian limestone and two thousand tons of Carrara marble were shipped out to India, carved by over 1500 sculptors, and then shipped back to London and assembled in a matter of weeks. Even more surprising is the fact that Lord Swaminarayan (1781–1830), to whom the temple is dedicated, is a relatively obscure and very recent Hindu deity. There are no more than ten thousand followers in Britain, mostly from Gujarat, and no more than a million worldwide.

To reach the temple, you must enter through the adjacent **Haveli**, or cultural complex, with its carved wooden portico and balcony, and its twin covered, carpeted courtyards. Shoes are the only thing that are sexually segregated inside the temple, so, having placed yours in the appropriate alcove, you can then proceed to the **Mandir** (temple) itself. The temple is carved entirely out of Carrara marble from the floor to the dome, with every possible surface transformed into a honeycomb of arabesques, flowers and seated gods. The pillars are intricately decorated with figures of gods and goddesses, while on three sides are alcoves sheltering serene life-sized **Murti** (gods), garish figures in resplendent clothes representing Rama, Sita, Ganesh the elephant god, Hanuman the monkey god, and, of course, Shri Swaminarayan himself. The Murti are only on display from 9am to 11am, and from 4pm to 6.30pm.

Beneath the Mandir, an **exhibition** (daily 9am–6pm; £2) explains the basic tenets of Hinduism through dioramas, extols the virtues of vegetarianism and details the life of Lord Swaminarayan, who became a yogi at the age of 11, and stood naked on one leg for three months amidst snowstorms and "torturing weather". At the end, there's a short video about the history of the building.

21

Southeast London: Brixton to Greenwich and beyond

S outheast London was a confirmed part of rural Kent until the late eighteenth century. Now largely built up into a patchwork of Victorian terraces, one area stands head and shoulders above all the others in terms of sightseeing: **Greenwich**, once home to the Tudor court. Its nautical associations are trumpeted by the likes of the *Cutty Sark* and the National Maritime Museum; its architecture, especially the Old Royal Naval College and the Queen's House, is some of the finest on the river; and its Royal Observatory is renowned throughout the world.

The rest of this chapter is really just a hotchpotch of scattered suburban sights, where, given the distances involved and the dire lack of tube lines south of the river, it pays to be selective. A few areas and sights do, however, stand out: **Dulwich**, whose public art gallery is even older than the National Gallery, and, way out on the very edge of London, the Arts and Crafts **Red House**, William Morris's former home, and **Down House**, the home of Charles Darwin.

Brixton

Brixton is a classic Victorian suburb, transformed from open fields into bricks and mortar in a couple of decades following the arrival of the railways in the 1860s. The viaducts still dominate the landscape of central Brixton, with shops and arcades hidden under their arches, but it's the West Indian community, who arrived here in the 1950s and 1960s, who still define the character of the place – Notting Hill may have Carnival, but it's Brixton that has the most upfront African-Caribbean consciousness. Brixton is also saddled with the reputation for violence it earned during the 1981, 1985 and 1995 riots, when tensions between the police and locals came to a head. Various government initiatives have attempted to get to the root of local discontent, racism and unemployment with varying degrees of success, though the visual fabric of the place has definitely improved.

Brixton's main axis is the junction of Brixton Road, Acre Lane and Coldharbour Lane, just to the south of the tube station and overlooked by the slender clock tower of the Edwardian **Lambeth Town Hall**; the dinky neo-Renaissance Tate Library; the Ritzy cinema from 1911; and, on the triangular traffic island, the Neoclassical church of **St Matthew**, with its grandiose Doric portico, its crypt now converted into a trendy bar, restaurant and theatre space.

The commercial lifeblood of Brixton, however, pulses most strongly through **Brixton Market** (Mon–Sat 8am–3pm), whose stalls spread out through the warren of streets and arcades east of Brixton Road. **Electric Avenue** – as in the Eddy Grant song – runs behind the tube station, and is so-called as it was one of the first London shopping streets to be lit by electricity in the 1880s. A network of shabby interwar arcades runs parallel with the avenue, culminating in the **Granville Arcade**, where you can buy bold African and Asian fabrics, jewellery, all manner of exotic fruit and meat, amazing wigs and much more besides. On the far side of the railway tracks, the market veers eastwards along Brixton Station Road, with stalls selling everything from cheap secondhand clothes to rap and reggae soundtracks.

Dulwich and Crystal Palace

Dulwich is just two stops from Brixton on the overland railway, but light years away in every other respect. This affluent, middle-class enclave is one of southeast London's prettier patches – its leafy streets boast handsome Georgian houses and even a couple of weatherboarded cottages, while the Soane-designed **Dulwich Picture Gallery** is one of London's finest small museums. If Dulwich has a fault, it's the somewhat cloying self-consciousness about its "village" status, with its rather twee little shops, rural signposts and fully functioning tollgate – the only one remaining in London.

A day out in Dulwich can be combined with a visit to the nearby **Horniman Museum**, an enjoyable ethnographic collection, and, for the very curious, the remnants of the old **Crystal Palace**, further south. The green spaces between these sights are also worth exploring. **Dulwich Park**, opposite the Picture Gallery, is a pleasant enough public park, but for something a bit wilder, **Sydenham Hill Wood**, a nature reserve south of Dulwich Common, is the one to head for.

Dulwich Village

Dulwich came to prominence in 1619 when its lord of the manor, actor-manager Edward Alleyn, founded the **College of God's Gift** (Ⓦwww.dulwich.org.uk) as a school for poor boys on the profits of his whorehouses and bear-baiting pits on Bankside. The college has long since outgrown its original buildings, which still stand to the north of the Picture Gallery, and is now housed in a fanciful Italianate complex designed by Charles Barry (son of the architect of the Houses of Parliament), south of Dulwich Common. The college is now a fee-paying public school, with an impressive roll call of old boys, including Raymond Chandler, P.G. Wodehouse and World War II traitor Lord Haw-Haw, though they tend to keep quiet about the last of the trio.

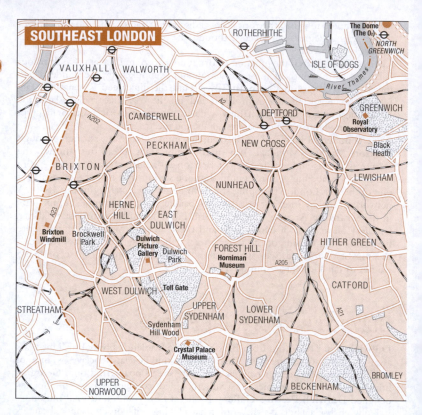

Dulwich Picture Gallery

Dulwich Picture Gallery (Tues–Sun 10am–5pm; £5; ☎020/8693 5254, Ⓦwww.dulwichpicturegallery.org.uk; West Dulwich train station from Victoria or North Dulwich train station from London Bridge), on College Road, is the nation's oldest public art gallery. Designed by John Soane in 1814, it houses, among other bequests, the collection assembled in the 1790s by the French dealer Noel Desenfans on behalf of King Stanislas of Poland, who planned to open a national gallery in Warsaw. In 1795, Poland disappeared from the map of Europe, Stanislas abdicated and Desenfans was left with the paintings. Neither the British nor Russians would buy the collection, so Desenfans proposed founding a national gallery. In the end it was left to his business partner, the landscape painter Francis Bourgeois, and Desenfans' widow, to complete the task and open the gallery in 1817.

Soane, who worked for no fee, created a beautifully spacious building, awash with natural light, and added a tiny **mausoleum** at the centre for the sarcophagi of the Desenfans family and of Francis Bourgeois. Based on an Alexandrian catacomb, it's suffused with golden-yellow light from the mausoleum's coloured glass – a characteristic Soane touch.

The gallery itself is crammed with superb paintings – elegiac landscapes by **Cuyp**, one of the world's finest **Poussin** series and splendid works by Hogarth, Murillo and Rubens. There's an unusually cloudy **Canaletto** of Walton Bridge

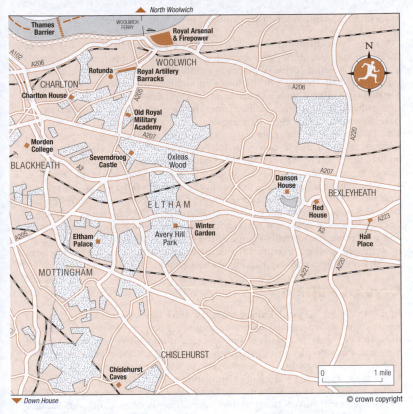

© crown copyright

on the Thames, **Rembrandt**'s tiny *Portrait of a Young Man*, a top-class portrait of poet, playwright and Royalist, the future Earl of Bristol, by **Van Dyck**, and a moving one of his much lamented kinswoman by marriage, Venetia Stanley, on her deathbed. Among the gallery's fine array of **Gainsborough** portraits are his famous *Linley Sisters*, sittings for which were interrupted by the elopement of one of them with the playwright Sheridan, and a likeness of Samuel Linley that's said to have been painted in less than an hour. Free guided tours of the permanent collection take place (Sat & Sun 3pm), and there are regular temporary exhibitions, for which there is an extra charge.

Horniman Museum

To the southeast of Dulwich Park, on the South Circular road, is the wonderful **Horniman Museum** (daily 10.30am–5.30pm; free; ☎020/8699 1872, ⓦwww.horniman.ac.uk; Forest Hill train station from Victoria or London Bridge), purpose-built in 1901 by Frederick Horniman, a tea trader with a passion for collecting. The building itself is a striking edifice designed by Charles Harrison Townsend, architect of the Whitechapel Gallery. Its most arresting features are the massive clock tower, with its smoothly rounded bastions and circular cornice, and the polychrome mosaic of allegorical figures in classical dress on the facade. Entry is from the gardens to the west, where you'll find turkeys, goats and hens, a sunken water garden and a

SOUTHEAST LONDON: BRIXTON TO GREENWICH AND BEYOND

Dulwich

www.roughguides.com

319

graceful Victorian conservatory, brought here from the Horniman mansion in Croydon.

A ramp leads down from the foyer to the **Natural History** collection of stuffed animals and birds – everything from a half-dissected pigeon to an ostrich – and their skeletons; pride of place goes to the Horniman Walrus, lying flat out on a mocked-up iceberg. On the lower ground floor, head first for the dimly lit **Centenary Gallery**, which contains an eclectic ethnographic collection, much of it gathered by Horniman himself, from the precious butterflies that started his obsession at the age of eight to a papier-mâché figure of Kali dancing on Siva. Equally arresting are the more recent acquisitions like the Nigerian puppets of Charles, Di and a British bobby, or the "ugly masks" used to chase the winter away in the Alps. The **African Worlds Gallery** contains a wide-ranging anthropological collection from African masks and voodoo altars to Egyptian sarcophagi and Sudanese dung bowls. In the **Music Gallery** you can see and hear more than 1500 instruments including Chinese gongs and electric guitars, or have a go at some of the instruments yourself in the hands-on room. Look out for the special sessions at the **Hands On Base**, which allow you to handle and learn more about a whole range of the museum's artefacts. And finally, don't miss the state-of-the-art **Aquarium** in the basement, featuring everything from British pond life to tropical jellyfish, sea horses and monkey frogs.

Crystal Palace

In the 1850s, the **Crystal Palace** from the 1851 Great Exhibition (see p.251) was enlarged and re-erected on the commanding heights of Sydenham Hill, to the south of Dulwich, a site affording spectacular views over London, Kent and Surrey. A fantastic pleasure garden was laid out around this giant glasshouse, with a complex system of fountains, some of which reached a height of 250ft. Exhibitions, funfairs, ballooning, a miniature railway and a whole range of events, including, from 1894 to 1924, the FA Cup Final, were staged here. Despite its initial success, though, the palace soon became a financial liability – then, in 1936, the entire structure burnt to the ground overnight.

All that remains now are the stone terraces, the triumphal staircase, a few sphinxes and a small **museum** on nearby Anerley Hill (Sat & Sun 11am–4.30pm; free; ☎020/8676 0700, ⓦwww.crystalpalacemuseum.org.uk; Crystal Palace train station from Victoria) that tells the history of the place. Nowadays, the **park** (daily 7.30am–dusk) is dominated by a TV transmitter, visible from all over London, and the **National Sports Centre**, whose tartan athletics track (Europe's first) was opened in the 1960s and where some 21 world records were set in the following two decades. There are further reminders of the park's Victorian heyday in and around **Lower Lake**, in the southeast corner of the park, whose islands feature around thirty life-sized **dinosaurs** lurking in the undergrowth, built out of brick and iron.

Greenwich

Greenwich is the one area in southeast London that draws tourists out from the centre in considerable numbers. At its heart is the outstanding architectural set piece of the **Old Royal Naval College** and the **Queen's House**, courtesy of Christopher Wren and Inigo Jones respectively. Most visitors, however, come

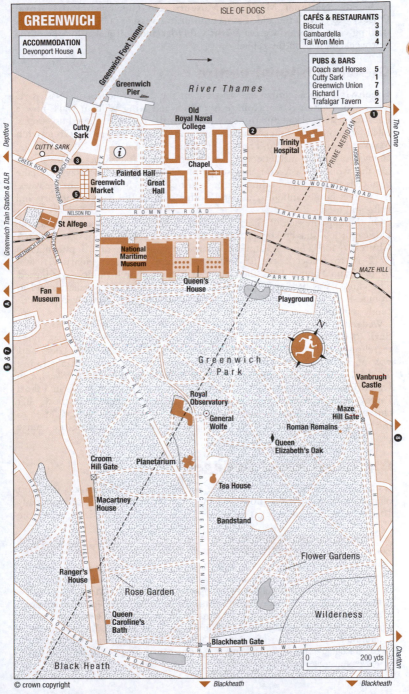

GREENWICH

ACCOMMODATION
Devonport House **A**

CAFÉS & RESTAURANTS
Biscuit	3
Gambardella	8
Tai Won Mein	4

PUBS & BARS
Coach and Horses	5
Cutty Sark	1
Greenwich Union	7
Richard I	6
Trafalgar Tavern	2

ISLE OF DOGS

River Thames

Greenwich Foot Tunnel

Greenwich Pier

Cutty Sark

CUTTY SARK

Old Royal Naval College

Trinity Hospital

PRIME MERIDIAN

HOSKINS STREET

The Dome

Deptford

CREEK ROAD

GREENWICH CHURCH ST

Greenwich Market

Painted Hall

Chapel

Great Hall

PARK ROW

OLD WOOLWICH ROAD

Greenwich Train Station & DLR

NELSON RD

St Alfege

GREENWICH HIGH ST

STOCKWELL ST

KING WILLIAM WALK

ROMNEY ROAD

TRAFALGAR ROAD

MAZE HILL

MAZE HILL

National Maritime Museum

Queen's House

PARK VISTA

Fan Museum

Playground

CROOM'S HILL

AVENUE

Greenwich Park

Vanbrugh Castle

Royal Observatory

General Wolfe

Maze Hill Gate

Roman Remains

Queen Elizabeth's Oak

MAZE HILL

Croom Hill Gate

Planetarium

BLACKHEATH AVENUE

Tea House

Macartney House

Bandstand

Flower Gardens

HYDE VALE

CHESTERFIELD WALK

Ranger's House

Rose Garden

Wilderness

SHOOTERS HILL ROAD

Queen Caroline's Bath

Blackheath Gate

Black Heath

CHARLTON WAY

Charlton

0   200 yds

© crown copyright

Blackheath

Blackheath

to see the **National Maritime Museum** and Greenwich Park's **Royal Observatory**. With the added attractions of its riverside pubs and walks – plus startling views across to Canary Wharf and Docklands – it makes for one of the best weekend trips in the capital.

Greenwich town centre

Greenwich town centre was laid out in the 1820s, hence the Nash-style terraces of Nelson Road, College Approach and King William Walk, now a one-way system plagued with heavy traffic. At the centre of these busy streets, filled with nautical knick-knack shops and bookshops, stands **Greenwich Market** (Wed 11am–7pm, Thurs & Fri 10am–5pm, Sat & Sun 10am–5.30pm; Ⓦ www.greenwich-market.co.uk), an old covered market where you can still see the wonderfully Victorian inscription on one of the archways: "A false balance is abomination to the Lord, but a just weight is his delight." In the week, the market houses antique, crafts and clothes stalls; at the weekend it's arts and crafts and food.

On the opposite side of Greenwich Church Street from the market rises the Doric portico and broken pediment of Nicholas Hawksmoor's **St Alfege's Church** (Mon–Thurs 9.30am–12.30pm; Ⓦ www.st-alfege.org). It was built in 1712–18 to replace a twelfth-century structure in which Henry VIII was baptized and Thomas Tallis, the "father of English church music", was buried. The church was flattened in the Blitz, but its lovely wooden galleries and its trompe-l'oeil coffered apse, originally by Thornhill, have since been magnificently restored.

Wedged in a dry dock by the Greenwich Foot Tunnel is the majestic **Cutty Sark** (Ⓣ 020/8858 2698, Ⓦ www.cuttysark.org.uk), the world's last surviving tea clipper. Launched from the Clydeside shipyards in 1869, the *Cutty Sark* was more famous in its day as a wool clipper, returning from Australia in just 72 days. The vessel's name comes from Robert Burns' *Tam O'Shanter*, in which Tam, a drunken farmer, is chased by Nannie, an angry witch in a short Paisley linen dress, or "cutty sark"; the clipper's figurehead shows her clutching the hair from the tail of Tam's horse. The ship is currently closed to the public for much needed repairs, but is due to reopen during the course of 2010.

Old Royal Naval College

It's entirely appropriate that the one London building that makes the most of its riverbank location should be the **Old Royal Naval College** (daily 10am–5pm; free; Ⓦ www.oldroyalnavalcollege.org), a majestic Baroque

---

Visiting Greenwich

The most scenic and leisurely way to reach Greenwich is to take a **boat** from one of the piers in central London. Greenwich can also be reached by **train** from Charing Cross, Waterloo East or London Bridge (every 15–30min), or by **Docklands Light Railway** (DLR) from Bank or Tower Gateway direct to *Cutty Sark*. For the best view of the Wren buildings, get out at Island Gardens station to admire the view across the river, and then take the Greenwich Foot Tunnel under the Thames. The local **tourist information office** (daily 10am–5pm; Ⓣ 020/8293 0673, Ⓦ www.greenwichwhs.org .uk) is located in the Pepys Building by the side of the *Cutty Sark*. Staff there can answer most queries.

▲ Old Royal Naval College

ensemble which opens out onto the Thames. Despite the symmetry and grace of the four buildings, which perfectly frame the Queen's House beyond, the whole complex has a strange and piecemeal history. The first of the four blocks was built in the 1660s as a palace for Charles II, but the money ran out. William and Mary eschewed the unfinished palace for Hampton Court and turned the Greenwich building into a hospital for disabled seamen, along the lines of the Royal Hospital in Chelsea. Wren, working for nothing, then had his original designs vetoed by the queen, who insisted the new development must not obscure the view of the river from the Queen's House – what you see now is Wren's revised plan, augmented by, among others, Hawksmoor and Vanbrugh.

The naval hospital moved out in 1869, to be replaced by the Royal Naval College, which, in turn, was supplanted by the current incumbents, the University of Greenwich and Trinity College of Music. The two grandest rooms, situated underneath Wren's twin domes, are open to the public and well worth visiting. The magnificent **Painted Hall**, in the west wing, is dominated by James Thornhill's gargantuan allegorical ceiling painting, which depicts William and Mary enthroned, with a vanquished Louis XIV clutching a broken sword. Equally remarkable are Thornhill's trompe-l'oeil fluted pilasters and decorative detailing, while on the far wall, behind the high table, Thornhill himself appears (bottom right) beside George I and family, with St Paul's in the background. Designed as the sailors' dining hall, it was later used for Nelson's lying-in-state in 1806 and then as a naval art gallery.

The **Chapel** (service Sun 11am), in the east wing, was designed by James Stuart, after a fire in 1779 destroyed its predecessor. However, it is Stuart's assistant, William Newton, whom we have to thank for the chapel's exquisite pastel and sky-blue plasterwork and spectacular decorative detailing, among the finest in London. The altarpiece, by Benjamin West, depicts St Paul wrestling with the viper that leapt out of the fire after he was shipwrecked off Malta.

The riverside

A fine vantage point for viewing the Old Royal Naval College is the **Five-Foot Walk**, which squeezes between the college railings and the riverbank. It was here that George I landed to take the throne on September 18, 1714, though it was estimated that 57 other cousins had a better claim. If you're in need of refreshment, drop into the Regency-style **Trafalgar Tavern** (see p.407), at the east end of the walk. Just beyond the pub down Crane Street is the **Trinity Hospital**, founded in 1613 by the Earl of Northampton for 21 pensioners; the entry requirements declared the hospital would admit "no common beggar, drunkard, whore-hunter, nor unclean person…nor any that is blind…nor any idiot". The cream-coloured mock-Gothic facade and chapel (which contains the earl's tomb) were rebuilt in the nineteenth century, but the courtyard of almshouses remains much as it was at its foundation. Beyond the Trinity Hospital, the Thames Path continues along the river all the way to the Dome (aka the O2).

National Maritime Museum

The main entrance to the excellent **National Maritime Museum** (daily 10am–5pm; free; ☏020/8858 4422, ⓦwww.nmm.ac.uk), which occupies the west wing of the former Naval Asylum, is on Romney Road, and brings you out into a glass-roofed central courtyard. The various themed galleries are ranged over three floors, and are imaginatively designed to appeal to visitors of all ages, with plenty of hands-on stuff to keep children amused. The courtyard has a gallery at its centre, and several "streets" along the sides, which house some of the museum's largest artefacts, among them the splendid 63-foot-long **Royal Barge**, a gilded Rococo confection designed by William Kent for Prince Frederick, the much-unloved eldest son of George II.

Level G: Explorers and Passengers

Explorers, on Level G, takes you from the Vikings to Franklin's attempt to discover the Northwest Passage; on display are the relics recovered from the Arctic by John Rae in 1854, many of which had to be bought from the local Inuit. In the central building, **Rank & Style** allows you to inspect various marine get-ups from naval uniforms to the survival suit that saved Tony Bullimore's life when his yacht capsized – each one hidden within a cupboard and accompanied by a brief audioguide. **Maritime London** has displays on the history of London's old docks, and Nelson's diminutive "undress coat", worn during the Battle of Trafalgar, with a tiny bullet hole made by the musket shot that killed him. **Passengers** relives the glory days of transatlantic shipping, which officially came to an end in 1957 when more people went by air than by sea. To their credit, the displays also touch on the role of shipping in immigration and in transporting refugees. Sponsors P&O get to display their wares at the end, with several huge models of P&O's *Grand Princess*, built in 1998 and, at 109,000 tons and over 950ft in length, at the time the largest passenger vessel ever built.

Level 1: Art, Trade & Empire and Nelson Gallery

The Upper Deck, on Level 1, houses the café, and is lined with cabinets filled with beautiful nauticalia from ship's badges and astrolabes to brass lamps and naval swords. Next door, **Art & the Sea** displays a wide range of artworks from eighteenth-century oils of historic naval encounters to Art Deco lithographs of submarine life by war artist Eric Ravilious. **Atlantic Worlds** focuses on the history of the trade links with the New World, from slavery to whaling. Lastly, don't miss the **stained glass** from the **Baltic Exchange**, a colourful 1920s memorial salvaged from the Baltic Exchange, after it was blown up by the IRA in 1992.

Level 2: Hands-on galleries

Level 2 is the place to head if you've got children, as it boasts two excellent hands-on galleries. **The Bridge** is aimed at all ages, as it really does take some skill to navigate a catamaran, a paddle steamer and a rowing boat to shore. **All Hands** is aimed at a younger audience, and gives kids a taste of life on the seas, loading miniature cargo, firing a cannon, learning to use Morse code and so forth. Also on this level is the **Oceans of Discovery** gallery, which concentrates on the voyages of Cook, Scott and Shackleton. Cook's K1 marine chronometer is here and there's a replica of the *James Caird*, in which Shackleton made the epic 700-mile journey from Elephant Island to South Georgia, plus lots of Scott memorabilia: his overshoes, his watch, his funky sledging goggles and a basic sketch of his planned route scrawled on some hotel notepaper. Also on Level 2 is **Ship of War**, the museum's collection of model sailing warships from 1650 to 1815, most of them made by the Navy Board at the same time as the ships they represent.

Queen's House

Inigo Jones's **Queen's House**, originally built on a cramped site amidst the Tudor royal palace, is now the focal point of the Greenwich ensemble. As royal residences go, it's an unassuming little Palladian country house, "solid... masculine and unaffected" in Jones's own words. Its significance in terms of British architecture, however, is immense. Commissioned in 1616, it was the first classical building in the country since Roman times, signifying a clear break with all that preceded it. The interior, exterior and setting of the Queen's House have all changed radically since Jones's day, making it difficult to imagine the impact the building must have had when it was built. The house is linked to its neighbouring buildings by open colonnades, added in the early part of the nineteenth century along the course of the muddy road which the H-shaped block originally straddled.

Inside, very few features survive from Stuart times. The **Great Hall**, a perfect cube, remains, but Orazio Gentileschi's ceiling paintings were removed to Marlborough House by the Duchess of Marlborough herself during the reign of Queen Anne. The southeastern corner of the hall leads to the beautiful **Tulip Staircase**, Britain's earliest cantilevered spiral staircase, whose name derives from the floral patterning in the wrought-iron balustrade. The only other significant interior decoration is upstairs, in the room intended as the bedchamber of Charles I and Henrietta Maria, which retains its ceiling decoration from the 1630s.

The rooms now house an exhibition on the history of royal Greenwich, stage various temporary exhibitions and provide a permanent home for the National Maritime Museum's vast **art collection**. Upstairs, in amongst the naval battles and portraits of admirals, there are works by the likes of Reynolds, Hogarth, Gainsborough, Lely, Kneller and Myrtens. Look out for Thornhill's portrait of an eldritch naval pensioner and Zoffany's unfinished, nightmarish *Death of Captain Cook*. There's a typically infatuated portrait of Lady Hamilton by

Romney, a Canaletto of Greenwich, painted from Island Gardens, and the only major British portrait of (a wistful and dreamy) Napoleon, painted while he was a prisoner on board the *Bellerophon*. Also of interest are the oil paintings by the official artists on board Cook's last two voyages to the Pacific. Back downstairs, one room is usually set aside for Turner's *Battle of Trafalgar, 21st October, 1805*, his largest work and only royal commission, which was intended for St James's Palace.

Greenwich Park and the Royal Observatory

Greenwich Park (daily 6am to dusk; Ⓦ www.royalparks.gov.uk) is one of the city's oldest royal parks, having been enclosed in the fifteenth century by the Duke of Gloucester, who fancied it as a hunting ground. Henry VIII was particularly fond of the place, introducing deer in 1515, as well as archery and jousting tournaments, and sword-fighting contests. The park was opened to the public in the eighteenth century, but it was only after the arrival of the railway in 1838 that it began to attract Londoners in great numbers. In 1894 Martial Bourdin, a young **French anarchist**, was killed in the park when the bomb he was carrying in a brown-paper bag exploded. The questions of whether he was planning to blow up the observatory, and whether he was a police informer, remain unresolved. Joseph Conrad used the episode as the inspiration for his novel *The Secret Agent*.

The park's chief delight is the view of Docklands from the steep hill crowned by a statue of **General James Wolfe** (1727–59), who lived near the park, and is buried in St Alfege. Wolfe is famed for the audacious campaign in which he captured Quebec in 1759, a battle in which he and his opposite number, the French general Montcalm, were both mortally wounded. Victory celebrations took place throughout England, but were forbidden in Greenwich out of respect for Wolfe's mother, who had also lost her husband only a few months previously.

Royal Greenwich

The history of Greenwich is replete with **royal connections**. Edward I appears to have been the first of the English kings to have stayed here, though there was nothing resembling a palace until Henry V's brother, the Duke of Gloucester, built **Bella Court** (later known as the Palace of Placentia) in 1447. Henry VI honeymooned here with his new wife, Margaret of Anjou, and eventually took over the place and rebuilt it in her honour. However, it was under the Tudors that the riverside palace enjoyed its royal heyday. **Henry VIII** was born there and made it his main base, pouring even more money into it than into Hampton Court. He added armouries, a banqueting hall and a huge tiltyard, hunted in the extensive grounds and kept a watchful eye over proceedings at the nearby **Royal Dockyards** in Deptford. His children, Mary and Elizabeth, were both born here.

Edward VI came to Greenwich in 1553 to try to restore his frail health, but died shortly afterwards. Mary came here rarely as queen, and on one of her few visits had the wall of her personal apartment blasted away by a cannonball fired in salute. For Elizabeth, Greenwich was the **chief summer residence**, and it was here in 1573 that she revived the Maundy Ceremony, washing the feet of 39 poor women (though only after three others had washed them first). The royal palace fell into disrepair during the 1650s Commonwealth, when it was turned into a biscuit factory, and was finally torn down by Charles II to make way for a new edifice, which eventually became the Royal Naval College.

The descendants of Henry's deer are now safely enclosed within **The Wilderness**, a fenced area in the southeast corner where they laze around "tame as children", in Henry James's words. Don't miss **Vanbrugh Castle**, halfway down Maze Hill, on the east side of the park, England's first mock-medieval castle, designed by the architect John Vanbrugh as his private residence in 1726. Note, too, **Queen Caroline's Bath**, by the park's southern wall, which is all that remains of the house where the queen used to hold her famous orgies – the rest of the house was destroyed by her estranged husband George IV after she left the country in 1804. If you're heading for the Ranger's House, the best approach is via the semicircular **Rose Garden**, laid out in front of it, which is worth a visit itself from June to August.

Royal Observatory

Established by Charles II in 1675, the **Royal Observatory** (daily 10am–5pm; free; ☎020/8312 6565, ⓦwww.nmm.ac.uk) is the longest-established scientific institution in Britain. The chief task of John Flamsteed, the first Astronomer Royal, was to study the night sky in order to discover an astronomical method of finding the longitude of a ship at sea, the lack of which was causing enormous problems for the emerging British Empire. Astronomers continued to work here at Greenwich until the postwar smog and light pollution forced them to decamp to Herstmonceux Castle in Sussex; the observatory, meanwhile, is now a very popular museum.

Greenwich's other great claim to fame is of course as the home of **Greenwich Mean Time** and the **Prime Meridian** – a meridian being any north–south line used as a basis for astronomical observations, and therefore also for the calculation of longitude and time. In 1884, the International Meridian Conference in Washington DC agreed to make Greenwich the Prime Meridian of the World – in other words, zero longitude. As a result, the entire world sets its clocks in relation to **GMT**.

The red strip in the main courtyard lies along the Greenwich Prime Meridian, and at night a green laser beam shines northwards along the meridian. Of course, the global standard for air and sea navigation is now the **Global Positioning System (GPS)**, which bases its calculations on the centre of the earth, not the surface, and places the meridian approximately 336ft to the east of the red strip.

Meridian route

The oldest part of the observatory is **Flamsteed House**, built by Wren (himself a trained astronomer) "for the observator's habitation and a little for pompe". The northeastern turret sports a bright-red Time Ball that climbs the mast at 12.58pm and drops at 1pm GMT precisely; it was added in 1833 to allow ships on the Thames to set their clocks. On the house's balcony overlooking the Thames, you can take a look at a **Camera Obscura**, of the kind which Flamsteed used to make safe observations of the sun. Inside, beyond the restored apartments in which the cantankerous Flamsteed lived, you eventually reach the impressive **Octagon Room**, built so that the king could show off his astronomical toys to guests. The ceiling plasterwork is all that remains of the original decor, but there are replicas of the precision clocks installed behind the original walnut panelling in 1676.

Beyond, the Time galleries focus on the search for longitude and display the first four marine chronometers built by **John Harrison**. Harrison eventually went on to win the £20,000 **Longitude Prize** in 1763 with his giant pocket watch, H4 – the only one that no longer functions – after much skulduggery

Greenwich

against his claims, most notably by the Astronomer Royal at the time, Nevil Maskelyne (a story wonderfully told by Dava Sobel in her book *Longitude*). Downstairs you can learn about the story of GMT, UTC and even GPS, as well as viewing the electrical contacts that used to provide the hourly six pips for the BBC and listening to three generations of the speaking clock.

Flamsteed carried out more than thirty thousand observations – "nothing can exceed the tediousness and ennui of the life" was his dispirited description of the job – in the Quadrant House, which now forms part of the **Meridian Building**. Edmond Halley, who succeeded Flamsteed as Astronomer Royal, bought more sophisticated quadrants, sextants, spyglasses and telescopes, which are among those displayed in the **Quadrant Room**. With the aid of his eight-foot iron quadrant he charted the comings and goings of the famous comet – though he never lived to see its return. Next door, you'll find **Bradley's Meridian**, used for Ordnance Survey maps since 1801. Finally, you reach a room that's sliced in two by the present-day Greenwich Meridian, fixed by the cross hairs in Airy's "Transit Circle", the astronomical instrument that dominates the room.

Astronomy route

The observatory has a new **Astronomy Centre**, housed in the fanciful, domed terracotta South Building. The hi-tech galleries here give a brief rundown of the Big Bang theory of the universe, allow you to conduct some hands-on experiments to explain concepts such as gravity and spectroscopy, and then invite you to consider the big questions of astronomy today. You can also choose to watch one of the thirty-minute presentations in the state-of-the-art **Planetarium** (daily 11am–4pm; £6), introduced by a Royal Observatory astronomer.

Ranger's House

Southwest of the observatory is the **Ranger's House** (April–Sept Mon–Wed guided tours 11.30am & 2.30pm, Sun 11am–5pm; EH; £5.70; ☎020/8853 0035; Greenwich DLR), a red-brick Georgian villa which looks out over Blackheath (see opposite). Built as a private residence in the early eighteenth century, it became the official residence of the park ranger (hence its name), a sort of top-notch grace-and-favour home. Entrance to the house is either from Croom's Hill, or from the doorway in the wall by the park's Rose Garden.

Pick up an audioguide and head upstairs to find out about **Julius Wernher**, the German-born millionaire Edwardian whose art collection is now displayed in the house. Wernher made his money by exploiting the diamond deposits of South Africa, and at his death in 1912 was one of the world's richest men. His taste in art is eclectic, ranging from medieval ivory miniatures to Iznik pottery, though he was definitely a man who placed technical virtuosity above artistic merit, and who, despite his Lutheran upbringing, amassed a vast array of Catholic bric-a-brac. Highlights on the top floor include Memlinc's *Virgin and Child*, the jewellery cabinet and the pair of sixteenth-century majolica dishes decorated with mythological scenes for Isabella d'Este, wife of the Marchese of Mantua and a great patron of the arts.

Downstairs, there's a sparkling Reynolds portrait of Lady Caroline Price, a top-notch de Hooch interior, and, in the splendid main gallery with its three bow windows and duck-egg-green coffered ceiling, a whole series of seventeenth-century French tapestries depicting life in the court of the Emperor of China. Finally, at the far end of the main gallery is Bergonzoli's striking *Love of Angels*, a highly charged sculpture that, despite weighing two tons, succeeds in appearing light and ethereal.

The Dome

[A] yellow-spiked Teflon tent... a genetically modified mollusc... The Dome is a blob of correction fluid, a flick of Tipp-Ex to revise the mistakes of nineteenth-century industrialists... a poached egg designed by a committee of vegans.

Iain Sinclair, *Sorry Meniscus*

Clearly visible from Greenwich's riverside and park, the **Dome** is the archetypal millennial cock-up. Architecturally, it's eye-catching enough: over half a mile in circumference and 160ft in height, it's the world's largest dome, held up by a dozen, 300ft-tall yellow steel masts. But it's best known for the £800 million that was poured into it, and for the millennium exhibition and show, which was panned by the critics and dismantled after one year.

Entertainment giants AEG have since spent yet more millions turning the Dome into a 23,000-seater events arena, known as the **O2** (Ⓦ www.theo2.co.uk). The venue is set to be the 2012 Olympic venue for gymnastics and basketball (with badminton and rhythmic gynastics in a temporary venue alongside). Meanwhile, the land to the southeast is being transformed into the Millennium Village, a conglomeration of riverside flats, plus the mini-wetlands of the Greenwich Peninsula ecology park (Wed–Sun 10am–5pm).

The easiest way to get to the Dome is to take the tube to **North Greenwich**, as the Dome has its very own Will Alsop-designed tube station (with a bus station by Norman Foster). It's also possible to walk or cycle the mile and a half along the riverside pathway from Greenwich or you can catch a boat to the QEII Pier by the Dome. The Dome itself is fenced off, but you can walk around the outside and admire the odd work of art: Anthony Gormley's very busy *Quantum Cloud* and Richard Wilson's *Slice of Reality*, the bridge of a boat cut away from its mother ship.

Fan Museum

At the bottom of Croom's Hill, the twisting road that runs along the western edge of the park and boasts some of Greenwich's finest seventeenth- and eighteenth-century buildings, you'll find the **Fan Museum** (Tues–Sat 11am–5pm, Sun noon–5pm; £4; Ⓣ020/8305 1441, Ⓦwww.fan-museum.org; Greenwich DLR) at no. 12. It's a fascinating little place (and an extremely beautiful house), revealing the importance of the fan as a social and political document. The permanent exhibition on the ground floor traces the history of the fan and the materials employed, from peacock feathers to straw, while temporary exhibitions on the first floor explore conditions of production, the fan's link with the Empire and changing fashion. Outside in the garden, there's a kitsch, hand-painted orangery.

Blackheath

Immediately south of Greenwich Park lies the well-to-do suburb of **Blackheath** (so-called because of the colour of the soil), whose bleak, windswept heath, crisscrossed with busy roads, couldn't be more different from the royal park. Nonetheless, with its pair of century-old pubs, the *Princess of Wales* and *Hare and Billet*, each set beside a pond, it can be quite pleasant on a summer afternoon. The odd fair takes place here on public holidays, and it's south London's premier kite-flying spot.

Down in Deptford

Deptford, just west of Greenwich, is never going to be high up anyone's list of places to visit in London. However, it does have a rich history thanks to the **Royal Dockyards** which existed here (and at Woolwich) from 1513 until 1869. It was at Deptford in 1581 that Drake moored the *Golden Hinde* (see p.234) after circumnavigating the globe, had Elizabeth I on board for dinner, and was knighted for his efforts. And, of course, it was in Deptford that the playwright **Christopher Marlowe** was murdered (possibly) in the company of three men who had links with the criminal underworld and the Elizabethan intelligence service.

All that remains of the old dockyards today are a few officers' quarters hidden in the Pepys housing estate, and the **Master Shipwright's House** of 1708, at the bottom of Watergate Street – a little downstream, there's even a waterfront statue of Peter the Great (flanked by a dwarf and an empty chair), who came to Deptford in 1798 to learn about shipbuilding. You can get an idea of how prosperous the area once was just off the High Street at **St Paul's Church** (Ⓦpaulsdeptford .org.uk), the local architectural gem, designed by Thomas Archer in 1720, whose interior Pevsner described as "closer to Borromini and the Roman Baroque than any other English church".

Lying on the main road to Dover, Blackheath was a convenient spot on which to pitch camp, as the Danes did in 1011, having kidnapped St Alfege. Their example was followed during the 1381 Peasants' Revolt by Wat Tyler's rebels, who were treated to a rousing revolutionary sermon by John Bull, which included the famous lines "When Adam delved and Eve span, who was then the gentleman?" The victorious Henry V was welcomed back from the Battle of Agincourt here in 1415, while Henry VII fought a pitched battle on this spot against Cornish rebels in 1497. It was at Blackheath, also, that Henry VIII was so disappointed on meeting his fourth wife, Anne of Cleves, in 1540; he famously referred to her as "the Flanders mare" and filed for divorce after just six months.

The heath's chief landmark is **All Saints' Church**, a Victorian church built in rugged Kentish ragstone which nestles in a slight depression in the south corner. The most striking residential development in Blackheath is **The Paragon**, east of the church, a crescent of four-storey Georgian mansions linked by Doric colonnades. An even earlier foundation, set in its own grounds further to the east, is **Morden College**, the aristocrat of almshouses, built in 1695 for "decayed Turkey merchants" who had lost their fortunes. The quadrangular red-brick building, built by Wren's master mason, was designed to reflect the lost status of its original inhabitants.

It's worth venturing down the charmingly named Tranquil Vale into the village-like centre of Blackheath, if only to visit the **Reminiscence Centre** (Mon–Fri 10am–5pm, Sat 10am–4pm; free; ☎020/8318 9105, Ⓦwww .age-exchange.org.uk; Blackheath train station from London Bridge), situated opposite the train station. A favourite with the older folks of Blackheath, the centrepiece is an old-fashioned shop counter, whose drawers are filled with two-pin plugs, wooden clothes pegs, chalk powder and a whole host of everyday objects now rarely seen. Ask for a demonstration of the shop's rare surviving example of a rapid-wire cash system, via which banknotes could be whizzed from cashier to till worker. Out the back, you can get a cuppa from the museum's period tuck shop.

Woolwich

In 1847, a visitor to **Woolwich** commented that it was the "dirtiest, filthiest and most thoroughly mismanaged town of its size in the kingdom". With its docks and factories defunct, Woolwich remains one of the poorest parts of the old Docklands. However, if you have a fascination for military history, it's worth exploring the old dockyards and arsenal, for their architecture and the **Firepower** artillery museum. The other reason to come to Woolwich is to visit the **Thames Barrier**, an awesome piece of modern engineering and the largest movable flood barrier in the world.

Thames Barrier

London has been subject to flooding from surge tides since before 1236, when it was reported that in "the great Palace of Westminster men did row with wherries in the midst of the Hall". A flood barrier was advocated as far back as the 1850s, but it was only after the 1953 flood that serious consideration was given to building tidal flood defences. Opened in 1983, the **Thames Barrier** is a mind-blowing feat of engineering, with its gleaming fins and movable steel gates weighing from 400 to 3700 tons. If you want to find out more, head for the **information centre** (daily: April–Sept 10.30am–4.30pm; Oct–March 11am–3.30pm; £3.50; ☎020/8305 4188), on Unity Way, where glossy models and macho videos help explain the basic mechanism of the barrier (something which is by no means obvious from above the water). If you want to see the barrier in action, phone ahead to find out the date of the monthly test. From the barrier you can walk inland, mostly through parks, to Charlton House (see p.333), just over a mile to the south.

Military Woolwich

Woolwich, like Deptford, owes its existence to the **Royal Dockyards**, which were established here in 1513 by Henry VIII. The men-of-war that established England as a world naval power were built in these dockyards, starting with the *Great Harry*, the largest ship in the world when it was launched from here in 1514, and Walter Ralegh and Captain Cook set out from Woolwich on their voyages of discovery. The docks closed in 1869, and the area is better known for the **Royal Arsenal**, which reached its heyday during World War I, when it stretched for three miles along the Thames, employed nearly 100,000 workers (half of whom were women) and had its own internal railway system. The ordnance factories were closed altogether in 1967, and council housing built over much of the site. However, a fine collection of mostly eighteenth-century buildings survives and has been converted into flats, plus a couple of museums.

Getting to Woolwich

The easiest way to reach Woolwich is by **DLR** from Canning Town tube; you can also take a **train** from London Bridge to Woolwich Dockyard (for the Royal Artillery Barracks) or Woolwich Arsenal (for the Royal Arsenal). During the week, there's a commuter **boat** service to and from Woolwich Arsenal, and at the weekend a more regular service; there are also boat trips that cruise round the barrier (see ⓦwww.tfl.gov.uk for details).

Royal Arsenal

Close to Woolwich Arsenal DLR station, on the market square is **Beresford Gateway**, built in 1828 as the Arsenal's main entrance, but now separated from the rest of the complex to the north by busy Beresford Street/Plumstead Road. Across the road, you enter **Dial Square**, overlooked by some of the Arsenal's most historic buildings, built by the likes of Vanbrugh, Wren and Hawksmoor: the Main Guard House, with its eighteenth-century Doric portico; Verbruggen's House, opposite, begun in 1772, and former residence of the Master Founder; and the Royal Brass Foundry, made of wood, but encased in brick, from 1717. To the north, the **Dial Arch Block** is distinguished by its central archway, which sports a sundial, pillars and a pile of cannonballs. A football on a plinth commemorates the fact that it was here in 1886 that a group of machinists formed Dial Square Football Club, later Woolwich Arsenal FC, and then just **Arsenal FC**, eventually moving to Highbury in north London. The team used to get changed in the toilets of the *Royal Oak* (now the *Pullman*), 27 Woolwich New Rd, right by Woolwich Arsenal train station.

If you head down Number One Street, towards the river, you'll come to the former bomb factory which now houses **Firepower** (April–Oct Wed–Sun 10.30am–5pm; Nov–March Fri–Sun 10.30am–5pm; £5; ℡020/8855 7755, Ⓦwww.firepower.org.uk), the Royal Artillery museum. To enjoy the museum, you do have to be seriously into **guns** – lots of them. Inevitably, there's a propaganda video on today's Royal Artillery, plus a twenty-minute multimedia show, *Field of Fire*, concentrating on the chief conflicts of the twentieth century. The main Gunnery Hall features ancient World War I field guns, old and new howitzers, anti-tank guns, Thunderbird guided-missile launchers and Rapier surface-to-air missiles used in the Gulf War, and allows you to play various war games, fire simulator guns and watch lots of wartime film clips. Upstairs, the History Gallery takes you through the history of artillery and rocket science, features the gun carriage used in the funeral cortège for Georges V and VI, and includes the Medals Gallery. Finally, at the **Camo Zone** (£1.50), you can have a go at the bungee run, test your marksmanship on the firing range and take part in a tank battle.

On the opposite side of the street is the distinctive eighteenth-century brown-brick building that served as the Royal Military Academy, from 1741 until 1806, when new barracks were built (see below). Next door, there's a small permanent exhibition on the history of the Arsenal in the **Greenwich Heritage Centre** (Tues–Sat 9am–5pm; free; ℡020/8854 2452, Ⓦwww.greenwichheritage.org).

Royal Artillery Barracks and around

Britain's first two artillery regiments were founded at the Arsenal in 1716, and are now housed half a mile to the south in the **Royal Artillery Barracks**, built in 1802 by James Wyatt. Its three-storey Georgian facade, interrupted by stucco pavilions and a central triumphal arch, runs for an amazing 1080ft, making it one of the longest in Europe. Appropriately enough, the barracks will host the shooting during the 2012 Olympics.

The barracks face south onto the grassy parade ground, to the east of which lies the abandoned **Garrison Church of St George**, built in neo-Romanesque style in 1863. Gutted in the last war, it's now an attractive husk, with fragments of its colourful interior decor still surviving. Further south still, on the other side of Woolwich Common, is Wyatt's former **Royal Military Academy**, built in 1806 in an imposing mock-Tudor style as a foil to the Royal Artillery Barracks. The 720-foot facade faces north onto a parade ground, with an imitation of the

Tower of London's White Tower as its centrepiece. The academy, known as "The Shop" in the British Army – because its first building was a converted workshop in the Arsenal – closed in 1939, and merged with Sandhurst after the war.

To the west of the Royal Artillery Barracks, off Repository Road, stands John Nash's bizarre Chinese-style **Rotunda** (closed to the public). Originally used as a marquee in the gardens of Carlton House during the celebrations at the end of the Napoleonic Wars, it was damaged by a gas explosion, repaired and re-erected on its present site.

Charlton to Bexleyheath and beyond

This final section is a real miscellany of sights, spread between **Charlton** and **Bexleyheath** and beyond, across considerable tracts of suburbia and country-side. Using the suburban railway system, your top targets are the Tudor **Eltham Palace**, William Morris's **Red House**, and Charles Darwin's home, **Down House**.

Charlton House

A little to the west of Woolwich, on Charlton Road, stands **Charlton House** (Mon–Fri 9am–9pm; free; Charlton train station from Victoria, Charing Cross or London Bridge) a splendid Jacobean mansion completed in 1612 as a "nest for his old age" by Adam Newton, tutor to the eldest son of James I, Prince Henry, who died in the same year. The house is owned by the local council, which means you need to call ☎020/8856 3951 to arrange a visit (in case there are any events taking place). Among the best surviving features inside is the wonderful oak staircase, to the left of the Great Hall, which boasts beauti-fully carved bulb- and plant-shaped newels and grotesque faces on the balusters. Off the wood-panelled Long Gallery on the top floor, with its strapwork ceiling, is the White Room, which harbours the finest of the house's period fireplaces, adorned with a relief of Perseus and several biblical scenes. The best of the strapwork ceilings, however, is to be found in the Grand Salon, featuring lovely pendants.

Eltham Palace

A mile or so west of Avery Hill Park lies **Eltham Palace** (Sun–Wed: April–Oct 10am–5pm; Nov to mid-Dec, Feb & March 10am–4pm; EH; £8.30, gardens only £5.30; ☎020/8294 2548, ⓦwww.elthampalace.org.uk; Eltham train station from Victoria, London Bridge or Charing Cross), one of the country's foremost medieval royal residences and even a venue for Parliament for some two hundred years from the reign of Edward II. All that remains now is the fifteenth-century bridge across what used to be the moat, and the **Great Hall**, built by Edward IV in 1479, with a fine hammerbeam roof hung with pendants, and two fan-vaulted stone oriels at the far end. The hall's two original fireplaces are now in Eltham's pubs; the best one, with its sixteenth-century Chinese tiles intact, can be seen in *The Greyhound* on the High Street.

Somewhat incredibly, in the 1930s, the millionaire Stephen Courtauld (of art-collecting fame) got permission to build his own "Wrenaissance"-style **house** onto the Great Hall, and convert the moat into landscaped gardens.

Courtauld lavished a fortune on the place, creating a sort of movie star's party palace for his glamorous half-Italian, half-Hungarian wife, Virginia (who sported a risqué tattoo of a snake above one ankle). The house was designed by Seely and Paget, furnished by the best Swedish and Italian designers, and kitted out with all the latest mod cons, including underfloor heating, a centralized vacuum cleaner, a tannoy system and ten en-suite bedrooms. Then, shortly before the end of the war, the family left for Rhodesia, taking most of the house's furniture with them.

The house and gardens have since been handsomely restored and the lost furnishings replaced. Inside, there are acres of exotic veneer, an onyx and gold-plated bathroom, and lots of quirky little Art Deco touches – check out the Alice in Wonderland relief above the door in the circular entrance hall, which is flooded with light from a spectacular glazed dome. The audiotours fill visitors in on the family's various eccentricities, which included keeping a pet ring-tailed lemur called Mah-Jongg, which had its own centrally heated bedroom approached by a bamboo ladder and was notorious for biting disliked male visitors.

Bexleyheath

Bexleyheath, three miles east of Eltham, is a pretty nondescript suburb, but it has three significant architectural attractions from the days when it was still mostly heath. The most impressive is **Danson House** (Easter–Oct Wed, Thurs & Sun 11am–5pm; £5; ☏020/8303 6699, ⓦwww.dansonhouse.com; Bexleyheath train station from Victoria, Charing Cross or London Bridge), a modest little Palladian villa, built in the 1760s as a country retreat for John Boyd, who'd made a fortune from the slave trade, and had a new 19-year-old bride to impress. The highlights of the *piano nobile* are the paintings telling the love story of Vertumnus and Pomona in the Dining Room, the Chinoiserie wallpaper in the octagonal Salon, and the built-in organ in the library, which is still used for recitals. It's also worth climbing up to inspect the trompe-l'oeil paintings of Jupiter's thunderbolts in the oval dome. There's a **tearoom** on the ground floor and a **restaurant-pub** in the old stables at the eastern edge of the park.

A short walk east of Danson House lies the **Red House** (March–Dec Wed–Sun 11am–4.45pm; NT; £6.90, garden only 50p; ☏020/8304 9878; Bexleyheath train station), a wonderful red-brick country house designed by Philip Webb in 1859 for his friend **William Morris**, following Morris's marriage to Pre-Raphaelite heart-throb Jane Burden. The mock-medieval exterior features pointed brick arches, steep gables, an oriel window and even a turreted well in the garden, and the whole enterprise stands as the embodiment of the Arts and Crafts movement. Sadly, after just five years, with "Janey" conducting an affair with Dante Gabriel Rossetti, the couple were forced to leave their dream home due to financial difficulties and move to Kelmscott in Oxfordshire. It has to be said the interior is a bit gloomy, half-finished even in Morris's time, still in need of much restoration and not at all cosy, with only a few of the larger interior furnishings still in place. Visits before 2pm are by pre-booked guided tour only. The tours are interesting, however, thanks to the various anecdotes about Morris and his entourage, about how they used to eat in the hallway, indulge in apple fights and wear medieval clothes at the weekend.

Finally, for those with the energy, there's an interesting Tudor mansion called **Hall Place** (Mon–Sat 10am–4.45pm, Sun 11am–4.45pm; Nov–March closes

4.15pm; free; ☎01322/526574, ⓦwww.hallplace.com; Bexley train station), right by the A2, about a mile east of the Red House. It's a mishmash of a place, but the Tudor half sports a wonderful chequerboard flintwork exterior and gardens full of top-class topiary, including an entire set of the Queen's Beasts wrought in yew. The house has a municipal feel (it's used by the local council), but there's an introductory gallery on the ground floor which gives you the background to the place. Downstairs, the wood-panelled Great Hall survives with its coved ceiling and carved bosses; upstairs, head for the principal bedroom which boasts an ornate Jacobean plasterwork ceiling featuring grotesques.

Down House

Down House (April–June, Sept & Oct Wed–Sun 11am–5pm; July & Aug daily 11am–5pm; March, Nov & Dec Wed–Sun 11am–4pm; EH; £8.80; ☎01689/859119; bus #146 from Bromley North or Bromley South train station), home of the scientist Charles Darwin, is situated eight miles south of Eltham in the village of Downe, overlooking the southeastern suburbs of London. Born in Shrewsbury in 1809, Darwin showed little academic promise at Cambridge. It was only after returning from his five-year tour of South America aboard HMS *Beagle* – in which he stopped off at the Galapagos Islands – that he began work on the theory he would eventually publish in 1859 as *On the Origin of Species*. Darwin moved to Down House in 1842, shortly after his marriage to his cousin Emma Wedgwood, who nursed the valetudinarian scientist here until his death forty years later. The house itself is set in lovely grounds, and is stuffed with Darwin memorabilia, though there's no sign (or smell) of the barnacles which Darwin spent eight years dissecting – he later moved on to the study of orchids (to the relief, no doubt, of his wife and children), several examples of which you can find in the glasshouse.

Out West: Hammersmith to Hampton Court

H ammersmith to **Hampton Court** – a distance of some seven miles overland (more by the river) – takes you from the traffic-clogged western suburbs of London to the touristed royal outpost of **Hampton Court**. In between, London seems to continue unabated, with only fleeting glimpses of the countryside, in particular the fabulous **Kew Gardens** and the two old royal hunting parks, **Richmond** and **Bushy Park** – though, as one nineteenth-century visitor observed, they are "no more like the real untrimmed genuine country than a garden is like a field". Running through the chapter, and linking many of the places described, is the **River Thames**, once known as the "Great Highway of London" and still the most pleasant way to travel in these parts during the summer.

Aside from the river and the parks, the chief attractions are the royal palaces and lordly mansions that pepper the riverbanks: textbook Palladian style at **Chiswick House**, unspoilt Jacobean splendour at **Ham House**, and Tudor and Baroque excess (and the famous maze) at **Hampton Court**. We kick off this chapter at **Hammersmith** – London's gateway to the west, by road or tube – which, with neighbouring **Chiswick**, and **Kew**, **Richmond** and **Twickenham** beyond, has the additional appeal of its riverside walks and pubs.

Hammersmith to Osterley

Most people experience the five-mile stretch of west London between **Hammersmith and Osterley** en route to or from Heathrow airport, either from the above confines of the train or tube (which runs overground at this point) or from the M4, which was driven through areas of parkland in the 1960s. The sights here – former country retreats now surrounded by suburbia – receive nothing like the number of visitors of Kew and Richmond, on the south bank of the Thames.

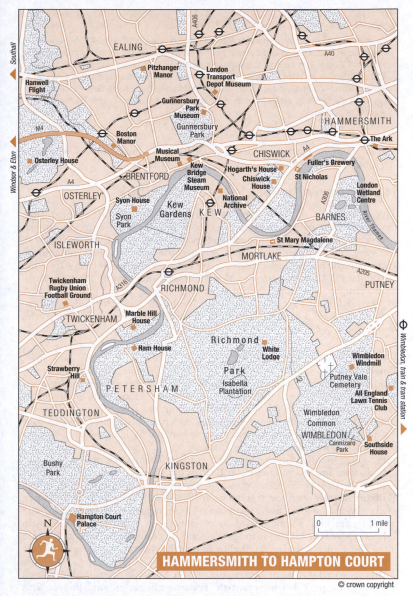

© crown copyright

HAMMERSMITH TO HAMPTON COURT

The Palladian villa of **Chiswick House** is the best known of these attractions, but you'll never see a crowd here and, though nearby Syon Park draws in the locals, most come for the garden centre rather than for the splendid **Syon House**, a showcase for the talents of Robert Adam and Capability Brown. There's more of Adam's work at **Osterley House**, another Elizabethan conversion, while **Pitzhanger Manor** is a must for fans of John Soane's architecture. Another attraction in these parts is the remarkable **Wetland Centre**, a

---

River transport

From April to October **Westminster Passenger Services** (☎020/7930 2062, ⓦwww
.wpsa.co.uk) run a scheduled service from Westminster Pier to Kew, Richmond and
Hampton Court. The full trip takes three hours one-way, and costs £13.50 single,
£19.50 return. In addition, Turks (☎020/8546 2434, ⓦwww.turks.co.uk) runs a regular
service from Richmond to Hampton Court (April to mid-Sept Tues–Sun) which costs
£6.70 single or £8.20 return. For the latest on boat services on the Thames, see
ⓦwww.tfl.gov.uk.

---

purpose-built landscaped haven for water birds and rare wildfowl, across the
river from Hammersmith in the sleepy suburb of Barnes.

Hammersmith Bridge to Chiswick Mall

This chapter starts in the hellhole of **Hammersmith**, for one simple reason:
the nearby tube station gives easy access to the Wetland Centre and to the
riverside walk to Chiswick. The riverside walk begins a short way southwest of
the tube, down Queen Caroline Street. First off, you pass underneath
Hammersmith Bridge, a graceful green and gold suspension bridge from the
1880s that the IRA have tried to blow up three times: first in 1939, as part of
their attempt to disrupt the British war effort, secondly by the Provisional IRA
in 1996, and finally four years later by the Real IRA. From the bridge, you can
walk all the way to Chiswick along the most picturesque stretch of riverbank
in the whole of London, much of it closed to traffic.

Lower Mall and Upper Mall

Lower Mall, the section just west of the bridge, is a mixture of Victorian pubs,
boathouses, Regency verandas and modern flats. An interesting array of boats
huddles around the marina outside the *Dove*, an atmospheric seventeenth-
century riverside pub (see p.407). This started out as a coffee house and has the
smallest back bar in the country, copious literary associations – regulars have
included Graham Greene, Ernest Hemingway and William Morris – and a
canopied balcony overlooking the Thames.

It's strange to think that this genteel part of the Thames was once a hotbed of
radicals, who used to congregate at **Kelmscott House** (Thurs & Sat 2–5pm;
free; ☎020/8741 3735, ⓦwww.morrissociety.org), at 26 Upper Mall, where
William Morris lived and worked from 1878 until his death in 1896. (Morris
used to berate the locals from a soapbox on Hammersmith Bridge.) From 1885
onwards, the local socialists used to meet here on a Sunday evening, with
Labour leader Keir Hardie, anarchist Prince Kropotkin, writer George Bernard
Shaw and Fabian founders the Webbs among the speakers – their photos now
line the walls.

Another socialist mate of Morris, the printer Emery Walker, lived just down
the riverbank at **7 Hammersmith Terrace** (Easter to mid-July & Sept
Thurs & Fri pre-booked guided tours only; £10; ☎020/8741 4104, ⓦwww
.emerywalker.org.uk), one of a line of tall Georgian houses built facing the
river sometime before 1755. The house has a well-preserved Arts and Crafts
interior and contains lots of Morris memorabilia as well as furniture by
Philip Webb, architect of Morris's Red House in Bexleyheath (see p.334) –
tours are very popular so book ahead online.

Chiswick Mall

Chiswick Mall continues for another mile or so along the river to the village of Chiswick. A riotous ensemble of seventeenth- and eighteenth-century mansions lines the north side of the Mall, which cuts them off from their modest riverside gardens. Halfway along, a particularly fine trio ends with **Walpole House**, once the home of Barbara Villiers, Duchess of Cleveland, Countess of Castlemaine and one of Charles II's many mistresses.

Chiswick Mall terminates at the church of **St Nicholas**, which retains its original fifteenth-century ragstone tower. The church lay at the heart of the riverside village of **Chiswick** from medieval times until the Victorian period, when the action moved north to Chiswick High Street, its modern heart. Lord Burlington and his architect friends William Kent and Colen Campbell are all buried in the graveyard, as is the aforementioned Barbara Villiers, though only the painters William Hogarth and James Whistler are commemorated by gravestones, the former enclosed by wrought-iron railings.

Nearby Church Lane was the medieval village high street. Its oldest building today is the Old Burlington, originally a sixteenth-century inn, now a private residence. Beyond lies **Fuller's Griffin Brewery**, dating back to the seventeenth century and still going strong. You can book yourself onto a ninety-minute guided tour (Mon–Fri 11am–3pm; £10; ☎020/8996 2063, ⓦwww.fullers.co.uk), which includes the inevitable tasting session, and also gives visitors the chance to see the country's oldest wisteria, which has clung to the brickwork for over 180 years.

Chiswick House and around

Chiswick House (April–Oct Mon–Wed & Sun 10am–5pm, Sat 10am–2pm; EH; £4.40; ☎020/8995 0508; Chiswick train station from Waterloo) is a

---

London Wetland Centre

For anyone even remotely interested in wildlife, the **London Wetland Centre** (daily: April–Oct 9.30am–6pm; July & Aug Thurs until 9pm; Nov–March 9.30am–5pm; £9.50; ☎020/8409 4400, ⓦwww.wwt.org.uk) in well-to-do Barnes is an absolute must. Lying on the site of four disused reservoirs, the Wildfowl & Wetlands Trust (WWT) has created a mosaic of wetland habitats. The easiest way to get here is to catch bus #283, the special "Duck Bus" from stand K at Hammersmith tube. On arrival – unless it's raining – skip the introductory audiovisual in the theatre, and head straight out to the ponds. If the weather's bad, head for the **Discovery Centre**, where kids can take part in a swan identification parade, or take a duck's-eye view of the world. You can also look out over the wetlands from the glass-walled **Bird Airport Observatory** next door, or from the tables of the *Water's Edge Café*.

The centre basically serves a dual function: to attract native species of bird to its watery lagoons, and to assist in the WWT's programme of breeding rare wildfowl in captivity. The **World Wetlands** area harbours a variety of extremely rare wildfowl – from White-faced Whistling Ducks to the highly endangered Blue Duck – whose wetland habitats have been re-created in miniature (3pm is feeding time). In the **Wildside** are the reedbeds and pools that attract native species, such as lapwing, tufted ducks, grebes and, if you're lucky, even the odd wintering bittern, all of which you can view from a moss-roofed hide. The **Waterlife** section includes a sustainable garden, a chance for younger children to get near some domesticated wildfowl and, best of all, do some pond-dipping. At the far end is the mother of all hides: a triple-decker octagonal one with a lift, allowing views over the whole of the reserve. There are also free guided tours daily at 11am and 2pm.

perfectly proportioned classical villa, designed by Richard Boyle, third Earl of Burlington, in the 1720s, as an extension of his Jacobean mansion, and set in a beautifully landscaped garden. Like its prototype, Palladio's Villa Capra near Vicenza, the house was purpose-built as a "temple to the arts" – an extension to Burlington's adjacent Jacobean mansion (which was torn down in 1788). Here, amid his fine art collection, Burlington used to entertain such friends as Swift, Handel and Pope, who lived in nearby Twickenham.

Guests and visitors (who could view the property on payment of an admission fee even in Lord Burlington's day) would originally have ascended the quadruple staircase and entered the *piano nobile* through the magnificent Corinthian portico. The public entrance today is via the **lower floor**, where the earl had his own private rooms and kept his extensive library. Here, you can pick up an audioguide, watch a short video, and peruse an exhibition on the history of the house and grounds.

Entertaining took place on the **upper floor**, a series of cleverly interconnecting rooms, each enjoying a wonderful view out onto the gardens – all, that is, except the Tribunal, the domed octagonal hall at the centre of the villa, where the house's finest paintings and sculptures are displayed, just as they would have been in Burlington's day. The other rooms retain much of their rich decor, in particular the ceilings, designed by William Kent. The most sumptuous is the Blue Velvet Room, decorated in a deep Prussian blue, with eight pairs of heavy gilded brackets holding up the ceiling.

The gardens

Like the villa, the house's extensive **gardens** (daily 8am–dusk; free) were influenced by descriptions of the gardens of classical Rome and, in their turn, became the inspiration for the English landscape garden. You can admire the northwest side of the house from the stone benches of the exedra, a set of yew-hedge niches harbouring lions and copies of Roman statuary, and overlooking a smooth carpet of grass, punctuated by urns and sphinxes, that sit under the shadow of two giant cedars of Lebanon. Other highlights include England's first **mock ruin** – the Kent-designed cascade – and the network of narrow yew-hedge avenues, each one ending at some diminutive building or statue. One of the most remarkable focal points is the grassy **amphitheatre**, by the side of the lake, centred on an obelisk in a pond and overlooked by an Ionic temple. To the north of the villa, beside a section of the gardens' old ha-ha, stands a grand stone gateway designed by Inigo Jones. Beyond lies a large conservatory, built to grow peaches, grapes and pineapples and now stuffed with camellias. It looks out onto the formal **Italian Garden**, laid out in the early nineteenth century by the sixth Duke of Devonshire, who also established a zoo (now gone) featuring an elephant, giraffe, elks and emus.

Hogarth's House

If you leave Chiswick House gardens by the northernmost exit, beyond the conservatory, it's a short walk (to the right) along the thunderous A4 road to **Hogarth's House** (April–Oct Tues–Fri 1–5pm, Sat & Sun 1–6pm, Nov–March closes one hour earlier; closed Jan; free; ☎020/8994 6757), where the artist spent each summer with his wife, sister and mother-in-law from 1749 until his death in 1764. Nowadays it's difficult to believe Hogarth came here for "peace and quiet", but in the eighteenth century the house was almost entirely surrounded by countryside. After Chiswick House, whose pretentious Palladianism and excess epitomized everything Hogarth loathed the most, the domesticity here comes as some relief. Among the scores of Hogarth's engravings, you can see copies of his satirical series – *An Election, Marriage à la Mode, A Rake's Progress* and *A Harlot's Progress* – and compare the modern view from the parlour with the more idyllic scene in *Mr Ranby's House*.

Gunnersbury Park and around

An even earlier Palladian villa, built by Inigo Jones's son-in-law, John Webb, once stood in **Gunnersbury Park**, a mile or so to the northwest of Chiswick House. Today, the park has been largely given over to sports pitches, but overlooking the boating pond, there's a Neoclassical temple erected by George II's daughter Amelia, who used to own the aforementioned villa. The temple was later used as a private synagogue by the Rothschilds, who bought up the estate in the nineteenth century. The park's large mansion, built shortly after the villa was pulled down in 1802, now houses the **Gunnersbury Park Museum** (daily: April–Oct 11am–5pm; Nov–March 11am–4pm; free; ☏020/8992 1612; Acton Town tube), with interesting temporary exhibitions on the local boroughs of Ealing and Hounslow, a fully restored set of Victorian kitchens, and a permanent collection of historical vehicles, including a tandem tricycle and the Rothschilds' own Victorian "chariot".

Ealing has a large Polish community and **Kensington Cemetery**, which adjoins the park's southeast corner, contains a black marble obelisk erected in 1976 to the 14,500 Polish POWs who went missing in 1940, when the Nazi–Soviet Pact carved up Poland. A mass grave containing 4500 was later discovered by the advancing Nazis at Katyn, near Smolensk, but responsibility for the massacre was denied by the Russians until fifty years later, as a new plaque bitterly records. Fifty yards to the south is the grave of General Komorowski, leader of the Polish Home Army during the ill-fated 1944 Warsaw Uprising, who lived in exile in Britain until his death in 1966. Also buried here is the film director Carol Reed, best known for *The Third Man*. There's no direct access to the graveyard from the park; the main entrance is a quarter of a mile further south down Gunnersbury Avenue.

Kew Bridge Steam Museum

Difficult to miss thanks to its stylish, tapered, Italianate standpipe tower, **Kew Bridge Steam Museum** (Tues–Sun 11am–5pm; £9.50; ☏020/8568 4757, ⓦwww.kbsm.org; bus #237 or #267 from Gunnersbury tube or Kew Bridge train station from Waterloo) occupies an old pumping station, 100yd west of Kew Bridge. At the heart of the museum is the Steam Hall, which contains a green triple-expansion steam engine, similar to the one used by the *Titanic*, and four gigantic nineteenth-century Cornish beam engines, while two adjoining rooms house the pumping station's original beam engines, including the world's largest.

The steam engines may be things of great beauty, but they are primarily of interest to enthusiasts. Not so the museum's wonderfully imaginative and educational Water for Life Gallery, situated in the basement and overlooked by a vast bank of ancient boilers, baths, sinks, taps and kettles. The exhibition tells the history of the capital's water supply: the section on rats and cockroaches goes down particularly well with kids, while the tales of the Victorian "toshers", who had to work the sewers in gangs of three to protect themselves from rat attacks, will make adults' stomachs turn. The best time to visit is at weekends, when each of the museum's industrial dinosaurs is put through its paces, and a narrow-gauge **steam railway** runs back and forth round the yard (April–Oct Sun).

Musical Museum

Just west of the Steam Museum is the superb **Musical Museum** (Tues–Sun 11am–5.30pm; ☎020/8560 8108, ⓦ www.musicalmuseum.co.uk; £7; bus #237 or #267 from Gunnersbury tube or Kew Bridge train station from Waterloo), packed with the world's largest collection of self-playing instruments. The best time to visit is on the weekend (or else phone ahead) when the enthusiastic staff will give noisy demonstrations of all the mechanical music-making machines from cleverly crafted music boxes, through badly tuned barrel organs, to the huge orchestrions that were once a feature of London cafés. The museum also boasts one of the world's finest collections of player-pianos, which can reproduce live performances of the great pianists. In addition, regular concerts are performed on the museum's enormous Art Deco Wurlitzer, which once graced the Regal cinema in Kingston upon Thames.

Syon Park

Syon Park, directly across the Thames from Kew Gardens, is one of the few aristocratic estates left intact in London, with a fantastically lavish stately home at its heart. It has been in the hands of the Percy family since Elizabethan times, although these days it's more of a working commercial concern than a family retreat. It started out as one of the richest monasteries in the country, established by Henry V after the Battle of Agincourt. Dissolved by Henry VIII, who incarcerated his fifth wife, Catherine Howard, here shortly before her execution in 1542, it was eventually granted to the Percys, earls (and later dukes) of Northumberland. To get here, take bus #237 or #267 to Brent Lea bus stop from Gunnersbury tube and train station or Kew Bridge train station, or else it's a fifteen-minute walk from Syon Lane train station.

Syon House

From its rather plain castellated exterior, you'd never guess that **Syon House** (Easter–Oct Wed, Thurs & Sun 11am–5pm; £9; ☎020/8560 0881, ⓦ www .syonpark.co.uk) contains the most opulent eighteenth-century interiors in London. The splendour of Robert Adam's refurbishment is immediately revealed, however, in the pristine **Great Hall**, where you can pick up the excellent audioguide. An apsed double cube with a screen of Doric columns at one end and classical statuary dotted around the edges, the hall has a chequered marble floor that cleverly mirrors the pattern of the coffered ceiling. It was in the hall's Tudor predecessor that Henry VIII's body lay in state en route to Windsor, and was discovered the next morning surrounded by a pack of hounds happily lapping the blood seeping from the coffin.

From the austerity of the Great Hall you enter the lavishly decorated **Ante Room**, with its florid scagliola floor (made from a mixture of marble-dust and resin) and its green-grey Ionic columns topped by brightly gilded classical statues. Here, guests could mingle before entering the **State Dining Room**, a compromise between the two preceding rooms, richly gilded with a double apse but otherwise calm in its overall effect. The remaining rooms are warmer and softer in tone, betraying their Elizabethan origins much more than the preceding ones. The **Red Drawing Room** retains its original red-silk wall hangings from Spitalfields, upon which are hung portraits of the Stuarts by Lely, Van Dyck and others, and features a splendid ceiling studded with over two hundred roundels set within gilded hexagons. Looking out to the Thames, the **Long Gallery** – 136ft by just 14ft – stretches the entire width of the house, decorated by Adam's busy pink and gold plasterwork and lined with 62 individually painted pilasters. It was in the Long Gallery that Lady Jane Grey was formally offered the crown by her father-in-law, John Dudley, the owner of Syon at the time; nine days later they were arrested and eventually beheaded.

The rest of the house pales in comparison with the first five rooms. However, there are still one or two highlights to look out for: more works by Lely and Van Dyck, as well as Gainsborough and Reynolds in the **Print Room**; a superb Adam fireplace and ornate fan-patterned ceiling, plus portraits by Holbein and Reynolds, in the **Green Drawing Room** – still used by the family; and a monster golden Sèvres vase at the foot of the modest principal **staircase**. Upstairs, past the delicate thousand-piece Sèvres dinner service, there are several plush bedrooms, including two refurbished in 1832 for the future Queen Victoria and her mother, the Duchess of Kent, with magnificent canopied beds, blue silk outside and yellow within.

The gardens

While Adam beautified Syon House, Capability Brown laid out its **gardens** (daily: March–Oct 10.30am–5pm or dusk; Nov–Feb 10.30am–4pm; £4.50; free with ticket to the house) around an artificial lake, surrounding it with oaks, beeches, limes and cedars. Since then, the gardens have been further enhanced by still more exotic trees, ranging from an Indian bean tree to a pagoda tree. Beside the lake, there's a stretch of lawn overlooked by a Doric column topped by a fibreglass statue of Flora, but the gardens' real highlight is the crescent-shaped **Great Conservatory**, an early nineteenth-century addition which is said to have inspired Joseph Paxton, architect of the Crystal Palace.

Osterley Park

Robert Adam redesigned another colossal Elizabethan mansion three miles northwest of Syon at **Osterley Park** (daily 8am–6pm; free) – one of London's largest surviving estate parks, which still gives the impression of being in the middle of the countryside, despite the M4 motorway to the north of the house. The main approach is along a splendid avenue of sweet chestnuts to the south, past the National Trust-sponsored **farmhouse** (whose produce you can buy all year round). The driveway curves past the southernmost of the park's three lakes, with a Chinese pagoda at one end. Cedars planted in the 1820s and oaks planted in Victorian times stand between the lake and the house, and to the north are the grandiose Tudor stables of first owner Thomas Gresham, now converted into a **café**.

Osterley House

Unlike Syon, **Osterley House** (March–Oct Wed–Sun 1–4.30pm; Dec Sat & Sun 12.30–3.30pm; NT; £8.40; ☎020/8232 5050; Osterley tube) was built with mercantile rather than aristocratic wealth: it was erected in 1576 by Thomas Gresham, the brains behind the City's Royal Exchange. Later it was bought by another City gent, the goldsmith and banker Francis Child, who used it merely as a kind of giant safe-deposit box – it was his grandsons who employed Robert Adam to create the house as it is today.

From the outside, Osterley bears some similarity to Syon, the big difference being the grand entrance portico, with a broad flight of steps rising to a tall, Ionic colonnade, which gives access to the central courtyard. From here, you enter Adam's characteristically cool **Entrance Hall**, a double-apsed space decorated with grisaille paintings and classical statuary. The finest rooms are the State Rooms of the south wing, where the *nouveaux riches* Childs hoped, in vain, to entertain royalty as Gresham had once done. The **Drawing Room** is splendid, with Reynolds portraits on the damask walls and a coffered ceiling centred on a giant marigold, a theme continued in the lush carpet and elsewhere in the house. The **Tapestry Room** is hung with Boucher-designed Gobelins tapestries, while the silk-lined **State Bedchamber** features an outrageous domed bed designed by Adam. Lastly, there's the **Etruscan Dressing Room**, in which every surface is covered in delicate painted trelliswork, sphinxes and urns, dubbed "Etruscan" by Adam (and Wedgwood), though it is in fact derived from Greek vases found at Pompeii.

The **Long Gallery** is much broader, taller and plainer than the one at Syon and, like much of the house, features Adam-designed furniture, as well as some fine Chinoiserie. Sadly, the Childs' Rubens, Van Dyck and Claude pictures no longer hang here, having been transported to the family's home in the Channel Islands (where they were destroyed by fire), and replaced instead by B-list works from the V&A. In the north wing, the whitewashed Library is worth a quick peek as is the Neoclassical **Great Staircase**, with its replica Rubens ceiling painting.

Boston Manor and Pitzhanger Manor

Two other country houses worth mentioning are dotted across the suburbs of west London. The first is the Jacobean **Boston Manor House** (April–Oct Sat & Sun 2.30–5pm; free; ☎0845/456 2800; Boston Manor tube), originally built by a wealthy widow who married into the Spencer family. It was bought by James Clitherow, a City merchant, in 1670 and remained in the family until taken over by the local council in the 1920s. With magnificent cedar trees and ornamental flowerbeds, the grounds (daily dawn–dusk) are well worth a visit, despite the presence of the M4. The highlight of the house is the Drawing Room on the first floor, which retains a sumptuous mantelpiece and an extraordinarily elaborate, original Jacobean plaster ceiling. In an unusual break with protocol, William IV and Queen Adelaide paid a visit to the Clitherows (mere commoners), and dined in the Dining Room, which also boasts a fine plaster ceiling, in 1834.

A couple of miles north of Boston Manor is Pitzhanger Manor, now known as the **PM Gallery & House** (Tues–Fri & Sun 1–5pm, Sat 11am–5pm; free; ☎020/8567 1227; Ealing Broadway tube). Designed in 1770 by George Dance, but later bought and extensively remodelled by John Soane, Pitzhanger is well worth a visit. The balustraded main facade, though small, is magnificent, its bays divided by Ionic pillars topped by terracotta statues. As soon as you enter the narrow vestibule, Soane stops you short with some spatial gymnastics by taking a section of the ceiling up through the first floor. To the right is the now book-less Library, which features a cross-vaulted ceiling, decorated with an unusual trelliswork pattern. Soane's masterpiece, though, is the **Breakfast Room**, with caryatids in the four corners and lush red porphyry and grey marbling on the walls.

An unexpected bonus is the house's **Martinware Gallery**, a display of the idiosyncratic stoneware pottery produced around 1900 by the four Martin brothers from the nearby Southall Pottery. Its centrepiece is their Moorish ceramic fireplace; the rest of the ware, including face mugs and bird jars, is more of an acquired taste. The manor's south wing is all that survives from the original house by George Dance (Soane's architectural teacher), the remainder of which Soane demolished. The rooms here are on a much larger scale, providing an interesting contrast to Soane's intimate and highly wrought style, while the Monk's Dining Room in the basement is the precursor of Soane's Monk's Parlour in Lincoln's Inn Fields.

Kew Gardens and around

Kew's **Royal Botanic Gardens** (daily 9.30am–6.30pm or dusk; £13; ☎020/8332 5000, ⓦwww.kew.org; Kew Gardens tube) manage the extremely difficult task of being both a world leader in botanic research and an extraordinarily beautiful and popular public park at the same time. Kew began life in the eighteenth century as the pleasure gardens of two royal estates, but it was Princess Augusta, the widow of Prince Frederick, eldest son of George II, who turned Kew into a first botanic gardens in the 1750s, with the help of her paramour, the Earl of Bute. Some of the earliest specimens were brought back from the voyages of Captain Cook, instantly establishing Kew as a leading botanical research centre. From its original eight acres Kew has grown into a 300-acre site in which more than 33,000 species are grown in plantations and glasshouses, a display that attracts nearly two million visitors annually, most of them with no specialist interest at all.

The glasshouses

The main shop and visitor centre are at the **Victoria Gate**, as is the distinctive **campanile**, which originally served as the chimney for the furnaces below the glassshouses. Beyond lies the Pond, home to two ten-ton Ming lions, and the best vantage point from which to appreciate Kew's magnificent **Palm House**. This distinctive, curvaceous mound of glass and wrought iron, designed by Decimus Burton in the 1840s, nurtures most of the known palm species in its drippingly humid atmosphere, while in the basement there's a small, but excellent, tropical aquarium. From the Palm House, head north to the diminutive **Waterlily House**, where a canopy of plants and creepers overhangs a circular pond boasting spectacular, giant water lilies.

Further north still, is the rather less graceful **Princess of Wales Conservatory**, opened in 1987. However, the cacti collection here is awesome, as are the giant koi fish that swim stealthily beneath the pathways – look out, too, for the bizarre plants in the insectivorous section. Immediately east, set amidst Kew's gargantuan Rock Garden, is the extraordinary **Alpine House**, a glasshouse shaped like the sail on the back of a dimetrodon.

> ### Visiting Kew Gardens
>
> There are four entry points to the gardens, but the majority of people arrive at Kew Gardens tube and overground station, a short walk east of the **Victoria Gate**, at the end of Lichfield Road. The only drawbacks with Kew are the hefty entry fee, and the fact that it's on the main flight path to Heathrow. That said, it's a wonderful place with something to see whatever the season. On a summer weekend, it's worth getting here early to avoid the queues. If you've **kids** with you, the good news is that they get in free. If it's raining, the aquarium beneath the Palm House usually goes down well, while under-10s will enjoy the indoor interactive play area, Climbers & Creepers. If the weather's good, head for the giant Badger Sett and the Beetle Loggery, home to stag beetles and the like.

▲ Kew Gardens

The largest of all the glasshouses is the **Temperate House**, another Decimus Burton structure, south (and twice the size) of the Palm House and almost forty years in the making. It contains plants from every continent, including one of the largest indoor palms in the world, the sixty-foot Chilean Wine Palm, first planted in 1846 and currently approaching the roof – and therefore the end of its life.

The eighteenth-century gardens

His mosque, waxworks, observatory and House of Confucius may be gone, but several of the buildings William Chambers created in the 1760s for the amusement of Princess Augusta remain dotted about the gardens. The most famous is his ten-storey, 163-foot-high **Pagoda**, Kew's most distinctive landmark, albeit minus the eighty enamelled dragons that used to adorn it. Standing nearby in a sort of miniature tea garden is the ornate **Japanese Gateway**, a scaled-down version of the one in Kyoto and a legacy of the 1911 Japanese Exhibition, built in cedar wood and topped by a copper roof.

To the north of the pagoda, you can walk through Chambers' **Ruined Arch**, purpose-built with sundry pieces of Roman masonry strewn about as if tossed there by barbarian hordes. (Close by is Kew's tallest object, a 225-foot-high flagpole fashioned from a single Canadian fir tree and erected in 1959.) Chambers is also responsible for the classical temples, the most picturesque being the **Temple of Aeolus**, situated close to Cumberland Gate on one of Kew's few hillocks, surrounded by a carpet of bluebells and daffodils in the spring.

Capability Brown's horticultural work has proved more durable than Chambers': his lake remains a focal point of the Syon vista from the Palm House, and the hidden **Rhododendron Dell** he devised survives to the south of it. More recent nearby additions include the **Bamboo Garden**, laid out in 1891, and the **Minka House**, a thatched wooden farmhouse built in the suburbs of Okazaki in Japan, and transferred here in 2001. The most recent addition to Kew is the **Treetop Walkway**, in the centre of the gardens – not a thing of beauty in itself but the views are good and it's quite novel to be among the tree canopy.

The thickly wooded, southwestern section of the park is the bit to head for if you want to lose the crowds, few of whom ever make it to **Queen Charlotte's Cottage** (June–Sept Sat & Sun 11am–4pm; free), a tiny thatched summerhouse built in brick and timber in the 1770s as a royal picnic spot for George III's wife. There's very little to see inside, beyond a room of Hogarth prints and a trompe-l'oeil pergola, but the surrounding native woodland is carpeted with bluebells in spring.

Kew Palace

In the north of the gardens stands the country's smallest royal residence, **Kew Palace** (Easter–Sept Mon 11am–5pm, Tues–Sun 10am–5pm; £5; ☎0844/482 7777, ⓦhrp.org.uk), a three-storey red-brick mansion measuring a mere 70ft by 50ft, and commonly known as the "Dutch House", after its fancy Flemish-bond brickwork and its curly Dutch gables. It's the smallest (and sole survivor) of the three royal residences that once stood at Kew and was bought from a City merchant by George II as a nursery and schoolhouse for his umpteen children. The only king to live here was George III, who was confined to the palace from 1801 onwards and subjected to the dubious attentions of doctors who attempted to find a cure for his "madness" by straitjacketing him and applying poultices of mustard and Spanish fly – only his strong constitution helped him to pull through. The ticket office and welcome centre, with an exhibition on the palace's history, stand apart. Inside the palace, there are one or two bits and bobs belonging to the royals, like the much-loved doll's house, on the ground floor, which belonged to George III's daughters. Upstairs, you can view the chair in which Queen Charlotte passed away in 1818, while the top floor has been left pretty much untouched since those days. Take time, too, to explore the secluded **Queen's Garden**, behind the palace, set out in a formal late seventeenth-century style, with a pleached hornbeam avenue and a lovely sunken nosegay garden.

The museum and art galleries

Kew's Museum No. 1, designed by Decimus Burton across the Pond from the Palm House (and now called **Plants and People**) provides an excellent wet-weather retreat. Inside, an exhibition shows the myriad uses to which humans have put plants, from food and medicines to clothes and tools. Along with the usual static glass-case displays, there are also touch-screen computers to hand, a scent station and various hands-on exhibits which should keep younger visitors happy. There's also a great 1886 model of an Indian indigo factory, with over one hundred clay figures and one colonial overseer in a pith helmet.

Kew also boasts three art galleries. To the south of Victoria Gate is the **Shirley Sherwood Gallery of Botanical Art**, a modern space that displays the most exquisitely executed botanical art from the last three centuries. Next door stands the resolutely old-fashioned **Marianne North Gallery**, purpose-built in 1882 to house the prolific output of the self-trained artist Marianne North. Over eight hundred paintings, completed in fourteen years of hectic world travel, are displayed end to end, filling every single space in the gallery. **Kew Gardens Gallery**, the largest of the lot, in the northeastern corner of the gardens, puts on temporary exhibitions often on more general botanical themes.

Kew Green and the National Archives

Kew's majestic **Main Gates**, designed by Decimus Burton, fulfilled their stated function until the arrival of the railway at Kew. Nowadays, you only get to see them if you're walking from Kew Bridge or exploring **Kew Green**, one of London's prettiest village greens. Lined with Georgian houses, the green is centred on the delightful church of **St Anne** (for opening times, visit ⓦwww .saintanne-kew.org.uk), an unusual building sporting a Victorian polygonal clock turret at one end and a peculiar Georgian octagonal cupola at the other; the painters Gainsborough and Zoffany lie in the churchyard. Inside, there's a royal Georgian gallery, held up by Tuscan columns, while at the east end is a rather fine late-Victorian chancel with scagliola columns and a top-lit dome.

Hidden in the residential backstreets of Kew is the Public Records Office, a rather nasty-looking beige and green premises housing the **National Archives** (Mon & Fri 9am–5pm, Tues & Thurs 9am–7pm, Wed 10am–5pm, Sat 9.30am–5pm; free; ☎020/8876 3444, ⓦwww.nationalarchives.gov.uk). Its research library is full of historians consulting primary source materials, while its exhibition gallery displays a changing rota of fascinating artefacts ranging from the likes of the Domesday Book and the trial record of Charles I, to Queen Victoria's 1851 census return and Elton John's Deed Poll certificate changing his name (wisely) from Reginald Kenneth Dwight.

Richmond and around

Richmond, upstream from Kew, basked for centuries in the glow of royal patronage, with Plantagenet kings and Tudor monarchs frequenting the riverside palace of Shene, as Richmond Palace was then called. In the eighteenth century Richmond enjoyed a brief life as a spa, and its agreeable locale began to attract City merchants, as well as successful artists, actors and writers: Pope, Gainsborough, Garrick and Reynolds are just some of the plaque-worthy names associated with the place. Although most of the courtiers and aristocrats have gone, as has the Tudor palace on the green, Richmond is still a wealthy district, with two theatres and highbrow pretensions. To appreciate its attractions fully, you need to visit the old village green, take in the glorious view from **Richmond Hill** and pay a visit to the vast acreage of **Richmond Park**, the old royal hunting grounds, still wild and replete with deer, and walk along the riverside to the nearby stately homes of **Ham House** and, across the river in Twickenham, **Marble Hill House**.

Richmond Green

George Street, Richmond's main street, is traffic-clogged and dominated by chain stores, but take one of the narrow pedestrianized alleyways, lined with arty shops and tearooms, and you'll emerge onto the wonderful open space of **Richmond Green**, one of London's finest village greens, and one of the most peaceful except for the planes using it as the main flight path into Heathrow. Handsome seventeenth- and eighteenth-century houses line the southwest and southeast sides of the green, with the most striking building of all, the flamboyant **Richmond Theatre**, designed by the great Frank Matcham in terracotta and brick in 1899, in the northeast corner.

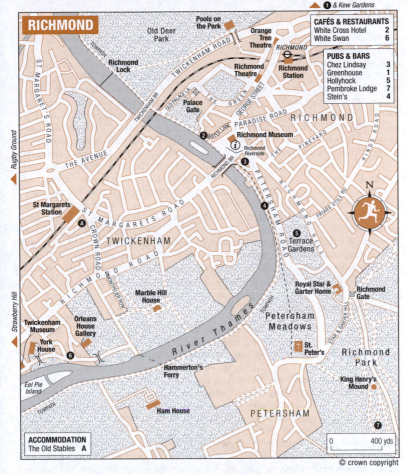

RICHMOND

Old Deer Park

Pools on the Park

Orange Tree Theatre

RICHMOND

TWICKENHAM ROAD

Richmond Lock

Richmond Theatre

Richmond Station

Palace Gate

THE GREEN

GEORGE STREET

OLD PALACE LA

TWICKENHAM BR

PARADISE ROAD

② WATER LANE

Richmond Museum

ⓘ Richmond Riverside

③

RICHMOND

THE AVENUE

RICHMOND BR

THE VINEYARD

KINGS ROAD

St Margarets Station

Ⓐ

ST MARGARET'S ROAD

④

FRIARS STILE RD

N

CROWN ROAD

TWICKENHAM

MONTPELIER ROW

⑤ Terrace Gardens

RICHMOND HILL

Marble Hill House

Royal Star & Garter Home

Richmond Gate

Orleans House Gallery

Petersham Meadows

Richmond Park

Twickenham Museum

York House

⑥

River Thames

Hammerton's Ferry

TOWPATH

STAR & GARTER HILL

St. Peter's

Eel Pie Island

TOWPATH

Ham House

PETERSHAM

King Henry's Mound

⑦

ACCOMMODATION
The Old Stables Ⓐ

0   400 yds

© crown copyright

CAFÉS & RESTAURANTS	
White Cross Hotel	2
White Swan	6
PUBS & BARS	
Chez Lindsay	3
Greenhouse	1
Hollyhock	5
Pembroke Lodge	7
Stein's	4

① & Kew Gardens

Rugby Ground

Strawberry Hill

OUT WEST: HAMMERSMITH TO HAMPTON COURT

The southwest corner is the site of medieval **Richmond Palace**, acquired by Henry I in 1125 (when it was known as Shene Palace). The first king to frequent the place was Edward III, who lay dying here in 1377 while his mistress urged the servants to prise the rings from his fingers. Seventeen years later a grief-stricken Richard II razed the place to the ground after his wife, Anne of Bohemia, died here of the plague. Henry V had it restored and Edward IV held jousting tournaments on the green, but it was Henry VII who, in an atypical burst of extravagance, constructed the largest complex of all, renaming it Richmond after his Yorkshire earldom. Henry VIII granted the palace to his fourth wife, Anne of Cleves, as part of their divorce settlement. Queen Mary and Philip of Spain spent part of their honeymoon here and Elizabeth I came here to die in 1603. A lot of history is attached to the place, but very little of Richmond Palace survived the Commonwealth and even less is visible now. The most obvious relic is the unspectacular **Tudor Gateway**, on the south side of the green.

Richmond Riverside

To the untrained eye, the buildings that form the backdrop to the pedestrianized terraces of **Richmond Riverside** look Georgian, but closer inspection reveals the majority to be a sham: the cupolas conceal air vents, the chimneys are decorative and the facades hide offices and flats. Still, Quinlan Terry's pastiche from the late 1980s has proved very popular. One of the few originals is **Heron House**, a narrow three-storey building where Lady Hamilton and her daughter Horatia came to live shortly after Trafalgar, the battle in which the girl's father died.

The old town hall, set slightly back from the riverside, to the north, now houses the **tourist office** (Mon–Sat 10am–5pm; ☎020/8940 9125, ⓦwww .visitrichmond.co.uk), a library and, on the top floor, the **Richmond Museum** (Tues–Sat 11am–5pm; free; ☎020/8332 1141, ⓦwww.museumofrichmond .com). The museum contains a small permanent exhibition on the history of the town, plus the lowdown on (and a model of) the old royal palace; temporary displays tend to focus on Richmond's past luminaries. To the south of the riverside development lies **Richmond Bridge**, an elegant span of five arches made from Purbeck stone in 1777, and cleverly widened in the 1930s, thus preserving London's oldest extant bridge. From April to September you can rent rowing boats from the nearby jetties, or take a boat trip to Hampton Court or Westminster (see p.338). If you continue along the towpath beyond Richmond Bridge, you will eventually come to Ham House.

Richmond Hill

If you're still wondering what's so special about Richmond, take a hike up **Richmond Hill**. To get there, head up Hill Rise from the top of Bridge Street, passing between the eighteenth-century antique shops and tearooms on your left, and the small sloping green on your right. Eventually you come to the **Terrace Gardens**, celebrated for the view up the thickly wooded Thames valley. Turner, Reynolds, Kokoschka and countless other artists have painted this view, which remains relatively unchanged and takes in six counties from Windsor to the North Downs. Richmond's wealthiest inhabitants have flocked to the hill's commanding heights over the centuries. The future George IV is alleged to have spent his secret honeymoon at **3 The Terrace**, after marrying Mrs Fitzherbert; twice divorced and a Catholic to boot, she was never likely to gain official approval, though she bore the prince ten children.

Further along, on the opposite side of the street, William Chambers built **Wick House** in 1772 as a summer residence for the enormously successful Joshua Reynolds. The building currently houses the nurses who work at the nearby **Royal Star & Garter Home** (ⓦwww.starandgarter.org), a rest home for war veterans built shortly after World War I, and now the dominant feature of the hillside. Disabled war veterans are also among the workforce at Richmond's **Poppy Factory** (☎020/8940 3305, ⓦwww.poppyfactory.org), who produce the thousands of poppies, petals and wreaths used during the build-up to Remembrance Day in November; the factory welcomes visitors and conducts regular ninety-minute guided tours (Mon–Thurs 10.30am & 1.30pm; free).

Richmond Park

Richmond's greatest attraction is the enormous **Richmond Park** (daily: March–Sept 7am–dusk; Oct–Feb 7.30am–dusk; free; ☎020/8948 3209, ⓦwww.royalparks.gov.uk), at the top of Richmond Hill – 2500 acres of undulating grassland and bracken, dotted with coppiced woodland and as wild as anything in London. Royal hunting ground since the thirteenth century (when it was known as Shene Chase), this is Europe's largest city park – eight miles across at its widest point. It's famous for its red and fallow deer, which roam freely – and breed so successfully, they have to be culled twice a year – and for its ancient oaks. Though for the most part untamed, there are a couple of deliberately landscaped plantations which feature splendid springtime azaleas and rhododendrons.

From Richmond Gate, at the top of Richmond Hill, it's a short walk south along the crest of the hill to **Pembroke Lodge** (originally known as The Molecatcher's), the childhood home of the philosopher Bertrand Russell. Set in its own lovely garden, the house is now a tearoom with outdoor seating and more spectacular views up the Thames valley. Close by, to the north, is the highest point in the park, known as **King Henry VIII's Mount**, where tradition has it the king waited for the flare launched from the Tower of London, which signalled the execution of his second wife, Anne Boleyn, though historians believe he was in Wiltshire at the time.

For a longer stroll through the park, head east from Pembroke Lodge into **Sidmouth Wood**, whose sweet chestnuts, oaks and beeches were planted during the nineteenth century. Originally established as pheasant cover, the wood is now a bird sanctuary, and walkers must keep to the central path, known as the Driftway. A little further east lie the **Pen Ponds**, the largest stretches of water in the park and a good spot for birdwatching. To the south is the park's extremely popular **Isabella Plantation**, a carefully landscaped woodland park, with a little rivulet running through it, two small artificial ponds, and spectacular rhododendrons and azaleas in the spring. The round trip from Richmond Gate is about four miles.

The two most important historic buildings in the park are both closed to the public. Of the two, the **White Lodge**, to the east of the Pen Ponds, is the more attractive, a Palladian villa commissioned by George II, and frequented by his wife, Queen Caroline, and their daughter, the aforementioned Amelia. Much altered over the years, it was also the birthplace of the ill-fated Edward VIII, and home to the Duke and Duchess of York (later George VI and the Queen Mother); it currently houses the Royal Ballet School. The **Thatched House Lodge**, in the southernmost corner of the park, was built in the 1670s for the park's rangers, and gets its name from the thatched gazebo in the garden. General Eisenhower hung out in the lodge during World War II, and it's now home to Princess Alexandra.

Ham and Twickenham

Ham lies just upriver from Richmond and **Ham House**, slightly off the beaten track, is one of the most appealing of all the historic houses along the river. The best approach is on foot from Richmond Riverside, heading south along the towpath, past the cows grazing on Petersham Meadows, leaving the rest of London far behind. **Twickenham**, on the other side of the river, is best known for its rugby – there's a museum if you're really keen (see p.353) – but also conceals a cluster of lesser-known sights close to the river, all of which repay a brief visit. It's a pleasant mile-long walk to Ham House from Richmond Riverside and, weather permitting, **Hammerton's Ferry** will take people (and bicycles) over to the Twickenham side (Feb–Sept Mon–Fri 10am–6pm, Sat & Sun 10am–6.30pm; Oct–Jan Sat & Sun 10am–6.30pm; £1).

Ham House

Hidden in the woods that line the south bank of the Thames lies the red-brick Jacobean mansion of **Ham House** (April–Oct Mon–Wed, Sat & Sun 1–5pm; NT; £9.90; ☎020/8940 1950; bus #371 or #65 from Richmond tube), home to the earls of Dysart for nearly three hundred years. The first Earl of Dysart was Charles I's childhood whipping boy (he literally received the punishment on behalf of the prince when the latter misbehaved), who was granted a peerage and the estate of Ham for his pains, but it is his ambitious daughter, **Elizabeth** – a Royalist spy during the Commonwealth and at one time Oliver Cromwell's lover – who is most closely associated with the place. With the help of her second husband, the Earl of Lauderdale, one of the most powerful ministers to Charles II, she added numerous extra rooms, "furnished like a great Prince's" according to diarist John Evelyn, and succeeded in shocking even **Restoration** society with her extravagance.

Elizabeth's profligacy, and a ruinous legal battle over her husband's inheritance, meant she died penniless and alone in 1698, having not ventured out of the house for eight years. She also left the family heavily in debt, so the later earls of Dysart could afford to make few alterations to one of the finest **Stuart interiors** in the country, prompting Horace Walpole (who lived across the river at Strawberry Hill) to describe Ham as a "Sleeping Beauty". The Great Staircase, off the Central Hall, is stupendously ornate, featuring huge bowls of fruit at the newel posts and trophies of war carved into the balustrade. The rest of the house is equally sumptuous, with lavish plasterwork, silverwork and parquet flooring, **Verrio ceiling paintings** and rich hangings, tapestries, silk damasks and cut velvets. The Long Gallery, in the west wing, features a Van Dyck self-portrait, a portrait of Elizabeth Dysart, and six "Court Beauties" by **Peter Lely**.

Another bonus is the formal seventeenth-century **gardens** (Mon–Wed, Sat & Sun 11am–6pm; £3.30), now restored to something like their former glory. To the east lies the Cherry Garden, laid out with a pungent lavender parterre, and surrounded by yew hedges and pleached hornbeam arbours. On the south terrace, the Lauderdales would display their citrus trees, considered the height of luxury at the time, while across the lawn lies the "Wildernesse" of hornbeam hedges and maple trees. Finally, to the west, you'll find the partially resurrected kitchen garden, overlooked by the Orangery, which currently serves as a tearoom.

Marble Hill House

On the Twickenham side of the river, not far from Hammerton's Ferry, is **Marble Hill House** (April–Oct Sat 10am–2pm, Sun 10am–5pm; EH; £4.40; ☎020/8892 5115; St Margarets train station from Waterloo), a stuccoed Palladian villa set in rolling green parkland. It was completed in 1729 for Henrietta Howard, Countess of Suffolk, mistress of George II for some twenty years and, conveniently, also a lady-in-waiting to his wife, Queen Caroline (apparently "they hated one another very civilly"). She was renowned not just for her "long chesnut tresses", but also for her wit and intelligence and she entertained the Twickenham Club of Alexander Pope, John Gay and Horace Walpole. The few original furnishings are being slowly added to with reproductions and the place is beginning to have the feel of an eighteenth-century villa. The Great Room, on the *piano nobile*, is a perfect cube whose coved ceiling carries on up into the top-floor apartments. Copies of Van Dycks decorate the walls as they did in Lady Suffolk's day, but the highlight is Lady Suffolk's Bedchamber, with its Ionic columned recess – a classic Palladian device – where she died in 1767 at the age of 79. In the grounds, there are open-air concerts on occasional summer evenings.

Orleans House Gallery

Set in a small wood to the west of Marble Hill is the **Orleans House Gallery** (April–Sept Tues–Sat 1–5.30pm, Sun 2–5.30pm; Oct–March closes 4.30pm; free; ☎020/8831 6000; Twickenham train station from Waterloo), in what began life as a villa built in 1710 for James Johnston, Secretary of State for Scotland. It was most famously occupied in 1815–17 by Louis-Philippe, the exiled Duke of Orléans (and later "King of the French"), who referred to it as "dear quiet Twick". In 1926, it was all but entirely demolished – all, that is, except for the **Octagon**, designed for Johnston by James Gibbs in 1720 in honour of a visit by Queen Caroline. The exhibitions staged in the old stables and the modern extension are interesting enough, but it's the Octagon that steals the limelight, an unusually exuberant Baroque confection celebrated for its masterly Italian stucco decoration.

York House to Eel Pie Island

A little further west, towards Twickenham town centre, is **York House**, an early seventeenth-century mansion that now belongs to the local council, though the **gardens** (Mon–Sat 7.30am to dusk, Sun 9am to dusk), laid out by the last private owner, the Indian prince Ratan Tata, are open to the public. The bit to head for is the riverside section – a great picnic spot – that lies beyond the sunken garden, on the other side of the delicate arched bridge spanning the road. Here, in amongst the yew hedges, you'll find the gardens' celebrated "naked ladies", seven larger-than-life marble nymphs frolicking in the water lilies of an Italian fountain, above which Venus rises up at the head of two winged horses.

To learn a bit more about this side of the river, pop into the **Twickenham Museum** (Tues & Sat 11am–3pm, Sun 2–4pm; free; ☎020/8408 0070, ⓦwww .twickenham-museum.org.uk; Twickenham train station from Waterloo), which puts on changing historical exhibitions. A few yards offshore, near York House, lies **Eel Pie Island**, the only inhabited island in the tidal Thames. Tea dances began at the island's *Eel Pie Hotel* back in the 1920s; bawdy jazz nights were the staple diet in the 1950s; rock and rhythm'n'blues followed in the 1960s. The hotel burned down in 1971 (ⓦwww.eelpie.org), and the island is now better known for its eccentric community of independent-spirited artisans, among them Trevor Baylis, inventor of the clockwork radio.

Twickenham World Rugby Museum

The English rugby fan's number-one pilgrimage site is the national stadium at Twickenham, and the pompously entitled **World Rugby Museum** (Tues–Sat 10am–5pm, Sun 11am–5pm; £6; ☎020/8892 8877, ⓦwww.rfu.com; Twickenham train station from Waterloo) in the East Stand. The exhibition is full of video footage and lots of memorabilia from the sport, which was famously invented in 1823, when W.W. Ellis picked up and ran with the ball during a game of football at Rugby School. There's not much here for the non specialist, however, save for the Calcutta Cup, an object of supreme beauty, having been made from 270 silver rupees, with great cobra handles and an elephant lid. You can also sign up for a **stadium tour** (£14), which allows you to see the dressing rooms and walk onto the pitch itself, and includes a visit to the museum. Note that on match days the museum is only open to match ticket-holders.

Strawberry Hill

One last oddity well worth making the effort to visit is **Strawberry Hill** (℡0870/626 0402, Ⓦwww.friendsofstrawberryhill.org; Strawberry Hill station from Waterloo), upriver from Eel Pie Island, on Waldegrave Road, a short walk from Strawberry Hill train station (trains from Waterloo). In 1747 writer, wit and fashion queen Horace Walpole, youngest son of former prime minister Robert Walpole, bought this "little play-thing house…the prettiest bauble you ever saw…set in enamelled meadows, with filigree hedges", renamed it Strawberry Hill and set about inventing the most influential building in the Gothic Revival. Walpole appointed a "Committee of Taste" to embellish his project with details from other Gothic buildings: screens from Old St Paul's and Rouen cathedrals, and fan vaulting from Henry VII's Chapel in Westminster Abbey.

The house quickly became the talk of London, a place of pilgrimage for royalty and foreign dignitaries alike. Walpole was forced to issue tickets in advance (never more than four and no children) to cut down the number of visitors. Those he wished to meet he greeted dressed in a lavender suit and silver-embroidered waistcoat, sporting a cravat carved in wood by Grinling Gibbons and an enormous pair of gloves that once belonged to James I. When he died in 1797, he left the house to his friend, the sculptor Anne Damer, who continued to entertain in the same spirit, giving lavish garden parties dressed in a man's coat, hat and shoes. The house is undergoing restoration but should open during 2010.

Wimbledon

Wimbledon is a dreary, high, bleak, windy suburb, on the edge of a threadbare heath.

Virginia Woolf

Nowadays, of course, **Wimbledon** is best known for its tennis tournament, the Wimbledon Championships, held every year in the last week of June and the first week of July, on the grass courts of the All England Lawn Tennis and Croquet Club – to give the ground its grand title. For the rest of the year, though, Wimbledon's vast **common** is its most popular attraction, worth a visit for its windmill alone, and for the remarkable **Southside House**.

Wimbledon Lawn Tennis Museum

If you've missed the tournament itself (see p.448), the next best thing for tennis fans is a quick spin around the state-of-the-art **Wimbledon Lawn Tennis Museum** (daily 10am–5pm; £8.50; ℡020/8946 6131, Ⓦwww.wimbledon .org; bus #493 from Southfields tube), situated by Gate 4, on Church Road. The museum traces the history of the game, which is descended from the *jeu de paume* played by the French clergy from the twelfth century onwards. The modern version, though, is considered to have been invented by a Victorian major, who called it "Sphairstike", a name that, not surprisingly, failed to stick. The new sport was initially seen as a genteel pastime, suitable for both gentlemen and ladies, and its early enthusiasts hailed almost exclusively from the aristocracy and the clergy – the museum's Edwardian dressing room is the epitome of upper-class masculinity. As well as the historical and fashion angles and the tennis-star memorabilia, there's also plenty of opportunity for watching vintage game footage. If you're keen for a behind-the-scenes **guided tour** (90min; £15.50) as well, you need to phone ahead.

Wimbledon Common

With none of the views of Richmond, **Wimbledon Common** (Ⓦwww
.wpcc.org.uk), to the southeast of Richmond Park, can appear rather bleak:
mostly rough grass and bracken punctuated by playing fields and golf courses,
and cut through by the busy A3. The chief reason to come here is the
Wimbledon Windmill (April–Oct Sat 2–5pm, Sun 11am–5pm; £2;
☏020/8947 2825, Ⓦwww.wimbledonwindmillmuseum.org.uk; bus #93 from
Wimbledon tube), situated at the end of Windmill Road in the northern half
of the common, with conveniently placed tearooms nearby. Built in 1817, the
mill was closed down in 1864, and converted into cottages, one of which was
home to Baden-Powell when he began writing his *Scouting for Boys* in 1908.
Subsequently restored and turned into a museum, the windmill is the last
remaining hollow-post flour mill in the country; you can also climb into the
first section of the wooden cap and see the giant chain wheel.

Putney Vale Cemetery

Beyond the attractive nearby pool of **Queen's Mere**, just to the west of the
windmill, lies **Putney Vale Cemetery**, worth a visit for its wonderful array of
Victorian angels and its peaceful Gardens of Remembrance, at their best in early
summer. Look out for the nautical grave of Bruce Ismay, *Titanic* survivor and
chairman of the ill-fated White Star Line. The cemetery's most illustrious
incumbent is Alexander Kerensky, leader of the Russian Revolution of
February 1917, which overthrew the tsar. Kerensky's downfall was his failure to
bring an end to the war, and he was forced to flee disguised as a Serb during
the October Revolution.

Cannizaro Park and the Buddhist temple

In the southeastern corner of the common is **Cannizaro Park** (Mon–Fri 8am
to dusk, Sat & Sun 9am to dusk; free; ☏020/8946 7349; bus #93 from
Wimbledon tube), a small, sheltered, wooded area, made up of the grounds of
Cannizaro House (now a hotel frequented by the tennis glitterati), and entered
from West Side Common. Within its walls are an ugly teapot fountain, a lovely
stretch of lawn for picnicking, a maze of paths, an aviary, an Italian garden,
occasional student art shows, and an open-air theatre and jazz festival every July.
Another peripheral but intriguing sight is the **Wat Buddhapadipa** (☏020/8946
1357, Ⓦwww.buddhapadipa.org), a startling, white-gabled Thai Buddhist
temple, east off the common on Calonne Road, richly decorated in red and
gold and set in four acres of grounds (daily 9am–6pm; free); the temple itself is
only accessible at the weekend.

Southside House

Hidden away behind high walls just round the corner from Cannizaro Park in
Woodhayes Road is the Dutch-Baroque mansion of **Southside House**
(Easter–Sept Wed, Sat & Sun 2, 3 & 4pm; £5; ☏020/8946 7643, Ⓦwww
.southsidehouse.com; bus #93 from Wimbledon tube), built in the late seventeenth century, and now hemmed in by Wimbledon's King's College School.
Visiting the house is an unforgettable experience, not least because you're
quite likely to be guided round, and fed with anecdotes, by the eccentric
descendants of the Pennington-Mellor-Munthe family who first built the
house – several of whom still live here in a kind of time warp, using only
candles for light and open fires for warmth, surrounded by the house's rich and

slowly disintegrating decor, and the family's ancestral hangings, many of which are extremely valuable.

Inside, the place has a ramshackle feel, partly because at heart it's still an old Tudor farmhouse, onto which a Dutch facade has been added, and partly because of bomb damage. Nevertheless, virtually every room is stuffed to the rafters with artworks and other sundry heirlooms. In the Dining Room alone, there are no fewer than 34, mostly full-length, portraits, including three by Van Dyck, one each by Hogarth and Goya, and a depiction of St George by Burne-Jones. Other treasures on show include the sapphire worn by the last king of Serbia on the day of his assassination, and, in a cabinet of curiosities in the royal bedroom upstairs, you can see the pearl necklace worn by Marie Antoinette on the day of her execution. Finally, in the Music Room, there's a portrait of Angelica Kauffmann, a Reynolds self-portrait, a Fragonard and one of George Romney's famous portraits of Emma, Lady Hamilton, who used to strike her "attitudes" in that very room.

Hampton Court Palace

Hampton Court Palace, a sprawling red-brick ensemble on the banks of the Thames, thirteen miles southwest of London, is the finest of England's royal abodes. The present building began life, however, as an ecclesiastical palace, built from 1516 onwards by the upwardly mobile **Cardinal Wolsey**, Henry VIII's high-powered, fast-living Lord Chancellor. Wolsey eventually fell from favour, due to his failure to secure a papal annulment for Henry's marriage to Catherine of Aragon, and, in a vain attempt to ingratiate himself, gifted the place to the king in 1528.

Like Wolsey, **Henry VIII** spent enormous sums of money on the palace, enlarging the kitchens, rebuilding the chapel and altering the rooms to suit the tastes of the last five of his six wives. Under Elizabeth I and James I, Hampton Court became renowned for its masques, plays and balls; during the Civil War, it was a refuge and then a prison for Charles I. The palace was put up for sale during the Commonwealth but, with no buyers forthcoming, Cromwell decided to move in and lived here on and off until his death in 1658. Charles II laid out the gardens, inspired by what he had seen at Versailles, but it was **William and Mary** who instigated the most radical alterations, hiring Christopher Wren to remodel the buildings. Wren intended to tear down the whole palace and build a new Versailles, but, in the end, had to content himself with rebuilding the east and south wings, adding the Banqueting House on the river and completing the chapel for Queen Anne.

George III eschewed the place, apparently because he associated it with the beatings he received here from his grandfather. Instead, he established grace-and-favour residences for indigent members of the royal household, which still exist today. The palace was opened to the public in 1838, and, along with the vast expanse of **Bushy Park**, it's now a major tourist attraction.

The Palace

The Tudor west front may no longer be moated but it positively prickles with turrets, castellations, chimneypots and pinnacles. The **Great Gatehouse** is impressive and would have been five storeys high in Wolsey's day. The first

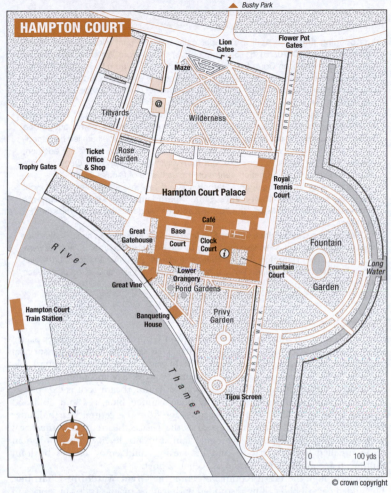

HAMPTON COURT

Bushy Park

Flower Pot
Gates

Lion
Gates

Maze

Tiltyards

@

Wilderness

B R O A D   W A L K

Rose
Garden

Ticket
Office
& Shop

Trophy Gates

Hampton Court Palace

Royal
Tennis
Court

Café

River

Great
Gatehouse

Base
Court

Clock
Court

ℹ

Fountain

Long
Water

Great Vine

Lower
Orangery
Pond Gardens

Fountain
Court

Garden

Hampton Court
Train Station

Banqueting
House

Privy
Garden

B R O A D   W A L K

Thames

Tijou Screen

N

0   100 yds

© crown copyright

and largest courtyard, **Base Court**, is reminiscent of an Oxbridge college and features another Tudor gateway known as Anne Boleyn's Gateway, though it too dates from the time of Wolsey. Beyond lies **Clock Court**, which has none of the uniformity of the other two quadrangles: to the north rises the Tudor Great Hall, to the south Wren's colonnade, announcing the new State Apartments, and to the east a fairly convincing mock-Tudor gateway by William Kent. Originally centred on a large fountain which was equipped by Elizabeth I with a nozzle that soaked innocent passers-by, the courtyard gets its current name from the **astronomical clock** on the inside of the Anne Boleyn Gateway, made in 1540 for Henry VIII, which was used to calculate the high tide at London Bridge (and thus the estimated time of arrival of palace guests travelling by boat). The last and smallest of the three courtyards is Wren's **Fountain Court**, which crams in more windows than seems possible.

Visiting Hampton Court

The **opening times** are April to October daily 10am to 6pm; November to March closes 4.30pm (☎0870/751 5175, ⊛hrp.org.uk). Trains from Waterloo take half an hour to reach Hampton Court train station, across the river from the palace. **Tickets** to the Royal Apartments cost £14, and cover entry to everything in the palace and grounds. Those who don't wish to visit the apartments can buy a separate ticket for the gardens (April–Sept only; £4.60) and the Maze (£3.50).

The **State Apartments** are divided into six thematic walking tours, which are numbered and colour-coded. There's not a lot of information in the rooms, but **guided tours**, lasting half an hour or so, are available at no extra charge; all are led by period-costumed historians, who do a fine job of bringing the place to life. In addition, **audioguides** are available (for all except the Wolsey Rooms and the Queen's State Apartments) from the information centre on the east side of Clock Court.

If your energy is lacking – and Hampton Court is a huge complex – the most rewarding sections are **Henry VIII's State Apartments**, the **King's Apartments** (remodelled by William III) and the **Tudor Kitchens**. And be sure not to miss out on the **Maze**.

The **Hampton Court Palace Flower Show** takes place in early July, rivals Chelsea for sheer snob factor, and is likewise organized by the Royal Horticultural Society (⊛www .rhs.org.uk). The **Hampton Court Palace Festival** (⊛www.hamptoncourtfestival .com) features stars from the classical and pop music worlds, and takes place each year in June.

Henry VIII's Apartments

Henry VIII lavished more money on Hampton Court than on any other palace except Greenwich (which no longer exists). That said, the only major survival from Tudor times is his **Great Hall**, which was completed with remarkable speed in 1534, Henry having made the builders work day and night – a highly dangerous exercise in candlelight. The double hammerbeam roof is exceptionally ornate, and would have originally been painted blue, red and gold and featured a louvre to allow the smoke to escape from the central hearth. Under Elizabeth I and James I, the hall served as the palace theatre, where theatrical troupes, among them Shakespeare's, entertained royalty. Even Cromwell had an organ installed here so that he and his family could enjoy recitals by John Milton, an accomplished musician as well as a poet.

Passing through the Horn Room, you enter the **Great Watching Chamber**. The gilded oak-ribbed ceiling is studded with leather-mâché Tudor insignia, and hung with tapestries that were part of Wolsey's collection. In these surroundings up to eighty yeomen would be stationed at any one time, guarding the principal entrance to the king's private chambers, which William and Mary found "old-fashioned and uncomfortable" and consequently demolished.

From here you come to the **Haunted Gallery**, built by Wolsey to connect his apartments to the chapel, and home to the ghost of Henry's fifth wife, 19-year-old Catherine Howard. The night before her arrest for high treason in November 1541, Catherine is alleged to have run down the gallery in an attempt to make a final plea for mercy to the king, who was praying in the chapel. Henry refused to see her, and she was dragged kicking and screaming back to her chambers – or so the story goes.

The Haunted Gallery leads into the Royal Pew in the chapel gallery, which was decorated for Queen Anne but has been a feature since Wolsey's day – it was here that Henry VIII was passed the note alleging that Catherine Howard was not in fact a virgin when he married her. From here, you can look down on the

Chapel Royal, and admire the colourful false-timber Tudor vaulting wrought in plaster, heavy with pendants of gilded music-making cherubs – one of the most memorable sights in the whole palace. It was here that Henry married the sixth of his wives (and the only one to outlive him), Catherine Parr.

Mary II's Apartments

These apartments remained unfinished at Queen Mary's death in 1694, and weren't fully furnished and decorated until the time of Queen Caroline, George II's wife. The main approach is via the grandiose **Queen's Staircase**, splendidly decorated with trompe-l'oeil reliefs and a coffered dome by William Kent.

One of the finest rooms here is the **Queen's Drawing Room**, decorated top to bottom with trompe-l'oeil paintings depicting Queen Anne's husband, George of Denmark – in heroic naval guise, and also, on the south wall, riding naked and wigless on the back of a "dolphin". Queen Anne takes centre stage on the ceiling as Justice, somewhat inappropriately given her habit of not paying her craftsmen, including Verrio, the painter of this room. After Anne's death in 1714, the Prince and Princess of Wales (later George II and Queen Caroline) took over the Queen's Apartments, though they hated the trompe-l'oeil paintings and hung Mantegna's works over the top of them. In 1717, the couple fell out with the king and moved to Kew; the ceiling painting in the **Queen's Bedroom** by James Thornhill predates the quarrel, with four portraits of a seemingly happy Hanoverian family staring at one another from the coving

The **Queen's Gallery** features one of the most ornate marble fireplaces in the palace – originally intended for the King's Bedchamber – with putti, doves and Venus frolicking above the mantelpiece; the walls, meanwhile, are hung with Gobelin tapestries depicting Alexander the Great's exploits and lined with Chinese vases and Delftware.

Georgian Private Apartments

The **Georgian Private Apartments** begin with the rooms of the **Cumberland Suite**, lived in by George II before his accession, then by his eldest son, Prince Frederick, and lastly by Frederick's brother, the Duke of Cumberland, better known as "Butcher Cumberland" for his ruthless suppression of the Jacobites in Scotland. The rooms were decorated by Kent, who added Gothic touches to the first two rooms and a grandiose Neoclassical alcove in the bedchamber.

Beyond here you'll find the tiny **Wolsey Closet**, which, although a Victorian invention, gives a tantalizing impression of the splendour of Wolsey's original palace. It's a jewel of a room – though at 12ft square it's easily missed – with brightly coloured early sixteenth-century paintings set above exquisite linenfold panelling and a fantastic gilded ceiling of interlaced octagons.

Next is the **Communication Gallery**, constructed to link the King's and Queen's apartments, now lined with Lely's "Windsor Beauties", flattering portraits of the best-looking women in the court of Charles II. The **Cartoon Gallery** was purpose-built by Wren to display the Raphael Cartoons – the originals are in the V&A, and what you see are late seventeenth-century copies. Tapestries made from the cartoons are scattered throughout William and Mary's apartments.

The next sequence of rooms is of minor interest, though they do include an excellent Gibbons overmantle in the Queen's Private Bedchamber. Last of all, you enter the **Queen's Private Oratory**, used by Queen Caroline for

▲ Hampton Court Palace

private worship – it's one of the few windowless rooms, hence the octagonal dome and skylight.

William III's Apartments

William III's Apartments are approached via the **King's Staircase**, the grandest of the lot thanks chiefly to Verrio's busy, militaristic trompe-l'oeil paintings glorifying the king, depicted here as Alexander the Great. The **King's Guard Chamber** is notable chiefly for its 3000-piece display of arms, arranged as they were laid out in the time of William III. William's rather modest throne still stands in the **King's Presence Chamber**, under a canopy of crimson damask. The sixteenth-century Brussels tapestries in the room were originally commissioned by Henry VIII for Whitehall Palace.

Further on, in the **King's Privy Chamber**, there's a much grander throne used by William, with a canopy that still retains its original ostrich feathers. The most impressive room here is the **King's Great Bedchamber**, which boasts a superb vertical Gibbons frieze and ceiling paintings by Verrio – just as you're leaving this floor, you'll catch a glimpse of a splendidly throne-like velvet toilet. Ground-floor highlights include a semi-nude portrait by Van Dyck of his mistress Margaret Lemon, in the East Closet, the **Orangery**, built to house the king's orange trees during the winter, and the only room in the palace lockable solely from the inside (a tryst room – highly unusual for the royals' very public life). Past here is the **King's Private Dining Room**, its table laden with pyramids of meringues and fruit and its walls hung with eight full-length portraits of Queen Mary's favourite ladies-in-waiting (known as the "Hampton Court Beauties"), for which the German-born painter Godfrey Kneller received a knighthood.

Young Henry VIII's Story

Several early Tudor rooms, with striking linenfold panelling and gilded strapwork ceilings, are now used to display **Young Henry VIII's Story**. This is a worthy attempt by the palace to portray Henry in his virile youth, during his happy, twenty-year marriage to his first wife, Catherine of Aragon. Interactive screens help tell the story of the Battle of the Spurs at Guinegate in 1613, when Henry led his troops from the front, and of the Field of the Cloth of Gold, Henry's famous meeting with the French king, François I, in 1620.

Henry VIII's kitchens

After a surfeit of opulent interiors, the workaday **Tudor Kitchens** come as something of a relief. Henry VIII quadrupled the size of the kitchens, large sections of which have survived to this day and have been restored and embellished with historical reconstructions. Past the Boiling Room and Flesh Larder (not for squeamish vegetarians) you come to the **Great Kitchen**, where a fire is still lit in the main hearth every day. This kitchen is only one of three Henry built to cope with the prodigious consumption of the royal court – six oxen, forty sheep and a thousand or more larks, pheasants, pigeons and peacocks were an average daily total. The tour ends in Henry's vast **Wine Cellar**, where the palace's Rhineland wine was stored. At each main meal, the king and his special guests would be supplied with eight pints of wine; courtiers had to make do with three gallons of beer.

The Gardens

The gardens' magnificent **Broad Walk** runs for half a mile from the Thames past Wren's austere East Front to the putti-encrusted Flower Pot Gate and is lined with some of the country's finest herbaceous borders. Halfway along lies the indoor **Royal Tennis Court**, established here by Henry VIII (a keen player of Real Tennis himself), but extensively restored by Charles II. If you're lucky, you might even catch a game of this arcane precursor of modern tennis, though the rules are incredibly tricky.

Fanning out from the Broad Walk is William's **Fountain Garden**, a grand, semicircular parterre, which in William's day featured box hedges, thirteen fountains and dwarf yew trees pruned to look like obelisks. A fair number of these "black pyramids", as Virginia Woolf called them, have been reduced to chubby cone shapes, while a solitary pool stands in place of the fountains, and the box hedges have become plain lawns. A semicircular canal separates the Fountain Garden from the Home Park beyond, its waters feeding Charles II's **Long Water**, Hampton Court's most Versaillean feature, which slices the Home Park in two.

Privy Garden

Overlooked by Wren's magnificent South Front is the formal **Privy Garden**, laid out as it would have been under William III; the twelve magnificent wrought-iron panels at the river end of the garden are the work of Jean Tijou. To the west, you can peek into the **Pond Gardens**, which were originally constructed as ornamental fish ponds stocked with freshwater fish for the kitchens, and feature some of the gardens' most spectacularly colourful flowerbeds. Further along, protected by glass, is the palace's celebrated **Great Vine**, grown from a cutting in 1768 by Capability Brown and averaging about seven hundred pounds of Black Hamburg grapes per year (sold at the palace in September).

Close by stands the **Lower Orangery**, designed by Wren and used as a dimly lit gallery for Andrea Mantegna's heroic canvases, *The Triumphs of Caesar*, bought by Charles I in 1629 and kept here ever since. Painted around 1486 for the

Ducal Palace in Mantua, Mantegna's home town, these nine richly coloured paintings, depicting the general's victory parade, are among his best works, characterized by his obsessive interest in archeological and historical accuracy. Beyond the South Gardens, beside the river, is William III's dinky little red-brick **Banqueting House**, built for intimate riverside soirees, with castellations and mouldings by Gibbons and exuberant paintings by Verrio.

The Maze

To the north of the palace, Henry VIII laid out a **Tiltyard** with five towers for watching jousting tournaments, one of which survives near the garden restaurant. William III transformed the tiltyard into a **Wilderness** – an informal park of evergreens – which now contains the most famous feature of the palace gardens, the deceptively tricky trapezoidal **Maze**, laid out in 1714. Mazes, or labyrinths as they were called at the time, were used by pilgrims, who used to crawl along on hands and knees reciting prayers, as penance for not making a pilgrimage to the Holy Land. They were all the rage among the eighteenth-century nobility, who used them primarily for amusement, secret conversations and flirtation. The maze was originally planted with hornbeam, but, with the onset of the tourist boom in the 1960s, the hornbeam had to be replaced with yew.

Bushy Park

Beyond the Lion Gates, to the north of the Maze, across Hampton Court Road, lies **Bushy Park**, the palace's semi-wild enclosure of over a thousand acres, which sustains copious herds of fallow and red deer. Wren's mile-long royal road, Chestnut Avenue, cuts through the park, and is at its best in May when the trees are in blossom. The main architectural feature of the park is the **Diana Fountain**, situated a third of the way along the avenue to help break the monotony. The statue – which, in fact, depicts Arethusa – was commissioned by Charles II from Francesco Fanelli and originally graced the Privy Garden; stranded in the centre of this vast pond, she looks ill-proportioned and a bit forlorn.

Off to the west, a little further up the avenue, you'll come upon the **Waterhouse Woodland Gardens**, created in 1949, and at their most colourful each spring when the rhododendrons, azaleas and camellias are in bloom. The crowds are fairly thin even here, compared with the crush around the palace, but if you really want to seek out some of the park's abundant wildlife head for its wilder western section, where few visitors venture.

Listings

Listings

Accommodation

There's no getting away from the fact that **accommodation** in London is expensive. Compared with most European cities, you pay over the odds in every category. The city's hostels are among the most costly in the world, while an astonishing number of hotels charge guests the very top international prices – from £300 per luxurious night. Demand for beds is so great that the city doesn't really have a **low season**, though things do slacken off a little in the months just after Christmas. The way to get the best price is to look around online far enough in advance – with any luck, you should be able to shave £50–100 off room rates at some of the more upmarket hotels.

Aside from the city's **campsites**, the cheapest place to stay is in one of the numerous **hostels**, where dorm beds start at around £12. Even the most basic **B&Bs** struggle to bring their tariffs below £60 for a double with shared facilities, which is why so many people head for the budget chain hotels. For a really decent **hotel** room, you shouldn't expect much change out of £100 a night. Most B&Bs and many hotels are housed in former residential properties, so rooms tend to be on the small side, and only the more upmarket places have lifts. That said, even the most basic **rooms** tend to have TVs, tea- and coffee-making facilities and telephones, and breakfast is nearly always included in the price.

All London **tourist offices** (listed on p.38) operate a room-booking service, for which a small fee is levied (they also take the first night's fee in advance). There are also **British Hotel Reservation Centre** (**BHRC**; 24hr helpline ☎020/7592 3055, ⓦwww.bhrc.co.uk) desks at Heathrow and Gatwick airports, and Paddington, King's Cross and Victoria stations, as well as at 13 Grosvenor Gardens, SW1. BHRC offices are open daily from 6am till midnight, and there's no booking fee – they can also get big discounts at the more upmarket hotels.

You can book accommodation for free **online** at ⓦwww.londontown.com; payment is made directly to the hotel on checking out and they offer discounts of over fifty percent. Other useful websites include ⓦwww.accommodation london.net and ⓦwww.hotelsengland.com, and for last-minute offers: ⓦwww .laterooms.com and ⓦwww.lastminute.com. ⓦwww.londonbb.com sources classy **B&B** options, while ⓦwww.couchsurfing.com puts travellers in touch with people to stay or hang out with. For gay and lesbian accommodation see p.416

Hostels, student halls and camping

Hostels run the gamut from the efficient, but a little soulless, official YHA hostels (see box, p.366), to much funkier and more relaxed independent hostels,

London's YHA hostels

London's seven **Youth Hostel Association (YHA)** hostels are guaranteed to be clean and efficiently run. Their rates depend on availability: dorm prices start at £18–20, doubles/twins at £50–60; breakfast is included and advanced booking recommended. You don't have to be a member of the YHA or an affiliated hostel association to stay, but nonmembers are charged a £3 surcharge or can join for £16. Note that you can book a bed in advance by phoning individual hostels or online at Ⓦwww.yha.org.uk.

Central 104 Bolsover St, W1 ☎0845/371 9154, Ⓔlondoncentral@yha.org.uk; Great Portland Street tube. See map, p.104. YHA's newest hostel is in a quiet location, and yet walking distance from the West End. Free wi-fi, kitchen and a 24hr café-bar. No groups. Dorms only (4–8 beds).

Earls Court 38 Bolton Gardens, SW5 ☎0845/371 9114, Ⓔearlscourt@yha.org.uk; Earl's Court tube. See map, p.254. Recently refurbished 150-bed hostel with small kitchen, café and patio garden. Small groups. Dorms (4–10 beds) and doubles/twins.

Holland House Holland Walk, W8 ☎0845/371 9122, Ⓔhollandhouse@yha.org.uk; Holland Park or High Street Kensington tube. See map, p.278. Idyllically situated in Holland Park and fairly convenient for the centre. Kitchen available and café. Popular with groups. Dorms only (4–10 beds).

Oxford Street 14 Noel St, W1 ☎0845/371 9133, Ⓔoxfordst@yha.org.uk; Oxford Circus or Tottenham Court Road tube. See map, p.104. The Soho location and modest size mean this hostel tends to be full year-round. No groups, no café, but a large kitchen. Dorms (4–6 beds) and doubles/twins.

St Pancras 79–81 Euston Rd, NW1 ☎0845/371 9344, Ⓔstpancras@yha.org.uk; King's Cross St Pancras tube. See map, p.127. Eight-floor hostel on the busy Euston Road. Rooms are very clean, bright, triple-glazed and have en-suite facilities. No kitchen; no groups. Dorms (3–6 beds) and doubles/twins.

St Paul's 36 Carter Lane, EC4 ☎0845/371 9012, Ⓔstpauls@yha.org.uk; St Paul's tube. See map, p.168. Large 190-bed hostel in a superb location opposite St Paul's Cathedral. Breakfast included and a café for dinner, but no kitchen. Small groups only. Dorms (4–8 beds) and twins.

Thameside 20 Salter Rd, SE16 ☎0845/371 9756, Ⓔthameside@yha.org.uk; Canada Water tube. See map, p.230. London's largest purpose-built hostel, with 320 beds, is located in a quiet spot near the river, fifteen minutes from the nearest tube. Can feel a bit out on a limb, but has space when more central places are full. Kitchen available, plus café. Dorms (4–10 beds) and doubles/twins.

some of which have a serious party attitude. Virtually all hostels have dispensed with a curfew, all have internet access (for a fee), and most include breakfast in the price – we've noted the exceptions to these rules. A good website for booking hostels online is Ⓦwww.hostellondon.com.

Outside term-time, it's also possible to stay in **student halls of residence** (see box, p.368). Prices are slightly higher than hostels because you usually get a room to yourself, and some locations are very central and attractive. The quality of the rooms varies enormously, but they tend to be small and basic and get booked up quickly. Some have shared kitchen facilities, some offer B&B – student and senior discounts are often available.

Finally, London has only a couple of **campsites** on the perimeter of the city. Pitches cost £3–6, plus a fee of around £5–7 per person per night, with reductions for children and during the winter months.

Hostels

Ashlee House 261–265 Gray's Inn Rd, WC1 ☏020/7833 9400, ⊛www.ashleehouse.co.uk; King's Cross tube. See map, p.127. A clean and friendly 170-bed hostel in a converted office block near King's Cross Station, with laundry and kitchen facilities. Breakfast included. Dorms (4–16 beds) from £14, singles £25, twins £50.

Clink Hostel 78 King's Cross Rd, WC1 ☏020/7183 9400, ⊛www.clinkhostel .com; King's Cross tube. See map, p.127. This 300-bed place is run by *Ashlee House*, but has funkier decor, bargain pod beds, and plenty of period features from the days when it was a Victorian courthouse, like the spacious internet courtroom – you can even stay in one of the old prison cells. Breakfast included; kitchen facilities from noon. Dorms (4–16 beds) from around £10, doubles/twins from £40.

Curzon House 158 Courtfield Gardens, SW5 ☏020/7581 2116, ⊛www.curzonhousehotel .co.uk; Gloucester Road tube. See map, p.254. Basic hostel in a leafy street of white stucco terraces in South Kensington. Small kitchen; breakfast included. Dorms (4–8 beds) from £17, singles from £35, doubles/twins £48, triples from £67.

Generator Compton Place, off Tavistock Place, WC1 ☏020/7388 7666, ⊛www.generator hostels.com; Russell Square or Euston tube. See map, p.127. A huge hostel, with over 800 beds, in a converted police barracks, tucked away down a cobbled street. The neon and UV lighting and postindustrial decor may not be to everyone's taste, but this is without doubt the best bargain in Bloomsbury. There's a young, party atmosphere with themed nights in the late-night bar. Laundry, but no kitchen; breakfast included, plus cheap café. Dorms (4–12 beds) from £15, singles/twins £50, triples £60, quads £80.

Globetrotter Inn Ashlar Court, Ravenscourt Gardens, W6 ☏020/8746 3112, ⊛www .globetrotterinns.com; Ravenscourt Park tube. Good, clean, dorm-only hostel, with friendly and helpful staff – not central, but close to the tube. Generous breakfast included, and kitchen available. Dorms from £19, doubles/ twins from £60.

Meininger Baden Powell House, 65–67 Queen's Gate, SW7 ☏020/3051 8173, ⊛www .meininger-hostels.com; Gloucester Road or South Kensington tube. See map, p.258. Bright and cheerful, modern hostel run with Teutonic efficiency by a German hostel chain. Located near the South Ken museums. Free wi-fi. Breakfast not included; kitchen, but no laundry. Dorms (4–6 beds) from £19, singles £33, twins from £45.

Palmers Lodge 40 College Crescent, NW3 ☏020/7483 8470, ⊛www.palmerslodge.co.uk; Swiss Cottage tube. Self-proclaimed boutique backpackers lodge in a vast Victorian mansion in south Hampstead with period features galore in the public rooms. Breakfast included, plus cheap meals in the scullery. Unique double dorm bunk-beds for couples (£30). Dorms (4–28 beds) from £15, en-suite doubles/twins from £50.

Piccadilly Backpackers 12 Sherwood St, W1 ☏020/7434 9009, ⊛www.piccadilly backpackers.com; Piccadilly Circus tube. See map, p.108. Vast, 700-bed hostel with small rooms and an institutional feel. Not the quietest place to crash out, but it's incredibly cheap and central. You can pay more for pod bunks and en-suite facilities. Breakfast not included; laundry but no kitchen. Dorms from £12, doubles/twins from £65.

Pickwick Hall International Backpackers 7 Bedford Place, WC1 ☏020/7323 4958, ⊛www .pickwickhall.co.uk; Russell Square tube. See map, p.127. Most accommodation is in twin-bed rooms, with 3- and 4-bed single-sex dorms also available, not all of them en suite. Kitchen facilities and a laundry. Breakfast included. Dorms from £25; singles, £55, doubles/twins £66.

Smart Backpackers ☏020/7221 7773, ⊛www .smartbackpackers.com. Hard-partying mini-chain of hostels, with basic, functional furnishings, and the city's cheapest dorm beds. Only the Russell Square hostel (see map, p.127) and the *Hyde Park Inn* (see map, p.278) have kitchens; *Smart Hyde Park View* also has en-suite doubles and a bar, and there are other branches in Camden and Bayswater. Dorm beds from around £12 (including breakfast), en-suite doubles from £80.

St Christopher's Inn ☏020/7407 1856, ⊛www .st-christophers.co.uk. *St Christopher's* run seven hostels across London, with no fewer than three near London Bridge (see map, p.234), with branches in Camden, Greenwich, Shepherd's Bush and Hammersmith. The decor is upbeat and cheerful, the

City University 15 Bastwick St, EC1 ☏020/7040 8037, ⓦwww.city.ac.uk/ems; Barbican tube. See map, p.168. City University has a modern hall of residence in Clerkenwell offering singles (from £21), with shared facilities, en-suite twins/doubles (£60) and 4–6 room apartments – all rooms have use of a shared kitchen and laundrette. The bulk of the rooms are available for just six weeks from mid-July, but some are available all year round.

International Students House 229 Great Portland St, W1 ☏020/7631 8310, ⓦwww .ish.org.uk; Great Portland Street tube. See map, p.104. Hundreds of beds in a vast complex near Regent's Park. No kitchen facilities. Dorms (6–10 beds) from around £13 (not including breakfast), B&B singles (from £36.50) and twins (from £56), with or without en suite, plus triples (around £70) and quads (around £83). Open all year.

King's College London ☏020/7848 1700, ⓦkcl.ac.uk. King's College offers rooms at four different locations. The **Great Dover Street Apartments** are in a Victorian building not far from Bankside (see map, p.234), while the **Stamford Street Apartments** are all singles in a purpose-built block close to the South Bank (see map, p.221) – both these places offer en-suite singles from £40, while Great Dover Street also has twins from £60. The **Hampstead Residence** is in a nice Victorian building on a tree-lined avenue, off Finchley Road, within walking distance of the West Heath – all rooms have shared facilities (and no kitchen), with B&B £32 for a single and £53 for a twin (no under-14s allowed). **King's College Hall** offers B&B singles for £25 per person, with shared facilities (and no kitchen), but it's in Denmark Hill in suburban south London. All rooms July–Sept only.

London Schoool of Economics (LSE) ☏020/7955 7575, ⓦwww.lsevacations.co.uk. LSE has a whole host of halls scattered across central London, offering B&B and self-catering – most are available Christmas, Easter & July–Sept, but several have rooms that can be booked all year round. **Bankside House** (see map, p.234), bang next door to Tate Modern, has everything from cheap B&B singles with shared facilities (from £43) to en-suite quads (£110), though if you want a kitchen, you'll have to book a self-catering apartment (from £140). Purpose-built **Butler's Wharf**, near Tower Bridge (see map, p.230), offers self-catering singles (£35) and twins (£55), while **Grosvenor House**, in Covent Garden (see map, p.140), has self-catering en-suite singles (£63), twins/doubles (£90) and apartments (from £99). **Northumberland House**, a grandiose building just off Trafalgar Square (see map, p.44), also offers self-catering en-suite singles (£59) and twins/doubles (from £79). **Carr-Saunders Hall** is an office block just north of Oxford Street (see map, p.104), with B&B singles (£33) and bargain twins/doubles (from £45), with shared facilities, including a kitchen. **Passfield Hall** is made up of ten attractive, late Georgian buildings in Bloomsbury (see map, p.127), and offers singles (£37), twins (£60) and triples (£75). Lastly, **High Holborn** is a modern block on a busy street (see map, p.151), close to the West End, with B&B singles (£37), twins (from £55) and triples (£99), plus kitchen facilities, and **Rosebery Hall** is in trendy Clerkenwell (see map, p.158), and has B&B singles (£33), twins (from £52) and triples (£64).

hostels are efficiently run and there's a party-animal ambience, fuelled by the hostel bars. The *London Bridge Village* hostel also has a nightclub and cinema, plus a rooftop hot tub and sauna, while the *Orient Express* branch is probably the quietest and has a women-only floor. Free breakfast and laundry facilities but no kitchen. Dorms from £18, doubles/twins from £50.

Campsites

Abbey Wood Federation Rd, Abbey Wood, SE2 ☏020/8311 7708, ⓦwww.caravanclub.co.uk; Abbey Wood train station from Charing Cross or London Bridge. Spacious, woody, well-equipped Caravan Club site, ten miles southeast of central London. Open all year.

Crystal Palace Crystal Palace Parade, SE19 ☎020/8778 7155, ⓦwww.caravanclub.co.uk; **Crystal Palace train station from Victoria or London Bridge.** A decent Camping & Caravanning Club site on south London's most famous woody hill, best suited for caravans and campervans. Station is five minutes' walk or bus #3 will take you all the way to Oxford St. Open all year.

Lea Valley Camping & Caravan Park Meridian Way, Edmonton N9 ☎020/8803 6900, ⓦwww .leevalleypark.org.uk; **Ponders End train station from Liverpool Street.** Well-equipped site at Pickett's Lock on the River Lea, backing onto a vast reservoir. Multiplex cinema and 18-hole golf course on your doorstep. Open all year.

Hotels and B&Bs

The bulk of the recommendations here cost between £50 and £150 a double, though a few are considerably more expensive. Many hotels quote expensive walk-in or rack rates, but there are usually deals to be had online or at the weekend, which can bring down prices considerably. Prices given are for the **cheapest double room** – if not all the rooms are en suite, this will be for rooms with shared facilities. Where a price range is given, the higher price will be the cheapest rack (or walk-in) rate, the lower price will be a weekend or discount rate which must be booked online in advance. Trawling the net may produce further savings, and of course there may be additional low-season discounts.

Whitehall & Westminster

The hotels in this section are marked on the map on p.44.

Westminster

The Grand/Club Quarters Trafalgar Square, WC2 ☎020/7839 9333, ⓦwww.clubquarters.com; **Covent Garden tube.** Grandiloquent building on Trafalgar Square itself, with fully equipped, modern rooms. *Club Quarters* is an American business-orientated chain that uses minimal staff – there's no check-in and no breakfast. Rates vary according to availability. £110.

Sanctuary House 33 Tothill St, SW1 ☎020/7799 4044, ⓦwww.fullershotels.co.uk; **St James's Park tube.** A Fuller's hotel, above a Fuller's pub, and decked out like one too, in comfortable pseudo-Victoriana. Breakfast is extra, and is served in the pub, but the location by St James's Park is terrific. Rates depend on availability – ask about the weekend deals. £120.

Victoria

B&B Belgravia 64–66 Ebury St, SW1 ☎020/7259 8570, ⓦwww.bb-belgravia .com; **Victoria tube.** A real rarity in this neck of the woods – a B&B with flair, very close to the train and coach stations. The rooms are boutique-hotel quality, with original features

as well as stylish modern touches. Communal spaces are light and well designed, and staff are welcoming and enthusiastic. Free in-room internet access. £115.

Cartref House 129 Ebury St, SW1 ☎020/7730 6176, ⓦwww.cartrefhouse.co.uk; **Victoria tube.** A clean, Georgian B&B with ten fresh and bright en-suite rooms as well as some with shared facilities. The family room (£156) with a double and bunk sleeps four. £95.

Cherry Court Hotel 23 Hugh St, SW1 ☎020/7828 2840, ⓦwww.cherrycourthotel.co.uk; **Victoria tube.** Bargain, mid-terrace Victorian B&B, with amiable staff. The rooms are very small, but all are en suite, there are several triples (£85) and the family room sleeps five (£120). Free internet. £60.

Luna & Simone Hotel 47–49 Belgrave Rd, SW1 ☎020/7834 5897, ⓦwww .lunasimonehotel.com; **Victoria tube. See map, p.254.** Inexpensive B&B with a bright foyer, very friendly staff and plain, well-maintained en-suite rooms. Big breakfasts. £85.

Morgan House 107 & 120 Ebury St, SW1 ☎020/7730 2384, ⓦwww.morganhouse.co.uk; **Victoria tube.** An above-average B&B in a Georgian building, run by a vivacious couple. Great breakfasts, patio garden, and a fridge for guests to use. Most rooms are en suite; the family room (£132) has a double and a bunk bed. £72.

Budget chain hotels

Chain hotels have pretty much got the **budget hotel** market sewn up. B&Bs may be able to offer a more personal touch and more character in the decor, but the franchises are often in unbeatable central locations. Although they will never really be more than perfunctory places to stay, on the whole they can be guaranteed to provide clean, anonymous rooms.

Bumping along at the bottom are easyHotel (⊛ www.easyhotel.com), whose prices start at just £25 for an en-suite double – if you want a window, TV use or room cleaning, it's extra; there are branches in Victoria, South Ken, Paddington and Earl's Court. Serious bargains can also be had at Travelodge, which has some very handily situated hotels in Covent Garden, Farringdon, Marylebone and Southwark; rooms are utilitarian, but if you book online well in advance, en-suite doubles can cost less than £50. Premier Inn is the other real budget option. It's generally considered a cut above Travelodge, though it doesn't have quite the online bargains; centrally located branches exist at the back of County Hall, near Tate Modern and by the Tower of London. The rest of the chain gang aren't worth considering as you can get better value elsewhere.

Look out, however, for nitenite (⊛ www.nitenite.com), a micro-boutique hotel chain which offers luxury "cabins" for as little as £50, and should have several London branches by 2010; ditto Yotel (⊛ www.yotel.com), a Japanese-style capsule chain, where rooms can be rented by the hour.

St James's

The Stafford Hotel 16–18 St James's Place, SW1 ☏ 020/7493 0111, ⊛ www.thestaffordhotel.co .uk; Green Park tube. See map, p.77. Tucked in a quiet backstreet off St James's St, The Stafford provides high-class rooms in the main building, with more expensive accommodation in the unique Carriage House, a row of eighteenth-century stables luxuriously converted to large guest rooms. The hotel also has the *American Bar*, founded to provide cocktails for pioneering American visitors in the early 1930s, and its courtyard terrace is a delight. £250–330.

Mayfair

The hotels in this section are marked on the map on p.87.

Claridge's Brook St, W1 ☏ 020/7629 8860, ⊛ www.claridges.co.uk; Bond Street tube. This famous and glamorous Art Deco Mayfair hotel is the chosen abode of visiting heads of state and media megastars. For your money you get wardrobes bigger than most bathrooms, showerheads the size of dinner plates and decor as plush as any vacationing potentate could wish for. £330.

Grosvenor House Park Lane, W1 ☏ 020/7499 6363, ⊛ www.londongrosvenorhouse.co.uk; Marble Arch tube. One of the capital's most historic hotels – the Queen learnt to skate in the hotel's ice rink (now the gargantuan Great Hall). Rooms are nicely understated and although rack rates are high, online deals are a five-star bargain. Breakfast not included. £150–290.

Marylebone

The hotels in this section are marked on the map on p.97.

Edward Lear Hotel 28–30 Seymour St, W1 ☏ 020/7402 5401, ⊛ www.edlear.com; Marble Arch tube. Lear's former home enjoys a great location close to Oxford St and Hyde Park, lovely flower boxes and a plush foyer. Rooms themselves need a bit of a makeover, but the low prices reflect both this and the fact that most only have shared facilities. Full English breakfast included. £80.

Lincoln House Hotel 33 Gloucester Place, W1 ☏ 020/7486 7630, ⊛ www.lincoln-house-hotel .co.uk; Marble Arch or Baker Street tube. Dark wood panelling gives this Georgian B&B in Marylebone a ship's-cabin feel: all the rooms are en suite and well equipped. Rates vary according to the size of the bed and length of stay. Breakfast not included. £75.

Weardowney 23 Ashbridge St, NW8 ☏ 020/7725 9694, ⊛ www.weardowney.com; Marylebone or

Edgware Road tube. Seven rooms above a former pub, now a knitwear boutique run by two former models. Most rooms share facilities and, naturally enough, feature arty knitted furnishings. There's a kitchen and roof terrace. £90.

Wigmore Court Hotel 23 Gloucester Place, W1 ☎020/7935 0928, ⓦwww.wigmore-court-hotel .co.uk; Marble Arch or Baker Street tube. The ruched curtains and floral decor may not be to everyone's taste, but this Georgian town house in Marylebone is a better-than-average B&B, boasting a high tally of returning clients. Comfortable rooms with en-suite facilities, plus two cheaper doubles with shared facilities. No lift, but there's a laundry and basic kitchen for guests' use. £89.

Soho and Fitzrovia

The hotels in this section are marked on the map on p.104.

Charlotte Street Hotel 15–17 Charlotte St, W1 ☎020/7806 2000, ⓦwww.firmdale.com; Goodge Street or Tottenham Court Road tube. Smart but comfortable town house hotel just north of Oxford St. Rooms are sumptuously decorated, but resolutely modern in style, with en-suite granite bathrooms complete with flatscreen TVs, and Tivoli radios at the bedsides. £240.

Hazlitt's 6 Frith St, W1 ☎020/7434 1771, ⓦwww.hazlittshotel.com; Tottenham Court Road tube. Located off the south side of Soho Square, this early eighteenth-century building is a hotel of real character and discreet charm, offering en-suite rooms exquisitely decorated with period furniture. There's a small sitting room, but no dining room; breakfast (served in the rooms) is not included. £230.

Soho Hotel 4 Richmond Mews, W1 ☎020/7559 3000, ⓦwww.firmdale.com; Tottenham Court Road tube. Once a multistorey car park made over by Kit Kemp's boutique hotel group Firmdale. The eclectic decor borders on the schizophrenic, from the Oriental lobby to the camp fuchsia boudoirs and a screening room done out in fake fur and scarlet leather. The penthouse suites (£2750 a night anyone?) have wonderful wraparound terraces and rooftop views, and the facilities are, as you'd expect, top-notch. £280.

Bloomsbury

The hotels in this section are marked on the map on p.127.

Alhambra Hotel 17–19 Argyle St, WC1 ☎020/7837 9575, ⓦwww.alhambrahotel.com; Goodge Street or Euston Square tube. Clean, modern, functional place just a stone's throw from St Pancras. Cheapest rooms have shared facilities and there's no lift, but breakfast is included and there's free wi-fi. £60.

Arosfa Hotel 83 Gower St, WC1 ☎020/7636 2115, ⓦwww.arosfalondon.com; Goodge Street or Euston Square tube. Well-maintained, simple B&B with en-suite rooms. Plain furnishings, TVs in all the rooms, with tea and coffee facilities in the lounge area, and a small garden out back. Free wi-fi. £82.

Arran House Hotel 77–79 Gower St, WC1 ☎020/7535 2186, ⓦwww.arranhotel-london .com; Goodge Street tube. Bright, cheerful and clean B&B, with doubles, triples, quads and even bargain hostel-style accommodation (£23–27). The cheaper rooms have shared facilities. Hearty breakfast included. £82.

Celtic Hotel 61–63 Guilford St, WC1 ☎020/7837 6737; Russell Square tube. Simply furnished family-run hotel just off Russell Square, with clean, light and airy singles, doubles, triples and quads; the cheaper rooms have shared facilities. Two resident lounges and a hotel cat… called "Dog". £65.

Jesmond Hotel 63 Gower St, WC1 ☎020/7636 1141, ⓦwww.jesmondhotel.org.uk; Goodge Street tube. Reliable Bloomsbury hotel with a lovely little garden at the back. Rooms are clean but can be on the small side; free internet, and they'll do your laundry for £5. Cheaper rooms have shared facilities. Breakfast included. £75.

Ridgemount Hotel 65–67 Gower St, WC1 ☎020/7636 1141, ⓦwww.ridgemounthotel .co.uk; Goodge Street tube. Old-fashioned, very friendly, family-run place, with small rooms (half with shared facilities), a garden, and free hot-drinks machine. A reliable, basic bargain for Bloomsbury. £60.

Hotel Russell 1–8 Russell Square, WC1 ☎020/7837 6470, ⓦwww.londonrussellhotel .co.uk; Russell Square tube. From its grand 1898 exterior to its opulent interiors of marble, wood and crystal, this late Victorian landmark fully retains its period atmosphere in all its public areas (though not in the rooms themselves). Service could often be better, and the rack rates are pretty high, but online you can get good deals. Breakfast not included. £125–230.

Covent Garden and the Strand

The hotels in this section are marked on the map on p.140.

Covent Garden Hotel 10 Monmouth St, WC2 ☎020/7806 1000, ⊛www.firmdale.com; Covent Garden tube. Stylish conversion of a former French hospital in the heart of the West End. Rooms are all individually decorated in luxurious and striking but tasteful furnishings. All mod cons including wi-fi and DVD/CD player. £240.

The Fielding Hotel 4 Broad Court, Bow St, WC2 ☎020/7836 8305, ⊛www.thefieldinghotel.co.uk; Covent Garden tube. Quietly situated on a traffic-free and gas-lit court, this excellent hotel is one of Covent Garden's hidden gems. Its en-suite rooms are a firm favourite with visiting performers, since it's just a few yards from the Royal Opera House. No lift and no breakfast. £130.

One Aldwych 1 Aldwych, WC2 ☎020/7300 1000, ⊛www.onealdwych.com; Covent Garden or Temple tube. On the outside, an Art Nouveau 1907 building, built for the *Morning Post*; on the inside a minimalist contemporary boutique hotel. The attractions include underwater music in the hotel's vast pool, oodles of modern art about the place and TVs in the bathrooms. £340.

Seven Dials Hotel 7 Monmouth St, WC2 ☎020/7681 0791, ⊛www.sevendialshotellondon.com; Covent Garden tube. Pleasant family-run B&B hotel on a lovely street in the heart of the West End. The staircase is narrow and winding (no lift) and the rooms are small, but all are en suite, with TV and tea/coffee-making facilities, and breakfast is included. £80.

Clerkenwell and Hoxton

The hotels in this section are marked on the map on p.158.

Fox & Anchor 115 Charterhouse St, EC1 ☎0845/347 0100, ⊛www.foxandanchor.com; Farringdon tube. This traditional Clerkenwell pub has six small, but luxuriously furnished rooms, up a narrow flight of stairs, with all the mod cons you could desire. Only issue

is noise from nearby clubs, so ask for a room at the back. Check-in is at *Malmaison* (see below). £95–165.

Hoxton Hotel 81 Great Eastern St, EC2 ☎020/7550 1000, ⊛www.hoxtonhotels.com; Old Street tube. Fittingly trendy hotel for über-hip Hoxton, with contemporary art on the walls and fashionably lugubrious decor in the rooms, with flat-screen TVs and duck-down duvets. Tiny breakfast delivered to your room. Free wi-fi and cheap phone calls. Price depends entirely on availability so you could pay as little as £30 or as much as £165 – occasionally they even sell rooms for £1.

Malmaison 18–21 Charterhouse Square, EC1 ☎020/7012 3700, ⊛www.malmaison-london.com; Farringdon tube. Set in a quiet, cobbled square in the heart of Clerkenwell, this is the London branch of a slowly expanding chain of British boutique hotels. The tone is dark, modern and quite clubby in deference to the nearby City. Service and facilities are difficult to fault. £125–250.

The Rookery 12 Peter's Lane, Cowcross St, EC1 ☎020/7336 0931, ⊛www.rookeryhotel.com; Farringdon tube. Rambling Georgian town house on the edge of the City in trendy Clerkenwell that makes a fantastically discreet little hideaway. Each room has been individually designed in a deliciously camp, modern take on the Baroque period, and all have super bathrooms with lots of character. £220.

The Zetter 86–88 Clerkenwell Rd, EC1 ☎020/ 7324 4444, ⊛www.thezetter.com; Farringdon tube. A warehouse converted with real style and a dash of 1960s glamour. Rooms are simple and minimalist, with fun touches such as lights which change colour and decorative floral panels; ask for a room at the back, overlooking quiet, cobbled St John's Square. Water for guests is supplied from *The Zetter*'s own well, beneath the building. £170.

The City

The hotels in this section are marked on the map on p.168.

Andaz 40 Liverpool St, EC2 ☎020/7618 5010, ⊛www.andaz.com; Liverpool Street tube. The venerable 1884 Great Eastern Hotel by Liverpool Street Station had a complete Conran makeover in 2000; the rooms are in the cool contemporary style, but the public areas have nevertheless retained some of the old-world clubby flavour. Service is so hi-tech and personal, there's not even a reception desk anymore. £250.

🏃 **Apex City of London Hotel** 1 Seething Lane, EC3 ☎020/7977 9593, ⓦwww .apexhotels.co.uk; Tower Hill tube. A swish hotel on a secluded City street, designed for corporate clientele – the rooms are very masculine, in black, grey and burgundy, with the pricier ones enjoying more light and better views. Rates vary enormously according to availability so book early. The gym, sauna and steam room are free for guests. £60–130.

Club Quarters 24 Ludgate Hill, EC3 ☎020/7651 2200, ⓦwww.clubquarters.com; St Paul's or Blackfriars tube. Designed for business folk, with smartly furnished, spacious rooms and suites fitted with all mod cons. *Club Quarters* currently have two other locations: another one in the City, and one on Trafalgar Square itself. £150.

🏃 **The King's Wardrobe** 6 Wardrobe Place, Carter Lane, EC4 ☎020/7792 2222, ⓦwww.bridgestreet.com; St Paul's tube. In a quiet courtyard just behind St Paul's Cathedral, this place is part of an international chain that caters largely for a business clientele. The apartments offer fully equipped kitchens and workstations, a concierge service and housekeeping. Though housed in a fourteenth-century building that once contained Edward III's royal regalia, the interior is modern. £130–210.

Threadneedles 5 Threadneedle St, EC2 ☎020/7657 8080, ⓦwww.theetoncollection .com; Bank tube. Magnificent former Midland Bank in the heart of the financial district, now a boutique hotel, with every mod con from plasma TVs to cordless digital telephones. Rack rates are stratospheric, but online, in advance, and at the weekend, a luxury double costs from £200–300.

Docklands

Four Seasons Hotel Canary Wharf 46 Westferry Circus, E14 ☎020/7510 1999, ⓦwww .fourseasons.com; Canary Wharf tube and DLR. A spectacular riverfront setting, funky modern interiors and good links to the City have made this hotel very popular with business folk, but weekend rates, which bring prices down, mean that it's an equally

good base for sightseeing. Pool, fitness centre, spa and tennis courts. Several rooms have superb Thames views. There's also the option of taking a boat into town. £195.

The South Bank

The hotels in this section are marked on the map on p.221.

Captain Bligh House 100 Lambeth Rd, SE1 ☎020/8769 3500, ⓦwww.bed-and-breakfast -london.co.uk; London Bridge tube. Former home of Captain Bligh is now a nautically flavoured Georgian B&B, a short walk from the South Bank, run by a friendly couple (and their two cats). There are just three rooms, two of which have self-catering facilities; breakfast is included and taken in your room. £90.

Mad Hatter 3–7 Stamford St, SE1 ☎020/7401 9222, ⓦwww.fullershotels.co.uk; Southwark or Blackfriars tube. Plush pseudo-Victorian Fuller's hotel, above a modern Fuller's pub on Blackfriars Rd. Breakfast is extra on weekdays, and is served in the pub, but this is a great location, a short walk from Tate Modern and the South Bank. Rates depend on availability – weekends are cheapest. £95–135.

London Marriott Hotel County Hall County Hall, SE1 ☎020/7928 5200, ⓦwww.marriott.com; Waterloo or Westminster tube. Historic County Hall, once home to London's government, stands right on the river with over three-quarters of its rooms offering river views, many with small balconies. It's all suitably pompous inside, and there's a full-sized indoor pool and well-equipped gym. £210.

Southwark

The hotels in this section are marked on the map on p.230.

London Bridge Hotel 8–18 London Bridge St, SE1 ☎020/7855 2200, ⓦwww.londonbridge hotel.com; London Bridge tube. Perfectly placed for Southwark and Bankside or the City, this is a comfortable, contemporary hotel right by the station with flat-screen TVs and wi-fi in the rooms. £100–170.

🏃 **Southwark Rose Hotel** 43–47 Southwark Bridge Rd, SE1 ☎020/7015 1480, ⓦwww.southwarkrosehotel.co.uk; London Bridge tube. The *Southwark Rose* has nice

▲ Southwark Rose Hotel

contemporary design touches that raise the rooms several notches above the bland chain hotels in the area. Giant aluminium lamps hover over the lobby, which is lined with funky photographs, while the penthouse restaurant offers breakfast with a rooftop view and free wi-fi. Rates depend on availability. £125–190.

South Kensington, Knightsbridge and Chelsea

The hotels in this section are marked on the map on p.254.

South Kensington

 Aster House 3 Sumner Place, SW7 ☎020/7581 5888, ⓦwww.asterhouse .com; South Kensington tube. Pleasant, award-winning B&B in a luxurious South Ken white-stuccoed street; there's a lovely garden at the back and a large conservatory, where breakfast is served. £180.
Baglioni 60 Hyde Park Gate, SW7 ☎020/7368 5700, ⓦwww.baglionihotels.com; High Street Kensington tube. A bit of Italian designer cool has arrived near the Albert Hall, overlooking Kensington Gardens. Decor is dark, brooding and out to impress. Butler service on every floor and every conceivable tasteful mod con. £320.

The Halkin 5 Halkin St, SW1 ☎020/7333 1000, ⓦwww.halkin.como.bz; Hyde Park Corner tube. A luxury hotel that spurns the chintzy country-house theme: elegant, East-meets-West minimalism prevails in each of the 41 rooms. The contemporary theme is continued in the Michelin-starred Thai restaurant, which overlooks a private garden. £250–450.
Milestone Hotel 1 Kensington Court, W8 ☎020/7917 1000, ⓦwww.milestonehotel.com; High Street Kensington tube. Luxury hotel, situated in two adjoining nineteenth-century town houses overlooking Kensington Palace and Gardens. Sumptuously decorated in period style and complete with butler, this place feels more like a stately home than a hotel. All mod cons, gym and sauna, too, plus conference facilities. £300.

Earl's Court and Fulham

Barclay House 21 Barclay Rd, SW6 ☎020/7384 3390, ⓦwww.barclayhouselondon.com; Fulham Broadway tube. Small, friendly Fulham B&B in a quiet street very close to the tube – it's run by genuine music lovers, with a grand piano for the use of guests. Continental breakfast is included, but it's worth paying the little extra for a cooked one. £85.
Merlyn Court Hotel 2 Barkston Gardens, SW5 ☎020/7370 1640, ⓦwww.merlyncourthotel .com; Earl's Court tube. Well-appointed and popular B&B in a quiet leafy street close to the tube. Clean, bright rooms, some with en-suite facilities; English breakfast is included. £68–75.
Parkcity Hotel 18–30 Lexham Gardens, SW5 ☎020/7341 7090, ⓦwww.theparkcity.com; Gloucester Road or Earl's Court tube. Reliably good small hotel, ten minutes' walk from the tube in the quiet backstreets of South Ken/ Earl's Court; staff are very helpful, rooms are clean. Book ahead to get the cheapest rates. £120.
Twenty Nevern Square 20 Nevern Square, SW5 ☎020/7565 9555, ⓦwww .twentynevernsquare.co.uk; Earl's Court tube. In an area of bog-standard B&Bs, this is a real winner, decked out in bold, warm colours and strewn with Oriental and European antiques. Rooms are en suite, comfortable and appealing. Buffet breakfast included. Apartments and family rooms available. £90–175.

The hotels in this section are marked on the map on p.278.

High Street Kensington

Vicarage Hotel 10 Vicarage Gate, W8 ☎020/7229 4030, ⓦwww.londonvicaragehotel .com; Notting Hill Gate or High Street Kensington tube. Ideally located B&B on a quiet street a step away from Kensington Gardens. Clean and smart floral rooms with shared facilities; full English breakfast included. £93.

Paddington

Caring Hotel 24 Craven Hill Gardens, W2 ☎020/7262 8708, ⓦwww.caringhotel.com; Bayswater, Paddington or Lancaster Gate tube. The decor isn't to all tastes, but the rooms are clean, the cheaper ones have shared facilities, and breakfast is included. £55.

Columbia Hotel 95–99 Lancaster Gate, W2 ☎020/7402 0021, ⓦwww.columbiahotel.co.uk; Lancaster Gate tube. This large hotel, once five Victorian houses, offers simply decorated rooms, some with views over Hyde Park, a spacious public lounge with a vaguely Art Deco feel, and a cocktail bar. Said to be a rock-star favourite, but surprisingly good value for all that. En-suite doubles, triples and quads also available. £89.

Pavilion Hotel 34–36 Sussex Gardens, W2 ☎020/7262 0905, ⓦwww.pavilionhoteluk.com; Paddington tube. A decadent rock star's home from home, with outrageously over-the-top decor and every room individually themed, from "honky-tonk Afro" to "Highland Fling". Service can be erratic but it's perfect for those who like their hotels a bit quirky. £100.

St David's Hotels 14–20 Norfolk Square, W2 ☎020/7723 3856/4963, ⓦwww.stdavidshotels .com; Paddington tube. A friendly welcome is assured at this inexpensive B&B, famed for its substantial English breakfast. Most rooms are en suite. The large family rooms make it a good option for families on a budget. £60.

Bayswater, Westbourne Grove and Notting Hill

Garden Court Hotel 30–31 Kensington Gardens Square, W2 ☎020/7229 2553, ⓦwww .gardencourthotel.co.uk; Bayswater or Queensway tube. Nicely refurbished family-run B&B close to Portobello Market; rooms are small, and the cheaper ones have shared facilities. English breakfast included. £75.

The Main House 6 Colville Rd, W11 ☎020/7221 9691, ⓦwww.themainhouse.co.uk; Ladbroke Grove/Notting Hill Gate tube. Bright and cheerful place that manages to be both homely – thanks to some lovely period furniture – and chic; smart, but without being pretentious. Perfectly placed for Portobello Rd. Breakfast not included. £110.

Miller's Residence 111a Westbourne Grove, W2 ☎020/7243 1024, ⓦwww.millersuk.com; Bayswater tube. Every inch of this grandiose and eccentric B&B is littered with nineteenth-century antiques, from the sumptuous baronial drawing room (much in demand for fashion shoots) to the bedrooms. Some rooms are a little small and dark for the price, but the welcome is warm and the ambience unique. Access from Hereford Rd. £150.

New Linden Hotel 59 Leinster Square, W2 ☎020/7221 4321, ⓦwww.mayflower-group .co.uk; Bayswater/Notting Hill Gate tube. Elegant on the outside and functional on the inside. Some rooms are on the small side, but imaginative use of fabrics and lighting gives them an enticing feel. Perks include flat-screen TVs, CD players, and proximity to Portobello Rd. £100–130.

Portobello Gold 95–97 Portobello Rd, W1 ☎020/7460 4910, ⓦwww.portobellogold.com; Notting Hill Gate or Holland Park tube. A fun and friendly option above a cheery modern pub/seafood restaurant. The seven rooms are plain and some are tiny, with miniature en-suite bathrooms, but the hotel also has a great apartment (sleeps 6 – at a bit of a pinch), with a dinky Caribbean-themed bathroom and a fantastic roof terrace (and putting green). Breakfast not included. £70.

Vancouver Studios 30 Prince's Square, W2 ☎020/7243 1270, ⓦwww.vancouverstudios .co.uk; Bayswater tube. Part of a growing trend away from standard hotel accommodation, *Vancouver Studios* offers self-contained apartments in a grand Victorian town house, with fully equipped kitchens and maid service. Decor is to a high standard and mixes modern trends with traditional period touches. £125.

The hotels in this section are marked on the map on p.286.

Hampstead Village Guesthouse 2 Kemplay Rd, NW3 ☏020/7435 8679, Ⓦwww.hampstead guesthouse.com; Hampstead tube. Lovely B&B in a freestanding Victorian house on a quiet backstreet between Hampstead Village and the Heath. Rooms (most en suite) are tiny, but characterful, crammed with books, pictures, and handmade and antique furniture. £75.

Langorf Hotel 20 Frognal, NW3 ☏020/7794 4483, Ⓦwww.langorfhotel.com; Finchley Road or Hampstead tube. Pristinely maintained if rather old-fashioned hotel in a trio of red-brick Victorian mansions, with a walled garden. Apartments (sleeping 3–4) also available. £90–100.

New Inn 2 Allitsen Rd, NW8 ☏020/7722 0726, Ⓦwww.newinnlondon.co.uk; St John's Wood tube. Landlady Jan runs an excellent B&B with just five rooms above a nice pub (with good Thai food), in a quiet street a few minutes' walk from the north edge of Regent's Park. Breakfast is £5–8 extra. £75.

The suburbs: Richmond, Hampton Court and Greenwich

Devonport House 81 Greenwich South St, SE10 ☏020/8283 3121, Ⓦwww.deverevenues.co.uk; Greenwich DLR or train station from Charing Cross. Right in the centre of Greenwich, these conference-centre rooms are functional, but worth it if you can find an online bargain. £80–170.

The Old Stables 1 Bridle Lane, Twickenham ☏020/8892 4507, Ⓦwww.oldstables.co.uk; St Margarets train station from Waterloo. Three bedrooms and one studio apartment in a lovely house in a quiet street right by the train station; walking distance to Richmond and the Thames. No on-site staff, but the manager is a phone call away. £75.

Paddock Lodge The Green, Hampton Court ☏020/8979 5254, Ⓦwww.paddocklodge.co.uk; Hampton Court train station from Waterloo. A secluded Palladian villa set down a leafy lane amidst wonderful gardens, with just two luxurious rooms. Excellent breakfast included; four-course dinner available by arrangement. £90.

24

Cafés and restaurants

L ondon is an exciting – though often expensive – place in which to eat out, and as it's home to people from all over the globe, you can sample pretty much any kind of cuisine here. The city boasts some of the best **Cantonese** restaurants in the whole of Europe, and is a noted centre for **Indian and Bangladeshi** food. As well as some excellent French, Greek, Italian, Japanese, Spanish and Thai restaurants, the capital also offers more unusual culinary options, from Polish and Peruvian to Sudanese and Brazilian. And of course, examples of **British** cuisine can be found all over town, from eel and pie caffs to Michelin-starred affairs.

This chapter covers the full range of eating places from unreconstructed cafés, known as "greasy spoons", which dish up traditional fried English breakfasts, fish and chips and other calorific treats, to London's top restaurants. Amongst the cafés, you'll find bakeries, brasseries, sandwich bars, coffee shops and several ethnic eating places where speedy service and low prices are the priority. Wherever you go, you should be able to fill up for under £10. In the restaurant listings, we've given price ranges for the main courses (though remember side dishes are often extra).

It's always best to **reserve a table**, and with some places you'll need to plan at least a week ahead. We've given the **opening hours**, but it's always worth calling to check. As for **prices**, you can pay an awful lot for a meal in London, and if you're used to North American portions you're going to feel short-changed. Tipping ten to fifteen percent for **service** is discretionary, but considered normal practice. However, some restaurants add the service charge to the bill, so it's always good to check to ensure you're not paying twice.

Chain coffee and sandwich options

A rash of chain coffee shops and sandwich outlets has emerged over the capital in the last decade or so. Best of the bunch for **coffee** is reckoned to be *Caffè Nero*, with well-trained and friendly baristas. Bottom of the pile, but easily the bargain-hunter's choice is cheap and cheerful Greggs (takeaway only), which offers a large tea for under a quid. It also dishes up sausage rolls, hot sarnies, pasties and cakes, as well as the full range of coffee options.

Home-grown **sandwich** chains *Pret à Manger* and *EAT* produce by far the best lunchtime food, with great sandwiches, salads and cakes made on the premises daily. *Pret*, all flash chrome and zingy service, does its own healthy canned drinks, while *EAT* outlets have a more muted feel and serve good soups, either "simple" (carrot, honey and ginger for example) or "bold" (such as beef and Guinness). *Pret* coffee is Fairtrade or ethically sourced, while *EAT* prides itself on using only organic milk.

The listings in this section are marked on the map on p.44.

Cafés

Café in the Crypt St Martin-in-the-Fields, Duncannon St, WC2 ☏020/7766 1129; Charing Cross tube. The self-service buffet food is standard fare, but there are regular veggie dishes, and the handy (and atmospheric) location – below the church in the crypt – makes this an ideal spot to fill up before hitting the West End. Fortnightly jazz nights (Wed 8pm). Mon–Wed 8am–8pm, Thurs–Sat 8am–10.30pm, Sun 11am–6pm.

Jenny Lo's Teahouse 14 Ecclestone St, SW1 ☏020/7259 0399; Victoria tube. Bright, bare and utilitarian yet somehow stylish and fashionable too, *Jenny Lo's* serves good Chinese food at low prices. Be sure to check out the therapeutic teas. Mon–Sat 11am–3pm & 6–10pm.

Restaurants

The National Dining Rooms Sainsbury Wing, The National Gallery, Trafalgar Square, WC2 ☏020/7747 2525, ⓦwww.thenationaldining rooms.co.uk; Charing Cross tube. An award-winning modern café and restaurant, with a top-notch menu of British dishes, including salmon and scallops; round off your meal with Eton Mess and British cheeses. There's also a kids' menu. Mon–Tues & Thurs–Sun 10am–5pm, Wed 10am-8.30pm. Mains £10–15.

The Vincent Rooms 76 Vincent Square ☏020/7802 8391, ⓦwww.westking.ac.uk; Victoria or St James's Park tube. Elegant brasserie serving up dishes cooked by the student chefs of Westminster Kingsway College (where Jamie Oliver learnt his trade). Mon–Fri noon–2pm, plus some eves 6–9pm; closed Easter, July, Aug & Christmas.

St James's

Cafés

Inn the Park St James's Park, W1 ☏020/7451 9999, ⓦwww.innthepark.com; St James's Park. See map, p.77. The panoramic windows of this curving wooden building look onto the park's lake. The restaurant serves delicious but pricey British food, while the classy takeaway section provides sandwiches, salads and cakes for a top-notch picnic. Mon–Fri 8am to dusk, Sat & Sun 9am to dusk.

Mayfair

The listings in this section are marked on the map on p.87.

Cafés

Mô 25 Heddon St, W1 ☏020/7434 4040, ⓦwww.momoresto.com; Piccadilly Circus tube. Serving reasonably priced and delicious snacks, this is London's ultimate Arabic pastiche tearoom, with tables and hookahs spilling out onto the pavement of a quiet Mayfair alleyway. Mon–Sat noon–11pm.

Sotheby's 34–35 New Bond St, W1 ☏020/7293 5077; Bond Street tube. Sotheby's café-restaurant is by no means cheap, but the lunches are exquisitely prepared, and the excellent afternoon teas are a fraction of the price of the nearby hotels. Mon–Fri 9.30am–4.45pm.

Tibits 12–14 Heddon St, W1 ☏020/7758 4110, ⓦtibits.co.uk; Piccadilly Circus tube. Spacious, modernist Swiss German veggie café serving up a vast range of salads and hot dishes from across the globe. Mon–Wed 9am–10.30pm, Thurs–Sat 9am–midnight, Sun 10am–10.30pm.

The Wolseley 160 Piccadilly, W1 ☏020/7499 6996, ⓦwww.thewolseley .com; Green Park tube. The lofty and stylish 1920s interior (built as the showroom for Wolseley cars) is the big draw. The Viennese-inspired food is good but pricey, and it's very popular so book ahead. Mon–Fri 7am–midnight, Sat 8am–midnight & Sun 8am–11pm.

Restaurants

Kiku Half Moon St, W1 ☎020/7499 4208, ⓦwww.kikurestaurant.co.uk; Green Park tube. "Kiku" translates as pricey, but at least this place serves up top-quality sushi and sashimi (£3–5). Take a seat at the traditional sushi bar and wonder at the dexterity of the knife man. Mon–Sat noon–2.30pm & 6–10.15pm, Sun 5.30–9.45pm. Set lunch £20.

Maze 10–13 Grosvenor Square, W1 ☎020/7107 0000, ⓦwww.gordonramsay.com; Bond Street tube. Very successful Gordon Ramsay restaurant, serving sublime *haute cuisine* with an Asian twist, in tiny, artfully presented portions. Four-course set lunch for around £30. Daily noon–2.30pm & 6–11pm. Mains £15–30.

Patterson's 4 Mill St, W1 ☎020/7499 1308, ⓦwww.pattersonsrestaurant.com; Oxford Circus or Bond Street tube. A very smart family-run restaurant serving mostly local and organic produce – the seafood is sourced from the chef's hometown of Eyemouth. The Modern European cooking looks and tastes superb. Mains (lunch) £10, (evening) £20.

Truc Vert 42 North Audley St, W1 ☎020/7491 9988, ⓦwww.trucvert.co.uk; Bond Street tube. An upmarket but friendly restaurant, offering robust provincial French food. The menu changes daily and begins early with breakfast; also has a small deli section. Mon–Sat 7.30am–midnight, Sun 9am–3pm. Mains £15–18.

Wild Honey 12 St George St, W1 ☎020/7758 9160, ⓦwww.wildhoneyrestaurant.co.uk; Baker Street or Bond Street tube. Very popular wood-panelled restaurant with friendly service, serving up slow-cooked, UK-sourced *haute cuisine*. Mon–Sat noon–2.30pm & 6–11pm, Sun noon–3pm & 6–10.30pm. Mains £14–20.

Marylebone

The listings in this section are marked on the map on p.97.

Cafés

Abu Ali 136–138 George St, W1 ☎020/7724 6338; Marble Arch tube. Lebanese equivalent of a working men's club, serving honest Lebanese fare that's terrific value for money, from the tabbouleh to the kebabs – wash it all down with fresh mint tea. Daily 9am–11pm.

Eat & Two Veg 50 Marylebone High St, W1 ☎020/7258 8595; Bond Street tube. A lively and modern veggie diner, with an eclectic menu featuring Thai, Greek and Italian dishes; some vegan and soya protein choices. Mon–Sat 9am–11pm, Sun 10am–10pm.

Golden Hind 73 Marylebone Lane, W1 ☎020/7486 3644; Bond Street tube. Marylebone's heritage fish-and-chip restaurant, founded in 1914, serves classic cod and chips from around a fiver, as well as slightly fancier fare. Bring your own wine. Mon–Fri noon–3pm & 6–10pm, Sat 6–10pm.

Patisserie Valerie at Sagne 105 Marylebone High St, W1 ☎020/7935 6240; Bond Street tube. Founded as Swiss-run Maison Sagne in the 1920s, and preserving its wonderful decor from those days, the café is now run by Soho's fab patisserie-makers, and is without doubt Marylebone's finest. Mon–Fri 7.30am–7pm, Sat 8am–7pm, Sun 9am–6pm.

Paul Rothe & Son 35 Marylebone Lane, W1 ☎020/7935 6783; Bond Street tube. Old-fashioned deli established in 1900, selling "English & Foreign Provisions" and serving inexpensive soups, toasties and sandwiches to customers at formica tables inside the shop. Mon–Fri 8am–6pm, Sat 11.30am–5.30pm.

Quiet Revolution 62–64 Weymouth St, W1 ☎020/7487 5683; Baker Street or Bond Street tube. Laid-back organic café attached to the Aveda natural cosmetics shop on the corner of Marylebone High St, serving mostly veggie fare, cakes and fresh juices. Mon–Sat 9am–6pm, Sun 11am–5pm.

Restaurants

Fairuz 3 Blandford St, W1 ☎020/7486 8108, ⓦwww.fairuz.eu; Bond Street tube. Busy, informal Lebanese restaurant, with an epic list of meze, a selection of charcoal grills and one or two oven-baked dishes. Get here early and secure one of the nook-and-crannyish, tent-like tables. Mon–Sat noon–11pm, Sun noon–10.30pm. Mains £12–20.

Phoenix Palace 3–5 Glentworth St, W1 ☎020/7486 3515, ⓦwww.phoenixpalace.uk.com; Baker Street or Marylebone tube.

There's plenty to choose from here with dishes from all over China. Better still, the cooking is good and the portions large. Mon–Sat noon–11.30pm, Sun 11am–10.30pm. Mains £8–11.

🏃 **The Providores** 109 Marylebone High St, W1 ⊕020/7935 6175, ⊛www .theprovidores.co.uk; Baker Street or Bond Street

Soho & Fitzrovia

Chinatown

The listings in this section are marked on the map on p.108.

Restaurants

Leong's Legends 4 Macclesfield St, W1 ⊕020/7287 0288; Leicester Square tube. Brusque service may be automatically added to your bill, but this multi storey teahouse-style restaurant dishes up excellent Taiwanese cuisine. Daily noon–11pm. Mains £8–14.

Misato 11 Wardour St, W1; Leicester Square tube. Modern, canteen-style Japanese place serving stomach-filling rice and noodle dishes, plus miso soup, sushi and bento boxes. Daily noon–midnight. Mains £5–8.

🏃 **Mr Kong** 21 Lisle St, WC2 ⊕020/7437 7923; Leicester Square tube. One of Chinatown's finest, with a huge choice of Cantonese dishes and friendly service. There's always something intriguing among the specials – anyone for jellyfish? Mon–Sat noon–2.45am, Sun noon–1.45am. £8–25.

Royal Dragon 30 Gerrard St, W1 ⊕020/7734 0935; Leicester Square tube. A varied menu, but the delicious dim sum is a speciality, and after your meal you can repair to the karaoke room upstairs. Mon–Sat noon–3am, Sun 11am–3am. Mains £8–23.

Tokyo Diner 2 Newport Place, WC2 ⊕020/7287 8777, ⊛www.tokyodiner.com; Leicester Square tube. Friendly eatery, on the edge of Chinatown, serving fast food, Tokyo style. Minimalist decor lets the (tuna-free) sushi do the talking. They don't accept tips. Daily noon–midnight. Mains £6–15.

Wong Kei 41–43 Wardour St, W1 ⊕020/7437 8408; Leicester Square tube. Famous for dispensing large portions of cheap Chinese washed down with free tea. The place is enormous; seating is communal; have a

tube. Outstanding fusion restaurant run by an amiable New Zealander and split into two: snacky Tapa Room downstairs and an elegant restaurant upstairs. In both the food, which may sound like an untidy assemblage on paper, is original and wholly satisfying. Mon–Fri 9am–11pm, Sat 10am–11pm, Sun 10am–10pm. Mains £18–26.

look at the Art Nouveau exterior on the way in. Mon-Sat noon–11.30pm, Sun noon–10.30pm. Mains £6–12.

Soho

The listings in this section are marked on the map on p.104 or p.108.

Cafés

🏃 **Bar Italia** 22 Frith St, W1 ⊕020/7437 4520, ⊛www.baritaliasoho.co.uk; Leicester Square tube. Tiny café that's a Soho institution, serving pricey coffee, croissants, beers and sandwiches more or less around the clock – as it has been since 1949. Popular with late-night clubbers and with fans of Italian soccer. Nearly 24hr; closed Mon–Fri 4–6am.

Beatroot 92 Berwick St, W1 ⊕020/7437 8591, ⊛beatroot.org.uk; Piccadilly Circus, Oxford Circus or Tottenham Court Road tube. Great little veggie café by the market, doling out hot savoury bakes, stews and salads (plus delicious cakes) in boxes of varying sizes – all around £5. Mon–Fri 9am–9pm, Sat 11am–9pm.

🏃 **Breakfast Club** 33 D'Arblay St, W1 ⊕020/7434 2571, ⊛www.thebreakfast clubsoho.com; Oxford Circus tube. With an appropriately egg-yolk yellow exterior, this laidback Aussie-style place, with its battered leather couches, offers substantial toasted sarnies, fresh juice, great coffee and free wi-fi. Branches in Islington and Hoxton. Mon–Fri 8am–6pm, Sat 9.30–5pm, Sun 10am–4pm.

Fernandez & Wells 73 Beak St, W1 ⊕020/287 8124, ⊛www.fernandezandwells.com; Piccadilly Circus or Oxford Circus tube. Superlative, freshly prepared sandwiches for around £5, and sweets for under £2 – most folk take away, but there are one or two tables. Mon–Fri 7.30am–7pm, Sat 8am–7pm, Sun 9am–7pm.

Gaby's 30 Charing Cross Rd, WC2 ☎020/7836 4233; Leicester Square tube. Small, clean café that stays open late serving home-cooked (non-kosher) Jewish specialities. Hard to beat for value or choice – the takeaway falafel is a central London bargain – and it's licensed, too. Mon–Sat 11am–midnight, Sun noon–10pm.

Jerk City 189 Wardour St, W1 ☎020/7287 2878; Tottenham Court Road tube. Small Carribean café that serves up big portions of jerk chicken and ackee and saltfish, as well as takeaway patties. Mon–Wed 10am–10pm, Thurs–Sat 10am–11pm

Kopi-Tiam 67 Charing Cross Rd, W1 ☎020/7287 1113; Leicester Square tube. Bright, cheap Malaysian coffee shop (*kopi tiam*) serving up curries, coconut rice, juices and "herbal soups" to local Malays, all for around a fiver. Mon–Thurs & Sun noon–11pm, Fri & Sat noon–11.30pm.

Maison Bertaux 28 Greek St, W1 ☎020/7437 6007; Leicester Square tube. Long-standing (established in 1871), old-fashioned and terribly French patisserie, with tables on two floors, plus one or two outside. A loyal clientele keeps the place busy all day long. Daily 8.30am–8pm.

Maoz Vegetarian 43 Old Compton St, W1 ☎020/7851 1586, Ⓦwww.maozusa.com; Leicester Square or Tottenham Court Road tube. Kosher, vegan, late-night place that special-ises in falafel in pitta, with a good salad bar and chips to boot. Mon–Thurs 11am–1am, Fri & Sat 11am–2am, Sun 11am–midnight.

Nordic Bakery 14a Golden Square, W1 ☎020/3230 1077, Ⓦwww.nordicbakery.com; Piccadilly Circus tube. Fill up on crispbreads, cinnamon rolls, rye-bread sandwiches and strong coffee, at this super-sharp minimalist Scandinavian café. Mon–Sat 8am–8pm, Sat 9am–7pm, Sun 11am–6pm.

Stockpot 18 Old Compton St, W1 ☎020/7287 1066; Leicester Square or Tottenham Court Road tube. Cheap and cheerful is the name of the game at this spartan Soho institution: large plates of pasta, omelettes and forgotten classic British dishes. Mon & Tues 11.30am–11.30pm, Wed–Sat 11.30am–midnight, Sun noon–11.30pm. Mains £4–6.

Restaurants

Chowki 2–3 Denman St, W1 ☎020/7439 1330, Ⓦwww.chowki.com; Piccadilly Circus tube. Large, cheap Indian restaurant serving authentic home-style food. The menu changes every month to feature three different areas of India, with the regional feast coming in at £18–20 Mon–Sat noon–11.30pm, Sun noon–10.30pm. Mains £8–12.

Mildred's 45 Lexington St, W1 ☎020/7494 1634, Ⓦwww.mildreds.co.uk; Oxford Circus or Piccadilly Circus tube. *Mildred's*, tucked away on a north Soho side street, has a fresher and more stylish feel than many veggie restaurants. The stir-fries, pasta dishes and meat-free burgers are wholesome and delicious. Can get very busy, but no bookings or credit cards. Mon–Sat noon–11pm. Mains £8–10.

Patara 15 Greek St, W1 ☎020/7437 1071, Ⓦwww.pataralondon.com; Leicester Square tube. A dimly lit and glamorous place, with orchids on the tables, fresh ingredients and fine Thai cooking. Mon–Sat noon–2.30pm & 6.30–10.30pm, Sun 6.30–10.30pm. Branches in Mayfair, South Kensington and elsewhere. Mains £7–20.

Thai Cottage 34 D'Arblay St, W1 ☎020/7439 7099; Oxford Circus tube. Tiny and resolutely unfashionable place, where the welcome is friendly and the decor simple. Follow the chicken satay with one of the terrific fried-noodle dishes. Mon–Wed noon–4pm & 5.30–10.30pm, Thurs 5.30–10.30pm, Fri noon–4pm & 5.30–11pm, Sat 5.30–11pm. Mains £7–20.

Yauatcha 15 Broadwick St ☎020/7494 8888, Ⓦwww3.yauatcha.com; Piccadilly Circus tube. Very popular, minimalist Chinese teahouse-restaurant serving up dim sum (£3.50–7) all day long. Mon–Sat noon–11.45pm, Sun 11am–10.30pm.

Fitzrovia

The listings in this section are marked on the map on p.104.

Cafés

Eagle Bar Diner 3 Rathbone Place, W1 ☎020/7637 1418, Ⓦwww.eaglebardiner.co.uk; Tottenham Court Road tube. Modern and elegant US diner, with cosy leather booths and a long bar serving cocktails, martinis and pick-me-ups. But the real reason to come here is the burgers – Aberdeen Angus beef, chicken, lamb and even emu and ostrich, with brownies and cheesecakes for afters. Come at lunchtime if you want to avoid the DJs (Wed–Sat). Mon–Wed

Most places in London will make some attempt to cater for **vegetarians**. Below is a list of exclusively veggie cafés and restaurants.

Beatroot 92 Berwick St, W1 (see p.380).

Eat & Two Veg 50 Marylebone Lane, W1 (see p.379).

Food for Thought 31 Neal St, WC2 (see p.384).

The Gate 51 Queen Caroline St, W6 (see p.395).

Manna 4 Erskine Rd, NW3 (see p.392).

Mildred's 45 Lexington St, W1 (see p.381).

Moaz Vegetarian 43 Old Compton St, W1 (see p.381).

The Place Below Church of St Mary-le-Bow, Cheapside, EC2 (see p.386).

Poetry Café 22 Betterton St, WC2 (see p.384).

Rasa 55 Stoke Newington Church St, N1 (see p.393).

Rootmaster Ely's Yard, up Dray Walk, E1 (see p.387).

Saf 152–154 Curtain Rd, E2 (see p.386).

Sakonis 127–129 Ealing Rd, Alperton, Middlesex (see p.394).

Tibits 12–14 Heddon St, W1 (see p.378).

Wild Cherry 241–247 Globe Rd, E2 (see p.388).

World Food Café 14 Neal's Yard, WC2 (see p.384).

noon–11pm, Thurs & Fri noon–1am, Sat 10am–1am, Sun 11am–6pm.

El Burrito 5 Charlotte Place, W1 ☎020/7580 5048; Goodge Street tube. Very popular Mexican diner that produces superb spicy fajitas, tacos and burritos filled with pork, chicken or beef. Mon–Fri 11am–4pm & 7–10pm, Sat 7–11pm.

Indian YMCA 41 Fitzroy Square, W1 ☎020/7387 0411; Warren Street tube. Ignore the signs saying the canteen is only for students – this place is open to all; just press the bell and pile in. The entire menu is portioned up into pretty little bowls; go and collect what you want and pay at the till. The food is great and the prices unbelievably low. Mon–Fri 7.30–9.15am, noon–2pm & 7–8.30pm, Sat & Sun 8–9.30am, 12.30–1.30pm & 7–8.30pm.

Rasa Express 5 Rathbone St, W1 ☎020/7637 0222, ⊛www.rasarestaurants.com; Goodge Street or Tottenham Court Road tube. This takeaway-only outlet, at the back of *Rasa Samudra* restaurant, hands out genuinely sophisticated South Indian dishes for next to nothing. Perfect for a Fitzrovia picnic. Mon–Fri noon–3pm.

Salumeria Dino 15 Charlotte Place, W1 ☎020/7580 3938; Goodge Street tube. Small and authentic Italian café-deli with a few outside tables on an appealing pedestrian

side street. Daily focaccia and pasta specials, served in generous quantities and with fine ingredients. Mon–Fri 9am–6pm.

Restaurants

 Hakkasan 8 Hanway Place, W1 ☎020/7927 7000, ⊛www.hakkasan.com; Tottenham Court Road tube. Impressive, atmospheric designer restaurant (complete with bouncers) serving novel Chinese dishes, with a long, fashionably crammed cocktail bar attached. It's expensive, so go at lunchtime for the dim sum. Mon–Fri noon–3pm & 6pm–midnight, Sat noon–5pm & 6pm–midnight, Sun 6–11pm. Mains £10–40.

Istanbul Meze 100 Cleveland St, W1 ☎020/7387 0785, ⊛www.istanbulmeze.co.uk; Great Portland Street or Warren Street tube. Gorgeous grills and friendly service are pretty much guaranteed at this inexpensive Turkish restaurant, popular on the weekend for the live music in the basement. Mon–Sat noon–11pm, Sun 5–11pm. Mains £7–12.

The Kerala 15 Great Castle St, W1 ☎020/7580 2125; Oxford Circus tube. Friendly, bargain Keralan restaurant serving up Syrian Christian specialities, coastal seafood dishes, Malabar biryanis, vegetable curries and special dosas. Daily noon–10.30pm. Mains £7–10.

Sardo 45 Grafton Way, W1 ☎020/7387 2521, ⊛www.sardo-restaurant.com;

Warren Street tube. Sardinian flagship restaurant with a light modern interior and spectacular local cuisine, guaranteed to make your taste buds tingle. Mon–Fri noon–3pm & 6–11pm, Sat 6–11pm. Mains £8–15.

Bloomsbury

The listings in this section are marked on the map on p.127.

Cafés

Abeno 47 Museum St, WC1 ☏020/7402 3211, Ⓦwww.abeno.co.uk; Tottenham Court Road or Holborn tube. Small Japanese place that specializes in *okonomiyaki* (£7–12), a cabbage, egg and dough pancake filled with pork, bacon, seafood or tofu, prepared before your very eyes. Branch on Great Newport St. Mon–Sat noon–11pm, Sun noon–10.30pm.

Hare & Tortoise 15–17 Brunswick Centre, WC1 ☏020/7278 9799, Ⓦwww.hareandtortoise.co.uk; Russell Square tube. Located in the Brunswick mall, this smart budget café-restaurant serves up tasty sushi, nigiri, chow mein and ramen dishes. Branches in Blackfriars, Kensington and elsewhere. Daily noon–11pm.

Hummus Bros 37–63 Southampton Row, WC1 ☏020/7404 7079, Ⓦwww.hbros .co.uk; Holborn tube. Hummus and a choice of topping with pitta bread on the side. You sit on benches at red lacquer tables; service is efficient and they often throw in mint tea on the house. Also takeaway. Branch on Wardour St in Soho. Mon–Fri 11am–9pm.

Patisserie Deux Amis 63 Judd St, WC1 ☏020/7383 7029; Euston or King's Cross tube. Small, civilized French-style bakery specializing in pastries, filled baguettes and coffee, with a great cheese shop next door – a real find near King's Cross. Mon–Sat 9am–6pm, Sun 9am–2pm.

Wagamama 4 Streatham St, WC1 ☏020/7323 9223; Tottenham Court Road tube; plus numerous branches. *Wagamama* was the pioneer when it comes to minimalist canteen-style noodle bars and this was the first branch. Diners share long benches and slurp huge bowls of noodle soup or stir-fried plates. Mon–Sat noon–11pm, Sun 12.30–10pm.

Restaurants

Busaba Eathai 22 Store St, WC1 ☏020/7299 7900, Ⓦwww.busaba.com; Goodge Street tube. This popular, expanding chain serves up very tasty Thai food in an atmospheric, modern, dark wood interior. Be prepared to share the huge tables with other diners. Branches in Soho and Marylebone. Mon–Thurs noon–11pm, Fri & Sat noon– 11.30pm, Sun noon–10pm. Mains £7–10.

Cigala 54 Lamb's Conduit St, WC1 ☏020/7405 1717, Ⓦwww.cigala.co.uk; Russell Square tube. Simple dishes, strong flavours, fresh ingredients and real passion are evident at this Iberian restaurant. The menu changes daily which makes for excellent seasonal dishes. There's also a tapas menu (£2–8). Mon–Fri noon–10.45pm, Sat 12.30– 10.45pm, Sun noon–9.45pm. Mains £12–18.

La Porchetta 33 Boswell St, WC1 ☏020/7242 2434; Holborn or Russell Square tube. Tiny, cramped, very loud, very Italian pizza and pasta place that dishes up huge portions. Branches in Clerkenwell, Islington and elsewhere. Mon–Fri noon–3pm & 5–11pm, Sat 5–11pm. Mains £6–10.

Covent Garden and the Strand

The listings in this section are marked on the map on p.140.

Cafés

Canela 33 Earlham St, WC2 ☏020/7240 6926, Ⓦwww.canelacafe.com; Leicester Square tube. A little Brazilian/Portuguese café-bar that serves up authentic snacks and cakes. The high-ceilinged, chandeliered interior makes it a nice place for a coffee, or you can sit outside and watch the action on Seven Dials. Branch in Soho. Mon–Wed 9.30am–10.30pm, Thurs & Fri 9.30am–11.30pm, Sat 10.30am–11.30pm, Sun 10.30am–8pm.

Food for Thought 31 Neal St, WC2 ☎020/7836 9072; **Covent Garden tube.** Long-established, minuscule, basement bargain veggie restaurant and takeaway counter – the food is good, with the menu changing twice daily, plus regular vegan and wheat-free options. Expect to queue and don't expect to linger at peak times. Mon–Sat noon–8.30pm, Sun noon–5pm.

Just Falafs 27b Covent Garden Piazza, WC2 ☎020/7240 3838, ⓦwww.justfalafs .com; **Covent Garden tube.** Mainly takeaway joint at the southeast corner of the piazza – wholesome falafel, mainly organic salad, yoghurt and seasonal beans rolled in a flatbread. Branch in Soho. Daily 9am–7pm.

Kastner & Ovens 52 Floral St, WC2 ☎020/7836 2700; **Covent Garden tube.** Minimalist lunching spot where the emphasis is on top-quality sandwiches and heart-warming savoury bakes, plus a wicked selection of cakes, all cooked on the premises. A few tables inside and lots of takeaway. Mon–Fri 8am–5pm.

Monmouth Coffee Company 27 Monmouth St, WC2 ☎020/7645 3516; **Covent Garden or Leicester Square tube.** The marvellous aroma is the first thing that greets you when you walk in. Pick and mix your coffee from a fine selection (or buy the beans to take home), then settle into one of the cramped wooden booths and flick through the daily newspapers on hand. Branch at Borough Market. Mon–Sat 8am–6.30pm.

Poetry Café 22 Betterton St, WC2 ☎020/7420 9887; **Covent Garden or Holborn tube.** The ground-floor veggie café is a pleasant place to relax and browse poetry magazines, with salads, quiche and cakes on offer as well as their excellent Portuguese custard tarts; the basement has had some fine poets grace its stage. Mon–Fri noon–11pm, Sat 7–11pm.

Rock & Sole Plaice 47 Endell St, WC2 ☎020/7836 3785; **Covent Garden tube.** A no-nonsense Turkish-run fish-and-chip shop in central London. Eat in or out at one of the pavement tables or takeaway. Mon–Sat 11.30am–11pm, Sun noon–10pm.

World Food Café 14 Neal's Yard, WC2 ☎020/7379 0298; **Covent Garden tube.** First-floor veggie café where the windows are flung open in summer and you can gaze down upon trendy humanity as you tuck into filling dishes from all corners of the globe: Mexican tortillas, Indian thalis or Turkish meze. Bring your own booze, or stick to the fruit juices. Mon–Fri 11.30am–4.30pm, Sat 11.30am–5pm.

Restaurants

J. Sheekey 28–32 St Martin's Court, WC2 ☎020/7240 2565, ⓦwww.caprice-holdings .co.uk; **Leicester Square tube.** Established in 1896, but elegantly refurbished since then, the atmosphere is formal and the traditional menu focused on fish. The weekend lunch three-course menu, at £24.50, is your best bet. Mon–Sat noon–3pm & 5.30pm–midnight, Sun noon–3.30pm, 6pm–11pm. Mains £14–28.

Masala Zone 48 Floral St, W1 ☎020/7379 0101, ⓦwww.masalazone.com; **Covent Garden tube.** Smart restaurant, decorated with Rajastani puppets, serving modern Indian food, including lots of veggie options. Start with little dishes of "street food", then move on to the well-balanced, richly flavoured curries. Branches in Soho, Camden, Islington and elsewhere. Mon–Sat noon–11pm, Sun 12.30–10.30pm. Mains £5–15.

Mon Plaisir 21 Monmouth St, WC2 ☎020/7836 7243, ⓦwww.monplaisir.co.uk; **Covent Garden tube.** Claims to be the oldest French restaurant in London and certainly feels French. Deco posters and a glamorous mirrored bar give a vintage feel, while the classic French dishes are reliably excellent. The pre- and post-theatre menu is a bargain at £13.50 for two courses, £15.50 for three. Mon–Fri noon–3pm & 5.45pm–midnight, Sat 5pm–midnight. Mains £17–25.

Clerkenwell and Hoxton

Clerkenwell

The listings in this section are marked on the map on p.158.

Cafés

Al's Café Bar 11–13 Exmouth Market, EC1 ☎020/7837 4821; **Angel or Farringdon tube.** A nouveau greasy spoon with a loyal, local arty clientele, which serves up Italian sandwiches, bagels, nachos, decent coffee and good soups alongside the chips and grills. In the evening, it's more DJ bar than café. Mon 9am–midnight, Tues–Sat 9am–2am, Sun 9am–11.30pm.

Clark & Sons 46 Exmouth Market, EC1
☎020/7837 1974; Angel or Farringdon tube.
Despite Exmouth Market's gentrification, this
genuine pie-and-mash shop is still going
strong – this is now the most central one in
the capital. Mon–Thurs 10.30am–4pm, Fri &
Sat 10.30am–5pm.

Clerkenwell Kitchen 27–31 Clerkenwell
Close, EC1 ☎020/7101 9959, ⓦwww
.theclerkenwellkitchen.co.uk; Farringdon tube.
Bright, modern, airy place decked in light
wood and brick. Open-plan kitchen
serves up everything from breakfast through
to afternoon tea. Menu is short and
admirably seasonal. Mon–Fri 8am–5pm,
Thurs until 11pm.

De Santis 11–13 Old St, EC1 ☎020/7689 5577;
Barbican tube. Swish Milanese *paninoteca*
with a great terrace at the back. Home-
baked paninis with top-class fillings, and
very good coffee. Mon–Fri 8.30am–11pm.

Kurz & Lang 1 St John St, EC1 ☎020/7253
6623, ⓦwww.kurzandlang.com;
Farringdon tube. An *echt* German Bratwurst in
a prominent corner site off Smithfield. Choose
from a variety of sausages, and help them
down with bread, mustard and sauerkraut.
Popular clubbers' pit-stop. Mon–Wed
11am–11.30pm, Thurs 11am–1am, nonstop
Fri 11am to Sun 7am, Sun noon–8.30pm.

Pho 86 St John St, EC1 ☎020/7253 7624,
ⓦwww.phocafe.co.uk; Farringdon or Barbican
tube. Small, bright, modern café serving up
standard Vietnamese noodle soups, washed
down with weasel coffee. Mon–Fri
noon–3pm & 6–10pm, Sat 6.30–10.30pm.

Smiths of Smithfield (SOS) 67–77 Charterhouse
St, EC1 ☎020/7251 7950, ⓦwww.smithsofsmith
field.co.uk; Farringdon tube. A big bustling
warehouse-style place on four levels. Not the
place for an intimate evening, but the ground-
floor café-bar serves up fine all-day breakfasts, superb bacon butties, salads, snacks,
ice cream and sundaes. Mon 7am–11pm,
Tues–Fri 7am–11.30pm, Sat 10am–11.30pm,
Sun 9.30am–5pm.

Restaurants

Cicada 132 St John St, EC1 ☎020/7608 1550;
Farringdon tube. Part bar, part restaurant,
Cicada offers an unusual pan-Asian menu
that allows you to mix and match from
small, large and side dishes ranging from
fishy *tom yum* to ginger noodles or sushi.
Mon–Fri noon–2.45pm, 6–10.45pm, Sat
6–10.45pm. Mains £10–17.

Fish Central 149–155 Central St, EC1; Old Street
tube. Sitting on the edge of the Barbican/
City and Clerkenwell's council estates, this
reliable fish-and-chip restaurant attracts
clientele from both. Mon–Sat 11am–2.30pm
& 5–10.30pm. Mains £8–15.

Medcalf 40 Exmouth Market, EC1 ☎020/7833
3533, ⓦwww.medcalfbar.co.uk; Farringdon or
Angel tube. A converted turn-of-the-century
butcher's shop, fashionably unchic, which
serves modern British cuisine, with fresh
ingredients and excellent puds. Mon–Thurs
& Sat noon–11pm, Fri noon–1am, Sun
noon–6pm. Mains £9–15.

Moro 34–36 Exmouth Market, EC1 ☎020/7833
8336, ⓦwww.moro.co.uk; Farringdon or Angel
tube. Attractive modern restaurant that's a
place of pilgrimage for disciples of the
restaurant's Moorish cookbooks. Food is
usually excellent, service sometimes less so
and you have to book well in advance.
Tapas (for around £4) are served throughout
the day. Daily 12.30–10.30pm. Mains
£16–19.

St John 26 St John St, EC1 ☎020/7251 0848,
ⓦwww.stjohnrestaurant.com; Farringdon
tube. Pared-down former smokehouse
close to Smithfield meat market that's
become famous for serving outstanding
British dishes often involving unfashionable
animal parts. Daily noon–midnight. Mains
£14–22.

Hoxton

The listings in this section are marked
on the map on p.158.

Cafés

Flavours 35 Charlotte Rd, E2 ☎020/7739 5345,
ⓦwww.kitchenflavours.co.uk. Tiny café with just
four stools, serving delicious Mediterranean
lunch options: big soups, grilled tuna, salads
and great pastries, all freshly prepared.
Mon–Fri 8.30am–3.30pm, Sat 9am–4pm.

Macondo 8–9 Hoxton Square, N1 ☎020/7729
1119, ⓦwww.macondo.co.uk; Old Street tube.
Small, laid-back, arty Spanish café that
serves up authentic tortillas and delicious
cakes, which morphs into more of a bar
in the evening. Branch in Islington. Mon–
Thurs & Sun 9.30am–11pm, Fri & Sat
9.30am–midnight.

Viet Hoa Café 72–74 Kingsland Rd, E2
☎020/7729 8293, ⓦwww.viethoarestaurant
.co.uk; Old Street tube. Large, chaotic

Vietnamese café in a street heaving with similar places. Big portions and lots of spicy noodle soups to choose from. Mon–Fri noon–3.30pm & 5.30pm–midnight, Sat & Sun 12.30pm–midnight.

Restaurants

Eyre Brothers 70 Leonard St, EC2 ☎020/7613 5346, Ⓦwww.eyrebrothers.co.uk; **Old Street or Liverpool Street tube.** Very large, very swish, very elegant. The food is hard to categorize – there are a few Iberian and Italian dishes, a lot of Portuguese specialities and some favourites from Mozambique. Also a tapas and *petiscos* (£4–7) menu. Mon–Fri noon–3pm & 6.30–10.45pm, Sat 7–10.45pm. Mains £10–26.

Real Greek 15 Hoxton Market, N1 ☎020/7739 8212, Ⓦwww.therealgreek.com; **Old Street tube.** Modern, attractive mini-chain with excellent service and a menu that shows off authentic Greek cooking with lots of dishes to share. Neighbouring *Mezedopolio*, in a sympathetically converted mission building, serves meze and has a glamorous marble bar. Daily noon–11pm. Dishes £5–7; sharers for two or more £19–25.

🏃 **Saf** 152–154 Curtain Rd, E2 ☎020/7613 0007, Ⓦwww.safrestaurant.co.uk; **Old Street tube.** Modern, shiny new and (totally unique) vegan restaurant which specializes in exquisitely presented (mostly uncooked) fruit and veg dishes. Daily 11am–3.30pm & 6–11pm. Mains £10–12.

The City

The listings in this section are marked on the map on p.168 or on p.181.

Cafés

Chilango 142 Fleet St ☎020/7353 6761, Ⓦwww.chilango.co.uk; **Blackfriars tube.** Busy, modern canteen-style Mexican place serving up fast, fresh, soft tortilla burritos and tacos, salads and great guacamole. Branch in Islington. Mon–Fri 11am–9pm.

De Gustibus 53–55 Carter Lane, EC2 ☎020/7236 0056, Ⓦwww.degustibus.co.uk; **St Paul's or Blackfriars tube.** Award-winning artisan bakery that creates a wide variety of sandwiches, *bruschette*, *croque-monsieur* and quiche to eat in or take away. Branches in Marylebone and Borough Market. Mon–Fri 7am–5pm.

🏃 **The Place Below** Church of St Mary-le-Bow, Cheapside, EC2 ☎020/7329 0789, Ⓦwww.theplacebelow.co.uk; **St Paul's or Bank tube.** A rare City gem: a café, set in a wonderful Norman church crypt, serving imaginative vegetarian dishes and delicious breakfast pastries. Mon–Fri 7.30am–3pm.

Restaurants

1 Lombard Street 1 Lombard St, EC3 ☎020/7929 6611, Ⓦwww.1lombardstreet.com; **Bank tube.** A former banking hall in the heart of the City with a spectacular glass dome above the buzzy circular bar-brasserie, and a more intimate restaurant beyond. Service can be iffy, but the French-inspired dishes are always artistically presented and

delicious. Mon–Fri 11am–11pm. Mains (brasserie) £17–25; (restaurant) £25–35.

Prism 147 Leadenhall St, EC3 ☎020/7256 3888, Ⓦwww.harveynichols.com; **Bank tube.** Another old banking hall, with the obligatory long bar, suave service and a menu comprising well-judged English favourites with modernist influences. The bar menu has Ploughman's and sausage and mash for

▲ 1 Lombard Street

around a tenner. Mon–Fri 8am–10am, 11.30am–3pm & 6–10pm. Mains (bar) £10–15, (restaurant) £20–30.

Rhodes Twenty Four 24th Floor, Tower 42, Old Broad St, EC2 ☎020/7877 7703, ⊛www .rhodes24.co.uk; Bank or Liverpool Street tube.

There's a smart, but bland corporate feel to the decor, and the prices are City-high, but the views from halfway up the old NatWest Tower are amazing and the British menu is well executed. Mon–Fri noon–2.30pm & 6–9pm. Mains £16–27.

The East End

Spitalfields, Brick Lane and Whitechapel

The listings in this section are marked on the map on p.202.

Cafés

Arkansas Café Unit 12, Old Spitalfields Market, E1 ☎020/7377 6999; Liverpool Street tube. American barbecue fuel stop, using only the very best free-range ingredients. Try chef Bubb's own smoked beef brisket and ribs, and be sure to taste his home-made barbie sauce. Mon–Fri noon–2.30pm, Sun noon–4pm.

Brick Lane Beigel Bake 159 Brick Lane, E1 ☎020/7729 0616; Whitechapel tube. Classic bagel takeaway shop in the heart of the East End – unbelievably cheap, even for your top-end filling, smoked salmon and cream cheese. Daily 24hr.

Café 1001 1 Dray's Lane, E1 ☎020/7247 9679, ⊛www.cafe1001.co.uk; Whitechapel tube. Just off Brick Lane, this café has a beaten-up studenty look, with lots of sofas to crash on, and simple snacks and delicious cakes to sample. DJ sets every night; live jazz every Wed. Mon–Sat 6am–midnight, Sun 6am–11.30pm.

Rootmaster Ely's Yard, up Dray Walk, E1 ☎07912/389314, ⊛www.root-master.co.uk; Liverpool Street tube. Tasty vegan food from all over the world, knocked up on the ground floor of an old red Routemaster bus; seating upstairs and outside. Mon–Sat 11am–11pm, Sun 11am–10.30pm.

Sweet & Spicy 40 Brick Lane, E1 ☎020/7247 1081; Aldgate East tube. Very basic self-service Bangladeshi café decorated with pictures of wrestlers, serving up cheap hot curries with a minimum of fuss. Daily 8am–10.30pm.

Restaurants

Café Naz 46–48 Brick Lane, E1 ☎020/7247 0234, ⊛www.cafenaz.co.uk; Aldgate East tube. Self-proclaimed contemporary Bangladeshi restaurant that cuts an imposing modern figure on Brick Lane. The menu has all the standards plus a variety of baltis, the kitchen is open-plan, and the prices keen. Daily noon–midnight. Mains £6–15.

Lahore Kebab House 2–10 Umberston St, E1 ☎020/7481 9737, ⊛www.lahore-kebabhouse .com; Aldgate East tube. A legendary BYO bargain Punjabi kebab house, just off Commercial Rd. Go for the lamb cutlets and roti. Daily noon–midnight. Mains £6–9.

Les Trois Garçons 1 Club Row, E1 ☎020/7613 1924, ⊛www.lestroisgarcons.com; Liverpool Street tube. The service can be iffy and the prices for the French cuisine are over-the-top, but then so is the whole experience: the decor's a surreal mixture of fantastic stuffed animals and art installations, and the punters aren't afraid to dress up. Mon–Sat 7pm–midnight. Set menus £42–50.

Rosa's 12 Hanbury St, E1 ☎020/7247 1093, ⊛www.rosaslondon.com; Liverpool Street tube. Clean-cut, simple, modern Thai restaurant serving up tasty, freshly prepared curries at very reasonable prices. Tables may well be shared unless you book ahead. Mon–Fri 11am–3pm & 6–11pm, Sat 11am–midnight, Sun 11am–11pm. Mains £6–10.

St John Bread & Wine 94–96 Commercial St, EC1 ☎020/7247 8924, ⊛www.stjohnrestaurant .co.uk; Aldgate East/Liverpool Street tube. White minimalist decor and a menu which offers a new twist on old British favourites – lots of offal, pig's cheek and squirrel followed by traditional puds. Does breakfasts, too. Mon–Fri 9am–11pm, Sat 10am–11pm, Sun 10am–10.30pm. Mains £8–12.

Tayyabs 83–89 Fieldgate St, E1 ☎020/7247 9543, ⊛www.tayyabs.co.uk; Aldgate East or Whitechapel tube. Opened in 1974, *Tayyabs* still offers the same straight-forward Pakistani fare: good, freshly cooked and served without pretension. Prices have remained low, booking is essential, and service is speedy and slick. BYO. Daily 5pm–11.30pm. Mains £6–10.

Bethnal Green

The listings in this section are marked on the map on p.201.

Cafés

E. Pellicci 332 Bethnal Green Rd, E2 ☎020/7739 4873; Bethnal Green tube. Famous East End caff with original 1940s decor intact, serving great fry-ups and good Anglo-Italian grub at low prices. Mon–Sat 6.30am–5pm.

🏃 **Frizzante@City Farm** 1a Goldsmith's Row, E2 ☎020/7729 2266, ⊛www.frizzanteltd .co.uk; Bethnal Green tube. Hackney City Farm's rustic café serves up great home-made family-friendly breakfasts and Italian-style lunches, all for around a fiver. Also does home-made ice cream. Tues–Sun 10am–4.30pm.

Jones Dairy 23 Ezra St, E2 ☎020/7739 5372, ⊛www.jonesdairy.co.uk; Bethnal Green tube. Take a detour from Sunday's Columbia Road Market (see p.206) to this gorgeous, busy little place, which sells great breads, bagels and fine cheeses. Fri & Sat 9am–3pm, Sun 8am–2pm.

Wild Cherry 241–245 Globe Rd, E2 ☎020/8980 6678; Bethnal Green tube. Buddhist veggie restaurant best known for its all-day Saturday breakfasts, just around the corner from the Museum of Childhood. Tues–Fri 10.30am–5pm, Sat 10.30am–4.30pm.

Docklands

The listings in this section are marked on the map on p.215.

Cafés

Hubbub 269 Westferry Rd, E14 ☎020/7515 5577, ⊛hubbub76.valuehost.co.uk; Mudchute DLR or bus #D7 from Westferry DLR. A real oasis in the desert of Docklands, this café-bar is housed in a former church, now arts centre, and does decent fry-ups, sandwiches and tapas. Weekend brunch till 5pm. Mon–Wed noon–11pm, Thurs & Fri noon–midnight, Sat 10am–midnight, Sun 10am–10.30pm.

Restaurants

Lotus Floating Chinese Restaurant 38 Limeharbour, E14 ☎020/7515 6445, ⊛www .lotusfloating.co.uk; Crossharbour DLR. As it says on the tin, this is a floating Chinese restaurant moored in Millwall Docks specializing in steaming hot, fresh dim sum (£2–3.50). Mains £5–12.

Mem Saheb on Thames 65–67 Amsterdam Rd, E14 ☎020/7538 3008, ⊛www.memsaheb.com; Crossharbour DLR. Decent riverside Indian restaurant in the cultural wasteland that is Docklands, with a superb view over the river to the Dome. Mon–Fri noon–2.30pm & 6–11.30pm, Sat & Sun 6–11.30pm. £6–12.

Royal China 30 Westferry Circus, W1 ☎020/7221 2535; Canary Wharf tube. You can eat well from the full menu, but it's the dim sum (£2.50–4) that is most enticing here – the roast pork bun and marinated chicken feet are famous. Branches in Marylebone and elsewhere. Mon–Thurs noon–11pm, Fri & Sat noon–11.30pm, Sun 11am–10pm. Mains £9–18.

South Bank

The listings in this section are marked on the map on p.221.

Cafés

🏃 **Ev** 97–99 Isabella St, SE1 ☎020/7620 6191, ⊛www.tasrestaurant.com; Waterloo tube. A Turkish deli/café and adjoining restaurant that's one of the prettiest places to eat in London: tucked under a railway arch, it has a lofty barrel-vaulted ceiling, low wooden seats and outside tables shaded by ferns and bamboo. Great salads and bread, dried fruit and an array of Turkish delight. Mon–Sat noon–11.30pm, Sun noon–10.30pm.

Marsh Ruby 30 Lower Marsh, SE1 ☎020/7620 0593, ⊛www.marshruby.com; Waterloo tube. Terrific filling lunchtime curries for under a fiver: the food is organic/free range and there's a basic but cheery communal dining area at the back. Mon–Fri 11.30am–3pm.

Restaurants

Livebait The Cut, SE1 ☎ 020/7928 7211, ⓦ www.livebaitrestaurants.co.uk; Waterloo tube. This bustling green-and-white-tiled restaurant dishes up seafood galore, from classic fish'n'chips to platters heaped with lobster, crab and prawns. Branch in Covent Garden. Mon–Sat noon–11pm, Sun 12.30–9pm. Mains £11–20.

Masters Super Fish 191 Waterloo Rd, SE1 ☎ 020/7928 6924; Waterloo tube. An old-fashioned, unpretentious fish-and-chip restaurant, which serves up huge portions

with all the trimmings: gherkins, pickled onions, coleslaw and a few complimentary prawns. Mon 5.30–10.30pm, Tues–Sat noon–3pm & 4.30–10.30pm. Mains £7–13.

RSJ 33 Coin St, SE1 ☎ 020/7928 4554, ⓦ www .rsj.uk.com; Waterloo tube. Regularly high standards of Anglo-French cooking make this a good spot for a meal before or after an evening at a South Bank theatre or concert hall. The set meals for £16–19 are particularly popular. Mon–Fri noon–2.30pm & 5.30–11pm, Sat 5.30–11pm. Mains £11–19.

Southwark

The listings in this section are marked on the map on p.230 or on p.234.

Cafés

Café 2 Tate Modern, Sumner St, SE1 ☎ 020/7401 5014, ⓦ www.tate.org.uk; Southwark or London Bridge tube. Tate Modern's café on Level 2 has modest riverside views, and offers sophisticated British cuisine for around £10 a main course, though you can snack for less. Kids' menu's good, too. Mon–Thurs & Sun 10am–5.30pm, Fri & Sat 10am–9.30pm.

El Vergel 8 Lant St, SE1 ☎ 020/7357 0057, ⓦ www.elvergel.co.uk; Borough tube. Small, very busy weekday café at the west end of Lant St, worth the quick stroll from the tube. The reason to come here is to sample the Latin American specialities such as *empanadas*, pasties filled with meat and spices or spinach and feta cheese. Mon–Fri 8.30am–3pm.

The Table 83 Southwark St, SE1 ☎ 020/7401 2760, ⓦ www.thetablecafe.com; London Bridge tube. Tucked behind the Tate, this self-service place has an excellent salad bar and

chunky canteen tables. Owned and designed by neighbouring architects, with a nice industrial-style, decked outside space. Mon–Fri 7am–5pm, Sat & Sun 9am–3pm.

Restaurants

Roast The Floral Hall, Borough Market, Stoney St, SE1 ☎ 020/7940 1300, ⓦ www.roast-restaurant .com; London Bridge tube. With a game and offal section on the menu, this is a place for those seeking truly British meat dishes. The glamorous contemporary dining room looks down on the bustle of Borough Market and it's open for breakfast. Mon–Fri 7–11am, noon–2.30pm & 5.30–11pm, Sat 8am–3.30pm & 6–11pm, Sun 11.30am–3.45pm. Mains £14–19.

Tentazioni 2 Mill St, SE1 ☎ 020/7237 1100, ⓦ www.tentazioni.co.uk; Bermondsey or Tower Hill tube. Smart, busy Italian restaurant serving high-quality, imaginative peasant fare. Mon–Fri noon–2.45pm & 6.30–10.45pm. Mains £11–19.

South Kensington, Knightsbridge and Chelsea

South Kensington & Knightsbridge

The listings in this section are marked on the map on p.254.

Cafés

Daquise 20 Thurloe St, SW7 ☎ 020/7589 6117; South Kensington tube. This old-fashioned Polish café right by the tube is something of

a South Ken institution and stands little changed since 1947, serving Polish home cooking or simple coffee, tea and cakes depending on the time of day. Daily 11.30am–11pm.

Gloriette 128 Brompton Rd, SW7 ☎ 020/7589 4750; South Kensington tube. Long-established Viennese café serving coffee and outrageous cakes as well as

sandwiches, Wiener schnitzel, pasta dishes, goulash, and fish and chips. Mon–Fri 7am–8pm, Sat 8am–8pm, Sun 9am–6pm.
Troubadour 263–267 Old Brompton Rd, SW5 ☎020/7370 1434, ⊛www.troubadour.co.uk; **Earl's Court tube**. A fine 1950s hangover, this cluttered boho café/club once played host to Hendrix, Bob Dylan and Joni Mitchell. It still runs terrific folk and blues nights, and dishes up omelettes, steaks and burgers. Daily 9am–midnight.

Restaurants

Bibendum Oyster Bar Michelin House, 81 Fulham Rd, SW3 ☎020/7589 1480, ⊛www .bibendum.co.uk; **South Kensington tube**. A glorious tiled affair built in 1911, this former garage is a great place to eat shellfish. You can snack in the café for under a fiver, splash out on a *plateau de fruits de mer* for £30 a head at the oyster bar or enjoy a three-course lunch in the restaurant for around £30. Mon–Sat noon–11pm, Sun noon–10.30pm. Mains £15–27.

O Fado 45–50 Beauchamp Place, SW3 ☎020/7589 3002, ⊛ofado.co.uk; **Knightsbridge tube**. Probably the oldest Portuguese restaurant in London, which speaks volumes for its authenticity. It can get rowdy, what with the live *fado* ballads (Mon–Sat) and the family parties, but that's half the enjoyment. You'll need to reserve a table. Mon–Sat noon–3pm & 6.30–11pm. Mains £15–18.

Racine 239 Brompton Rd, SW3 ☎020/7584 4477; **Knightsbridge or South Kensington tube**. The food here is French – not just any old French, but familiar, delicious, nostalgic dishes from the glory days of French cooking, with friendly service. Booking is imperative. Daily noon–3pm & 6–10.30pm. Mains £12–20.

Chelsea

The listings in this section are marked on the map on p.258 or p.270.

Cafés

New Culture Revolution 305 King's Rd, SW3 ☎020/7352 9281, ⊛www.newculturerevolution .co.uk; **Sloane Square tube**. Great name, great concept – big bowls of freshly cooked noodles in sauce or soup, or dumplings and rice dishes, inspired by northern China, all offering a one-stop meal at bargain prices in simple, minimalist surroundings. Not a place to linger. Branches in Notting Hill and Islington. Daily noon–11pm.

Poilâne 46 Elizabeth St, SW1 ☎020/7808 4910; **Sloane Square tube**. Tiny London outlet of the legendary French boulangerie, which produces the city's best Parisian bread, croissants and sourdough. Mon–Fri 7.30am–7.30pm, Sat 7.30am–6pm.

Restaurants

Chutney Mary 535 King's Rd, SW10 ☎020/7351 3113, ⊛www.chutneymary.com; **Fulham Broadway tube**. *Chutney Mary* turns out superb gourmet Indian food – complicated dishes, that were developed for the Maharajas, with silky textured sauces, subtle flavours and authentic spicing. Mon–Fri 6.30–11pm, Sat 12.30–2.30pm & 6.30–11pm, Sun 12.30–3pm & 6.30–10pm. Mains £16–22.

Gordon Ramsay 68 Royal Hospital Rd, SW3 ☎020/7352 4441, ⊛www.gordonramsay .com; **Sloane Square tube**. The great man may be nowhere to be seen, but his small Chelsea restaurant is a class act through and through – book well in advance and dress up. Mon–Fri noon–2.30pm & 6.30–11pm. Three-course lunch £45, dinner £90.

Hunan 51 Pimlico Rd, SW1 ☎020/7730 5712, ⊛www.hunanlondon.com; **Sloane Square tube**. Very popular, expensive Chinese restaurant, where a vast array of small dishes are brought to your table for the £40 a head "leave-it-to-us feast", which lets the chef, Mr Peng, show what he can do. Mon–Sat 12.30–2pm & 6.30–11pm. £40.

High Street Kensington to Notting Hill

The listings in this section are marked on the map on p.278.

Cafés

Books for Cooks 4 Blenheim Crescent, W11 ☎020/7221 1992, ⊛www.books forcooks.com; **Ladbroke Grove or Notting Hill**

Gate tube. Tiny café/restaurant within London's top cookery bookshop. Conditions are cramped, but this is an experience not to be missed. Just wander in and have a coffee while browsing, or get there in time to grab a table for the set-menu lunch (noon–1.30pm). Tues–Sat 10am–6pm.

Exeter Street Bakery 18 Argyll Rd, W8 ☎020/7937 8484, ⊛www.exeterstreetbakery .co.uk; High Street Kensington tube. Tiny bakery (not in Exeter St) selling unbelievably superb Italian bread, home-made soup, plus sweet and savoury pizzas and coffee, stand-up or takeaway. Mon–Sat 8am–7pm, Sun 9am–6pm.

Hummingbird Bakery 133 Portobello Rd, W11 ☎020/7229 6446, ⊛www.hummingbirdbakery .com; Notting Hill tube. A cute and kitsch stop halfway down Portobello Rd, selling quality American home-baking, from prettily garish cupcakes to sumptuous Brooklyn Blackout Cake. Wrought-iron chairs and tables outside make for great people-watching. Branch in South Kensington. Mon–Sat 10.30am–5.30pm, Sun 11am–5pm.

Lisboa Patisserie 57 Golborne Rd, W10 ☎0871/3327 7010; Ladbroke Grove tube. Authentic and basic Portuguese *pastelaria*, with the best *pasteis de nata* (custard tarts) this side of Lisbon – also coffee, cakes and a friendly atmosphere. *Café O'porto* at no. 62a Golborne Rd is a good fall-back if this place is full. Daily 8am–8pm.

Restaurants

Al Waha 75 Westbourne Grove, W2 ☎020/7229 0806, ⊛www.alwaharestaurant.com; Bayswater or Queensway tube. Arguably London's best

Lebanese restaurant; delicious meze, but also mouthwatering main-course dishes. Daily noon–11.30pm. Mains £10–13.

Costas Fish Restaurant Hillgate St, W8 ☎020/7727 4310; Notting Hill tube. One of the best fish-and-chips experiences in London can be had at this old-fashioned Greek-Cypriot outfit. Head past the takeaway counter and grab a seat. Tues–Sat noon–2.30pm & 5.30–10.30pm.

Galicia 323 Portobello Rd, W10 ☎020/8969 3539; Ladbroke Grove or Westbourne Park tube. *Galicia* is a pleasant Spanish restaurant without pretension and with a regular Spanish clientele who enjoy the straightforward traditional tapas (£3–7) at the bar. Tues–Sat noon–3pm & 7–11.30pm, Sun noon–3pm & 7–10.30pm. Mains £8–14.

Mandalay 444 Edgware Rd, W2 ☎020/7258 3696, ⊛www.mandalayway .com; Edgware Road tube. Pure and unexpurgated Burmese cuisine – a melange of Thai, Malaysian and a lot of Indian. The portions are huge, the service friendly and the prices low. Booking essential in the evening. Mon–Sat noon–2.30pm & 6–10.30pm. Mains £4–8.

Mandarin Kitchen 14–16 Queensway, W2 ☎020/7727 9012; Bayswater or Queensway tube. People come here specially for its lobsters. Waiters deftly wheel four-foot-diameter tabletops around like giant hoops as they set up communal tables for parties of Chinese. Daily noon–11.30pm. Mains £6–25.

North London

Camden Town

The listings in this section are marked on the map on p.288.

Cafés

Garden Café Inner Circle, Regent's Park, NW1 ☎020/7935 5729, ⊛www.thegardencafe.co.uk; Baker Street or Regent's Park tube. A classic modernist building from the 1960s with a copper-domed roof. The food is as retro as the decor, with mains such as fish pie and ribeye steak, and Bakewell tart or crumble for afters. Daily noon–3pm.

Marine Ices 8 Haverstock Hill, NW3 ☎020/7482 9003, ⊛www.marineices.co.uk; Chalk Farm tube. Situated halfway between Camden

and Hampstead, this is a splendid and justly famous old-fashioned Italian ice-cream parlour established here in 1930; pizza and pasta are served in the adjacent kiddie-friendly restaurant. Tues–Sat noon–11pm, Sun noon–10pm.

Primrose Patisserie 136 Regent's Park Rd, NW1 ☎020/7722 7848; Chalk Farm tube. Very popular pastel-pink and sky-blue patisserie in fashionable Primrose Hill, offering superb East European cakes and pastries. Daily 8am–10pm.

Restaurants

Mango Room 10–12 Kentish Town Rd, NW1 ☎020/7482 5065, ⊛www.mangoroom.co.uk; Camden Town tube. An engaging, laid-back,

Afternoon tea

The classic English **afternoon tea** – assorted sandwiches, scones and cream, cakes and tarts, and, of course, lashings of tea – is available all over London. The best venues are the capital's top hotels and most fashionable department stores; a selection of the best is given below. To avoid disappointment it's essential to book in advance, sometimes as far as twelve weeks ahead. Expect to spend £20–40 a head, and leave your jeans and trainers at home – most hotels will expect "smart casual attire", though only *The Ritz* insists on jacket and tie. All the places listed below are marked on the Mayfair map on p.87.

Cadogan 75 Sloane St, SW1 ☎020/7235 7141, ⊛www.cadogan.com; Sloane Square or Knightsbridge tube. Daily 3pm.

Claridge's Brook St, W1 ☎020/7409 6307, ⊛www.savoy-group.co.uk; Bond Street tube. Daily 3–5.30pm.

▲ Afternoon tea at *The Ritz*

Fortnum & Mason 181 Piccadilly, W1 ☎0845/602 5694, ⊛www.fortnumandmason.com; Green Park/Piccadilly Circus tube. Mon–Sat 2–7pm, Sun 2–5pm.

Lanesborough Hyde Park Corner, SW1 ☎020/7259 5599, ⊛www.lanesborough.com; Hyde Park Corner tube. Daily 3.30–6pm.

The Ritz Piccadilly, W1 ☎020/7493 8181, ⊛www.theritzhotel.co.uk; Green Park tube. Daily 11.30am, 1.30, 3.30, 5.30 & 7.30pm.

The Wolseley 160 Piccadilly, W1 ☎020/7499 6996, ⊛www.thewolseley.com; Green Park tube. Mon–Sat 3.30–5.30pm, Sun 3.30–6.30pm.

Camden-cool Caribbean place whose cooking is consistent and whose presentation is first class. Daily noon–11pm. Mains £10–13.

Manna 4 Erskine Rd, NW3 ☎020/7722 8028, ⊛www.manna-veg.com; Chalk Farm tube. Smart vegetarian restaurant serving large portions of very good veggie and vegan food from around the world. Tues–Sun noon–3pm, daily 6.30–10.30pm. Mains £10–13.

Odette's 130 Regent's Park Rd, NW3 ☎020/7586 8569, ⊛www.odettesprimrosehill.com; Chalk Farm tube. Top-notch modern British food is served at this Primrose Hill restaurant, which opens out onto the street and has a conservatory at the back. Tues–Sat noon–2.30pm & 6.30–10.30pm, Sun noon–3.30pm. Mains £15–22.

Trojka 101 Regent's Park Rd, NW1 ☎020/7483 3765, ⊛www.trojka.co.uk; Chalk Farm tube. The East European food is inexpensive, filling and tasty: blinis and caviar, schnitzel and stroganoff, *pierogi* and *pelmeni*. Service can be a bit East European as well. Live Russian music (Fri & Sat eve). Daily 9am–10.30pm. £6–9.

Islington

The listings in this section are marked on the map on p.288.

Cafés

Afghan Kitchen 35 Islington Green, N1 ☎020/7359 8019; Angel tube. Austere, two-floor café featuring a short menu of cheap, spicy stews with rice. Tues–Sat noon–3.30pm & 5.30–11pm.

Alpino 97 Chapel Market, N1 ☎020/7837 8330; Angel tube. A classic caff, with teak-veneer formica tables, shiny wooden booths and glorious light fittings dating back to 1959. Tues–Sat noon–3.30pm & 5.30–11pm.

M. Manze 74 Chapel Market, N1 ☎020/7837 5270; Angel tube. With their tiled interiors and unchanging menus, pie-and-mash shops are a unique experience, though the rewards are often more architectural than culinary. Tues–Sat 11am–5pm.

Restaurants

Elk in the Woods 39 Camden Passage ☎020/7226 3535, Ⓦwww.the-elk-in-the-woods .co.uk; Angel tube. A sort of bare-brick-and-wood pub/café/restaurant cross, with a stuffed elk looking down on proceedings. Mains can include ribeye steaks, lamb stew and aubergine and coconut curry, but they do breakfasts, sandwiches and burgers too. Daily 10.30am–11pm. Mains £9–17.

Ottolenghi 287 Upper St, N1 ☎020/7288 1454, Ⓦwww.ottolenghi.co.uk; Angel tube. An elegant space – halfway between a café and a restaurant – with long white communal tables and takeaway available. The food is wonderful, with imaginative and varied salads, and fantastic cakes, tarts and pastries. They do breakfast, too, with at-table toasters and piles of newspapers. The downside is that it's not, in any way, cheap. Branches in Notting Hill, Kensington and Belgravia. Mon–Sat 8am–11pm, Sun 9am–7pm. Mains £10–13.

Pasha 301 Upper St, N1 ☎020/7226 1454, Ⓦwww.pasharestaurant.co.uk; Angel or Highbury & Islington tube. This modern Turkish restaurant serves more than just Ottoman dishes, but has enough of the authentic for the discerning. Mon–Sat 11am–11.30pm, Sun 11am–11pm. Mains £8–14.

Stoke Newington

The listings in this section are marked on the map on p.297.

Cafés

Blue Legume 101 Stoke Newington Church St, N16 ☎020/7923 1303; bus #73 or #476 from King's Cross or Angel tube. Buzzy atmosphere, arty decor, mosaic tables and delicious chocolate cakes, teas and coffee. Good breakfasts too – smoked fish, wild

mushrooms on toast and the like. Mon–Sat 9.30am–11pm, Sun 9.30am–6.30pm.

Restaurants

🏃 **Rasa** 55 Stoke Newington Church St, N1 ☎020/7249 0344, Ⓦwww.rasarestaurants .com; Stoke Newington train station. Small, local restaurant, with attentive service and delicious well-priced South Indian vegetarian dishes. *Rasa Travancore* across the road specializes in Syrian Christian cooking, serving some meat and fish dishes. Mon–Thurs 6–10.45pm, Fri 6–11.30pm, Sat noon–3pm & 6–11.30pm, Sun noon–3pm, & 6–10.45pm. Mains £4–6.

Walthamstow

Cafés

L. Manze 76 Walthamstow High St, E17 ☎020/8520 2855; Walthamstow Central tube. Still boasting its original 1929 decor, this is probably London's finest pie-and-mash shop, architecturally speaking, and the grub's not bad, too, including the jellied eel. Mon–Wed 10am–4pm, Thurs–Sat 10am–5pm.

Hampstead and Highgate

The listings in this section are marked on the map on p.302.

Cafés

Brew House Kenwood House, Hampstead Lane, NW3 ☎020/8341 5384; Highgate tube or bus #210 from Archway tube. Everything from full English breakfast to lunches, cakes and teas, all served in the old laundry at Kenwood, or enjoyed in the sunny garden courtyard. Daily 9am–6pm.

Café Mozart 17 Swains Lane, N6 ☎020/8348 1384; Gospel Oak Overground. Conveniently located on the southeast side of Hampstead Heath, the best thing about this café is the Viennese cake selection and soothing classical music. Mon–Fri 8am–10pm, Sat & Sun 9am–10pm.

Camden Arts Centre Arkwright Rd, NW3 ☎020/7472 5516, Ⓦwww.camdenartscentre .org; Finchley Road tube. A pleasing, light modern space with a Gaggia machine providing excellent coffee. Daily lunch specials, soup, snacks and generous slabs of cake. Newspapers and free wi-fi. Tues–Sun 10am–5.30pm, Wed until 8.30pm.

High Tea of Highgate 50 Highgate High St, N6 ☎020/8348 3162, Ⓦwww.highteaofhighgate .co.uk; Highgate tube. Half-modern, half-retro

tearoom run by the fragrant Georgina, serving proper loose-leaf tea and lovely home-made cakes. Tues–Sun 11am–5pm.
Lauderdale House Waterlow Park, Highgate Hill, N6 ⊕020/8341 4807; Archway tube. Handily located café with a terrace overlooking the park, offering full meals as well as exceptional strawberry-and-cream scones on summer weekends. Tues–Sun 8am–dusk.

🏃 **Louis Patisserie** 32 Heath St, NW3 ⊕020/7435 9908; Hampstead tube. Tiny, understated, old-fashioned Hungarian tearoom serving sticky cakes, tea and coffee to a mixed crowd. There's another branch at 12 Harben Parade, Finchley Rd, NW3. Daily 9am–6pm.

Restaurants

Czechoslovak Restaurant 74 West End Lane, NW6 ⊕020/7372 1193, ⓦwww.czechoslovak -restaurant.co.uk; West Hampstead tube. Classic, unreconstructed Czech & Slovak meat and dumplings washed down with Czech beer. Set in a lovely house with a

garden out back, and very popular with Czech expats – book ahead if you want to come for Sunday lunch. Tues–Fri 5–11pm, Sat & Sun noon–10pm. Mains £6–12.
Jin Kichi 73 Heath St, NW3 ⊕020/7794 6158, ⓦwww.jinkichi.com; Hampstead tube. A vast menu with almost every Japanese dish, *Jin Kichi* is cramped, homely and very busy (so book ahead) and specializes in grilled skewers of meat. Tues–Fri 6–11pm, Sat 12.30–2pm & 6–11pm, Sun 12.30–2pm & 6–10.30pm. Mains £6–12.

Wembley

Restaurants

Sakonis 127–129 Ealing Rd, Alperton, Middlesex ⊕020/8903 9601, ⓦwww.sakonis.co.uk; Alperton or Wembley Central tube. Top-notch vegetarian food factory, crowded with Asian families and serving terrific food, especially good *pani puri and aloo bhajia*, deep-fried delights and wonderful juices. Branch in Harrow. Daily noon–10pm, Sat & Sun 9am–11pm. Mains £5–7.

Southeast London

Brixton

Cafés

🏃 **Franco Manca** 4 Market Row, SW9 ⊕020/7738 3021, ⓦwww.francomanca .co.uk; Brixton tube. Very popular, tiny Italian place in Brixton Market that dishes up inexpensive sourdough pizzas from a wood-fired oven washed down with cheap house wine. Mon–Sat noon–5pm.
Rosie's 14e Market Row, Brixton Market, entrance Coldharbour Lane ⊕020/7733 0054, ⓦwww.rosiesdelicafe.com; Brixton tube. A cute and friendly lunch option, with freshly made sandwiches, ciabattas, tarts and great coffee. The deli section contains artisan cheese, handmade pasta and charcuterie. Mon, Tues & Thurs–Sat 9.30am–5.30pm, Wed 9.30am–3pm.

Restaurants

Asmara 386 Coldharbour Lane, SW9 ⊕020/7737 4144; Brixton tube. A welcoming, if slightly spartan Eritrean restaurant; you sit at circular wicker tables and your food arrives on a large tray: the idea is to eat communally, with your

hands. The food – delicately spiced stews and *injera* – is subtle and delicious – and you can wash it down with honey wine. Daily 5.30pm–midnight. £5–8.
Upstairs Bar and Restaurant 89b Acre Lane, SW9 ⊕020/7733 8855, ⓦwww.upstairslondon .com; Brixton tube. A small and hidden arrival on the Brixton scene, with white leather seats and real fires. Delicious mains often include steak tartare and sea bream. Tues–Thurs 6.30–9.30pm, Fri & Sat 6.30–10.30pm. Two courses £22, three courses £26, four courses £30.

Greenwich

The listings in this section are marked on the map on p.321.

Cafés

Biscuit 3–4 Nelson Rd, SE10 ⊕020/8858 8588; Cutty Sark DLR. This quirky modern café is great for those with kids: as well as serving soup, toast and cakes, you can paint your own design on their blank ceramics and they'll fire it for you within a week. Mon–Sat 11am–6pm, Sun 11am–5pm.

Gambardella 48 Vanbrugh Park, SE3
☎020/8858 0327; Maze Hill or Blackheath
train station from Charing Cross. Good old
caff to the southeast of Greenwich Park,
serving filling comfort food in a beautiful
Art Deco interior with lots of chrome and
formica. Mon–Fri 7am–5.30pm, Sat
7am–2.30pm.

Tai Won Mein 39 Greenwich Church St, SE10
☎020/8858 1668; Cutty Sark DLR. Good-
quality fast-food noodle bar that gets very
busy at weekends. Decor is functional and
minimalist; choose between rice, soup or
various fried noodles, all for under a fiver.
Daily 11.30am–11.30pm.

West London

Hammersmith and Chiswick

Restaurants

Azou 35 King St, W6 ☎020/8563 7266, 🖰www
.azou.co.uk; Stamford Brook tube. Small,
informal and atmospheric North African
restaurant where you can enter into the spirit
and end up sitting on a cushion on the floor.
A warm welcome is assured and the classics
– tagines and couscous – are presented with
panache. Daily 6–11pm. Mains £8–12.
The Gate 51 Queen Caroline St, W6 ☎020/8748
6932, 🖰www.thegate.tv; Hammersmith tube.
Located in a converted church with an
outside courtyard that's lovely in summer, *The
Gate* serves excellent and original vegetarian
and vegan dishes with intense and satisfying
tastes and textures. Mon–Fri noon–3pm &
6–11pm, Sat 6–11pm. Mains £10–14.
La Trompette 5–7 Devonshire Rd, W14
☎020/8747 1836, 🖰www.latrompette.co.uk;
Turnham Green tube. A pleasant dining room
with a good deal of light oak and chocolate
leather on show. The French food is very
good, the menu changes on a day-to-day
basis and the prix fixe arrangements are
straightforward. Mon–Sat noon–2.30pm &
6.30–10.30pm, Sun 12.30–3pm &
7–10pm. Three courses from £23.50.
Patio 5 Goldhawk Rd, W12 ☎020/8743 5194;
Goldhawk Road or Shepherd's Bush tube.
Good, solid Polish food in a friendly,
comfortable atmosphere, for a relatively
small amount of money. The four-course set
menu (including a vodka shot) for around
£16 is the trump card. Mon–Fri noon–3pm
& 6pm–11.30pm, Sat & Sun 12.30–3pm,
6pm–midnight. Mains £7–10.

Ealing and Southall

Cafés

Café Grove 65 The Grove, W5 ☎020/8810 0364;
Ealing Broadway tube. Polish café serving

English fry-ups as well as a whole range of
traditional Polish food. Mon–Sat
11am–11pm, Sun 11am–10pm.

Kew and Richmond

The listings in this section are marked
on the map on p.349.

Cafés

Greenhouse 1 Station Parade, Kew ☎020/8940
0183; Kew Gardens tube/rail. A deliciously
old-fashioned and pretty place near Kew
Gardens, with cream teas and home-made
tarts. Daily 8am–dusk.
Pembroke Lodge Richmond Park ☎020/8940
8207; Richmond tube/rail. Popular wedding
venue, this park café has one of the best
views in London, looking west over the
Thames valley. Daily 9.30am–5.30pm or
dusk.

🏃 **Stein's** Richmond Towpath, Richmond
☎20/8948 8189; Richmond tube/rail.
An authentic Bavarian beer garden,
serving up *wurst* and sauerkraut
washed down with *echt* beers and finished
off with strudel. Outdoor seating only, so
closed in wet weather. May to mid-Oct
Mon–Fri noon–10pm, Sat & Sun
10am–10pm; mid-Oct to April Fri–Sun
noon–10pm.

Restaurants

Chez Lindsay 11 Hill Rise, Richmond, Surrey
☎020/8948 7473, 🖰www.chezlindsay.co.uk;
Richmond tube. Small, bright, authentic
Breton *creperie*, with a loyal local following.
There's a wide choice of galettes, crepes or
more formal French main courses, including
lots of fresh fish and shellfish. Mon–Sat
noon–10.45pm, Sun noon–10pm. Mains
£10–19.

Pubs and bars

There's no escaping the fact that the number of traditional **pubs** is declining. Despite this, however, the pub remains one of the country's most enduring social institutions, and is still the place where folk of all ages choose to meet up of an evening, and the majority will be drinking alcohol. Most decent pubs serve at least two or three **real ales** (see below) **of varying strength**, as well as the usual array of drinks. The emergence of **gastropubs**, where the food is as important as the drink, has had a knock-on effect on all pubs; it's meant all pubs can now charge (and make) a lot more money out of food, but also that the overall standard of cooking has improved enormously.

London's great period of pub building took place under the Victorians, and genuine examples survive all over the capital, while the rest usually pay some kind of homage to the era. Chain pubs can now be found everywhere – branches of *All Bar One*, *Pitcher & Piano* and *Slug & Lettuce* are the most obvious, as they all share the chain name. Others, like Young's, Fuller's, Nicholson and J.D. Wetherspoon, do at least vary the names of their pubs. With a pint now often costing £3 or more, it's worthwhile knowing that you can pay half that at Sam Smith's pubs, and at Wetherspoon's, who can also be relied on to provide a wide range of real ales.

Alongside pubs, we've also listed a selection of the capital's **bars**, which go in and out of fashion with incredible speed. These are very different places to your average pub, with designer interiors and drinks; they also tend to be more expensive. Note that this chapter covers pubs and bars that are good for drinking – and, sometimes, eating – in. It doesn't include club-bars or pubs and bars that are primarily live-music venues, which you'll find in Chapter 26, or gay and lesbian pubs and bars, which are covered in Chapter 27.

Whitehall and Westminster

The listings in this section are marked on the map on p.44.

The Chandos 29 St Martin's Lane, WC2 ☏020/7836 1401; Charing Cross tube. If you can get one of the booths downstairs, or the leather sofas upstairs in the more relaxed Opera Room Bar, then you'll find it difficult to leave this Sam Smith's pub. Mon–Sat 11am–11pm, Sun noon–10.30pm.

Red Lion 48 Parliament St, SW1 ☏020/7930 5826; Westminster tube. Classic old pub with good grub, convenient for Westminster Abbey and Parliament. Popular with MPs, who are called to votes by a division bell in the bar. Mon–Fri 11am–11pm, Sat 11am–9.30pm, Sun noon–10.30pm.

St Stephen's Tavern 10 Bridge St, SW1 ☏020/7925 2286; Westminster tube. A beautifully restored, opulent Victorian pub, built in 1867, wall to wall with civil servants and MPs (there's a division bell), and serving good real ales. Mon–Fri 11am–11pm, Sat 11am–8pm, Sun noon–6pm.

English beer

Although lager has now overtaken bitter in popularity, the classic pub drink is **real ale**. It was CAMRA (Campaign for Real Ale; Ⓦ www.camra.org.uk), that first coined the term, to differentiate traditional ale from processed keg beer. Real ale is an uncarbonated and dark beverage that matures in barrels or casks in the cellar and is pumped by hand fresh from the cellar. Most real ales are also referred to as **bitter**; terms like Mild, Best and Special merely refer to the strength; the acronym IPA (India Pale Ale) refers to bitter's colonial precursor. Real ales are brewed all over the country, and in one or two brew-pubs within the capital, but the only large-scale London brewery of distinction left is Fuller's, producer of London Pride.

St James's

The listings in this section are marked on the map on p.77.

ICA Bar The Mall, SW1 ℡ 020/7930 3647, Ⓦ www.ica.org.uk; **Piccadilly Circus or Charing Cross tube.** Cool late-opening drinking venue, with a noir dress code observed by the arty crowd and staff. Sweaty DJ nights at the weekends. Mon noon–11pm, Tues–Sat noon–1am, Sun noon–10.30pm.

Red Lion 23 Crown Passage, SW1 ℡ 020/7930 4141; **Green Park tube.** Hidden away in a passageway off Pall Mall, this is a genuinely warm and cosy local, with super friendly bar staff, well-kept beer and excellent sandwiches. Mon–Sat 11.30am–11pm.

Red Lion 2 Duke of York St, SW1 ℡ 020/7321 0782; **Piccadilly Circus tube.** Genuine old Victorian gin palace with elegant etched mirrors, lots of polished wood and a great ceiling. Offers a commendable selection of ales, including a weekly guest choice as voted for by its customers. Mon–Sat 11.30am–11pm.

Mayfair

The listings in this section are marked on the map on p.89.

Audley 41 Mount St, W1 ℡ 020/7499 1843; **Hyde Park Corner or Bond Street tube.** A grand Mayfair pub, with original Victorian burgundy lincrusta ceiling, beautiful wood-panelled walls, chandeliers and clocks. Mon–Sat 11am–11pm, Sun noon–10.30pm.

Guinea 30 Bruton Place, W1 ℡ 020/7409 1728; **Bond Street or Oxford Circus tube.** Pretty, old-fashioned, flower-strewn mews pub, serving good Young's bitter, and excellent steak-and-kidney pies. Invariably packed to its tiny rafters. Mon–Fri 11am–11pm, Sat 6–11pm.

Shepherd's Tavern 50 Hertford St, W1 ℡ 020/7499 3017; **Green Park or Hyde Park Corner tube.** A comfortable, low-key boozer in a quiet area off Piccadilly, with decent food in the antique pine-panelled room upstairs. Daily 11am–11pm.

The Windmill 6–8 Mill St, W1 ℡ 020/7491 8050; **Oxford Circus tube.** Convivial, well-regarded pub just off Regent St, and a perfect retreat for exhausted shoppers. The Young's beers are top-notch, as are the steak and kidney pies, for which the pub has won numerous awards. Mon–Fri 11am–midnight, Sat noon–4pm.

Marylebone

The listings in this section are marked on the map on p.97.

Dover Castle 43 Weymouth Mews, W1 ℡ 020/7580 4412; **Regent's Park or Great Portland Street tube.** A traditional, quiet, cheap Sam Smith's boozer hidden away down a labyrinthine and picturesque Marylebone mews. Green upholstery, dark wood and a nicotine-stained lincrusta ceiling add to the atmosphere. Mon–Sat 11.30am–11pm, Sun noon–10.30pm.

Golden Eagle 59 Marylebone Lane, W1 ℡ 020/7935 3228; **Bond Street tube.** Proper old one-room, neighbourhood pub, with a good range of real ales, and singalongs on the old "Joanna" (Tues, Thurs & Fri). Mon–Sat 11am–11pm, Sun noon–7pm.

Windsor Castle 27–29 Crawford Place, W1 ℡ 020/7723 4371; **Edgware Road tube.** Bizarre, slightly mad, one-of-a-kind pub stuffed to the brim with royalty- and celebrity-related ephemera collected by the landlord. Decent Thai food, too. Mon–Thurs 11am–11pm, Fri & Sat noon–10.30pm, Sun noon–10.30pm.

Soho

The listings in this section are marked on the map on p.104 or p.108.

Argyll Arms 18 Argyll St, W1 ☎020/7734 6117; Oxford Circus tube. Mobbed by shoppers and tourists alike, but this Victorian pub has preserved its beautifully crafted snugs, separated by mahogany and etched glass partitions, and offers a good range of real ales. Mon–Sat 11am–11.30pm, Sun noon–10.30pm.

De Hems 11 Macclesfield St, W1 ☎020/7437 2494; Leicester Square tube. London's official Dutch pub since 1890, the frequently jam-packed downstairs bar is a simple wood-panelled affair, while the contempo-rary upstairs space is good for more relaxed drinking. Good selection of mainly Belgian and Dutch beers and food. Mon–Sat noon–midnight, Sun noon–10.30pm.

Dog & Duck 18 Bateman St, W1 ☎020/7494 0697; Tottenham Court Road tube. Tiny Soho pub that retains much of its old character, beautiful Victorian tiling and mosaics, a good range of real ales and a loyal clientele. If it gets too busy downstairs, head upstairs to the George Orwell Bar (he used to drink here). Mon–Sat 11am–11pm, Sun noon–10.30pm.

French House 49 Dean St, W1 ☎020/7437 2799; Leicester Square tube. This tiny French pub has been a Soho institution since Belgian Victor Berlemont bought the place shortly before World War I. Free French and literary associations galore, and half-pints only at the bar (no real ale). Mon–Fri noon–11pm, Sat & Sun noon–10.30pm.

LAB 12 Old Compton St, W1 ☎020/7437 7820, ⓦ www.lab-townhouse.com; Leicester Square tube. Two-floor retro cocktail bar that's considered one of the best in London; cocktail-school graduates serve up classics and new concoctions. DJs on Fridays and every other Wednesday. Mon–Sat 4pm–midnight, Sun 4pm–10.30pm.

Fitzrovia

The listings in this section are marked on the map on p.104.

Annex 3 6 Little Portland St, W1 ☎020/7631 0700, ⓦ www.annex3.co.uk; Oxford Circus tube. *Annex Trois* (bien sûr!) is a bizarre bar, decked with high-camp kitsch and fuelled

by an imaginative range of cocktails. Mon–Fri 5pm–midnight, Sat 6pm–midnight.

Bradley's Spanish Bar 42–44 Hanway St, W1 ☎020/7636 0359; Tottenham Court Road tube. Appealingly unpretentious backstreet bar, set over two very small floors, with a mixed but faithful clientele and an excellent vinyl jukebox full of old favourites. Mon–Sat noon–11pm, Sun 3–10.30pm.

Newman Arms 23 Rathbone St, W1 ☎020/7636 1127; Tottenham Court Road or Goodge Street tube. Intimate, extremely friendly, family-run local, popular with a mixed and loyal crowd. Upstairs you can sample one of the pub's fabulous pies, with every sort from lamb-and-rosemary to steak-and-kidney. Mon–Fri noon–12.30am.

The Social 5 Little Portland St, W1 ☎020/7636 4992, ⓦ www.thesocial.com; Oxford Circus tube. Industrial club-bar and diner, with great DJs playing everything from rock to rap, a truly hedonistic-cum-alcoholic crowd. Mon–Wed noon–midnight, Thurs–Sat 1pm–midnight, Sun 5pm–midnight.

The listings in this section are marked on the map on p.127.

The Duke 7 Roger St, WC1 ☎020/7242 7230, ⓦ www.dukepub.co.uk; Russell Square tube. Lovely little neighbourhood gastropub, without the pretensions often associated with the breed, and an unusual Art Deco bent to the decor. Mon–Sat noon–11pm, Sun noon–10.30pm.

The Lamb 94 Lamb's Conduit St, WC1 ☎020/7405 0713; Russell Square tube. Marvellously well-preserved Victorian pub of mirrors, polished wood and etched glass "snob" screens. Deep green leather banquettes and small circular tables with dinky brass balustrades round things off splendidly. Excellent Young's beers. Mon–Sat 11am–midnight, Sun noon–10.30pm.

Lincoln Lounge 52 York Way, N1 ☎020/7837 9339; King's Cross tube. Very useful find a short walk from King's Cross: a very friendly, slightly offbeat but unpretentious pub with decent real ales. Mon–Fri 11am–11pm, Sat noon–11.30pm, Sun noon–10.30pm.

Museum Tavern 49 Great Russell St, WC1 ☎020/7242 8987; Tottenham Court Road or Russell Square tube. The erstwhile drinking hole of Karl Marx is a handsome old pub right opposite the main entrance to the

British Museum. A choice range of ales available. Mon–Sat 11am–11pm, Sun noon–10.30pm.

Covent Garden and the Strand

The listings in this section are marked on the map on p.140.

Coal Hole 91 Strand, WC2 ☎020/7379 9883; **Charing Cross or Embankment tube.** Popular Edwardian pub next to *The Savoy*. Take a look up at the high wooden beams and stone friezes as you sip one of the fine ales on offer, or head to the cellar bar for wine. Decent pies, too. Mon–Sat 11am–midnight, Sun noon–10.30pm.

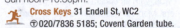 **Cross Keys** 31 Endell St, WC2 ☎020/7836 5185; **Covent Garden tube.** Stuffed with copper pots, brass instruments, paintings and memorabilia, this most welcoming of West End pubs attracts an appealing blend of older Covent Garden residents, young workers and tourists – you'll do well to find a seat. Mon–Sat 11am–11pm, Sun noon–10.30pm.

Gordon's 47 Villiers St, WC2 ☎020/7930 1408, ⓦwww.gordonswinebar.com; **Charing Cross or Embankment tube.** Cavernous, shabby, atmospheric family-run wine bar specializing in ports, sherries and Madeiras. The genial atmosphere makes this a favourite with local office workers, who spill outdoors in the summer. Mon–Sat 11am–11pm, Sun noon–10pm.

Lamb & Flag 33 Rose St, WC2 ☎020/7497 9504; **Leicester Square tube.** Over 300 years old, this agreeably tatty pub, tucked away down an alley between Garrick and Floral streets, was where John Dryden was attacked in 1679 (see p.144). Mon–Sat 11am–11pm, Sun noon–10.30pm.

The Salisbury 90 St Martin's Lane, WC2 ☎020/7836 5863; **Leicester Square tube.** One of the capital's most beautifully preserved Victorian pubs, with etched and engraved windows, bronze figures and Art Nouveau light fittings. A wide and unusual range of ales and unusually attentive staff add to the general joy of this place. Mon–Fri 11am–11pm, Sat noon–midnight, Sun noon–10.30pm.

Holborn

The listings in this section are marked on the map on p.151.

Bar Polski 11 Little Turnstile, WC1 ☎020/7831 9679; **Holborn tube.** Modern Polish bar hidden in an alleyway behind Holborn tube, with a wicked selection of flavoured vodkas and beers, and good, cheap Polish food. Mon 4–11.30pm, Tues–Fri 12.30–11.30pm, Sat 6–11pm, Sun 6–10.30pm.

Cittie of Yorke 22 High Holborn, WC1 ☎020/7242 7670; **Chancery Lane tube.** A venerable London lawyers' pub now run by Sam Smith's. Head for the vaulted cellar bar or the grand quasi-medieval wine hall at the back with its rows of cosy cubicles. Mon–Fri 11.30am–11pm, Sat noon–11pm.

Old Bank of England 194 Fleet St, EC4 ☎020/7430 2255; **Temple or Chancery Lane tube.** Not the actual Bank of England, but the former Law Courts' branch, this imposing High Victorian banking hall is now a magnificently opulent Fuller's ale-and-pie pub. Mon–Fri 11am–11pm.

Princess Louise 208 High Holborn, WC1 ☎020/7405 8816; **Holborn tube.** Architecturally, this is one of London's most impressive Victorian pubs, featuring gold-trimmed mirrors, gorgeous mosaics and a fine moulded ceiling. The Sam Smith's beer is very reasonably priced and there's always a lively crowd. Mon–Fri 11am–11pm, Sat noon–11pm.

Seven Stars 53–54 Carey St, WC1 ☎020/7242 8521; **Holborn tube.** This diminutive and gloriously dishevelled boozer dates from 1602, and despite the legal crowd, it oozes charm, and attracts a surprisingly mixed clientele. Mon–Fri 11am–11pm, Sat noon–11pm, Sun noon–10.30pm.

Ye Olde Mitre 1 Ely Court, EC1 ☎020/7405 4751; **Farringdon tube.** Hidden down a tiny alleyway off Ely Place or Hatton Garden, this wonderfully atmospheric pub dates back to 1546, although it was actually rebuilt in the eighteenth century. The low-ceilinged, wood-panelled rooms are packed with history and the real ales are excellent. Mon–Fri 11am–11pm.

Clerkenwell and Hoxton

The listings in this section are marked on the map on p.158.

Clerkenwell

Café Kick 43 Exmouth Market, EC1 ☎020/7837 8077, ⓦwww.cafekick.co.uk; **Farringdon or Angel tube.** This chaotic, very popular

French-style café/bar is great fun, enlivened by three busy table-football games. Branch (*Bar Kick*) at 127 Shoreditch High St, E1. Mon–Sat noon–11pm, Sun noon–10.30pm.

Dovetail 9 Jerusalem Passage, EC1 ☎020/7490 7321; Farringdon tube. Marvellous, understated Belgian bar offering 101 varieties of beer (including a dozen or so on tap). The curious decor comprises pew-style seating, green-tiled tables and kitchen-style wall tiling. First-rate Belgian food, too. Mon–Sat noon–11pm.

Eagle 159 Farringdon Rd, EC1 ☎020/7837 1353; Farringdon tube. The first (and still one of the best) of London's gastropubs, this place is often heaving for lunch and dinner, but you should be able to find a seat at other times. Mon–Sat noon–11pm, Sun noon–5pm.

Jerusalem Tavern 55 Britton St, EC1 ☎020/7490 4281; Farringdon tube. Converted Georgian coffee house – the frontage dates from 1810 – that has retained much of its original character. Better still, the excellent draught beers are from St Peter's Brewery in Suffolk. Something of a gem in these parts. Mon–Fri 11am–11pm.

Queen Boadicea 292–294 St John St, EC1 ☎020/7278 9990; Angel tube. The immaculately restored exterior – green and brown Georgian tiling and a statue of Boadicea herself – of this cool pub, is complemented by an equally striking interior, comprising floral patterned wallpaper, deep leather sofas and grand chandeliers. Mon–Wed & Sun 11.30am–11pm, Thurs 11.30am–midnight, Fri & Sat 11.30am–2am.

Slaughtered Lamb 34–35 Great Sutton St, EC1 ☎020/7253 1516, ⊛www.theslaughteredlamb pub.co.uk; Barbican or Farringdon tube. Self-consciously trendy former art gallery, filled with sofas and old furniture. Lots of live music and events – moustaches must be worn on Saturday evenings. Ironically old-fashioned pub grub. Mon–Thurs noon–midnight, Fri & Sat noon–1am, Sun noon–10.30pm.

Vinoteca 7 St John St, EC1 ☎020/7253 8786, ⊛www.vinoteca.co.uk; Farringdon tube. Small, laid-back wine bar (and shop) with a vast and impressive selection of wines. Also serves very good, Moorish-influenced food. Bookings taken for lunch but not dinner. Mon–Sat noon–midnight.

Hoxton

Callooh Callay 65 Rivington St, EC2 ☎020/7739 4781, ⊛www.calloohcallaybar.com; Old Street or Liverpool Street tube. Hidden away off Shoreditch High St, this Jabberwocky-inspired camp-kitsch bar has a Narnia-style wardrobe separating its wacky rooms. Cocktails and wines are the drinks of choice. Mon–Wed 5–11pm, Thurs noon–11pm, Fri noon–1am, Sat 6pm–1am, Sun 6–11pm.

Cantaloupe 35 Charlotte Rd, EC2 ☎020/7613 4411, ⊛www.cantaloupe.co.uk; Old Street tube. One of the pioneers of the Hoxton transformation, this place still manages to pull in the crowds, with its cocktails, tapas and bottled beers. Mon–Fri noon–4pm & 6pm–11pm, Sat 6pm–11pm.

Charlie Wright's International Bar 45 Pitfield St, N1 ☎020/7490 8345, ⊛www.charliewrights .com; Old Street tube. Part of old-style – rather than trendy – Hoxton, this convivial bar-club, serving decent Thai food, has regular jazz nights and a useful late licence. Mon–Wed noon–1am, Thurs & Fri noon–4am, Sat 5pm–4am, Sun 5pm–2am.

Three Blind Mice 5 Ravey St, EC2 ☎020/7739 7746; Old Street tube. A tiny, tatty but atmospheric basement bar, it has a good range of vodka and a music policy that departs from the usual Hoxton scene with Country & Western, Northern Soul, Mod and reggae. There's no sign – it's located next to the small *Casita* bar. Tues–Thurs 5–11pm, Fri & Sat 6pm–midnight, Sun 6.30–10.30pm.

The City

The listings in this section are marked on the map on p.168.

Fleet Street and St Paul's

The Black Friar 174 Queen Victoria St, EC4 ☎020/7236 5474; Blackfriars tube. A gorgeous, utterly original pub, with Art Nouveau marble friezes of boozy monks and a highly decorated alcove – all original, dating from 1905. A lovely fireplace, and an unhurried atmosphere make this a relaxing place to drink. Mon–Fri 11am–11pm, Sat 11am–11.30pm, Sun noon–10.30pm.

Viaduct Tavern 126 Newgate St, EC1 ☎020/7600 1863; St Paul's tube. Fuller's pub situated across from the Old Bailey, with a glorious Victorian interior from 1869. The red ceiling and walls are adorned with oils of

The Thames

If it weren't for the Thames, there would be no London – after all, the city grew up around the river crossing. The river had its heyday in the Victorian era when London was the busiest port in the world. The Thames may be a lot quieter nowadays, but it's just as interesting, and easier than ever before to explore, thanks to the Thames Path, which runs along both banks all the way to Greenwich, and beyond to the Thames Barrier in Woolwich.

Thames transport

Up until 1750 London Bridge was the only bridge over the Thames. Everywhere else, the river was crossed by **ferry**, so all the way along the banks there were stairs and landing places for picking up passengers and even horses and carts. The Thames watermen became extremely important, and took advantage of this by overcharging customers. Competition was fierce, too, and accidents between poorly qualified men in unsuitable boats frequent. Until the street improvements ushered in by the late Victorian and Edwardian period, and the expansion of the tube, it was, of course, much quicker to get from A to B via the river, than fight through the city's muddy crowded streets. Today, only one such ferry remains: Hammerton's Ferry, taking foot passengers and bicycles from Ham to Twickenham (see p.351), though Thames Clippers, a fleet of modern catamarans, also provide an impressively fast service for commuters travelling between Greenwich, Docklands and central London (see p.26).

Houseboats near Docklands ▲

The Thames Path at Hammersmith ▼

Thames Clipper approaching Blackfriars Bridge ▼

I walk my beat before London Town,
Five hours up and seven down.
Up I go till I end my run
At Tide-end-town, which is Teddington.
Down I come with the mud in my hands
And plaster it over the Maplin Sands.
But I'd have you know that these waters of mine
Were once a branch of the River Rhine,
When hundreds of miles to the East I went
And England was joined to the Continent.

The River's Tale, Rudyard Kipling

Frost Fairs

Until the eighteenth century, long-living Londoners could hope to experience at least one or two **Frost Fairs** in their lifetime. Diarist John Evelyn witnessed the Frost Fair of 1684: "The Thames before London was planted with booths in formal streets as in a city, or continual fair, all sorts of trades and shops furnished and full of commodities even to a printing press… Coaches plied from Westminster to the Temple, and from several other stairs too and fro, as in the streets, also on sleds, sliding with skates; there was likewise bull-baiting, horse and coach races, puppet plays and interludes, cooks, tippling and lewder places, so that it seemed to be a bacchanalian triumph, or carnival on the water".

As Europe's "**Little Ice Age**" came to an end, the last Frost Fair was held in 1814, during which an elephant was led across the river below Blackfriars Bridge. It was changes to the river, rather than the climate, that initially put paid to the celebrations. Uncontrolled, unembanked and undredged, the current was a lot slower in days gone by, and the narrow piers of old **London Bridge** acted as a sort of natural dam. With the removal of old London Bridge in 1831, the river flowed faster and no longer froze sufficiently, although in recent years a "Frost Fair" Christmas market has been relaunched, on dry land, along the South Bank.

▲ The Thames winds its way past the O2

▼ Frost Fair on the Thames, 1683–4

▼ Frost Fair Christmas market

Millennium Bridge ▲

Golden Jubilee Bridge ▼

Tower Bridge ▼

From Tower to Westminster Bridge

▶▶ **Tower Bridge (1894)** London's most spectacular bridge, its bascules are still raised hundreds of times a year to let tall ships pass through.

▶▶ **London Bridge (1972)** London's first river crossing – the famous medieval bridge has long since gone and the current concrete structure is without doubt the ugliest yet.

▶▶ **Southwark Bridge (1921)** This remains the quietest of London's bridges; to the east, note the wonderful fluted Doric piers of the nearby Cannon Street railway bridge (1866).

▶▶ **Millennium Bridge (2000)** The first new river crossing in London for a century and the first pedestrian-only bridge. The bridge wobbled when it first opened and was closed after only two days, reopening after repairs.

▶▶ **Blackfriars Bridge (1869)** Upstaged by the wonderfully ornate, nearby piers of the (now defunct) London, Chatham & Dover Railway bridge. Blackfriars is where the financier Roberto Calvi, known as "God's Banker", was found hanging in 1972 with bricks in his pockets, murdered by the Mafia.

▶▶ **Waterloo Bridge (1942)** Built mostly by women during World War II, the view from here was made famous by The Kinks' 1967 song, *Waterloo Sunset*.

▶▶ **Hungerford Bridge (1864 & 2002)** An old Victorian steel-truss railway bridge now flanked by two snazzy pedestrian sections, officially named the Golden Jubilee Bridges, which are attached by a succession of white pylons and cables.

▶▶ **Westminster Bridge (1862)** Sadly, Wordsworth's poem, "Earth has not anything to show more fair. . ." and so on – was addressed to the bridge's predecessor and not this solid cast-iron Victorian one.

faded ladies representing Commerce, Agriculture and the Arts. Mon–Fri 11am–11pm.

🏃 **Ye Olde Cheshire Cheese** Wine Office Court, 145 Fleet St, EC4 ☎020/7353 6170; Temple or Blackfriars tube. A famous seventeenth-century watering hole – chiefly because of patrons such as Dickens and Dr Johnson – with several snug, dark-panelled bars and real fires. Popular with tourists, but by no means exclusively so. Mon–Fri 11am–11pm, Sat noon–11pm, Sun noon–5pm.

▲ Ye Olde Cheshire Cheese

Bank and around

The Counting House 50 Cornhill, EC2 ☎020/7283 7123; Bank tube. Another inspired Fuller's bank conversion, the magnificent interior features high ceilings, marble walls, mosaic flooring, and a large, oval island bar, above which is an enormous glass dome. Mon–Fri 11am–9pm.

Jamaica Wine House St Michael's Alley, EC3 ☎020/7929 6972; Bank tube. Located down a narrow alleyway, on the site of London's first coffee house (1652), this old City institution is known locally as the "Jam Pot". Despite the name, it is really just a pub, divided into four large "snugs" by original, high wood-panelled partitions. Mon–Fri 11am–11pm.

The Lamb Tavern 10–12 Leadenhall Market, EC3 ☎020/7626 2454; Monument tube. Situated in the middle of beautiful Leadenhall Market,

it's almost exclusively standing room only (both inside and out) at this super Young's pub. Excellent roast beef, pork and sausage sandwiches at lunchtime. Mon–Fri 11am–11pm.

The East End

The listings in this section are marked on the map on p.202.

Loungelover 1 Whitby St, E1 ☎020/7012 1234, ⓦwww.loungelover.co.uk; Liverpool Street tube. Behind the unprepossessing facade of this former meat-packing factory lies a bizarre array of opulently camp bric-a-brac, expertly slung together to create an extraordinary-looking and unique cocktail bar. Mon–Thurs & Sun 6pm–midnight, Fri 5.30pm–1am, Sat 6pm–1am.

Ten Bells 84 Commercial St, E1 ☎020/7366 1721; Liverpool Street tube. Stripped-down, pleasantly ramshackle pub (with Jack the Ripper associations), with some great Victorian tiling. Attracts a relentlessly hip and young crowd these days. Mon–Thurs & Sun noon–midnight, Fri & Sat noon–1am.

Vibe Bar Old Truman Brewery, 91–95 Brick Lane, E1 ☎020/7377 2899, ⓦwww.vibe-bar.co.uk; Liverpool Street tube. Trendy bar in an old brewery with good sofas and DJs and live bands in the evenings. Great covered beer garden with summer barbecues at weekends, which is also used as a festival venue. Mon–Thurs & Sun 11am–11.30pm, Fri & Sat 11am–1am.

🏃 **Water Poet** 9 Folgate St, E1 ☎020/7426 0495; Liverpool Street tube. Large, appealingly unorthodox pub with big bay windows, deep leather sofas and Dalí-esque decor, but also a side bar with Sky TV, and a tidy little pool room with two tables. Lovely beer garden, too. Mon–Fri 11am–11pm, Sat noon–10.30pm.

Docklands

The listings in this section are marked on the map on p.215.

The Grapes 76 Narrow St, E14 ☎020/7987 4396; Westferry DLR. A lovely, narrow, little pub on a quiet street, with lots of seafaring paraphernalia and a great riverside balcony out back. The ales are good and there's an expensive fish restaurant upstairs. Mon–Fri noon–3.30pm & 5.30–11pm, Sat noon–11pm, Sun noon–10.30pm.

The Gun 27 Coldharbour, E14 ☎020/7515 5222, ⓦwww.thegundocklands.com; Canary Wharf tube or South Quay or Blackwall DLR. Legendary dockers' pub, once the haunt of Lord Nelson, *The Gun* is now a classy gastropub, with a cosy back bar with a couple of snugs, and an outside deck offering an unrivalled view of the Dome. Mon–Sat 11am–midnight, Sun 11am–11pm.

Prospect of Whitby 57 Wapping Wall, E1 ☎020/7481 1095; Wapping tube. Steeped in history, this is London's most famous riverside pub, with a pewter bar, flagstone floor, ancient timber beams and stacks of maritime memorabilia. Decent beers and terrific views out across the Thames. Mon–Sat noon–11pm, Sun noon–10.30pm.

Town of Ramsgate 62 Wapping High St, E1 ☎020/7264 0001; Wapping tube. Dark, narrow, medieval pub located by Wapping Old Stairs, which once led down to Execution Dock. Captain Blood was discovered here with the Crown Jewels under his cloak, "Hanging" Judge Jeffreys was arrested here trying to flee, and Admiral Bligh and Fletcher Christian were regular drinking partners in pre-mutiny days. Mon–Sat noon–midnight, Sun noon–10.30pm.

South Bank

The listings in this section are marked on the map on p.221.

Anchor & Hope 36 The Cut, SE1 ☎020/7928 9898; Southwark tube. *The Anchor* is a gastropub that dishes up truly excellent, yet simple grub: soups, salads and mains such as slow-cooked pork with *choucroute*, as well as mouthwatering puds. You can't book a table, so the bar is basically the waiting room. Mon 5–11pm, Tues–Sat 11am–11pm, Sun 12.30–5pm.

Baltic 74 Blackfriars Rd, SE1 ☎020/7928 1111, ⓦwww.balticrestaurant.co.uk; Southwark tube. Very stylish modern bar (with a restaurant at the back) situated opposite Southwark tube in an old Georgian coachworks: serves an incredible array of vodka shots and Baltic snacks. Live jazz some evenings. Daily noon–3.30pm & 6–11pm.

Kings Arms 25 Roupell St, SE1 ☎020/7207 0784; Waterloo tube. Sited on a quiet Victorian terraced street, this terrific local is divided into two parts; the front part is a traditional drinking area, while the rear is a tastefully cluttered, glass and wood conservatory-style space adorned with bric-a-brac and featuring a large open fire and long wooden table. Thai food. Mon–Sat 11am–11pm, Sun noon–10.30pm.

Southwark

Bankside

The listings in this section are marked on the map on p.234.

The Anchor 34 Park St, SE1 ☎020/7407 1577; London Bridge tube. First built in 1770, this sprawling pub retains only a few vestiges of the past, but it does have one of the few riverside terraces in the centre of town – inevitably it's often mobbed by tourists. Mon–Sat 11am–11pm, Sun noon–10.30pm.

Founders Arms 52 Hopton St, SE1 ☎020/7928 1899; Southwark or Blackfriars tube. A modern Young's pub, wholly undistinguished except for its position by the river, with outside tables and superlative views across to St Paul's and the City. Mon–Thurs 10am–11pm, Fri 10am–midnight, Sat 9am–midnight, Sun 9am–11pm.

Borough

The listings in this section are marked on the map on p.230 or p.234.

George Inn 77 Borough High St, SE1 ☎020/7407 2056; Borough or London Bridge tube. London's only surviving galleried coaching inn (see p.235), dating from the seventeenth century and now owned by the National Trust; mobbed by tourists, but it does serve a good range of real ales. Mon–Thurs 11am–11pm, Fri & Sat 11am–midnight, Sun noon–10.30pm.

Lord Clyde 27 Clennam St, SE1 ☎020/7407 3397; Borough tube. A genuinely hospitable, family-run boozer, with a good choice of ales, obliging staff and lots of good chatter. Before entering, take a look at the superb frontage, with its cream-and-green glazed earthenware dating from 1913. Mon–Fri 11am–11pm, Sat noon–11pm, Sun noon–6pm.

Market Porter 9 Stoney St, SE1 ☎020/7407 2495; London Bridge tube. Handsome semicircular pub by Borough Market, with an interesting range of real ales and decent food. Outrageously popular, as evidenced by the masses that spill out onto the surrounding pavements. Mon–Fri

6–8.30am & 11am–11pm, Sat noon–11pm, Sun noon–10.30pm.

The Rake 14 Winchester Walk, SE1 ☎020/7407 0557; London Bridge tube. Sleek, bright, little bar whose enthusiastic staff are happy to advise on half a dozen (very strong and very expensive) draught beers from Germany, America, Belgium and Holland, as well as over a hundred bottled beers from around the globe. There's also a pleasant decked terrace. Mon–Fri noon–11pm, Sat 10am–11pm.

Royal Oak 44 Tabard St, SE1 ☎020/7357 7173; Borough tube. Beautiful, lovingly restored Victorian pub that eschews jukeboxes and one-armed bandits and opts simply for serving a superb stock of real ales (mild, pale and old) from Harvey's brewery in Sussex and some good pub grub. Mon–Fri 11am–11pm, Sat 6–11pm, Sun noon–6pm.

Rotherhithe

The listings in this section are marked on the map on p.230.

The Angel 101 Bermondsey Wall East, SE16 ☎020/7394 3214; Rotherhithe tube. Comprehensively refurbished, historic pub that stands on its own in the middle of nowhere on the path between Butler's Wharf and Rotherhithe. Wonderful riverside terrace and cheap Sam Smith's ale on tap. Mon–Sat noon–11pm, Sun noon–10.30pm.

The Mayflower 117 Rotherhithe St, SE16 ☎020/7237 4088, ⊛themayflowerpub.co.uk; Rotherhithe tube. This eighteenth-century pub, in the heart of old Rotherhithe, is steeped in history. The blackened brick walls, wonky timber frames and creaky floorboards give it genuine character, while the wooden terrace offers splendid views out across the Thames. Decent real ales and pub food. Daily 11am–11pm.

South Kensington, Knightsbridge and Chelsea

The listings in this section are marked on the map on p.254 or on p.258.

Belgravia and Knightsbridge

Grenadier 18 Wilton Row, SW1 ☎020/7235 3074; Hyde Park Corner or Knightsbridge tube. Located in a private mews, this quaint little pub was Wellington's local (his horse block survives outside) and his officers' mess; the

original pewter bar survives, while there's plenty of military paraphernalia to gawp at. Classy but pricey bar food. Mon–Sat noon–11pm, Sun noon–10.30pm.

The Nag's Head 53 Kinnerton St, SW1 ☎020/7235 1135; Hyde Park Corner or Knightsbridge tube. A convivial, quirky and down-to-earth little pub in a posh cobbled mews, with dark wood panelling, china handpumps and old prints on hunting, shooting and fishing. The unusual sunken back room has a flagstone floor and fires in winter. The pub grub's good and the landlord doesn't like mobiles. Mon–Sat 11am–11pm, Sun noon–10.30pm.

Star Tavern 6 Belgrave Mews West, SW1 ☎020/7235 3019; Hyde Park Corner or Knightsbridge tube. Quiet two-storey mews pub with a large open sitting room and a murky past: allegedly, it was from here that the Great Train Robbery was planned. Fine Fuller's beer and traditional pub grub. Mon–Sat 11am–11pm, Sun noon–10.30pm.

South Kensington

Anglesea Arms 15 Selwood Terrace, SW7 ☎020/7373 7960; South Kensington tube. Charming little local, with hanging flower baskets on the outside and dark wooden tables and green leather benches inside. In addition, there's an elegant dining area to the rear of the bar and a very pleasant courtyard area. There are half a dozen first-class ales on offer, including Brakspear and Hog's Back. Mon–Sat 11am–11pm, Sun noon–10.30pm.

Chelsea

Cooper's Arms Bar 87 Flood St, SW3 ☎020/7376 3120; Sloane Square tube. Very fine, popular, easy-going neighbourhood pub, with an attractively understated spacious interior, decorated with vintage travel posters and grandfather clocks and offering first-rate beer and food. Mon–Sat 11am–11pm, Sun noon–10pm.

Fox and Hounds 29 Passmore St, SW1 ☎020/7730 6367; Sloane Square tube. On a quiet street near Sloane Square, this tiny Young's pub provides a perfect winter retreat. With an open fire, faux books, oil paintings and a flagstone floor, plus plenty of hunting memorabilia, it feels as if you've stumbled into a country squire's living room. Mon–Sat 11am–11pm, Sun noon–10.30pm.

The Pig's Ear 35 Old Church St, SW1
☎020/7352 2908, ⓦwww.thepigsear.co.uk;
Sloane Square tube. Deep in Chelsea village,
The Pig's Ear is a sympathetically converted
and stylish panelled pub, where you can
enjoy a leisurely board game, a pint of Pig's
Ear or some classy pub grub. Mon–Sat
noon–11pm, Sun noon–10.30pm.

High Street Kensington to Notting Hill

The listings in this section are marked
on the map on p.278.

Paddington

Victoria 10a Strathearn Place, W2
☎020/7724 1191; **Lancaster Gate or
Paddington tube.** Fabulously ornate corner
pub, with two open fires, much Victorian
brass and tilework, and gold-trimmed
mirrors. The Fuller's beer is excellent, too.
Mon–Sat 11am–11pm, Sun noon–10.30pm.

Notting Hill

Churchill Arms 119 Kensington Church St, W8
☎020/7229 4242; **Notting Hill Gate tube.**
Justifiably popular, flower-festooned pub
serving Fuller's beers, superb Guinness,
and good Thai food. Mon–Wed
11am–11pm, Thurs–Sat 11am–midnight,
Sun noon–10.30pm.
Cock & Bottle 17 Needham Rd, W11 ☎020/7229
1550; **Westbourne Park or Notting Hill Gate tube.**
Remarkably unpretentious two-room corner
pub – given the area – with a warm and
friendly staff, smart Victorian fittings and
good ales. Mon–Sat noon–11pm, Sun
noon–10.30pm.
The Cow 89 Westbourne Park Rd, W2
☎020/7221 0021, ⓦwww.thecowlondon.co.uk;
Westbourne Park or Royal Oak tube. Owned by
Tom Conran, son of gastro-magnate
Terence, this pub pulls in the beautiful W11
types, thanks to its spectacular food,
including a daily supply of fresh oysters.
Mon–Thurs noon–11pm, Fri & Sat noon–
midnight, Sun noon–10.30pm.
Windsor Castle 114 Campden Hill Rd, W8
☎020/7243 9551; **Notting Hill tube.** Pretty,
popular, early Victorian wood-panelled
English pub with a great courtyard, more
like something you might find in the country
than tucked away in the backstreets of one
of London's poshest residential neighbourhoods. Mon–Sat noon–11pm, Sun
noon–10.30pm.

Notting Hill

Paradise by Way of Kensal Green 19 Kilburn
Lane, W10 ☎020/8969 0098, ⓦwww
.theparadise.co.uk; **Kensal Green tube.** Giant
gastropub near the Kensal Green Cemetery,
with an artfully and theatrically dishevelled
interior. Mon–Wed 12.30pm–midnight, Thurs
12.30pm–1am, Fri & Sat 12.30pm–2am,
Sun noon–11.30pm.

North London

Maida Vale and St John's Wood

The listings in this section are marked
on the map on p.288.

Bridge House 13 Westbourne Terrace Rd, NW8
☎020/7432 1361; **Warwick Avenue tube.**
Theatre pub right by the canal at Little
Venice, this is a positively bohemian
hangout considering the area. Excellent real
ales and good food too. Mon–Thurs
noon–11pm, Fri & Sat noon–11.30pm, Sun
noon–10.30pm.
Prince Alfred 5a Formosa St, W9 ☎020/7286
3027; **Warwick Avenue tube.** A period-piece
Victorian pub with all its original 1862 fittings
intact, right down to the glazed "snob
screens" that divide the bar into a series of
"snugs". Along with the heritage, the pub
also runs a pricey Modern European restaurant at the back. Daily noon–11pm.
Warrington Hotel 93 Warrington Crescent, W9
☎020/7286 2929; **Warwick Avenue or Maida
Vale tube.** Grandiose (former hotel) pub with
a flamboyant Edwardian Art Nouveau
interior. Worth it for the architecture alone.
Pricey Gordon Ramsay restaurant upstairs.
Daily noon–1am.

Camden Town

Bartok 78–79 Chalk Farm Rd, NW1
☎020/7916 0595; **Chalk Farm tube.**
Beautifully stylish bar where punters can
sink into one of the deep-red leather sofas
and listen to a superb and quite unusual
programme of live music, ranging from jazz
and world to classical and opera. Acoustic
evenings and DJ sets, too. Mon–Thurs
5pm–3am, Fri 5pm–4am, Sat noon–4am,
Sun noon–3am.
Edinboro Castle 57 Mornington Terrace, NW1
☎020/7255 9651; **Camden Town tube.** A large,
high-ceilinged pub with an attractively
glammed-up interior. The main draw,
though, is the large, leafy beer garden which

hosts summer weekend barbecues. Above-average selection of draught continental lagers and a couple of real-ale options. Mon–Sat noon–11pm, Sun noon–10.30pm.

Lock Tavern 35 Chalk Farm Rd, NW1 ☏020/7482 7163, ⓦwww.lock-tavern.co.uk; **Chalk Farm tube.** Rambling pub with large, battered wooden tables, comfy sofas, a leafy upstairs terrace and beer garden down below, as well as posh pub grub and DJs playing anything from punk funk and electro to rock. Effortlessly cool. Mon–Thurs noon–midnight, Fri & Sat noon–1am, Sun noon–11pm.

Princess of Wales 22 Chalcot Rd, NW1 ☏020/7722 0354; **Chalk Farm tube.** Primrose Hill's most genuine pub, with everything you want from a local: real ales, reasonably priced food, good age range, Sunday evening live jazz and a little garden out the back. Mon–Thurs & Sun noon–11pm, Fri & Sat noon–midnight.

The Queen's 49 Regent's Park Rd, NW1 ☏020/7586 0408; **Chalk Farm tube.** A light, airy and posh Young's pub in Primrose Hill, with tasteful decor and above-average food for above-average prices. Mon–Sat 11am–11pm, Sun noon–10.30pm.

Sir Richard Steele 97 Haverstock Hill, NW3 ☏020/7483 1261; **Belsize Park or Chalk Farm tube.** The cluttered and oddball decor and clientele here make for a fun, laid-back atmosphere; Thai food, occasional live music and small beer-garden. Mon–Sat 11am–midnight, Sun noon–11.30pm.

Islington

The listings in this section are marked on the map on p.288.

Camden Head 2 Camden Walk, N1 ☏020/7359 0851; **Angel tube.** In the midst of Islington's antique market on a dainty street, the *Camden Head* is a fabulous-looking Victorian boozer, with engraved glass fittings and frosted mirrors. Cracking atmosphere, enlivened by regular comedy nights upstairs. Mon & Tue 11am–11pm, Wed & Thurs 11am–midnight, Fri & Sat noon–1am, Sun noon–11pm.

Compton Arms 4 Compton Ave, N1 ☏020/7359 6883; **Highbury & Islington tube.** Akin to a village local, this fabulous little pub, hidden away down a mews, is a welcome alternative to the boisterous places on Upper St. Good ales and a very

pleasant, summery beer garden. Mon–Sat noon–11pm, Sun noon–10.30pm.

Duke of Cambridge 30 St Peter's St, N1 ☏020/7359 3066, ⓦwww.sloeberry.co.uk; **Angel tube.** The focus at this bright and hip corner pub is most definitely organic, with an award-winning organic food menu, as well as half a dozen organic beers (including real ales), wine and soft drinks. Unsurprisingly, none of it comes cheap. Mon–Sat noon–11pm, Sun noon–10.30pm.

King's Head 115 Upper St, N1 ☏020/7226 0364, box office ☏020/7226 1916; **Angel tube.** The original pub-theatre in the heart of Islington, with two real fires, large spotlights, big curtains and lots of theatrical posters and photos. Live music pretty much every night (jazz, Cajun, blues and folk). Mon–Thurs 11am–1am, Fri & Sat 11am–2am, Sun noon–12.30am.

Island Queen 87 Noel Rd, N1 ☏020/7704 7631; **Angel tube.** Beautiful, weathered, wood-panelled Victorian pub in the backstreets of Islington, with lovely etched glass and high ceilings. Good range of beers and excellent pub food. Mon & Sun noon–11pm, Tues & Wed noon–11.30pm, Thurs–Sat noon–midnight.

Hackney

The listings in this section are marked on the map on p.297.

Dove Freehouse 24–28 Broadway Market ☏020/7275 7617; **London Fields or Cambridge Heath train station from Liverpool Street.** Cosy, low-lit and plant-filled, this characterful pub offers a stupendous selection of draught and bottled Belgian beers, plus a few real ales; also does specially made sausages and burgers, as well as *moules frites*. Mon–Thurs noon–11pm, Fri & Sat noon–midnight, Sun noon–10.30pm.

Royal Inn on the Park 111 Lauriston Rd, E9 ☏020/8985 3321; **bus #277 from Mile End tube.** Big, grand Victorian pub with laid-back tunes, real ale, beer garden and, as the name suggests, a location right on the edge of Victoria Park. Mon–Sat noon–11pm, Sun noon–10.30pm.

Hampstead and Highgate

The listings in this section are marked on the map on p.302.

The Flask 14 Flask Walk, NW3 ☏020/7435 4580; **Hampstead tube.** Convivial Young's pub that retains much of its original Victorian interior, tucked down one of Hampstead's more atmospheric lanes. Mon–Sat 11am–11pm, Sun noon–10.30pm.

The Flask 77 Highgate West Hill, N6 ☏020/8348 7346; bus #210 from Archway tube. Ideally situated at the heart of Highgate village green – with a rambling, low-ceilinged interior and a summer terrace – and, as a result, very, very popular on the weekend. Mon–Sat noon–11pm, Sun noon–10.30pm.

The Holly Bush 22 Holly Mount, off Holly Hill, NW3 ☏020/7435 2892; Hampstead tube. A lovely old pub, with a real fire in winter, tucked away in the steep backstreets of Hampstead village. Some fine real ales on offer, as well as decent food (particularly the sausages and pies), though it can get pretty mobbed at weekends. Mon–Sat noon–11pm, Sun noon–10.30pm.

The Spaniards Inn Spaniards Rd, NW3 ☏020/8731 6571; Hampstead tube or bus #210 from Golders Green tube. Big, atmospheric sixteenth-century coaching inn near Kenwood and the Heath, frequented by everyone from Dick Turpin to John Keats. Extremely busy on Sunday afternoons. Mon–Thurs 11am–11pm, Fri & Sat 11am–midnight, Sun 11am–11pm.

Prince of Wales 53 Highgate High St, N6 ☏020/8340 0445; bus #210 from Archway tube. If *The Flask* is mobbed, this is a great alternative: a cosy, tiny local with good real ales, Thai food and a nice terrace out the back. Quiz night (Tues) is crazily popular. Mon–Thurs noon–11pm, Fri & Sat noon–midnight, Sun noon–10.30pm.

Southeast London

Brixton and Clapham

Bread & Roses 68 Clapham Manor St, SW4 ☏020/7498 1779, ⓦwww .breadandrosespub.com; Clapham North or Clapham Common tube. One good reason for venturing into Clapham, this Workers' Beer Company pub serves fine ales, has comedy and cabaret evenings, political events and occasional live music. It's also very welcoming to those with kids. Mon–Thurs 5–11pm, Fri & Sat noon–midnight, Sun noon–10.30pm.

The Effra 38a Kellet Rd, SW2 ☏020/7274 4180; Brixton tube. Tucked down a quiet residential street, *The Effra* is the perfect local, with a vibrant cultural/age mix, handsome Victorian

looks and great live music, predominantly jazz. Jamaican pub food. Daily 3–11pm.

Trinity Arms 45 Trinity Gardens, SW2 ☏020/7274 4544; Brixton tube. Attractively sited on a quiet square in the backstreets off Acre Lane, this local institution is a low-key place, frequented by die-hard regulars and popular with gig-goers attending the nearby Brixton Academy. Mon–Thurs 11am–11pm, Fri & Sat 11am–midnight, Sun noon–11pm.

Dulwich

Crown & Greyhound 73 Dulwich Village, SE21 ☏020/8299 4976; North Dulwich train station from London Bridge. Grandiose Victorian pub, convenient for the Picture Gallery, with an ornate plasterwork ceiling and lots of polished wood and stained glass. The two-tiered beer garden is perfect for the summer barbecues that take place here. Young's, Harvey's and Pride on tap. Mon–Wed 11am–11pm, Thurs–Sat 11am–midnight, Sun noon–10.30pm.

Greenwich

The listings in this section are marked on the map on p.321.

Coach and Horses 13 Greenwich Market, SE10 ☏020/8293 0880; Cutty Sark DLR. Occupying a prime spot on the corner of Greenwich's wonderful covered market, this smart pub is particularly appealing in winter, the simple interior features a roaring fire and squishy brown leather sofas. Good real ales and decent food. Mon–Thurs noon–11pm, Fri & Sat noon–midnight, Sun noon–10.30pm.

Cutty Sark Ballast Quay, off Lassell St, SE10 ☏020/8858 3146; Cutty Sark DLR or Maze Hill train station from Charing Cross. This Georgian pub is the nicest place for a proper riverside pint in Greenwich, and much less touristy than the *Trafalgar Tavern* (see p.323). Mon–Sat 11am–11pm, Sun noon–10.30pm.

Greenwich Union 56 Royal Hill, SE10 ☏020/8692 6258; Greenwich DLR & train station. A modern, laid-back place with a youthful, unpretentious feel, fine gastro grub and a nice garden. Go for free samples of blonde ale, raspberry beer, chocolate stout or the house Union, before committing yourself to a pint. Mon–Fri 11am–11pm, Sat 10am–11pm, Sun noon–6pm.

Richard I 52–54 Royal Hill, SE10 ☏020/8692 2996; Greenwich DLR & train station. Popular and very traditional Greenwich local tucked away on an attractive street. Good Young's beers and a lovely, spacious garden make it an ideal post-market/museum retreat. Mon–Sat 11am–11pm, Sun noon–10.30pm.

Trafalgar Tavern 5 Park Row, SE10 ⊤020/8858 2437; **Cutty Sark DLR or Maze Hill train station from Charing Cross.** Great riverside position and a mention in Dickens' *Our Mutual Friend* have made this Regency-style inn a firm tourist favourite. Good whitebait and other snacks. Mon–Thurs noon–11pm, Fri & Sat noon–midnight, Sun noon–10.30pm.

Blackheath

Hare & Billet 1a Eliot Cottages, SE3 ⊤020/8852 2352; **Blackheath train station from Charing Cross.** A ten-minute walk from the village up on the heath, this pleasantly refurbished, comfortable, rustic Greene King pub is the place to visit for a slow, quiet drink. Mon–Sat 11am–11pm, Sun noon–10.30pm.

Zerodegrees 29–31 Montpelier Vale, SE3 ⊤020/8852 5619; **Blackheath train station from Charing Cross.** The somewhat hollow atmosphere at this popular microbrewery is more than compensated for by the beer – Black, Pale, Pilsner and Wheat are the four main varieties, in addition to some speciality offerings. Appealing wood-fired pizzas in the adjoining dining area. Mon–Sat noon–midnight, Sun noon–11.30pm.

Bexleyheath

Robin Hood & Little John 78 Lion Rd, Bexleyheath ⊤020/8303 1128; **Bexleyheath train station from Charing Cross.** This small pub, in the residential side streets of Bexleyheath, has an impressive range of very well-kept ales, and is the perfect place for a post-Red House pint. Mon–Sat 11am–3pm & 7–11pm, Sun noon–3pm & 7–10.30pm.

Out West

Hammersmith and Chiswick

Blue Anchor 13 Lower Mall, W6 ⊤020/8748 5774; **Hammersmith or Ravenscourt Park tube.** First of Hammersmith's riverside pubs, with a boaty theme and a beautiful pewter bar; the upstairs room offers good views of Hammersmith Bridge, though most people sit outside and enjoy the river. Mon–Sat 11am–11pm, Sun noon–10.30pm.

Dove 19 Upper Mall, W6 ⊤020/8748 5405; **Ravenscourt Park tube.** Wonderful low-beamed, old riverside pub with literary associations – Ernest Hemingway and

Graham Greene used to drink here – the smallest bar in the UK (4ft by 7ft), and very popular Sunday roast dinners. Take time to look at the fine selection of black-and-white photos. Mon–Sat 11am–11pm, Sun noon–10.30pm.

Acton and Ealing

George & Dragon 183 High St, W3 ⊤020/8992 3712; **Acton Central tube.** Dark wood-panelled interior, with real fires and – in the back rooom – high ceilings and Art Nouveau statues. Fuller's beers and great pub food. Mon–Sat 11am–11pm, Sun noon–10.30pm.

Red Lion 13 St Mary's Rd, W5 ⊤020/8567 2541; **South Ealing or Ealing Broadway tube.** A good mixed crowd frequents this grand Fuller's pub, decorated with mementoes from the days when the Ealing Studios stood opposite. Mon–Sat 11am–11pm, Sun noon–10.30pm.

Kew, Richmond, Twickenham and Wimbledon

Fox & Grapes 9 Camp Rd, SW19 ⊤020/8946 5599; **Wimbledon tube.** Right on the edge of Wimbledon Common, with good real ales, this place is great in summer, when you can sit outside on the grass. Mon–Thurs 11am–11pm, Fri & Sat 11am–midnight, Sun noon–10.30pm.

The Railway Kew Gardens Station Parade, Kew ⊤020/8332 1162; **Kew Gardens tube.** Convenient pub in Kew Gardens station's former ticket office. Real ales, good pub grub and very convenient for the botanic gardens. Mon–Sat 11am–midnight, Sun noon–10.30pm.

White Cross Hotel Water Lane, Richmond ⊤020/8940 6844; **Richmond tube. See map, p.349.** With a longer pedigree and more character than its rivals, the *White Cross* has a very popular, large garden overlooking the river. In winter, you can decamp to the lovely upstairs lounge with its big bay windows and open fire. Mon–Sat 11am–midnight, Sun noon–10.30pm.

White Swan Riverside, Twickenham ⊤020/8892 2166; **Twickenham train station from Waterloo. See map, p.349.** Filling pub food, draught beer and a quiet riverside location – except on rugby match days – make this a good halt on any towpath ramble. The excellent summer Sunday barbecues are a big draw. Mon–Sat 11am–11pm, Sun noon–10.30pm.

26

Live music and clubs

Genres, venues, fashions and intoxicants come and go, but London's nightlife – sprawling, chaotic, buzzing and impossibly varied – carries on regardless. The last few years have seen much-loved venues like King's Cross's *Canvas* and the West End's *Astoria* close down, the Docklands-set O2 sell more tickets than any other venue in the world and Shoreditch's supercool punters inch east and north to Whitechapel, Bethnal Green and Dalston.

Clubs play everything from pop to house, techno to punk, and drum'n'bass to r'n'b on virtually any night of the week. **Gigs** are equally wide-ranging, encompassing rock, roots, hip-hop and world music, while London's jazz clubs host a highly individual scene of home-based artists supplemented by top-name visiting players. Dividing these scenes into concrete categories makes them easier to navigate, but shouldn't obscure the cross-pollination: club nights take over music venues once gigs have finished, DJ sets are enlivened by percussion and live performers, gay venues (see p.420) host mixed nights and jazz acts play at rock venues. Don't ignore venues outside the centre, either – Brixton or Kilburn can be just as cutting edge as Clerkenwell or Hoxton.

Live music

Few cities in the world can match London for the sheer volume and diversity of its **live music**. Quite apart from its array of fine venues and impressive homegrown talent, the city's media spotlight makes it pretty much *the* place for young **bands** to break into the global mainstream. Those acts who've already made it head for the bright lights and vast seating plans of Wembley Arena (Ⓦ www.livenation .co.uk/wembley), Wembley Stadium (Ⓦ www.wembleystadium.com), Earl's Court (Ⓦ www.eco.co.uk) and the O2 (Ⓦ www.theo2.co.uk). The Royal Albert Hall (Ⓦ www.royalalberthall.com) – traditionally a classical music venue – and the beautiful courtyard at Somerset House (Ⓦ www.somerset-house.org.uk) are smaller, more atmospheric alternatives.

London's small and medium-sized venues may be pub backrooms, converted warehouses or old cinemas; you might get in free to see an unknown band or pay £80 for a visiting legend, but most acts on the circuit will set you back £10–30, not counting drinks. You may get cheaper tickets if you book online, although booking fees can nullify any saving – the real advantage is that you can be sure of getting in. Try sites such as Ⓦ www.seetickets.com, Ⓦ www.gigsandtours.com or Ⓦ www.ticketmaster.co.uk. Radio stations Xfm (Ⓦ www.xfm.co.uk) and 6 Music (Ⓦ www.bbc.co.uk/6music) are also worth tuning into for gig info, while magazines *NME* (Ⓦ nme.com) and *Time Out* (Ⓦ www.timeout.com/london /music/) deliver news and listings.

General venues

Academy Brixton 211 Stockwell Rd, SW9 ℡020/7771 3000, ⊛www.brixton-academy.co.uk; Brixton tube. The Academy has seen them all, from mods and rockers to Madonna. The four-thousand-capacity Victorian hall doesn't always deliver perfect sound quality, but remains a cracking place to see mid-level bands. Upstairs has seats, downstairs has a sloping floor for standing and bags of atmosphere.

Academy Islington N1 Centre, 16 Parkfield St, N1 ℡020/7288 4400, ⊛www.islington-academy.co.uk; Angel tube. Despite its location in a modern shopping centre, the Islington Academy has some good up-and-coming bands, as well as club nights in *Bar Academy* (in the same building). Good views from the main venue's mezzanine level, which opens for well-attended gigs.

Cargo 83 Rivington St, EC2 ℡020/7739 3440, ⊛www.cargo-london.com; Old Street tube. Small and groovy venue in what was once a railway arch, with an attached restaurant and chillsome garden area. Hosts a variety of live acts, including jazz, hip-hop, indie and folk, and an excellent line-up of club nights (see p.412).

Coronet 28 New Kent Rd, SE1 ℡020/7701 1500, ⊛www.coronettheatre.co.uk; Elephant and Castle tube. Theatre-turned-cinema-turned-music venue, with a gorgeous Deco interior and an often heroically long cloakroom queue. Live acts, DJ nights and talent shows.

Forum 9–17 Highgate Rd, NW5 ℡0207/428 4099, ⊛www.meanfiddler.com; Kentish Town tube. One of the capital's best medium-sized venues, with a decent mix of successful new acts and groups inching their way onto the nostalgia circuit.

Hammersmith Apollo 45 Queen Caroline St, W6 ℡020/8563 3800, ⊛www.hammersmithapollo.net; Hammersmith tube. The former Hammersmith Odeon is a cavernous, theatre-style venue, featuring everyone from Nick Cave to Kenny Rogers, plus stand-up and popular theatre.

Roundhouse Chalk Farm Rd, NW1 ℡0844/482 8008, ⊛www.roundhouse.org.uk; Chalk Farm tube. Originally dating from 1846, this magnificent Grade II listed building is one of London's premier performing arts centres; its programme includes regular appearances by artier rock acts and world music stars.

Shepherds Bush Empire Shepherd's Bush Green, W12 ℡0844/477 2000, ⊛www.shepherds-bush-empire.co.uk; Shepherd's Bush tube. Yet another grand old theatre, the Empire now plays host to a fine cross-section of mid-league UK and US bands in the capital. There's often a superb atmosphere downstairs, while the upstairs balconies provide some of the best stage views around.

▲ P.J. Harvey at the Shepherds Bush Empire

Union Chapel Compton Terrace, N1 ℡020/7226 1686, ⊛www.unionchapel.org.uk; Highbury & Islington tube. Wonderful, intimate venue that doubles as a church, hence the pew-style seating arrangements; the eclectic array of artists ranges from contemporary stars to world-music legends.

Rock, blues and indie

12 Bar Club Denmark St, WC2 ℡020/7240 2622, ⊛www.12barclub.com; Tottenham Court Road tube. Tiny, atmospheric bar, café and venue offering up-and-coming and often pleasantly eccentric indie acts as well as blues and folk.

93 Feet East 150 Brick Lane, E2 ℡020/7053 2029, ⊛www.93feeteast.co.uk; Old Street tube. An intimate live venue during the week and a club at weekends (see p.413), this is a good place to catch electronic, punk and indie gigs.

London's festivals

Noisy, densely populated and about as bucolic as a tube door in the face, London might not seem an obvious place to hold a **music festival**. But recent years have seen a number of events draw on the capital's enthusiasm and pulling power. Perhaps the most entertaining of the bunch is Groove Armada's **Lovebox** (July; Ⓦwww.lovebox.net), held in East London's Victoria Park, which mixes dance and rock in exhilarating style – Duran Duran, Sly and the Family Stone and Hot Chip have all played in recent years. **Field Day** (Aug; Ⓦwww.fielddayfestivals.com), an indier-than-thou freakout that uses the same patch of grass, has hosted everyone from Four Tet to Lightspeed Champion. Hyde Park, fittingly enough, is the venue for more mainstream events that make up in headliner clout what they lose in underground cred: **Hard Rock Calling** (June; Ⓦwww.hardrockcalling.co.uk) featured the Police in 2008 and Bruce Springsteen in 2009, while the slightly groovier **Wireless** (July; Ⓦwww.wirelessfestival.co.uk) grabbed Basement Jaxx in 2009. As at any festival, the acts lower down the bill can be more entertaining than the big names – check the websites and arrive early.

You'll have to book in advance for most of the big events, but free festivals are well worth your time: North London's **Rise** (July; Ⓦwww.risefestival.org) is among the best. The hipper events will always have an afterparty, sometimes with live acts as well as DJs, at nearby venues, while the **Notting Hill Carnival** (see p.282) stops traffic in West London with DJ sets as well as parades.

The sunshine is never guaranteed, sadly, but various events use London's plethora of clubs and halls to great effect. The **Camden Crawl** (April; Ⓦwww.thecamdencrawl.com), a seemingly chaotic mass of gigs and DJs spilling through London's indie-rock capital in the spring, is the highest profile of an ear-bursting bunch.

Barfly 49 Chalk Farm Rd, NW1 ☎0207/424 0800, Ⓦwww.barflyclub.com; Chalk Farm tube. Decent Camden venue offering a relentless roster of gigs (three nightly), typically indie, rock, punk and metal bands. *The Fly*, 36–38 New Oxford St (same web address), has a similarly rambunctious line-up.

Borderline Orange Yard, Manette St, W1 ☎020/7734 5547, Ⓦwww.meanfiddler.com; Tottenham Court Road tube. Small and slightly ramshackle basement joint with a great sound and a diverse musical policy.

Bull & Gate 389 Kentish Town Rd, NW5 ☎020/7093 4820, Ⓦwww.bullandgate.co.uk; Kentish Town tube. Decent-enough pub that's also one of London's key venues for unsigned indie bands. Gigs nightly.

Dingwalls Middle Yard, Camden Lock, NW1 ☎020/7428 0010, Ⓦwww.dingwalls.com; Camden Town tube. This split-level music/club venue is a good place to catch up-and-coming talent, though the views aren't always great.

Dublin Castle 94 Parkway, NW1 ☎020/7485 1773; Ⓦwww.bugbearbookings.com; Camden Town tube. Grungy music pub offering a solid diet of indie-rock gigs most nights.

Half Moon Putney 93 Lower Richmond Rd, SW15 ☎020/8780 9383, Ⓦwww.halfmoon.co.uk; Putney Bridge tube. Long-running pub venue, good for blues, rock and soul. Acoustic on Monday, Jazz on Sunday afternoon, folk on Sunday night, plus regular cover bands and unsigned showcases.

Hope and Anchor 207 Upper St, N1 ☎020/7354 1312, Ⓦwww.bugbearbookings.com; Angel tube. This cramped venue is popular with punkish indie acts, many playing their first gigs here.

Luminaire 311 High Rd, NW6 ☎020/7372 7123, Ⓦwww.theluminaire.co.uk; Kilburn tube. With a cracking music policy that incorporates electronica, world music and the groovier end of indie and a "no talking when the band's on" rule, this intimate space is one of London's best small venues.

Monto Water Rats 328 Grays Inn Rd, WC1 ☎020/7336 7326, Ⓦwww.plumpromotions.co.uk; King's Cross tube. Indie and indie/electronica crossover bands trying to make it big in the biz, plus the odd established act. Bob Dylan played his first UK gig here almost five decades ago.

Underworld 174 Camden High St, NW1 ☎020/7482 1932, ⓦwww.theunderworld camden.co.uk; Camden Town tube. Popular, scruffy warren under the *World's End* pub that's a great place to check out metal, hardcore and heavy-rock bands.

Windmill 22 Blenheim Gardens, SW2 ☎020/8671 0700, ⓦwww.windmillbrixton .co.uk; Brixton tube. A fine, leftfield mix of bands play at this poky pub halfway up Brixton Hill. Entry for everything from swirly electronica to throbbing post-rock is rarely much over £5.

Jazz

100 Club 100 Oxford St, W1 ☎020/7636 0933, ⓦwww.the100club.co.uk; Tottenham Court Road tube. Fun jazz venue whose history stretches back to 1942 and takes in Louis Armstrong, Glen Miller and the Sex Pistols. Now mixes mostly trad bands with DJ-led nights.

606 Club 90 Lots Rd, SW10 ☎020/7352 5953, ⓦwww.606club.co.uk; Fulham Broadway tube. Located just off the King's Rd, this rare all-jazz venue has a particular focus on home-bred talent. Licensing restrictions mean alcohol can only be served to non-members if they have a meal.

Bull's Head Barnes Barnes Bridge, SW13 ☎020/8876 5241, ⓦwww.thebullshead.com; bus #209 from Hammersmith tube or Barnes Bridge train station from Waterloo. This relaxed riverside alehouse has been attracting Britain's finest jazz musicians for almost fifty years. Live music nightly and Sunday lunchtimes. Good Thai restaurant here too.

Dover Street 8–10 Dover St, W1 ☎020/7629 9813, ⓦwww.doverst.co.uk; Green Park tube. London's largest jazz restaurant has music and dancing every night until 3am, plus Modern British food. Attracts an older crowd; dress smart.

Jazz Café 5 Parkway, NW1 ☎0207/485 6834, ⓦwww.jazzcafelive.com; Camden Town tube. Buzzing venue with an adventurous music policy exploring Latin, funk and hip-hop. If you fancy a sit-down book a seat at the restaurant tables. The clubbier late sessions start at 11pm on Fri and Sat.

Pizza Express 10 Dean St, W1 ☎0845/602 7017, ⓦwww.pizzaexpresslive.com; Tottenham Court

Road tube. Also known as *Jazz Club Soho*, this restaurant hosts consistent quality – with both established and new jazz artists. The associated *Pizza on the Park* (11 Knightsbridge, SW1, same website; Hyde Park Corner tube) is a little more middle-of-the-road.

Ronnie Scott's 47 Frith St, W1 ☎020/7439 0747, ⓦwww.ronniescotts .co.uk; Leicester Square tube. The most famous jazz club in London, this small and atmospheric place has smartened up its decor and stretched its remit to more pop-oriented acts in recent years. Book for the big names; Wednesday's midweek jam sessions give the flavour of the place.

The Vortex 11 Gillett St, N16 ☎020/7254 4097, ⓦwww.vortexjazz.co.uk; Dalston Kingsland train station or buses #67, #149 from Liverpool Street or #243 from Liverpool Street. Sat in snazzy Dalston Cultural House, this small venue is a serious player on the live jazz scene, managing to combine a touch of urban style with a cosy, friendly atmosphere.

World music, folk and roots

Barbican Silk St, EC2 ☎020/7638 4141, ⓦwww.barbican.org.uk; Barbican tube. It's easy to lose yourself in the expansive Barbican, a focal point for the best world-music bands and orchestras, plus one-off contemporary music events and festivals. There's often free music in the foyer.

Blackheath Halls 23 Lee Rd, SE3 ☎020/8463 0100, ⓦwww.blackheathhalls.com; Blackheath train station from Charing Cross. This polished, medium-sized venue hosts some of the best world and roots bands alongside classical events.

Cecil Sharp House 2 Regent's Park Rd, NW1 ☎020/7485 2206, ⓦwww.efdss.org; Camden Town tube. Headquarters of the English Folk Dance and Song Society, with singing and dancing performances as well as workshops and classes.

Southbank Centre South Bank, SE1 ☎0870/ 663 2501, ⓦwww.royalfestivalhall.org.uk; Waterloo tube. The all-seater Royal Festival Hall, Queen Elizabeth Hall and Purcell Room host imaginative programmes of world music, jazz and folk, as well as classical concerts and the odd pop event.

Clubs

Twenty years after acid house irreversibly shook up British **clubs**, London remains *the* place to come if you want to party after dark. The so-called super-clubs may be dying out, and 2008–9 in particular saw a raft of closures – some venues are just too valuable as real estate for promoters to hang onto – but, in their place, there's more variety than ever, both in terms of music being played and the small to mid-sized venues available. The relaxation of late-night licensing laws has encouraged many places to keep serving until 6am or even later, and the resurgence of alcohol in clubland has – much to the relief of the breweries – been echoed by the rise of the club-bar.

House music's myriad genres still dominate, with specialist nights aplenty, and **electro**'s shimmering synths and up-front basslines providing the sound of the last few years. **Drum'n'bass** is as popular as ever, experiencing a new lease of life thanks to the influx of vocal cuts and Latin influences. In addition, **reggae**, **ragga** and the US-led fusion of **r'n'b** and **hip-hop** still command a loyal following. **Latin**, **African**, **Indian** and **world music** fans have their own clubs too, and there's also a healthy and vibrant alternative **rock** and **punk** scene.

For nearly all clubs, **opening time** is between 10pm and midnight, with most favouring the 11pm slot. Some keep irregular days, others just open at the weekend, and others host a different club on each night of the week. Sunday clubs are increasingly popular: some starting in the wee hours to catch the Saturday-night crew who can't face going home, some featuring a mellow Sunday-afternoon vibe, while others are geared towards the total hedonists who party on until Monday morning.

Admission charges vary enormously, with small midweek nights starting at around £3–5 and large weekend events charging as much as £30; around £10–15 is the average, but bear in mind that profit margins at the bar can be even more outrageous than at live-music venues. London's scene is fairly **dressed down** – West End clubs may want you to wear smart shoes, and a few venues discourage baseball caps, but trainers are generally fine – although in some Shoreditch clubs you may feel underdressed if you haven't made at least some effort to look like a wacky hipster.

Club venues

93 Feet East 150 Brick Lane, E2 ⓣ020/7247 5293, ⓦwww.93feeteast.co.uk; Old Street tube. Perched cheerfully in Brick Lane's buzzing epicentre, this engaging small venue hosts indie, soul, electro and funk nights alongside its gigs, particularly on weekend nights – there's a daytime session on Saturday too.

333 333 Old St, EC1 ⓣ020/7739 5949, ⓦwww.333mother.com; Old Street tube. Rumours of closure haven't dented the popularity of this dressed-down, mashed-up Hoxton club. It's actually two venues – *Mother* and the *333*, each spinning drum'n'bass, breakbeats and solid, scuzzy four/four.

Aquarium 256–264 Old St, EC1 ⓣ020/7253 3558, ⓦwww.clubaquarium.co.uk; Old Street tube. Big, mainstream (disco, house and pop) venue with a splendid selling point – a good-sized pool and jacuzzi. The rather more hardcore afterhours (typically 4am–11am) Saturday and Sunday events are dominated by electro and minimal techno.

Bar Music Hall 134 Curtain Rd, EC2 ⓣ020/7729 7216, ⓦwww.barmusichall.com; Old Street tube. Free to get in – although you'll have to queue, and it pays to wear your craziest threads – this draws wild club kids for electro (check out Sat's Foreign), filthy disco and live electronica.

Bar Rumba 36 Shaftesbury Ave, W1 ⓣ020/7287 6933, ⓦwww.barrumba.co.uk; Piccadilly Circus tube. Fun, smallish West End basement club – one of the few quality venues in the area – whose slant has edged towards guitars since 2008, when long-running indie night Blow Up took over the Saturday residency. Tuesday is salsa and reggaeton, Thursday r'n'b, Friday live bands.

Bethnal Green Working Men's Club 44–46 Pollard Row, E2 ⓣ020 7739 7170, ⓦwww.workersplaytime.net; Bethnal Green tube. As old school as they come, this working men's club caught the mid-noughties trend for burlesque and rode it with style. Expect disco, rock'n'roll, stand-up comedy and merrily kitsch decor, plus a whole lot of dressing up.

Cargo 83 Rivington St, EC2 ⓣ020/7739 3440, ⓦwww.cargo-london.com; Old Street tube. *Cargo* (see p.409) plays host to a variety of excellent and often innovative club nights, from deep house to jazz, and often features live bands alongside the DJs.

Corsica Studios 5 Elephant Rd, SE17 ⓣ020/7703 4760, ⓦwww.corsicastudios.com; Elephant & Castle tube. Grubby but likeable mid-sized venue that pretty much worships the bass, with breaks, dubstep, electro and reggae dominating the speakers and frequent live sessions.

EGG 200 York Way, N7 ⓣ020/7609 8364, ⓦwww.egglondon.net; King's Cross tube. Two exposed-brick, medium-sized rooms, a smart loft-style bar and a decent outdoor space (used to full effect on the breakfast sessions, which start at 5am on Sun) play host to techno through to grime and breaks.

Electric Ballroom 184 Camden High St, NW1 ⓣ020/7485 9006, ⓦwww.electricballroom.co.uk; Camden Town tube. Long-running and large club that hosts rock and metal (most Fri) and disco nights (Sat), plus several gigs a week.

Fabric 77a Charterhouse St, EC1 ⓣ020/7336 8898, ⓦwww.fabriclondon.com; Farringdon tube. Despite big queues (arrive early or late) and a confusing layout that means you may take hours to find friends, jackets and some of its numerous rooms, this 1600-capacity club remains one of the world's finest. Sounds booming from the devastating soundsystem include drum'n'bass (most Fri) and techno (most Sat), but live bands and lengthy DJ line-ups means you can hear a huge variety of acts – usually underground, and almost always quality.

Herbal 10–14 Kingsland Rd, E2 ⓣ020/7613 4462, ⓦwww.herbaluk.com; Old Street tube. This intimate venue, with a cool New York-style loft and sweaty ground-floor club, is a great place to check out drum'n'bass and breaks (Fri) and dirty house and electro (Sat).

KOKO 1a Camden High St, NW1 ⓣ09062/100200, ⓦwww.koko.uk.com; Mornington Crescent tube. The old Camden Palace has slipped effortlessly back into London's indie club-and-gig scene, with Club NME combining the two in raucous style on Fri nights.

Madame JoJo's 8–10 Brewer St, W1 ⓣ020/7734 3040, ⓦwww.madamejojos.com; Piccadilly Circus tube. Louche, enjoyable Soho institution, known for its wickedly diverse range of entertainment – alongside variety and comedy, you'll find electronica, disco, rock and funk – the big nights here are Deep Funk (Fri), and indie White Heat (Tues).

Matter Peninsula Square, SE10 ☏020/7549 6686, ⓦwww.matterlondon.com; North Greenwich tube or boat from Waterloo or London Bridge. Big, new and super-snazzy club with a top-notch weekend roster majoring on house and electro. Its Dome location can make the trip home quite a mission, though.

Ministry of Sound 103 Gaunt St, SE1 ☏020/7378 6528, ⓦwww.ministryofsound.com; Elephant & Castle tube. The vast headquarters of this clubbing brand may sometimes seem peopled largely by corporate clubbers and gawping visitors, but the soundsystem is exceptional and it gets the pick of visiting DJs.

Notting Hill Arts Club 21 Notting Hill Gate, W11 ☏020/7460 4459, ⓦwww.nottinghill artsclub.com; Notting Hill Gate tube. Groovy, arty basement club that's popular for everything from Latin-inspired funk, jazz and disco through to soul, house and indie; Saturday afternoon has gigs courtesy of Rough Trade records.

Plan B 418 Brixton Rd, SW9 ☏08701/165421, ⓦwww.plan-brixton.co.uk; Brixton tube. Slicker and more style-conscious than the average Brixton club, with a good soundsystem, friendly staff, a great bar and a house-oriented music policy.

Plastic People 147–149 Curtain Rd, EC2 ☏020/7739 6471, ⓦwww.plasticpeople.co.uk; Old Street tube. Scuzzy, thumping basement club whose cheeringly broad booking policy stretches through punk, funk, rock'n'roll, Afro-jazz and dubstep.

Rhythm Factory 16–18 Whitechapel Rd ☏020/7375 3774, ⓦwww.rhythmfactory.co.uk; Aldgate East or Whitechapel tube. This textile-factory-turned-cutting-edge club houses a bar area serving Thai food and two medium-sized rooms. Live bands play Tuesday and Thursday; drum'n'bass and techno dominate the weekends.

Scala 275 Pentonville Rd, N1 ☏020/7833 2022, ⓦwww.scala-london.co.uk; King's Cross tube. Once a cinema (it was forced to shut down after illegally showing Kubrick's *A Clockwork Orange*), the *Scala* stages some top-quality gigs, usually from established bands, while the weekend club nights take in hardcore rock, dubstep, tech-house and the nostalgia-fest that is School Disco.

Sosho 2 Tabernacle St, EC2 ☏020/7920 0701, ⓦwww.sosho3am.com; Old Street tube. Smart club-bar with good cocktails, some impressive beers and decent food; the ambience is chilled until the DJs kick in, playing house, disco and electronica. Wed & Thurs noon–1am, Fri noon–6am, Sat 7pm–6am, Sun 10pm–5.30am.

South London Pacific 340 Kennington Rd, SE11 ☏020/7820 9189, ⓦwww.southlondonpacific .com; Kennington tube. From the outlandish exterior to the range of fruity cocktails on offer inside, there's no escaping the South Pacific theme at this exuberant little bar/club. DJs play funk, soul, rock'n'roll and Latin, and there's cabaret and bingo. Tues–Thurs 5pm–1am, Fri & Sat 6pm–3am, monthly Sun.

Lesbian and gay London

Lleft ondon's **lesbian and gay scene** is so huge, diverse and well established that it's easy to forget just how much – and how fast – it has grown and moved into the mainstream over the last couple of decades. Political progress has been accompanied by a certain amount of depoliticization of the scene, so that pink power has given way to the pink pound, gay liberation to gay lifestyle, and the central lesbian and gay "village" of Soho is vibrant, self-assured and unashamedly commercial. As a result of this high-profile activity, straight Londoners tend to be a fairly homo-savvy bunch and, on the whole, happy to embrace and even dip into the city's queer offerings.

When it comes to exploring the London scene, **Soho** is the obvious place to start; **Old Compton Street** is, so to speak, its main drag. Here, traditional gay pubs rub alongside cafés and bars selling expensive designer beers and lattes, while hairdressers, letting agencies, sex boutiques and spiritual health centres offer a range of gay-run services. A good introduction to Soho's lesbian and gay history is offered by the Sunday **walking tour** (2–4pm) organized by Kairos (☏020/7437 6063, Ⓦwww.kairosinsoho.org.uk; £5) – meet outside the *Admiral Duncan* pub (see p.416).

There are **clubs** to cater for just about every musical, sartorial and sexual taste and, while the bigger ones congregate on the river's south bank in **Vauxhall**, there are well-established venues all over the city. Gay men still enjoy the best permanent facilities London-wide, but today's **lesbian scene** is bigger and more eclectic than ever, and the cruisey girl-bars which took up prize pitches on the boys' Soho turf a few years ago are here to stay.

You can also find pockets of queer activity away from the centre in the city's funkier residential areas, most notably Shoreditch, and, especially for dykes, Stoke Newington and Hackney. Anti-gay **hostility** is rare in London, but there have been high-profile homophobic attacks so it's probably wise not to hold hands or smooch too obviously in areas you don't know well.

The main **outdoor event** of the year is **Pride London** in late June or early July, encompassing a rally in Trafalgar Square, a colourful, whistle-blowing march through the city streets, live cabaret in Leicester Square and a women's stage in Soho. For up-to-date information, festival plans and transport news, visit the website Ⓦwww.pridelondon.org. The **Pride Festival Fortnight**, staged at venues throughout London, is a mix of theatre, concerts, sports, film and visual arts that takes place in the run-up to Pride itself.

In March and April, the National Film Theatre hosts the annual **Lesbian and Gay Film Festival** (Ⓦ www.llgff.org.uk), which celebrates new cinema from around the world. Elsewhere, queer theatre and arts events take place all year round in the city's many fringe theatres, arts centres, galleries and clubs. If none of this appeals, there are also a huge number of **gay groups and organizations** which offer everything from ballroom dancing to spanking seminars.

Hotels

London's best-known gay accommodation options cater mostly for men, though all are lesbian friendly, and a full breakfast is almost always included. Self-catering **apartments** are available through the gay-run Outlet Gay Accommodation, 32 Old Compton St, W1 (Ⓣ020/7287 4244, Ⓦwww .outlet4holidays.com).

Garth Hotel 69 Gower St, WC1 Ⓣ020/7636 5761, Ⓦwww.garthhotel-london.com; Goodge St tube. See map, p.127. Small, privately owned Bloomsbury hotel. This Grade II-listed Georgian townhouse features many original antiques in its seventeen mostly en-suite bedrooms. Doubles from £69.

Griffin House Holiday Apartments 22 Stockwell Green, SW9 Ⓣ020/7096 3332, Ⓦwww.griffin house.Info; Stockwell tube. Highly rated self-catering accomodation with an emphasis on providing a home-from-home. Convenient for the Vauxhall and Clapham scenes. Apartments from £90.

Number 16 16 St Alfege Passage, SE10 Ⓣ020/8853 4337, Ⓦwww.st-alfeges.co.uk. Cutty Sark DLR. Charming, tiny gay-run B&B in a peaceful location in historic Greenwich, with tasteful yet quirky Victorian decor. A good hideaway. From £75.

Cafés, bars and pubs

There are loads of lesbian and gay eating and watering holes in London, many of them operating as cafés by day and transforming into drinking dens by night. Lots have cabaret or disco nights and are open until the early hours, making them a fine (and affordable) alternative to the big clubs. Most of these cafés and bars have free admission, though a few levy a charge after 10.30pm (usually £3–5) if there's music, cabaret or a disco.

The places below represent a selective list of the best and most accessible, from self-consciously minimalist eateries to shabby old pubs. We use "mixed" to mean places for both gays and lesbians, though many "mixed" places are mostly frequented by men.

Mixed cafés, bars and pubs

The Admiral Duncan 54 Old Compton St, W1 Ⓣ020/7437 5300; Leicester Square tube. See map, p.108. Unpretentious, traditional-style gay bar in the heart of Soho, popular and busy with the post-work crowd, and now fully restored after the blast that ripped through it in 1999.

Balans 34 Old Compton St, W1 Ⓣ020/7439 3309; 60 Old Compton St, W1 Ⓣ020/7439 2183; Ⓦwww.balans.co.uk.; Leicester Square tube. See map, p.108. The two branches of this enduringly busy Soho institution are open into the small hours during the week and 6am at weekends. The menu includes a lengthy hangover-busting breakfast and brunch section.

The Black Cap 171 Camden High St, NW1 Ⓣ020/7485 0538, Ⓦwww.theblackcap.com; Camden Town tube. See map, p.288. Venerable north London establishment offering cabaret and dancing almost every night. The upstairs bar is quieter, and opens onto the Fong Terrace in the summer.

The Box 32–34 Monmouth St, WC2 Ⓣ020/7240 5828, Ⓦwww.boxbar.com; Covent Garden or Leicester Square tube. See map, p.140. Popular, bright café-bar serving hearty portions of simple food for a gay/straight crowd during the day, and attracting a muscly pre-clubbing crowd as the night goes on.

Central Station 37 Wharfdale Rd, N1 020/7278 3294, www.centralstation.co.uk; King's Cross tube. See map, p.127. Award-winning, late-opening community pub offering cabaret, cruisey club nights and the UK's only gay sports bar. Mainly men, but Tuesdays see the ladies invade with Bar Wotever.

The Duke of Wellington 77 Wardour St, W1 020/7439 1274; Piccadilly Circus tube. See map, p.108. Pub in the traditional style on two floors, with cheap lager and real ale on pump and a down-to-earth, male-dominated crowd, keen on chatting and socializing.

Escape 10a Brewer St, W1 020/7734 2626, www.escapesoho.com; Piccadilly Circus tube. See map, p.108. Trendy DJ bar in the heart of Soho, attracting a young, mixed crowd and open until 3am Monday to Saturday.

First Out 52 St Giles High St, WC2 020/7240 8042, www.firstoutcafebar.com; Tottenham Court Road tube. See map, p.140. The West End's original gay café-bar, serving good veggie food. Upstairs is airy, downstairs dark. Girl Friday is a pre-club session for grrls; gay men allowed as guests.

▲ First Out

Freedom 66 Wardour St, W1 020/7734 0071, www.freedombarsoho.com; Piccadilly Circus tube. See map, p.108. Hip metrosexual place,

popular with a straight/gay Soho crowd. The basement becomes an intimate club at night, complete with pink banquettes and glitter balls.

Friendly Society Tisbury Court, 79 Wardour St, W1 020/7434 3805. See map, p.108. Enjoyably offbeat, cultish and trendy pre-clubbing bar with sweetly kitsch decor, tucked into a Soho cellar and with a strictly "word of mouth" approach to advertising.

G-A-Y Bar 30 Old Compton St, W1 020/7494 2756, www.g-a-y.co.uk; Tottenham Court Road or Leicester Square tube. See map, p.108. Vast, pinky-purple video bar that attracts a young, fashionable, pre-G-A-Y crowd. The basement bar is for women and guests only in the evening.

George & Dragon 2–4 Hackney Rd, E2 020/7012 1100; Old Street tube. See map, p.158. Dandies, fashionistas and locals meet in this lively, often rammed east London hangout. The interior set-up is traditional, but then adorned with a fabulous collection of odd trinkets and curios.

The Green 74 Upper St, N1 020/7226 8895, www.thegreenislington.co.uk; Angel tube. Relaxed, stylish bar/restaurant fronting Islington Green, with interesting food, wine, beers and cocktails, plus regular themed nights with DJs and drag.

Green Carnation 5 Greek St, W1 020/7434 3323, www.greencarnation.co.uk; Tottenham Court Road tube. See map, p.108. Inspired by Oscar Wilde, the bar attracts quirky types who lend the venue a bohemian air, to go with its richly coloured flock wallpaper and sumptuous upholstery.

Halfway 2 Heaven 7 Duncannon St, WC2 020/7484 0736; Charing Cross tube. See map, p.56. Friendly, traditional pub off Trafalgar Square, featuring pub quizzes, karaoke and occasional cabaret. Attracts a largely male crowd slightly older than that in Soho.

Joiners Arms 116–118 Hackney Rd, E2 020/7739 9397; Old Street tube. Atmospheric bar with regular DJs and funky dance floor. Open late at weekends, it attracts a diverse crowd, with everything from East End stalwarts to pre-clubbing, loft-living trendies.

Kazbar 50 Clapham High St, SW4 020/7622 0070; Clapham Common or Clapham North tube. Modern, mostly boyz, split-level bar, with a video screen playing happy, poppy hits. Upstairs is a lounge area, and there is seating out front on the street.

Print

Though they carry excellent entertainment listings, most lesbian- and gay-oriented **newspapers and magazines** these days tend towards the glossy and consumerist, with celebrity features, fashion, lifestyle and the inevitable eye candy. Monthly newsstand magazines aimed at gay men include **Attitude** (ⓦwww.attitudemag .couk) **Axm** (ⓦwww.axm-mag.com) and **reFRESH** (ⓦwww.refreshmag.co.uk). **Gay Times** (ⓦwww.gaytimes.co.uk) is the longest-established glossy, and is also read by lesbians. **Diva** (ⓦwww.divamag.co.uk) is aimed squarely at the lesbian market.

Free magazines have made inroads into the market, with glossies **Bent** (ⓦwww .bent.com), **Out** (ⓦwww.outmag.co.uk) and **G3** (ⓦwww.g3mag.co.uk) serving gay males and lesbians each month. In addition to these, listings-based freesheets like **Boyz** (ⓦwww.boyz.co.uk) and **qx** (ⓦwww.qxmagazine.com) abound in clubs and bars. They give the most up-to-date and accurate club and bar listings and information. **The Pink Paper** (ⓦwww.pinkpaper.com), also free, is the UK's only serious weekly newspaper addressing lesbian and gay issues.

Online

While print media is still the best place to find the freshest news and information, the last few years have seen a proliferation of online resources.

ⓦ**www.pinknews.co.uk** Award-winning website putting an LGBT slant on news from the UK and abroad.

ⓦ**www.gayuknews.com** Up-to-date-news digest, with entertainment, scene and Pride sections.

ⓦ**www.gaytoz.com** Directory of gay, lesbian, bisexual and TV/TS-friendly organizations and businesses. A print version (£3) is also available from Gay to Z Directories, 41 Cooks Rd, London SE17 3NG.

ⓦ**www.rainbownetwork.com** Lifestyle e-zine with news on events, interviews with scene faces, listings and message boards.

ⓦ**www.gingerbeer.co.uk** Regularly updated website for London dykes, offering listings and reviews of bars, clubs and events.

ⓦ**www.gaydargirls.com** Online dating for queer girls nationwide. Tempting but often a little disappointing in the flesh.

ⓦ**www.gaydar.co.uk** If you like to order a date like you order a pizza, it's the place to meet up-for-it guys of all persuasions.

ⓦ**www.transgenderzone.com** Transsexual and transvestite site offering news plus national club and venue listings.

King Edward VI 25 Bromfield St, N1 ☎020/7704 0745; Angel tube. Long-established, loud-and-proud 1980s-style gay bar, with deafening music and a loyal local crowd. The Edward is particularly popular for its garden at the back, which is heated, lit and open until 11pm.

Ku Bar 30 Lisle St, WC2; 25 Frith St, W1; ☎020/7437 4303, ⓦwww.ku-bar.co.uk; Leicester Square tube. See map, p.108. The Lisle St original, with a downstairs club open late, is one of Soho's largest and best-loved gay bars, serving a scene-conscious yet low-on-attitude clientele. It's now joined by a stylish sibling bar on Frith St.

Kudos 10 Adelaide St, WC2 ☎020/7379 4573, ⓦwww.kudosgroup.com; Charing Cross tube.

See map, p.140. Popular among smart, besuited post-work boys and London's gay Chinese community, with a café and a basement theatre bar. Mixed during the day but gayer at night.

Retro Bar 2 George Court (off Strand), WC2 ☎020/7839 8760; Charing Cross tube. See map, p.140. Tucked down a quiet alleyway off the Strand, this friendly, indie/retro bar plays 1970s, 80s, rock, pop, goth and alternative sounds, and features regular DIY DJ nights.

The Royal Vauxhall Tavern 372 Kennington Lane, SE11 ☎020/7820 1222, ⓦwww.rvt.org .uk; Vauxhall tube. This huge, disreputable, divey drag and cabaret pub is home to legendary alternative night Duckie. The rest of the week brings bingo, comedy and a changing calendar of performance.

Rupert Street 50 Rupert St, W1 ☎020/7292 7140, ⦿www.rupertstreet.com; Piccadilly Circus tube. See map, p.108. Smart, mainstream bar attracting a mixed after-work crowd, but with a more pre-club vibe at weekends when they remove the furniture and it's frequently packed to the rafters.

Shadow Lounge 5 Brewer St, W1 ☎020/7287 7988, ⦿www.theshadowlounge.co.uk; Piccadilly Circus tube. See map, p.108. Glitzy gay lounge and members bar (non-members can pay at the door) which attracts celebrity punters. More fag hag than leather lez, and the boys rule the school.

The Stag 15 Bressenden Place, SW1 ☎020/7828 7287; Victoria tube. See map, p.44. Now with a fifty-seat theatre above it which looks to stage new writing on gay issues, this tucked-away bar plays pop and dance and hosts regular karaoke, drag and cabaret nights.

Trash Palace 58 Old St, EC1 ☎020/7287 3726, ⦿www.trashpalace.co.uk; Barbican tube. See map, p.108. Alternative, glam/punk/indie/pop/electro bar above *Ghetto*, open until 5am Fridays and Saturdays. Book-reading group Trash Fiction meets one Monday a month.

Two Brewers 114 Clapham High St, SW4 ☎020/7819 9539, ⦿www.the2brewers.com; Clapham Common/Clapham North tube. Big, long-established and popular south London pub, with nightly cabaret in the front bar and a more cruisey dance floor in the back.

Village Soho 81 Wardour St, W1 ☎020/7439 4089, ⦿www.village-soho.co.uk; Piccadilly Circus tube. See map, p.108. Elegant café-bar attracting pretty boyz: clean and modern on the ground floor, with a Moroccan-themed basement and the plush, comfortable upstairs Boudoir.

The Yard 57 Rupert St, W1 ☎020/7437 2652, ⦿www.yardbar.co.uk; Piccadilly Circus tube. See map, p.108. Attractive bar with courtyard, loft areas and a laid-back, sociable atmosphere. *The Yard* attracts a post-work crowd and in fine weather it's one of the best spots in the village for alfresco drinking.

Lesbian cafés, bars and pubs

Blush 8 Cazenove Rd, Stoke Newington, N16 ☎020/7923 9202, ⦿www.blushbar .co.uk; bus #73 from King's Cross or Angel tube. Two floors of fun with quizzes, games nights and lazy Sundays with roast dinners

and the newspapers make this local popular among lesbians.

Candy Bar 4 Carlisle St, WC2 ☎020/7494 4041, ⦿www.candybarsoho.com; Tottenham Court Road tube. This Sapphic magnet has been in operation since 1996 and still has the same crucial, cruisey vibe that makes it the hottest girl bar in central London. Pole dancing is a regular feature.

The Oak Bar 79 Green Lanes, N16 ☎020/7354 2791, ⦿www.oakbar.co.uk; Manor House tube. Friendly, spacious local pub with a dance floor and pool table, mixed but a female favourite. It hosts a range of club nights and events, including the wildly popular Lower the Tone.

Star at Night 22 Great Chapel St, W1 ☎020/7494 2488, ⦿www.thestaratnight.com; Tottenham Court Rd tube. See map, p.108. Comfortable venue open from 6pm Tues–Sat, popular with a slightly older crowd who want somewhere to sit, a decent glass of wine and good conversation.

Gay men's cafés, bars and pubs

79CXR 79 Charing Cross Rd, WC2 ☎020/7734 0769, ⦿www.79cxr.co.uk/home.htm; Leicester Square tube. See map, p.108. Big, busy, cruisey men-den on two floors, with indus-trial decor, late licence and a no-messing atmosphere. Popular with businessmen, mature men and those who like them.

BarCode Soho 3–4 Archer St, W1 ☎020/7734 3342, ⦿www.bar-code.co.uk; Piccadilly Circus tube. See map, p.108. Busy, stylish cruise and dance bar on two floors, attracting a buff, masculine crowd. On Tuesdays it hosts Comedy Camp, an award-winning gay comedy club.

BarCode Vauxhall Arch 69, Albert Embankment, SE11 ☎020/7582 4180, ⦿www.bar-code.co.uk; Vauxhall tube. Slick, spacious outpost of the cruisey gay men's bar in the heart of Vauxhall's clubbing quarter, convenient for Area and Fire.

Comptons of Soho 51–53 Old Compton St, W1 ☎020/3238 0163; Leicester Square or Piccadilly Circus tube. See map, p.108. This large, traditional-style pub attracts a butch, cruising yet relaxed 25-plus crowd. Upstairs is more chilled and draws younger folks.

The Kings Arms 23 Poland St, W1 ☎020/7734 5907; Oxford Circus tube. See map, p.104. London's best-known and perennially popular bear bar, with a traditional London pub atmosphere, DJ on Sat and karaoke night Sun.

The Quebec 12 Old Quebec St, W1 ☎020/7629 6159; Marble Arch tube. See map, p.244.

Long-established and busy gay venue with downstairs disco and a late licence. Especially popular with the older crowd, and believed to be the oldest gay pub in London.

Clubs

London's clubs tend to open up and shut down with surreal frequency, so do check the gay press, listings magazines and individual websites for up-to-date times and prices before you plan your night out.

Places are listed by club name if this is well known and long-lived, and by venue where there's a variety of changing theme nights. Entry **prices** start at around £3–5, but are more often between £8 and £15, rising to around £35 or even £50 for special events like New Year's Eve extravaganzas. A few places offer concessions for students and those on benefits, and some extend discounts if you've managed to pick up the right flyer from a bar earlier in the evening. Most **clubs open** at around 11pm (although some don't get going until the small hours) and close between 3am and 5am, sometimes later. When it's throwing-out time and you need a guaranteed harassment-free **cab service**, Liberty Cars, 330 Old St, EC1 (☎020/7739 9080), offers a reasonably priced, London-wide, 24-hour ride home; you can order a cab direct from its car marshal in Old Compton Street between *Balans* and *Balans Café*.

Mixed clubs

Area 67–68 Albert Embankment, SE1 ☎07500/667874, ⓦwww.areaclublondon.com; Vauxhall tube. With two dancefloors, chic decor and impressive laser and light displays, it hosts the after-hours club Beyond, as well as offering a London venue for big-name international DJs.

Bootylicious Club Colosseum, 1 Nine Elms Lane, SW8 ⓦwww.bootylicious-club.co.uk; Vauxhall tube. Despite London's large black community, this is the capital's only dedicated gay and lesbian urban music night, featuring r'n'b, hip-hop, dancehall, house and classic vibes.

Club Kali The Dome, 1 Dartmouth Park Hill, N19 ⓦwww.clubkali.com; Tufnell Park tube. Held

Saunas

London's burgeoning male sauna scene runs from small, intimate affairs with just a steam room and jacuzzi, to labyrinthine venues with swimming pools and gyms. They all charge around £10–14.

Chariots 57 Cowcross St, EC1 ☎020/7251 5553, Farringdon tube; 1 Fairchild St, EC2 ☎020/7247 5333, Old Street tube; 63–64 Albert Embankment, SE1 ☎020/7247 5333, Vauxhall tube; 101 Lower Marsh, SE1 ☎020/7401 8484, ⓦwww.gaysauna .co.uk; Waterloo tube. London's Roman sauna chain has four main locations: the Waterloo branch never closes, while the other three are open daily. Expect steam, sweat and saucy videos, plus private rest rooms to retire to with your man of choice. The Shoreditch branch is the largest and has a heated pool.

Pleasuredrome Sauna Arch 124, Cornwall Rd, SE1 ☎020/7633 9194 ⓦwww .pleasuredrome.com; Waterloo tube. Facilities here include two saunas, two steam rooms, dark rooms and private rooms, plus café-bar and jacuzzi. Mixed ages, fast turnover, highly rated. Open 24/7.

The Sauna Bar 29 Endell St, WC2 ☎020/7836 2236; Covent Garden tube. Very central, this friendly place offers the usual facilities, along with masseurs, a bar, and video entertainment. Sun–Thurs 11am–midnight, Fri & Sat 11– 2.30am.

on the first and third Friday of every month, Kali is a huge multiethnic extravaganza offering bhangra, Bollywood, Arabic, swing, Hindi and house flavours for a friendly, attitude-free crowd.

Duckie Royal Vauxhall Tavern, 372 Kennington Lane, SE11 ☏020/7737 4043, ⓦwww.duckie.co.uk; Vauxhall tube. Duckie's modern, rock-based hurdy-gurdy provides a Saturday antidote to gay dance domination. Cult DJs The Readers Wifes play everything from Kim Wilde to The Velvet Underground. Regular live art performances, occasional bouncy castles and theme nights.

Exilio Latino Rez Bar, Club Colosseum, 1 Nine Elms Lane, SW8 ☏07931/374391, ⓦwww.exilio.co.uk; Vauxhall tube. Every Friday night, Exilio erupts in a lesbian and gay Latin frenzy, spinning salsa, cumbias and merengue, and also features live acts.

Fire South Lambeth Rd, SW8 ⓦwww.fireclub.co.uk; Vauxhall tube. Fire is London's superclub of choice for a mixed though mostly male crowd of disco bunnies. The party runs from Saturday night to Sunday morning, then on Sunday afternoon, and from Monday night to Monday morning.

G-A-Y Late 5 Goslett Yard, W1 ☏020/7734 9858, ⓦwww.g-a-y.co.uk; Tottenham Court Road tube. Nocturnal sister of Old Compton St's *G-A-Y Bar*, the venue attracts a similar young, trendy, fun crowd who enjoy drinking, lounging about chatting and lurching to pop music on the dancefloor.

Ghetto 58 Old St, EC1 ☏020/7287 3726, ⓦwww.ghetto-london.com; Barbican tube. Relocated eastwards due to Crossrail works, Ghetto is claiming a less familiar part of the capital for its clientele of indie boys, club kids, riot grrrls and electro trash. Saturday nights see the madness of Wig Out.

Hard-On Hidden, 100 Tinworth St, SE11 ☏07533/402 985, ⓦwww.hardonclub.co.uk; Vauxhall tube. Suzy Krueger's celebrated, raunchy, mixed gay, lesbian and bisexual fetish/dance club has a strict dress code and is members only: you can apply for membership online.

Heaven Under the Arches, Villiers St, WC2 ☏020/7930 2020, ⓦwww.heaven-london.com; Charing Cross or Embankment tube. Said to be the UK's most popular gay club, this 2000-capacity venue is now home to G-A-Y at the weekend, the queen of London's scene nights, with big-name DJs, PAs and shows. More Muscle Mary than Diesel Doris.

Lo-Profile 84-86 Wardour St, W1 ☏020/7734 1053, ⓦwww.profilesoho.com; Piccadilly Circus tube. The physical manifestation of hook-up website gaydar.co.uk, this industrial-chic basement bar glows with neon-lit stars and circles and attracts a masculine crowd.

Madame Jojo's 8–10 Brewer St, W1 ☏020/7734 3040, ⓦwww.madamejojos.com; Piccadilly Circus tube. Lush, louche club offering cabaret and drag shows for office girls, gay boys and those in between, plus a variety of dance nights. Surrender your gender at Trannyshack on Wednesdays.

Popstarz The Den, 18 West Central St, WC1 ☏020/7240 1083, ⓦwww.popstarz.org; Tottenham Court Rd tube. The ground-breaking Friday-night indie club's still-winning formula of alternative tunes, 1970s and 80s trash, cheap beer and no attitude attracts a mixed, studenty crowd.

Unskinny Bop The Star of Bethnal Green, 359 Bethnal Green Rd, E2 ☏020/7729 0167, ⓦwww.unskinnybop.co.uk; Bethnal Green tube. Monthly indie night that describes itself as offering "disco dancing opportunities for girls, gays and misfits" in an increasingly popular pub. Every third Sat.

WayOut Club Charlie's 9 Crosswall, off Minories, EC3; ☏07778/157 290, ⓦwww.thewayoutclub.com; Tower Hill or Aldgate tube. Long-established Saturday night for gays, straights, cross-dressers, drag queens, TVs, TSs and friends offers a warm welcome, changing rooms, video screen and cabaret.

Lesbian clubs

100% Babe The Roxy, 3 Rathbone Place, W1 ⓦwww.myspace.com/hundredpercentbabe. Babelicious dance parties held several times a year on Bank Holiday Sundays in this plush, central London venue.

Chicks Rock!! Zenith Bar, 125 Packington St, N1 ☏07817/989 368; Angel tube. Second and fourth Thursday monthly, bringing together girls who like getting up and giving it a go. The formula involves an open mike and a melange of music, comedy, dancing and rock'n'roll air guitar.

Rumours Minories, 64–73 Minories, EC3 ☏07949/477 804, ⓦwww.girl-rumours.co.uk; Tower Hill or Aldgate tube. There's room for 500 grrrls at this monthly, women-only Saturday-nighter. The popular and cheap club night offers two bars, quiet lounges and a dancefloor until 3am.

Helplines and information

The following services provide information, advice and counselling, and can point you in the direction of specific organizations and community or support groups.

Antidote ☎020/7437 3523, ⓦwww.thehungerford.org/antidote.asp. Despite their illegality, drugs are a part of London's queer clubbing scene. Antidote provides a lesbian, gay, bi and transgender-specific drugs counselling and support service, including a weekly drop-in at 32a Wardour St, W1 (Thurs 6.30–8.30pm).

London Lesbian & Gay Switchboard ☎020/7837 7324, ⓦwww.llgs.org.uk. Huge database on everything you might ever want to know, plus legal advice and counselling. Lines are open 24hr: keep trying if you can't get through.

Sexual Health Line ☎0800/567123, ⓦwww.playingsafely.co.uk. Freephone 24hr service for anyone worried about HIV- and AIDS-related issues and other sexually transmitted infections.

A Taste of Honey The Cape Bar, 10 Aldermanbury, EC2 ☎07961/715 024, ⓦwww.tasteof honeyclubnight.co.uk; St Paul's tube. Fun, retro party atmosphere with a mix of music spanning the 1970s, 80s and 90s, plus requests for more recent songs. Third Sat of the month.

Waltzing with Hilda Jacksons Lane Arts Centre, 269a Archway Rd, N6 ⓦwww.hildas.org.uk; Highgate tube. Women-only Latin and ballroom dancing club with classes for beginners and the more experienced. Twice monthly on the second and last Sat (7.30–11.30pm). Closed Aug.

Gay men's clubs

The Eagle 349 Kennington Lane, SE11 ☎020/7793 0903, ⓦwww.eaglelondon .com; Vauxhall tube. Home to the excellent disco Sunday-nighter Horse Meat Disco, the vibe here is a loose, friendly re-creation of late 1970s New York, complete with facial hair, checked shirts and a pool table.

The Fort 131 Grange Rd, SE1 ☎020/7237 7742, ⓦwww.thefortlondon.com; London Bridge tube.

There's no set dress code at this sleazy, sexy cruise bar but check the free press or phone for details about special themed nights such as the frequent boots-only nights.

The Hoist Railway Arches, 47b–47c South Lambeth Rd, SW8 ☎020/7735 9972, ⓦwww .thehoist.co.uk; Vauxhall tube. London's biggest and best-known leather/dress code bar for men with few inhibitions. *The Hoist* also hosts regular skinhead and rubber nights, plus SM Gays monthly.

Union 66 Albert Embankment, SE1 ⓦwww .clubunion.co.uk; Vauxhall tube. With semiclothed, arousing nights such as MA1 Club, Growl and Fitladz, this venue appeals to the unabashedly cruisey. Fans of corporal punishment are served by the weekly Club CP.

XXL The Arches, 51/53 Southwark St, SE1 ☎020/7403 9643, ⓦwww.xxl-london.com; London Bridge tube. Massively popular Wednesday and Saturday dance club for big, burly men and their fans, attracting a diverse crowd with its two dance floors, two bars and outside chillout area.

28

Classical music, opera and dance

With the Southbank Centre, the Barbican and Wigmore Hall offering year-round appearances by generally first-rate musicians, and numerous smaller venues providing a stage for less-established or more specialized performers, the capital should satisfy most devotees of **classical music**. What's more, in the annual Promenade Concerts at the Royal Albert Hall, London has one of the world's greatest, most democratic music festivals.

Despite its elitist image, **opera** in the capital has an enthusiastic following. While the Royal Opera House (ROH) can attract top international stars to perform here, the downside is the prohibitive price (and availability) of most of the tickets. The nearby English National Opera (ENO) is better value, and can be more adventurous in its repertoire and productions. Apart from the two major companies, there are also outfits like the Almeida Theatre and Battersea Arts Centre that are extending the boundaries of contemporary music theatre in lively and adventurous ways.

The more modest economic demands of **dance** mean that you'll often find a broad spectrum of ambitious work on offer, with some of the world's outstanding companies appearing regularly at Sadler's Wells. Meanwhile, fans of classicism can revel in the Royal Ballet, a company with some of the most accomplished dancers in Europe.

Classical music

London is spoilt for choice when it comes to **orchestras**. On most days you should be able to catch a concert by one of the five major orchestras based in the capital or one of the more specialized ensembles. Unless a glamorous guest conductor is wielding the baton, or one of the world's high-profile orchestras is giving a performance, full houses are a rarity, so even at the biggest concert halls you should be able to pick up a ticket for around £12 (the usual range is about £10–40).

During the week there are numerous **free concerts** by students or professionals, often at lunchtimes (usually around 1pm), in London's churches (Ⓦwww.cityevents.co.uk), the best of which are listed below. London's two leading conservatoires, the Royal College of Music and Royal Academy of Music, also give regular concerts of an amazingly high standard, with programming that is often more adventurous than in commercial venues.

The Proms

BBC Henry Wood Promenade Concerts (the "Proms") Royal Albert Hall ☎0845/401 5040, ⓦwww.bbc.co.uk/proms; South Kensington tube. The Proms tend to be associated with the raucous "Last Night", when the flag-waving audience sings its patriotic heart out, but this jingoistic knees-up is untypical of the season (mid-July to mid-Sept), which features an exhilarating mix of favourites and new or recondite works. The unique aspect of the Proms is that the stalls seats are removed to create hundreds of standing places costing around £5 and purchased on the day. The upper gallery is similarly packed with people sitting on the floor or standing. The acoustics aren't the world's best – OK for orchestral blockbusters, less so for small-scale works – but the performers

▲ Royal Albert Hall

are usually outstanding, the atmosphere is great, and the hall is so vast that the likelihood of being turned away if you turn up on the night is slim. A handful of lunchtime concerts are also held in Cadogan Hall, just off Sloane Square.

The **Proms** provide a feast of music at bargain-basement prices (see box above), and there are several other regular **music festivals** throughout the year. The most prestigious is probably the City of London Festival (ⓦwww.colf.org), which takes place in the City's churches and livery halls from mid-June to early August. Christ Church, Spitalfields, is at the centre of several music events, the largest of which is its summer festival in June (ⓦwww.spitalfieldsfestival.org.uk). Other annual musicfests to look out for include the Festival of Baroque Music (ⓦwww.lufthansafestival.org.uk), held in May in St John's Smith Square and Westminster Abbey, and the Early Music Festival, held in Greenwich's beautiful Old Royal Naval College.

Concert venues

Barbican Centre Silk St, EC2 ☎020/7638 8891, ⓦwww.barbican.org.uk; Barbican or Moorgate tube. With the outstanding resident London Symphony Orchestra, and with top foreign orchestras and big-name soloists in regular attendance, the Barbican is one of the outstanding arenas for classical music. The free music in the foyer is often very good.
BMIC (British Music Information Centre) First Floor, 26 Berners St, W1 ☎020/7580 3869, ⓦwww.bmic.co.uk; Tottenham Court or Goodge Street tube. The BMIC promotes British contemporary classical music, has an impressive library and organizes a concert

series of innovative work, The Cutting Edge, in Oct/Nov at The Warehouse, 13 Theed St, SE1 (Waterloo tube).
Cadogan Hall Sloane Terrace, SW1 ☎020/7730 4500, ⓦwww.cadoganhall.com; Sloane Square tube. This handsome neo-Byzantine building, originally built in 1901 as a Christian Science church, now serves as a 900-seat concert hall with outstanding acoustics. The Royal Philharmonic is its resident orchestra and it's the venue for the Proms chamber concerts (see box above).
Kings Place 90 York Way, N1 ☎0844/264 0321, ⓦwww.kingsplace.co.uk; King's Cross tube. Home of the London Sinfonietta, one of the world's finest contemporary music groups,

and the Orchestra of the Age of Enlighten-ment, who play on period instruments, this impressive, purpose-built venue, by the canal behind King's Cross, has two performance spaces and online "saver" tickets for around £10.

LSO St Luke's 161 Old St, EC1 ⊕ 020/7490 3939, ⓦ lso.co.uk/lsostlukes; Old Street tube. Hawksmoor church beautifully converted into a 370-seat concert hall for the London Symphony Orchestra, but also used for a wide variety of recitals from chamber music to free jazz.

St John's Smith Square, SW1 ⊕ 020/7222 1061, ⓦ www.sjss.org.uk; Westminster tube. Firebombed in 1941, this striking Baroque church (from the outside) serves as an austere concert hall, with fine acoustics and a great organ. Its varied musical menu includes orchestral and choral concerts, chamber music and solo recitals. There's a good restaurant in the crypt.

Southbank Centre South Bank, SE1 ⊕ 0871/663 2500, ⓦ www.southbankcentre.co.uk; Waterloo or Embankment tube. The SBC has three concert venues, none of which is exclusively used for classical music. The 3000-seat Royal Festival Hall (RFH) is a gargantuan space, tailor-made for large-scale choral and orchestral works, and home to the Philharmonia and the London Philharmonic. The lugubrious Queen Elizabeth Hall (QEH) is the prime location for chamber concerts, solo recitals and contemporary work; while the Purcell Room is the most intimate venue, excellent for chamber music and recitals by up-and-coming instrumentalists and singers.

Wigmore Hall 36 Wigmore St, W1 ⊕ 020/7935 2141, ⓦ www.wigmore-hall.org.uk; Bond Street or Oxford Circus tube. With its near-perfect acoustics, the intimate Wigmore Hall – originally built as a hall for the adjacent Bechstein piano showroom – is a favourite with artists and audiences alike so book well in advance. Brilliant for piano recitals and chamber music, but best known for its song recitals by some of the world's greatest singers. Tickets for the Monday lunchtime concerts and Sunday mid-morning concerts cost around £10.

Free concerts

BBC Maida Vale Concerts Delaware Rd, W9 ⊕ 0370/901 1227, ⓦ www.bbc.co.uk; Warwick Avenue or Maida Vale tube. The BBC Symphony Orchestra hosts free concerts, performed by various BBC ensembles and artists, at the Maida Vale Studios. All concerts are later broadcast. Booking opens six weeks in advance.

Royal Academy of Music Marylebone Rd, NW1 ⊕ 020/7873 7300, ⓦ www.ram.ac.uk; Regent's Park or Baker Street tube. During term time, there are masterclasses, free lunchtime concerts, and early evening recitals for around £6, either at the RAM itself or at nearby venues.

Royal College of Music Prince Consort Rd, SW7 ⊕ 020/7591 4314, ⓦ www.rcm.ac.uk; South Kensington tube. During term time, free lunchtime concerts are held, and fee-paying evening concerts, either in the RCM or in nearby venues.

St Anne and St Agnes Gresham St, EC2 ⊕ 020/7606 4986, ⓦ www.stanneslutheran church.org; St Paul's tube. As well as lunchtime recitals (Mon & Fri), this Lutheran church has a week-long Bach Festival in July.

St Bride Fleet St, EC4 ⊕ 020/7427 0133, ⓦ www.stbrides.com; Blackfriars tube. Lunchtime concerts every week (Tues & Fri), usually by professional musicians. A good professional choir sings at two services every Sunday.

St Giles-in-the-Fields St Giles High St, WC2 ⊕ 020/7240 2532, ⓦ www.stgilesonline.org; Tottenham Court Road tube. Free lunchtime organ recitals or chamber music (Fri) in the spring and autumn, plus the occasional fee-paying evening concert.

St James Piccadilly, W1 ⊕ 020/7734 4511, ⓦ www.st-james-piccadilly.org; Piccadilly Circus tube. Wren church with free lunchtime concerts (Mon, Wed & Fri), plus fee-paying evening concerts. The restaurant in the crypt is good for before or after.

St Lawrence Jewry Guildhall, EC2 ⊕ 020/7600 9478, ⓦ www.slj.btik.com; Bank or St Paul's tube. As well as weekly organ recitals on an impressive new instrument (Thurs), there are occasional free lunchtime concerts on other weekdays.

St Magnus the Martyr Lower Thames St, EC3 ⊕ 020/7626 4481, ⓦ www.stmagnusmartyr.org .uk; Monument tube. There are regular recitals on the 1712 Jordan organ as well as a chamber or instrumental concert (Wed). A good choir provides sung Mass every Sunday (11am).

St Margaret Lothbury Lothbury, EC2 ⊕ 020/7726 4878, ⓦ www.stml.org.uk; Bank tube.

Lunchtime recitals (Thurs) on the church's 200-year-old organ all year except August.
St Martin-in-the-Fields Trafalgar Square, WC2 ☎020/7839 8362, ⓦwww.stmartin-in-the-fields.org; Charing Cross or Leicester Square tube. Free lunchtime recitals (Mon, Tues & Fri), plus fee-charging evening concerts, which occasionally feature the top-notch orchestra or chamber ensemble of the Academy of St Martin-in-the-Fields.
St Martin-within-Ludgate Ludgate Hill, EC4 ☎020/7248 6054, ⓦwww.stmartin-within-ludgate.org.uk; St Paul's or Blackfriars tube. This Wren church hosts a varied lunchtime recital programme (Wed) throughout the year except August.
St-Mary-le-Bow Cheapside, EC2 ☎020/7248 5139, ⓦwww.stmarylebow.co.uk; St Paul's tube. A varied programme of mainly chamber and solo recitals (Thurs), except in August and September.
St-Mary-le-Strand Strand, WC2 ☎020/7836 3126, ⓦstmarylestrand.org; Covent Garden or Temple tube. Lunchtime recitals (Wed) with young professional or student musicians providing a respite from the surrounding traffic in this eighteenth-century gem by James Gibbs.

St Michael Cornhill, EC3 ☎020/7248 3826, ⓦwww.st-michaels.org.uk; Bank tube. Organ recitals (Mon) on an instrument first played by Henry Purcell in 1684, and a choral Sunday service followed by a glass of wine in the vestry.
St Olave Hart St, EC3 ☎020/7488 4318, ⓦwww.sanctuaryinthecity.net; Tower Hill tube. Atmospheric medieval setting for chamber pieces or solo recitals (Wed & Thurs), except in August, plus fee-paying evening concerts.
St Sepulchre-without-Newgate Holborn Viaduct, EC1 ☎020/7248 3826, ⓦwww.st-sepulchre.org.uk; Chancery Lane or St Paul's tube. A church with a strong association with musicians, it holds regular chamber or organ concerts (Wed).
St Stephen Walbrook Walbrook, EC4 ☎020/7626 9000, ⓦststephenwalbrook.net; Bank tube. Lunchtime organ recitals (Fri) at the earlier than normal time of 12.30pm in one of the finest of all Wren's churches, plus regular choral Eucharist (Thurs eve).
Temple Church Fleet St, EC4 ☎020/7353 0172, ⓦwww.templechurch.com; Temple tube. Lunchtime organ recitals (Wed), except in August and September, usually by leading organists.

Opera

Of the two main companies, the **Royal Opera House** is the place to go to see the top international stars, while **English National Opera** continues to show what can be achieved with largely home-grown talent and lively, radical productions.

Opera

Barbican Centre Silk St, EC2 ☎020/7638 8891, ⓦwww.barbican.org.uk; Barbican or Moorgate tube. Concert performances of operas are frequently performed at the Barbican, usually employing top soloists supported by the resident London Symphony Orchestra.
English National Opera Coliseum, St Martin's Lane, WC2 ☎0871/911 0200, ⓦwww.eno.org; Leicester Square or Charing Cross tube. All operas at the ENO are sung in English, the repertoire is more adventurous (and occasionally includes musicals), productions more experimental, and the cost far less (£16–80); day seats (£10–15), in the balcony, are also available to personal callers after 10am on the day of the

performance; standbys (£10–30) go on sale three hours before a performance for students, senior citizens, under-16s and the unemployed.
Opera Holland Park Holland Park, Kensington High St, W8 ☎0845/230 9769, ⓦwww.ohp.rbkc.gov.uk; High Street Kensington or Holland Park tube. Opera takes to the great outdoors in green and pleasant Holland Park (June–Aug). Standard repertoire is the order of the day, and productions range unpredictably from the inspired to the workaday. There's a canopy to cover you in case of rain. Tickets start at £10.
Royal Opera House Bow St, WC2 ☎020/7304 4000, ⓦwww.roh.org.uk; Covent Garden tube. The ROH is one of the world's leading opera houses and puts on lavish productions of

the standard opera repertoire. More innovative productions are staged in the Linbury Studio Theatre. Most tickets are expensive (£30–180), with just 67 day seats (at various prices) going on sale from 10am on the day of a performance; these are restricted to one per person, and you need to get there before 9am for popular shows. Student standby tickets (subject to availability) can be bought for £10 online. In summer, some performances are relayed live to screens in Covent Garden Piazza, Trafalgar Square and Canary Wharf. All operas are performed in the original language but are surtitled.

Dance

For classical ballet lovers, the **Royal Ballet** possesses a number of truly outstanding soloists, while those interested in more cutting-edge work can choose between the intimacy of **The Place** or the larger **Sadler's Wells**, both venues for the best contemporary work. London also has a good reputation for international dance festivals showcasing the work of a wide range of companies. The biggest of the annual events is the **Dance Umbrella** (℡020/8741 5881, ⊛www.danceumbrella.co.uk), a season (Sept–Nov) of often groundbreaking new work at various venues across town. The newest kid on the block is **Breakin' Conventions** (⊛www.breakinconventions.com), a five-day festival of hip-hop dance held in May at Sadler's Wells.

Dance companies and venues

Barbican Centre Silk St, EC2 ℡020/7638 8891, ⊛www.barbican.org.uk; Barbican or Moorgate tube. As part of its mixed programming the Barbican regularly stages contemporary dance by top international companies. It's also used as a venue for Dance Umbrella events.

English National Ballet ℡020/7581 1245, ⊛www.ballet.org.uk. English National Ballet tours nationally, but also regularly performs seasons at the Coliseum (home of the ENO – see opposite), with occasional appearances at the Royal Festival Hall and the Royal Albert Hall.

Laban Creekside, SE8 ℡020/8691 8600, ⊛www.laban.org; Deptford train station from Charing Cross. This funky Herzog & de Meuron building in deepest Deptford includes a 300-seat theatre. The venue showcases many leading names in contemporary dance as well as staging work by Laban students.

The Place 17 Duke's Rd, WC1 ℡020/7387 0031, ⊛www.theplace.org.uk; Euston tube. The Place has a small theatre that presents the work of contemporary choreographers and student performers.

Royal Ballet Royal Opera House, Bow St, WC2 ℡020/7304 4000, ⊛www.roh.org.uk; Covent Garden tube. The Royal Ballet is a world-renowned classical company, whose outstanding principals include Carlos Acosta, Alina Cojocaru and Zenaida Yanowsky. Tickets for the main house are cheaper than for opera (£5–100), and there are two small performing spaces, the Linbury Studio Theatre and the Clore Studio, where more experimental work can be seen. Sellouts are frequent so book early (see Royal Opera House, opposite, for details of day tickets and standbys).

Sadler's Wells Theatre Rosebery Ave, EC1 ℡0844/412 4300, ⊛www.sadlerswells.com; Angel tube. Sadler's Wells is home to Britain's best contemporary dance companies, including the Rambert, and many of the finest international companies are also regular visitors. The Lillian Baylis Theatre, tucked around the back, puts on smaller-scale shows, while the Peacock Theatre in the West End is where Sadler's Wells stages more populist dance, including flamenco and tango.

Southbank Centre South Bank, SE1 ℡0871/663 2500, ⊛www.southbankcentre.co.uk; Waterloo or Embankment tube. The Southbank Centre's three venues all stage dance performances; the Dance Umbrella festival visits every year in the autumn and it's also the main centre for large-scale Asian dance in the capital.

29

Theatre, comedy and cinema

L ondon has enjoyed a reputation for quality **theatre** since the time of Shakespeare and, despite the continuing dominance of blockbuster musicals and revenue-spinning star vehicles, the city still provides a platform for innovation. The **comedy** scene in London is so big that the capital now boasts more comedy venues than any other city in the world, while comedians who have made the transition to television also stage shows in major theatres.

Cinema is dominated by multiscreen complexes which show mainstream Hollywood fare a few months behind America. Nevertheless, there remain a few excellent independent cinemas, the charge led by the BFI Southbank, which is the focus of the huge and richly varied **London Film Festival** in November.

Current details of **what's on** can be found in a number of publications, the most comprehensive being the weekly *Time Out*. Other good sources of information include *The Guardian*'s *The Guide* section (free with the paper on Saturdays) and Friday's *Evening Standard*.

Theatre

The **West End** is the heart of London's "Theatreland", with Shaftesbury Avenue its most congested drag, but the word is more of a conceptual pigeon-hole than a geographical term. On any given night in the West End there are more people watching **musicals** than all other forms of theatre put together, and the trend shows no sign of abating, despite the fact that only half the shows actually make money. *Les Misérables* is the longest-running musical at the moment, on the go since 1985, closely followed by *The Phantom of the Opera*, which opened in 1986. Both of these are mere babies, though, compared with *The Mouserap* by Agatha Christie, which began its West End run in 1952. For details (and tickets) for all the West End's long runners, see Ⓦwww.albemarle-london.com.

The **Royal Shakespeare Company** and **National Theatre** often put on extremely original performances of mainstream masterpieces, while some of the most exciting work is found in what have become known as the **Off-West End** theatres, which consistently stage interesting and frequently challenging productions. Further down the financial ladder still are the **Fringe** theatres,

The drama schools

The London drama schools each mount as many as ten productions per term, giving you a chance to indulge in a bit of talent-spotting for very little outlay – indeed, plays at the Guildhall are free. The following are the main schools:

Central School of Speech and Drama 64 Eton Ave, NW3 ☎020/7722 8183, ⓦwww .cssd.ac.uk; Swiss Cottage tube.

Guildhall School of Music and Drama Silk St, Barbican, EC2 ☎020/7628 2571, ⓦwww.gsmd.ac.uk; Barbican or Moorgate tube.

London Academy of Music and Dramatic Art 155 Talgarth Rd, W14 ☎020/8834 0500, ⓦwww.lamda.org.uk; Barons Court tube.

Royal Academy of Dramatic Art 18–22 Chenies St, WC1 ☎020/7908 4800, ⓦwww .rada.org; Goodge St tube.

more often than not pub venues, where ticket prices are lower, and quality more variable. Look out, too, for London's two main theatre festivals: the **Mimefest** (ⓦwww.mimefest.co.uk), a feast of puppetry, mime and physical theatre which takes place in January, and **LIFT** (ⓦwww.liftfest.org.uk), an international theatrical jamboree held in August.

Tickets for £10 are restricted to the Fringe; the box-office average is closer to £15–25, with £30–50 the usual top price. It's worth looking out for special deals: cheap Monday tickets or standby tickets. Tickets for the durable musicals and well-reviewed plays are like gold dust so book ahead. The cheapest way to buy your ticket is to go to the theatre box office in person; if you book over the phone or online, you may be charged a booking fee. Students, senior citizens and the unemployed can get **concessionary rates** on tickets for most shows, and many theatres offer reductions on standby tickets to these groups.

Whatever you do, avoid the touts and the ticket agencies that abound in the West End – there's no guarantee that the tickets are genuine. Ticket agencies such as Ticketmaster (☎0161/385 1138, ⓦwww.ticketmaster.co.uk) or Keith Prowse (☎0844/209 0381, ⓦwww.keithprowse.com) can get seats for most West End shows, but add as much as twenty percent on the ticket price.

The Society of London Theatre (ⓦwww.officiallondontheatre.co.uk) runs **tkts** (Mon–Sat 10am–7pm, Sun noon–3pm), in Leicester Square, which sells on-the-day tickets for all the West End shows at discounts of up to fifty percent, though they tend to be in the top end of the price range, are limited to four per person, and carry a service charge of £3 per ticket.

The venues

What follows is a list of West End theatres which offer a changing roster of good plays, along with the most consistent of the Off-West End and Fringe venues. This by no means represents the full tally of London's stages, as there are scores of Fringe places that present work intermittently – the weekly listings magazine *Time Out* provides the most comprehensive and detailed up-to-the-minute survey.

West End

Barbican Silk St, EC2 ☎020/7638 8891, ⓦwww.barbican.org.uk; Barbican or Moorgate tube. The Barbican's two venues – the excellently designed Barbican Theatre and the much smaller Pit – put on a wide variety of theatrical spectacles from puppetry and musicals to new drama works, plus the Royal Shakespeare Company who perform here (and elsewhere in London) on and off from autumn to spring each year.

National Theatre Southbank Centre, South Bank, SE1 ☎020/7452 3000, ⓦwww .nationaltheatre.org.uk; Waterloo tube. The NT consists of three separate theatres: the 1100-seater Olivier, the proscenium-arched Lyttelton and the experimental Cottesloe. Standards set by the late Laurence Olivier, founding artistic director, are maintained by the country's top actors and directors in a programme ranging from Greek tragedies to Broadway musicals. Some productions sell out months in advance, but £10 day seats go on sale at 9.30am on the morning of each performance – get there by 8am for the popular shows.

Old Vic The Cut, SE1 ☏0870/060 6628, ⊛www.oldvictheatre.com; Waterloo tube. The ancient Old Vic, established in 1811, is currently under the stewardship of Oscar-winning American actor Kevin Spacey, who occasionally treads the boards himself.

Open Air Theatre Regent's Park, Inner Circle, NW1 ☏0844/826 4242, ⊛www.openairtheatre .org; Baker Street tube. If the weather's good, there's nothing quite like a dose of alfresco drama. This beautiful space in Regent's Park hosts a tourist-friendly summer programme of Shakespeare, musicals, plays and concerts.

Royal Court Sloane Square, SW1 ☏020/7565 5000, ⊛www.royalcourttheatre.com; Sloane Square tube. The Royal Court is one of the best places in London to catch radical new writing, either in the proscenium arch Theatre Downstairs, or the smaller-scale Theatre Upstairs studio space.

Shakespeare's Globe New Globe Walk, SE1 ☏020/7401 9919, ⊛www.shakespeares -globe.com; London Bridge, Blackfriars or Southwark tube. This thatch-roofed replica Elizabethan theatre uses only natural light and the minimum of scenery, and puts on fun Shakespearean shows from mid-May to mid-September, with "groundling" tickets (standing-room only) for around a fiver.

Off-West End

Almeida Almeida St, N1 ☏020/7359 4404, ⊛www.almeida.co.uk; Angel or Highbury & Islington tube. Deservedly popular Off-West End venue in Islington that continues to premiere excellent new plays and excitingly reworked classics, and has attracted some big Hollywood names.

Battersea Arts Centre 176 Lavender Hill, SW11 ☏020/7223 2223, ⊛www.bac.org.uk; Clapham Junction train station from Victoria or Waterloo.

The BAC is a triple-stage building, housed in an old town hall in south London, and has acquired a reputation for excellent productions, from straight theatre to comedy and cabaret.

Bush Shepherd's Bush Green, W12 ☏020/8743 5050, ⊛www.bushtheatre.co.uk; Shepherd's Bush tube. This minuscule above-pub theatre is London's most reliable venue for new writing after the Royal Court, and it has turned out some great stuff.

Donmar Warehouse Thomas Neal's, 41 Earlham St, WC2 ☏0870/060 6624, ⊛www .donmarwarehouse.com; Covent Garden tube. A small, central performance space, noted for new plays and top-quality reappraisals of the classics.

The Gate The Prince Albert, 11 Pembridge Rd, W11 ☏020/7229 0706, ⊛www.gatetheatre.co .uk; Notting Hill Gate tube. A small pub-theatre noted for its excellent revivals of neglected European classics.

Hampstead Theatre Eton Ave, NW3 ☏020/7722 9301, ⊛www.hampsteadtheatre.com; Swiss Cottage tube. A prestigious zinc-and-glass-fronted theatre in Swiss Cottage (not in Hampstead proper) whose productions often move on to the West End.

Menier Chocolate Factory 51–53 Southwark St, SE1 ☏020/7907 7060, ⊛www.menierchocolate factory.com; London Bridge tube. Great name, great venue in an old Victorian factory; consistently good shows and has a decent bar and restaurant attached.

Soho Theatre 21 Dean St, W1 ☏020/7478 0100, ⊛www.sohotheatre.com; Tottenham Court Road tube. Great Off-West End theatre that specializes in new writing from around the globe, as well as putting on regular comedy acts.

Theatre Royal Stratford East Gerry Raffles Square, E15 ☏020/8534 0310, ⊛www .stratfordeast.com; Stratford tube. Beautiful, small Victorian theatre in the East End, which puts on community-pleasing shows, including consistently excellent Christmas panto.

Tricycle Theatre 269 Kilburn High Rd, NW6 ☏020/7328 1000, ⊛www.tricycle.co.uk; Kilburn tube. One of London's most dynamic fringe venues, showcasing a mixed bag of new plays, often aimed at the theatre's multicultural neighbourhood, and often with a sharp political focus.

Young Vic The Cut, SE1 ☏020/7922 2922, ⊛www.youngvic.org; Waterloo tube. The Young

Vic opened in 1970 as a temporary structure with a five-year lifespan – 37 years later, it has finally been rebuilt from scratch and looks set to go from strength to strength.

Fringe and occasional venues

Arcola Theatre 27 Arcola St, E8 ☎020/7503 1646, 🅦www.arcolatheatre.com; Dalston Kingsland or Junction Overground. Fringe theatre deep in Dalston/Stoke Newington borders, which puts on some challenging, uncompromising shows.

King's Head 115 Upper St, N1 ☎0844/209 0326, 🅦www.kingsheadtheatre.org; Angel or Highbury & Islington tube. The oldest and probably most famous of London's thriving pub-theatres (with a useful late licence). Adventurous performances in a pint-sized room, at lunchtimes and in the evening.

New End Theatre 27 New End, NW3 ☎0870/033 2733, 🅦www.newendtheatre.co.uk; Hampstead tube. Cosy neighbourhood venue in literary-minded Hampstead that offers a reliable programme of Fringe-like fare.

Roundhouse Chalk Farm Rd, NW1 ☎0844/482 8008, 🅦www.roundhouse.org.uk; Chalk Farm tube. Camden's barn-like former engine shed puts on theatrical spectacles and circus stuff interspersed with live gigs.

Shunt 20 Stainer St, SE1 ☎020/7378 7776, 🅦www.shunt.co.uk; London Bridge tube. The brick vaults under London Bridge Station are the venue for strange nightly happenings – theatre, film, music – put together by a different curator each week. It's £5 (Wed & Thurs) or £10 (Fri & Sat) – take ID.

Wilton Music Hall Grace's Alley, off Cable St, E1 ☎020/7702 2789, 🅦www.wiltons.org.uk; Tower Hill tube. A crumbling Victorian music hall, built in 1858, with barley-sugar wrought-iron columns holding up the gallery, intermittently provides a wonderful venue for theatre and opera performances.

Comedy

The **comedy scene** continues to thrive in London, with the leading funny-persons catapulted to unlikely stardom on both stage and screen. The Comedy Store is the best known and most central venue on the circuit, but just about every London suburb has a pub stage giving a twenty-minute platform to a handful of young hopefuls (full listings appear on 🅦www.chortle.co.uk and in *Time Out*) or a nearby purpose-built venue. Note that many venues operate only on Friday and Saturday nights, and that August is a lean month, as much of London's talent heads north for the Edinburgh Fringe. Tickets at smaller venues can be had for £7–10, but in the more established places, you're looking at over £10.

Amused Moose Soho 17 Greek St, W1 ☎020/7287 3727, 🅦www.amusedmoose.com; Tottenham Court Road tube. Top stand-up, and comedy courses too. Every Sat, plus other occasional nights. Branches in Covent Garden and Chalk Farm.

Banana Cabaret The Bedford, 77 Bedford Hill, SW12 ☎020/8682 8940, 🅦www.bananacabaret .co.uk; Balham tube. This double-stage pub is one of London's most welcoming comedy venues – well worth the trip out from the centre of town. Fri & Sat from 9pm, followed by a DJ.

Canal Café Theatre The Bridge House, Delamere Terrace, W2 ☎020/7289 6056, 🅦www .canalcafetheatre.com; Warwick Ave tube. Perched on the water's edge in Little Venice, this venue is good for improvisation acts and is home to the NewsRevue team of topical gagsters; there's usually something going on from Thursday to Sunday.

Chuckle Club Tutu's, KCLSU, Fourth Floor, Macadam Building, Surrey St, WC2 ☎020/7476 1672, 🅦www.chuckleclub.com; Holborn tube. Student comedy club of some standing, with subsidized bar and a great vibe. Sat doors open 7.45pm.

Comedy Café 66–68 Rivington St, EC2 ☎020/ 7739 5706, 🅦www.comedycafe.co.uk; Old Street tube. Long-established, purpose-built club in Shoreditch/Hoxton, often with impressive line-ups, and free admission for the new-acts slot on Wednesday nights. Wed–Sat.

Comedy Camp Barcode, 3–4 Archer St, W1 ☎020/7483 2960, 🅦www.comedycamp.co.uk; Leicester Square or Piccadilly Circus tube.

▲ Comedy Café

Cracking gay comedy night every Tuesday at 8.30pm.

Comedy Store 1a Oxendon St, SW1 ☎0844/847 1728, ⓦwww.thecomedystore.co.uk; Piccadilly Circus tube. Widely regarded as the birthplace of alternative comedy, the Comedy Store has catapulted many a stand-up onto primetime TV. Improvisation by in-house comics on Wednesdays and Sundays, in addition to a stand-up bill; Friday and Saturday are the busiest nights, with two shows, at 8pm and midnight – book ahead.

The Funny Side The Corner Store, 33–35 Wellington St, WC2 ☎0870/446 0616, ⓦwww.thefunnyside.info. Upmarket, well-run comedy club offering a reliably good roster of stand-ups (Wed–Sun), with a branch in the City.

Cinema

There are an awful lot of **cinemas** in the West End, but very few places committed to independent films, and even fewer repertory cinemas programming serious films from the back catalogue. **Tickets** at the major screens in the West End cost £8–10, although afternoon shows are usually discounted. The suburban screens run by the big companies (see *Time Out* for full listings) tend to be a couple of pounds cheaper, as do independent cinemas. Students, senior citizens and the unemployed can get concessionary rates for some shows at virtually all cinemas, usually all day Monday or at other off-peak times on weekdays.

Big screens

Empire Leicester Square, WC2 ☎0871/471 4714, ⓦwww.empirecinemas.co.uk; Leicester Square tube. Victorian former variety theatre whose 2000-seat main auditorium is one of London's largest, and the place where blockbusters tend to premiere, and royalty and celebs occasionally turn up.

Odeon Leicester Square Leicester Square, WC2 ☎0871/224 4007, ⓦwww.odeon.co.uk; Leicester Square tube. Another gargantuan cinema, with 1700 seats, and a favourite for celeb-packed premieres. There's just one screen here, so don't mistakenly enter the adjacent Odeon Mezzanine, which crushes five into a far smaller space, or Odeon West End, which is on the south side of the square.

Repertory cinemas

Barbican Silk St, EC2 ☎020/7638 8891, ⓦwww.barbican.org.uk; Barbican or Moorgate tube. Comfy seats, three tiny screens and a regular rota of obscure classics, plus the odd mini-festival.

BFI IMAX South Bank, SE1 ☎0870/787 2525, ⓦwww.bfi.org.uk; Waterloo tube. This glazed drum, in the middle of Waterloo roundabout, houses Europe's largest screen. It's stunning, state-of-the-art stuff alright, showing 2D and 3D films on a massive screen, but, like all IMAX cinemas, it suffers from the paucity of good material that's been shot in the format.

BFI Southbank Belvedere Rd, South Bank, SE1 ☎020/7928 3232, ⓦwww.bfi.org.uk; Waterloo tube. Known for its attentive audiences and an exhaustive, eclectic programme that includes directors' seasons and thematic series. Around six films daily are shown in the vast NFT1 and the smaller NFT2 and NFT3.

Ciné Lumière 17 Queensberry Place, SW7 ☎020/7073 1350, ⓦwww.institut-francais.org.uk; South Kensington tube. Predominantly,

Film festivals

Birds Eye View Film Festival ⓦ www.birds-eye-view.co.uk. Nine-day film festival with films by women directors from all over the globe.

London Film Festival ⓦ www.lff.org.uk. A huge event, held over a fortnight in late October, and shown across half a dozen West End cinemas, so popular that many of the films sell out soon after publication of the festival's programme.

London International Animation Festival ⓦ www.liaf.org.uk. Over 200 animation shorts from all over the world are shown during this ten-day festival.

London Short Film Festival ⓦ www.shortfilms.org.uk. The LSSF is a nine-day orgy of weird and wonderful short films shown at a variety of trendy venues.

Portobello Film Festival ⓦ www.portobellofilmfestival.com. Fortnight-long free film festival showing innovative works by British filmmakers in the middle of September.

Raindance Festival ⓦ www.raindance.co.uk. Two-week independent film festival, held in late September/early October, showing new work by first-time directors from all over the globe.

but by no means exclusively, French films, both old and new (sometimes with subtitles), put on by the Institut Français.

Electric 191 Portobello Rd, W11 ☎020/7908 9696, ⓦ www.the-electric.co.uk; Notting Hill Gate or Ladbroke Grove tube. One of the oldest cinemas in the country (opened 1910), the Electric has been filled out with luxury leather armchairs, footstools and two-seater sofas.

Everyman Hollybush Vale, NW3 ☎0870/066 4777, ⓦ www.everymancinema.com; Hampstead tube. The city's oldest rep cinema, and still one of its best, with strong programmes of classics, cultish crowd-magnets and directors' seasons. Two screens and some very plush seating.

Goethe Institut 50 Princes Gate, Exhibition Rd, SW7 ☎020/7596 4000, ⓦ www.goethe.de/london; South Kensington tube. Sporadic showings of German cinematic masterpieces.

ICA Cinema Nash House, The Mall, SW1 ☎020/7930 3647, ⓦ www.ica.org.uk; Piccadilly Circus or Charing Cross tube. Vintage and underground movies shown on one of two tiny screens in the avant-garde HQ of the Institute of Contemporary Arts.

Prince Charles 2–7 Leicester Place, WC2 ☎020/7494 3654, ⓦ www.princecharlescinema .com; Leicester Square or Piccadilly Circus tube. The Downstairs screen here is the bargain basement of London's cinemas (entry for most shows is just £4–5), with a programme of newish movies, classics and cult favourites, plus participatory "singalong" romps.

Riverside Studios Crisp Rd, W6 ☎020/8237 1111, ⓦ www.riversidestudios.co.uk; Hammersmith tube. A converted film studio in West London, this art cinema is worth checking out for its mini-festivals and innovative programming.

Shops and markets

30

From the *folie de grandeur* that is Harrods to the frenetic street markets of the East End, London is a shopper's playground. As befits a city of villages, London's **shopping districts** all have their own flavour, with some known for their specialities and others simply for their location. In the sections that follow, we've listed shops according to what they sell, rather than by area.

Where to shop

In the centre of town, **Oxford Street** is the city's hectic chain-store heartland and, together with **Regent Street**, offers pretty much every mainstream clothing label you could wish for. Just off Oxford Street expensive designer outlets clutter **St Christopher's Place** and **South Molton Street**, with even pricier designers and jewellers lining chic **Bond Street**. To the north, **Marylebone High Street** offers a pretty village oasis in the middle of town – a laid-back place to get all your labels, treats and gifts away from the bustle.

  Tottenham Court Road is the place for electrical goods, sportswear and, in its northern section, furniture and design shops, while **New Oxford Street** has a range of shops selling new and used camera equipment. **Charing Cross Road** is the centre of London's book trade, both new and secondhand. At its north end, particularly on **Denmark Street** (once the heart of Britain's music industry), music shops sell everything from instruments to sound equipment and sheet music. On the other side of Charing Cross Road, stretching down to Piccadilly, **Soho** offers an offbeat mix of sex shops, specialist record stores and fabric retailers, while the streets surrounding **Covent Garden** yield art and design, mainstream fashion, designer wear and camping gear; **Neal Street** is the place to go to indulge a shoe-shopping habit.

  Just off Piccadilly, **St James's** is the domain of the quintessential English gentleman, with the shops of **Jermyn Street** in particular dedicated to his grooming. Stultifyingly swanky **Knightsbridge**, further west, is home to Harrods and the big-name fashion stores of **Sloane Street** and **Brompton Road**. On the South Bank, east of the National Theatre, you'll find the craft market of **Gabriel's Wharf** and the appealing design shops of the **OXO Tower**. Less well known, and just a stone's throw from the bustle of Waterloo, **Lower Marsh** harbours a fantastic variety of one-off shops and studios on either side of the daily local street market.

  Hampstead, in a luxurious and leafy world of its own to the north of the centre, is a great place to spend an afternoon browsing upmarket fashion stores, posh delicatessens and patisseries, antiquarian booksellers and tasteful arts and crafts. **Greenwich**, south of the river, has an eclectic range of shops and markets, while **Richmond**, out to the west, has the mainstream staples and one-off boutiques in a swanky riverside setting. For an edgier experience, head for the east, where independent stores and markets in **Brick Lane**, **Hoxton** and **Spitalfields** specialize in quirky one-offs for hip young things. Other popular market areas, like **Camden**, **Greenwich** and **Portobello Road**, are good for small independent stores selling offbeat gear. At the other end of the scale, the **Westfield shopping centre**, which opened in 2008 in unlovely White City, is Europe's largest indoor shopping mall, with more than 250 chains from Topshop to Tiffany.

When to shop

Opening hours for central London shops are generally Monday to Saturday 9.30am to 6pm, although some stores stay open later, especially on Thursdays and in the weeks leading up to Christmas. Many shops also open on Sundays, generally from around noon to 5pm. If in doubt, phone ahead to check.

The cheapest time to shop in London is during one of the two big annual **sale seasons**, centred on January and July, when prices are routinely slashed by anything between twenty and seventy percent. The best place to find details of other discount events is in *Time Out* magazine's "Sell Out" section.

How to pay

Some stores, notably Selfridges and Harrods, will take payment in **euros**, although this is still quite rare. Market stalls tend to take cash only, or personal cheques in sterling (supported by a guarantee card) for more expensive items. Always keep receipts: whatever the shop may tell you, the law allows a full refund or replacement on purchases which turn out to be faulty. There's no such legal protection if you just decide you don't like something, but most retailers will offer a credit note.

Finally, non-UK visitors can sometimes claim back the **value-added tax** (VAT) that applies to most goods sold in British shops, although you will need to spend well over £100 for this to be worthwhile. On request, participating stores (there should be a Tax Free Shopping sticker in the window) will issue you with a form that you should hand in to Customs on your way out of the country – a simple till receipt will not do. There's a six-week wait for reimbursement.

Clothes and shoes

The listings below concentrate on the home-grown rather than the ubiquitous international names, but if it's **designer wear** you're after, bear in mind that nearly all the department stores below stock lines from major and up-and-coming names. For designer-style fashion at lower prices, try the more upmarket high-street **chains** such as Jigsaw and Whistles. Mango, Zara, Monsoon, H&M, Warehouse and Topshop are a good bet for cheaper versions of the same, while Primark is able to offer bargain-basement prices. For street, club, secondhand and vintage gear, also try London's **markets** (see p.444).

Although all London's **department stores** offer a huge range of high-quality goods under one roof, most specialize in fashion and food. Many of them are worth visiting just to admire the scale, architecture and interior design, and the majority have cafés or restaurants.

Fortnum & Mason 181 Piccadilly, W1 ☎020/7734 8040, ⓦwww.fortnumandmason .com; Green Park or Piccadilly Circus tube. A beautiful and eccentric 300-year-old store with heavenly murals, cherubs, chandeliers and fountains as a backdrop to its perfectly English offerings. Justly famous for its fabulous, pricey food, it also specializes in the best and most upmarket designer clothes, furniture, luggage and stationery.

Harrods 87–135 Brompton Rd, Knightsbridge, SW1 ☎020/7730 1234, ⓦwww .harrods.com; Knightsbridge tube. An enduring landmark of quirks and pretensions – don't wear shorts, a sleeveless t-shirt or a backpack, or you may fall foul of the draconian dress code. Harrods has everything, but is most notable for its Art Nouveau tiled food hall, the huge toy department and its range of designer labels.

Harvey Nichols 109–125 Knightsbridge, SW1 ☎020/7235 5000, ⓦwww.harveynichols .com; Knightsbridge tube. Absolutely fabulous, darling, with all the latest designer collections and shop assistants who look like models. The gorgeous cosmetics department is frequented by A- and Z-listers alike, while the fifth-floor food hall offers frivolous goodies at high prices.

John Lewis 278–306 Oxford St, W1 ☎020/7629 7711, ⓦwww.johnlewis.co.uk; Oxford Circus tube. Famous for being "never knowingly undersold", this reliable institution can't be beaten for basics. Every kind of button, stocking, pen and rug can be found here, along with reasonably priced and well-made clothes, furniture and household goods.

Liberty 210–220 Regent St, W1 ☎020/7734 1234, ⓦwww.liberty.co.uk; Oxford Circus tube. A fabulous emporium of luxury, this exquisite store, with its mock-Tudor exterior, is most famous for its fabrics, design and accessories, but also has an excellent reputation for both mainstream and high fashion. The perfume, cosmetics, gift and household departments are recommended, too.

Marks & Spencer 458 Oxford St, W1 ☎020/7935 7954, ⓦwww.marksandspencer .co.uk; Marble Arch tube. London's largest branch of this everyday British institution offers a huge range of own-brand clothes, food, homeware and furnishings. The underwear is essential, the ready-meals good value, and the clothes well made and reliable.

Selfridge's 400 Oxford St, W1 ☎0800/123 400, ⓦwww.selfridges.com; Bond Street tube. This huge, airy palace of clothes, food and furnishings was London's first great department store and remains its best. The vast mens- and womenswear departments offer mainstream designers and casual lines alongside hipper, younger names and labels. The food hall is superb, too.

Designer fashion

Browns 23–27 South Molton St, W1 ☎020/7514 0000, ⓦwww.brownsfashion.com; Bond Street tube. London's biggest range of designer wear, with international names and hip young things catering for women and men. Across the way, Browns Labels for Less (50 South Molton St, W1 ☎020/7514 0052) offers discounts.

Dover Street Market 17–18 Dover St, W1 ☎020/7518 0680, ⓦwww.doverstreetmarket .com; Green Park tube. Uber-cool six-floor megastore, showcasing directional designers such as Comme des Garçons, Hussein Chalayan and Azzedine Alaia.

Koh Samui 65 Monmouth St, WC2 ☎020/7240 4280, ⓦwww.kohsamui .co.uk; Leicester Square or Covent Garden tube. This elegant, eclectic and feminine one-stop boutique offers a highly selective range of designer womenswear – Chloe, Phillip Lim, Marc Jacobs – with stunning (and pricey) vintage pieces.

Paul Smith Westbourne House, 122 Kensington Park Rd, W11 ☏020/7727 3553, Notting Hill Gate tube, and 40–44 Floral St, WC2 ☏020/7379 7133, Covent Garden tube; ⓦwww.paulsmith .co.uk. Both the cosily contemporary Covent Garden store and the Notting Hill shop-in-a-house are worth a visit: they're ever so English in Smith's quirky way, and sell the range of his well-tailored and whimsical clothes and accessories for men, women and children. The Paul Smith Sale Shop (23 Avery Row, W1 ☏020/7493 1287; Bond Street tube) offers huge discounts, and is especially good for blokes.

Precious 16 Artillery Passage, E1 ☏020/7377 6668, ⓦwww.precious-london.com; Liverpool Street tube. An elegant little store tucked away in a narrow street near Spitalfields. Cool designer gear with a dressed-up feel, including accessories.

Vivienne Westwood 44 Conduit St, W1, and other branches ☏020/7439 1109, ⓦwww .viviennewestwood.com; Oxford Circus tube. Revered by the international fashion pack, this quintessentially English maverick is going strong. Punks-at-heart with money to burn should make for the historic World's End branch (430 King's Rd, SW10 ☏020/7352 6551; Sloane Square tube).

Budget and mid-range fashion

Equa 28 Camden Passage, N1 ☏020/7359 0955, ⓦwww.equaclothing.com; Angel tube. A fair trade and organic boutique for women, with a fresh and elegant feel.

Joy 432 Coldharbour Lane, SW9, and other branches ☏020/7787 9616, ⓦwww.joythestore .com; Brixton tube. A joy indeed, this lively store features fantastic imported designer fashion at high-street prices, from sassy streetwear to ballgowns, well-cut menswear to kitsch gifts.

The Laden Showroom 103 Brick Lane, E1 ☏020/7247 2431, ⓦwww.laden.co.uk; Aldgate East tube. Beloved of the hipper London celebs, the showroom showcases loads of independent designers, and is great for exuberant dressers on a budget. There is a small men's department.

New Look 500–502 Oxford St, W1 ☏020/7290 7860, ⓦwww.newlook.co.uk; Oxford Circus

tube. Unlike many of the pile 'em high stores, New Look is a member of the ETI (Ethical Trading Initiative), so you needn't feel guilty as you wade through the catwalk-inspired garments.

Oliver Bonas 22 Kensington Park Rd, W11 ☏020/7727 4932. A pretty store, with branches in most of the more villagey London neighbourhoods, selling vibrant, feminine clothing at very reasonable prices, along with bright homewares and accessories.

Topshop 214 Oxford St, W1, and many other branches ☏0844/848 7487, ⓦwww.topshop .co.uk or www.topman.co.uk; Oxford Circus tube. A big hit with both celebs and mere mortals, Topshop's flagship store is the place to go for this season's must-haves – with a vintage section and maternity gear, as well as the high-profile Kate Moss range – at a snip of the designer prices.

Vintage, retro and secondhand

Absolute Vintage 15 Hanbury St, E1 ☏020/7247 3883, ⓦwww.absolutevintage.co.uk; Liverpool Street/Aldgate East tube. A Spitalfields treasure trove of 1920s to 1980s clobber, with one of the biggest collections of vintage shoes in the UK. Its sister store, Blondie, a slightly more glamorous outfit filled with pre-loved designer gear, is around the corner at 114–118 Commercial St (☏020/7247 0050; Liverpool Street tube).

Annie's Vintage Costume & Textiles 10 Camden Passage, N1 ☏020/7359 0796; Angel tube. This well-stocked shop, draped in shimmering fabrics and specializing in fabulous 1920s and 1930s glamour – from party dresses and embroidered Chinese jackets to handmade shoes and suitcases – is a favourite with stylists and movie production artists.

The Antiques Clothing Shop 282 Portobello Rd, W10 ☏020/8964 4830; Ladbroke Grove tube. Lots of treasures in this store, with affordable Victoriana and vintage menswear a speciality.

🏃 **Beyond Retro** 110–112 Cheshire St (off Brick Lane), E2 ☏020/7613 3636, ⓦwww.beyondretro.com; Liverpool St tube. Cavernous warehouse of twentieth-century classics, with thousands of goodies including vintage jeans, 1950s frocks, battered cowboy boots, punk gear and disco-dolly gewgaws. Sister store Beyond

Retro Soho, 58 Great Marlborough St, glams it up a bit with a boudoir ambience (℡020/7434 1406; Oxford Circus tube).

The Emporium 330–332 Creek Rd, SE10 ℡020/8305 1670; Cutty Sark DLR or Greenwich train station from Charing Cross. Swanky retro store specializing in 1940s to 1960s clothes for men and women, and featuring kitsch and well-preserved bras, stockings, compacts and cigarette-holders.

The Loft 35 Monmouth St, WC2 ℡020/7240 3807, Ⓦwww.the-loft.co.uk; Covent Garden tube. A huge array of used designer clothes for men and women. Many are sourced from film shoots or the catwalk, so are in good nick. Labels include Jimmy Choo, Chanel and Alexander McQueen.

Modern Age Vintage Clothing 65 Chalk Farm Rd, NW1 ℡020/7482 3787, Ⓦwww.modern-age .co.uk; Chalk Farm tube. Splendid clobber (mostly menswear) for lovers of 1940s and 1950s American-style gear. The best bargains are on the rails outside.

Rokit 105–107 Brick Lane, E1 ℡020/7375 3864, Ⓦwww.rokit.co.uk; Aldgate East tube. Quintessential Brick Lane retro, nicely presented – you'll find sparkly knits, jeans, legwarmers and 1970s shades the size of dinnerplates, plus a host of goodies for the boys. Also at 225 Camden High St (℡020/7267 3046; Camden Town tube) and 42 Shelton St (℡020/7836 6547; Covent Garden tube).

Lingerie

Agent Provocateur 6 Broadwick St, W1 ℡020/7439 0229, Oxford Circus tube, plus other branches; Ⓦwww.agentprovocateur.com. Kitschy, glamorous undies displayed in a shamelessly sexy setting. From gingham bikinis with wet-look bows to fluffy mules with marabou trim, there's something to appeal to the diva in every girl.

Coco de Mer 23 Monmouth St, WC2 ℡020/7836 8882, Covent Garden tube; 108 Draycott Ave, SW3 ℡020/7584 7615, South Kensington tube; Ⓦwww.coco-de-mer.co.uk. Upmarket and stylish, this sex shop for women has an inviting boudoir feel, and Ann Summers it most certainly isn't. The lingerie ranges from floaty to filthy minded, but is always in the best possible taste. Pick up a feather tickler while you're here.

Rigby & Peller 2 Hans Rd, SW3 (Knightsbridge tube); 13 Kings Rd, SW3 (Sloane Square tube); 22a Conduit St, W1 (Oxford Circus tube);

℡0845 076 5545, Ⓦwww.rigbyandpeller.com. Corsetières to HM the Queen, if that can be counted as a recommendation, this old-fashioned store stocks a wide range of beautiful lingerie and swimwear, including designer names and its own range, for all shapes and sizes. The personal fitting service is deemed to be London's best.

Shoes

Birkenstock 70 Neal St, WC2 ℡020/7240 2783, Ⓦwww.birkenstock.co.uk; Covent Garden tube. Comfortable, well-crafted sandals and shoes in leather, suede, nubuck and vegan styles; for a spin on the classic designs, check the pretty Papillo range, the funky Footprints, and the extra-comfy Birkis.

Camper 39 Floral St, WC2, and many other branches ℡020/7379 8678, Ⓦwww.camper.es; Covent Garden tube. A Spanish store selling well-made, colourful and quirky shoes, many of which have different designs for the left and right feet.

Georgina Goodman 44 Old Bond St, W1 ℡020/7493 7673, Ⓦwww.georginagoodman .com; Green Park tube. Racy and eccentric women's shoes in a splash of colours, materials and styles – all trend-setting and covetable.

Manolo Blahnik 49–51 Old Church St, SW3 ℡020/7352 3833; Sloane Square tube. This secluded, exclusive store on a leafy street off the King's Rd is perfect for fantasy window-shopping, with the slender footwear worshipped by *Sex and the City*'s Carrie dramatically lit and theatrically framed.

Natural Shoe Store 13 Neal St, WC2, and other branches ℡020/7836 5254, Ⓦwww .thenaturalshoestore.com; Covent Garden tube. Worthy, socially responsible and ecologically sound shoes – stylish, comfortable and sometimes strange. Good value, but not cheap.

Sniff 1 Great Titchfield St, W1 ℡020/7299 3560, Oxford Circus tube; 115 Commercial St, E1 ℡020/7375 1580, Liverpool Street tube. Eclectic footwear boutique, with funky designer one-offs and big-name classics, all personally selected. Pop in for high-heeled Doc Marten boots, pretty Birkenstocks, Vivienne Westwood creations and Hoxton hipster wedges, all at reasonable prices.

Terra Plana 124 Bermondsey St, SE1 ℡020/7407 3758, Ⓦwww.terraplana .com, London Bridge tube; and 64 Neal St, WC2

ⓣ**020/7379 5959.** A brilliant option for ecofriendly shoe fetishists, Terra Plana make exuberant use of recycled materials. Proceeds from the Soul of Africa range go to fund facilities for AIDS orphans, and the innovative "barefoot" range uses a uniquely thin sole that claims to both strengthen your feet and increase your sex drive.

Books

As well as the big-name chain bookstores, most of which have branches throughout the city, London is blessed with a wealth of local, independent and specialist bookshops.

General interest

Blackwell's 100 Charing Cross Rd, WC2 ⓣ020/7292 5100, ⓦwww.bookshop.blackwell.co.uk; Tottenham Court Road or Leicester Square tube. The London flagship of Oxford's best academic bookshop is bigger than it looks and has a much wider range than you might expect. Its academic stock is, unsurprisingly, excellent, but so too is its range of computing, travel and fiction titles.

Borders Books & Music 203 Oxford St, W1, and other branches ⓣ020/7292 1600, ⓦwww.borders.co.uk; Oxford Circus tube. Enormous London flagship of the American import, boasting four floors of books alongside a huge range of CDs and magazines. Good range of titles, with staff recommendations and reviews, a solid children's section, regular readings and a coffee bar.

Foyles 113–119 Charing Cross Rd, WC2 ⓣ020/7437 5660, ⓦwww.foyles.co.uk; Tottenham Court Road tube. Long-established, huge and famous London bookshop with a big feminist section (Silver Moon) and Ray's Jazz Shop and café. There's a second, riverside, branch outside the Royal Festival Hall on the South Bank (ⓣ020/7440 3212; Waterloo tube).

Hatchards 187 Piccadilly, W1 ⓣ020/7439 9921, ⓦwww.hatchards.co.uk; Piccadilly Circus tube. A little overshadowed by the colossal Waterstone's down the road, the venerable Hatchards holds its own when it comes to quality fiction, biography, history and travel. The regal interiors are all you'd expect of a bookseller by appointment to HM the Queen.

Waterstone's 203–206 Piccadilly, W1, and other branches ⓣ020/7851 2400, ⓦwww.waterstones.co.uk; Piccadilly Circus tube. This flagship bookstore – Europe's largest – occupies the former Simpson's department store building and boasts a café, bar, gallery and events rooms as well five floors of books.

Independent and specialist

Arthur Probsthain Oriental & African Bookseller 41 Great Russell St, WC1 ⓣ020/7636 1096, ⓦwww.oriental-african-books.com; Tottenham Court Road tube. Connected to the nearby School of Oriental and African Studies, this impressive academic store covers all relevant aspects of art, history, science and culture.

Bookmarks 1 Bloomsbury St, WC1 ⓣ020/7637 1848, ⓦwww.bookmarks.uk.com; Tottenham Court Road tube. Leftist and radical fare in the heart of Bloomsbury, with a wide range of political biography, history, theory and assorted political ephemera. There's even a children's section.

Books for Cooks 4 Blenheim Crescent, W11 ⓣ020/7221 1992, ⓦwww.booksforcooks.com; Ladbroke Grove tube. Anything and everything to do with food at this wonderful new and used bookshop, which also has a tiny café (see p.290) offering cookery demonstrations, coffee and lunch (ring ahead to book).

The Calder Bookshop 51 The Cut, SE1 ⓣ020/7620 2900, ⓦwww.calderpublications.com; Waterloo tube. A fine little bookshop specializing in foreign fiction in translation. The weekly programme of talks and play- and poetry-readings draws a loyal audience of intellectuals.

Daunt Books 83 Marylebone High St, W1, and other branches ⓣ020/7224 2295, ⓦwww.dauntbooks.co.uk; Bond Street or Baker Street tube. Wide and inspirational range of travel literature as well as the usual guidebooks, presented by expert staff in the beautiful, galleried interior of this famous Edwardian shop.

European Bookshop 5 Warwick St, W1 ⓣ020/7734 5259, ⓦwww.europeanbookshop.com; Piccadilly Circus tube. This place has an excellent range of European-language (except Italian) books, and very helpful staff. For Italian books, head for The Italian Bookshop, 5 Cecil Court, W1 (☎020/7240 1634; Leicester Square tube).

Forbidden Planet 179 Shaftesbury Ave, WC2 ☎020/7420 3666, ⓦwww.forbiddenplanet.com; Tottenham Court Rd tube. Two jam-packed floors of all things science fiction- and fantasy-related, ranging from comics and graphic novels to books, games and ephemera.

Gay's the Word 66 Marchmont St, WC1 ☎020/7278 7654, ⓦfreespace.virgin.net/gays .theword; Russell Square tube. Long-established, renowned community bookshop, famed for the weekly lesbian discussion groups and readings held in the shop, and offering an extensive collection of lesbian and gay classics, pulps, contemporary fiction and nonfiction, plus cards and calendars.

Gosh! 39 Great Russell St, WC1 ☎020/7636 1011, ⓦwww.goshlondon.com; Tottenham Court Rd tube. All kinds of comics for the casually curious to the serious collector, with gorgeous vintage items, Manga, small-press oddities and superhero standards.

Housmans 5 Caledonian Rd, N1 ☎020/7837 4473, ⓦhousmans.com; King's Cross tube. Dilapidated and friendly store established in 1945, specializing in black, lesbian and gay fiction, plus socialism, anarchism and ecology, with cheap secondhand titles.

ICA Bookshop The Mall, SW1 ☎020/7766 1452, ⓦwww.ica.org.uk; Piccadilly Circus or Charing Cross tube. Tiny, artsy store with a strong style bent and lots of funky magazines, postcards and book imports.

🏃 **London Review Books** 14 Bury Place, WC1 ☎020/7269 9030, ⓦwww.lrbshop .co.uk; Tottenham Court Rd tube. All the books reviewed in the august literary journal and many, many more in this superb, tranquil Bloomsbury bookstore. Particularly strong on literary fiction, poetry, history, politics and current affairs, it hosts regular readings and events and has a nice little tearoom.

🏃 **Persephone Books** 59 Lamb's Conduit St, WC1 ☎020/7242 9292, Russell Square tube; and 109 Kensington Church St, W8 ☎020/7221 2201, Notting Hill Gate tube; ⓦwww.persephonebooks.co.uk. Lovely bookshop offspring of a publishing house that specializes in neglected early twentieth-century writing, mostly by women. The books (all £10) are beautifully produced, all

with endpapers in a textile design from the relevant period.

The School of Life Shop 70 Marchmont St, WC1 ☎020/7833 1010, ⓦwww.theschooloflife.com; Russell Square tube. A bijou little store, part of the ingenious and delightful School of Life concept, which aims to offer "good ideas for everyday living" – relationships, work, play, politics, philosophy – with its books, short courses, meals, "sermons" and holidays. Its "bibliotherapy" service can design you a bespoke reading list, on any subject or theme.

Stanford's Map and Travel Bookshop 12–14 Long Acre, WC2 ☎020/7836 1321, ⓦwww .stanfords.co.uk; Covent Garden tube. The world's largest specialist travel bookshop, selling pretty much any map of anywhere, plus a huge range of books, guides, literature, travel accessories and gifts.

Zwemmer Arts & Architecture 24 Litchfield St, WC2 ☎020/7240 4158, ⓦwww.zwemmerbooks .co.uk; Leicester Square tube. Specialist art bookstore with a fantastic and expert selection.

Secondhand and antiquarian

Any Amount of Books 56 Charing Cross Rd, WC2 ☎020/7836 3697, ⓦwww.anyamountofbooks .com; Leicester Square or Charing Cross tube. Wonderful, sprawling secondhand bookshop stocking everything from obscure fifty-pence bargains to rare and expensive first editions. Especially strong on fiction, the arts and literary biography.

Halcyon Books 1 Greenwich South St, SE10 ☎020/8305 2675, ⓦwww.halcyonbooks.co.uk; Greenwich DLR or train station from Charing Cross. A little stuffy, but packed with scholarly gems. Lots on military history, travel and languages, with some cheap paperback fiction.

Quinto 48a Charing Cross Rd, WC2 ☎0207/379 7669; Covent Garden tube. Another Charing Cross Rd treasure, this secondhand bookshop has a huge choice from battered paperbacks to precious first editions.

Riverside Walk under Waterloo Bridge on the South Bank, SE1; Waterloo or Embankment tube. An attractive book market by the Thames, offering everything from current and pulp fiction to obscure psychology textbooks and modern European poetry – most of it reasonably priced, although rarely a complete bargain.

Food and drink

As you'd expect of a city that has some of the best restaurants in the world, London offers great shopping for even the most discerning of food buffs. In the centre of town, **Soho and Covent Garden**, in particular, are a gourmand's delight: the former replete with Chinese supermarkets and Italian delicatessens, the latter harbouring health-conscious **Neal's Yard**. Numerous **supermarkets** line the high streets of nearly every residential area with the two biggest, Tesco and Sainsbury's, also making forays into the city centre; with late (and even 24hr) opening hours, all offer a good range of groceries and fresh foods and inexpensive lunch-on-the-go options. **Marks & Spencer** is excellent for fresh foods and quality ready-meals, as are the major department-store food halls (see box, p.436), while **specialist stores** and the many local **food markets** (see "Markets", p.444) offer a more atmospheric shopping experience.

The specialist **beer, wine and spirits** outlets listed are the pick of central London's numerous retailers, but you'll also find ever-improving ranges in the main supermarkets. Relaxed **licensing laws** mean that outlets no longer have to close between 3pm and 7pm on Sundays, although some – usually local, family-run places – still do.

Bakeries and patisseries

Konditor & Cook 22 Cornwall Rd, SE1 ☎020/7261 0456; Waterloo tube. A cut above your average bakery, *Konditor & Cook* (with five branches) make the most wonderful cakes, cupcakes, meringues and biscuits, as well as offering a choice of sandwiches, coffee and tea.

Louis' Patisserie 32 Heath St, NW3 ☎020/7435 9908; Hampstead tube. This fabulous old Hungarian patisserie has changed little since it opened in 1963. Breads, pastries and creamy European cakes galore, plus a very splendid tearoom.

Maison Bertaux 28 Greek St, W1 ☎020/7437 6007; Leicester Square tube. Delightful and eccentric old Soho hangout, selling fancy French cakes, tartlets, éclairs, croissants and the like, as well as savoury snacks. There's a hip little fashion store, Shop at Maison Bertaux, downstairs.

Patisserie Valerie 44 Old Compton St, W1 ☎020/7437 3466, Leicester Square tube; plus many other branches; ⓦwww.patisserie -valerie.co.uk. This beloved old Soho café dates back to the 1920s and still sells croissants, mousses and gooey cakes to die for.

Treacle 110 Columbia Rd, E2 ☎020/7729 5657, ⓦwww.treacleworld.com. Avoiding the supermodel smugness that came with the cupcake craze, this cute little tearoom in the heart of the flower market keeps things real, celebrating British

baking with scrumptious fairy cakes, Victoria sponges and fruit loaves, with a host of nostalgic crockery and cake stands to boot.

Cheese

Neal's Yard Dairy 17 Shorts Gardens, WC2 ☎020/7240 5700, Covent Garden tube; 6 Park St, Borough Market, SE1 ☎020/7367 0799, Borough tube; ⓦwww .nealsyarddairy.co.uk. Fragrant store packed to the rafters with quality cheeses from around the British Isles, with a few exceptionally good choices from further afield. You can taste before you buy.

Paxton & Whitfield 93 Jermyn St, SW1 ☎020/7930 0259, ⓦwww.paxtonandwhitfield .co.uk; Green Park or Piccadilly Circus tube. Quintessentially English, 200-year-old cheese shop offering a very traditional range of English and European varieties, plus fine wines and ports.

Coffee and tea

Monmouth Coffee Company 27 Monmouth St, WC2 ☎020/7379 3516, Covent Garden or Leicester Square tube; 2 Park St, Borough, SE1 ☎020/7940 9960, Borough tube; ⓦwww.monmouthcoffee.co.uk. A wonderful range of coffees, all roasted in the Covent Garden store, where they're served up with delicious chocolate-coated coffee beans in the tiny sampling room at the back.

R. Twining & Co 216 Strand, WC2 ☎020/7353 3511, ⊛www.twinings.com; Temple tube. The oldest established tea company in Britain has traded from these premises since the early eighteenth century. It stocks the full Twinings range and also hosts a small museum on the history of the company.
The Tea House 15a Neal St, WC2 ☎020/7240 7539; Covent Garden tube. The distinctive red-tiled facade conceals two fragrant floors of teas – black, green, white and caffeine-free – with a wealth of accessories including infusers, teapots and cosies.

Confectionery

Charbonnel et Walker 1 Royal Arcade, 28 Old Bond St, W1 ☎020/7491 0939, ⊛www .charbonnel.co.uk; Green Park or Piccadilly Circus tube. It might sound French, but this is a very English affair dating from 1875, offering beautifully presented chocolates, truffles and peppermint creams.
The Chocolate Society 36 Elizabeth St, SW1 ☎020/7259 9222, ⊛www.chocolate.co.uk; Sloane Square tube. A toney Belgravia "chocolate boutique" proffering precious handmade goodies, Valhrona treats, luxury hampers and creamy drinking chocolate.
Thorntons 2 The Market, WC2, and many other branches ☎020/7836 2173, ⊛www.thorntons .co.uk; Covent Garden tube. Massively popular chain selling good-quality chocolates, truffles, fudges and the like at affordable prices.

Delicatessens

The Delicatessen Shop 23 South End Rd, NW3 ☎020/7435 7315; Belsize Park tube. Small shop stuffed to the rafters with all manner of delights. Sells handmade chocolates and freshly made sandwiches alongside the cheeses and olives.
Verde's 40 Brushfield St, E1 ☎020/7247 1924, ⊛www.jeanettewinterson.com/verdes.asp; Liverpool Street tube. Tasteful if slightly precious Spitalfields deli owned by author Jeanette Winterson, who has preserved the original eighteenth-century shopfront and bareboard interior. All manner of classy deli goods including sumptuous fresh pasta and posh preserves. It also trades a few well-chosen antiques on the side. Next door, A. Gold is a similarly classy old establishment selling British foodstuffs: spiced ginger wine, sugar mice, Scotch eggs and black pudding.

World food

Brindisa Floral Hall, Stoney St, Borough Market, SE1, ☎0207/407 1036, ⊛www .brindisa.com, Borough tube. If you're craving pimientos, manchego, habas fritas and chorizo, this superb and stylish Spanish deli is the place for you.
G. Gazzano & Son 167 Farringdon Rd, EC1 ☎020/7837 1586; Farringdon tube. This fabulous Clerkenwell establishment has been keeping the area in Italian fare for a century, and the old wooden cabinets are still holding up under the weight of all that good-quality food.
I. Camisa & Son 61 Old Compton St, W1 ☎020/7437 7610; Leicester Square tube. The whole classic Italian deli range packed into one small Soho space. Excellent cheeses, salamis, pastas and dried foods, plus all the essential wines and spirits.
London Oriental Foods 122 Drummond St, NW1 ☎020/7387 3740; Euston or Euston Square tube. Excellent Bengali food store in London's most central Asian shopping and eating enclave; check out the rest of the street for more good Indian food stores.
Loon Fung Supermarket 42–44 Gerrard St, W1 ☎020/7437 7332; Leicester Square tube. This warren of a supermarket in the heart of Chinatown offers every kind of Chinese food item you can imagine, and probably some you can't. There's also a huge range of foods and groceries in the shops of neighbouring Newport St, Newport Place and Lisle St.
Taj Stores 112 Brick Lane, E1 ☎020/7377 0061; Aldgate East tube. Big South-Asian food store established in 1936, offering everything from halal meats, herbs and spices to fish, fruit and vegetables.

Wine, beer and spirits

Berry Bros & Rudd 3 St James's St, SW1 ☎0800 280 2440, ⊛www.bbr.com; Green Park tube. This well-stocked, 300-year-old establishment houses a huge range of fine wines from £5 to £5000.
Gerry's 74 Old Compton St, W1 ☎020/7734 4215, ⊛www.gerrys.co.uk; Leicester Square tube. Characterful old Soho store, crammed with the best, most eclectic and sometimes downright weird range of spirits you'll find anywhere in London; vodka is a speciality.

Royal Mile Whiskies 3 Bloomsbury St, WC1 ☎020/7436 4763, ⊛www.royalmilewhiskies .com; Tottenham Court Rd tube. Wide range of whiskies, brandies, gins and other spirits, with some bottled Scottish beers.

The Vintage House 42 Old Compton St, W1 ☎020/7437 2592, ⊛www.vintagehouse.co.uk; Leicester Square tube. Wines, brandies and more than seven hundred whiskies line the shelves of this family-run drinker's paradise in the heart of Soho.

Music

While the **megastores** collapse under the might of the MP3 – only HMV, at 150 Oxford St (☎020/7631 3423; Oxford Circus tube) remains, selling not only the latest releases but also an impressive backlist, a reassuring amount of vinyl and a good classical section – plenty of mainstream, independent and specialist **music shops** in London cater for the CD bulk-buyer and the obsessive rare-vinyl collector. London's markets, especially Camden, are also good sources of vinyl (see "Markets").

Independent, specialist and secondhand

Brill 27 Exmouth Market ☎020/7833 9757; Farringdon tube. Tiny CD store/café with a small but well-chosen selection of rock, pop, dance, country, soul and reggae. Good Fairtrade coffee, too.

Cheapo Cheapo Records 53 Rupert St, W1 ☎020/7437 8272; Piccadilly Circus tube. Not everything in this tiny spot is totally cheapo cheapo – but there's a lot that is. CDs, vinyl and most musical tastes catered for.

Dub Vendor 274 Lavender Hill, SW11 ☎020/7223 3757, ⊛www.dubvendor.co.uk; Clapham Junction train station from Victoria or Waterloo. Essential reggae outlet, with up-to-the-minute imports and good advice.

Gramex 25 Lower Marsh, SE1 ☎020/7401 3830; Lambeth North tube. A splendid find for classical-music lovers, this new and second-hand record store features CDs and vinyl, with some jazz, and comfy leather armchairs to sample or discuss your finds at leisure.

Honest Jon's 278 Portobello Rd, W10 ☎020/8969 9822, ⊛www.honestjons.com; Ladbroke Grove tube. Jazz, soul, funk, R&B, rare groove, dance, world music and much more, with current releases, secondhand finds and reissues.

MDC Classic Music Royal Festival Hall, SE1 ☎020/7620 0198, ⊛www.mdcmusic.co.uk; Waterloo tube. South Bank store stocking classical, world music and jazz CDs. Its sister store, at 31 St Martin's Lane, WC2

(☎020/7240 0270; Leicester Square tube), specializes in opera.

Music & Video Exchange 38 Notting Hill Gate, W11, and many other branches ☎08456/441 442, ⊛www.mveshops.co.uk; Notting Hill Gate tube. This enduring, expanding and busy secondhand and collectors' chain always has some unexpected finds.

Nudge Records 20 Hanbury St, E1 ☎020/7655 4823; Liverpool Street tube. A friendly store off Brick Lane, stocking reggae, roots, blues and ska – both vinyl and CDs – with lots of bargains.

Ray's Jazz Shop Foyles, 113–119 Charing Cross Rd, WC2 ☎020/7440 3205, ⊛www.foyles.co.uk; Leicester Square or Tottenham Court Road tube. Though now squeezed into a tiny section of the huge bookshop, the once great jazz store still has a fine selection of jazz and blues on vinyl and CD – but prices aren't low.

Rough Trade 130 Talbot Rd, W11 ☎020/7229 8541, ⊛www.roughtrade.com; Ladbroke Grove tube. Also in the Old Truman Brewery, 91 Brick Lane, E1 ☎020/7392 7788; Aldgate East tube. Historic indie specialist with knowledgeable, friendly staff and a dizzying array from electronica to hardcore and beyond.

Trax Records 55 Greek St, W1 ☎020/7734 0795, ⊛www.traxrecords.co.uk; Tottenham Court Road tube. Tiny but legendary record store specializing in gay-oriented dance music, including hi-NRG, trance, hard house and club classics.

Markets

London's **markets** are more than just a cheap alternative to high-street shopping: the best of them are significant holdouts for communities endangered by the heedless expansion of the city. You haven't really got to grips with London unless you've rummaged through the junk at Brick Lane on a Sunday morning, or haggled over a leather jacket at Camden. Do keep an eye out for **pickpockets**, however.

Bermondsey (New Caledonian) Bermondsey St and Long Lane, SE1; London Bridge tube. **Fri 5am–noon.** Huge antique market offering everything from obscure nautical instruments to pricey furniture. The real collectors arrive at dawn to pick up the bargains.

Berwick Street Berwick and Rupert streets, W1; Piccadilly Circus tube. **Mon–Sat 9am–6pm.** This famous and chaotic fruit and veg market is a piece of living Soho history, with ferociously fast vendors working the crowds like showmen. There's bread, fish, cheese and herbs, too, all very cheap after 4pm. You'll also find cheap clothes, tapes and CDs aplenty along Berwick Street's southerly extension, Rupert St.

Borough Market 8 Southwark St, SE1 ☎020/7407 1002, ⊛www.boroughmarket .org.uk; London Bridge or Borough tube. **Thurs 11am–5pm, Fri noon–6pm, Sat 9am–4pm.** Fine-food heaven – suppliers from all over the UK converge here to sell piles of organic

▲ Borough Market

veg, venison, fish, wines and home-baked goodies. The Victorian structure itself, with its slender grass-green wrought-iron columns, is lovely. Saturdays can be a crush.

Brick Lane Brick Lane, Cygnet and Sclater streets, E1; Bacon, Cheshire and Chilton streets, E2; Aldgate East or Liverpool Street tube. **Sun 6am–2pm.** Huge, sprawling, cheap and frenzied, this famous East End market is well worth getting up early for. Fruit and veg, household goods, clothes, antique furniture, scratched records and broken spectacles – it's hard to say what you can't find here, most of it going for a song.

Brixton Electric Ave, Pope's, Brixton Station and Atlantic rds, SW9 ⊛www.brixtonmarket.net; Brixton tube. **Mon, Tues & Thurs–Sat 8am–6pm, Wed 8am–3pm.** Based in the arcades just off Atlantic Rd, but spilling out along nearly all of the neighbouring streets, this huge, energetic market is the centre of Brixton life, offering a vast range of African and Caribbean foods, beauty products, records, clothes, fabrics and even triple-fast-action spiritual-cleanser-cum-floor-wash.

Broadway Market Broadway Market, E8 ⊛www .broadwaymarket.co.uk; London Fields rail. **Sat 9am–5pm.** This is a "farmers' style" foodies' market, so beware the distinction – you're not buying straight from the growers, as prices suggest. But the organic produce is terrific, and you can pick up some hip clothes and accessories, too.

Camden Camden High St to Chalk Farm Rd, NW1; Camden Town tube. The Goths' favourite is actually a gaggle of markets, segueing into each other and supplemented by lively stores and restaurants in the surrounding streets. Nearest Camden tube, Camden Market (Camden High St at Buck St; daily, but most action Thurs–Sun 9.30am–5.30pm) has around 200 stalls selling new, used, retro and young designer clothes, as well as jewellery, records and ephemera. Camden Lock (Camden Lock Place, off Chalk Farm Rd; daily 10am–6pm; outdoor stalls Sat & Sun 10am–6pm) offers mainly arts, crafts and clothes, with the shops adding a few hip designers, antique dealers and booksellers to the mix. Stables Yard (leading off from Camden Lock or from Chalk Farm Rd; daily, but most stalls Sat & Sun 10.30am–6pm) is a sprawling adventure of clubwear, more young designers, furniture, retro design, trinkets and antiques.

Columbia Road Columbia Rd, E2 ⓦ www .columbiaroad.info; Liverpool Street tube then bus #26 or Old St tube then bus #55. Sun 8am–2pm. Fabulous, funky flower market in the heart of the East End, with bargains galore, especially late in the day, for the serious plant-lover. Get here early, have breakfast in one of the many cafés or coffee stalls, and check out the increasingly hip shops while you're at it.

Greenwich Greenwich High Rd, Stockwell St and College Approach, SE10; Greenwich train station from Charing Cross or Cutty Sark DLR. Sprawling set of flea markets selling crafts, modern antiques, vintage clothes, bric-a-brac and furniture in a rather more scenic setting than Camden. Many places are open daily, but there's most activity at the weekends; antiques are the speciality on Thursday and Friday, with Thursday the best for unusual and distinctive collectibles. The surrounding streets, and the shops inside the covered market, offer more treasures, with lots of secondhand books and retro clothes.

Petticoat Lane Middlesex St and around, E1; Liverpool Street tube. Mon–Fri & Sun 9am–2pm. Cheap, cheerful and heaving, this famous clothes and bric-a-brac market (there's a lot of tat) is like any other local offering – but much, much bigger.

Portobello Road Portobello and Golborne rds, W10 and W11 ⓦ www.portobelloroad.co.uk; Ladbroke Grove or Notting Hill Gate tube. Antique market Sat 4am–6pm; surrounding shops Mon–Sat. Probably the best way to approach this enormous market is from the Notting Hill end, working your way through the antiques and bric-a-brac down to the fruit and veg stalls, and then under the Westway to the hip new and secondhand clothes stalls and shops. Friday is better than Saturday to pick up a bargain here. Still further up again, beyond Portobello Green, the secondhand becomes pure boot-sale material, laid out on rugs on the road. The Golborne Rd market is cheaper and less crowded, with some very attractive antique and retro furniture.

Ridley Road Ridley Rd, E8; Dalston Kingsland train station or Marble Arch tube then bus #30, or Old St tube then bus #67, #76, #149 or #236. Mon–Wed 9am–3pm, Thurs 9am–noon, Fri & Sat 9am–5pm. A great food and clothes market in the heart of Hackney, Ridley Rd, like Brixton Market, is worth travelling to for the sheer diversity of goods on display. African and Caribbean fruit, veg and fish predominate, but there are also Turkish and Asian staples and a long line of shops offering fabrics, hair and beauty products, old gospel albums, cheap shoes and clothes, and much else.

Spitalfields Commercial St, between Brushfield and Lamb streets, E1 ⓦ www.visitspitalfields .com; Liverpool St tube. Main market Mon–Fri 10am–4pm, Sun 9am–5pm; food market 10am–4pm. The East End's historic Victorian fruit and veg hall now houses an organic food, crafts and secondhand goods market. Lots of tasty food stalls and fabulous gifts.

Sunday Upmarket Old Truman Brewery, Brick Lane/Hanbury St, E1; Aldgate East or Liverpool Street tube. Sun 10am–5pm. Hip fashion and accessories for trendy Eastenders – vintage jewellery, limited edition t-shirts, handmade handbags – plus contemporary lighting, art and homewares, and some great food stalls.

31

Activities and sports

M any of the crucial international fixtures of the **football**, **rugby and cricket** seasons take place in the capital, and London also hosts one of the world's top tennis tournaments, **Wimbledon**. London will host the **2012 Olympics**, using several of the capital's existing venues such as Wembley, Wimbledon, Lord's and the Dome, as well as a number of new arenas built specifically for the Games in the Olympic Park in East London (see p.210), all of which should help to improve the city's less-than-brilliant sporting facilities.

On the domestic front, **football** (**soccer**) is the most popular sport, with London clubs Chelsea and Arsenal among Europe's top teams. The rest of the sporting calendar is chock-full of other quality events, ranging from the sedate pleasures of **county cricket** to the thrills of **greyhound racing** at Wimbledon. For up-to-the-minute details of sporting events in London, check *Time Out* or the *Evening Standard*.

For those who'd rather compete than spectate, London offers a wide range of reasonable facilities: council-run leisure centres and parks provide inexpensive access to **swimming pools**, **gyms**, **tennis courts** and so forth, while a host of private establishments cater for everyone from the pool-hall shark to the amateur canoeist – even **golf** enthusiasts can find a course within the city limits.

Spectator sports

For the top international events, it can be almost impossible to track down a ticket without paying over the odds through a ticket agency. Should you be thwarted in your attempts to gain admission, you can often fall back on **TV or radio coverage**. BBC Radio 5 Live (909 & 685 Mhz) has live commentaries on almost all major sporting events, while one of the free-to-view TV channels nearly always carries live transmission of international rugby and soccer. To watch some sports (including Premiership football), you'll need to find a TV that has the Sky stations – many pubs show Sky games (sometimes on big screens) to draw in custom.

Football

The English **football** (or **soccer**) season runs from mid-August to early May, when the **FA Cup Final** at Wembley finishes off the season. There are four professional leagues: at the top is the twenty-club Premiership, followed by the Championship and leagues one and two. There are London clubs in every single division, with around five or six in the Premiership at any one time.

Over the decades, London's most successful club by far has been **Arsenal**. However, since the arrival of Russian oil tycoon Roman Abramovich, fellow London club **Chelsea** have had a resurgence, winning the league for the first time in fifty years in 2005. Tickets for most Premiership games start at £30–40 and are virtually impossible to get hold of on a casual basis, though you may be able to see one of the Cup fixtures. It's a lot easier and cheaper to see a game in one of the lower leagues.

Most Premiership fixtures kick off at 3pm on Saturday, though there's also an early and late kick-off on Saturday, plus a couple on Sunday; all matches apart from the Saturday 3pm kick-offs are broadcast live on Sky TV.

National stadium

Wembley Stadium Wembley Way ☏0844/800 2755, ⓦwww.wembleystadium.com; Wembley Park or Wembley Central tube. The new 90,000-seat stadium, designed by Norman Foster and featuring a massive steel arch, is the most expensive soccer stadium in the world. The old stadium was the sole survivor of a much larger complex, constructed for the 1924 British Empire Exhibition, and served as the main focus for the 1948 Olympic Games. The most famous features of the old place were the now-demolished "twin towers", forever associated with England's historic victory here in the 1966 World Cup Final. Erected as a mute reference to the old Raj, they were, in fact, only added in 1963, to celebrate the hundredth anniversary of the Football League. Guided tours are available (daily 10am–4.30pm; £15).

Football clubs

Arsenal Emirates Stadium, Ashburton Grove, N7 ☏020/7704 4040, ⓦwww.arsenal.com; Arsenal tube.

Barnet Underhill Stadium, Barnet Lane, Barnet ☏020/8449 6325, ⓦwww.barnetfc.com. High Barnet tube.

Brentford Griffin Park, Braemar Rd ☏0845/345 6442, ⓦwww.brentfordfc.co.uk; Brentford train station from Waterloo.

Charlton Athletic The Valley, Floyd Rd, SE7 ☏0871/226 1905, ⓦwww.cafc.co.uk; Charlton train station from Charing Cross.

Chelsea Stamford Bridge, Fulham Rd, SW6 ☏020/7386 9373, ⓦwww.chelseafc.com; Fulham Broadway tube.

Crystal Palace Selhurst Park, Whitehorse Lane, SE25 ☏0871/200 0071, ⓦwww.cpfc.co.uk; Selhurst train station from Victoria.

Dagenham & Redbridge Glyn Hopkins Stadium, Victoria Rd, Dagenham ☏020/8592 1549, ⓦwww.daggers.co.uk; Dagenham East tube.

Fulham Craven Cottage, Stevenage Rd, SW6 ☏0870/442 1234, ⓦwww.fulhamfc.com; Putney Bridge tube.

Leyton Orient Matchroom Stadium, Brisbane Rd, E10 ☏0871/310 1883, ⓦwww.leytonorient .co.uk; Leyton tube.

Millwall The Den, Zampa Rd, SE16 ☏020/7231 9999, ⓦwww.millwallfc.co.uk; South Bermondsey train station from London Bridge.

Queens Park Rangers Loftus Road Stadium, South Africa Rd, W12 ☏0870/112 1967, ⓦwww .qpr.co.uk; White City tube.

Tottenham Hotspur White Hart Lane Stadium, Tottenham High Rd, N17 ☏0870/420 5000, ⓦwww.tottenhamhotspur.com; White Hart Lane train station from Liverpool Street.

West Ham United Upton Park, Green St, E13 ☏0870/112 2700, ⓦwww.whufc.co.uk; Upton Park tube.

Cricket

The **cricket** season runs from April to September. If you're new to cricket,

▲ Wembley Stadium

the best introduction is to go to an inter-county **Twenty20** knock-out match, which lasts three to four hours and represents the game at its most frenetic. The other option is to attend a match, either in one of the fast and furious **one-day competitions** or in the old-fashioned **county championship**. Games in the latter take place over the course of four days and are never sold out; tickets for all the above games cost in the region of £15–20. Two county teams are based in London: **Middlesex**, who play at Lord's, and **Surrey**, who play at The Oval.

Two international sides visit each summer and play a series of **Test matches** against England, which last up to five days. Tickets can be difficult unless you book months in advance, and cost £30 and upwards. However, not all matches last the full five days, so tickets for the fifth day are usually sold on the day and can cost as little as £10. In tandem with the full-blown five-day Tests, there's also a series of **one-day internationals**, two of which are usually held in London.

Cricket grounds

Lord's St John's Wood, NW8 ☎020/7432 1000, ⓦwww.lords.org; St John's Wood tube.
The Oval Kennington Oval, SE11 ☎0871/2461 100, ⓦwww.britoval.com; Oval tube.

Rugby

There are two types of rugby played in England. Thirteen-a-side **Rugby League** is played almost exclusively in the north of England. However, the Super League does feature one London club, **Harlequins**, who play at the Stoop Memorial Ground in Twickenham. The season runs from February to September, and games traditionally take place on Sundays at 3pm, but there are also matches on Friday and Saturday nights. The final of the knock-out Challenge Cup is traditionally held at Wembley Stadium (see p.447).

In London, however, virtually all rugby clubs play fifteen-a-side **Rugby Union**, which has upper-class associations and only went professional in 1995. **Harlequins**, who play at the same stadium as their Rugby League namesake, are the only Premiership team to actually play in London. Despite their names, **London Wasps** and **London Irish** play outside London. Matches are traditionally on Saturdays at 3pm and the season runs from September until May, finishing off with the two knock-out finals for the European Rugby Cup (better known as the Heineken Cup) and the European Challenge Cup.

International matches are played at **Twickenham Stadium**, but unless you're affiliated to a rugby club, it's tough (and expensive) to get a ticket. A better bet is to go and see a Premiership game, where there's bound to be an international player or two on display – you can usually get in for £20–40.

Major rugby stadiums and clubs

Harlequins Twickenham Stoop Stadium, Langhorn Drive, Twickenham ☎020/8410 6000, ⓦwww.quins.co.uk; Twickenham train station from Waterloo.
Twickenham Stadium Whitton Rd, Twickenham ☎0870/405 2000, ⓦwww.rfu.com; Twickenham train station from Waterloo.

Tennis

Tennis in England is synonymous with **Wimbledon**, the only Grand Slam tournament played on grass. The Wimbledon championships last a fortnight, in the last week of June and the first week of July. Getting hold of a **ticket** is a bit of a palaver. On weekdays, if you arrive early enough, you might get one of the 500 day tickets for the show courts (prices from around £40–100); otherwise, if you get there by 9am, you should get admission to the outside courts (where you'll catch some top players in the first week of the tournament), which costs £15–20. Avoid the middle Saturday, when thousands of people camp overnight.

An easier opportunity to see big-name players is the Men's Championship at **Queen's Club** in Hammersmith, which finishes a week before Wimbledon. Many of the male tennis stars use this tournament to acclimatize themselves to English grass-court conditions. As with Wimbledon, you have to apply for tickets in advance, although there are a limited number of returns on sale at 10am each day.

Tennis clubs

All England Lawn Tennis and Croquet Club
Church Rd, Wimbledon, SW19 ☎020/8971 2473, ⓦwww.wimbledon.org; Southfields or Wimbledon Park tube. For public-ballot tickets, you have to send a stamped, addressed envelope to the club for an application form (available from the August preceding the championship) and return it by December 31.

Queen's Club Palliser Rd, Hammersmith, W14 ☎020/7385 3421, ⓦwww.queensclub.co.uk; Barons Court tube. For priority booking for the Championships, you need to put your name on the Mailing List and you will be sent an application form in January.

Greyhound racing and motorsport

The most central London venue for watching greyhound racing is **Wimbledon** (Tues, Fri & Sat evenings; ☎0870/840 8905, ⓦwww.lovethe dogs.com; Wimbledon Park tube). Trackside admission costs £5. Evening meetings usually start around 7.30pm and finish at 10.30pm, and generally include around a dozen races. The stadium also hosts stock-car and banger races, every other Sunday from September to April (ⓦwww.spede worth.co.uk).

Participating sports

The following section lists most of the **sporting activities** possible in the capital. As a rule, the most reasonably priced facilities are provided by community leisure and sports centres, where you can simply turn and pay to use the facilities. Most boroughs also have membership schemes that allow you to use the facilities for free or give discounts to regular users.

Golf

At most places, you don't need to be a member – a pay-and-play round usually costs in the region of £15 – but it's often advisable to book ahead if you're playing at the weekend. There are also a few places closer to the city centre, where you can hone your driving and putting for considerably less. Below is a selection of the city's golf courses; for more information visit ⓦwww.londongolf.info.

Climbing walls

Indoor climbing centres are run by serious climbers, and you must be a registered climber to climb unsupervised. Registration is a fairly straightforward process, however, and you can rent helmet, harness and footwear when they get there; total novices should book themselves on a course. The hippest place to climb is at **The Castle**, Green Lanes, N4 (☎020/8211 7000, ⓦwww.castle -climbing.co.uk; Mon–Fri 2–10pm, Sat & Sun 10am–7pm), an old Victorian water pumping station that looks like a Hammer Horror Gothic castle. Another large-scale operation is the **Westway Climbing Centre**, Crowthorne Rd, W10 (☎020/8969 0992, ⓦwww.westwaysportscentre.org.uk; Mon–Wed & Fri 9.30am–10pm, Thurs 8am–10pm, Sat & Sun 10am–8pm), and there's also the smaller **Mile End Climbing Wall**, Haverfield Rd, E3 (☎020/8980 0289, ⓦwww.mileendwall.org .uk), in an old pipe-bending factory in the East End.

Central London Golf Centre Burntwood Lane, SW17 ☎020/8871 2468, ⓦwww.clgc.co.uk; Earlsfield train station from Vauxhall tube. Nine-hole course and a floodlit driving range.

Lee Valley Golf Course Picketts Lock Lane, N9 ☎020/8803 6900, ⓦwww.leevalleypark.org.uk; Ponders End train station from Liverpool Street. Eighteen-hole course.

Richmond Park Roehampton Gate, Richmond Park, SW15 ☎020/8876 3205, ⓦwww.richmondparkgolfclub.org.uk; Barnes train station from Waterloo, bus #371 or #65 from Richmond tube or bus #85 from Putney Bridge tube. Two eighteen-hole courses and a driving range.

Horseriding

Strange though it might seem, there are places in the metropolis where you can **saddle up**, though at quite a price – £25 per hour is the average. It's usually possible to borrow a hard hat, but you must wear shoes or boots with a heel.

Hyde Park Stables 63 Bathurst Mews, W2 ☎020/7823 2813, ⓦwww.hydeparkstables.com; Lancaster Gate tube. The only stables in central London, situated on the north side of Hyde Park. An hour's ride or lesson in a group costs £55–59, or £64–95 for a private lesson.

Lee Valley Riding Centre 71 Lea Bridge Rd, E10 ☎020/8556 2629, ⓦwww.leevalleypark.org.uk; bus #48, #55 or #56. Stables in northeast London by the River Lea. A one-hour class will cost £25, whereas private lessons cost upwards of £30 for half an hour.

Wimbledon Village Stables 24 High St, SW19 ☎020/8946 8579, ⓦwww.wvstables.com; Wimbledon tube. Hack over the wilds of Wimbledon Common and Richmond Park for £50–55 per hour. Private lessons available from British Horse Society-approved instructors at £70–75 per hour. Closed Mon.

Tennis

There are loads of reasonably priced outdoor **tennis courts** in London in council-run parks, which cost £5–10 an hour outdoors; the downside is that they are rarely maintained to perfect standard. If you want to book a court in advance, you sometimes have to join the local borough's registration scheme (£10–20 per year); we've given the phone numbers for the courts in the main central London parks or you could visit ⓦwww.londontennis.co.uk. However, during the day it's generally possible simply to turn up and get a court within half an hour or so, except during July and August, when the Wimbledon tournament spurs a mass of couch potatoes into activity.

Battersea Park SW11 ☎020/8871 7542, ⓦwww.batterseapark.org; Battersea Park train station from Victoria.

Highbury Fields N1 ☎020/7226 2334; Highbury & Islington tube.

Holland Park W8 ☎020/7361 3003; High Street Kensington tube.

Hyde Park W2 ☎020/7262 3474, ⓦwww.royalparks.gov.uk; South Kensington tube.

Islington Tennis Centre Market Rd, N7 ☎020/7700 1370, ⓦwww.aquaterra.org; Caledonian Road tube. Outdoor and indoor courts.

Paddington Recreation Ground W9 ☎020/7625 4303; Maida Vale tube.

Regent's Park W9 ☎020/7486 4216, ⓦwww.royalparks.gov.uk; Maida Vale tube.

Swimming pools, gyms and leisure centres

Below is a selection of the best-equipped and most central of London's multipurpose **leisure centres**. Of the city's many council-run indoor swimming pools, almost all also have fitness classes and gyms; for local addresses visit ⓦwww.yell.com. Wherever you go, an indoor swim will usually cost you around £4. For an alfresco dip, see the box opposite.

Ironmonger Row Baths Ironmonger Row, EC1 ☎020/7253 4011, ⓦwww.aquaterra.org; Old St tube. An old-fashioned kind of place that attracts all shapes and sizes, with a steam room, sauna, small plunge pool, masseurs, a lounge area with beds, and a large pool. Admission for a three-hour weekday morning steam room session is a bargain £8 (Mon–Fri) or around £14 (weekday from noon & all day weekends). Men: Tues & Thurs 9am–9.30pm, Sat 9am–6.30pm; women: Wed & Fri 9am–9.30pm, Sun 10am–6.30pm; mixed: Mon 2–9.30pm.

Open-air swims

If you fancy an alfresco dip, check out the places listed below and visit Ⓦwww .londonpoolscampaign.com.

Brockwell Lido Brockwell Park, SE24 Ⓣ020/7274 3088, Ⓦwww.brockwelllido.com; Herne Hill train station. Laid-back lido at the heart of Brixton's Brockwell Park. May & Sept Mon–Fri 6.30–10am & 4–8pm, Sat & Sun 10am–6pm; June–Aug Mon–Fri 6.30am–8pm or later, Sat & Sun 10am–6pm.

Hampstead Ponds Hampstead Heath, NW3 Ⓦ020/7485 5757, Ⓦwww.cityoflondon .gov.uk; Hampstead tube. The Heath has three natural ponds: the Women's and Men's ponds are on the Highgate side, while the Mixed Bathing Pond is nearer Hampstead. Daily 7 or 8am–9pm or dusk.

Hampton Pool Hampton High St, Hampton Ⓣ020/8255 1116, Ⓦwww.hamptonpool .co.uk; bus #R68, #111, #R70 & #285. Heated outdoor pool on the western edge of Bushy Park, about a mile's walk from Hampton Court Palace. Open all year; phone for hours.

London Fields Lido London Fields, E8 Ⓣ020/7254 9038, Ⓦwww.gll.org; London Fields train station from Liverpool Street. Refurbished interwar lido with a 164ft heated outdoor pool. Open daily all year round, but hours vary.

Oasis 32 Endell St, WC2 Ⓣ020/7831 1804, Ⓦwww.gll.org; Tottenham Court Rd tube. The outdoor pool is small, but the water is heated to a bath-like temperature and it's open all year. Mon–Fri 6.30am–10pm, Sat & Sun 9.30am–6pm.

Parliament Hill Lido Gordon House Road, NW5 Ⓣ020/7485 5757. Beautiful 200ft by 90ft open-air pool with Art Deco touches and notoriously chilly water. Daily: May to mid-Sept 7am–8pm; mid-Sept to April 7am–noon.

Pools on the Park Old Deer Park, Richmond Ⓣ020/8940 0561. Not in fact in Richmond Park, but in the Old Deer Park near the Thames, adjacent to modern leisure centre. Easter to Sept Mon–Fri 6.30am–8pm, Sat & Sun 8am–5.45pm.

Serpentine Lido Hyde Park, W2 Ⓣ020/7706 3422, Ⓦwwwserpentinelido.com. Offers 110yd of swimming in Hyde Park's lake, plus a paddling pool; deck chairs and sun loungers for rent. Mid-June to mid-Sept daily 10am–6pm.

Tooting Bec Lido Tooting Bec Rd, SW16 Ⓣ020/8871 7198. At 300ft by 100ft, this is England's (and one of Europe's) largest freshwater, open-air swimming pools. Mid-May to Aug daily 6am–8pm, Sept 6am–5pm.

Oasis Sports Centre 32 Endell St, WC2 Ⓣ020/7831 1804, Ⓦwww.gll.org; Covent Garden tube. Oasis has two pools, one of which is the only heated outdoor pool in central London, open in all weather. Other facilities include a gym, a health suite with sauna and sunbed, massage and squash courts. Pools: Mon–Fri 6.30am–10pm, Sat & Sun 9.30am–6pm.

Porchester Spa 225 Queensway, W2 Ⓣ020/7792 3980, Ⓦwww.courtneys.co.uk; Bayswater or Queensway tube. Built in the 1920s, the Porchester's baths are well worth a visit for the Art Deco tiling alone. Admission is around £22 for a three-hour session, and entitles you to use the saunas, steam rooms, plunge pool, jacuzzi and swimming pool. Men: Mon, Wed & Sat 10am–10pm; women: Tues, Thurs, Fri 10am–10pm, Sun 10am–4pm; couples Sun 4–10pm.

The Sanctuary 12 Floral St, WC2 Ⓣ01442/430 330, Ⓦwww.thesanctuary.co.uk; Covent Garden tube. For a day of serious self-indulgence, this women-only club in Covent Garden is the place to go: the interior is filled with lush tropical plants and you can swim naked in the pool. It's a major investment at £45–80 for day/eve membership, but your money gets you unlimited use of the pool, jacuzzi, sauna and steam room, plus one sunbed session. Mon & Tues 9.30am–6pm, Wed–Fri 9.30am–8pm, Sat & Sun 9.30am–8pm.

32

Kids' London

London is a great place for children and it needn't overly strain the parental pocket. **Covent Garden**'s buskers and jugglers provide no-cost entertainment in a car-free setting (see p.139). Another great area to head for is the **South Bank** (see p.220) and Southwark, which are connected by a traffic-free riverside walk that stretches from the **London Eye** (see p.224) to Tower Bridge. And if you don't fancy the walk, there are now plenty of **boats** stopping off at piers along the way (see p.26).

Don't underestimate the value of London's **public transport** as a source of fun, either – and remember kids travel free (see p.24). The Underground is a buzz for a lot of kids, and you can get your bearings while entertaining your offspring by installing them in the front seats on the top deck of a **red double-decker bus**. The driverless **Docklands Light Railway** (see p.25) is another source of amusement, too – grab a seat at the front of the train and pretend to be driver; at Island Gardens, you can take the foot tunnel under the river to Greenwich. Alternatively, you can go transport-mad at the **London Transport Museum** (see p.141), which has been redesigned with kids in mind.

The spread of **shows** on offer is at its best during school holidays, when even the biggest theatres often stage family entertainment. This is also the case at Christmas, when there's a glut of traditional British **pantomimes**, stage shows based on folk stories or fairy tales, invariably featuring a showbiz star or two, and often with an undercurrent of innuendo aimed at the adults. If that's too passive for you, there are plenty of indoor **play centres** where children can burn off some excess energy. And of course, **London Zoo** (p.291) and the **Aquarium** (see p.225) are surefire winners.

Museums

Museums are an obvious diversion and many of the big museums are free of charge. The **Science Museum** (see p.264), the **Natural History Museum** (see p.266) and the **National Maritime Museum** (see p.324), in particular, have hi-tech, hands-on sections that will keep young kids busy for hours, and they might even learn something while they're at it. At the other end of the scale, the **London Dungeon** (see p.237) and **Madame Tussaud's**, with its infamous Chamber of Horrors (see p.102), remain very popular with teenagers, but are among the most expensive sights in the entire city.

Smaller museums specifically designed with children in mind include the **Horniman Museum** (see p.319), which houses an aquarium, and **Kew Bridge Steam Museum**, which runs a miniature steam train at the weekends. There are also museums devoted to childhood and toys, from the atmospheric

City farms

Free fun is available at the city's various working farms, the majority of them located in London's East End. The website ⓦ www.farmgarden.org.uk is also worth a visit for details of other, smaller gardens and wildlife havens in London.

Brooks Farm Skelton's Lane Park, Leyton, E10 ⓣ020/8539 4278, ⓦwww.lbwf.gov .uk; Leyton tube. Very much a community resource, this farm has pigs, goats, Shetland ponies, llamas and more, as well as its own allotments and an adventure playground. Tues–Sun: April–Oct 10.30am–12.30pm & 1.30–5.30pm; Nov–March 9.30am–12.30pm & 1.30–4.30pm.

Freightliners Farm Sheringham Road, N7 ⓣ020/7609 0467, ⓦwww.freightlinersfarm .org.uk; Highbury & Islington or Holloway Road tube. Small farm (and café) with cows, pigs, goats, hens, ducks, geese, sheep and giant rabbits. Tues–Sun 10am–4.45pm; winter closes 4pm.

Hackney City Farm 1a Goldsmith's Row, E2 ⓣ020/7729 6381, ⓦwww.hackney cityfarm.co.uk; Bethnal Green tube. Converted brewery that's now a small city farm (with an excellent café), housing cows, sheep, pigs, hens, turkeys, chinchillas, degus, rabbits and a donkey; also has an organic garden. Weekend kids' activities. Tues–Sun 10am–4.30pm.

Kentish Town City Farm 1 Cressfield Close, Grafton Rd, NW5 ⓣ020/7916 5421, ⓦwww.aapi.co.uk/cityfarm; Chalk Farm or Kentish Town tube. Five acres of farmland with cows, horses, pigs, goats, sheep and chickens. Tues–Sun 9.30am–5.30pm.

Mudchute City Farm Pier St, E14 ⓣ020/7515 5901, ⓦwww.mudchute.org; Mudchute, Crossharbour or Island Gardens DLR. Covering some 35 acres, this is London's largest city farm, with farmyard animals, llamas, pets' corner, equestrian centre and café. Fantastic location with great views of Canary Wharf. Tues–Sun 9.30am–4.30pm.

Spitalfields City Farm Weaver St, E1 ⓣ020/7247 8762, ⓦwww.spitalfieldscityfarm .org; Shoreditch tube. Another tiny East End farm (with a shop and café) housing sheep, donkeys, goats, pigs, ducks, geese, rabbits and guinea pigs. Also runs a propagation scheme and organic vegetable garden. Tues–Sun: April–Sept 10am–4.30pm; Oct–March 10am–4pm.

Stepping Stones Farm Stepney Way, E1 ⓣ020/7790 8204, ⓦwww.stepping stonesfarm.org.uk; Stepney Green tube. A rural haven in the East End, with cows, pigs, goats, sheep, rabbits, ferrets and hamsters. Also has a coffee shop, nature trail and toddlers' play area. Tues–Sun 10am–4pm.

Surrey Docks Farm Rotherhithe Street, SE16 ⓣ020/7237 6525, ⓦwww.surrey docksfarm.org; Surrey Quays tube. A corner of southeast London set aside for goats, sheep, donkeys, chickens, pigs, ducks and bees in hives, with a smithy and a dairy. Tues–Sun 10am–5pm.

Vauxhall City Farm Tyers St, SE11 ⓣ020/7582 4204, ⓦwww.vauxhallcityfarm .org.uk; Vauxhall tube. Little city farm with sheep, pigs, ducks, ponies and donkeys. Activities at weekends and on holidays. Wed–Sun 10.30am–4pm.

Pollock's Toy Museum (see p.112) to the much larger V&A outpost, the **Museum of Childhood** (see p.211).

Parks

Right in the centre of the city, there are plentiful green spaces, such as **St James's Park** (see p.76) and **Regent's Park** (see p.289), providing playgrounds and ample room for general mayhem, as well as a diverting array of city wildlife. If you want something more unusual than ducks and squirrels, head for one of London's several **city farms** (see box, p.453), which provide urbanites with a free taste of country life. Below is a list of the best parks and playgrounds.

Battersea Park Albert Bridge Rd, SW11 ☎020/8871 7539 (playground), ⓦwww .batterseapark.org; Battersea Park or Queens-town Road train station from Victoria. The park has an excellent free adventure playground, a boating lake and a children's zoo (ⓦwww .batterseaparkzoo.co.uk). Playground: term time weekdays 3.30–7pm, Sat 11am–6pm; holidays Mon–Sat 11am–6pm. Zoo: daily 10am–5pm; adults £6.50, children 3–12 £4.95. See p.275.

Camley Street Natural Park 12 Camley St, NW1 ☎020/7833 2311, ⓦwww.wildlondon.org.uk; King's Cross St Pancras tube. Canalside wildlife haven, run by the London Wildlife Trust, with pond dipping and a good info centre. Daily 10am–5pm; free. See p.138.

Coram's Fields 93 Guilford St, WC1 ☎020/7837 6138, ⓦwww.coramsfields.org; Russell Square tube. Very useful, centrally located playground with lots of water and sand play plus mini-farm with hens, horses, sheep, goats and ducks. Adults admitted only if accompa-nied by a child. Veggie café. Daily 9am–7pm or dusk; free. See p.138.

Hampstead Heath NW3 ☎020/7485 4491, ⓦwww.cityoflondon.gov.uk; Hampstead tube, Gospel Oak or Hampstead Heath train station. Nine hundred acres of grassland and woodland, with superb views of the city. Excellent kite-flying potential, too, and plenty of playgrounds, sports facilities, music

events and fun days throughout the summer. Open daily 24hr. See p.307.

Hyde Park/Kensington Gardens W8 ☎020/7298 2100, ⓦwww.royalparks.gov.uk; Hyde Park Corner, Knightsbridge, Lancaster Gate or Queensway tube. Hyde Park is central London's main open space and now features the Diana Fountain in which the kids can dip their feet; in Kensington Gardens (daily 6am to dusk), adjoining its western side, you can find the famous Peter Pan statue and a groovy playground also dedicated to Princess Diana. Daily 5am–midnight. See p.249.

Kew Gardens Richmond, Surrey ☎020/8332 5000, ⓦwww.kew.org; Kew Gardens tube. Come here for the edifying open spaces, though the glasshouses usually go down well too, and there's a small aquarium in the basement of the Palm House. Daily 9.30am–5.30pm or dusk; adults £13, children under 17 free. See p.345.

Richmond Park Richmond, Surrey ☎020/8948 3209, ⓦwww.royalparks.gov.uk; Richmond tube or train station from Waterloo. A fabulous stretch of countryside, with opportunities for duck-feeding, deer-spotting, mushroom-hunting and cycling. Playground situated near Petersham Gate or toddlers' play area near Kingston Gate. Daily: March–Sept 7am–dusk; Oct–Feb 7.30am–dusk. See p.350.

Theatre, puppetry and circuses

Shows that appeal to children play in the West End all the time. What follows is a pretty selective rundown of theatre, puppetry and circuses that are consist-ently aimed at kids. For the latest listings, check out the "Children" section of *Time Out*.

Half Moon Young People's Theatre 43 Whitehorse Rd, E1 ☎020/7709 8900, ⓦwww.halfmoon.org .uk; Limehouse DLR, Stepney Green tube. Well-established theatre that hosts touring youth shows, puts on its own productions, and runs a programme of workshops and theatre sessions for over-5s. Sept–April Sat 11.30am & 2pm; all tickets £5.

Little Angel Puppet Theatre 14 Dagmar Passage, off Cross St, N1 ☎020/7226 1787,

ⓦwww.littleangeltheatre.com; Angel tube. London's only permanent puppet theatre, with shows usually on Saturdays and Sundays at 11am and 2pm. Extra perform-ances during holidays. No babies are admitted. Adults £10, children £8.

Polka Theatre 240 The Broadway, SW19 ☎020/8543 4888, ⓦwww.polkatheatre.com; Wimbledon or South Wimbledon tube. Aimed at kids aged up to around 12, this is a

Music

There are plenty of **free music** options worth looking out for: the Barbican (see p.179) puts on excellent weekend foyer concerts; the Royal Festival Hall (see p.222) and the National Theatre (see p.223) run regular seasonal festivals where you can catch some world-class music. In addition, most of the established orchestras run special **children's concerts**: look out for the London Philharmonic Orchestra (Ⓦwww.lpo.org.uk), London Symphony Orchestra (Ⓦlso.co.uk) and National Children's Orchestra (Ⓦwww.nco-gb.org.uk).

specially designed junior arts centre, with two theatres, a playground, a café and a toyshop. Storytellers, puppeteers and mime artists make regular appearances. Tickets £10–16.

Puppet Theatre Barge Little Venice, W2 Ⓣ020/7249 6876 or 07836/202745, Ⓦwww.puppetbarge.com; **Warwick Avenue tube.** Wonderfully imaginative marionette shows on a unique fifty-seat barge moored in Little Venice from October to July, and at Richmond in August and September. Shows usually start at around 3pm at weekends and in the holidays. Adults £10, children £8.50.

Tricycle Theatre 269 Kilburn High Rd, NW6 Ⓣ020/7328 1000, Ⓦwww.tricycle.co.uk; **Kilburn tube.** High-quality children's shows Sept–June Saturdays at 11.30am & 2pm. Budding thespians can also attend drama and dance workshops after school and during the holidays; for toddlers, a performance workshop/playgroup. Tickets £5.

Unicorn Theatre Tooley St, SE1 Ⓣ020/7645 0560, Ⓦwww.unicorntheatre.com; **London Bridge tube.** The oldest professional children's theatre in London now lives in purpose-built premises near City Hall in Southwark. Shows run the gamut from story-telling sessions and traditional plays to creative-writing workshops and mime and puppetry. Tickets £10.

Zippo's Circus Ⓣ0871/210 2100, Ⓦwww.zipposcircus.co.uk. Zippo's Circus performs in and around London for much of the year. It's a totally traditional, big-top circus offering a variety of standard acts from clowning and tightrope walking to acrobatic budgies and equine tricks, compered by an old-fashioned ringmaster. Adults £8–20, children £6–14.

▲ Puppet Theatre Barge

Indoor adventure play centres and swimming pools

Most local leisure centres offer "soft play" sessions for pre-school toddlers during the week. Listed below are some of the bigger operations which also cater for older children.

Bramley's Big Adventure 136 Bramley Rd, W10 ☎020/8960 1515, ⓦwww.bramleysbig.co.uk; **Latimer Road or Ladbroke Grove tube.** Indoor play centre with sophisticated equipment suitable for children up to 11 and magazines for bored adults. Tues–Fri 10.30am–6pm, Sat & Sun 10am–6.30pm; £3.50–5.50 for 2hr or more.

Discover 1 Bridge Terrace, E15 ☎020/8536 5555, ⓦwww.discover.org.uk; **Stratford tube.** A hands-on interactive creative learning centre with a great outdoor play garden, aimed at story-building for under-11s. Tues–Fri noon–1pm & 3–5pm, Sat & Sun 11am–5pm; £4.

Waterfront Leisure Centre High St, Woolwich, SE18 ☎020/8317 5000, ⓦwww.gll.org; **Woolwich Arsenal train station from Charing Cross.** Massive Wild and Wet adventure swimming pool with 100ft-plus slide, wave machine, waterfall and all the usual aquatic high-jinks. Under-3s free; 3–15s from £2; adults £5.40. Term time Mon–Thurs 4–8pm, Fri 4–6pm, Sat 9am–1pm & 2–5pm, Sun 9am–5pm; holidays Mon–Fri 10am–8pm, Sat & Sun 2–5pm.

Contexts

Contexts

History

The citizens of London are universally held up for admiration and renown for the elegance of their manners and dress, and the delights of their tables…The only plagues of London are the immoderate drinking of fools and the frequency of fires.

William Fitzstephen, companion of Thomas Becket

Conflagrations and drunkenness certainly feature strongly in London's complex two-thousand-year history. What follows is a highly compressed account featuring riots and revolutions, plagues, fires, slum clearances, lashings of gin, Ken Livingstone and the London people. For more detailed histories, see p.476.

Legends

Until Elizabethan times, most Londoners believed that London had been founded around 1000 BC as New Troy or *Troia Nova* (later corrupted to Trinovantum), capital of Albion (aka Britain), by the Trojan prince **Brutus**. At the time, according to medieval chronicler Geoffrey of Monmouth, Britain was "uninhabited except for a few giants", several of whom the Trojans subsequently killed. They even captured one called Goemagog (more commonly referred to as Gogmagog), who was believed to be the son of Poseidon, Greek god of the sea, and whom one of the Trojans, called Corineus, challenged to unarmed combat and defeated.

For some reason, by late medieval times, Gogmagog had become better known as two giants, **Gog and Magog**, whose statues can still be seen in the Guildhall (see p.180) and on the clock outside St Dunstan-in-the-West (see p.170). According to Geoffrey of Monmouth's elaborate genealogical tree, Brutus is related to Leir (of Shakespeare's *King Lear*), Arthur (of the Round Table) and eventually to **King Lud**. Around 70 BC, Lud is credited with fortifying New Troy and renaming it *Caer Ludd* (Lud's Town), which was later corrupted to Caerlundein and finally London.

So much for etymology and mythology. Archeologists and historians tell a different story, and though there is evidence of scattered Celtic settlements along the Thames, no firm proof exists to show that central London was permanently settled before the arrival of the Romans.

Roman Londinium

Julius Caesar led several small cross-Channel incursions in 55 and 54 BC, but it wasn't until nearly a century later, in **43 AD**, that a full-scale invasion force of some forty thousand Roman troops landed in Kent. Britain's rumoured mineral wealth was certainly one motive behind the Roman invasion, but the immediate spur was the need of Emperor Claudius, who owed his power to the army, for an easy military triumph. The Romans defeated the main Celtic tribe of southern Britain, the Catuvellauni, on the Medway, southeast of London, crossed the Thames and then set up camp to await the triumphant arrival of Claudius, his elephants and the Praetorian Guard.

It's now thought that the site of this first Roman camp was, in fact, in Westminster – the lowest fordable point on the Thames – and not in what is now the City. However, around 50 AD, when the Romans decided to establish the permanent military camp of **Londinium** here, they chose a point further downstream, building a bridge some 50 yards east of today's London Bridge. London became the hub of the Roman road system, but it was not the Romans' principal colonial settlement, which remained at **Camulodunum** (modern Colchester) to the northeast.

In 60 AD, the East Anglian people, known as the Iceni, rose up against the invaders under their queen **Boudicca** (or Boadicea) and sacked Camulodunum, slaughtering most of the legion sent from Lindum (Lincoln) and making their way to the ill-defended town of Londinium. According to archeological evidence, Londinium was burnt to the ground and, according to the Roman historian, Tacitus, whose father-in-law was in Britain at the time (and later served as its governor), the inhabitants were "massacred, hanged, burned and crucified". The Iceni were eventually defeated, and Boudicca committed suicide (62 AD).

In the aftermath, Londinium emerged as the new commercial and administrative (though not military) **capital of Britannia**, and was endowed with an imposing basilica and forum, a governor's palace, temples, bathhouses and an amphitheatre (see p.181). Archeological evidence suggests that Londinium was at its most prosperous and populous from around 80 AD to 120 AD, during which time it is thought to have evolved into the empire's fifth largest city north of the Alps.

Between 150 AD and 400 AD, however, London appears to have sheltered less than half the former population, probably due to economic decline. Nevertheless, it remained strategically and politically important and, as an imperial outpost, actually appears to have benefited from the chaos that engulfed the rest of the empire during much of the third century. In those uncertain times, **fortifications** were built, three miles long, 15ft high and 8ft thick, with a large fort, whose ragstone walls can still be seen near today's Museum of London (see p.180), home to many of the city's most significant Roman finds.

In 406 AD, the Roman army in Britain mutinied for the last time and invaded Gaul under the self-proclaimed Emperor Constantine III. The empire was on its last legs, and the Romans were never in a position to return, officially abandoning the city in **410 AD** (when Rome was sacked by the Visigoths), and leaving the country and its chief city at the mercy of the marauding Saxon pirates, who had been making increasingly persistent raids on the coast since the middle of the previous century.

Saxon Lundenwic and the Danes

Roman London appears to have been more or less abandoned from the first couple of decades of the fifth century until the ninth century. Instead, the **Anglo-Saxon** invaders, who controlled most of southern England by the sixth century, appear to have settled, initially at least, to the west of the Roman city. When Augustine was sent to reconvert Britain to Christianity, the Saxon city of **Lundenwic** was considered important enough to be granted a bishopric, in 604, though it was Canterbury, not London, that was chosen as the seat of the Primate of England. Nevertheless, trade flourished once more during this period, as attested by the Venerable Bede, who wrote of London in 730 as "the mart of many nations resorting to it by land and sea".

In 841 and 851 London suffered Danish Viking attacks, and it may have been in response to these raids that the Saxons decided to reoccupy the walled Roman city. By 871 the **Danes** were confident enough to attack and established London as their winter base, but in 886 Alfred the Great, King of Wessex, recaptured the city, rebuilt the walls and formally re-established London as a fortified town and a trading port. After a lull, the Vikings returned once more during the reign of Ethelred the Unready (978–1016), attacking unsuccessfully in 994, 1009 and 1013. The following year, the Danes, under Swein Forkbeard, finally recaptured London, only for Ethelred to reclaim it later that year, with help from King Olaf of Norway. In 1016, following the death of Ethelred, and his son, Edmund Ironside, the Danish leader Cnut (or Canute), son of Swein, became King of All England, and made London the national capital (in preference to the Wessex base of Winchester), a position it has held ever since.

Danish rule lasted only 26 years, and with the death of Cnut's two sons, the English throne returned to the House of Wessex, and to Ethelred's exiled son, **Edward the Confessor** (1042–66). Edward moved the court and church upstream to Thorney Island (or the Isle of Brambles), where he built a splendid new palace so that he could oversee construction of his "West Minster" (later to become Westminster Abbey). Edward was too weak to attend the official consecration and died just ten days later: he is buried in the great church he founded, where his shrine has been a place of pilgrimage for centuries. Of greater political and social significance, however, was his geographical separation of power, with royal government based in **Westminster**, while the **City of London** remained the commercial centre.

1066 and all that

On his deathbed in the new year of 1066, the celibate Edward made Harold, Earl of Wessex, his appointed successor. Having crowned himself in the new abbey – establishing a tradition that continues to this day – Harold went on to defeat his brother Tostig (who was in cahoots with the Norwegians), but was himself defeated by **William of Normandy** (aka William the Conqueror) and his invading army at the Battle of Hastings. On Christmas Day of 1066, William crowned himself king in Westminster Abbey. Elsewhere in England, the Normans ruthlessly suppressed all opposition, but in London, William granted the City a charter guaranteeing to preserve the privileges it had enjoyed under Edward. However, as an insurance policy, William also built three forts in the city, of which the sole remnant is the White Tower, now the nucleus of the **Tower of London**. As a further precaution, he also established another castle, a day's march away at **Windsor** and, like his predecessor, Edward, based the court at Westminster.

Over the next few centuries, the City waged a continuous struggle with the monarchy for a degree of self-government and independence. After all, when there was a fight over the throne, the support of London's wealth and manpower could be decisive, as **King Stephen** (1135–54) discovered, when Londoners attacked his cousin and rival for the throne, Mathilda, daughter of Henry I, preventing her from being crowned at Westminster. Again, in 1191, when the future **King John** (1199–1216) was tussling with William Longchamp over the kingdom during the absence of Richard the Lionheart (1189–99), it was the Londoners who made sure Longchamp remained cooped up in the Tower. For this particular favour,

London was granted the right to elect its own sheriff, or lord mayor, an office that was officially acknowledged in the Magna Carta of 1215.

Occasionally, of course, Londoners backed the wrong side, as they did when they turned up at Old St Paul's to accept **Prince Louis of France** (the future Louis VIII) as ruler of England during the barons' rebellion against King John in 1216, and again with Simon de Montfort, when he was engaged in civil war with **Henry III** (1216–72) during the 1260s. As a result, the City found itself temporarily stripped of its privileges. In any case, London was chiefly of importance to the medieval kings as a source of wealth, and traditionally it was to the Jewish community, which arrived in 1066 with William the Conqueror, that the sovereign turned for a loan. By the second half of the thirteenth century, however, the Jews had been squeezed dry, and in 1290, after a series of increasingly bloody attacks, **London's Jews** were expelled by Edward I (1272–1307), who turned instead to the City's Italian merchants for financial assistance.

From the Black Death to the Wars of the Roses

London backed the right side in the struggle between Edward II (1307–27) and his queen, Isabella, who, along with her lover Mortimer, succeeded in deposing the king. The couple's son Edward III (1327–77) was duly crowned, and London enjoyed a period of relative peace and prosperity, thanks to the wealth generated by the wool trade. All this was cut short, however, by the arrival of the Europe-wide bubonic plague outbreak, known as the **Black Death**, in 1348. This disease, carried by black rats and transmitted to humans by flea bites, wiped out something like two-thirds of the capital's 75,000 population in the space of two years. Other epidemics followed in 1361, 1369 and 1375, creating a volatile economic situation that was worsened by the financial strains imposed on the capital by having to bankroll the country's involvement in the Hundred Years' War with France.

Matters came to a head with the introduction of the poll tax, a head tax imposed in the 1370s on all men regardless of means. During the ensuing **Peasants' Revolt** of 1381, London's citizens opened the City gates to Wat Tyler's Kentish rebels and joined in the lynching of the archbishop, plus countless rich merchants and clerics. Tyler was then lured to meet the boy-king Richard II at Smithfield, just outside the City, where he was murdered by Lord Mayor Walworth, who was subsequently knighted for his treachery. Tyler's supporters were fobbed off with promises of political changes that never came, as Richard unleashed a wave of repression and retribution.

Parallel with this social unrest were the demands for clerical reforms made by the scholar and heretic **John Wycliffe**, whose ideas were keenly taken up by Londoners. His followers, known as **Lollards**, made the first translation of the Bible into English in 1380. Another sign of the elevation of the common language was the success enjoyed by Geoffrey Chaucer (c.1340–1400), a London wine merchant's son, whose *Canterbury Tales* was the first major work written in English and was later one of the first books to be printed.

After the Peasants' Revolt, the next serious disturbance was **Jack Cade's Revolt**, which took place in 1450. An army of 25,000 Kentish rebels – including gentry, clergy and craftsmen – defeated King Henry VI's forces at Sevenoaks, marched to Blackheath, withdrew temporarily and then eventually reached Southwark in early July. Having threatened to burn down London Bridge, the insurgents entered the City and spent three days wreaking vengeance on their enemies before being ejected. A subsequent attempt to enter the City via London Bridge was repulsed, and the army was dispersed with yet more false promises. The reprisals, which became known as the "harvest of heads", were as harsh as before – Cade himself was captured, killed and brought to the capital for dismemberment.

A decade later, the country was plunged into more widespread conflict during the so-called **Wars of the Roses**, the name now given to the strife between the rival noble houses of Lancaster and York. Londoners wisely tended to sit on the fence throughout the conflict, only committing themselves in 1461, when they opened the gates to the Yorkist king Edward IV (1461–70 and 1471–83), thus helping him to depose the mad Henry VI (1422–61 and 1470–71). In 1470, Henry, who had spent five years in the Tower, was proclaimed king once more, only to be deposed again a year later, following Lancastrian defeats at the battles of Barnet and Tewkesbury.

Tudor London

The **Tudor** family, which with the coronation of **Henry VII** (1485–1509) emerged triumphant from the mayhem of the Wars of the Roses, reinforced London's pre-eminence during the sixteenth century, when the Tower of London and the royal palaces of Whitehall, St James's, Richmond, Greenwich, Hampton Court and Windsor provided the backdrop for the most momentous events of the period. At the same time, the city's population, which had remained constant at around fifty thousand since the Black Death, increased dramatically, trebling in size during the course of the century.

One of the crucial developments of the century was the English **Reformation**, the separation of the English Church from Rome, a split initially prompted not by doctrinal issues, but by the failure of Catherine of Aragon, first wife of **Henry VIII** (1509–47), to produce a male heir. In fact, prior to his desire to divorce Catherine, Henry, along with his lord chancellor, Cardinal Wolsey, had been zealously persecuting Protestants. However, when the Pope refused to annul Henry's marriage, Henry knew he could rely on a large amount of popular support, as anti-clerical feelings were running high. By contrast, Henry's new chancellor, Thomas More, wouldn't countenance divorce, and resigned in 1532. Henry then broke with Rome, appointed himself head of the English Church and demanded both citizens and clergy swear allegiance to him. Very few refused, though More was among them, becoming the country's first Catholic martyr with his execution in 1535.

Henry's most far-reaching act, by far, though, was his **Dissolution of the Monasteries**, a programme commenced in 1536 in order to bump up the royal coffers. The Dissolution changed the entire fabric of both the city and the country: previously dominated by its religious institutions, London's property market was suddenly flooded with confiscated estates, which were quickly snapped up and redeveloped by the Tudor nobility.

Henry may have been the one who kickstarted the English Reformation, but he was, in fact, a religious conservative, and in the last ten years of his reign he succeeded in executing as many Protestants as he did Catholics. Religious turmoil only intensified in the decade following Henry's death. First, Henry's sickly son, **Edward VI** (1547–53), pursued a staunchly anti-Catholic policy. By the end of his short reign, London's churches had lost their altars, their paintings, their relics and virtually all their statuary. After an abortive attempt to secure the succession of Edward's Protestant cousin, Lady Jane Grey, the religious pendulum swung the other way for the next five years with the accession of "**Bloody Mary**" (1553–58). This time, it was Protestants who were martyred with abandon at Tyburn and Smithfield.

Despite all the religious strife, the Tudor economy remained in good health for the most part, reaching its height in the reign of **Elizabeth I** (1558–1603), when the piratical exploits of seafarers Walter Ralegh, Francis Drake, Martin Frobisher and John Hawkins helped to map out the world for English commerce. London's commercial success was epitomized by the millionaire merchant Thomas Gresham, who erected the **Royal Exchange** in 1572, establishing London as the premier world trade market.

The 45 years of Elizabeth's reign also witnessed the efflorescence of a specifically **English Renaissance**, especially in the field of literature, which reached its apogee in the brilliant careers of **Christopher Marlowe**, **Ben Jonson** and **William Shakespeare**. The presses of **Fleet Street**, established a century earlier by William Caxton's apprentice Wynkyn de Worde, ensured London's position as a centre for the printed word. Beyond the jurisdiction of the City censors, in the entertainment district of Southwark, whorehouses, animal-baiting pits and theatres flourished. The carpenter-cum-actor James Burbage designed the first purpose-built playhouse in 1576, eventually rebuilding it south of the river as the **Globe Theatre**, where Shakespeare premiered many of his works (the theatre has since been reconstructed; see p.232).

From Gunpowder Plot to Civil War

On Elizabeth's death in 1603, James VI of Scotland became **James I** (1603–25) of England, thereby uniting the two crowns and marking the beginning of the **Stuart dynasty**. His intention of exercising religious tolerance after the anti-Catholicism of Elizabeth's reign was thwarted by the public outrage that followed the **Gunpowder Plot** of 1605, when Guy Fawkes and a group of Catholic conspirators were discovered attempting to blow up the king at the state opening of Parliament. James, who clung to the medieval notion of the divine right of kings, inevitably clashed with the landed gentry who dominated Parliament, and tensions between Crown and Parliament were worsened by his persecution of the Puritans, an extreme but increasingly powerful Protestant group.

Under James's successor, **Charles I** (1625–49), the animosity between Crown and Parliament came to a head. From 1629 to 1640 Charles ruled without the services of Parliament, but was forced to recall it when he ran into problems in Scotland, where he was attempting to subdue the Presbyterians. Faced with extremely antagonistic MPs, Charles attempted unsuccessfully to arrest several of their number at Westminster. Acting on a tip-off, the MPs fled by river to the City, which sided with Parliament. Charles withdrew to Nottingham, where he raised his standard, the opening military act of the **Civil War**.

London was the key to victory for both sides, and as a Parliamentarian stronghold it came under attack almost immediately from Royalist forces. Having defeated the Parliamentary troops to the west of London at Brentford in November 1642, the way was open for Charles to take the capital. Londoners turned out in numbers to defend their city, some twenty-four thousand assembling at Turnham Green. A stand-off ensued, Charles hesitated and in the end withdrew to Reading, thus missing his greatest chance of victory. A complex system of fortifications was thrown up around London, but was never put to the test. In the end, the capital remained intact throughout the war, which culminated in the execution of the king outside Whitehall's Banqueting House in January 1649.

For the next eleven years England was a **Commonwealth** – at first a true republic, then, after 1653, a Protectorate under **Oliver Cromwell**, who was ultimately as impatient of Parliament and as arbitrary as Charles had been. London found itself in the grip of the Puritans' zealous laws, which closed down all theatres, enforced observance of the Sabbath and banned the celebration of Christmas, which was considered a papist superstition.

Plague and fire

Just as London proved Charles I's undoing, so its ecstatic reception of **Charles II** (1660–85) helped ease the **Restoration** of the monarchy in 1660. The "Merry Monarch" immediately caught the mood of the public by opening up the theatres, and he encouraged the sciences by helping the establishment of the **Royal Society** for Improving Natural Knowledge, whose founder members included **Christopher Wren**, **John Evelyn** and **Isaac Newton**.

The good times that rolled in the early period of Charles's reign came to an abrupt end with the onset of the **Great Plague** of 1665. Epidemics of bubonic plague were nothing new to London – there had been major outbreaks in 1593, 1603, 1625, 1636 and 1647 – but the combination of a warm summer and the chronic overcrowding of the city proved calamitous in this instance. Those with money left the city (the court moved to Oxford), while the poorer districts outside the City were the hardest hit. The extermination of the city's dog and cat population – believed to be the source of the epidemic – only exacerbated the situation by allowing the flea-carrying rat population to explode. In September, the death toll peaked at twelve thousand a week, and in total an estimated hundred thousand lost their lives.

A cold snap in November extinguished the plague, but the following year London had to contend with yet another disaster, the **Great Fire** of 1666. As with the plague, outbreaks of fire were fairly commonplace in London, whose buildings were predominantly timber-framed, and whose streets were narrow, allowing fires to spread rapidly.

Within five years, nine thousand houses had been rebuilt with bricks and mortar (timber was banned), and fifty years later **Christopher Wren** had almost single-handedly rebuilt all the City churches and completed the world's first Protestant cathedral, **St Paul's**. Medieval London was no more, though the grandiose masterplans of Wren and other architects had to be rejected due to the legal intricacies of property rights within the City. The **Great Rebuilding**, as it was known, was one of London's most remarkable achievements – and all achieved in spite of a chronic lack of funds, a series of very severe winters and continuing wars against the Dutch.

Religious differences once again came to the fore with the accession of Charles's Catholic brother, **James II** (1685–88), who successfully put down the Monmouth Rebellion of 1685, but failed to halt the "Glorious Revolution" of 1688, which brought the Dutch king William of Orange to the throne, much to most people's relief. **William** (1689–1702) and his wife **Mary** (1689–95), daughter of James II, were made joint sovereigns, having agreed to a Bill of

The Great Fire

In the early hours of September 2, 1666, the **Great Fire** broke out at Farriner's, the king's bakery in Pudding Lane. The Lord Mayor refused to lose any sleep over it, dismissing it with the line "Pish! A woman might piss it out." Pepys was also roused from his bed, but saw no cause for alarm. Four days and four nights later, the Lord Mayor was found crying "like a fainting woman", and Pepys had fled, having famously buried his Parmesan cheese in the garden: the Fire had destroyed some four-fifths of the City of London, including 87 churches, 44 livery halls and 13,200 houses. The medieval city was no more.

Miraculously, there were only eight recorded fatalities, but 100,000 people were made homeless. "The hand of God upon us, a great wind and the season so very dry", was the verdict of the parliamentary report on the Fire, but Londoners preferred to blame Catholics and foreigners. The poor baker eventually "confessed" to being an agent of the pope and was executed, after which the following words, "but Popish frenzy, which wrought such horrors, is not yet quenched", were added to the Latin inscription on the Monument (see p.226), and only erased in 1830.

Rights defining the limitations of the monarch's power and the rights of his or her subjects. This, together with the Act of Settlement of 1701 – which among other things barred Catholics, or anyone married to one, from succession to the throne – made Britain the first country in the world to be governed by a **constitutional monarchy**, in which the roles of legislature and executive were separate and interdependent. A further development during the reign of **Anne** (1702–14), second daughter of James II, was the Act of Union of 1707, which united the English and Scottish parliaments.

Georgian London

When Queen Anne died childless in 1714 (despite having given birth seventeen times), the Stuart line ended, though pro-Stuart or Jacobite rebellions continued on and off until 1745. In accordance with the Act of Settlement, the succession passed to a non-English-speaking German, the Duke of Hanover, who became **George I** (1714–27) of England. As power leaked from the monarchy, the king ceased to attend cabinet meetings (which he couldn't understand anyway), his place being taken by his chief minister. Most prominent among these chief ministers or "prime ministers", as they became known, was **Robert Walpole**, the first politician to live at **10 Downing Street**, and effective ruler of the country from 1721 to 1742.

Meanwhile, London's expansion continued unabated. The shops of the newly developed **West End** stocked the most fashionable goods in the country, the volume of trade more than tripled, and London's growing population – it was by now the largest city in the world, with a population rapidly approaching one million – created a huge market for food and other produce, as well as fuelling a building boom. In the City, the **Bank of England** – founded in 1694 to raise funds to conduct war against France – was providing a sound foundation for the economy. It could not, however, prevent the mania for financial speculation that resulted in the fiasco of the **South Sea Company**, which in 1720 sold shares in its monopoly of trade in the Pacific and along the east coast of South America. The "bubble" burst when the shareholders took fright at the extent of their own investments, and the value of the shares dropped to nothing, reducing many to penury and almost wrecking the government, which was saved only by the astute intervention of Walpole.

Wealthy though London was, it was also experiencing the worst mortality rates since records began in the reign of Henry VIII. Disease was rife in the overcrowded immigrant quarter of the East End and other slum districts, but the real killer during this period was **gin**. It's difficult to exaggerate the effects of the gin-drinking orgy which took place among the poorer sections of London's population between 1720 and 1751. At its height, gin consumption was averaging two pints a week for every man, woman and child, and the burial rate exceeded the baptism rate by more than 2:1. The origins of this lay in the country's enormous surplus of corn, which had to be sold in some form or another to keep the landowners happy. Deregulation of the distilling trade was Parliament's answer, thereby flooding the urban market with cheap, intoxicating liquor, which resulted in an enormous increase in crime, prostitution, **child mortality** and general misery among the poor. Papers in the Old Bailey archives relate a typical story of the period: a mother who "fetched her child from the workhouse, where it had just been 'new-clothed', for the afternoon. She strangled it and left it in a ditch in Bethnal Green in order to sell its clothes. The money was spent on gin." Eventually, in the face of huge vested interests, the government was forced to pass an Act in 1751 that restricted gin retailing and brought the epidemic to a halt.

Policing the metropolis was an increasing preoccupation for the government. It was proving a task far beyond the city's three thousand beadles, constables and nightwatchmen, who were, in any case, "old men chosen from the dregs of the people who have no other arms but a lantern and a pole", according to one French visitor. As a result, crime continued unabated throughout the eighteenth century, so that, in the words of Horace Walpole, one was "forced to travel even at noon as if one was going into battle". The government imposed draconian measures, introducing **capital punishment** for the most minor misdemeanours. The prison population swelled, transportations began, and 1200 Londoners were hanged at Tyburn's gallows.

Despite such measures, and the passing of the Riot Act in 1715, rioting remained a popular pastime among the poorer classes in London. Anti-Irish riots had taken place in 1736; in 1743 there were further riots in defence of cheap liquor; and in the 1760s there were more organized mobilizations by supporters of the great agitator **John Wilkes**, calling for political reform. The most serious insurrection of the lot, however, were the **Gordon Riots** of 1780, when up to fifty thousand Londoners went on a five-day rampage through the city. Although anti-Catholicism was the spark that lit the fire, the majority of the rioters' targets were chosen not for their religion but for their wealth. The most dramatic incidents took place at Newgate Prison, where thousands of inmates were freed, and at the Bank of England, which was saved only by the intervention of the military – and John Wilkes, of all people. The death toll was in excess of three hundred, 25 rioters were subsequently hanged, and further calls were made in Parliament for the establishment of a proper police force.

Nineteenth-century London

The **nineteenth century** witnessed the emergence of London as the capital of an empire that stretched across the globe. The world's largest enclosed **dock system** was built in the marshes to the east of the City, Tory reformer **Robert**

Peel established the world's first civilian **police force**, and the world's first public-transport network was created, with horse-buses, trains, trams and an underground railway.

The city's population grew dramatically from just over one million in 1801 (the first official census) to nearly seven million by 1901. **Industrialization** brought pollution and overcrowding, especially in the slums of the East End. Smallpox, measles, whooping cough and scarlet fever killed thousands of working-class families, as did the cholera outbreaks of 1832 and 1848–49. The **Poor Law** of 1834 formalized **workhouses** for the destitute, but these failed to alleviate the problem, in the end becoming little more than prison hospitals for the penniless. It is this era of slum life and huge social divides that Dickens evoked in his novels.

Architecturally, London was changing rapidly. **George IV** (1820–30), who became Prince Regent in 1811 during the declining years of his father, George III, instigated several grandiose projects that survive to this day. With the architect **John Nash**, he laid out London's first planned processional route, Regent Street, and a prototype garden city around **Regent's Park**. The Regent's Canal was driven through the northern fringe of the city, and Trafalgar Square began to take shape. The city already boasted the first secular public museum in the world, the **British Museum**, and in 1814 London's first public art gallery opened in the suburb of Dulwich, followed shortly afterwards by the National Gallery, founded in 1824. London finally got its own university, too, in 1826.

The accession of **Queen Victoria** (1837–1901) coincided with a period in which the country's international standing reached unprecedented heights, and as a result Victoria became as much a national icon as Elizabeth I had been. Though the intellectual achievements of Victoria's reign were immense – typified by the publication of Darwin's *The Origin of Species* in 1859 – the country saw itself above all as an imperial power founded on industrial and commercial prowess. Its spirit was perhaps best embodied by the great engineering feats of **Isambard Kingdom Brunel** and by the **Great Exhibition** of 1851, a display of manufacturing achievements from all over the world, which took place in the Crystal Palace, erected in Hyde Park.

Despite being more than twice the size of Paris, London did not experience the political upheavals of the French capital – the terrorists who planned to wipe out the cabinet in the **1820 Cato Street Conspiracy** were the exception (see p.105). Mass demonstrations and the occasional minor fracas preceded the passing of the **1832 Reform Act**, which acknowledged the principle of popular representation (though few men and no women had the vote), but there was no real threat of revolution. London doubled its number of MPs in the new parliament, but its own administration remained dominated by the City oligarchy.

The **Chartist movement**, which campaigned for universal male suffrage (among other things), was much stronger in the industrialized north than in the capital, at least until the 1840s. Support for the movement reached its height in the revolutionary year of 1848. In March, some ten thousand Chartists occupied Trafalgar Square and held out against the police for two days. Then, on April 10, the Chartists organized a mass demonstration on Kennington Common. The government panicked and drafted in eighty thousand "special constables" to boost the capital's four thousand police officers, and troops were garrisoned around all public buildings. In the end, London was a long way off experiencing a revolution: the demo took place, but the planned march on Parliament was called off.

The birth of local government

The first tentative steps towards a cohesive form of metropolitan govern-ment were taken in 1855 with the establishment of the **Metropolitan Board of Works** (**MBW**). Its initial remit only covered sewerage, lighting and street maintenance, but it was soon extended to include gas, fire services, public parks and slum clearance. The achievements of the MBW – and in particular those of its chief engineer, **Joseph Bazalgette** – were immense, creating an underground sewer system (much of it still in use), improving transport routes and wiping out some of the city's more notorious slums. However, vested interests and resistance to reform from the City hampered the efforts of the MBW, which was also found to be involved in widespread malpractice.

In 1888 the **London County Council** (**LCC**) was established. It was the first directly elected London-wide government, though as ever the City held on jealously to its independence (and in 1899, the municipal boroughs were set up deliberately to undermine the power of the LCC). The arrival of the LCC coincided with an increase in working-class militancy within the capital. In 1884, 120,000 gathered in Hyde Park to support the ultimately unsuccessful London Government Bill, while a demonstration held in 1886 in Trafalgar Square in protest against unemployment ended in a riot through St James's. The following year the government banned any further demos, and the resultant protest brought even larger numbers to Trafalgar Square. The brutality of the police in breaking up this last demonstration led to its becoming known as "Bloody Sunday".

In 1888 the Bryant & May matchgirls won their landmark **strike action** over working conditions, a victory followed up the next year by further successful strikes by the gasworkers and dockers. Charles Booth published his seventeen-volume *Life and Labour of the People of London* in 1890, providing the first clear picture of the social fabric of the city and shaming the council into action. In the face of powerful vested interests – landlords, factory owners and private utility companies – the LCC's Liberal leader-ship attempted to tackle the enormous problems, partly by taking gas, water, electricity and transport into municipal ownership, a process that took several more decades to achieve. The LCC's ambitious housing programme was beset with problems, too. Slum clearances only exacerbated overcrowding, and the new dwellings were too expensive for those in greatest need. Rehousing the poor in the suburbs also proved unpopular, since there was a policy of excluding pubs, traditionally the social centre of working-class communities, from these developments.

While half of London struggled to make ends meet, the other half enjoyed the fruits of the richest nation in the world. Luxury establishments such as The Ritz and Harrods belong to this period, which was personified by the dissolute and complacent Prince of Wales, later **Edward VII** (1901–10). For the masses, too, there were new entertainments to be enjoyed: music halls boomed, public houses prospered, and the circulation of populist newspapers such as the *Daily Mirror* topped one million. The first "Test" cricket match between England and Australia took place in 1880 at the Kennington Oval in front of twenty thousand spectators, and during the following 25 years nearly all of London's professional football clubs were founded.

From World War I to World War II

Public patriotism peaked at the outbreak of **World War I** (1914–18), with crowds cheering the troops off from Victoria and Waterloo stations, convinced the fighting would all be over by Christmas. In the course of the next four years London experienced its first aerial attacks, with Zeppelin raids leaving some 650 dead, but these were minor casualties in the context of a war that destroyed millions of lives and eradicated whatever remained of the majority's respect for the ruling classes.

At the war's end in 1918, the country's social fabric was changed drastically as the voting franchise was extended to all men aged 21 and over and to women of 30 or over. The tardy liberalization of women's rights – largely due to the radical **Suffragette** movement led by Emmeline Pankhurst and her daughters – was not completed until 1928, the year of Emmeline's death, when women were at last granted the vote on equal terms with men.

Between the wars, London's population increased dramatically, reaching close to nine million by 1939, and representing one-fifth of the country's population. In contrast to the nineteenth century, however, there was a marked shift in population out into the **suburbs**. Some took advantage of the new "model dwellings" of LCC estates in places such as Dagenham in the east, though far more settled in "Metroland", the sprawling new suburban districts that followed the extension of the Underground out into northwest London.

In 1924 the **British Empire Exhibition** was held, with the intention of emulating the success of the Great Exhibition. Some 27 million people visited the show, but its success couldn't hide the tensions that had been simmering since the end of the war. In 1926, a wage dispute between the miners' unions

The Blitz

The Luftwaffe bombing of London in World War II – commonly known as the **Blitz** – began on September 7, 1940, when in one night alone some 430 Londoners lost their lives, and over 1600 were seriously injured. It continued for 57 consecutive nights, then intermittently until the final and most devastating attack on the night of May 10, 1941, when 550 planes dropped over 100,000 incendiaries and hundreds of explosive bombs in a matter of hours. The death toll that night was over 1400, bringing the total killed during the Blitz to between 20,000 and 30,000, with some 230,000 homes wrecked. Along with the East End, the City was particularly badly hit: in a single raid on December 29 (dubbed the "Second Fire of London"), 1400 fires broke out across the Square Mile. Some say the Luftwaffe left St Paul's standing as a navigation aid, but it came close to destruction when a bomb landed near the southwest tower; luckily the bomb didn't go off, and it was successfully removed to the Hackney marshes where the 100ft-wide crater left by its detonation is still visible.

The authorities were ready to build mass graves for potential victims, but were unable to provide adequate air-raid shelters to prevent widespread carnage. The corrugated steel **Anderson shelters** issued by the government were of use to only one in four London households – those with gardens in which to bury them. Around 180,000 made use of the tube, despite initial government reluctance, by simply buying a ticket and staying below ground. The cheery photos of singing and dancing in the Underground which the censors allowed to be published tell nothing of the stale air, rats and lice that folk had to contend with. And even the tube stations couldn't withstand a direct hit, as occurred at Bank in January 1941, when over a hundred died. The vast majority of Londoners – some sixty percent – simply hid under the sheets and prayed.

and their bosses developed into the **General Strike**. For nine days, more than half a million workers stayed away from work, until the government called in the army and thousands of volunteers to break the strike.

The economic situation deteriorated even further after the crash of the New York Stock Exchange in 1929, with unemployment in Britain reaching over three million in 1931. The Jarrow Marchers, the most famous protesters of the **Depression** years, shocked London on their arrival in 1936. In the same year thousands of British fascists tried to march through the predominantly Jewish East End, only to be stopped in the so-called **Battle of Cable Street** (see p.204). The end of the year brought a crisis within the Royal Family, too, when Edward VIII abdicated following his decision to marry Wallis Simpson, a twice-divorced American. His brother, **George VI** (1936–52), took over.

There were few public displays of patriotism with the outbreak of **World War II** (1939–45), and even fewer preparations were made against the likelihood of aerial bombardment. The most significant step was the evacuation of six hundred thousand of London's most vulnerable citizens (mostly children), but around half that number had drifted back to the capital by the Christmas of 1939, the midpoint of the "phoney war". The Luftwaffe's bombing campaign, known as the **Blitz**, lasted from September 1940 to May 1941. Further carnage was caused towards the end of the war by the pilotless V-1 "doodlebugs" and V-2 rockets, which caused another twenty thousand casualties.

Postwar London

The end of the war in 1945 was followed by a general election, which brought a landslide victory for the Labour Party under **Clement Attlee**. The Attlee government created the **welfare state**, and initiated a radical programme of **nationalization**, which brought the gas, electricity, coal, steel and iron industries under state control, along with the inland transport services. London itself was left with a severe accommodation crisis, with some eighty percent of the housing stock damaged to some degree. In response, prefabricated houses were erected all over the city, some of which were to remain occupied for well over forty years. The LCC also began building huge housing estates on many of the city's numerous bombsites, an often misconceived strategy which ran in tandem with the equally disastrous New Towns policy of central government.

To lift the country out of its gloom, the **Festival of Britain** was staged in 1951 on derelict land on the south bank of the Thames, a site that was eventually transformed into the Southbank Arts Centre. Londoners turned up at this technological funfair in their thousands, but at the same time many were abandoning the city for good, starting a slow process of population decline that has continued ever since. The consequent labour shortage was made good by mass **immigration** from the former colonies, in particular the Indian subcontinent and the West Indies. The first large group to arrive was the 492 West Indians aboard the SS *Empire Windrush*, which docked at Tilbury in June 1948. The newcomers, a large percentage of whom settled in London, were given small welcome, and within ten years were subjected to **race riots**, which broke out in Notting Hill in 1958.

The riots are thought to have been carried out, for the most part, by "Teddy Boys", working-class lads from London's slum areas and new housing estates, who formed the city's first postwar youth cult. Subsequent cults, and their accompanying music, helped turn London into the epicentre of the so-called

Swinging Sixties, the Teddy Boys being usurped in the early 1960s by the "Mods", whose sharp suits came from London's Carnaby Street. Fashion hit the capital in a big way, and, thanks to the likes of The Beatles, The Rolling Stones and Twiggy, London was proclaimed hippest city on the planet on the front pages of *Time* magazine.

Life for most Londoners, however, was rather less groovy. In the middle of the decade London's local government was reorganized, the LCC being supplanted by the **Greater London Council** (**GLC**), whose jurisdiction covered a much wider area, including many Tory-dominated suburbs. As a result, the Conservatives gained power in the capital for the first time since 1934, and one of their first acts was to support a huge urban motorway scheme that would have displaced as many people as did the railway boom of the Victorian period. Luckily for London, Labour won control of the GLC in 1973 and halted the plans. The Labour victory also ensured that the Covent Garden Market building was saved for posterity, but this ran against the grain. Elsewhere, whole areas of the city were pulled down and redeveloped, and many of London's worst tower blocks were built.

Thatcherite London

In 1979 **Margaret Thatcher** won the general election for the Conservatives, and the country and the capital would never be quite the same again. Thatcher went on to win three general elections, steering Britain into a period of ever greater social polarization. While taxation policies and easy credit fuelled a consumer boom for the professional classes (the yuppies of the 1980s), the erosion of the manufacturing industry and weakening of the welfare state created a calamitous number of people trapped in long-term unemployment, which topped three million in the early 1980s. The Brixton riots of 1981 and 1985 and the Tottenham riot of 1985 were reminders of the price of such divisive policies, and of the long-standing resentment and feeling of social exclusion rife among the city's black youth.

Nationally, the Labour Party went into sharp decline, but in London the party won a narrow victory in the GLC elections on a radical manifesto that was implemented by its youthful new leader **Ken Livingstone**, or "Red Ken" as the tabloids dubbed him. Under Livingstone, the GLC poured money into projects among London's ethnic minorities, into the arts and, most famously, into a subsidized fares policy which saw thousands abandon their cars in favour of inexpensive public transport. Such schemes endeared Livingstone to the hearts of many Londoners, but his popular brand of socialism was too much for the Thatcher government, who, in 1986, abolished the GLC, leaving London as the only European capital without a directly elected body to represent it.

Abolition exacerbated tensions between the poorer and richer boroughs of the city. Rich Tory councils like Westminster proceeded to slash public services and sell off council houses to boost Tory support in marginal wards. Meanwhile in impoverished Labour-held Lambeth and Hackney, millions were being squandered by corrupt council employees. **Homelessness** returned to London in a big way for the first time since Victorian times, and the underside of Waterloo Bridge was transformed into a "Cardboard City", sheltering up to two thousand vagrants on any one night. Great efforts were made by nongovernmental organizations to alleviate homelessness, not least the establishment of a weekly magazine, the *Big Issue*, which continues to be sold by the homeless right across London, earning them a small wage.

At the same time as homelessness and unemployment were on the increase, the so-called "**Big Bang**", which abolished a whole range of restrictive practices on the Stock Exchange, took place. The immediate effect of this deregulation was that foreign banks began to take over brokers and form new, competitive conglomerates. The side effect, however, was to send stocks and shares into the stratosphere, shortly after which they inevitably crashed, ushering in a recession that dragged on for the best part of the next ten years. The one great physical legacy of the Thatcherite experiment in the capital is the **Docklands** development (see p.212), a new business quarter in the derelict docks of the East End, which came about as a direct result of the Big Bang.

Thatcher's greatest folly, however, was the introduction of the **Poll Tax**, a head tax levied regardless of means, which hit the poorest sections of the community hardest. The tax also highlighted the disparity between the city's boroughs. In wealthy, Tory-controlled Wandsworth, Poll Tax bills were zero, while those in poorer, neighbouring, Labour-run Lambeth were the highest in the country. In 1990, the Poll Tax provoked the first full-blooded riot in central London for a long time, and played a significant role in Thatcher's downfall later that year.

Twenty-first-century London

On the surface at least, **twenty-first-century London** has come a long way since the bleak Thatcher years. Funded by money from the National Lottery and the Millennium Commission, the face of the city has certainly changed for the better: the city's national museums have been totally transformed into state-of-the-art visitor attractions, and all of them are free; there are new pedestrian bridges over the Thames; and Tate Modern towers like a beacon of optimism over the South Bank.

The most significant political development for London has been the creation of the **Greater London Assembly** (**GLA**), along with an American-style Mayor of London, both elected by popular mandate. The Labour government, which came to power on a wave of enthusiasm in 1997, did everything it could to prevent the election of the former GLC leader Ken Livingstone as the first mayor, but, despite being forced to leave the Labour Party and run as an independent, he won a resounding victory in the 2000 mayoral elections and was successfully re-elected in 2004.

Livingstone's lasting legacy has been in **transport**. As well as creating more bus routes and introducing more buses, he successfully introduced a **congestion charge** for every vehicle entering central London (see p.26). As a result, traffic levels in central London have been reduced, and, although the congestion charge hasn't solved all the city's problems, at least it showed that, with a little vision and perseverance, something concrete can be achieved.

Livingstone was also instrumental in helping London win the **2012 Olympics** (see p.210). The bid emphasized its regenerative potential for a deprived, multicultural area of London's East End and, against all the odds, beat Paris in the final head-to-head vote. For a moment, London celebrated wildly. Unfortunately, the euphoria was all too brief. A day after hearing the news about the Olympics, on **July 7, 2005**, London was hit by four **suicide bombers** who killed themselves and over fifty innocent commuters in four separate explosions: on tube trains at Aldgate, Edgware Road and King's Cross

London in film through the decades

As early as 1889 Wordsworth Donisthorpe made a primitive motion picture of Trafalgar Square, and since then London has been featured in countless films. Below is a snapshot selection of films culled from each decade since the 1920s.

Blackmail (Alfred Hitchcock, 1929). The first British talkie feature film, this thriller stars the Czech actress Anny Ondra and has its dramatic finale on the dome of the British Museum.

The Adventures of Sherlock Holmes (Alfred Werker, 1939). The Baker Street detective has made countless screen appearances, but Basil Rathbone remains the most convincing incarnation. Here Holmes and Watson (Nigel Bruce) are pitted against Moriarty (George Zucco), out to steal the Crown Jewels.

Passport to Pimlico (Henry Cornelius, 1948). The quintessential Ealing Comedy, in which the inhabitants of Pimlico, discovering that they are actually part of Burgundy, abolish rationing and closing time. Full of all the usual eccentrics, among them Margaret Rutherford in particularly fine form as an excitable history don.

The Ladykillers (Alexander Mackendrick, 1955). Delightfully black comedy set somewhere at the back of King's Cross (a favourite location for filmmakers). Katie Johnson plays the nice old lady getting the better of Alec Guinness, Peter Sellers and assorted other crooks.

Blow-Up (Michelangelo Antonioni, 1966). Swinging London and some less obvious backgrounds (notably Maryon Wilson Park, Charlton) feature in this metaphysical mystery about a photographer (David Hemmings) who may unwittingly have recorded evidence of a murder.

Jubilee (Derek Jarman, 1978). Jarman's angry punk collage, in which Elizabeth I finds herself transported to the urban decay of late twentieth-century Deptford.

My Beautiful Laundrette (Stephen Frears, 1985). A surreal comedy of Thatcher's London, offering the unlikely combination of an entrepreneurial Asian (Gordon Warnecke), his ex-National Front boyfriend (Daniel Day-Lewis) and a laundrette called Powders.

Naked (Mike Leigh, 1993). David Thewlis is brilliant as the disaffected and garrulous misogynist who goes on a tour through the underside of what he calls "the big shitty" – life is anything but sweet in Leigh's darkest but most substantial film.

Dirty Pretty Things (Stephen Frears, 2002). Entertaining romantic thriller set in London's asylum-seeking, multicultural underbelly, shot through with plenty of humour and lots of pace.

and one on a bus in Tavistock Square. Two weeks later a similar attack was unsuccessful after the bombers' detonators failed. Despite everyone's worst fears, however, these two attacks have proved to be isolated incidents and not the beginning of a concerted campaign.

Books

G iven the enormous number of books on London, the list below is necessarily a selective one, with books marked 🏃 being particularly recommended. London's bookshops are covered in detail on p.439. The best known online bookshop is ⊛www.amazon.com, but if you're looking for a particular book in the UK, ⊛www.bookbrain.co.uk will tell you which online bookshop is selling it for the cheapest price. Most of the books recommended are in paperback, but the more expensive books can often be bought secondhand online these days.

Travel, journals and memoirs

Paul Bailey (ed) *The Oxford Book of London*. Large anthology of musings on London, arranged in chronological order from twelfth-century monks via Dostoevsky and Van Gogh to Hanif Kureishi and Angela Carter.

John Betjeman *Betjeman's London*. A selection of writings and poems by the then Poet Laureate, who spearheaded the campaign to save London's architectural heritage in the 1960s.

🏃 **James Boswell** *London Journal*. Boswell's diary, written in 1792–93 when he was lodging in Downing Street, is remarkably candid about his frequent dealings with the city's prostitutes, and is a fascinating insight into eighteenth-century life.

Richard Broad (ed) *Nella's Last's War: the Second World War Diaries of 'Housewife 49'*. An account written for Mass Observation, which reveals the minute details of the struggles of everyday life from a woman's point of view.

John Evelyn *The Diary of John Evelyn*. In contrast to his contemporary, Pepys, Evelyn gives away very little of his personal life, but his diaries cover a much greater period of English history and a much wider range of topics.

Ford Madox Ford *The Soul of London*. Experimental, impressionist portrait of London published in 1905.

Tarquin Hall *Salaam Brick Lane: A Year in the New East End*. The stories of a colourful cast of immigrant characters, met by the author when living above a sweatshop in modern-day Brick Lane.

Doris Lessing *Walking in the Shade 1949–62*. The second volume of Lessing's autobiography, set in London in the 1950s, deals with the writing and theatre scenes and party politics, including her association with the Communist Party, with which she eventually became disenchanted.

George Orwell *Down and Out in Paris and London*. Orwell's tramp's-eye view of the 1930s, written from firsthand experience. The London section is particularly harrowing.

🏃 **Samuel Pepys** *The Shorter Pepys*; *The Illustrated Pepys*. Pepys kept a voluminous diary while he was living in London from 1660 until 1669, recording the fall of the Commonwealth, the Restoration, the Great Plague and the Great Fire, as well as describing the daily life of the nation's capital. Penguin's *The Shorter Pepys*, although abridged from eleven volumes, is still massive; *The Illustrated Pepys* is made up of the choicest extracts accompanied by contemporary illustrations.

Christopher Ross *Tunnel Visions*. Witty and perceptive musings of popular philosopher Ross as he spends a year working as a station master on the Tube.

Iain Sinclair *Hackney, That Rose-Red Empire: a Confidential Report*; *Liquid City*; and *London Orbital*. Sinclair is one of the most original (and virtually unreadable) London writers of

his generation. His latest work is an absorbing autobiography of the author and his favourite borough. *Liquid City* contains beautiful photos and entertaining text about London's hidden rivers and canals; and *London Orbital* is an account of his walk round the M25, delving into obscure parts of the city's periphery.

Brian Thompson *Keeping Mum – A Wartime Childhood*. In spite of the difficult circumstances of his family life, this is a heart-warming book set mostly during the Blitz.

History, society and politics

Peter Ackroyd *Dickens*; *Blake*; *Sir Thomas More*; *Thames: Sacred River* and *London: The Biography*. Few writers know quite as much about London as Ackroyd does, and London is central to all three of his biographical subjects – the result is scholarly, enthusiastic and eminently readable. *London: The Biography* is the massive culmination of a lifetime's love affair with a living city and its intimate history.

Paul Begg *Jack the Ripper: The Definitive History*. This book, whose author has given talks to the FBI on the subject, sets the murders in their Victorian context and aims to debunk the myths.

Angus Calder *The Myth of the Blitz*. A timely antidote to the backs-against-the-wall, "London can take it" tone of most books on this period. Calder dwells instead on the capital's internees – Communists, conscientious objectors and "enemy aliens" – and the myth-making processes of the media of the day.

Piers Dudgeon *Our East End: Memoirs of Life in Disappearing Britain*. Packed with extracts from written accounts and diaries as well as literary

sources, this is a patchwork of the East End with its legendary community spirit and a dash of realism.

Markman Ellis *The Coffee House*. Tracing the unlikely connection between the strange bitter drink from Turkey, which reached London in the seventeenth century, and today's ubiquitous Starbucks and the like.

Clive Emsley *The Newgate Calendar*. Grim and gory account of the most famous London criminals of the day – Captain Kidd, Jack Sheppard, Dick Turpin – with potted biographies of each victim, ending with an account of his execution. Starting out as a collection of papers and booklets, *The Newgate Calendar* was first published in 1828 and was second in popularity only to the Bible at the time of publication, but is now difficult to get hold of.

Jonathan Glancey *London Bread and Circuses*. In this small, illustrated book, the *Guardian*'s architecture critic extols the virtues of the old LCC and visionaries like Frank Pick, who transformed London's transport in the 1930s, discusses the millennium projects (the "circuses" of the title), and bemoans the city's creaking infrastructure.

Ed Glinert *The London Compendium*. Glinert dissects every street, every park, every house and every tube station and produces juicy anecdotes every time. The same author's *East End Chronicles: 300 Years of Mystery and Mayhem* is a readable revelation of all the nefarious doings of the East End, sorting myth from fact, and hoping the spirit will somehow survive in spite of Docklands.

Rahila Gupta *From Homebreakers to Jailbreakers: Southall Black Sisters*. The story of a radical Asian women's group which, against all the odds, was founded in London in 1979 and became internationally famous for campaigning for all disempowered black women.

Sarah Hartley *Mrs P's Journey: The Remarkable Story of the Woman Who Created the A–Z Map*. The tale of Phyllis Pearsall, the indomitable woman who survived a horrific childhood and went on to found London's most famous mapmaking company – you won't feel the same about the A–Z again.

Rachel Lichtenstein and Iain Sinclair *Rodinsky's Room*. A fascinating search into the Jewish past of the East End, centred on the nebulous figure of David Rodinsky.

Peter Linebaugh *The London Hanged*. Superb, Marxist analysis of crime and punishment in the eighteenth century, drawing on the history of those hanged at Tyburn.

Jack London *The People of the Abyss*. The author went undercover in 1902 to uncover East End poverty.

Henry Mayhew *London Labour and the London Poor*. Mayhew's pioneering study of Victorian London, based on research carried out in the 1840s and 1850s.

Roy Porter *London: A Social History*. This immensely readable history is one of the best books on London published since the war. It is particularly strong on the continuing saga of the capital's government and includes an impassioned critique of the damage done by Thatcher.

Stephen Porter *London's Plague Years: Lord Have Mercy Upon Us*. Drawing on various contemporary sources, Porter paints a vivid picture of what it was like to live with a horror which killed 70,000 Londoners.

Winston G. Ramsey (ed) *The East End Then and Now*. Massive tome full of black-and-white photos of the East End before and after the Blitz – it covers all the legends from the Ripper to the Krays.

Maude Pember Reeves *Round About a Pound a Week*. From 1909 to 1913, the Fabian Women's Group, part of the British Labour Party, recorded the daily budget of thirty families in Lambeth living in extreme poverty. This is the accompanying comment, which is both enlightening and enlightened.

John Stow *A Survey of London*. Stow, a retired tailor, set himself the unenviable task of writing the first-ever account of the city in 1598, for which he is now revered, though at the time the task forced him into penury.

Judith R. Walkowitz *City of Dreadful Delight: Narratives of Sexual Danger in Late-Victorian London*. Weighty feminist tract on issues such as child prostitution and the Ripper murders, giving a powerful overview of the image of women in the fiction and media of the day.

Maureen Waller *1700: Scenes from London Life*. Fascinating minutiae of the crazy, everyday life of eighteenth-century London. Equally enthralling is *London 1945: Life in the Debris of War* which explores a very different era.

Ben Weinreb & Christopher Hibbert *The London Encyclopaedia*. More than a thousand pages of concisely presented information on London past and present, accompanied by the odd illustration. The most fascinating book on the capital.

Jerry White *London in the Nineteenth Century*; *London in the Twentieth Century*. Comprehensive and history of the most momentous centuries in the city's history.

Sarah Wise *The Blackest Streets: The Life and Death of a Victorian Slum*. A meticulously researched work which reveals the depths of poverty in the area north of Bethnal Green Road.

Art, architecture and archeology

Ken Allinson & Victoria Thornton *A Guide to London's Contemporary Architecture*. Comprehensive gazetteer to the new buildings, great and small, erected all over Greater London in the 1980s and 1990s, with a black-and-white photo for each entry.

Felix Barker & Peter Jackson *The History of London in Maps*. A beautiful volume of maps, from the earliest surviving chart of 1558 to the new Docklands, with accompanying text explaining the history of the city and its cartography.

Bill Brandt *London in the Thirties*. Brandt's superb black-and-white photos bear witness to a London lost in the Blitz.

Elaine Harwood & Andrew Saint *London*. Part of the excellent Exploring England's Heritage series, sponsored by English Heritage. It's highly selective, though each building is discussed at some length and is well illustrated.

Edward Jones & Christopher Woodward *A Guide to the Architecture of London*. Straightforward illustrated catalogue of London's 1920s buildings, each one accompanied by a black-and-white photo, and with useful maps at the beginning of each chapter.

Derek Kendall *The City of London Churches*. A beautifully illustrated book, comprised mostly of colour photos, covering the remarkable City churches, many of them designed by Wren after the Great Fire.

Andrew Richard Kershman *London's Monuments*. A stroll around some of the well-known and the more obscure monuments of the city.

Nikolaus Pevsner and others *The Buildings of England*. Magisterial series, started by Pevsner, to which others have added, inserting newer buildings but generally respecting the founder's personal tone. The latest of the London volumes (there are now five in the series) is a paperback edition devoted to London Docklands.

Arnold Schwartzman *London Art Deco: A Celebration of the Architectural Style of the Metropolis During the Twenties and Thirties*. Generously illustrated, this book bears witness to the British version of Art Deco in the likes of the Savoy and the Hoover building.

Anthony Sutcliffe *Architectural History of London*. A weighty tome, extensively illustrated, which traces the history of building in London from the Romans to the twenty-first century.

Richard Trench & Ellis Hillman *London under London*. Fascinating book revealing the secrets of every aspect of the capital's subterranean history, from the lost rivers of the underground to the gas and water systems.

London in fiction

Peter Ackroyd *English Music*; *Hawksmoor*; *The House of Doctor Dee*; *The Great Fire of London*; and *Dan Leno and the Limehouse Golem*. Ackroyd's novels are all based on arcane aspects of London, wrapped into thriller-like narratives, and conjuring up kaleidoscopic visions of various ages of English culture. *Hawksmoor*, about the great church architect, is the most popular and enjoyable.

Monica Ali *Brick Lane*. Acute, involving, and slyly humorous, novel about a young Bengali woman who comes over with her husband to live in London's East End.

Hanan Al-Shaykh *Only in London*. An amusing and sympathetic tale of four people from different parts of the Arab world who arrive in London on the same flight.

Martin Amis *London Fields*; *Yellow Dog*. Short sentences and cartoon characters, Amis's novels tend to provoke extreme reactions in readers. Love 'em or hate 'em, these two are set in London.

J.G. Ballard *Concrete Island*; *High Rise*; *The Drowned World*; *The Millennium People*. Wild stuff. In *Concrete Island*, a car crashes on the Westway, leaving its driver stranded on the central reservation, unable to flag down passing cars. In *The Millennium People* the middle classes turn urban terrorist. In *High Rise*, the residents of a high-rise block of flats in East London go slowly mad. *The Drowned World*, Ballard's first novel, is set in a futuristic, flooded and tropical London.

Samuel Beckett *Murphy*. Nihilistic, dark-humoured vision of the city, written in 1938, and told through the eyes of anti-hero Murphy.

Elizabeth Bowen *The Heat of the Day*. Bowen worked for the Ministry of Information during World War II, and witnessed the Blitz first-hand from her Marylebone flat; this novel perfectly captures the dislocation and rootlessness of wartime London.

Anthony Burgess *A Dead Man in Deptford*. Playwright Christopher Marlowe's unexplained murder in a tavern in Deptford provides the background for this historical novel, which brims over with Elizabethan life and language.

Angela Carter *The Magic Toyshop*; *Wise Children*. *The Magic Toyshop* was Carter's most celebrated 1960s novel, about a provincial woman moving to London, while *Wise Children* was published in 1992, the year of her untimely death.

G.K. Chesterton *The Napoleon of Notting Hill*. Written in 1904, but set eighty years in the future, in a London divided into squabbling independent boroughs – something prophetic there – and ruled by royalty selected on a rotational basis.

Clare Clark *The Great Stink*; *The Nature of Monsters*. You need a very strong stomach for either of these historical novels, the first set in Victorian sewers and the second in the eighteenth century.

J.M. Coetzee *Youth*. Claustrophobic, semi-autobiographical novel by South African Booker Prize-winner, centred on a self-obsessed colonial, struggling to find the meaning of life and become a writer in London in the 1960s.

Arthur Conan Doyle *The Complete Sherlock Holmes*. Deerstalkered sleuth Sherlock Holmes and dependable sidekick Dr Watson penetrate all levels of

Victorian London, from Limehouse opium dens to millionaires' pads. *A Study in Scarlet* and *The Sign of Four* are based entirely in London.

Joseph Conrad *The Secret Agent*. Conrad's wonderful spy story, based on the botched anarchist bombing of Greenwich Observatory in 1894, and exposing the hypocrisies of both the police and the anarchists.

Daniel Defoe *Journal of the Plague Year*. An account of the Great Plague seen through the eyes of an East End saddler, written some sixty years after the event.

Charles Dickens *Bleak House*; *A Christmas Tale*; *Little Dorrit*; *Oliver Twist*. The descriptions in Dickens' London-based novels have become the clichés of the Victorian city: the fog, the slums and the stinking river. *Little Dorrit* is set mostly in Borough and contains some of his most trenchant pieces of social analysis. Much of *Bleak House* is set around the Inns of Court that Dickens knew so well.

Maureen Duffy *Capital*. First published in 1975, the novel is like a many-layered sandwich full of startling flavours, as the focus shifts from the central character, an unbalanced squatter with an obsession with London's past and future, to vivid slices of history.

Nell Dunn *Up the Junction*; *Poor Cow*. Perceptive and unsentimental account of the downside of south London life in the 1950s after the hype of the Festival of Britain.

Sally Gardner *I, Coriander*. That rare thing, a really good historical read for children (10+), this book tells the story of a young girl living in Puritan London and involved in a magic world.

George Gissing *New Grub Street*. Classic 1891 story of intrigue and jealousy among London's Fleet Street hacks.

Graham Greene *The Human Factor*; *It's a Battlefield*; *The Ministry of Fear*; *The End of the Affair*. Greene's London novels are all fairly bleak, ranging from *The Human Factor*, which probes the underworld of the city's spies, to *The Ministry of Fear*, which is set during the Blitz.

Patrick Hamilton *Hangover Square*; *Twenty Thousand Streets Under the Sky*. The first is a story of unrequited love and violence in Earl's Court in the 1940s, while the latter is a trilogy of stories set in seedy 1930s London.

Neil Hanson *The Dreadful Judgement*. A docu-fiction account in which modern scientific methods and historical knowledge are applied to the Fire of London so vividly you can almost feel the heat.

Nick Hornby *High Fidelity*. Hornby's extraordinarily successful second book focuses on the loves and life of a thirty-something bloke who lives in North London; his first, *Fever Pitch*, is the autobiography of an Arsenal supporter.

Aldous Huxley *Point Counter Point*. Sharp satire of London's high-society wastrels and dilettantes of the Roaring Twenties.

Henry James *The Awkward Age*. Light, ironic portrayal of London high society at the turn of the century.

Hanif Kureishi *The Buddha of Suburbia*; *Love in a Blue Time*; *My Ear at His Heart*. *The Buddha of Suburbia* is a raunchy account of life as an Anglo-Asian in late-1960s suburbia, and the art scene of the 1970s; *Love in a Blue Time* is a collection of short stories set in 1990s London; *My Ear at His Heart* is a biography of Kureishi's father from his privileged childhood in Bombay to a life in Bromley.

Andrea Levy *Small Island*. A warm-hearted novel in which postwar London struggles to adapt to the influx of Jamaicans who in turn find that the land of their dreams is full of prejudice.

Colin MacInnes *Absolute Beginners*; *Omnibus*. *Absolute Beginners*, a story of life in Soho and Notting Hill in the 1950s (much influenced by Selvon – see below), is infinitely better than the film of the same name. *Omnibus* is set in 1957, in a Victoria Station packed with hopeful black immigrants; white welfare officer meets black man from Lagos with surprising results.

Somerset Maugham *Liza of Lambeth*. Maugham considered himself a "second-rater", but this book on Cockney lowlife is packed with vivid local colour.

Ian McEwan *Saturday*. Set on the day of a protest march against the war in Iraq, this book captures the mood of London post-9/11, as the main character is forced to consider his attitude to this and many other issues.

Timothy Mo *Sour Sweet*. Very funny and very sad story of a newly arrived Chinese family struggling to understand the English way of life in the 1970s, written with great insight by Mo, who is himself of mixed parentage.

Michael Moorcock *Mother London*. A magnificent, rambling, kaleidoscopic portrait of London from the Blitz to Thatcher by a once-fashionable, but now very much underrated, writer.

Iris Murdoch *Under the Net*; *The Black Prince*; *An Accidental Man*; *Bruno's Dream*. *Under the Net* was Murdoch's first, funniest and arguably her best novel, published in 1954, starring a hack writer living in London. Many of her subsequent works are set in various parts of middle-class London and span several decades of the second half of the twentieth century.

George Orwell *Keep the Aspidistra Flying*. Orwell's 1930s critique of Mammon is equally critical of its chief protagonist, whose attempt to rebel against the system only condemns him to poverty, working in a London bookshop and freezing his evenings away in a miserable rented room.

Jonathan Raban *Soft City*. An early work from 1974 that's both a portrait of, and paean to, metropolitan life.

Derek Raymond *Not till the Red Fog Rises*. A book which "reeks with the pervasive stench of excrement" as Iain Sinclair (see below) put it, this is a lowlife spectacular set in the seediest sections of the capital.

Ruth Rendell *The Keys to the Street*. The mystery centres on the homeless who are being spiked on the railings around rich Regent's Park.

Barnaby Rogerson (ed) *London: Poetry of Place*. A delightful pocket-sized book complete with potted biographies of the poets.

Edward Rutherford *London*. A big, big novel (perhaps too big) that stretches from Roman times to the present and deals with the most dramatic moments of London's history. Masses of historical detail woven in with the story of several families.

Samuel Selvon *The Lonely Londoners*. "Gives us the smell and feel of this rather horrifying life. Not for the squeamish", ran the quote from the *Evening Standard* on the original cover. This is, in fact, a wry and witty account of the Afro-Caribbean experience in London in the 1950s.

Iain Sinclair *White Chappell, Scarlet Tracings*; *Downriver*; *Radon Daughters*. Sinclair's idiosyncratic and richly textured novels are a strange mix of Hogarthian caricature, New

Age mysticism and conspiracy-theory rant. Deeply offensive and highly recommended.

Stevie Smith *Novel on Yellow Paper.* Poet Stevie Smith's first novel takes place in the publishing world of 1930s London.

Zadie Smith *White Teeth.* Highly acclaimed and funny first novel about race, gender and class in the ethnic melting pot of North London.

John Sommerfield *May Day.* Set in the revolutionary fervour of the 1930s, this novel is "as if Mrs Dalloway was written by a Communist Party bus driver", in the words of one reviewer.

Muriel Spark *The Bachelors*; *The Ballad of Peckham Rye.* Two London-based novels written one after the other by the Scots-born author, best known for *The Prime of Miss Jean Brodie.*

Graham Swift *Last Orders.* Four friends recall the East End as it was during the war, in an unsentimental view of Cockney life.

Edith Templeton *Gordon.* A tale of sex and humiliation in postwar London, banned in the 1960s when it was published under a pseudonym (Louisa Walbrook).

Rose Tremain *The Road Home.* The moving story of Lev, an Eastern European economic migrant, who heads for London and finds the streets are not paved with gold.

Sarah Waters *Affinity, Fingersmith,* and *Tipping the Velvet* are racy modern novels set in Victorian London: *Affinity* is set in the spiritualist milieu, *Fingersmith* focuses on an orphan girl, while *Tipping the Velvet* is about lesbian love in the music hall. Waters' latest, *The Night Watch*, is a tale of London during World War II.

Evelyn Waugh *Vile Bodies.* Waugh's target, the "vile bodies" of the title, are the flippant rich kids of the Roaring Twenties, as in Huxley's *Point Counter Point* (see p.480).

Patrick White *The Living and the Dead.* Australian Nobel Prize-winner's second novel is a sombre portrait of family life in London at the time of the Spanish Civil War.

Angus Wilson *The Wrong Set.* A collection of short stories written in 1949 satirizing contemporary upper-middle-class characters in Knightsbridge and Kensington.

P.G. Wodehouse *Jeeves Omnibus.* Bertie Wooster and his stalwart butler, Jeeves, were based in Mayfair, and many of their exploits take place with London showgirls and in the Drones gentlemen's club.

Virginia Woolf *Mrs Dalloway.* Woolf's novel relates the thoughts of a London society hostess and a shell-shocked war veteran, with her "stream-of-consciousness" style in full flow. *The London Scene* consists of six musings on Woolf's favourite London walks, originally written for *Good Housekeeping* in 1932.

Specialist guides

Jill Billington *London's Parks and Gardens.* An expensive coffee-table item, but the photos are beautiful.

Judi Culbertson & Tom Randall *Permanent Londoners.* An illustrated guide to the finest of London's cemeteries, from Westminster Abbey and St Paul's to the Victorian splendours of Highgate and Kensal Green. Very good on biographical histories of the deceased, too.

Andrew Duncan *Secret London*. With boundless enthusiasm, Duncan takes you along the lost rivers, unmasks the property tycoons, exposes dead tube stations and uncovers just about every undiscovered nook and cranny in the city.

Bob Gilbert *The Green London Way*. This hundred-mile walk (also cyclable) circles the capital, taking in favourites like Greenwich and Kew Gardens, but also covering more unusual urban landscapes such as the Northern Outfall Sewerway. Politically astute and ecologically sound text, too.

Paul Goldsack *River Thames: In the Footsteps of the Famous*. Written in conjunction with English Heritage this is a racy romp up the river, spotting connections with the famous and the infamous.

Andrew Richard Kerschman *The London Market Guide*. A must for bargain hunters, packed with useful information and a few warnings for the unwary.

Jean Moorcroft Wilson *Virginia Woolf's London*. A book of place, tracing Woolf's connections with Kensington, Bloomsbury and Richmond, and the footsteps of some of her characters.

Christian Wolmar *The Subterranean Railway*. A fascinating history of the Tube, the world's first underground railway and product of the vision of Victorian pioneers.

Glossary of architectural terms

Aisle Clear space parallel to the nave of a church, usually with lower ceiling than the nave.

Altar Table at which the Eucharist is celebrated, at the east end of a church. (When the church is not aligned to the geographical east, the altar end is still referred to as the "east" end.)

Ambulatory Passage behind and around the chancel.

Apse The curved or polygonal east end of a church.

Arcade Row of arches on top of columns or piers, supporting a wall.

Baldachin Canopy over an altar.

Barbican Defensive structure built in front of main gate fortress.

Barrel vault Continuous rounded vault, like a semi-cylinder.

Blue plaque English Heritage plaques placed on a building associated with a prominent figure (who must have been dead for at least 25 years).

Boss A decorative carving at the meeting point of the lines of a vault.

Buttress Stone support for a wall; some buttresses are wholly attached to the wall, others, known as "flying buttresses", take the form of a tower with a connecting arch.

Capital Upper section of a column or pier, usually carved.

Chancel Section of a church where the altar is located.

Choir Area in which the church service is conducted; next to or same as chancel.

Clerestory Upper storey of nave, containing a line of windows.

Coffering Regular recessed spaces set into a ceiling.

Corbel Jutting stone support, often carved.

Crenellations Battlements with square indentations.

Fan vault Late Gothic form of vaulting, in which the area between walls and ceiling is covered with stone ribs in the shape of an open fan.

Finial Any decorated tip of an architectural feature.

Gallery A raised passageway.

Hammerbeam Type of internal roofing in which horizontal beams support vertical timbers that connect to and support the roof.

Lady Chapel Chapel dedicated to the Virgin, often found at the east end of major churches.

Lantern Structure on top of a dome or tower, often glazed to let in light.

Listed building A building which has been put on English Heritage's protected list; buildings are classed (in descending order of importance) Grade I, Grade II★ and Grade II.

Misericord Carved ledge below a tip-up seat, usually in choir stalls.

Nave The main part of a church on the other (usually western) side of the crossing from the chancel.

Oriel Projecting window.

Palladian Eighteenth-century classical style adhering to the principles of Andrea Palladio.

Pediment Triangular space above a window or doorway.

Perpendicular Late Gothic style, about 1380–1550.

Piano nobile Principal floor of a large house usually located above the ground floor.

Pilaster Flat column set against a wall.

Reredos Painted or carved panel at the back of an altar.

Rood screen Wooden screen supporting a crucifix (or rood), separating the choir from the nave; few survived the Reformation.

Rose window Large, circular window, divided into vaguely petal-shaped sections.

Stalls Seating for clergy in the choir area of a church.

Tracery Pattern formed by narrow bands of stone in a window or on a wall surface.

Transept Sections of the main body of a church at right angles to the choir and nave.

Tympanum Panel over a doorway, often carved in medieval churches.

Vault Arched ceiling.

Glossary of British terms

Bill	Restaurant check
Biscuit	Cookie or cracker
Bonnet	Car hood
Boot	Car trunk
British Rail	State railways (1945–1997)
Caravan	Trailer
Car park	Parking lot
Cheap	Inexpensive
Chemist	Pharmacist
Chips	French fries
Coach	Bus
Crisps	Potato chips
Dodgy	Suspect or unreliable
Dustbin	Trash can
First floor	Second floor
Fiver	Five-pound note
Flat	Apartment
Fortnight	Two weeks
Ground floor	First floor
High Street	Main Street
Hire	Rent
Jam	Jelly
Jelly	Jell-O
Jumper	Sweater
Leaflet	Pamphlet
Lift	Elevator
Lorry	Truck
Motorway	Highway
NHS	National Health Service
Off-licence	Liquor store
Pants	Underwear
Petrol	Gasoline
Pudding	Dessert
Queue	Line
Quid	Pound (money)
Return ticket	Round-trip ticket

Cockney rhyming slang

The term **Cockney** originally meant cock's egg or misshapen egg such as a young hen might lay, in other words, a lily-livered townie as opposed to a strong countryman. From the seventeenth century, it was used as a pejorative term for any Londoner, but was later appropriated by Londoners to describe themselves (and their accent). Traditionally, to be a true Cockney, you had to be born within earshot of the **Bow Bells** (see p.183), an area estimated to be roughly a five-mile radius around the City. However, with increased traffic noise, and no maternity ward in the near vicinity, this traditional definition is of little use nowadays. As for **Cockney rhyming slang**, it's basically a coded language, where a word is replaced by two or more words, the last one of which rhymes with the original. For example, instead of the word "stairs" you have "apples and pears"; a piano (pronounced "pianner") is a "Joanna"; and pinch becomes "half-inch".

The general theory is that it evolved in the criminal underworld of the **East End** as a secret means of communication, and many folk nowadays think of Cockney rhyming slang as a bit of a joke. In actual fact, it's alive and well, you just need to know a few basic rules. For a start, Londoners often don't use the part of the phrase which rhymes with the original at all. In other words, rather than say "butcher's hook" (for "look"), they say "Have a butcher's at that"; instead of "loaf of bread" (for "head"), you hear "Use your loaf!", and when it's cold, it's "'tat'ers" not "potatoes in the mould". Rhyming slang is constantly evolving, too, with public figures providing rich pickings: Brad Pitt (shit), Posh & Becks (specs) and Gordon Brown (clown). For the latest rhyming slang, and all the old favourites, visit ⓦ www.cockneyrhymingslang.co.uk.

Roundabout	Rotary interchange	**Tenner**	Ten-pound note
Single ticket	One-way ticket	**Tights**	Pantyhose
Stalls	Orchestra seats	**Tory**	Conservative (politics)
Stone	Fourteen pounds (weight)	**Trainers**	Sneakers
Subway	Pedestrian passageway	**Trousers**	Pants
Sweets	Candy	**Tube/Underground**	Subway (train)
Tap	Faucet	**Whig**	Liberal (politics)

Travel store

Travel

Andorra The Pyrenees, Pyrenees & Andorra Map, Spain
Antigua The Caribbean
Argentina Argentina, Argentina Map, Buenos Aires, South America on a Budget
Aruba The Caribbean
Australia Australia, Australia Map, East Coast Australia, Melbourne, Sydney, Tasmania
Austria Austria, Europe on a Budget, Vienna
Bahamas The Bahamas, The Caribbean
Barbados Barbados DIR, The Caribbean
Belgium Belgium & Luxembourg, Bruges DIR, Brussels, Brussels Map, Europe on a Budget
Belize Belize, Central America on a Budget, Guatemala & Belize Map
Benin West Africa
Bolivia Bolivia, South America on a Budget
Brazil Brazil, Rio, South America on a Budget
British Virgin Islands The Caribbean
Brunei Malaysia, Singapore & Brunei [1 title], Southeast Asia on a Budget
Bulgaria Bulgaria, Europe on a Budget
Burkina Faso West Africa
Cambodia Cambodia, Southeast Asia on a Budget, Vietnam, Laos & Cambodia Map [1 Map]
Cameroon West Africa
Canada Canada, Pacific Northwest, Toronto, Toronto Map, Vancouver
Cape Verde West Africa
Cayman Islands The Caribbean
Chile Chile, Chile Map, South America on a Budget
China Beijing, China,

Hong Kong & Macau, Hong Kong & Macau DIR, Shanghai
Colombia South America on a Budget
Costa Rica Central America on a Budget, Costa Rica, Costa Rica & Panama Map
Croatia Croatia, Croatia Map, Europe on a Budget
Cuba Cuba, Cuba Map, The Caribbean, Havana
Cyprus Cyprus, Cyprus Map
Czech Republic The Czech Republic, Czech & Slovak Republics, Europe on a Budget, Prague, Prague DIR, Prague Map
Denmark Copenhagen, Denmark, Europe on a Budget, Scandinavia
Dominica The Caribbean
Dominican Republic Dominican Republic, The Caribbean
Ecuador Ecuador, South America on a Budget
Egypt Egypt, Egypt Map
El Salvador Central America on a Budget
England Britain, Camping in Britain, Devon & Cornwall, Dorset, Hampshire and The Isle of Wight [1 title], England, Europe on a Budget, The Lake District, London, London DIR, London Map, London Mini Guide, Walks In London & Southeast England
Estonia The Baltic States, Europe on a Budget
Fiji Fiji
Finland Europe on a Budget, Finland, Scandinavia
France Brittany & Normandy, Corsica, Corsica Map, The Dordogne & the Lot, Europe on a Budget, France, France Map, Languedoc & Roussillon, The Loire, Paris, Paris DIR,

Paris Map, Paris Mini Guide, Provence & the Côte d'Azur, The Pyrenees, Pyrenees & Andorra Map
French Guiana South America on a Budget
Gambia The Gambia, West Africa
Germany Berlin, Berlin Map, Europe on a Budget, Germany, Germany Map
Ghana West Africa
Gibraltar Spain
Greece Athens Map, Crete, Crete Map, Europe on a Budget, Greece, Greece Map, Greek Islands, Ionian Islands
Guadeloupe The Caribbean
Guatemala Central America on a Budget, Guatemala, Guatemala & Belize Map
Guinea West Africa
Guinea-Bissau West Africa
Guyana South America on a Budget
Holland see The Netherlands
Honduras Central America on a Budget
Hungary Budapest, Europe on a Budget, Hungary
Iceland Iceland, Iceland Map
India Goa, India, India Map, Kerala, Rajasthan, Delhi & Agra [1 title], South India, South India Map
Indonesia Bali & Lombok, Southeast Asia on a Budget
Ireland Dublin DIR, Dublin Map, Europe on a Budget, Ireland, Ireland Map
Israel Jerusalem
Italy Europe on a Budget, Florence DIR, Florence & Siena Map, Florence & the best of Tuscany, Italy, The Italian Lakes, Naples & the Amalfi Coast, Rome, Rome DIR, Rome Map, Sardinia, Sicily, Sicily Map, Tuscany & Umbria, Tuscany Map,

Venice, Venice DIR, Venice Map
Jamaica Jamaica, The Caribbean
Japan Japan, Tokyo
Jordan Jordan
Kenya Kenya, Kenya Map
Korea Korea
Laos Laos, Southeast Asia on a Budget, Vietnam, Laos & Cambodia Map [1 Map]
Latvia The Baltic States, Europe on a Budget
Lithuania The Baltic States, Europe on a Budget
Luxembourg Belgium & Luxembourg, Europe on a Budget
Malaysia Malaysia Map, Malaysia, Singapore & Brunei [1 title], Southeast Asia on a Budget
Mali West Africa
Malta Malta & Gozo DIR
Martinique The Caribbean
Mauritania West Africa
Mexico Baja California, Baja California, Cancún & Cozumel DIR, Mexico, Mexico Map, Yucatán, Yucatán Peninsula Map
Monaco France, Provence & the Côte d'Azur
Montenegro Montenegro
Morocco Europe on a Budget, Marrakesh DIR, Marrakesh Map, Morocco, Morocco Map,
Nepal Nepal
Netherlands Amsterdam, Amsterdam DIR, Amsterdam Map, Europe on a Budget, The Netherlands
Netherlands Antilles The Caribbean
New Zealand New Zealand, New Zealand Map

DIR: Rough Guide **DIRECTIONS** for short breaks

Available from all good bookstores

ROUGH GUIDES
Don't Just Travel

Computers Cloud Computing, FWD this link, The Internet, iPhone, iPods & iTunes, Macs & OS X, Website Directory
Film & TV American Independent Film, British Cult Comedy, Comedy Movies, Cult Movies, Film, Film Musicals, Film Noir, Gangster Movies, Horror Movies, Sci-Fi Movies, Westerns
Lifestyle Babies & Toddlers, Brain Training, Food, Girl Stuff, Green Living, Happiness, Men's Health, Pregnancy & Birth, Running, Saving & Selling Online, Sex, Weddings
Music The Beatles, The Best Music You've Never Heard, Blues, Bob Dylan, Book of Playlists, Classical Music, Heavy Metal, Jimi Hendrix, Led Zeppelin, Nirvana, Opera, Pink Floyd, The Rolling Stones, Soul and R&B, Velvet Underground, World Music
Popular Culture Anime, Classic Novels, Conspiracy Theories, Crime Fiction, The Da Vinci Code, Graphic Novels, Hidden Treasures, His Dark Materials, Hitchhiker's Guide to the Galaxy, The Lost Symbol, Manga, Next Big Thing, Shakespeare, True Crime, Tutankhamun, Unexplained Phenomena, Videogames
Science The Brain, Climate Change, The Earth, Energy Crisis, Evolution, Future, Genes & Cloning, The Universe, Weather

For more information go to www.roughguides.com

Who do you want to meet?

The images shown depict wax figures created and owned by Madame Tussauds

Book online at
www.madametussauds.com

Madame Tussauds LONDON

 Next to Baker Street Tube Station

Small print and
Index

A Rough Guide to Rough Guides

Published in 1982, the first Rough Guide – to Greece – was a student scheme that became a publishing phenomenon. Mark Ellingham, a recent graduate in English from Bristol University, had been travelling in Greece the previous summer and couldn't find the right guidebook. With a small group of friends he wrote his own guide, combining a highly contemporary, journalistic style with a thoroughly practical approach to travellers' needs.

The immediate success of the book spawned a series that rapidly covered dozens of destinations. And, in addition to impecunious backpackers, Rough Guides soon acquired a much broader and older readership that relished the guides' wit and inquisitiveness as much as their enthusiastic, critical approach and value-for-money ethos.

These days, Rough Guides include recommendations from shoestring to luxury and cover more than 200 destinations around the globe, including almost every country in the Americas and Europe, more than half of Africa and most of Asia and Australasia. Our ever-growing team of authors and photographers is spread all over the world, particularly in Europe, the US and Australia.

In the early 1990s, Rough Guides branched out of travel, with the publication of Rough Guides to World Music, Classical Music and the Internet. All three have become benchmark titles in their fields, spearheading the publication of a wide range of books under the Rough Guide name.

Including the travel series, Rough Guides now number more than 350 titles, covering: phrasebooks, waterproof maps, music guides from Opera to Heavy Metal, reference works as diverse as Conspiracy Theories and Shakespeare, and popular culture books from iPods to Poker. Rough Guides also produce a series of more than 120 World Music CDs in partnership with World Music Network.

Visit www.roughguides.com to see our latest publications.

Rough Guide travel images are available for commercial licensing at www.roughguidespictures.com

Rough Guide credits

Text editor: Ann-Marie Shaw
Layout: Umesh Aggarwal
Cartography: Rajesh Chhibber
Picture editor: Mark Thomas
Production: Rebecca Short
Proofreader: Diane Margolis
Cover design: Chloë Roberts
Editorial: Ruth Blackmore, Andy Turner, Keith
Drew, Edward Aves, Alice Park, Lucy White,
Jo Kirby, James Smart, Natasha Foges, Róisín
Cameron, Emma Traynor, Emma Gibbs, Kathryn
Lane, Monica Woods, Mani Ramaswamy, Harry
Wilson, Lucy Cowie, Amanda Howard, Lara
Kavanagh, Alison Roberts, Joe Staines, Peter
Buckley, Matthew Milton, Tracy Hopkins, Ruth
Tidball; **Delhi** Madhavi Singh, Karen D'Souza,
Lubna Shaheen
Design & Pictures: London Scott Stickland,
Dan May, Diana Jarvis, Nicole Newman, Sarah
Cummins, Emily Taylor; **Delhi** Ajay Verma, Jessica
Subramanian, Ankur Guha, Pradeep Thapliyal,
Sachin Tanwar, Anita Singh, Nikhil Agarwal,
Sachin Gupta
Production: Vicky Baldwin

Cartography: London Maxine Repath, Ed
Wright, Katie Lloyd-Jones; **Delhi** Ashutosh Bharti,
Rajesh Mishra, Animesh Pathak, Jasbir Sandhu,
Karobi Gogoi, Alakananda Roy, Swati Handoo,
Deshpal Dabas
Online: London George Atwell, Faye Hellon,
Jeanette Angell, Fergus Day, Justine Bright, Clare
Bryson, Aine Fearon, Adrian Low, Ezgi Celebi,
Amber Bloomfield; **Delhi** Amit Verma, Rahul Kumar,
Narender Kumar, Ravi Yadav, Debojit Borah,
Rakesh Kumar, Ganesh Sharma, Shisir Basumatari
Marketing & Publicity: London Liz Statham,
Niki Hanmer, Louise Maher, Jess Carter, Vanessa
Godden, Vivienne Watton, Anna Paynton, Rachel
Sprackett, Libby Jellie, Laura Vipond, Vanessa
McDonald; **New York** Katy Ball, Judi Powers,
Nancy Lambert; **Delhi** Ragini Govind
Manager India: Punita Singh
Reference Director: Andrew Lockett
Operations Manager: Helen Phillips
PA to Publishing Director: Nicola Henderson
Publishing Director: Martin Dunford
Commercial Manager: Gino Magnotta
Managing Director: John Duhigg

Publishing information

This eighth edition published January 2010 by
Rough Guides Ltd,
80 Strand, London WC2R 0RL
14 Local Shopping Centre, Panchsheel Park,
New Delhi 110017, India
Distributed by the Penguin Group
Penguin Books Ltd,
80 Strand, London WC2R 0RL
Penguin Group (USA)
375 Hudson Street, NY 10014, USA
Penguin Group (Australia)
250 Camberwell Road, Camberwell,
Victoria 3124, Australia
Penguin Group (Canada)
195 Harry Walker Parkway N, Newmarket, ON,
L3Y 7B3 Canada
Penguin Group (NZ)
67 Apollo Drive, Mairangi Bay, Auckland 1310,
New Zealand
Cover concept by Peter Dyer.

Typeset in Bembo and Helvetica to an original
design by Henry Iles.
Printed in Singapore
© Rob Humphreys, 2010
Maps © Rough Guides
No part of this book may be reproduced in any
form without permission from the publisher except
for the quotation of brief passages in reviews.
504pp includes index
A catalogue record for this book is available from
the British Library
ISBN: 978-1-84836-278-9
The publishers and authors have done their best
to ensure the accuracy and currency of all the
information in **The Rough Guide to London**,
however, they can accept no responsibility for
any loss, injury, or inconvenience sustained by
any traveller as a result of information or advice
contained in the guide.

1   3   5   7   9   8   6   4   2

Help us update

We've gone to a lot of effort to ensure that the
eighth edition of **The Rough Guide to London**
is accurate and up-to-date. However, things
change – places get "discovered", opening hours
are notoriously fickle, restaurants and rooms raise
prices or lower standards. If you feel we've got it
wrong or left something out, we'd like to know,
and if you can remember the address, the price,
the hours, the phone number, so much the better.

Please send your comments with the subject
line "**Rough Guide London Update**" to ⓒmail
@roughguides.com. We'll credit all contributions
and send a copy of the next edition (or any other
Rough Guide if you prefer) for the very best
emails.
    Have your questions answered and tell others
about your trip at ⓦwww.roughguides.com

SMALL PRINT

www.roughguides.com

495

Acknowledgements

The author would like to thank Val for help with the listings and biblio and Annie for introducing Kate to the mosh pit.

The editor would like to thank Umesh for his stylish typesetting, Rajesh Chhibber for the maps, Diane Margolis for her painstaking proofreading, Mark for great pictures, Monica Woods for her kindness and support, and Rob for all the giddy emails.

Index

Map entries are in colour.

Q

R

Map symbols

– – –	Chapter division boundary		◆	Place of interest
	Main road		🕌	Mosque
	Minor road		🏛	Stately home
	Pedestrianized street		⚘	Gardens/fountain
	Tunnel		@	Internet café
	Railway		○	Train station
- - - -	Footpath		⊖	Underground station
	River/canal		✡	Synagogue
— —	Ferry route		✉	Post office
= = = =	Walkway		ⓘ	Tourist information
ⅢⅢⅢⅢ	Steps		⊞	Hospital
)(	Bridge		⛴	Boat
———	Wall		⬭	Stadium
⚱	Museum		✚	Church
⊙	Statue			Building
⊠	Gate			Cemetery
▲	Mountain peak			Park
⌂	Cave			

Before you book your
London hotel
check the
London hotel map
on LondonTown.com

London's hotels all on one map

Visually compare best hotel rates and availability

See real customer feedback on all hotels

View entertainment, including ticket prices and availability

Hotel Price Guarantee: "Find it cheaper, get £100"

full screen, fully interactive
**The new ∧ hotel map
on LondonTown.com**
www.londontown.com/hotelmap

LONDONTOWN.com
Your Best Friend in London

Key bus routes in central London

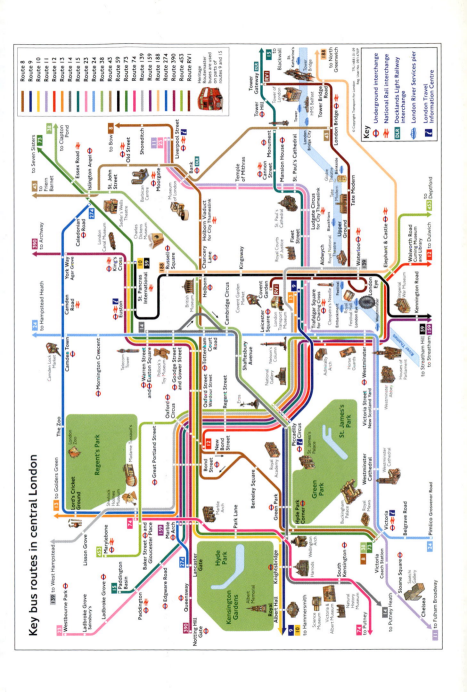

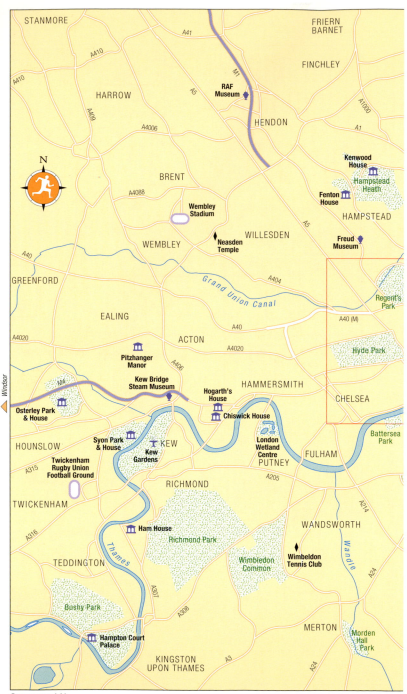

STANMORE

FRIERN BARNET

A41

A410

FINCHLEY

A410

HARROW

A5

M1

RAF Museum

HENDON

A1000

A1

A409

A4006

Kenwood House

N

BRENT

A4088

Fenton House

Hampstead Heath

HAMPSTEAD

Wembley Stadium

A5

WEMBLEY

WILLESDEN

Neasden Temple

Freud Museum

A40

GREENFORD

Grand Union Canal

A404

Regent's Park

EALING

A40

A40 (M)

Hyde Park

A4020

ACTON

A4020

Windsor

Pitzhanger Manor

A406

Kew Bridge Steam Museum

HAMMERSMITH

M4

Hogarth's House

CHELSEA

Osterley Park & House

Chiswick House

Battersea Park

HOUNSLOW

Syon Park & House

Kew Gardens

KEW

London Wetland Centre

FULHAM

Twickenham Rugby Union Football Ground

A315

PUTNEY

A205

RICHMOND

A316

TWICKENHAM

Ham House

Richmond Park

WANDSWORTH

A214

Thames

TEDDINGTON

Wimbledon Common

Wimbledon Tennis Club

Wandle

A24

A307

Bushy Park

A308

MERTON

Morden Hall Park

Hampton Court Palace

A3

KINGSTON UPON THAMES

A24

© crown copyright

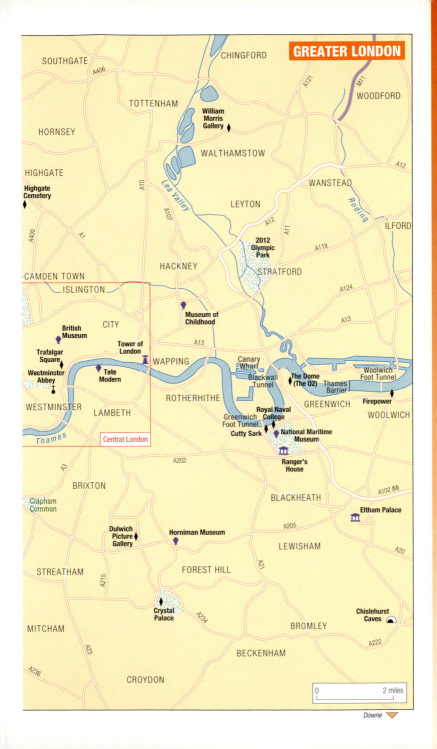

GREATER LONDON

SOUTHGATE

A406

CHINGFORD

A121

M11

WOODFORD

TOTTENHAM

HORNSEY

William
Morris
Gallery

WALTHAMSTOW

A12

HIGHGATE

Highgate
Cemetery

A400

A1

A10

Lea Valley

A107

WANSTEAD

Roding

A12

ILFORD

A118

A13

LEYTON

A12

A11

CAMDEN TOWN

ISLINGTON

2012
Olympic
Park

HACKNEY

STRATFORD

A124

CITY

British
Museum

Museum of
Childhood

Trafalgar
Square

Tower of
London

A13

WAPPING

Westminster
Abbey

Tate
Modern

ROTHERHITHE

Canary
Wharf

Blackwall
Tunnel

The Dome
(The O2)

Thames
Barrier

Woolwich
Foot Tunnel

Firepower

WESTMINSTER

LAMBETH

Thames

Central London

Greenwich
Foot Tunnel

Royal Naval
College

GREENWICH

WOOLWICH

Cutty Sark

National Maritime
Museum

A202

Ranger's
House

A3

BRIXTON

Clapham
Common

BLACKHEATH

A102 (M)

Eltham Palace

Dulwich
Picture
Gallery

Horniman Museum

A205

LEWISHAM

A20

STREATHAM

A215

FOREST HILL

A21

Crystal
Palace

A234

Chislehurst
Caves

MITCHAM

A23

BROMLEY

A222

BECKENHAM

A236

CROYDON

0   2 miles

Downe

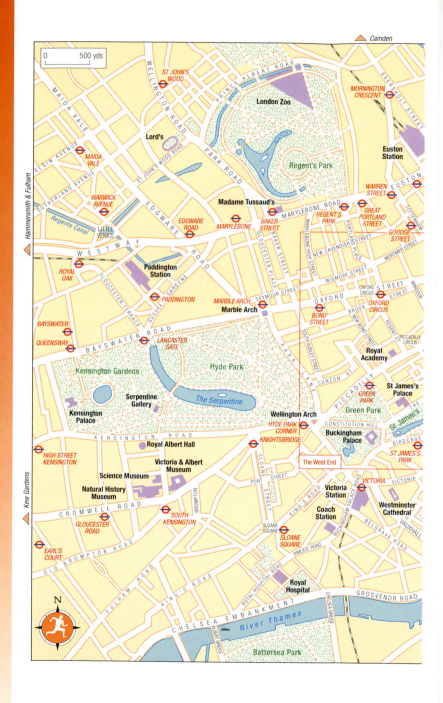

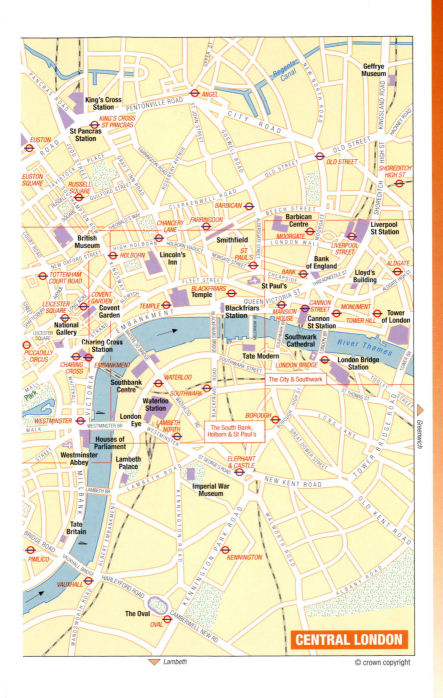

CENTRAL LONDON

© crown copyright

Lambeth

Greenwich

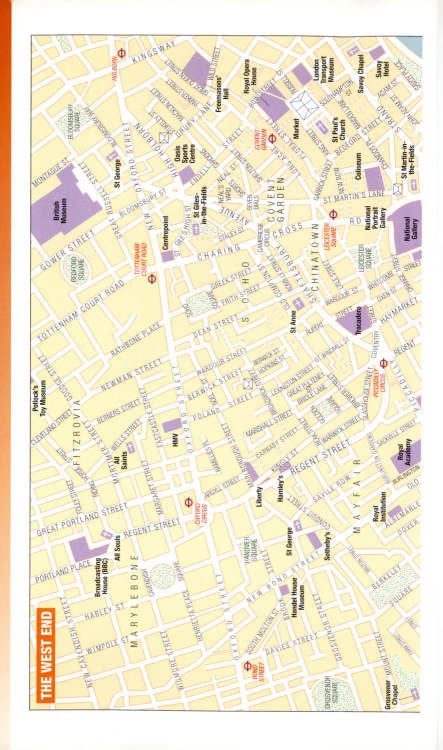

THE WEST END

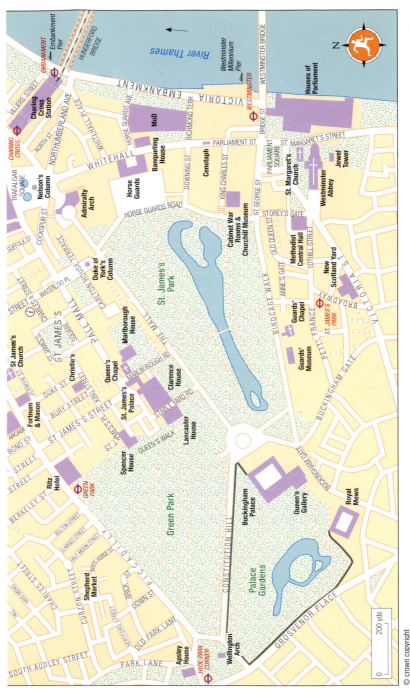

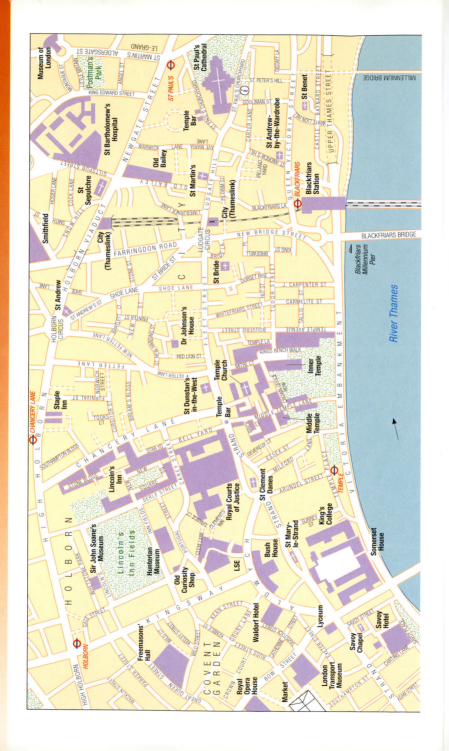

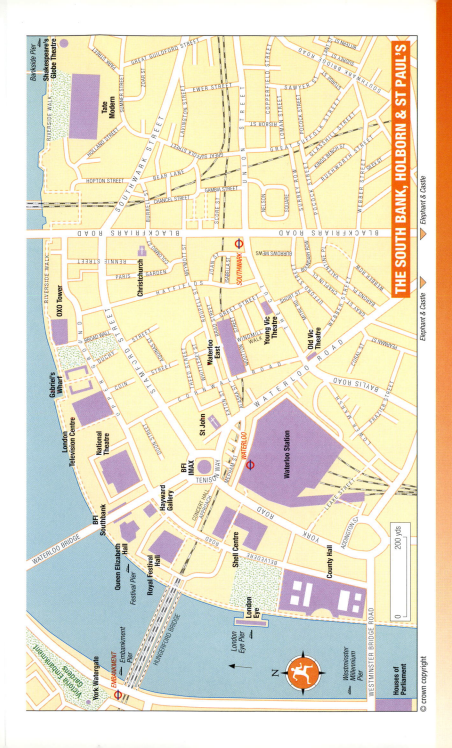

THE SOUTH BANK, HOLBORN & ST PAUL'S

Bankside Pier

Shakespeare's Globe Theatre

RIVERSIDE WALK

Tate Modern

PARK STREET

GREAT GUILDFORD STREET

ZOAR ST

SUMNER STREET

EWER STREET

HOLLAND STREET

HOPTON STREET

BEAR LANE

GAMBIA STREET

CHANCEL STREET

SOUTHWARK STREET

GREAT SUFFOLK STREET

GREAT SUFFOLK STREET

LAVINGTON STREET

UNION STREET

RISBOR ST

COPPERFIELD STREET

SAWYER ST

LOMAN STREET

POCOCK STREET

RISBOR ST

NELSON SQUARE

SURREY ROW

POCOCK STREET

KINGS BENCH ST

GLASSHILL STREET

RUSHWORTH STREET

WEBBER STREET

SILEX ST

SOUTHWARK BRIDGE ROAD

SUDREY ST

LANT ST

BITTERN ST

STURGE ST

WEBBER ROW

BLACKFRIARS ROAD

BLACKFRIARS ROAD

RIVERSIDE WALK

OXO Tower

RENNIE STREET

Christchurch

PARIS GARDEN

PARIS GARDEN

COLOMBO ST

MEYMOTT ST

HATFIELDS

JOAN ST

ISABELLA ST

BURROWS MEWS

SOUTHWARK

GROUND

BROAD WALL

UPPER

STAMFORD STREET

DUCHY STREET

ROUPELL ST

WHITTLESEY ST

BRAD STREET

GREET STREET

SHORT ST

THE CUT

WINDMILL WALK

WOOTTON STREET

Waterloo East

Young Vic Theatre

Old Vic Theatre

WATERLOO ROAD

WEBBER ST

CHAPLIN CL

BARONS PL

UPTON CL

MORLEY ST

GRAY ST

VALENTINE PL

MARCIA RD

WEBBER ROW

PEARMAN ST

BAYLIS ROAD

COBALT ST

Gabriel's Wharf

London Television Centre

National Theatre

COIN STREET

CORNWALL ROAD

EXTON ST

ALASKA ST

ROAD

St John

LOWER MARSH

FRAZIER STREET

BFI Southbank

Hayward Gallery

BFI IMAX

TENISON WAY

WATERLOO

MEPHAM ST

Waterloo Station

LEAKE STREET

ADDINGTON ST

WATERLOO BRIDGE

Queen Elizabeth Hall

Royal Festival Hall

CONCERT HALL APPROACH

Shell Centre

BELVEDERE ROAD

YORK ROAD

County Hall

Festival Pier

HUNGERFORD BRIDGE

London Eye Pier

London Eye

WESTMINSTER BRIDGE ROAD

York Watergate

Victoria Embankment Gardens

EMBANKMENT

Embankment Pier

Westminster Millennium Pier

Houses of Parliament

N

0   200 yds

© crown copyright

Elephant & Castle

Elephant & Castle

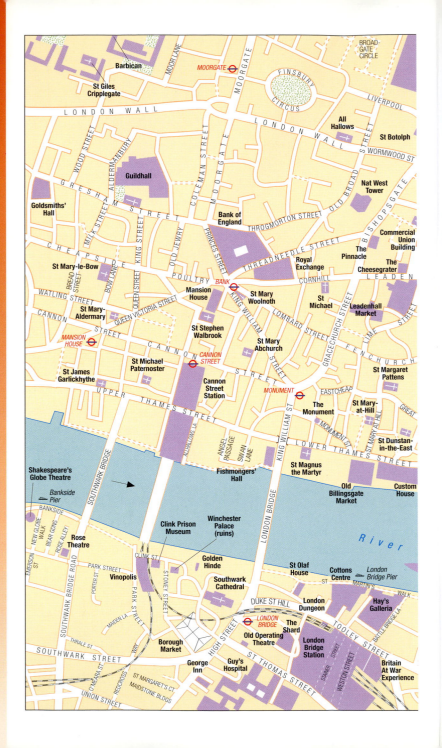

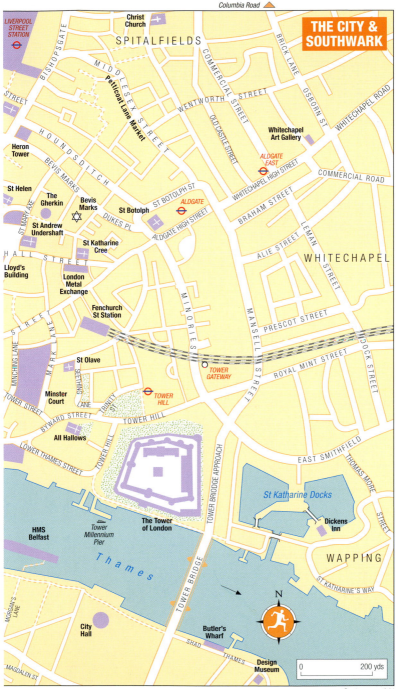

Columbia Road

THE CITY & SOUTHWARK

LIVERPOOL STREET STATION

SPITALFIELDS

Christ Church

BISHOPSGATE

MIDDLESEX STREET

Petticoat Lane Market

BRICK LANE

OSBORN ST

WHITECHAPEL ROAD

WENTWORTH STREET

COMMERCIAL STREET

STREET

HOUNDSDITCH

Heron Tower

BEVIS MARKS

Whitechapel Art Gallery

OLD CASTLE STREET

ALDGATE EAST

WHITECHAPEL HIGH STREET

COMMERCIAL ROAD

St Helen

The Gherkin

Bevis Marks

St Botolph

ST BOTOLPH ST

ALDGATE

BRAHAM STREET

ST MARY AXE

St Andrew Undershaft

DUKES PL

ALDGATE HIGH STREET

LEMAN STREET

St Katharine Cree

ALIE STREET

WHITECHAPEL

HALL STREET

Lloyd's Building

London Metal Exchange

MINORIES

MANSELL STREET

PRESCOT STREET

Fenchurch St Station

STREET

MARK LANE

MINCHING LANE

SEETHING LANE

TOWER GATEWAY

ROYAL MINT STREET

DOCK STREET

St Olave

TOWER HILL

Minster Court

TRINITY ST

TOWER HILL

BYWARD STREET

TOWER STREET

TOWER HILL

EAST SMITHFIELD

THOMAS MORE

All Hallows

LOWER THAMES STREET

St Katharine Docks

STREET

TOWER BRIDGE APPROACH

Dickens Inn

HMS Belfast

Tower Millennium Pier

The Tower of London

WAPPING

MORGAN'S LANE

Thames

TOWER BRIDGE

N

ST KATHARINE'S WAY

City Hall

Butler's Wharf

SHAD

THAMES

Design Museum

MAGDALEN ST

0   200 yds

© crown copyright

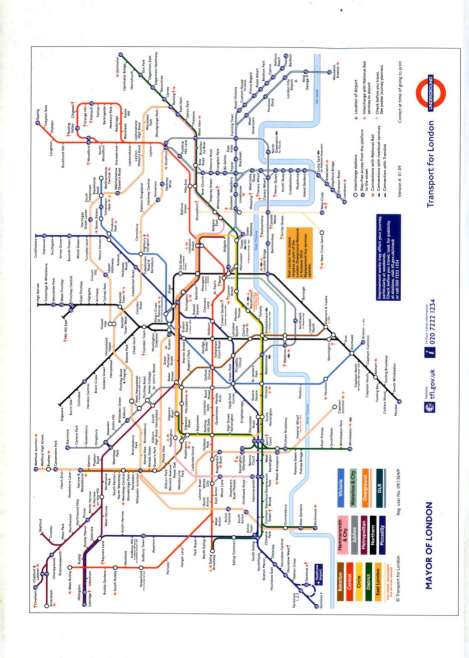

MAYOR OF LONDON

Transport for London

Version A 01.09

Correct at time of going to print